CHESS OPENINGS

Printed in the United States of America

PREFACE TO THE SIXTH EDITION

In the Sixth Edition of this book there is a notable change, which we are sure that all our supporters will appreciate. While we were considering the advisability of bringing it out in the current year we were approached by Mr. Reuben Fine with a suggestion that he should undertake the task of revision; and we gladly agreed.

Reuben Fine needs no introduction to those who are interested in the game of chess. His past achievements had already made him famous; and he added another glorious chapter to the story of his career, just as he had finished his work for us, by tieing for the first place in the great "A.V.R.O." Tournament towards the end of 1938.

Naturally we gave our reviser a free hand in dealing with his task, merely reserving to ourselves the editorial right of making such slight changes in his text as might seem to us necessary. Mr. Fine, however, scrupulously adhered to the traditions of *Modern Chess Openings*, while availing himself fully of the privilege which must be conceded to a master of his rank of expressing his personal opinions on the lines of play which are illustrated in the book, and altering as he thought fit the introductions to the various openings.

In comparing this new edition with its predecessor we may note that it contains 332 pages and 1,215 columns, as against 300 pages and 1,060 columns of seven years ago. We have gladly got rid of the cumbrous device of *Addenda,* which was forced upon us by circumstances of production in 1932. We have also, in deference to Mr. Fine's wishes, abandoned the use of " starred " columns to indicate what appears to be the best line of play for both sides. In his preface the reviser explains the system adopted by him in appraising lines of play, so no comment on it is needed from us.

PREFACE TO THE SIXTH EDITION

The only difficulty which arose in the completion of this edition was caused by our desire to introduce new variations from the "A.V.R.O." Tournament after the manuscript had been sent to the printers and was in process of being set up. The printer's work was held back sufficiently to permit the mention of the most important of these; and it so happened that this delay made it possible to put in some of the novelties from the Hastings Tournament of 1938-39 and a few from the Leningrad-Moscow Tournament this year.

In conclusion we should like to convey our personal thanks to Mr. Fine for the admirable way in which he has carried out his revision (on which point we think our readers will agree), and to acknowledge how little he left us to do. The manuscript was typed by his wife, and the printers had no difficulty on the score of illegibility. We desire also to express our gratitude to all who have helped us in the preparation of this new edition, and especially to our assistants in the exacting work of reading the proofs, with particular mention of Messrs. F. J. Camm and R. Hutter, and Sir Gilbert Jackson.

THE EDITORS.

London, January, 1939.

PREFACE

THE task of revising *Modern Chess Openings* has been both arduous and pleasant; arduous because of the almost endless ramifications of modern opening theory, which necessitated the examination of the openings of thousands of games; pleasant because the result is a solution, albeit an incomplete one, to the complicated labyrinth. I have been guided by the principle of the earlier editions, that this work is intended to be both modern and practical. For that reason I have enlarged the sections on the Queen's side openings and the Ruy Lopez, as these are the *sine qua non* of contemporary tournaments, although I have refrained from paying too much attention to any particular variation in these openings, since the practical player must be acquainted with a great number of different lines.

I wish to express my grateful thanks to various friends who have helped me; particularly to Mr. Fred Reinfeld for his countless invaluable suggestions, and to Mr. Sidney Bernstein for reading the manuscript.

REUBEN FINE.

New York, December 20th, 1938.

PREFATORY NOTES

THE arrangement of openings in alphabetical order seems to us most suitable for a book on Chess Openings. At the same time there is the difficulty of finding irregular openings or those infrequently played. For such the student must refer to the general index, which has been considerably altered for this new edition.

We have evaluated the variations by means of a number of symbols which are extensively used in all chess publications. For those who are unfamiliar with their exact meaning we append a short glossary.

    ++   (after White move) White has a winning advantage.

    ++   (after Black move) Black has a winning advantage.

    +   (after White move) White has a distinct superiority, but there is no question of a forced win.

    +   (after Black move) Black has a distinct superiority, but there is no question of a forced win.

    ±   White stands slightly better.

    ∓   Black stands slightly better.

    =   The position is even.

Where a variation is given without any evaluating symbol or comment, it can be assumed that the position reached is one where both sides have good chances, and that considerable analysis is required to come to a definite conclusion. In doubtful cases we would not recommend our readers to forego their own judgment; for an attacking player with a Pawn to the bad might consider his position to be an adequate return, whereas a more cautious player might come to the opposite conclusion.

For the benefit of the student unfamiliar with a particular opening, who wishes to acquaint himself with the leading variations, we would recommend in the first place a careful study of the introductory remarks. To obtain a preliminary view of the opening, the variations given in the footnotes may frequently be neglected for the time being. It is particularly advisable that a player should endeavour to ascertain for himself the why and wherefore of certain moves, the habit of playing a series of book-moves by heart leading to disaster when the opponent deviates from the book.

We have endeavoured to arrange the columns in the simplest possible form for reference, and this has rendered necessary a considerable amount of transposition of the opening moves, mainly in the sections dealing with the Queen's side openings and the Ruy Lopez. It is necessary to state this in order to avoid being charged with erroneous records of actual games. We have drawn attention, as far as possible, to the cases where one opening transposes into another.

NOTATION

FOR the benefit of such of our readers as are not familiar with the English notation of the chessboard and the names of the pieces, we give a diagram of the board showing the (English) descriptive and the algebraic names of the squares and a table of equivalents in various foreign languages for the symbols of the English chess pieces.

The Board:

(BLACK)

	A	B	C	D	E	F	G	H	
8	QR8	QKt8	QB8	Q8	K8	KB8	KKt8	KR8	8
7	QR7	QKt7	QB7	Q7	K7	KB7	KKt7	KR7	7
6	QR6	QKt6	QB6	Q6	K6	KB6	KKt6	KR6	6
5	QR5	QKt5	QB5	Q5	K5	KB5	KKt5	KR5	5
4	QR4	QKt4	QB4	Q4	K4	KB4	KKt4	KR4	4
3	QR3	QKt3	QB3	Q3	K3	KB3	KKt3	KR3	3
2	QR2	QKt2	QB2	Q2	K2	KB2	KKt2	KR2	2
1	QR1	QKt1	QB1	Q1	K1	KB1	KKt1	KR1	1
	A	B	C	D	E	F	G	H	

(WHITE)

The Symbols:

Eng.	Ger.	Fr.	It.	Span.	Dut.	Flem.	Hun.	Czech.	Pol.	Russ.
K	K	R	R	R	K	K	K	K	K	Kp
Q	D	D	D	D	D	D	V	D	H	Φ
R	T	T	T	T	T	T	B	V	W	Λ
B	L	F	A	A	L	L	F	S	G	C
Kt	S	C	C	C	P	P	H	J	S	К
	(B)	P	P	P	(B)	(B)	(G)	(P)	(P)	(π)

ALEKHINE'S DEFENCE

This defence to 1 P—K 4, which in our 1925 edition was characterized as "bizarre," has met with the fate which often awaits openings that at first seem bizarre, and has now come to be regarded as normal.

1..., Kt—K B 3, although known as a playable move long before the present Champion's days, was introduced as a tournament weapon by Alekhine at Budapest in 1921, and quickly grew in favour. In this decade the defence has lost much of its erstwhile popularity, but it is still often adopted by Euwe, Flohr, Reshevsky, and Fine.

The distinguishing feature of the defence is that, contrary to all the tenets of the classical school, Black allows his King's Knight to be driven about the board in the early stages of the game, in the expectation of provoking a weakness in White's centre Pawns. Tartakover aptly remarks that White has his initiative to defend; but if he is successful Black's position remains fearfully cramped.

The variations which were the earliest to assume a certain appearance of regularity are represented in cols. 1 to 3. They give rise to extremely difficult positions in which White's centre proves difficult to maintain. Black's development, apart from the Knight temporarily misplaced on Q Kt 3, leaves little to be desired. The simplifying variation in cols. 4 and 5 is easier for White to play, but yields him no advantage whatsoever. The line in col. 6, played by Alekhine in the highly important 29th match game against Euwe in 1935, has since been exhaustively analysed and need not be feared by Black. The simple continuation in col. 7 is one of the few lines where prevailing theory prefers White.

Dr. Lasker's move 4 P—B 5 is shown in cols. 8 to 10. If White wishes to avoid equality, he can adopt the complicated attacking variation in col. 10. Lajos Steiner's

move 4 P—Q Kt 3 (col. 11) is also worthy of attention.
Black does best to adopt the simplifying line in note (*b*).

In cols. 12 to 17 White omits for the time being a
second driving move against Black's Knight by P—Q B 4.
Botvinnik scored a memorable success against Flohr with
this line at Moscow, 1936, but in a later game Flohr
improved upon his earlier play. Böök's move (col. 12,
note (A)) is a recent attempt to avoid Flohr's equalising line.

In cols. 18 to 20 White does not even make the first
drive by P—K 5, substituting quiet development. Thereby
he avoids the weakness attendant on the advance of his
Pawn, without, however, placing such difficulties in Black's
way as in the earlier columns.

Notes for cols. 1 to 5 (p. 3) ctd.

(*h*) 15 R×Kt, R P×B; 16 P×P, B×P; 17 Q×Q ch, B×Q; 18 R×P,
B —Kt 2 ∓. Lafora—Treer, correspondence, 1927.

(*i*) 12 P×P, B×P; 13 Q—Q 2, Q—K 2; 14 Q R—Q 1, Q R—Q 1; 15 Q—K 1,
Kt—Kt 5; 16 P—Q R 3 !, Kt—B 7; 17 Q—B 2, Kt×B; 18 Q ⟨ Kt, P—B 3 (better
than 18.., Kt—Q 2; 19 P—B 5!+. Rauser—Fine, Leningrad, 1937) with even
prospects.

(*j*) Continued 16 Q×P, Kt—Q 2; 17 K—R 1 (better than 17 Kt—R 4,
P—Q Kt 4 !; 18 P×P, B—Q 3 with a strong attack. Spielmann—Colle, Dortmund,
1928)±. Znosko-Borovsky—Colle, Paris, 1929. All other Kt moves on move 14
are bad, *e.g.* 14 , Kt—Kt 1 ; 15 P—B 5, Kt—B 1 ; 16 Q—Kt 3+. Or 14 , Kt—R 4 ;
15 B×Kt, R P×B; 16 P—Q R 3+. Or 14.., Kt—Kt 5 ; 15 Q—Kt 3 +. (Analysis
by Yates and Winter).

(*k*) Other possibilities are less satisfactory : (1) 5.., B P×P ; 6 B—K 3, P—Kt 3 ;
7 Kt—Q B 3, B—Kt 2 ; 8 Kt—B 3, Kt—B 3 ; 9 P—K R 3, O—O ; 10 Q—Q 2,
P—Q 4 (better is 10.., P—K 4!; 11 P×P, Kt×K P ; 12 Kt×Kt, B×Kt=); 11 P—B 5,
Kt—B 5 ; 12 B×Kt, P×'3 ; 13 O—O, Kt—Kt 5 ; 14 B—R 6, B—B 4 ; 15 B×B,
K×B ; 16 Kt—K 2, B—Q 6 ; 17 K R—Q 1 ±. Yates—Alekhine, Dresden, 1926.
(2) 5.., Q×P; 6 B—K 3, Q—Q 1; 7 B—Q 3, P—Kt 3 ; 8 Kt—K B 3, B—Kt 2;
9 Kt—B 3, O—O; 10 P—K R 3 ±. Zubareff—Grünfeld, Moscow, 1925.

(*l*) If instead 6 P—Q 5, B—K 2 (or 6.., B—B 4 ; 7 Kt—K B 3, Kt (Kt 3)—Q 2;
8 Kt—B 3, B—Kt 5 ; 9 P—K R 3, B×Kt; 10 Q×B, Kt—K 4 ; 11 Q—K 4, Q—K 2 ;
12 P—Q Kt 3, P—K B 4 ; 13 Q—K 3, P—K Kt 3 ; 14 B—K 2, B—Kt 2 ; 15 B—Q 2,
P—B 5+. Tarrasch—Vukovic, Vienna, 1922) ; 7 Kt—Q B 3, O—O ; 8 B—Q 3,
R—K 1 ; 9 K Kt—K 2, Q Kt—Q 2 ; 10 P—Q Kt 3, Kt—B 4 ; 11 B—B 2, B—Kt 5;
12 O—O, B—B 3 ; 13 P—B 3, B—R 4 ; 14 Kt—Q 4, P—Q R 4=. Horowitz—
Kashdan, 1926.

(*m*) Continued 16 B—Kt 5, Q—Q 2 ; 17 Kt—Q 4, P—Q B 4 ; 18 Kt—B 3,
Kt—B 4 ; 19 Q R—K 1, P—Q R 3. Petrov—Flohr, Kemeri, 1937.

(*n*) 16 R×B, Kt—K 2. Nimzovitch—Kmoch, Semmering, 1926.

1 P—K 4, Kt—K B 3 ; 2 P—K 5, Kt—Q 4 ; 3 P—Q B 4, Kt—Kt 3 ;
4 P—Q 4, P—Q 3.

	1	2	3	4	5
5	P—B 4 . . . . P×P			P×P	
	P×P			K P×P (*k*)	
6	B P×P			Kt—Q B 3 (*l*)	
	Kt—B 3			Kt—Q B 3	
7	B—K 3 (*a*)			B—K 3	
	B—B 4			B—K 2	
8	Kt—Q B 3			B—Q 3	
	P—K 3			O—O	
9	Kt—B 3			K Kt—K 2	
	Kt—Kt 5 (*b*) . Q—Q 2 . . . . . . B—K 2			B—Kt 5	
10	R—B 1	B—K 2	B—K 2	O—O	
	P—B 4	O—O—O	O—O	R—K 1	
11	B—K 2 (*c*)	O—O	O—O	P—K R 3 . . . P—Q R 3	
	P×P (*d*)	P—B 3 (*f*)	P—B 3	B—R 4	B—R 4
12	Kt×P	P×P	Kt—K R 4 (*i*)	Q—Q 2	Q—B 2
	B—Kt 3	P×P	P×P	B—Kt 3	B—Kt 3
13	P—Q R 3	P—Q 5 (*g*)	Kt×B	B×B	P—Q Kt 3
	Kt—B 3	Kt—K 4	P×Kt	R P×B	B—B 3
14	Kt×Kt	B×Kt	P—Q 5	P—Q Kt 3	Q R—Q 1
	P×Kt	Kt×Kt ch	Kt—Q 5	B—B 1	Kt—Q 2
15	Q×Q ch = (*e*)	(*h*)	B×Kt	P—Q 5	B—B 1
			P×B (*j*)	Kt-K 2 = (*m*)	B×B = (*n*)

(*a*) A remarkable line is 7 Kt—K B 3, B—Kt 5 ; 8 P—K 6 !?, P×P ; 9 P—B 5,
Kt—Q 4 (Simpler is 9 .., P—K 4 !; 10 P×Kt, P—K 5 ; 11 P—K R 3, B—R 4 ;
12 P—K Kt 4, P×Kt ; 13 P×B, P—K 4 ! with a strong attack. Sorokin) ;
10 B—Q Kt 5, Q—Q 2 ; 11 Q Kt—Q 2, P—K Kt 3 !; 12 Q—R 4, B—Kt 2 ;
13 Kt—K 5, B×Kt ; 14 P×B, Kt—K 6 ; 15 Q—K 4, Q—Q 5 !; 16 B×Kt ch,
P×B ; 17 Q×Q, Kt—B 7 ch=. Ilyin-Zhenevsky—Lövenfisch, Leningrad, 1936.

(*b*) If 9 .., B—K Kt 5 ; 10 B—K 2, B×Kt ; 11 P×B (11 B×B, Kt×B P ;
12 B×Kt ch, P×B ; 13 Q—R 4 !, Kt—Kt 3 ! leads to a draw), Q—R 5 ch ;
12 B—B 2, Q—B 5 ; 13 Q—B 1 ! ±.

(*c*) 11 P—Q R 3, P×P ; 12 B—Kt 5 !? (12 P×Kt and 12 Kt×P are both
probably better), P×Kt !; 13 B×Q, R×B ; 14 Q—Kt 3, P×P +, although the game
ended in a draw. Znosko-Borovsky—Alekhine, Paris, 1925.

(*d*) 11 ., B—K 2 ; 12 O—O, O—O ; 13 P—Q R 3, P×P ; 14 Kt×P, Kt—B 3 ;
15 Kt×B, P×Kt ; 16 R×P, P—Kt 3 ; 17 R—B 1, B—Kt 4=. Petrov—Fine,
Kemeri, 1937.

(*e*) 15 .., K×Q (15 .., R×Q is bad because of 16 B×Kt, P×B ; 17 B—B 3,
R—B 1 ; 18 Kt—R 4+. Kmoch) ; 16 B×Kt, P×B ; 17 B—B 3, R—Q B 1 ;
18 Kt—R 4, K—B 2. Negyesy—Lokvenc, Vienna, 1925.

(*f*) A good alternative is 11 .., Q B—Kt 5 ; 12 P—B 5 (but not 12 Kt—K Kt 5 ?,
Kt×B P !; 13 Kt×P or 13 B×B, Kt×P B+), Kt—Q 4 ; 13 Kt×Kt, Q×Kt=.
However, 11 ., B—K 2 ? is a mistake because of 12 P—Q 5 !, P×P ; 13 B×Kt,
R P×B ; 14 P×P, Kt—Kt 5 ; 15 Kt -Q 4 !, P—Kt 3 (or 15 .., B—B 4 ; 16 R×B !!,
Kt×Q P ; 17 Kt—Kt 5 ! and wins) ; 16 Kt×B, P×Kt ; 17 R×P !, Kt×Q P (or 17 ..,
K—Kt 1 ; 18 B—Kt 4, Kt×Q P ; 19 P—K 6 ! and wins) ; 18 P—K 6 !, P×P ;
19 R×Kt ! and if 19 ., P×R ; 20 B—Kt 4 wins the Queen. (Analysis by Znosko-
Borovsky and Grünfeld).

(*g*) Or 13 Q—Q 2, R—Kt 1 ; 14 K R—Q 1, Q—Kt 2 ; 15 B—B 1, Kt—K 4 !=.
Naegeli—Euwe, Berne, 1932.

Notes ctd. on p. 2.

1 P—K4, Kt—KB3; 2 P—K5, Kt—Q4; 3 P—QB4, Kt—Kt3.

	6	7	8	9	10
4	(P—Q4)................P—B5				
	(P—Q3)		Kt—Q4		
5	Kt—KB3		Kt—QB3...............B—B4		
	B—Kt5		Kt×Kt		P—K3
6	B—K2......P×P		QP×Kt (g)		Kt-QB3 (m)
	P×P	KP×P	P—Q3 (h)...P—K3		Kt×Kt
7	P—B5 (a)	B—K2 (e)	BP×P (i)	B—K3	QP×Kt (n)
	P—K5	B—K2	KP×P	P—QKt3	B×P
8	P×Kt	Kt—B3	Kt—B3	P×P	Q—Kt4
	P×Kt	O—O	Kt—B3 (j)	RP×P	K—B1
9	B×P	P—QKt3	B—QB4	Kt—B3	B—B4 (o)
	B×B	R—K1	B—K2	Kt—B3	P—Q4
10	Q×B	O—O	B—B4	B—Q3	O—O—O
	RP×P (b)	B—B3	O—O	B—R3	Kt—Q2
11	Q×P	B—K3	O—O	O—O	B—Q3
	Kt—Q2	Kt—B3	P×P	B—K2	B—K2
12	B—B4	R—B1	Kt×P= (k)	R—K1= (l)	P—KR4
	P—K4!	P—Q4			P—QB4
13	B×P (c)	P—B5			R—R3
	Kt×B	Kt—B1			P—KR4 (p)
14	P×Kt	P—KR3			
	B-Kt5 ch=	± (f)			
	(d)				

(a) The sacrificial variation 7 Kt×P?, B×B; 8 Q×B, Q×P; 9 O—O, QKt—Q2; 10 Kt×Kt is refuted by 10.., Q×Kt (and not 10.., Kt×Kt; 11 Kt—B3, P—QB3; 12 B—K3, Q—K4; 13 QR—Q1, P—K3; 14 Q—B3, O—O—O; 15 B×P, Q—QR4; 16 B—Q4, Q—KB4; 17 Q—Kt3, P—K4; 18 B—K3 ±. Alekhine—Reshevsky, Kemeri, 1937); 11 Kt—B3, P—K3; 12 B—K3, B—K2; 13 QR—Q1, Q—B3; 14 Q—Kt4, O—O; 15 P—QKt3, P—B4+. Sir G. A. Thomas—Flohr, Antwerp, 1932.

(b) This is good enough to draw, but 10.., Kt—B3 was better. Alekhine maintains that after 11 O—O, Kt×P; 12 Q×P, RP×P; 13 B—K3, Black has only slight drawing chances, but after 13.., R—QKt1; 14 Q—K4, Kt—Kt4! Black certainly has a clear advantage.

(c) 13 P×P, B—Kt5 ch; 14 Kt—B3, B×Kt ch; 15 P×B, O—O; 16 O—O, Kt—B4; 17 Q—B3, R—R6 offered even less winning chances (Alekhine).

(d) Continued 15 Kt—B3, B×Kt ch; 16 P×B, O—O; 17 O—O, Q—K2. Alekhine—Euwe, 29th match game, 1935. Black drew fairly easily, despite the Pawn minus.

(e) Or 7 P—KR3, B—R4; 8 B—K2, Kt—B3; 9 P—Q5, B×Kt; 10 B×B, Kt—K4; 11 B—K2, Q—R5; 12 O—O, P—Kt4; 13 Kt—Q2, R—K Kt1; 14 Q—B2, P—Kt5; 15 P×P, Kt×KtP (Kashdan—Euwe, Hastings, 1931-32) and now 16 Kt—B3, Q—R4; 17 B—B4!± (Kashdan).

(f) Continued 14.., B—R4; 15 P—QR3, B—Kt3; 16 P—QKt4, P—QR3; 17 Q—Kt3. Maróczy—Keres, Dresden, 1936.

(g) If 6 KtP×Kt, P—Q3; 7 BP×P, KP×P; 8 Kt—B3 (8 B—B4, P×P; 9 Q—R5, Q—B3; 10 Kt—B3, Kt—B3; 11 O—O, P—KKt3; 12 Q—Kt5, B—Kt2; 13 B—R3 gives White some attack for the Pawn. P. W. Sergeant—R. H. Newman, City of London Championship, 1932), B—K2; 9 B—B4, O—O; 10 O—O, Kt—B3; 11 P×P, B×P; 12 P—Q4, B—K Kt5=. Gruber—Grünfeld, Vienna, 1923.

Notes ctd. on p. 7.

1 P—K 4, Kt—K B 3 ; 2 P—K 5, Kt—Q 4.

	11	12	13	14	15
3	(P—Q B 4).. (Kt—Kt 3)	P—Q 4 P—Q 3	....	....	B—B 4 Kt—Kt 3
4	P—Q Kt 3 P—Q B 4 (a)	Kt—K B 3 B—Kt 5 (d)	....	P×P K P×P (k)	B—Kt 3 P—Q B 4
5	B—Kt 2 Kt—B 3	B—K 2 (e) P—QB3!(f) ..Kt—Q B 3		Kt—K B 3 B—Kt 5	Q—K 2 (m) Kt—B 3
6	Kt—K B 3 P—Q 4	O—O (A) B×Kt (g)	O—O P—K 3	B—K 2 B—K 2	Kt—K B 3 P—Q 4
7	P×P e.p. Q×P	B×B P×P	P—Q B 4 Kt—Kt 3 (i)	O—O Kt—K B 3	P×P e.p. P—K 3
8	P—Q 4 B—Kt 5 (b)	P×P P—K 3	P×P P×P	R—K 1 O—O	Kt—B 3 B×P
9	P—Q 5 O—O—O	Q—K 2 Q—B 2	P—Q Kt 3 B—K 2	Q Kt—Q 2 Q Kt—Q 2	Kt—K 4 B—K 2
10	B—K 2 Q—B 5 ?	P—B 4 Kt—K 2 !	B—K 3 O—O	Kt—B 1 P—Q 4	P—Q 3 Kt—Q 5 ∓
11	Q Kt—Q 2 B×Kt	B—Kt 4 Kt—Q 2	Kt—B 3 P—Q 4	B—K Kt 5 P—B 3	
12	B×B Kt—K 4	P—B 4 P—K R 4	P—B 5 Kt—Q 2	P—K R 3 B×Kt	
13	B—K 4+ (c)	B—R 3 =(h)	P—Kt 4+ (j)	B×B= (l)	

(a) Or 4.., P—K Kt 3; 5 B—Kt 2 (5 P—B 5, Kt—Q 4; 6 B—B 4, P—K 3; 7 P—Q 4, P—Kt 3; 8 P×P, Kt×P; 9 B—Q 3, B—Kt 5 ch; 10 B—Q 2, Kt—B 3; 11 Kt—K B 3=. A. Steiner—Pikler, Budapest, 1931), B—Kt 2; 6 Q—B 3, P—K 3; 7 P—K R 4, Kt—B 3; 8 Q—K 3, P—Q 3; 9 Kt—K B 3, Kt×K P; 10 Kt×Kt, B×Kt; 11 B×B, P×B. Richter—Danielsson, Zoppot, 1935.

(b) Better is 8.., Q Kt×P; 9 Kt×Kt, P×Kt; 10 Q×P, Q×Q; 11 B×Q, B—B 4; 12 Kt—B 3?, P—K 4!; 13 B×P, O—O—O; 14 B—K 2, P—B 3; 15 B—B 4, B—Q Kt 5+. Tartakover—Colle, Bled, 1931.

(c) 13.., P—K 3; 14 P—Kt 3, Q—B 3; 15 Q—B 2. L. Steiner—Pikler, Budapest, 1931.

(d) 4.., P×P; 5 Kt×P, P—K 3; 6 B—Q 3, Q Kt—Q 2; 7 O—O, Kt×Kt; 8 P×Kt, B—Q 2; 9 Q—K 2, Q—R 5; 10 P—Q B 3, O—O—O. R. P. Michell—Réti, Margate, 1923.

Inferior is 4 ., B—B 4, because of 5 B—Q 3, Q—Q 2 (5.., B—Kt 3?: a P—B 4, Kt—Kt 3; 7 B×B, R P×B; 8 P—K 6!+. Bogoljuboff—Tarrasch, Breslau, 1925); 6 O—O, Kt—Q B 3; 7 P—B 4, B×B; 8 Q×B, Kt—Kt 3; 9 P×P, K P×P; 10 R—K 1 ch, Kt—K 2; 11 P—Q R 4!, Q—B 3; 12 P—Q Kt 3, P—K R 3; 13 Kt—B 3, O—O—O; 14 P—R 5+. Becker—Grünfeld, Vienna, 1927.

(e) Or 5 P—K R 3, B×Kt; 6 Q×B, P×P; 7 P×P, P—K 3; 8 P—K Kt 3, Kt—Q B 3; 9 B—Q Kt 5, Q—Q 2; 10 Q—K 4, B—B 4; 11 P—Q B 3, O—O+. Rubinstein—Spielmann, Moscow, 1925.

(f) A satisfactory alternative is 5.., P—K 3; 6 P—B 4, Kt—K 2; 7 Kt—B 3, Kt—B 4 (7.., Q Kt—B 3 transposes to note (i)); 8 P—K R 3, B×Kt; 9 B×B, Kt—B 3; 10 B×Kt ch, P×B; 11 B—B 4, B—K 2=. Sir G. A. Thomas—Fine, Hastings, 1937-38.

(g) If 6.., P×P; 7 Kt×P, B×B; 8 Q×B, P—K 3 (or 8.., Kt—Q 2; 9 P—K B 4, P—K 3; 10 P—B 4, K Kt—Kt 3; 11 B—K 3, B—K 2; 12 Q Kt—B 3, O—O; 13 R—B 3 ±. Botvinnik—Flohr, Moscow, 1936); 9 P—Q Kt 3, Kt—Q 2; 10 P—Q B 4, K Kt—B 3; 11 Kt—Q B 3, B—Kt 5; 12 B—Kt 2, O—O; 13 K R—Q 1, Q—B 2; 14 R—Q 3, K R—Q 1; 15 Q R—Q 1, Kt—B 1; 16 Kt—K 4 ±. Sir G. A. Thomas—Euwe, Nottingham, 1936.

Notes ctd. on p. 7.

1 P—K 4, Kt—K B 3.

	16	17	18	19	20
2	(P—K 5)		Kt—Q B 3		P—Q 3
	(Kt—Q 4)		P—Q 4 (A)		P—K 4 (o)
3	Kt—Q B 3		P×P	P—K 5	P—K B 4
	Kt×Kt (a)		Kt×P	K Kt—Q 2 (i)	Kt—Q B 3 (p)
4	Kt P×Kt...	Q P×Kt	B—B 4	Kt×P (j)	P×P
	P—Q 3	P—Q 3 (c)	Kt—Kt 3 (e)	Kt×P	O Kt×P
5	P—K B 4	Kt—B 3	B—Kt 3	Kt—K 3	Kt—K B 3
	P—K Kt 3	P×P	P—Q B 4	P—Q B 4	Kt×Kt ch
6	Kt—B 3	Q×Q ch	P—Q 3 (f)	P—K B 4 (k)	Q×Kt
	B—Kt 2 .	K×Q	P—K 3 (g)	K Kt—B 3	P—Q 4
7	P—Q 4	Kt×P	Kt—B 3	B—B 4	P—K 5
	P—Q B 4	K—K 1	Kt—B 3	P—K Kt 3	Q—K 2
8	B—Q 3	B—Q B 4	O—O	Kt—B 3	P—Q 4
	O—O	P—K 3	B—K 2	B—Kt 2	Kt—K 5
9	O—O	B—B 4	Kt—K 4	O—O	B—Q 3
	Q—B 2	B—Q 3	O—O	Kt—Q 5	Q—R 5 ch
10	Q—K 1	B—K Kt 3	B—K 3	P—B 3	P—Kt 3
	B P×P	Kt—Q 2	Kt—Q 2 (h)	Kt—B 4 (l)	Q—Kt 5
11	B P×P	Kt—B 3	P—Q 4	P—Q 4 !	Kt—Q 2
	Kt—B 3	Kt—Kt 3	P—Q Kt 3	Q—Q 3 (m)	Q×Q
12	P—B 3= (b)	B—K 2= (d)	P×P+	Kt—Kt 5+ (n)	Kt×Q= (q)

(a) 3 ., P—K 3; 4 Kt×Kt, P×Kt; 5 P—Q 4, P—Q 3; 6 Kt—B 3, Kt—B 3; 7 B—K 2, B—K 2; 8 B—K B 4, O—O; 9 O—O, P—B 3; 10 P×Q P, B×P=. Sämisch—Alekhine, Budapest, 1921.

(b) 12.., Kt—R 4; 13 Kt—Kt 5, P—K R 3; 14 Kt—K 4. Grob—Grünfeld, Meran, 1926.

(c) Or 4.., P—Q 4; 5 Kt—B 3, P—Q B 4; 6 B—K B 4, Kt—B 3; 7 Q—Q 2, B—Kt 5=. Yates—Capablanca, Moscow, 1925.

(d) 12.., B—Q 2; 13 Kt—K 5, P—K B 3; 14 Kt×B, Kt×Kt. Tarrasch—Réti, Baden-Baden, 1925.

(A) 2 ., P—K 4 is the simplest reply, transposing, if 3 Kt—B 3, into the Three Knights' Game, or, if 3 P—B 4 or 3 B—B 4, into the Vienna.

(e) Or 4.., P—K 3; 5 Kt—B 3, P—Q B 4; 6 O—O, B—K 2; 7 P—Q 4 (if 7 R—K 1, O—O), Kt×Kt; 8 P×Kt, O—O; 9 Kt—K 5, Q—B 2. Hromadka—Grünfeld, Mährisch-Ostrau, 1923. Or 4.., Kt×Kt; 5 Q—B 3, P—K 3=.

(f) Rarely played, but nevertheless strong, is 6 Q—R 5, e.g. 6.., P—K 3; 7 P—Q 3, Kt—B 3; 8 B—K 3, Kt—Q 5; 9 K Kt—K 2, Kt×B; 10 R P×Kt, Kt—Q 4; 11 Kt×Kt, Q×Kt; 12 Q×Q, P×Q; 13 P—Q 4, P—B 5; 14 Kt—B 4+. Maróczy—Landau, Zandvoort, 1936.

(g) If 6 ., B—B 4; 7 Q—B 3, Q—B 1; 8 Q—Kt 3+ (Kmoch). The column is Vadja—Kmoch, Budapest, 1926.

(h) Preferable is 10.., Kt—Q 5.

(i) Safer is 3.., P—Q 5; 4 P×Kt, P×Kt; 5 Kt P×P, Kt P×P, with about an equal game.

(j) 4 P—B 4, P—K 3; 5 Kt—B 3, P—Q B 4; 6 P—K Kt 3, Kt—Q B 3; 7 B—Kt 2, B—K 2; 8 O—O, O—O; 9 P—Q 3. Nimzovitch—Alekhine, Semmering, 1926. 9.., P—B 3 is Black's best continuation, and if 10 P×P, B×P.
A promising sacrificial line is 4 P—K 6 !, e.g. 4.., P×P; 5 P—Q 4, Kt—K B 3;

Notes ctd. on p. 7.

Notes for cols. 6 to 10 ctd.

(h) 6.., Kt—B 3 ; 7 Kt—B 3, P—K Kt 3 ; 8 B—Q B 4, B—Kt 2 ; 9 B—B 4, O—O ; 10 Q—Q 2, P—Kt 3 ; 11 P—K R 4, P—K R 4 ; 12 O—O—O, P—K 3 ; 13 B—K Kt 5, P—B 3 ; 14 P×B P, B×P ; 15 Q—B 2+. Stoltz—Colle, Bled, 1931.

(i) Or 7 B—Q B 4, P—Q 4 (Simpler is 7. , Kt—B 3 ; and if 8 Kt—B 3 ?, P×K P, tor 9 B×P ch is unsound : 9 , K×B ; 10 Kt—Kt 5 ch, K—Kt 1 ! ; 11 Q—Kt 3 ch, P—K 3 ; 12 Kt×K P, Kt—R 4 ! ; 13 Kt×Q dis. ch, Kt×Q ; 14 P×Kt, B—K 2 and wins) ; 8 Q×P, Q×Q ; 9 B×Q, P—K 3=. Alekhine—Fine, Pasadena, 1932.

(j) Better than 8 ., B—K 2 ; 9 B—K B 4, P×P ; 10 Kt×P, Q×Q ch ; 11 R×Q, B—K 3 and now 12 B—B 4 !, B×B ; 13 Kt×B, Kt—R 3 ; 14 Kt—R 5 !+ (Tartakover).

(k) H. Golombek—T. H. Tylor, London, 1932.

(l) Maróczy—Colle, Bled, 1931.

(m) 6 Q—Kt 4 !, P—Q 3 ; 7 B P×P, B P×P ; 8 P—Q 4, P×P ; 9 P×P, Kt—Kt 5 ; 10 Q—K 2, P—Q R 3 with advantage for White. Prins—Llorens, Sitges 1934.

(n) 7 Kt P×Kt, P—Q 3 (7. , B×P ; 8 Q—Kt 4, K—B 1 ; 9 P—Q 4 gives White a strong attack) ; 8 B P×P, P×P ; 9 P×P, B×P ; 10 Kt—K B 3, O—O ; 11 P—Q 4, Q—B 2=. Tartakover and Weenink—Takacs and Landau, 1934.

(o) If 9 B—K Kt 5, B—K 2 ; 10 B×B, Q×B ; 11 O—O—O, P—Q 4 ; 12 B×P, P—K R 4 ; 13 Q—R 3, Kt—Q 2 ; 14 B—K 4, Kt×P ; 15 P—B 4, Kt—Kt 5+. Prins—Mulder, 1933.

(p) White has a strong attack. Schwarz—Herzog, correspondence, 1926-28.

Notes for cols. 11 to 15 ctd.

(h) Continued 13.., O—O—O ; 14 B—K 3, Kt—K B 4 ; 15 B×Kt, P×B ; 16 Q—K B 2, Q—R 4 ; 17 Kt—Q 2, Kt—Kt 3 ; 18 P—Q R 3, R—Q 6. Botvinnik—Flohr, Nottingham, 1936.

(i) Or 7 , K Kt—K 2 ; 8 P×P, Q×P ; 9 Kt—B 3, B×Kt ; 10 B×B, O—O—O ; 11 P—Q 5, Kt—K 4 ; 12 P×P, Kt×B ch ; 13 Q×Kt ±. E. G. Sergeant—Réti, Hastings, 1927.

(j) 13.., P—Q R 3 ; 14 R—Kt 1. Tartakover—Takacs, Budapest, 1926.

(k) More aggressive is 4.., Q×P ; 5 Kt—K B 3, B—Kt 5 ; 6 B—K 3, Kt—Q B 3 ; 7 Kt—B 3, O—O—O ; 8 Kt×Kt, Q×Kt ; 9 B—K 3, P—K 4 ; 10 O—O (or 10 P v P, B×Kt ; 11 P×B, Q—R 4 ch ; 12 B—Q 2, Q×K P+. Ilyin-Zhenevsky—Réti, Moscow, 1925), P×P ; 11 Kt×P, B×B ; 12 Kt×B, Q—Q Kt 4 ! ∓.

(l) 13.., B—Q 3 ; 14 Q—Q 2, Q—B 2 ; 15 Kt—K 3 (Yates—Sacconi, Meran, 1926), B—B 5=.

(m) Better is 5 P—Q 3, Kt—B 3 ; 6 Kt—K B 3, P—Q 4 ; 7 P×P e.p., P—K 3 ; 8 Kt—B 3, B×P ; 9 Kt—K 4, B—K 2 ; 10 B—K 3 (Kmoch). The column is Yates—Rubinstein, Dresden, 1926.

(A) An interesting attempt here is 6 Kt—Kt 5 !, B—B 4 ; 7 B—Q 3, B×B ; 8 Q×B, P—K R 3 ; 9 Kt—K B 3, P—K 3 ; 10 O—O, P×P ; 11 P×P, Kt—Q 2 ; 12 R—Q 1+. Böök—Reshevsky, Kemeri, 1937.

Notes for cols. 16 to 20 ctd.

6 Kt—B 3, P—B 4 ; 7 P×P, Kt—B 3 ; 8 B—Q Kt 5 (better than 8 B—K B 4, Q—R 4 ; 9 P—Q R 3, Kt—K 5+. Mieses—Colle, Frankfurt, 1930), B—Q 2 ; 9 O—O, Q—B 2 ; 10 Kt—B 3, P—K R 3 ; 11 B v Kt, P v B ; 12 Kt—K 5, P—K 4 ; 13 Q—Q 3, R—K Kt 1 ; 14 P—Q Kt 4+. Spielmann—Landau, 3rd match game, 1935.

(k) 6 Kt—B 3, Kt v Kt ch ; 7 Q v Kt, Kt—B 3 ; 8 B—Kt 5, B—Q 2 ∓. Von Holzhausen—Kmoch, Giessen, 1928. 6 P—K B 4 is Brinckmann's innovation.

(l) Better Kt×Kt ch (Brinckmann).

(m) Better is 11.., P×P ; 12 Kt×Kt, B×Kt ; 13 Kt×P, B—Q 2.

(n) 12.., O—O ; 13 Kt—K 4. Brinckmann—Takacs, Rogaska-Slatina, 1929.

(o) Or 2. , P—Q B 4 ; 3 P—Q B 4, Kt—Q B 3 ; 4 P—B 4, P—Q 3 ; 5 Kt—Q B 3, P—K Kt 3 ; 6 B—K 2, B—Kt 2 ; 7 B—K 3, Kt—Q 5 ; 8 Q—Q 2, Kt—Kt 5 ; 9 K B×Kt, B×Kt ; 10 B v Kt, B×B ; 11 K Kt—K 2, B—Kt 2 ; 12 O—O, O—O. Nimzovitch—Vukovitch, Kecskemét, 1927.

(p) Or 3.., P—Q 4 ; 4 B P×P, Kt—Kt 5 (Alekhine).

(q) Nimzovitch—Alekhine, New York, 1927.

8

BIRD'S OPENING

THE opening which begins with P—K B 4, known in Holland and Germany as the Dutch Attack, is, in spite of White's move in hand, subject to the objection that Black experiences no difficulties in development; and it is for that reason rarely tried by modern masters.

Schlechter's variation (cols. 1 and 2) and the line in col. 3, played by Dr. Lasker recently in an important game, may be recommended as a simple method of defence for the second player. The King's fianchetto development for Black is another excellent line. Here Black not only avoids the dangers which an early development of his Queen's Knight involves, but also nullifies the effect of the White Queen's Bishop on the long diagonal.

With Bird's favourite Queen's fianchetto for White in this opening should be compared the manœuvre in Nimzovitch's Attack. See page 110, where the similarity of the plans of campaign is noted. The old English master had conceived the general idea of the attack long before the great modern exponent of enterprise in the chess openings.

In the From Gambit Black sacrifices a Pawn for a counter-attack. In the light of recent games and analysis (notably by Tartakover) the main variation beginning with P—K Kt 4 is insufficient against best play, and the gambit must consequently be considered unsound. Col. 10 is a recent example of an unusual gambit line.

Notes for cols. 1 to 5 (p. 9) ctd.

(k) Capablanca suggested later the continuation 8 , Kt × Kt ; 9 P × Kt, Kt—Q 2 ; 10 B × P ch, K—R 1 ; 11 P—Q 4, P—K 3 ; 12 B × K P, Kt—B 4 (or Kt × P) ; 13 P × Kt, B × P.

(l) 12 Kt—R 4, Kt—K 5 ; 13 Kt × P, Kt × Kt ; 14 P × Kt, Q—B 3 ! ; 15 B—B 3, B × B ch ; 16 Q × B, R—Q 1 ; 17 O—O, B—Kt 2 ; 18 R—B 2, Q × B P. Tartakover—Capablanca, Carlsbad, 1929.

(m) 3.., B—Kt 2 ; 4 P—Q 4, Kt—K B 3 ; 5 B—Q 3, O—O ; 6 Q Kt—Q 2, P—Q B 4 ; 7 P—Q B 3, P—Q Kt 3 ; 8 Q—K 2, B—Kt 2 ; 9 Kt—K 5, Q—B 2 ; 10 O—O, Kt—B 3 ; 11 Q Kt—B 3, Kt—K 5 ; 12 B—Q 2, Kt × Kt ; 13 Q P × Kt, P—B 3 ; 14 P × P, P × P ; 15 P—B 4, K R—K 1 ∓. Lilienthal—Tartakover, 2nd match, 1933.

(n) 12 Kt—K 2, B—Kt 2 ; 13 P—B 3, P × P ; 14 Kt × B P, P—R 6. Capablanca—I. S. Turover, New York, 1931

1 P—K B 4.

	1	2	3	4	5
1	P—Q 4				
2	P—K 3				
	Kt—K B 3			P—K Kt 3	
3	Kt—K B 3 (a)			P—B 4......	Kt—K B 3
	B—Kt 5 (b)..............	P—Q B 4		Kt—K B 3	P—Q B 4 (m)
4	B—K 2......	P—K R 3 (e)	P—Q Kt 3 (g)	Kt—Q B 3	B—Kt 5 ch
	B×Kt	B×Kt	P—K 3	B—Kt 2	B—Q 2
5	B×B	Q×B	B—Kt 2	Kt—B 3	B×B ch
	Q Kt—Q 2 (c)	Q Kt—Q 2	B—Q 3 (h)	O—O	Kt×B
6	P—B 4	P—Q 4	B—Q 3	Q—Kt 3	Kt—B 3
	P—K 3	Kt—K 5	P—Q R 3	P×P (j)	P—K 3
7	P×P	B—Q 3	O—O	B×P	P—K 4 ?
	P×P	P—K B 4 (f)	Kt—B 3	Kt—B 3	P—Q 5
8	Kt—B 3	O—O	P—B 4	Kt—K 5	Kt—K 2
	P—B 3	P—K 3	P×P !	P—K 3 (k)	K Kt—B 3
9	O—O	P—B 4	B×B P	Kt×Kt	Kt—Kt 3
	B—K 2	P—B 3	O—O	P×Kt	P—K R 4 !
10	P—Q 3	B—Q 2	Kt—K 5	P—Q 4	P—Q 3
	Kt—Kt 3	B—Q 3	Kt—K 2	Q—Q 3	B—R 3
11	P—K 4	P—B 5	Kt—Q B 3	B—Q 2	O—O
	P×P = (d)	B—B 2	Kt—Kt 3	P—B 4	P—R 5
12		P—Q Kt 4	= (i)	= (l)	∓ (r)
		Q—B 3 =			

(a) 3 P—Q Kt 3 is premature. Black securing the better endgame by P—Q 5 !; 4 B—Q 3, P×P; 5 P×P, P—Q 4 !: 6 P×P, Kt—Kt 5; 7 B—Kt 5 ch, P—B 3; 8 Q×Q ch, K×Q; 9 B—K 2, Kt×P (h 7) ∓. Nimzovitch—L. Steiner, Kecskemet, 19 27.

(b) Schlechter's Variation, threatening B×Kt and an early advance of the K P.

(c) 5.., P—B 3; 6 O—O, Q Kt—Q 2; 7 P—Q 4, P—K 3; 8 B—Q 2, B—K 2; 9 P—B 4, O—O; 10 Q—B 2, R—B 1; 11 P—Q B 5, Kt—K 1, 12 P—Q Kt 4, P—B 4; 13 P—K Kt 4, P—K Kt 3=. Reti—Kaufmann, Vienna, 1914.

(d) 12 P×P, B—B 4 ch. Tartakover—Grünfeld, Vienna 1917.

(e) Other continuations are: (1) 4 P—B 4, P—K 3; 5 Kt—B 3, P—B 3; 6 P—Q Kt 3, P—Q 5; 7 P×P, B×Kt; 8 Q×B, Q×P=. F. Becker—J. Mihalek, correspondence, 1931. (2) 4 P—Q Kt 3, P—K 3; 5 B—Kt 2 B—K 2; 6 B—Q 3, Q Kt—Q 2; 7 P—K R 3, B×Kt; 8 Q×B, Kt—B 4; 9 O—O, O—O; 10 Kt—B 3, P—Q 5. Tartakover—Schlechter, Vienna, 1917.

(f) The position has become a Stonewall Defence in the Queen's Pawn Game. The column is Brinckmann—Kmoch, Kecskemet, 1927.

(g) On 4 B—Kt 5 ch, B—Q 2 equalises most easily for Black, but 4.., Kt—B 3; 5 B×Kt ch, P×B; 6 Kt—K 5, Q—B 2; 7 O—O, P—K 3 (Bird—Janowski, Hastings, 1895) leads to White's ideal position in this opening.

(h) 5.., Kt—B 3; 6 B—Kt 5, Q—Kt 3; 7 Q—K 2, B—Q 2; 8 B×Kt, B×B; 9 Kt—K 5, B—K 2; 10 O—O, B—Kt 4. Eliskases—Lichtenstein. Vienna, 1935.

(i) Continued 12 P—Q 4, P×P; 13 P×P, P—Q Kt 4; 14 B—Q 3, B—Kt 2; 15 Q—K 2, Q—Kt 3; 16 Kt—K 4, K Kt×Kt; 17 B×Kt, Q R—Q 1; and the game was soon drawn. Tartakover—Lasker, Nottingham, 1936.

(j) Both 6.., P—K 3 (J. H. Blake) and 6.., P—B 3 (Tartakover) are good alternatives.

Notes ctd. on p. 8.

1 P—KB4

	6	7	8	9	10
1	Kt—KB3..	P—K4 (c)	....		P—KB4
2	P—K3	PxP			P—K4
	P—KKt3	P—Q3			PxP
3	P—QKt3	PxP			P—Q3 (k)
	B—Kt2	BxP			P—K6
4	B—Kt2	Kt—KB3			BxP
	P—Q3	P—KKt4!			Kt—KB3
5	Kt—KB3	P—Q4.................	P—KKt3		P—Q4
	O—O	P—Kt5	P—KR4 (i)		P—K3
6	B—K2	Kt—K5....	Kt—Kt5	P—Q4	B—Q3
	QKt—Q2(a)	BxKt	Q—K2 (f)	P—Kt5	Kt—B3
7	O—O	PxB	Q—Q3	Kt—R4	P—QR3
	P—B4	QxQ ch	P—KB4	B—K2	Kt—K2
8	P—B4	KxQ	P—KR3	Kt—Kt2	Kt—R3
	P—QKt3	Kt—QB3	Kt—QB3 (g)	P—R5	P—QKt3
9	Q—B1	B—Kt5 (d)	PxP	B—B4	O—O
	B—Kt2	KtxP	Kt—Kt5	B—KB4	B—Kt2
10	P—Q3	Kt—B3	Q—QKt3	Kt—B3	Kt—Q2
	KR—K1	B—K3	P—B5	PxP	P—Kt3
11	Kt—B3	P—K3	RxP	BxKtP	B—B2
	P—QR3	P—KB3	RxR	Kt—KB3	B—Kt2
12	P—K4	∓ (e)	QxKt+ (h)	Kt—B4+ (j)	±(l)
	P—K4= (b)				

(a) 6. , P—B4 (6.., Kt—B3; 7 Q—B1?, P—K4!; 8 O—O, PxP; 9 PxP, R—K1; 10 Kt—B3, P—Q4; 11 B—Kt5, B—Q2; 12 BxKt, BxB; 13 Kt—K5?, P—Q5; 14 Kt—K2, Kt—Kt5!+. Miss Menchik—Romanovsky, Moscow,1935); 7 O—O, Kt—B3; 8 P—B4, Q—B2; 9 Q—B1, P—K4; 10 PxP, PxP; 11 P—Q3, B—Kt5; 12 KR—Q1; 13 P—KR3, B—B1; 14 P—K4, Kt—Q5; 15 R—B2, Q—Q3. Eliskases—Miss Menchik, Hastings, 1933-34.

(b) 13 PxP, QKtxP; 14 KtxKt, PxKt; 15 Kt—Q5, B—QB1. Eliskases—Grünfeld, Vienna, 1933.

(c) The From Gambit.

(d) 9 Kt—B3, B—K3; 10 B—Kt5, P—QR3!; 11 P—K4, KtxP; 12 Kt—Q5, BxKt; 13 PxB, P—KR3= (Handbuch). If, however, 9 B—B4, B—K3; 10 P—KR3, KKt—K2; 11 B—QKt5, O—O—O ch; 12 K—B1, B—Q4; 13 R—Kt1, P—QR3; 14 B—K2, B—K3+. Bird—Lasker, match, 1892.

(e) 12 B—R4 and now 12.., O—O—O ch equalises, while if 12.., K—B2; 13 B—Q3, KtxB; 14 PxKt, Kt—K2; 15 Kt—K4, B—B4; 16 R—KB1, KR—KB1; 17 R—B1±. Brinckmann—Tartakover, Kecskemét, 1927.

(f) If 6.., P—KB4; 7 P—K4!(but not 7 P—Q5?, Q—K2; 8 Q—Q4, B—K4; 9 Q—QB4, P—KR3; 10 Kt—K6, BxKt+. Bird and Lee-Mason and Cook, consultation, 1890), P—KR3; 8 P—K5, B—K2; 9 Kt—KR3, PxKt; 10 Q—R5ch, K—B1; 11 B—QB4, Q—K1 (or 11.., R—R2; 12 Q—Kt6, R—Kt2; 13 BxP+. Hromadka—Gilg, Podebrady, 1936); 12 QxP(R3) and White has a strong attack (Smirnoff—Jacobson, 1926).

(g) If 8.., Kt—KB3; 9 P—B3, Kt—B3; 10 PxP, KKtxP; 11 Kt—QR3!, BxKt; 12 PxB, B—Q2; 13 P—Kt3, O—O—O; 14 B—KKt2+. Hromadka—Danielsson, Munich, 1936.

(h) 12.., K—Q2; 13 KtxR, KtxPch; 14 K—Q1, KtxR; 15 P—K4, PxP e.p. 16 BxP+. (Analysis by Alekhine).

Notes ctd. on p.11.

Notes for cols. 6 to 10 ctd.

(*i*) 5. , P—Kt 5 ; 6 Kt—R 4, P—K B 4 (For 6.., B—K 2 ; 7 Kt—Kt 2, P—K R 4, see the column) ; 7 P—K 3, Kt—K 2 ; 8 B—Q 3, Q Kt—B 3 ; 9 O—O, Kt—K 4, 10 Kt×P, Kt×Kt ; 11 B×Kt, Kt—B 6 ch ; 12 R×Kt, P×R ; 13 Q×P, O—O ; 14 Q—Kt 4 ch, K—R 1 ; 15 B×B, R×B. Chekhover—E. Rabinovitch, 1934.

(*j*) 12.., Kt—K 5 ; 13 Kt×Kt, B×Kt ; 14 B—Kt 2+. Hellman—Strautmanis, The Hague, 1928.

(*k*) The alternative is 3 Kt—Q B 3, Kt—K B 3 ; 4 P—K Kt 4 (the Swiss Gambit), P—K Kt 3 (4. , P—K R 3 is also good) ; 5 P—Kt 5, Kt—R 4 ; 6 P—Q 3, P—Q 4 ; 7 B—K 2, Kt—Kt 2 ; 8 P×P, P×P ; 9 Q×Q ch, K×Q ; 10 Kt×P, B—B 4 ; 11 B—Q 3, Kt—Q 2 ; 12 Kt—K B 3, B×Kt ; 13 B×B, Kt—Q B 4. E. Hold—R. Müni, 1913. The position is about even.

(*l*) Continued 12 P—B 3, O—O ; 13 Q—K 2, P—Q R 4 ; 14 P—Q R 4 ? K Kt—Q 4 ; 15 B—R 4, Q—K 1. Pelikan—Alekhine, Podebrady, 1936.

BISHOP'S OPENING

THIS method of development is, in its distinctive variations, a branch of the open game, leading to attractive combination-play without emphasizing the advantage of the move. Black having at his disposal a choice of three good replies in 2..., Kt—K B 3, 2..., B—B 4, and 2..., P—Q B 3. Black should be on his guard against attempts to transpose into prepared variations of other débuts, this being one of the chief characteristics of the Bishop's Opening.

The Berlin Defence, 2..., Kt—K B 3 (cols. 1 to 6), is the one approved by the majority of present-day players, and the most analysed. It gives Black good prospects, should he successfully ward off the various sacrificial attacks White can inaugurate at the cost of a Pawn. The enduring and somewhat cramping attack in col. 1 is adequate compensation for the material given up. The Boden-Kieseritzky Gambit (col. 6) is unsound, White being confronted with an unbreakable barrier of Black Pawns.

The Classical Defence, 2..., B—B 4 (cols. 7 and 8), limits White's opportunity for speculative attack, and yields equality of chances. Black may obtain a safe game without any risks, by the adoption of the defence based on 2..., P—Q B 3 (cols. 9 and 10), a move which forestalls White's intention of building up a Pawn-centre.

Notes for cols. 1 to 5 (p. 13) ctd.

(*k*) Less favourable is 4.., Q—R 5 ch; 5 P—Kt 3, Kt x P; 6 Kt—K B 3, Q—R 4; 7 R—Kt 1, Kt—B 4; 8 R—Kt 5, Q—R 6; 9 B x P ch!, K x B; 10 R—R 5!, Q—Kt 7; 11 R x Kt ch. The column is analysis.

(*l*) Better is 3 ., Kt—B 3; 4 P—B 4, P x P! (but not 4.., P—Q 4; 5 K P x P, Kt x P; 6 P x P, Kt x P; 7 Q—K 2, B—Kt 5 ch; 8 K—B 1+); 5 B x P, P—Q 4! 6 P x P, Kt x P=. 3. , P—Q 4 is inferior because of 4 P x P, Kt x P; 5 Kt—K B 3, Kt—Q B 3; 6 O—O, B—K Kt 5; 7 R—K 1 + (see Two Knights' Defence).

(*m*) 5.., P—Q 4!; 6 K P x P (6 B P x P, Kt x P!), K P x P; 7 B x P, O—O; 8 Kt—Q 2, P x P; 9 B—Q Kt 3, P—Q R 4! (Alekhine).

(*n*) Not 10 P x P, P x P; 11 B x P (Q Kt x P is worse), B—Kt 5!; 12 B—Q B 4, Kt—Kt 3+ (Becker).

(*o*) 13.., P—K Kt 3; 14 K—R 1, Kt—B 4; 15 B—Q 2, P—Q 5; 16 Kt—R 4!. Spielmann—Grüber, Vienna, 1929.

1 P—K 4, P—K 4 ; 2 B—B 4.

	1	2	3	4	5
2	Kt—KB3(a)				
3	P—Q 4			P—B 4	P—Q 3
	P x P			Kt x P (j)	P—B 3 (l)
4	Kt—K B 3			P—Q 3	Q—K 2
	Kt x P	B—B 4	Kt—B 3	Kt—Q 3 (k)	B—K 2
5	Q x P (b)	P—K 5	B—KKt5(h)	B—Kt 3	P—B 4
	Kt—K B 3	P—Q 4	P—K R 3	Kt—B 3	P—Q 3 (m)
6	B—KKt5(c)	P x Kt	B—R 4	Kt—K B 3	Kt—K B 3
	B—K 2	P x B	P—K Kt 4	P x P	Q Kt—Q 2
7	Kt—B 3	Q—K 2 ch	Q B—Kt 3	B x P	Kt—B 3
	Kt—B 3 (d)	B—K 3	P—Q 3	B—K 2	Q—B 2
8	Q—R 4	P x P	O—O	O—O	P—Q R 4
	P—Q 3	R—Kt 1	B—Kt 5	O—O	O—O
9	O—O—O	B—Kt 5	P—B 3	Kt—B 3	P—B 5 !
	B—K 3	B—K 2 (f)	P x P	Kt—B 4	P—Q 4
10	B—Q 3 (A)	B x B	Q Kt x P	P—Q 4	B—R 2 (n)
	Q—Q 2	K x B !	B—Kt 2	P—Q 3	P—Q R 3
11	B—Kt 5	Kt—R 4 !	P—K R 4	P—Q 5	P—K Kt 4 !
	O—O	Q—Q 4	Q—Q 2	Kt—R 4	B—Kt 5
12	Kt—Q 4	P—B 4	R—K 1	B—R 4	P—Kt 5
	P—Q R 3	Kt—B 3 ! (g)	O—O—O (i)	B—Q 2 ∓	Kt—R 4
13	B—Q 3 = (e)				O—O+ (o)

(a) The Berlin Defence.

(b) If 5 O—O, B—K 2 !; 6 R—K 1, P—Q 4.

(c) Or 6 Kt—B 3, Kt—B 3 ; 7 Q—R 4, B—Kt 5 ; 8 O—O, B x Kt ; 9 P x B; O—O ; 10 B—Q 3, Kt—K 2 ; 11 B—K Kt 5, Kt—Kt 3 ; 12 Q—Kt 3, P—Q R 4. Marshall—Torre, New York, 1925.

(d) 7.., O—O ; 8 O—O—O, P—B 3 ; 9 K R—K 1, P—Q 4 ; 10 Q—R 4 Q Kt—Q 2 ; 11 B—Q 3, P—K Kt 3 ; 12 Kt—K 5, Kt—B 4 !. Mieses—von Holzhausen, Duisberg, 1929. Or 7.., P—B 3 ; 8 O—O—O, P—Q 4 ; 9 Q—R 4, B—K 3 ; 10 B—Q 3, Q Kt—Q 2 ; 11 Kt—Q 4, Kt—B 4 ; 12 P—B 4, Kt—Kt 1 ; 13 K R—K 1, K—B ? (Torre—Tholfsen, New York, 1924) ; 14 P—Q Kt 4, Kt x B ch ; 15 R x Kt, Q—Q 3

(A) 10 R—K 1, B x B ; 11 Q x B, O—O ; 12 R—K 3, Kt—Q 2 : 13 P—K R 4 (13 R x B, Kt x R ; 14 R—K 1, R—K 1 ; 15 Kt—Q 5, Kt—Q Kt 3 ! K. Richter), R—K 1 Berlin—Budapest, correspondence, 1938.

(e) 13.., Kt—K 4 ; 14 P—B 4. Mieses—Rubinstein, Breslau, 1912.

(f) 9.., Q—Q 4 ; 10 Kt—B 3 !, P x Kt ; 11 R—Q 1, P x P ; 12 O—O+.

(g) 13 P—B 5, P—Q 6 ; 14 Q—K 3, Kt—Q 5 ; 15 O—O ! and if Kt x Q B P. 16 Q—Kt 3 (analysis by J. H. Morrison). Cp. Max Lange, pp. 106-9.

(h) For 5 Kt—Kt 5 see Two Knights' Defence, pp. 302-4. 5 P—K 5, P—Q 4 6 B—Q Kt 5, Kt—K 5 ; 7 Kt x P, B—Q B 4 ; 8 B—K 3, B—Q 2 ; 9 B x Kt, P x B 10 O—O is Torre—Bigelow, New York, 1925.

(i) Marshall—Smirka, New York, 1925.

(j) Or 3.., P—Q 4 ; 4 K P x P (4 B P x P, Kt x P ; 5 Q—B 3, B—Q B 4 . 6 Kt—K 2, B—B 7 ch ; 7 K—B 1, B—Kt 3 ; 8 B x P, Q x B ; 9 P—Q 3, Q x K P + S. Mlotkowski), Kt x P (4.., P—K 5 ; 5 P—Q 3, B—K Kt 5 ; 6 Kt—K 2, B—Q B 4 7 P—Q 4, B—Q 3 ; 8 O—O+) ; 5 B x Kt (If 5 Q—K 2, Kt x P ; 6 Q x P ch, Kt—K 3, 7 Kt—K B 3, Kt—Q B 3 ; 8 Q—Q B 3, B—Q 3 ; 9 O—O, O—O ; 10 P—B 3, R—K 1 ; 11 Q—B 2, Kt—R 4 ∓), Q x B ; 8 Q—K 2, Kt—Q B 3 ; 7 Kt—Q B 3, Q—K 3 ; 8 P x P, B—B 4 ; 9 Kt—B 3, O—O ; 10 Kt—K 4, B—Kt 3 ; 11 P—B 3, Kt x P ; 12 Kt x Kt, Q x Kt=.

Notes ctd on p. 12.

1 P—K 4, P—K 4 ; 2 B—B 4.

	6	7	8	9	10
2	Kt—K B 3	...B—B 4 (f)	....	P—Q B 3	
3	Kt—K B 3	P—Q B 3 (g)		P—Q 4......	Q—K 2
	Kt×P (a)	P—Q 4 (h)	...Kt—K B 3	P—Q 4	B—B 4
4	Kt—B 3 (b)	B×P	P—Q 4	K P×P	B×P ch (j)
	Kt×Kt	Kt—K B 3	P×P	B P×P	K×B
5	Q P×Kt	Q—B 3	P—K 5	B—Kt 5 ch	Q—B 4 ch
	P—K B 3! (c)	O—O	P—Q 4	B—Q 2	P—Q 4
6	Kt—R 4 (d)	P—Q 4 (i)	P×Kt	B×B ch	Q×B
	P—K Kt 3	P×P	P×B	Kt×B	P×P
7	P—K B 4	B—Kt 5	Q—R 5	P×P	Q×K P
	P—B 3	P×P	O—O	Kt×P	Kt—B 3
8	P—B 5	B×Kt	Q×B	Q—K 2	Kt—K 2
	P—Q 4	P—B 7	R—K 1 ch	Q—K 2	B—Kt 5
9	P×P	Kt—Q B 3	Kt—K 2	Kt—Q B 3	Q Kt—B 3
	P×B	Q×Q B	P—Q 6	O—O—O	R—K 1
10	Q—R 5	Q×Q	B—K 3	B—B 4	Q—K Kt 5
	K—Q 2	P×Q	P×Kt	Kt—Kt 3 ⇌	Q Kt—Q 2
11	P×P	Kt—B 3	Kt—Q 2		O—O
	Q—K 1	P—B 3	Kt—R 3		Kt—K 4
12	Kt—Kt 6	B—Kt 3	Q×P (B 4)		P—Q Kt 3
	K—B 2+ (e)	P—B 4 ⇌	Q×P ⇌		P—Q Kt 4 ∓

(a) For 3.., Kt—B 3 see Two Knights' Defence.

(b) Correct is 4 P—Q 3, with approximate equality. The column is the Boden-Kieseritzky Gambit, sometimes arising from the Vienna Game or Petroff's Defence.

(c) 5.., P—Q 3?; 6 Kt×P, Q—K 2 (6.., P×Kt?; 7 B×P ch+ +); 7 B×P ch, K—Q 1; 8 O—O, Q×Kt; 9 R—K 1+.

(d) 6 O—O, Q—K 2; 7 R—K 1, P—Q 3; 8 Kt—R 4, B—K 3; 9 B—Q 3, Q—B 2; 10 P—K B 4, Kt—Q 2, 11 P—Q Kt 3, O—O—O; 12 P—B 4, Kt—B 4+.

(e) 13 P—K Kt 4, B×P. Analysis by S. Mlotkowski.

(f) 2 , P—K B 4 (the Calabrese Counter-Gambit) is refuted by 3 P—Q 3, Kt—K B 3; 4 P—B 4, P—Q 3; 5 Kt—K B 3, B P×P; 6 Q P×P, B—Kt 5; 7 P×P, B×Kt; 8 Q×B, P×P; 9 Q—Q Kt 3, Q—B 1; 10 B—K Kt 5+. The text is the Classical Defence.

(g) White has the choice of the following alternative lines: (1) 3 Kt—Q B 3 transposes into Vienna Game and 3 Kt—K B 3, Kt—Q B 3 into Vienna Game. (2) 3 P—Q Kt 4, B×P; 4 P—B 4 (4 P—Q B 3, B—R 4; 5 Kt—B 3, Kt—Q B 3 leads to the Evans Gambit), P—Q 4 (4 ., P×P, known as M'Donnell's Double Gambit, gives White a very strong attack by 5 Kt—K B 3, B—K 2; 6 P—Q 4, B—R 5 ch; 7 P—Kt 3, P×P; 8 O—O, P×P ch; 9 K—R 1, P—Q 4); 5 K P×P, P—K 5; 6 Kt—K 2, Kt—K B 3; 7 O—O, O—O; 8 Q Kt—B 3, P—B 3; 9 P×P, Kt×P. (3) 3 P—Q 4, B×P (not 3 , P×P; 4 B×P ch!); 4 Kt—K B 3, Kt—Q B 3+. (4) 3 Q—Kt 4, K—B 1 (or 3 ., P—K Kt 3; 4 Q—Kt 3 or 3 , Q—B 3; 4 Kt—Q B 3!, Q×P ch; 5 K—Q 1+); 4 Q—Kt 3, Kt—Q B 3; 5 Kt—Q B 3, as in the Vienna Game.

(h) The Lewis Counter Gambit. If 4 P×P, B×P ch!.

(i) Handbuch, 1913, gives 6 B—B 4, B—K Kt 5; 7 Q—Q 3, Q—K 2; 8 Q—B 2, B—K 3; 9 B×B, P×B; 10 Kt—B 3, Kt—B 3; 11 P—Q 3, Kt—K Kt 5; 12 R—B 1 (if 12 O—O, R×Kt, 13 P×R, Q—R 5 draws at least) as in favour of White, but Black seems to have the better game after 12.., R×Kt; 13 P×R, Kt×R P; 14 R—K 1, Q—R 5!; 15 Q—K 2, B×P ch; 16 K—Q 1, Q—Kt 6. This and the next two columns are analysis.

(j) 4 Kt—K B 3 is safest for White, leading to equality. The column is analysis in Handbuch, 1913.

CARO-KANN DEFENCE

THIS reply to 1 P—K 4 has had numerous fluctuations in favour with the masters. We wrote in 1925 that, after being held for a considerable time the best of the irregular replies, it had fallen into desuetude again, while in 1932 we wrote that it had once more taken its place as a fairly frequent resource for Black in master-play. With the introduction of the Panoff-Botvinnik Attack at the end of 1933 the defence again passed through a critical period. However, at the end of the following year it returned to the tournament arena, and there are now many who consider it the best of the irregular defences to 1 P—K 4.

The Caro-Kann has the superiority over the other defences that the development of Black's Queen's Bishop is not obstructed (as in the French Defence), that there are few main variations, and that it is almost impossible for White to build up a strong attack. On the other hand, P—Q B 3 does not attack an important centre point (as does the Sicilian, P—Q B 4), nor does it facilitate the development of an important piece (as does the French, P—K 3). Consequently, if White develops naturally, Black is often burdened with a lifeless position.

Normally the game opens 1 P—K 4, P—Q B 3; 2 P—Q 4, P—Q 4, when White has four continuations :—

(i) 3 Kt—Q B 3 (cols. 1 to 10). Black has the choice for his 4th move of Kt—B 3 or B—B 4; Kt—Q 2 (col. 10) being practically a sub-variation of Kt—B 3. 4..., Kt—B 3 (the older line) is now rarely seen. After 5 Kt × Kt ch Black remains with a theoretical disadvantage, although White's superiority is seldom of great weight in practice. 4..., B—B 4 (cols. 6 to 9) has had the support of Flohr for many years. In the best variation (cols. 6 and 7) White retains the initiative throughout the whole game. The attack in col. 9 is based on Russian analysis. It can lead to a wild game, and may be recommended for those who are fond of enterprising chess.

(ii) 3 P × P (the Exchange Variation) now has 12 columns devoted to it instead of the three in our last edition. This is due to the Panoff-Botvinnik attack (cols. 11 to 19), where it is by no means easy for Black to maintain equality. It is advisable for the second player, as in col. 18, to give up the centre at an early stage and maintain control of his Q 4; this manœuvre takes most of the sting out of White's attack. Against the older continuation in the Exchange Variation, where White omits the attack on Black's centre by P—Q B 4 (cols. 20 and 22), Black has no difficulty in equalising.

(iii) 3 P—K 5 (cols. 23 and 24) is weak for the first player, who is often hard pressed to maintain equality.

(iv) 3 P—K B 3 (cols. 25 and 26), advocated by Tartakover, involves some very tricky play. The second player must not accept the Pawn-sacrifice (col. 25), but should develop quietly, as in col. 26. This leads to a kind of French Defence, where Black's position is satisfactory.

2 P—Q B 4 (cols. 27 and 28) has been successfully played in recent tournaments. Against this move it is not easy for Black to develop harmoniously, and the variation will doubtless receive a good deal of attention in the next few years. 2 Kt—Q B 3 (cols. 29 and 30) avoids the more regular lines, but leads to no advantage for White.

Notes for cols. 1 to 5 (p. 17) ctd.

(h) 8. , Q—K 2 ; 9 Q×Q ch, B×Q ; 10 K Kt—B 5 would leave White with the advantage of the two Bishops. The column is Alekhine—Tartakover, Kecskemet, 1927.

(i) Black's only good line is 9.., O—O ; 10 O—O—O, Q—R 4 ; 11 K—Kt 1, Kt—Q 4 (Alekhine).

(j) Best. Alternatives are (1) 5.., B—Kt 5 ; 6 Q—Q 3, Q Kt—Q 2 ; 7 P—K R 3, ᵭ—R 4 ; 8 Kt×B, Kt×Kt ; 9 Kt—B 3, P—K 3 ; 10 P—K Kt 3, B—Q 3 ; 11 B—Kt 2±. Spielmann—Capablanca, New York, 1927. (2) 5.., P—K R 4 ; 6 P—K R 4, B—Kt 5 ; 7 B—K 2, B×B ; 8 K Kt×B, Q Kt—Q 2 ; 9 Q—Q 3 ±. Spielmann—Alekhine, Carlsbad, 1911. Not, however, 6 B—K Kt 5, P—R 5 ; 7 B×Kt, P×Kt ; 8 B—K 5 R×P ; 9 R×R, Q—R 4 ch ; 10 P—Q B 3, Q×B ch ; 11 P×Q, P×R+ +. A game won by Torre.

(k) Spielmann—Hönlinger, Vienna, 1929. 12.., B—Kt 2 equalises.

1 P—K 4, P—Q B 3 ; 2 P—Q 4, P—Q 4 ; 3 Kt—Q B 3, P×P ;
    4 Kt×P (A), Kt—B 3.

	1	2	3	4	5
5	Kt×Ktch (B)			Kt—Kt 3	
	K P×Kt................		Kt P×Kt	P—K 4.....	P—K 3 (j)
6	B—Q B 4....P—Q B 3		P—Q B 3 (e)	Kt—B 3	Kt—B 3
	B—Q 3	B—Q 3	B—B 4	P×P	P—B 4
7	Q—K 2 ch	B—Q 3	Kt—K 2	Kt×P (g)	B—Q 3
	B—K 2 (a)	Q—K 2 ch (c)	P—K 3	B—Q B 4	Kt—B 3
8	Kt—B 3	Q—K 2	Kt—Kt 3	Q—K 2 ch	P×P
	O—O	B—K 3	B—Kt 3	B—K 2 (h)	B×P
9	O—O	Kt—B 3	P—K R 4	B—K 3	P—Q R 3
	B—Q 3	Kt—Q 2	P—K R 3	P—B 4 (i)	O—O
10	R—K 1	O—O	B—Q 3	K Kt—B 5	O—O
	P—Q Kt 4	O—O	B×B	O—O	P—Q Kt 3
11	B—Q 3	R—K 1	Q×B	Q—B 4	P—Q Kt 4
	Kt—R 3	K R—K 1	Kt—Q 2	R—K 1	B—K 2
12	P—Q R 4	Q—K 4	Q—B 3	B—Q 3	B—Kt 2 (k)
	Kt—Kt 5	Kt—B 1	Q—R 4	P—Q Kt 3	
13	P×P	B—K B 4	Kt—K 4	O—O—O	
	Kt×B	Kt—Kt 3	Q—Q 4	B—R 3	
14	Q×Kt	B×B	B—B 4	Kt—R 6 ch+	
	P×P	Q×B	O—O—O		
15	= (b)	Kt—R 4	Kt—Q 6 ch		
		B—Q 2	B×Kt (f)		
		= (d)			

(A) The gambit 4 P—B 3, P×P ; 5 Kt×P, B—Kt 5 ; 6 B—Q B 4, P—K 3 gives White some attack. 4 B—Q B 4, Kt—B 3 ; 5 P—B 3, P—K 6 ; 6 B×K P, B—B 4 ; 7 K Kt—K 2, P—K 3 ; 8 P—K Kt 4, B—Kt 3 ; 9 P—K R 4, P—K R 3 is J. H. O. v. d. Bosch—Flohr, match, 1932.

(B) A gambit alternative which is difficult for Black to meet is 5 B—Q 3 !, Q×P ; 6 Kt—K B 3, Q—Q 1 ; 7 Q—K 2, Kt×Kt ; 8 B×Kt, Kt—Q 2 (better is 8.., B—B 4 ; 9 B×B, Q—R 4 ch ; 10 B—Q 2, Q×B ; 11 O—O—O, Kt—Q 2) ; 9 O—O, Kt—B 4 ; 10 R—Q 1, Q—B 2 ; 11 Kt—K 5. Alekhine—Winter, Hastings, 1936-37.

(a) Best. The exchange of Queens is in favour of White because of his Pawn majority on the Queen's side.

(b) 15 Q×P, Q—B 2 ; 16 Q—Q 3, B—Kt 2 ; 17 P—Q 5, K R—B 1 ; 18 P—B 3, P—Q R 4 ; 19 B—K 3, P—R 5 ; 20 K R—Q 1, R—R 4. Nimzovitch—Réti, Berlin, 1928.

(c) If 7.., O—O ; 8 Q—B 2, P—K Kt 3 ; 9 Kt—K 2, Q—B 2 ; 10 P—K R 4, R—K 1 ; 11 P—R 5 ±. Znosko-Borovsky—Tartakover, Paris, 1925.

(d) 16 Kt—B 5, Q—B 1. Mattison—Sterk, Paris, 1924.

(e) Or 6 P—K Kt 3, B—B 4 ; 7 B—Kt 2, P—K 3 ; 8 Kt—K 2, Kt—Q 2 ; 9 O—O, Kt—Kt 3 ; 10 P—Q Kt 3, B—Q 3 ; 11 P—Q B 4, B—B 2 ; 12 B—K 3, Q—Q 2 ; 13 P—Q R 4, P—Q R 4 ; 14 R—R 2, Kt—B 1 ; 15 R—Q 2 ±. H. H. Cole—Winter, Hastings, 1919.

(f) 16 Q×Q, K P×Q=. Lövenfisch—Zubareff, Moscow, 1925.

(g) Weaker is 7 Q×P, Q×Q ; 8 Kt×Q, B—Q B 4 ; 9 K Kt—B 5, O—O ; 10 B—K 3, B×B ; 11 Kt×B, B—K 3 ; 12 O—O—O, Q Kt—Q 2 ; 13 B—B 4, Kt—B 4 ; 14 B×B=. Alekhine—Capablanca, New York, 1927.

Notes ctd. on p. 16.

1 P—K 4, P—Q B 3; 2 P—Q 4, P—Q 4; 3 Kt—Q B 3, P×P; 4 Kt×P.

	6	7	8	9	10
4	B—B 4				Kt—Q 2
5	Kt—Kt 3 B—Kt 3				Kt—K B 3 K Kt—B 3
6	P—K R 4 .... P—K R 3		Kt—B 3 (d) Kt—Q 2	Kt—R 3 P—K 3 (e)	Kt—Kt 3 P—K 3
7	Kt—B 3 (A) Kt—Q 2		B—Q 3 P—K 3	Kt—B 4 Q—R 5	B—Q 3 P—B 4
8	B—Q 3 (B) B×B		O—O K Kt—B 3	Kt×B (f) R P×Kt	P—B 3 (i) B—K 2
9	Q×B P—K 3		R—K 1 Q—B 2	Q—Q 3 Kt—Q 2	O—O O—O
10	B—Q 2 K Kt—B 3		P—B 4 B—Kt 5	Kt—K 4 Q—Q 1 !	Kt—K 5 P×P
11	O—O—O Q—B 2		R—K 2 B×B	B—K 2 Q Kt—B 3	P×P Kt—Kt3
12	K—Kt 1 ..... B—Q 3 (a)	K R—K 1 B—Q 3	Q×B O—O	Kt×Ktch (g) P×Kt	B—K Kt 5 Q Kt—Q 4
13	Kt—K 4 Kt×Kt	Kt—K 4 Kt×Kt	P—B 5 B—R 4	B—Q 2 Q—B 2	R—B 1 (j)
14	Q×Kt Kt—B 3	Q×Kt Kt—B 3	R—Kt 1 Q—Q 1	P—K Kt 3 O—O—O	
15	Q—K 2 ± (b)	Q—K 2 = (c)	=	∓ (h)	

(A) 7 Kt—R 3, threatening 8 Kt—B 4, is refuted by 7.., P—K 4 (Capablanca).

(B) An almost forgotten line, which is nevertheless quite strong, is 8 P—R 5, B—R 2; 9 B—Q 3, B×B; 10 Q×B, P—K 3; 11 B—Q 2, K Kt—B 3; 12 O—O—O, B—Q 3; 13 Q R—K 1, B×Kt; 14 P×B, O—O; 15 R—R 4 ±. Chajes—Réti, Carlsbad, 1923.

(a) Better is 12.., O—O—O; 13 P—B 4, P—B 4; 14 B—B 3, P—Q R 3; 15 Q—K 2, B—Q 3; 16 Kt—K 4, Kt×Kt; 17 Q×Kt, Kt—B 3; 18 Q—K 2, P×P; 19 Kt×P, B—B 4=.

(b) Continued 15.., O—O—O; 16 P—B 4, P—B 4; 17 B—B 3, K—Kt 1; 18 K R—K 1, P×P; 19 Kt×P. Maróczy—Keres, Zandvoort, 1936.

(c) 15. , B—B 5; 16 Kt—K 5, B×B ch. Spielmann—Capablanca, New York, 1927.

(d) If 6 P—K B 4, P—K 3; 7 Kt—B 3, B—Q 3; 8 B—Q 3, Kt—K 2; 9 O—O, Kt—Q 2; 10 K—R 1, Q—B 2; 11 Kt—K 5, R—Q 1; 12 Q—K 2, B×B=. Marshall—Capablanca, New York, 1927. The column is Kashdan—Flohr, London, 1932.

(e) Or 6.., Kt—Q 2; 7 Kt—B 4, P—K 4! (also good is 7.., K Kt—B 3; 8 P—K R 4, P—K 4 for if 9 P×P, Kt×P; 10 Q—K 2, Q—K 2; 11 P—R 5?, B×B P!); 8 Kt×B, R P×Kt; 9 P×P, Q—R 5!; 10 P—K 6, P×P; 11 Q—K 2, O—O—O!; 12 B—Q 2, K Kt—B 3; 13 O—O—O, B—B 4!; 14 B—K 3, Kt—Kt 5+. L. Steiner—Opocensky, Lodz, 1935.

(f) If 8 Q—K 2, Kt—Q 2!; 9 P—Q B 3, O—O—O; 10 Kt×B, R P×Kt, 11 Kt—K 4, Q—K 2; 12 B—Kt 5, Q Kt—B 3; 13 O—O—O, Q—B 2; 14 Q—B 3; Q—R 4; 15 K B—B 4, B—K 2=. Ragosin—Flohr, Moscow, 1935.

(g) Better was 12 Kt—Kt 5, Q—B 2; 13 Kt—B 3, with a slight advantage for White (Bogatyrchuk).

(h) Continued 15 Q—B 4, B—R 3!; 16 O—O—O, B×B ch; 17 R×B, Kt—K 2; 18 B—B 3, Kt—Q B 3. Bogatyrchuk—Flohr, Moscow, 1935.

(i) 8 P×P transposes to col. 5.

(j) Becker—Döry, Vienna, 1928. White has some attacking chances on the King's side.

1 P—K4, P—QB3; 2 P—Q4, P—Q4; 3 P×P, P×P; 4 P—QB4 (A), Kt—KB3; 5 Kt—QB3, Kt—B3.

	11	12	13	14	15
6	B—Kt5				Kt—B3
	P×P		P—K3 (g)		B—Kt5
7	P—Q5		Kt—B3 (h)..	P—B5	B—K2
	Kt—K4....Kt—QR4		P×P	B—K2	P—K3 (m)
8	Q—Q4	Kt—B3! (e)	B×P	B—Kt5	P—B5
	Kt—Q6 ch	P—K3	B—K2	O—O	Kt—K5! (n)
9	B×Kt	Kt—K5!	O—O	Kt—B3 (k)	P—KR3
	P×B	P×P	O—O	Kt—K5	B×Kt
10	Kt—B3 (a)	Q—R4 ch	R—B1	B×B	B×B
	P—KKt3 (b)	Kt—B3	P—QR3	Kt×B	Kt×Kt
11	B×Kt	O—O—O	B—Q3 (i)	R—QB1	P×Kt
	P×B	B—K2	P—KR3	P—QKt3!	B—K2
12	O—O	Kt×Kt	B—R4 (j)	P—QKt4	O—O
	B—K2 (c)	P×Kt	R—K1	P—QR4	O—O
13	QR—Q1	B×Kt	P—QR3	P—QR3	R—K1
	O—O	B×B	Kt—Q4	P×KtP	P—QKt3
14	R×P	Q×P ch	B—Kt3	RP×P	P×P
	B—KB4	B—Q2	Kt×Kt	P×P	P×P
15	R—Q2	Q×QP+ (f)	R×Kt	QP×P	B—K2
	B—Q3		B—B3	Kt×Kt	B—Q3
16	P—KKt4!		B—K5!±	R×Kt	B—Q3
	+ (d)			R—Kt1+	Q—R5
			(l)		=

(A) The Panoff—Botvinnik Attack, which almost demolished the whole defence in 1931-35.

(a) A decided improvement on 10 B×Kt, KP×B!; 11 Q×QP, B—Q3; 12 K Kt—K2, O—O; 13 O—O, R—K1!; 14 QR—Q1, B—K Kt5=. Botvinnik—Flohr, 1st match game, 1933.

(b) Other possibilities are likewise unsatisfactory, e.g. 10., P—KR3; 11 B×Kt, KP×B; 12 O—O, B—K2; 13 Kt—K4, Q—Kt3; 14 Q×QP+. Znosko-Borovsky—B. Reilly, Nice, 1934. Or 10.., P—K3; 11 B×Kt, Q×B; 12 Q×P, with a great advantage in development for White.

(c) Easier to refute is 12.., Q—Kt3; 13 KR—K1 ch, K—Q1; 14 Q—KR4!+. Botvinnik—Flohr, 9th match game, 1933.

(d) 16.., B—B1; 17 Kt—K4 with an overwhelming position. Analysis by Botvinnik.

(e) White must continue as aggressively as possible. If 8 B×P, Kt×B; 9 Q—R4 ch, B—Q2; 10 Q×Kt, P—Kt4!; 11 Q—K2, Q—Kt3!; 12 R—Q1, P—Kt5; 13 Kt—K4, Kt×Kt; 14 Q×Kt, P—K3=. Pitschak—Herzog, Liebwerda, 1934.

(f) Analysis by Yudovitch.

(g) 6. ; Q—Kt3 is met by 7 P×P, and if 7.., Q×Kt P?; 8 R—B1!, Kt—Q Kt5?; 9 Kt—R4!, Q×RP; 10 B—QB4, B—Kt5; 11 Kt—B3, Resigns! Botvinnik—Spielmann, Moscow, 1935. However, 7.., Q Kt×P; 8 B—K3, P—K4; 9 P×P e.p., B—B4 gives Black a strong attack at the cost of a Pawn. Best for White on 7.., Q Kt×P is 8 K Kt—K2!, when he is better developed.

(h) If 7 P×P, P×P; 8 B×Kt, Q×B; 9 Kt×P, Q—Q1; 10 Kt—QB3, Q×P; 11 Q×Q, Kt×Q; 12 O—O—O, B—QB4=.

Notes ctd. on p. 23.

1 P—K 4, P—Q B 3 ; 2 P—Q 4, P—Q 4 ; 3 P×P, P×P.

	16	17	18	19	20
4	(P—Q B 4)				B—Q 3 (j)
	(Kt—K B 3)				Q Kt—B 3
5	(Kt—Q B 3)				P—Q B 3
	(Kt—B 3)		P×P	P—K Kt 3	Kt—B 3
6	Kt—B 3		B×P	Q—Kt 3 !	B—K B 4
	B—Kt 5 (A)		P—K 3	B—Kt 2	B—Kt 5
7	P×P		Kt—B 3	P×P	Q—Kt 3
	K Kt×P		P—Q R 3	O—O	Kt—Q R 4
8	B—Q Kt 5...	Q—Kt 3	P—Q R 4 (f)	B—Q B 4 (h)	Q—R 4 ch
	R—B 1 (a)	B×Kt	Kt—B 3	Q Kt—Q 2	B—Q 2
9	P—K R 3	P×B	O—O	K Kt—K 2	Q—B 2
	B×Kt	P—K 3 (c)	B—K 2	Kt—Kt 3	Q—Kt 3
10	Q×B	Q×P	B—K 3	O—O	Kt—B 3 (k)
	P—K 3	Kt×P	O—O	Kt×B	P—K 3
11	O—O	B—Kt 5 ch	R—B 1	Q×Kt	O—O
	P—Q R 3	Kt×B	Q Kt—Kt 5	P—Kt 3	B—Kt 4
12	Kt×Kt	Q—B 6 ch	Kt—K 5	B—Kt 5	Q Kt—Q 2
	Q×Kt	K—K 2	K Kt—Q 4	B—Kt 2	B×B
13	Q×Q	Q×Kt (Kt 5)	Q—B 3	Kt—B 4	Q×B=(l)
	P×Q	Kt×Kt (d)	P—K B 3	Q—Q 2	
14	B—R 4	P×Kt	Kt—Q 3	K R—K 1	
	B—K 2 (b)	Q—Q 4 (e)	Kt (Kt 5) ×	K R—Q 1	
			= Kt (g)	=(i)	

(A) 6 , B—K 3; 7 P—B 5, P—K Kt 3; 8 B—Q Kt 5, B—Kt 2; 9 Kt—K 5, Q—B 1 ; 10 Q—R 4, B—Q 2; 11 O—O, O—O; 12 B—K B 4, P—Q R 3; 13 B×Kt±. Dake—Alekhine, Pasadena, 1932.

(a) In the sensational game Nimzovitch—Alekhine, Bled, 1931, 8.., Q—R 4 led to a quick victory for Black after 9 Q—Kt 3, B×Kt; 10 P×B, Kt×Kt; 11 B×Kt ch ?, P×B; 12 Q—Kt 7 ?, Kt—Q 4 dis ch; 13 B—Q 2, Q—Kt 3; 14 Q×R ch, K—Q 2 followed by .., Kt—B 2. But Alekhine himself later refuted 8.., Q—R 4; by 9 Q—Kt 3, B×Kt; 10 P×B, Kt×Kt; 11 P×Kt, P—K 3; 12 O—O+. Alekhine—Winter, London, 1932.

(b) Continued 15 B—K 3, B—Q 3; 16 B—Kt 3, Kt—K 2. Krause—Nimzovitch, correspondence, 1924-25.

(c) 9 , Kt×Kt; 10 Q×P !, Kt×Q P; 11 P×Kt+ (Panoff). If 9 ., Kt×P?; 10 B—Kt 5 ch wins a piece.

(d) If 13. , Q—Q 2; 14 Kt×Kt ch, P×Kt; 15 Q—K 2 ch, Q—K 3; 16 B—K 3, P—K B 3; 17 R—Q B 1 with the better ending. Panoff Sergeieff, Moscow, 1930.

(e) 15 Q×Q, P×Q; 16 R--Kt 1. Analysis by Becker. White has a minimal advantage.

(f) The opening transposes to a Queen's Gambit Accepted.

(g) Alekhine—Tartakover, Paris, 1925.

(h) Better is B—K 2—B 3, with advantage for White.

(i) Alekhine—Euwe, Berne, 1932.

(j) This must be played as soon as possible. Inferior, e.g. is 4 P—Q B 3, Kt—Q B 3; 5 B—K B 4, B—B 4; 6 Kt—B 3, P—K 3; 7 Q—Kt 3 (better 7 B—Q 3=), Q—Q 2; 8 Q Kt—Q 2, P—B 3; 9 B—K 2, P—K Kt 4 !; 10 B—Kt 3, P—K R 3, K Kt—K 2; 12 O—O, B—R 3 !+. Spielmann—Nimzovitch, Carlsbad, 1923.

(k) Or 10 Kt—Q 2, B—Kt 4; 11 K Kt—B 3, B×B; 12 Q×B, P—K 3=. Maróczy—Nimzovitch, Bled, 1931.

(l) Maróczy—Capablanca, Lake Hopatcong, 1926.

1 P—K 4, P—Q B 3 ; 2 P—Q 4, P—Q 4.

	21	22	23	24	25
3	(P × P)		P—K 5		P—K B 3
	(P × P)		B—B 4		P × P ?
4	(B—Q 3)		B—Q 3 (*i*)		P × P
	(Kt—Q B 3)		B × B		P—K 4
5	(P—Q B 3)		Q × B		Kt—K B 3
	Kt—B 3		P—K 3		P × P
6	B—K B 4 (*a*)		Kt—Q B 3...	Kt—K 2 (*k*)	B—Q B 4
	B—Kt 5	P—K Kt 3	Q—Kt 3	Q—Kt 3	B—K 2 (*n*)
7	Kt—B 3 (*b*)	Kt—B 3	K Kt—K 2	O—O	O—O !
	P—K 3 (*c*)	B—Kt 2	P—Q B 4	P—Q B 4	Kt—B 3
8	Q—Kt 3 (*d*)	P—K R 3 (*f*)	P × P	P—Q B 3	Kt—Kt 5
	Q—B 1	B—B 4 (*g*)	B × P	Q Kt—B 3	O—O
9	Q Kt—Q 2	O—O	O—O	Kt—Q 2	Kt × B P
	B—K 2	B × B	Kt—K 2	R—B 1 (*l*)	R × Kt
10	O—O	Q × B	Kt—R 4	Kt—B 3	B × R ch
	O—O	O—O	Q—B 3	P × P !	K × B
11	P—K R 3	Q Kt—Q 2	Kt × B	K Kt × P	P—K 5
	B—R 4	Q—Kt 3 !	Q × Kt	B—B 4	K—Kt 1
12	Q R—K 1	Q R—Kt 1	B—K 3	Kt—Kt 3	P × Kt
	B—Kt 3	Q R—B 1	Q—B 2	K Kt—K 2	B × P
13	B × B	K R—K 1	P—K B 4	Kt × B	Kt—Q 2
	R P × B	K R—K 1	Kt—B 4	Q × Kt	B—K 3
14	Kt—K5 ± (*e*)	Kt—K 5	P—B 3	K R—K 1	Kt—K 4
		P—K 3 (*h*)	Q Kt—B 3	Kt—Kt 3	+ (*o*)
	—		∓ (*j*)	= (*m*)	

(*a*) If 6 Kt—K 2, B—Kt 5 ; 7 O—O, P—K 3 ; 8 P—B 3, B—R 4 ; 9 Kt—Kt 3, B—Kt 3 ; 10 P—B 4, B × B ; 11 Q × B, B—Q 3 ; 12 Q—K 2, Q—B 2 ∓. Lilienthal—Flohr, Ujpest, 1934. And if 6 P—K R 3, P—K 4! ; 7 P × P, Kt × P ; 8 Q—K 2, Q—K 2 ; 9 B—Kt 5 ch, B—Q 2 ; 10 B—K 3, B × B ; 11 Q × B ch, Q—Q 2=. Wagner—Nimzovitch, Breslau, 1925.

(*b*) 7 Q—Kt 3, Kt—R 4 transposes to. col. 20.

(*c*) Passive play is disadvantageous for Black. Correct is 7.., Q—Kt 3 ! ; *e.g.* 8 Q—Kt 3, B × Kt ; 9 P × B, P—K 3 ; 10 Kt—Q 2, Kt—Q 2 ; 11 R—K Kt 1, P—Kt 3 ; 12 P—Q R 4, O—O—O ; 13 O—O—O, B—Kt 2=. P. S. Milner-Barry—Flohr, Hastings, 1934-35.

(*d*) Better than 8 Q Kt—Q 2, B—Q 3 ; 9 B × B, Q × B ; 10 P—K R 3, B—R 4 ; 11 Q—K 2, P—Q R 3 ; 12 O—O, O—O ; 13 Q—K 3, B × Kt ; 14 Kt × B, Kt—Q 2=. Spielmann—Capablanca, Moscow, 1925.

(*e*) P. S. Milner-Barry—Znosko-Borovsky, Tenby, 1928.

(*f*) Or 8 Q Kt—Q 2, B—B 4 ; 9 B × B, P × B ; 10 Kt—K 5, Q—Kt 3 ; 11 O—O !, O—O= ; 12 Kt—Kt 3, P—K 3 ; 13 Q—K 2, K R—Q 1 ; 14 Kt—B 5, Kt × Kt ; 15 B × Kt, Kt—K 5 ! ∓. Spielmann—Sämisch, Berlin, 1920.

(*g*) 8 , O—O ; 9 Q Kt—Q 2, P—Q R 3 ; 10 O—O, Kt—K R 4 ; 11 B—R 2 is not advisable for Black (H. Steiner—Kashdan, Györ, 1930). Similarly, 8 ., Kt—K 5 is weak, because of 9 Q Kt—Q 2, O—O, O—O ; 11 Kt—K 5!, Kt × Kt ; 12 B × Kt, B × B ; 13 P × B, Kt × Kt ; 14 Q × Kt, P—B 5 ; 15 Q R—Q 1+. Lasker—Tartakover, Mährisch-Ostrau, 1923.

(*h*) Bogatyrchuk—Tartakover, Moscow, 1925. The order of moves has been changed somewhat.

Notes ctd. on p. 23.

B

1 P—K 4, P—Q B 3.

	26	27	28	29	30
2	(P—Q 4)	....P—Q B 4	....	Kt—Q B 3	
	(P—Q 4)	P—Q 4	......P—K 4	P—Q 4	
3	(P—K B 3)	K P×P	Kt—KB3(e)	Kt—B 3	
	P—K 3	P×P	P—Q 3	P×P (g)	
4	B—K 3	P×P	P—Q 4	Kt×P	
	Kt—B 3	Kt—KB3(c)	B—Kt 5	B—Kt 5 (h)	..Kt—B 3
5	Kt—B 3	B—Kt 5 ch	Kt—B 3	Kt—Kt 3	Kt—Kt 3 (j)
	B—Kt 5 (a)	Q Kt—Q 2	Q Kt—Q 2	Kt—B 3	P—B 4
6	P—K 5	Q Kt—B 3	B—K 2	B—K 2	P—Q 4
	K Kt—Q 2	P—K Kt 3	Kt—B 3	P—K 3	P×P
7	P—B 4	Kt—B 3	O—O	Kt—K 5	Q×P
	P—Q B 4	B—Kt 2	B—K 2	B×B	Q×Q
8	Kt—B 3	P—Q 6!	B—K 3	Q×B	Kt×Q
	Kt—Q B 3	P×P	O—O	Q—Q 4	P—Q R 3
9	P—Q R 3	O—O	Kt—Q 2	Kt—B 3	B—K 2
	P×P	O—O	B×B	P—B 4	B—Kt 5
10	Kt×P	P—Q 4	Q×B	P—Q 3	B—Q 3
	B—B 4	P—K R 3	Q—R 4	Kt—B 3	P—K 4
11	Q—Q 2	B—K B 4	P—K Kt 4	O—O	Kt(Q4)—B5
	P—Q R 3	Kt—Kt 3	P×P	B—K 2	P—K Kt 3
12	Q—B 2	Q—Q 2	Kt—Kt3 ± (f)	B—Q 2	Kt—K 3
	Q—R 4= (b)	± (d)		O—O= (i)	Q Kt—Q2 ■
					(k)

(a) Or 5.., B—K 2; 6 P—K 5, K Kt—Q 2; 7 P—B 4, P—Q B 4; 8 Kt—B 3, Kt—Q B 3; 9 B—Kt 5, Q—Kt 3; 10 O—O, O—O; 11 K—R 1, P—Q R 3=. Torre—Fine, Monterrey, 1934.

(b) 13 Kt—Kt 3, B×B; 14 Q×B, Q—Kt 3; 15 Q×Q, Kt×Q; 16 O—O—O. Kostich—Pirc, Bled, 1931.

(c) 4.., Q×P; 5 Kt—Q B 3, Q—Q R 4 (5.., Q—Q 1 is simpler, leading to a variation of the Q.G.D.); 6 B—B 4, Kt—K B 3; 7 Kt—B 3, P—K 3; 8 O—O, B—K 2; 9 P—Q 4, O—O; 10 B—B 4 ±. L. Steiner—Carls, The Hague, 1928. A strong alternative is 4 , P—Q R 3; 5 Q—Kt 3, Kt—K B 3; 6 Kt—Q B 3, Q Kt—Q 2; 7 B—K 2 (L. Steiner—Flohr, Hastings, 1932-33), and now 7.., Kt—B 4!; 8 Q—B 4, P—K 3; 9 B—B 3, P×P; 10 Kt×P, B—K 3 with a good attack (Flohr).

(d) 12.., P—R 3; 13 B—Q 3, K—R 2; 14 P—K R 3, B—K 3; 15 K R—K 1, Q—Q 2; 16 B—R 2. Alekhine—Feigin, Kemeri, 1937.

(e) Or 3 P—Q 4, P—Q 3; 4 Kt—Q B 3, Q—B 2; 5 B—K 2, B—K 2; 6 B—K 3, Kt—B 3; 7 P—K R 3, O—O; 8 Kt—B 3, Q Kt—Q 2; 9 O—O, R—K 1; 10 R—B 1, B—B 1; 11 Q—B 2, P—K Kt 3; 12 P—Q 5, Kt—R 4; 13 Q—Q 2, Kt—Kt 2; 14 P—K Kt 4±. C. H. Alexander—Flohr, Hastings, 1937-38.

(f) 12.., Q—R 3; 13 Kt×P, Kt—K 4; 14 P—Kt 5. Mikenas—Flohr, Hastings, 1937-38.

(g) 3. , Kt—B 3; 4 P—K 5, Kt—K 5; 5 Q—K 2, Kt×Kt; 6 Q P×Kt, P—Q Kt 3; 7 Kt—Q 4, P—Q B 4? (7 , P—K 3 is necessary); 8 P—K 6! and wins. Spielmann—Walter, Trentschin-Teplitz, 1928.

(h) Weak is 4 , B—B 4?; 5 Kt—Kt 3, B—Kt 3; 6 P—K R 4, P—K R 3; 7 Kt—K 5, B—R 2; 8 Q—R 5, P—K Kt 3; 9 Q—B 3, Kt—B 3. Lasker—Muller, Zürich, 1934. And now 10 B—B 4, P—K 3; 11 P—Q 4! is overwhelming.

(i) Lasker—Flohr, Zürich, 1934.

(j) If 5 Kt×Kt ch, K P×Kt; 6 P—Q 4, B—Q 3; 7 B—Q 3, O—O; 8 O—O, B—K Kt 5; 9 P—K R 3, B—R 4; 10 B—K 3, Kt—Q 2=. Ragosin—Flohr, Semmering-Baden, 1937.

(k) 13 Kt—K4, B—Kt 5 ch; 14 P—B 3, B—K 2. Sir G. A. Thomas—Nimzovitch, Frankfurt, 1930. A typical Nimzovitch game with its restraining moves 5, 8 and 13.

B *

Notes for cols. 11 to 15 ctd.

(*i*) 11 P—Q R 3, P—Kt 4 ; 12 B—R 2, B—Kt 2 ; 13 Q—Q 3, Kt—Q 4 ; 14 Kt—K 4 ? (14 B—Kt 1 !, P—Kt 3 ; 15 B—R 6, R—K 1 ; 16 Kt—K 4 with a strong attack), Kt (B 3)—Kt 5 !+. Hasenfuss—Flohr, Kemeri, 1937.

(*j*) Better than 12 B—K 3, when the game Botvinnik—Euwe, Hastings, 1934–35, continued 12 ., Q Kt—Kt 5 ; 13 B—Kt 1, P—Q Kt 4 ; 14 Kt—K 5, B—Kt 2 ; 15 Q—Q 2, R—K 1 ; 16 P—B 4 (16 P—B 3 is safer), Q Kt—Q 4 ; 17 Kt × Kt, Q × Kt ; 18 P—B 5, B—Q 3 !+. The column is Weiss—Podhorzer, Vienna, 1934.

(*k*) Better is 9 K Kt—K 2, and if 9.., Kt—K 5 ; 10 B × B, Kt × B ; 11 O—O, P—Q Kt 3 ; 12 P—Q Kt 4, P—Q R 4 ; 13 P—Q R 3 with a good game.

(*l*) 17 Q—K 2, B—Q 2 ; 18 B × B, Q × B ; 19 R—Kt 3, Q—R 5 and Black wins a Pawn. Analysis by Lajos Steiner.

(*m*) 7.., P × P ; 8 P—Q 5, B × Kt ; 9 B × B, Kt—K 4 ; 10 O—O, with a strong attack : 10 .., Q—Q 2 ; 11 Q—K 2, Kt × B ch ; 12 Q × Kt, O—O—O ; 13 P—Q Kt 3 ! P—K 3 ; 14 Kt P × P. Mikenas—Flohr, Folkestone, 1933.

(*n*) Weaker is 8.., B—K 2 ; 9 O—O, O—O ; 10 B—K 3, Kt—K 5 ; 11 Q—Kt 3 !, Q—Q 2 ; 12 K R—Q 1, P—B 4 ; 13 P—K R 3 ±. Alekhine—Turover and Wimsatt, Washington, 1933. The column is Nimzovitch—Gygli, Zürich, 1934.

Notes for cols. 21 to 25 ctd.

(*i*) On 4 P—K Kt 4 !? the safest reply is 4.., B—Q 2 followed by .., P—K 3, .., P—Q B 4, .., Kt—Q B 3, .., P—K R 4, etc.; when White's weakened Pawn position will be a liability. On 4.., B—Kt 3 ; 5 P—K R 4, P—K R 4 ; 6 P—K 6 !, P × P ; 7 B—Q 3, B × B ; 8 Q × B gives White some attack, although the game Mieses—Speyer, Scheveningen, 1923, continued in Black's favour : 8.., P × P ; 9 Q—Kt 6 ch, K—Q 2 ; 10 Q × P (Kt 4), Kt—B 3 ; 11 Q—R 3, R—R 4 !; etc.

(*j*) Nimzovitch—Capablanca, New York, 1927.

(*k*) On 6 Kt—K B 3 Black should proceed as in the text. Weak, however, is 6.., Q—Kt 3 ; 7 O—O, Q—R 3 ? ; 8 Q—Kt 3 !, Kt—K 2 ; 9 B—Q 2, Kt—Kt 3 ? ; 10 B—Kt 4 !, B × B ; 11 Q × B, Q—Kt 3 ; 12 Q—R 3 ! ±. Tarrasch—Nimzovitch, San Sebastian, 1912.

(*l*) Also good is 9.., P × P ; 10 P × P, K Kt—K 2 ; 11 Kt—K B 3, P—K R 4=. H. Wolf-Tartakover, Carlsbad, 1923.

(*m*) Sämisch—Tartakover, Pistyan. 1922.

(*n*) If 6.., B—K 3 ; 7 B × B, P × B ; 8 O—O, B—K 2 ; 9 Kt × P, Q—Q 2 ; 10 Q—R 5 ch, K—Q 1 ; 11 B—K 3+. Tartakover—Przepiorka, Budapest, 1929.

(*c*) Teichmann—Mieses, match game, Berlin, 1913.

CENTRE GAME

THIS opening presents great difficulties for match-play. The early manœuvres of White's Queen, though embarrassing to an opponent not familiar with the defence, when correctly met often result in a congestion of forces unfavourable to White.

The general object of the exchange of Pawns on the second move is to clear the way for an advance of the King's and King's Bishop's Pawns and, after Castling on the Queen's side, to use the Rook on the open file.

The " Centre Game " covers both the variations where White on his 3rd move immediately recaptures the Pawn and those in which he defers or renounces recapture. The former variations constitute the Centre Game proper (cols. 1 to 8 below); the latter Centre Gambits '(cols. 9 and 10), and the Danish Gambit, which is an offshoot of the Centre Game.

Very recent examples of the Centre Game in masterplay are few. Col. 4 with note (k) presents two, arising from the line 5..., B—Kt 5 for Black, which aims at a counter-attack on the Queen's side.

In the more frequently seen line, beginning with 5..., B—Kt 5, there are three replies to 7..., R—K 1, given in cols. 2 to 5 :—

(i) 8 Q—Kt 3, defeated by the line adopted by Capablanca in col. 2.

(ii) 8 B—B 4, met by the variation given in col. 4, but relatively best.

(iii) 8 P—B 3, inferior, as in col. 5.

The early advance of P—K 5 for White has been proved premature (col. 6). In col. 7, the move 4..., P—K Kt 3, in spite of its adoption in important games, is nevertheless inferior. The line given in col. 8 appears good for Black, but has fallen into disuse. The sacrifice of a Pawn in cols. 9 and 10 gives White attacking chances, but Black's defence should be sufficient to turn the gain in material to account.

1 P—K 4, P—K 4 ; 2 P—Q 4, P×P ;
3 Q×P (a), Kt—Q B 3 ; 4 Q—K 3 (b), Kt—B 3.

	1	2	8	4	5
5	Kt—Q B 3				
	B—K 2	B—Kt 5			
6	B—Q 2	B—Q 2			
	P—Q 4	O—O (f)			
7	P×P	O—O—O			
	Kt×P	R—K 1			
8	Kt×Kt	Q—Kt 3	B—B 4		P—B 3
	Q×Kt	Kt×P (g)	B×Kt	P—Q 3	P—Q 4
9	Kt—K 2 (c)	Kt×Kt	B×B	Kt—B 3 (j)	Q—B 2
	B—Kt 5	R×Kt	Kt×P	B—K 3	P×P
10	Kt—B 4	B—K B 4	Q—B 4	B×B	Kt×P
	Q—Q 2	Q—B 3 !	Kt—B 3	R×B	B×B ch
11	P—K B 3	Kt—R 3	Kt—B 3	K Kt—Kt 5	R×B
	O—O—O	P—Q 3	P—Q 3	R—K 1	Q—K 2
12	O—O—O (d)	B—Q 3 (h)	Kt—Kt 5	P—B 4	Kt×Kt ch
	B—K B 4 (e)	R—K 1 +	B—K 3	P—K R 3	Q×Kt
13	B—Q 3		B—Q 3	P—K R 4	B—B 4
	B—B 3 ∓		P—K R 3 =	Q—B 1 ! + (k)	Kt—K 4 ∓
			(i)		(l)

(a) If 3 Kt—K B 3, Black can transpose by Kt—K B 3 into Petroff's Defence ;
by P—Q 3 into Philidor's Defence ; by Kt—Q B 3 or B—Kt 5 ch into the Scotch Game.
Or he can play 3.., B—B 4 ; 4 Kt×P (for 4 B—B 4, see Bishop's Opening,
column 2), Kt—K B 3 ; 5 B—K Kt 5, P—K R 3 ; 6 B×Kt, Q×B ; 7 P—Q B 3,
Kt—B 3 ; 8 Kt—B 3, O—O=. Mieses—Alekhine, The Hague, 1921. For 3 P—Q B 3,
see Danish Gambit.

(b) If 4 Q—B 4, Kt—B 3 ; 5 Kt—Q B 3, P—Q 4 ! ; 6 Kt×P, Kt×Kt ; 7 P×Kt,
Kt—Kt 5 ∓. Mieses—Leonhardt, Berlin, 1920. 4 Q—Q R 4 leads to a variation of
the Centre Counter with colours reversed, where White has a move in hand.

(c) 9 B—B 3, O—O ; 10 Q—Kt 3, P—K Kt 3 ; 11 B—Q 3, B—Q 3 ∓. Edinburgh—
Liverpool, correspondence, 1901. 9 P—Q B 4 ?, Q—Q B 4 ; 10 O—O—O, B—B 4 ! ;
11 Q×Q, B×Q ; 12 R—K 1 ch, B—K 3 ; 13 B—K 3, B—K 2 ; 14 Kt—B 3, O—O—O ;
15 Kt—Kt 5 ? (better is 15 B—K 2), B—K B 4 ! +. F. Meller—Kashdan, Györ, 1930.
Becker commends 9 Kt—B 3.

(d) If 12 P×B ?, K R—K 1 ; 13 Q—Q 3, Q×P ; 14 B—K 2, B—Kt 4 ; 15 K—Q 1,
R×B ; 16 Q×R, Q×Kt+ +.

(e) 12.., K R—K 1 ? ; 13 P×B, B—Kt 5 ; 14 Q—B 2 !+ +. Sultan Khan—
Marshall, Liège, 1930.

(f) Or 6.., P—Q 3 ; 7 P—B 4, B—Q B 4 : 8 Q—Kt 3, Kt—K R 4 : 9 Q—B 3,
Kt—B 3 ; 10 B—B 4, B—K Kt 5 ∓. Mieses—Englund, Scheveningen, 1913.

(g) If 8.., P—Q 3 ; 9 P—B 3, B—K 3 ; 10 Kt—R 3, Q—K 2 ; 11 Kt—B 4,
Q R—Q 1 ; 12 K—Kt 1 !, P—Q R 3 ; 13 B—Q 3, Kt—K 4 ; 14 Q Kt—Q 5, B×Kt ;
15 B×B, B—K 3 ; 16 K R—K 1 ±. Mieses—Spielmann, Berlin, 1914.

(h) Mieses—Capablanca, Berlin, 1913.

(i) 14 P—K R 4, Kt—Q 4 ; 15 B—R 7 ch, K—R 1 ; 16 R×Kt, B×R ; 17 B—K 4
(Winawer—Steinitz, Nuremberg, 1896) and now as recommended by Tarrasch, 17..,
R×B ! ; 18 Kt×R, Kt—K 4 ; 19 Kt×P, Q×Kt ; 20 B×Kt, Q—Q B 3 ; 21 R—Q 1,
B×R P ? (21.., B—K 5=) ; 22 R—Q 6 !+ +. W. F. de Greef—M. Seibold, corres-
pondence, 1931.

(j) Or 9 P—B 3, Kt—K 4 ; 10 B—Kt 3, B—K 3 ; 11 P—Kt 4, P—B 3 ; 12 P—Kt 5,
K Kt—Q 2 ∓. Spielmann—Eliskases, 1st match game, 1937.

(k) Continued 14 O—B 3, K—B 1 ! ; 15 Kt—Q 5, Kt×Kt. Tartakover—
Reshevsky, Stockholm, 1937.

(l) 14 B—Kt 3, P—Q R 4. Meisling—Dr. Em. Lasker. 1920

1 P—K 4, P—K 4 ; 2 P—Q 4, P×P.

	6	7	8	9	10
3	(Q×P)................................			P—K B 4	
	(Kt—Q B 3)			B—B 4	B—Kt 5 ch
4	(Q—K 3)			Kt—K B 3	B—Q 2 (*k*)
	(Kt—B 3) (*a*)	.P—K Kt 3 ...B	B—Kt 5 ch	Kt—Q B 3	B×B ch (*l*)
5	P—K 5 (*b*)	Kt—Q B 3	P—B 3 (*e*)	B—Q 3	Q×B
	Kt—K Kt 5	B—Kt 2	B—K 2 (*f*)	Kt—B 3	Kt—Q B 3
6	Q—K 2 (*c*)	B—Q 2	Kt—B 3	Q Kt—Q 2	Kt—K B 3
	P—Q 3 !	Kt—B 3 ! (*d*)	Kt—B 3	P—Q 3 (*i*)	Kt—B 3
7	P—K R 3	O—O—O	B—Kt 5	P—Q R 3	B—Q 3
	K Kt×K P	O—O	O—O	P—Q R 4	P—Q 4
8	P—K B 4	B—B 4	O—O	Q—K 2	P—K 5
	Kt—Q 5	P—Q 3	P—Q 4	O—O	Kt—K 5
9	Q—K 4	P—B 3	P×P	O—O	Q—K 2
	P—Q B 4	Kt—K 4	Kt×P	B—Q 2+ (*j*)	B—B 4
10	P×Kt	B—Kt 3	Q—K 2		Q Kt—Q 2
	P—Q 4	B—K 3 =	B—Q 3		Kt×Kt
11	Q—Q 3		R—Q 1		Q×Kt
	B—B 4		R—K 1		B—K 5
12	Q—K Kt 3		Q—B 2 (*g*)		O—O
	Kt×P ch+		B-K Kt5 ∓ (*h*)		O—O = (*m*)

(*a*) If 4. , B—K 2; 5 Q—K Kt 3, Kt—B 3; 6 P—K 5, Kt—K R 4; 7 Q—K 3, P—K Kt 3; 8 Kt—K B 3 ±.

(*b*) 5 B—Q 2, Kt—K Kt 5 (B—K 2: 6 Kt—Q B 3 transposes into Col. 1); 6 Q—K Kt 3, P—Q 4!; 7 P—K R 3, Kt—B 3; 8 P×P, Kt×P; 9 Kt—Q B 3, B—K 3; 10 O—O—O, Q—Q 3=. Analysis by Dr. Landau.

(*c*) 6 Q—K 4, P—Q4!; 7 P×P *e.p.* ch, B—K 3; 8 P×P, Q—Q 8 ch; 9 K×Q, Kt×P ch+. Or 8 B—Q R 6, Q×P; 9 B×P, Q—Kt 5 ch+ (Alekhine).

(*d*) Inferior is 6 , K Kt—K 2; 7 O—O—O, O—O; 8 B—B 4, P—Q 3; 9 P—K R 4! ±. Mieses—Spielmann, Breslau, 1912.

(*e*) 5 B—Q 2 is safer.

(*f*) Charousek's improvement on the older 5.., B—R 4.

(*g*) Better was 12 Q—B 1.

(*h*) Winawer—Charousek, Berlin, 1897. 13 Q Kt—Q 2 seems White's best continuation. Neither 13 R×Kt, nor 13 Kt—Kt 5 answers.

(*i*) If 6.., Kt—K Kt 5; 7 Kt—B 1, P—Q 3; 8 Q—K 2 ±.

(*j*) Analysis by Marshall.

(*k*) If 4 P—B 3, P×P; 5 P×P, B—B 4+.

(*l*) Superior is 4.., B—B 4, with a position similar to that in col. 9.

(*m*) 13 Q R—K 1, B×B; 14 Q×B, Kt—Kt 5; 15 Q—B 5, Q—B 1; 16 Q×Q, Q R×Q; 17 Kt×P.

CENTRE COUNTER GAME

THIS method of defence on the first move is not popular, and never has been popular, though advocated in the past by some masters, mostly from Northern Europe—whence its name on the Continent of Scandinavian Defence. The noted American analyst Fred Reinfeld has recently attempted to rehabilitate the opening, but he has not found any support among tournament players.

The Centre Counter has two main lines, according as after the moves 1 P—K 4, P—Q 4; 2 P × P, Black plays 2..., Q × P or 2..., Kt—K B 3.

The first line is open to the theoretical objections that the early development of the Queen is a violation of principle, that the centre is abandoned to White, and that, as in most of the irregular defences to 1 P—K 4, there is no good square for Black's Queen's Bishop. White's 3 Kt—Q B 3 is the simple and natural reply, and 3..., Q—Q R 4 (cols. 1 to 5) the continuation generally held best for Black. White has then a choice of four variations, of which 4 P—Q 4 is the strongest.

The second line, wherein the Pawn is not at once recaptured, was once thought analytically unsound, on account of 3 B—Kt 5 ch, apparently holding the Pawn. But, as seen in col. 10, Black can win the Pawn, with a slight shade of disadvantage in the position.

1 P—K 4, P—Q 4; 2 P×P, Q×P; 3 Kt—Q B 3, Q—Q R 4.

	1	2	3	4	5
4	P—Q 4 .... Kt—K B 3	 	 P—K 4	Kt—B 3 .... Kt—Q B 3	P—QKt4 (i) Q×Kt P
5	Kt—B 3 B—Kt 5		Kt—B 3 (f) B—Q Kt 5	B—Q Kt 5 B—Q 2	R—Kt 1 Q—Q 3
6	B—K 2 ..... Kt—B 3	P—K R 3! B—R 4	B—Q 2 B—Kt 5	O—O P—K 3	Kt—B 3 Kt—K B 3
7	B—K 3 (a) O—O—O	P—K Kt 4 B—Kt 3	B—K 2 P×P	P—Q 4 B—Kt 5	P—Q 4 P—Q R 3 (j)
8	Kt—Q 2 B×B	Kt—K 5 P—B 3	Kt×P Q—K 4	Q—Q 3 B×Kt	Q—Q 3 (k) Kt—Q B 3
9	Q×B Q—K B 4	P—K R 4 Kt—K 5 (c)	Q Kt—Kt 5 ! Q B×B	P×B P—Q R 3	B—K 2 P—K Kt 3
10	Kt—Kt 3 P—K 3 (b)	B—Q 2 (d) Q—Kt 3 (e)	Q×B B×B ch	B—Q B 4 K Kt—K 2	Kt—Q 1 B—B 4
11	P—Q R 3 B—Q 3	Kt×B Kt×Kt	K×B Q×Q ch	R—Kt 1 R—Q Kt 1	Q—Kt 3 P—Q Kt 4
12	O—O—O Kt—Q 4	B×Kt R P×Kt	K×Q Kt—Q R 3	Kt—Kt 5 Q—K B 4	B—R 3 Q—K 3
13	Kt—R 4 P—K 4	Q—Q 2 P—K 3	K R—K 1 O—O—O	Q—Kt3± (h)	Q—Kt 2 B—R 3
14	P×P B×K P	O—O—O Q—B 2	Kt×P ch! K—Kt 1		Kt—B 3 O—O
15	Q Kt—B5±	R—K 1 ±	Q Kt—B6ch! + (g)		O—O Kt—Q 4 ∓ (l)

(a) If 7 O—O, O—O—O; 8 Kt—K Kt 5!? (8 B—K 3, P—K 4!; 9 P—Q 5, Kt×P; 10 Kt×P?, Kt×B!; 11 B×B ch, P—B 4! and wins. Cohn—Tartakover, Ostend, 1907), and now 8 , R×P gives Black the better of it, e.g. 9 B×B ch, Kt×B; 10 Q—B 3, Q—K 4; 11 P—K Kt 3, P—B 3! and if 12 Kt—B 7?, Q—K R 4 wins.

(b) Better is 10 ., P—K 4. The column is Duras—Spielmann, Vienna, 1907.

(c) Or (1) 9 ., B—K 5; 10 Kt—B 4, Q—Q 1; 11 Kt×B, Kt×Kt; 12 P—Q B 3, P—K 3; 13 B—Q 3, Kt—Q 3; 14 Kt—K 5 ±. Balogh—Fahrni, correspondence, 1928-29. (2) 9 ., Q Kt—Q 2; 10 Kt—B 4, Q—B 2; 11 P—R 5, B—K 5; 12 Kt×B, Kt×Kt; 13 Q—B 3±. Analysis by Dr. Lasker.

(d) Inferior is 10 Q—B 3, Kt×Kt; 11 B—Q 2, Kt—Q 2; 12 Kt×Kt, K×Kt 13 B—Q B 4, B—K 5; 14 Q×B, Kt×Q; 15 B×Q, P—K 3; 16 P—K B 3, Kt—B 3= (Fred Reinfeld). The column to the 14th move is analysis by C. J. S. Purdy.

(e) Or 10.., Kt×Kt; 11 B×Kt, Q—Q 4; 12 P—B 3 ±. Or 10 ., Kt×B; 11 Q×Kt, P—B 3; 12 Kt×B, P×Kt; 13 B—Q 3, P—K Kt 4; 14 P—R 5, Kt—Q 2; 15 B—Kt 6 ch ±.

(f) If 5 P×P, B—Q Kt 5; 6 Kt—B 3, B—Kt 5; 7 B—K 2, Kt—Q B 3; 8 O—O, K Kt—K 2=.

(g) White won the ending. Tarrasch—Mieses, Gothenburg, 1920.

(h) Réti—Rubinstein, Teplitz-Schönau, 1922.

(i) 4 B—B 4, Kt—K B 3; 5 P—Q 3 leads only to equality, Black having a safe continuation in 5 ., P—B 3.

(j) Weaker is 7 ., P—B 3; 8 B—Q 3, P—Q Kt 3; 9 O—O, P—K 3; 10 Q—K 2, B—K 2; 11 Kt—K 4, Kt×Kt; 12 Q×Kt, Q—Q 4?; 13 Q—Kt 4, B—B 3; 14 P—B 4 with an overwhelming attack. Mieses—Leonhardt, Prague, 1908.

(k) If instead 8 B—Q B 4, P—K 3; 9 O—O, B—K 2; 10 R—K 1, P—Q Kt 4; 11 B—Kt 3, B—Kt 2; 12 B—Kt 5, Q Kt—Q 2; 13 Q—K 2, R—Q B 1∓. Sir G. A. Thomas—J. du Mont, Tunbridge Wells, 1912.

(l) Dr. Schumer—Sir G. A. Thomas, City of London Championship, 1912.

1 P—K4, P—Q4; 2 P×P.

	6	7	8	9	10
2	(Q×P)......Kt—KB3				
3	(Kt—QB3)	P—Q4................................			B-Kt5 ch (j)
	Q—Q1	Kt×P			B—Q2
4	P—Q4	P—QB4.................		Kt—KB3	B—B4 (k)
	Kt—KB3 (a)	Kt—KB3..Kt—Kt3		B—Kt5	B—Kt5
5	B—K3 (b)	Kt—KB3	Kt—QB3 (e)	P—B3	P—KB3
	P—B3	P—B3	P—K4 (f)	P—QB3	B—B4
6	B—Q3	Kt—B3	P—Q5 (g)	Q Kt—Q2	Kt—B3
	B—Kt5	B—Kt5	B—QKt5	Kt—Q2	Q Kt—Q2
7	K Kt—K2	B—K3	B—Q2	B—B4	Q—K2 (l)
	P—K3	P—K3	P—QB3	P—K3	Kt—Kt3
8	Q—Q2	Q—Kt3	Kt—K4	Kt—K4	B—Kt3
	B—Q3	Q—Kt3	B×B ch	B—K2	Q—Q2 (m)
9	Kt—Kt3	Kt—K5	Q×B	Kt—Kt3	P—Q3
	Q—B2	Q×Q	P×P	K Kt—Kt3	Q Kt×P
10	P—KR3	P×Q	P×P	B—K2	B—Q2
	K B×Kt	Q Kt—Q2	O—O	O—O	P—K3
11	R P×B	B—Q3	R—Q1	O—O	Q—B2
	Kt×P	Kt×Kt	B—B4 =	Q—B2	B—Q Kt5
12	P×B	P×Kt	(h)	P—KR3	K Kt—K2
	Q×P ch	Kt—Q2 = (d)		B×Kt	=
13	B—B2 ± (c)			B×B =	
				(i)	

(a) Or 4., P—QB3; 5 Kt—B3, B—Kt5; 6 B—K2, B×Kt; 7 B×B, P—K3; 8 O—O, Kt—B3; 9 R—K1, B—K2; 10 Q—Q3 ±. Teichmann—Lee, match, 1901.

(b) An equally strong alternative is 5 B—QB4, P—K3; 6 Kt—B3, B—K2; 7 O—O, O—O; 8 Q—K2, Q Kt—Q2; 9 R—K1, Kt—Kt3; 10 B—Kt3, P—B3. Alekhine—Schlechter, Carlsbad, 1911.

(c) Tarrasch—Pillsbury, Monte Carlo, 1903.

(d) Réti—Tartakover, match, 1920.

(e) Somewhat stronger is 5 Kt—KB3, B—Kt5; 6 Kt—B3, P—K4; 7 P—B5, P×P? (better 7.., K Kt—Q2—Tarrasch); 8 Kt—K4, K Kt—Q2; 9 Q×P, Q—K2; 10 B—Q Kt5 ±. Lasker—Alekhine, St. Petersburg, 1914. 10.., P—B4; 11 O—O gives White a winning attack now. The game continued 10.., Kt—B3; 11 B×Kt, P×B; 12 O—O, B×Kt; 13 P×B, O—O—O; 14 Q—R4, etc.

(f) The Kiel Variation.

(g) 3 P×P, Q×Q ch; 7 Kt×Q, Kt—B3; 8 P—B4, B—K3; 9 P—Q Kt3, O—O—O; 10 Kt—KB3, Q—B4; 11 P—Q R3, K R—K1 ∓. Treybal—Bogoljuboff, Pistyan, 1922.

(h) Spielmann—Walter, Mährisch-Ostrau, 1923.

(i) Bogatyrchuk—Rabinovitch, Moscow, 1925.

(j) 3 P—QB4 deserves more attention than it has received, if only for the reason that after 3., P—B3; 4 P—Q4, P×P; 5 Kt—QB3 White has transposed to the Panoff Attack against the Caro-Kann! The continuation 3 P—QB4, P—B3; 4 P×P, Kt×P; 5 Kt—KB3, P—K4; 6 P—Q3, B—KB4; 7 Kt—B3, B—B4; 8 B—K3, B×B; 9 P×B, Q—Kt3; 10 Q—B2, P—K5; 11 P×P, Kt×P; 12 B—K2 is playable for White but gives Black good attacking possibilities.

(k) 4 B×B ch, Q×B; 5 Kt—QB3, Kt×P; 6 Kt×Kt, Q×Kt; 7 Q—B3, P—QB3; 8 Q×Q, P×Q=. Krejcik—Rethy, Vienna-Budapest, match, 1931.

(l) Somewhat better is 7 K Kt—K2, Kt×Kt; 8 B—Kt3, Q Kt×P; 9 Kt×Kt, Kt×Kt; 10 Kt—Kt3, B—Kt3; 11 O—O, P—K3; 12 P—KB4, Kt—K2; 13 P—Q4 ±. Maróczy—Walter, Györ, 1924.

(m) Best. If 8.., P—QR3; 9 P—Kt4, B—Kt3; 10 P—B4 +. The column is Bogatyrchuk—Torre, Moscow, 1925.

DANISH GAMBIT

In this interesting branch of the Centre Game, White offers his Queen's Bishop's and Queen's Knight's Pawns for the sake of rapid development, obtaining long diagonals for his Bishops and considerable control of the board.

What is considered by the majority of experts the best defence is based upon the capture of three Pawns, followed by the immediate counter-sacrifice of the Queen's Pawn (col. 1). This plan, preached and practised by Schlechter, and endorsed by Amos Burn, was adopted, with excellent results from Black's point of view, at the Baden Gambit Tournament of 1914 and refutes White's opening strategy, for the analysis has not yet been controverted. The remaining forms of the Gambit Accepted (cols. 3 to 4) yield White an attack sufficiently compensating him for his two Pawns.

In the variations where Black captures two Pawns, retaining one—a plan which has its supporters—the development with K Kt—K 2 is inferior (col. 5), but the alternative lines, where White posts his pieces normally (cols. 6 to 8), are quite satisfactory for the first player. In cols. 9 and 10 White does not sacrifice a second Pawn (a variation recommended by Alekhine); by transposing into col. 6 Black can obtain at least equality.

The forms of the opening in which Black contents himself with equality of development rather than superiority in material (belonging to the Centre Game rather than to the Danish) are illustrated in cols. 11 to 15. Col. 11 is a simple equalising line for the second player, but col. 12 frequently results in positional advantage for him. Col. 13 is one of the very rare examples of a Danish in tournament-play after the War.

Mieses has recommended col. 15 as the best way of declining the Gambit, an opinion in which the *Lärobok* concurs; nevertheless, White's attack is not easily frustrated in over-the-board play.

1 P—K4, P—K4; 2 P—Q4, P×P; 3 P—QB3.

3.., P×P; 4 B—QB4.

	1	2	3	4	5
4	P×P				Kt-KB3 (k)
5	B×P				Kt×P
	P—Q4! (a)		Q—K2	Kt—KB3 (h)	Kt—B3
6	K B×P	P×P	Kt—Q B3	Kt—QB3 (i)	K Kt—K2
	Kt—K B3	Kt—K B3	P—Q B3	Kt—B3	B—B4 (l)
7	B×P ch (b)	Kt—KB3 (d)	Q—B2 (f)	Kt—B3	O—O
	K×B	B—Q3	P—Q3	B—Kt5	P—Q3
8	Q×Q	O—O	O—O—O	Q—B2	B—K Kt5
	B—Kt5 ch	O—O	B—K3	P—Q3	P—K R3
9	Q—Q2	Kt—B3	Kt—Q5!	O—O—O	B—R4
	B×Q ch	B—K Kt5	P×Kt	B×Kt	Kt—K4
10	Kt×B	Q—Q4	P×P	Q×B	B—Q Kt3
	P—B4∓(c)	Q Kt—Q2	Q—Kt4 ch	B—K3	Kt—Kt3
11		K R—K1	R—Q2	K R—K1	B—Kt3
		R—K1	B—B4	B×B	O—O
12		Kt—Kt5	Q—Kt3	Q×B	K—R1
		R—K4	Kt—Q2	O—O	B—K3 ∓
13		K Kt—K4	Kt—B3	P—K5	
		Q—K2	Q—R3	Kt—K1	
14		R—K3	Q×P (g)	R—K3	
		Q B-B4+ (e)		Q—B1=(j)	

(a) Introduced by Schlechter.

(b) 7 Kt—K B 3, B—Kt 5 ch!; 8 K—B 1, O—O; 9 Q—Kt 3 (9 B×P ch, K—R 1!; 10 Q×Q, R×Q+), Kt—B 3; 10 Kt—B 3, Q—K 2; 11 P—Q R 3, B—Q 3+. Nyholm—Réti, Baden, 1914.

(c) Followed by B—K3 and R—Q 1 with the better end-game (Schlechter). Marco gives the alternative 10.., R—K 1; 11 P—B3, P—B 4; 12 Kt—B 4, R—Q 1; 13 P—K 5, Kt—K 1+. If 10.., R—K 1; 11 P—B 3, Kt—B 3?; 12 R—B 1!, B—K 3 : 13P—Q R 3, Q R—Q 1; 14 Kt—K 2, R—K 2; 15 Q Kt—B 4 (15 K Kt—B 4 was even stronger) ±. Nyholm—Tartakover, Baden, 1914.

(d) Or 7 Kt—Q B 3, Q Kt—Q 2 (or 7.., B—Q 3; 8 Q—B 2, Q—K 2 ch; 9 K Kt—K 2, O—O; 10 O—O—O, B—Q R 6+. Tartakover); 8 Kt—B 3, B—Q Kt 5; 9 O—O, O—O+. Nyholm—Spielmann, Baden, 1914.

(e) Opocensky—Réti, Baden, 1914.

(f) 7 K Kt—K 2 (7 Q—K 2 has also been played), P—Q Kt 4!; 8 B—Kt 3, P—Q R 4; 9 R—Q B 1, Kt—Q R3; 10 O—O, Kt—B 4; 11 Kt—Q 4, Kt×B+. Mieses—Tchigorin, Cambridge Springs, 1904.

(g) 14.., R—Kt 1; 15 Q—B 7. Lärobok, 1921. White has a strong attack.

(h) 5.., B—Kt 5 ch; 6 Kt—B 3 (or 6 K—B 1, Kt—K B 3; 7 P—K 5, P—Q 4; 8 Q—R 4 ch+), Kt—Q B 3 (Mieses says that the best answer to 6.., Q—K 2 or Kt—K B 3 is 7 Q—B 2); 7 Kt—B 3, P—Q 3; 8 Q—Kt 3, Kt—R 3; 9 O—O—O, O—O; 10 P—Kt 4, B×P; 11 K R—Kt 1 with a powerful attack (11..,B×Kt?; 12 Kt—Q 5+).

(i) 6 P—K 5, Kt—Kt 5!; 7 P—K 6 (7 Q×Kt, P—Q 4+), P—K B 4; 8 P×P ch, B×P; 9 Kt—K B 3, Q—K 2 ch+ (Alapin).

(j) White's excellent development is sufficient compensation for the two Pawns minus.

(k) Both 4.., B—Kt 5; 5 P×P, Q—B 3; 6 Kt—K 2, B—B 4 (White threatens to entrap the Queen by 7 P×B, Q×R; 8 Kt—B 3); 7 O—O, P—Q 3; 8 Kt—B 4, Kt—R 5 ± (P. Johner—Breyer, Baden, 1914); and 4.., P—Q 3; 5 Kt×P, B—K 3; 6 B×B, P×B; 7 Q—R 5 ch, P—Kt 3; 8 Q—Kt 5 ch, Kt—B 3; 9 Q×P, Kt—Q 5; 10 B—Kt 5 are indifferent continuations for Black.

(l) If 6.., B—Kt 5; 7 O—O, B×Kt; 8 Kt×B, P—Q 3; 9 B—K Kt 5, Kt—K 4; 10 B—K 2, O—O : 11 P—B 4 ±.

1 P—K 4, P—K 4; 2 P—Q 4, P×P; 3 P—QB 3, P×P.

	6	7	8	9	10
4	(B—QB 4)................................Kt×P (i)				
	P—Q 3......Kt—QB 3...Kt—KB 3			B—Kt 5 (j)	..Kt—QB 3
5	Kt×P	Kt—B 3	Kt×P	B—QB 4	B—QB 4
	Kt—QB 3	B—B 4	Kt—B 3	P—Q 3	P—Q 3
6	Kt—B 3	Kt×P (c)	Kt—B 3 (f)	Kt—B 3	Kt—B 3
	B—K 3 !	P—Q 3	B—Kt 5	B×Kt ch	Kt—B 3 (n)
7	B—Q 5	Q—Kt 3	P—K 5 (g)	P×B	Q—Kt 3 (o)
	B×B (a)	Q—Q 2	P—Q 4	Kt—QB 3	Q—Q 2
8	P×B	Kt—Q 5	P×Kt	O—O	Kt—KKt 5
	Kt—K 4	K Kt—K 2	P×B	Kt—B 3	Kt—K 4 (p)
9	O—O !	Q—B 3	Q×Q ch	B—R 3 (h)	B—Kt 5
	Kt—KB 3	O—O	Kt×Q	O—O (l)	P—B 3
10	Q—K 2	O—O	P×P	P—K 5	P—B 4 !
	B—K 2	Kt—Kt 3	R—K Kt 1	Kt—K Kt 5	P×B
11	Kt×Kt	P—Q Kt 4	O—O	P×P	P×Kt
	P×Kt	B—Kt 3	B×Kt	P×P	P×P
12	Q×P	P—Q R 4 (d)	P×B	B×P	B—K 3+
	O—O	Q Kt—K 4 !	Kt—K 3 !	R—K 1	
13	B—Kt 5	Kt×B	R—K 1	R—K 1 !+ (m)	
	P—K R 3	R P×Kt	B—Q 2 = (h)		
14	B—R 4	B—Kt 2 ± (e)			
	Q—Q 2 = (b)				

(a) But this is not the logical continuation. Correct was 7.., Kt—B 3; 8 O—O, B—K 2 ∓. B×B, P×B; Q—Kt 3 would be met by .., Q—B 1.

(b) Opocensky—Fahrni, Baden, 1914.

(c) If 6 B×P ch, K×B; 7 Q—Q 5 ch, K—B 1; 8 Q×B ch, Q—K 2; 9 Q×Q ch, K Kt×Q; 10 Kt×P, P—Q 4 !=. Schlechter—Spielmann, Baden, 1914.

(d) Stronger was 12 B—Kt 2, e.g. 12.., Q Kt—K 4; 13 Kt×B, R P×Kt; 14 Kt×Kt, P×Kt; 15 P—B 4 !+ (Marco).

(e) Schlechter—Hromadka, Baden, 1914.

(f) If 6 B—K 3 ?, B—Kt 5; 7 Q—B 2, Q—K 2; 8 P—B 3, P—Q 4; 9 B—Q Kt 5, O—O+. Dr. Smith and others—P. W. Sergeant and others, consultation, London, 1921.

(g) 7 O—O, O—O; 8 P—K 5, B×Kt; 9 P×B, P—Q 4; 10 P×Kt (10 B—R 3, P×B; 11 B×R, Q×Q; 12 K R×Q, Kt—K 5 ∓), P×B; 11 P×P=. A good alternative for White here is 10 B—Kt 3, Kt—Kt 5; 11 R—K 1, B—K 3; 12 P—K R 3, Kt—R 3; 13 P—K Kt 4.

(h) Analysis by R. J. Loman.

(i) Alekhine warmly recommends this and, if B—Kt 5; 5 B—Q B 4, on the ground that White has thus better attacking chances than those shown in col. 1.

(j) Better is 4.., P—Q 3; transposing into col. 6.

(k) More in harmony with the opening is 9 P—K 5, P×P; 10 Q—Kt 3, with a strong attack (Alekhine).

(l) 9. , B—Kt 5 !; 10 Q—Kt 3, Kt—Q R 4; 11 B×P ch, K—B 1; 12 Q—R 4 B×Kt; 13 P×B, K×B; 14 Q×Kt, R—K 1, with a satisfactory game (Alekhine).

(m) Alekhine—Issakoff, Moscow, 1919.

(n) 6.., B—K 3 again transposes into col. 6.

(o) 7 Kt—Kt 5, Kt—K 4; 8 B—Kt 5 ch, P—B 3; 9 P—B 4, Q Kt—Kt 5. 10 B—B 4, P—Q 4=. Selman—Ford, New York, 1932.

(p) Better Kt—Q 1 (Alekhine). The column is Alekhine—Verlinsky, Odessa, 1918.

1 P—K 4, P—K 4 ; 2 P—Q 4, P×P ; 3 P—Q B 3.

	11	12	13	14	15
3	P—Q 4 (a)			P—Q 6	Q—K 2 (i)
4	K P×P / Kt—K B 3 !	..Q×P		B×P / B—B 4	P×P (j) / Q×P ch
5	P×P (b) / B—Kt 5 ch	P×P / Kt—Q B 3 (d)		Kt—K B 3 / P—Q 3	B—K 2 ! / Q×Kt P
6	B—Q 2 / B×B ch	Kt—K B 3 / B—K Kt 5		Q—B 2 / Kt—Q B 3	B—B 3 / Q—Kt 3
7	Q×B / O—O	B—K 2 / Kt—B 3	Kt—B 3 / B—Kt 5	Q Kt—Q 2 / P—Q R 3	Kt—B 3 / B—Kt 5
8	Kt—K B 3 / Kt—K 5	Kt—B 3 / Q—Q R 4 (e)	B—K 2 / B×Kt	Kt—Kt 3 / B—R 2	Kt—K 2 / Kt—K 2
9	Q—B 4 / Q×P	O—O / O—O—O	B×B / Q—Q R 4	Q Kt—Q 4 / Kt—B 3	Kt—B 4 / Q—B 4
10	B—Q 3 / Q—R 4 ch	B—K 3 / B—Q B 4	B—K 3 / B×Kt ch	B—K Kt 5 / P—R 3	B—K 3 / P—Q 4
11	Q Kt—Q 2 / Kt×Kt	Q—Kt 3 / B×P	P×B / Q×P ch	B—R 4 / B—Kt 5	R—K Kt 1 / O—O
12	Q×Kt / R—K 1 ch	Kt×B / Kt×Kt	K—B 1 / Q—B 5 ch	Kt×Kt / P×Kt	B—Kt 4 (k) / Q—K 5
13	Kt—K 5 / Q×Q ch =	B×B ch / Kt×B	K—Kt 1 / K Kt—K 2	O—O—O / Q—K 2	B—B 3 / Q—B 4
14	(c)	Q×P / K R—B 1 ∓ (f)	R—B 1 / Q×R P (g)	Q—R 4 ± (h)	B—Kt 4 =

(a) The "Danish Declined."

(b) Blumich says that 5 Kt—B 3 is much the best move, though after 5.., Kt×P; 6 Q×P, Kt—Q B 3; 7 B—Q Kt 5, B—K 2 Black stands well enough. Lárobok considers 5 B—Q B 4 best. 5 Q—R 4 ch (or 5 P—Q B 4, P—B 4!), P—B 3; 6 Q P×P, Kt×P; 7 B—Q Kt 5, B—Q 2; 8 Kt—B 3, Q—K 2 ch; 9 K—B 1, P—Q 6!+ is Nyholm—Breyer, Baden, 1914. Marshall recommends 5 B—Kt 5 ch.

(c) Réti—Schlechter, Baden, 1914.

(d) 5.., P—Q B 4; 6 Kt—Q B 3, Q×Q P; 7 B—Kt 5 ch !, Kt—B 3; 8 Q—K 2 ch, B—K 3; 9 Kt—B 3+ (Mieses).

(e) This is a better square for the Queen than K R 4 (Mieses). If 8.., B—Kt 5, 9 O—O leaves White with the superior game.

(f) Schlechter—Opocensky, Baden, 1914.

(g) 15 R—R 1, Q—B 5; 16 R—B 1, Q—R 7; 17 R—R 1, Q—B 5; 18 R—B 1, Q—R 7. Drawn. Marshall—Capablanca, Lake Hopatcong, 1926.

(h) Nyholm—Schlechter, Baden, 1914. 11.., B—Q 2 was better.

(i) 3.., Kt—K 2; 4 Kt—B 3, P—Q 4; 5 Q×P, Q Kt—B 3; 6 B—Q Kt 5, B—Q 2; 7 Q—K 3=.

(j) 4 B—Q 3, P—Q 4; 5 Q—K 2 (5 P—K 5, Kt—Q B 3!), P×K P; 6 B×P, Kt—K B 3; 7 B—B 3, Q×Q ch; 8 Kt×Q, P×P+. Or 4 Kt—K B 3, Q×P ch; 5 K—Q 2, Kt—K B 3; 6 B—Q 3, Q—Q 4; 7 R—K 1 ch, B—K 2; 8 K—K 2, P—Q 3+. Or 4 Q—K 2, Kt—K B 3; 5 Kt—Q 2, P—Q 4; 6 P—K 5, P—Q 6!+. Réti—Spielmann, Baden, 1914. If 4 Q×P, Black can equalise by 4.., P—K B 4.

(k) If 12 Kt—R 5, Kt—Kt 3; 13 R—Kt 5, Q—R 6; 14 B×P, P—B 3; 15 B—Kt 2, Q×P; 16 Q—B 3, P—K R 3; 17 R—Kt 3, B—Q 3; 18 O—O—O (analysis by Rosentreter), Q—R 5 ∓.

ENGLISH OPENING

THE popularity of the English Opening has steadily been increasing in the last few years and is due largely to a desire for variety in the openings. The début derives its name from its vogue at the time of the London Tournament of 1851 and its association with Howard Staunton.

The best reply for Black to 1 P—Q B 4 is 1..., P—K 4, which leads to a Sicilian Defence with a move in hand. In the Four Knights' Variation (cols. 1 to 7) White has four possible lines on his 4th move :—

(i) 4 P—Q 4 (cols. 1 to 3) is the most important. White generally obtains the two Bishops, but must submit to a serious weakening of his Pawn position.

(ii) 4 P—K 4 was championed by Nimzovitch, but has rarely been seen since his death. It leads to unusual positions, where the player with more imagination is at home.

(iii) 4 P—Q 3 leads after P—Q 4 into the well-known "Dragon" Variation of the Sicilian with colours reversed. The tempo gives White a strong initiative and, although Black's disadvantage is not serious, it can prove very annoying.

(iv) 4 P—K 3 (col. 7). Here White omits or postpones the central advance P—Q 4; Black can equalise easily.

It was formerly thought that the order in which White develops his Knights is of no consequence. Alekhine and others have shown that this opinion is faulty, for after 2 Kt—K B 3, P—K 5 is a strong reply (cols. 9 and 10).

The King's fianchetto development in cols. 13 to 15 has had the support of Capablanca and Flohr. An early advance on the King's Bishop's file (col. 13) makes it difficult for Black to equalise, while an early advance of White's Queen's Pawn (col. 15) is the invitation to an early draw.

Other first moves for Black are shown in cols. 16 to 25. The symmetrical defence with P—Q B 4* (cols. 16 to 18) is definitely unfavourable for Black. The line where Black prefers a quiet development of his pieces (cols. 19 to 21) leads to equality.

In the lines in cols. 22 to 24 (sometimes called Flohr's Attack) White attempts to profit from the absence of a Pawn on Black's centre squares. If Black has played P—K 3 the advance of White's King's Pawn leads to a position where White's Pawns are weak, but Black's King is insecure. In the best line (col. 23) the chances are even. Against P—B 3 (col. 24) the attack with the King's Pawn is inferior.

It should be noted that by playing P—Q 4 at an early stage in cols. 19 to 25 White can transpose into Queen's Pawn Game, or into the Queen's Gambit.

---

* The variations with 1 P—Q B 4, P—Q B 4 have not been assigned a separate column because they transpose into 1 P—Q B 4, Kt—K B 3 ; 2 Kt—K B 3, P—B 4.

1 P—Q B 4, P—K 4 ; 2 Kt—K B 3, Kt—Q B 3 ; 3 Kt—B 3, Kt—B 3

	1	2	3	4	5
4	P—Q 4..........................			P—K 4	
	P×P (a)			B—Kt 5.....	B—B 4
5	Kt×P			P—Q 3	Kt×P
	B—Kt 5................		B—B 4	P—Q 3	Kt×Kt
6	B—Kt 5 (A)		Kt×Kt	P—K R 3 (h)	P—Q 4
	O—O......	P—K R 3	Kt P×Kt	P—K R 3	B—Kt 5
7	R—B 1	B—R 4	P—K Kt 3	B—K 3	P×Kt
	R—K 1	B×Kt ch (c)	P—Q 4	B—Q 2	Kt×P
8	P—K 3	P×B	B—Kt 2	P—R 3	Q—Q 4
	P—Q 3	Kt—K 4 (d)	B—K 3	B×Kt ch	P—K B 4
9	B—K 2	P—K 3	O—O	P×B	P×P e.p.
	Kt—K 4	P—Q 3	O—O	Kt—K 2	Kt×P (B 3)
10	O—O	B—K 2	Q—R 4	R—Q Kt 1	P—B 5
	B×Kt	Kt—Kt 3	B—Q 2	P—Q Kt 3	Q—K 2 ch
11	R×B	B—Kt 3	B—Kt 5 !	P—Kt 3	B—K 3
	Kt—Kt 3 (b)	Kt—K 5	B—K 2	O—O	B×Kt ch
12	Kt—Kt 5 ! ±	Q—B 2	KR-Q 1 ± (g)	B—Kt 2	P×B
		Q—K 2 (e)		Q—B 1	O—O
13		B—Q 3		= (i)	= (j)
		= (f)			

(a) Or 4.., P—K 5 ; 5 Kt—Q 2 (if 5 Kt—K Kt 5, P—K R 3 ; 6 P—Q 5, P×Kt ; 7 P×Kt, B—B 4 ; 8 P×Kt P, B×P ; 9 P—K 3, Q—K 2 ; 10 P—Q R 3, P—Q R 4 ; 11 B—K 2, B—B 3 ; 12 B—Q 2, Q—K 4 ; 13 P—R 3, P—R 5=. Kostich—Opocensky, Prague, 1931), Kt×P ; 6 K Kt×P, Kt—K 3 ; 7 P—K Kt 3, Kt×Kt ; 8 Kt×Kt, B—Kt 5 ch ; 9 B—Q 2, B×B ch ; 10 Q×B, O—O ; 11 B—Kt 2, P—Q 3 ; 12 O—O, B—Q 2 ; 13 Kt—B 3, B—B 3 ; 14 Kt—Q 5, P—Q R 4 ; 15 P—K 4 ±. Botvinnik—Flohr, 5th match game, 1933.
(b) 11.., P—K R 3 ; 12 B—R 4, Kt—Kt 3 ; 13 B×Kt ± transposes into Flohr—H. Johner, Zurich, 1934. The column is Alekhine—Yates, Semmering, 1926.
(c) 7.., P—Q 3 ; 8 P—K 3 (8 Kt×Kt, P×Kt ; 9 Q—R 4, B×Kt ch ; 10 P×B, O—O !=. Botvinnik), Q—K 2 ; 9 B—K 2, P—K Kt 4 ; 10 B—Kt 3, Kt—K 5 ; 11 Kt×Kt (11 R—B 1, O—O ; 12 O—O, B×Kt ; 13 P×B, Kt×B ; 14 R P×Kt, Kt—K 4 ; 15 Q—B 2 ±. Botvinnik), P×Kt ; 12 R—B 1, O—O ; 13 O—O, B×Kt ; 14 P×B, Kt×B ; 15 R P×Kt, B—B 4 !=. Botvinnik—Flohr, 7th match game, 1933.
(d) 8.., P—Q 3 ; 9 P—B 3, O—O ; 10 P—K 4, Kt—K 4 ! ; 11 B—K 2, Kt—Kt 3 ; 12 B—B 2, Kt—Q 2 ; 13 Q—Q 2, Kt—Kt 3 ; 14 Kt—Kt 3, B—K 3 ; 15 P—B 5 ±. Botvinnik—Pirc, Moscow, 1935.
(e) 12.., Kt×B ; 13 R P×Kt, Kt—K 4 ; 14 R—Q 1, Q—K 2 ; 15 Q—K 4, P—Q R 3 ; 16 R—R 5, Kt—Q 2 ; 17 Q—B 4, Kt—B 3=. Lövenfisch—Botvinnik, Leningrad, 1934.
(f) Lasker—Lisitzin, Moscow, 1935.
(g) Réti—Przepiorka, Marienbad, 1925.
(h) Or I. 6 P—K Kt 3, O—O ; 7 B—Kt 2, Kt×Q 5 ; 8 Kt×Kt, P×Kt ; 9 P—Q R 3, B×Kt ch ; 10 P×B, P×P ; 11 Q—B 2, Kt—Kt 5 ; 12 Q×P, Q—B 3 ; 13 Q×Q, Kt×Q=. Nimzovitch—Spielmann, Bled, 1931. II. 6 B—K 2, O—O ; 7 O—O, B×Kt ; 8 P×B, Q—K 2 ; 9 Kt—K 1, Kt—K 1 ; 10 Kt—B 2, P—B 4 ; 11 P×P, B×P ; 12 Kt—K 3, B—K 3 ; 13 P—Q 4, B—B 2=. Fine—Dake, Mexico City, 1935.
(i) Nimzovitch—Naegeli, exhibition game, Berne, 1931.
(j) List—Colle, Berlin, 1926.
(A) If 6 Kt×Kt, 6 .., B×Kt ch (better than 6 .., Kt P×Kt ; 7 Q—Kt 3, B—B 4 ; 8 P—K 3, O—O ; 9 B—K 2, R—K 1 ; 10 O—O, Q—K 2 ; 11 Q—B 2, Q—K 4 ; 12 Kt—R 4. Tartakover—Grünfeld, match, 1922. Or 6.., Q P×Kt ; 7 Q×Q ch, K×Q ; 8 B—Q 2+) ; 7 P×B, Q P×Kt (7.., Kt P×Kt ; 8 B—R 3, P—Q 3 ; 9 P—B 5, P—Q 4 ; 10 P—K 3, O—O ; 11 P—Q B 4 ±) ; 8 Q×Q ch (8 Q—Q 4 ?, Q—K 2 ; 9 B—Kt 5, O—O ; 10 B×Kt, P×B ; 11 P—K 3, R—Q 1 ; 12 Q—B 4, Q—R 6 ! and wins H. Golombek—Flohr, Hastings, 1935-36), K×Q=. Hanauer—Reinfeld, New York, 1938.

1 P—Q B 4, P—K 4; 2 Kt—K B 3.

	6	7	8	9	10
2	(Kt—Q B 3).........................P—K 5				
3	(Kt—B 3).............. (Kt—B 3)		P—Q 4 P—Q 3 (g)	Kt—Q 4 Kt—Q B 3	
4	P—Q 3...... P—Q 4 (a)	P—K 3 B—Kt 5 (d)	Kt—B 3 B—Kt 5	Kt—B 2 (i) Kt—B 3	
5	P×P Kt×P	Q—B 2 (e) O—O	P—Q 5 Kt—Kt 1	Kt—B 3 B—B 4	
6	P—K Kt 3 B—K 3 (b)	B—K 2 R—K 1	P—K Kt 3 Kt—K B 3	P—Q Kt 3 O—O	
7	B—Kt 2 B—K 2	O—O P—Q 3	B—Kt 2 B—K 2	P—Kt 3 (j) P—Q 4......R—K 1	
8	O—O O—O	Kt—K 1 B—K 3	O—O' O—O	P×P Q Kt-Kt5 (k)	B—K Kt 2 P—Q R 4
9	P—Q R 3 Q—Q 2	P—Q R 3 B×Kt	=(h)	Kt×Kt B×Kt	O—O P—Q 3
10	B—Q 2 Q R—Q 1	Q×B P—Q R 4		K B—Kt 2 R—K 1	Kt—K 3 Kt—Q 5
11	P—Q Kt 4 Kt×Kt	P—Q Kt 3 Q—Q 2		O—O B—K B 4	P—Q 3 P×P
12	B×Kt B—B 3	P—Q 3 P—Q 4		B—Kt 2 Kt×P	Q×P ± (m)
13	Q—B 2 ± (c)	Q—B 2 =(f)		Kt × Kt=(l)	

(a) 4.., B—Kt 5; 5 B—Q 2, P—Q 4; 6 P×P, Kt×P; 7 P—K Kt 3, O—O; 8 B—Kt 2, Kt—Kt 3; 9 O—O, P—K R 3; 10 R—K 1, Q—K 2; 11 P—Q R 3, B—Q 3; 12 Kt—Q Kt 5, B—K 3; 13 P—Q Kt 4, P—R 3; 14 Kt×B, P×Kt; 15 P—K 4! ±. Capablanca—Reshevsky, Semmering-Baden, 1937.

(b) 6 ., P—B 3; 7 B—Kt 2, B—K 3; 8 P—Q R 3, Kt—Kt 3; 9 O—O, B—K2; 10 B—K 3, Kt—Q 5?; 11 P—Q Kt 4, Q—Q 2; 12 B×Kt, P×B; 13 Kt—K 4, Kt—R 5!?; 14 Kt×Q P! ±. Ragosin—Keres, Semmering-Baden, 1937.

(c) 13.., Kt—Q 5; 14 B×Kt, P×B; 15 Kt—Q 2, B—K 2; 16 Q R—Kt 1. Ragosin—Petrov, Semmering-Baden, 1937.

(d) 4.., P—Q 4; 5 P×P, Kt×P; 6 B—Kt 5, Kt×Kt; 7 Kt P×Kt, B—Q 2; 8 P—Q 4, B—Q 3; 9 B×Kt, B×B; 10 P×P, B×Kt; 11 Q×B, B×P; 12 O—O, P—Q B 3; 13 B—R 3, Q—R 4=. Flohr—Petrov, Semmering-Baden, 1937. Or 4., B—K 2; 5 Q—B 2, O—O; 6 P—Q R 3, P—Q 3; 8 B—K 2, R—K 1; 8 O—O, B—B 1; 9 P—Q 4, B—Kt 5; 10 P—Q 5, Kt—K 2 (Tartakover—Dr. Em. Lasker, New York, 1924) and now 11 P—K 4 followed by B—K 3 with a promising position for White (Tartakover).

(e) If 5 Kt—Q 5, P—K 5!; 6 Kt×B, Kt×Kt; 7 Kt—Q 4, O—O; 8 B—K 2, P—Q 4; 9 P—Q R 3, Kt—Q 6 ch; 10 B×Kt, P×B; 11 P—B 5, Kt—K 5 ∓. Eliskases—L. Steiner, Budapest, 1933.

(f) Flohr—Fine, Nottingham, 1936.

(g) If 3.., P×P; 4 Kt×P, B—Kt 5 ch; 5 B—Q 2, B×B ch; 6 Q×B, K Kt—K 2; 7 P—K Kt 3, O—O; 8 B—Kt 2, P—Q 3 (stronger than 8 ., Kt—K 4; 9 P—Kt 3, P—Q 4; 10 P×P, Kt×P; 11 Kt—Q B 3, Kt×Kt; 12 Q×Kt, P—Q B 3; 13 O—O, P—K B 4; 14 P—B 4 +. Fine—Berg, Kemeri, 1937); 9 O—O,B—Q 2; 10 Kt—Q B 3, R—K 1; 11 Q R—B 1, Kt×Kt; 12 Q×Kt, B—B 3; 13 P—K 4 ±. Chekhover—Rabinovitch, Tiflis, 1937.

(h) Nimzovitch—Tarrasch, Baden-Baden, 1925.

Notes ctd on p 41.

1 P—Q B 4, P—K 4; 2 Kt—Q B 3.

	11	12	13	14	15
2	Kt—K B 3	Kt—Q B 3			
3	P—KKt3 (a)	Kt—K B 3 ..	P—K Kt 3		
	P—Q 4	P—B 4	P—KKt3 (h)		
4	P×P	P—Q 4	B—Kt 2		
	Kt×P	P—K 5	B—Kt 2		
5	B—Kt 2	Kt—Q 2 (e)	P—Q 3		P—K 3
	Kt—Kt 3	Kt—B 3 (f)	P—Q 3	K Kt—K 2	P—Q 3
6	Kt—B 3	P—K 3	P—B 4 (i)	Kt—Q 5	K Kt—K 2
	Kt—B 3	B—Kt 5	K Kt—K 2	O—O	K Kt—K 2
7	O—O (b)	Q—Kt 3	Kt—B 3	P—K R 4	O—O (l)
	B—K 2	O—O	B—Kt 5	Kt—Q 5	O—O
8	P—Q 3	P—Q 5	O—O	B—Kt 5	P—Q 4 (m)
	O—O	B×Kt	O—O	P—K B 3	P×P
9	B—K 3	Q×B	P—K R 3	B—Q 2	Kt×P
	B—K Kt 5 (c)	Kt—K 2	B×Kt	P—B 3	Kt×Kt
10	Kt—Q R 4	P—Q Kt 3	B×B	Kt×Kt ch	P×Kt
	Q—Q 2	P—Q 3	Kt—B 4	Q×Kt	Kt—B 4
11	R—B 1	B—Kt 2	K—R 2	P—K 3	P—Q 5
	P—B 3	Kt—Kt 3	P×P	Kt—K 3	R—K 1
12	B—B 5	O—O—O	B×P	Kt—K 2	Kt—K 4
	Kt—Q 1	Q—K 2	R—K 1	P—K B 4	P—K R 3
13	B×B	B—K 2 ± (g)	Q—Q 2 ± (j)	Q—B 2	R—Kt 1
	Q×B=(d)			P—Kt3=(k)	R-Kt 1=(n)

(a) 3 P—K 4!, Kt—B 3; 4 P—B 4, P—Q 3; 5 P—Q 3, B—Kt 5; 6 B—K 2, P—K R 4; 7 Kt—B 3, B—K 2; 8 B—K 3, Q—Q 2; 9 P—K R 3, B×Kt; 10 B×B, P×P; 11 B×B P, Kt—Q 5; 12 B—K 3! ±. Alekhine—Lilienthal, Hastings, 1933-34.

(b) 7 P—Q R 3, P—Q R 4; 8 O—O, B—K 2; 9 P—Q 3, O—O; 10 B—K 3, B—K 3; 11 B×Kt, P×B; 12 Kt—Q 2. Opocensky—Flohr, Podebrady, 1936.

(c) 9 ., B—K 3; 10 R—B 1, Kt—Q 4 (better is P—B 3); 11 Kt×Kt, B×Kt; 12 Q—R 4, P—B 3; 13 B—B 5, B×B; 14 R×B, Kt—K 2; 15 K R—B 1, P—B 3; 16 P—K 4! ±. Kan—Chekhover, Moscow, 1936.

(d) Alexander—Euwe, Nottingham, 1936.

(e) 5 Kt—K 5!, P—Q 3; 6 Kt×Kt, P×Kt; 7 P—B 3, P—Q 4; 8 P×K P, B P×P; 9 Q—R 4, B—Q 2; 10 Q—R 5, R—Kt 1; 11 P—Q R 3, Kt—B 3; 12 P×P ±. Kevitz—Marshall, New York, 1935.

(f) If 5 ., B—Kt 5; 6 Kt—Q 5!, B×Kt ch; 7 Q×B ±. Poiland—Morton, Boston, 1938.

(g) Continued , P—Q R 4; 14 Q R—Kt 1, P—B 3; 15 P×P, P×P; 16 P—B 4, R—B 2; 17 P—K R 3 with a strong attack. Fine—H. Steiner, Mexico City, 1934.

(h) 3 ., B—B 4 (4. , P—Q 3; 5 P—K 3, K Kt—K 2; 6 P—Q R 3, P—Q R 4; 7 K Kt—K 2, O—O; 8 P—Q 4, B—Kt 3; 9 O—O, B—Q 2; 10 P—Kt 3, Q—B 1; 11 B—Kt 2, B—R 6=. Nimzovitch—Alekhine, Baden-Baden, 1925; 5 Kt—B 3, P—Q R 3; 6 O—O, P—Q 3; 7 P—K 3, O—O; 8 P—Q 4, B—R 2; 9 P—K R 3, P—K R 3; 10 P—Kt 3, B—K B 4; 11 B—R 3 ±. Tartakover—Grünfeld, Marienbad, 1925.

(i) Weaker is 6 B—Q 2, P—B 4; 7 R—Q Kt 1 (7 Kt—B 3, Kt—Q 5; 8 O—O, P—Q B 3; 9 R—B 1, Kt—K 2; 10 P—Q Kt 4, Kt×Kt ch=. Lasker—Alexander, Nottingham, 1936), Kt—K 2; 10 P—Q Kt 4, O—O; 9 P—Kt 5, Kt—K 2; 10 Q—Q 2, P—K R 3; 11 P—K 3, P—Q R 3; 12 P—Q R 4, P—B 4; 13 P×P, R×P; 14 K Kt—K 2, Kt—B 3 ∓. Capablanca—Bogoljuboff, Nottingham, 1936.

(j) Flohr—Euwe, 3rd match game 1932.

(k) Capablanca—Alexander, Nottingham, 1936.

Notes ctd. on p. 41.

1 P—Q B 4, Kt—K B 3; 2 Kt—K B 3.

	16	17	18	19	20
2	P—B 4............................			P—K 3	
3	P—K Kt 3... Kt—B 3	..... P—Q 4		Kt—B 3	
	P—Q Kt 3	P—Q 4	P×P	P—Q 4	
4	Kt—B 3	P×P	Kt×P	P—K 3	
	Kt—B 3	Kt×P	P—Q 4 (f)	P—Q B 4.... Kt—K 5	
5	B—Kt 2	P—K 4	P×P	P×P	Q—B 2
	B—Kt 2	Kt—Kt 5 (b)	Kt×P	Kt×P (h)	P—K B 4
6	O—O	B—B 4	P—K 4	B—K 2	P—Q 3
	P—K 3	Kt-Q6 ch (c)	Kt—Kt 5	B—K 2	Kt×Kt
7	P—Q Kt 3	K—K 2	Q—R 4 ch	O—O	P×Kt
	B—K 2	Kt×B ch	Q Kt—B 3	O—O	P—B 3
8	B—Kt 2	R×Kt	Kt×Kt	P—Q 3	P—Q 4
	O—O	P—Q R 3 (d)	Kt×Kt	P—Q Kt 3	B—Q 3
9	P—Q 4	P—Q 4	Kt—B 3	B—Q 2	P×P
	Kt×P	P×P	B—Q 2	Kt—Q B 3	K P×P
10	Kt×Kt	Q×P	B—K 3	R—B 1	B—Q 3
	B×B	Q×Q	P—K 3	B—Kt 2	O—O
11	K×B	Kt×Q	R—B 1	P—Q R 3	O—O
	P×Kt	P—K 3	B—Q 3	Kt×Kt	B—K 3
12	Q×P	Kt—R 4	B—K 2	B×Kt	P—B 4
	Q—B 2	Kt—Q 2	B—K 4	B—B 3	Kt—Q 2
13	P—K 4 ± (a)	K R-Q 1! ± (e)	O—O ± (g)	Q—B 2 = (i)	R-Kt 1 = (j)

(a) Botvinnik—Capablanca, Moscow, 1936.

(b) Better is 5.., Kt×Kt; 6 Kt P×Kt, P—K Kt 3 with a position analogous to the Grünfeld Defence in the Q.P. opening; or 6.., P—K 3; 6 P—Q 4, P×P; 7 P×P, B—Kt 5 ch with a satisfactory variation of the Q.G.D.

(c) 6.., P—K 3; 7 O—O, Q Kt—B 3; 8 P—Q 3, Kt—Q 5; 9 Kt×Kt, P×Kt; 10 Kt—K 2 ±. Nimzovitch—Rubinstein, Dresden, 1926.

(d) If 8.., Kt—B 3; 9 Q—Kt 3, P—K 3; 10 B—Kt 5, B—Q 2; 11 B×Kt, B×B; 12 K R—Q 1 followed by P—Q 4 ± (Becker).

(e) 13.., P—Q Kt 4 ?; 14 Kt×K P !, B P×Kt; 15 B×K P, P×Kt; 16 R×B ch, R×R; 17 B×Kt ch, K—Q 1; 18 B—Kt 4 ch and wins. Takacs—Rubinstein, Rogaska-Slatina, 1929 (1st Brilliancy Prize).

(f) 4.., Kt—Q B 3; 5 Kt—Q B 3, P—K Kt 3; 6 P—K 4 transposes to a variation of the Sicilian Defence which is in White's favour.

If 4.., P—Q Kt 3; 5 Kt—Q B 3, B—Kt 2; 6 B—Kt 5 !, Kt—K 5; 7 Kt×Kt, B×Kt; 8 P—B 3, B—Kt 2; 9 P—K 4 +. Alekhine—Sämisch, Baden-Baden, 1925.

An unusual alternative is 4. , P—K 4 !?; 5 Kt—Kt 5, B—Kt 5 ch; 6 B—Q 2 (better 6 Q Kt—B 3 and if 6.., O—O; 7 B—Kt 5 ±), B—B 4; 7 B—B 3, Q—Kt 3; 8 P—K 3, P—Q R 3; 9 K Kt—R 3 ? (9 P—Q Kt 4 was necessary), Kt—B 3; 10 B—Q 3, O—O; 11 O—O, P—Q 3; 12 Kt—B 2, B—K 3 ∓. Dake—Fine, 6th match game, New York, 1933.

(g) Dake—H. Müller, Folkestone, 1933.

(h) 5.., P×P; 6 P—Q 4, Kt—B 3; 7 B—Kt 5, P—Q R 3; 8 B×Kt ch, P×B; 9 Kt—K 5, B—Q 3; 10 P—B 4 ±. Opocensky—Alekhine, Podebrady, 1936.

(i) Flohr—Thomas, Nottingham, 1936.

(j) White has no appreciable advantage. Flohr—Tartakover, Nottingham, 1936.

ENGLISH OPENING

1 P—Q B 4.

	21	22	23	24	25
1	(Kt—K B 3) (A)				
2	(Kt—K B 3) (P—K 3)	Kt—Q B 3 P—K 3	.....	P—B 3	P-K Kt 3 (»»)
3	(Kt—B 3) B—Kt 5	P—K 4 P—Q 4 (c)		P—K 4 P—Q 4	P—K Kt 3 B—Kt 2
4	Q—B 2 P—B 4	P—K 5 P—Q 5 (d)		P—K 5 P—Q 5	B—Kt 2 P—Q 3
5	P—Q R 3 (a) B—R 4	P×Kt P×Kt		P×Kt P×Kt	P—Q 3 P—B 3
6	P—K 3 Kt—B 3	Kt P×P (e) Q×P		P×Kt P (k) P×P ch	B—Q 2 Q Kt—Q 2
7	P—Q 4 P—Q 3	P—Q 4 P—Q Kt 3 (f)		B×P B×P	Q—B 1 P—K R 3
8	B—K 2 O—O	Kt—B 3 B—Kt 2		Q—B 2 Q—B 2	R—Kt 1 P—K 4
9	O—O Q—K 2	B—K 2 Kt—Q 2....	P—K R 3	P—B 4 Kt—R 3	P—Q Kt 4 Kt—B 1
10	P—Q Kt 3 B×Kt	O—O B—Q 3	Kt—K 5! (h) B—Q 3	Kt—B 3 B—Kt 5	Kt—B 3 Kt—K 3
11	Q×B P—Q Kt 3	B—Kt 5 Q—B 4	Q—R 4 ch K—K 2 (i)	B—K 2 O—O—O	O—O P—K Kt 4
12	B—Kt 2 Kt—K 5 =	Q—R 4 P—Q B 3	B—B 3 B×B	O—O—O P—K3! ∓ (l)	Kt—K 4 O—O ∓ (n)
13	(b)	P—B 5! + (g)	Kt×B = (j)		

(A) 1.., P—Q B 3; 2 P—K 4, P—Q 4 (as in Botvinnik-Flohr, Leningrad, 1934) transposes into the Caro-Kann.

(a) 5 P—K 4, P—Q 3; 6 P—Q R 3, B—R 4: 7 P—Q 3, Kt—Q B 3; 8 B—K 3, O—O; 9 O—O—O, Kt—K Kt 5; 10 B—Kt 5, P—B 3; 11 B—R 4, K Kt—K 4= Bogoljuboff—Ahues, Berlin, 1927.

(b) 13 Q—B 2, P—B 4; 14 Kt—Q 2, Kt—B 3; 15 B—K B 3, B—Kt 2. Kmoch—Alekhine, Kecskemét, 1927.

(c) A good alternative is 3.., P—Q B 4; 4 P—K Kt 3, P—Q 4; 5 P—K 5, P—Q 5, 6 P×Kt, P×Kt; 7 Q P×P (Nimzovitch prefers 7 Kt P×P, Q×P; 8 P—Q 4 since Black cannot win a Pawn by 8.., P×P; 9 P×P, B—Kt 5 ch; 10 B—Q 2, Q×P, 11 B×B, Q—K 5 ch; 12 B—K 2, Q×R; 13 Q—Q 6, Kt—B 3; 14 B—K B 3!+ +), Q×P; 8 Kt—B 3, P—K R 3; 9 B—Kt 2, B—Q 2; 10 Kt—Q 2, B—B 3; 11 Kt—K 4, Q—Kt 3; 12 Q—K 2, B—K 2=. Bogoljuboff—Nimzovitch, London, 1927.

(d) If 4.., Kt—K 5; 5 Kt×Kt, P×Kt; 6 Q—Kt 4, P—K B 4; 7 P×P e.p., Q×P (K 4); 8 Q×P (K 4), B—B 4; 9 Kt—B 3, B—B 3; 10 B—K 2, B—Q 2; 11 O—O, O—O—O; 12 P—Q 3, Kt—Q 5? (P—K R 3 was necessary); 13 B—Kt 5!+. Flohr—Sir G. A. Thomas, Hastings, 1931.

(e) 6 P×Kt P, P×P ch; 7 B×P, B×P; 8 Q—B 2, Kt—B 3= (Kashdan).

(f) 7.., P—B 4; 8 Kt—B 3, P—K R 3; 9 B—K 2, P×P; 10 P×P, B—Kt 5 ch; 11 B—Q 2, B×Bch; 12 Q×B, O—O=. Eliskases—Kessner, Vienna, 1932.

(g) Flohr—Kashdan, Folkestone.

(h) Or 10 O—O, B—Q 3; 11 Q—R 4 ch, B—B 3; 12 Q—B 2, O—O; 13 B—K 3, Kt—Q 2; 14 Q R—Q 1, Q R—Q 1; 15 Kt—Q 2, P—K 4=. Kevitz—Fine, New York, 1933.

Notes ctd. on p 41.

Notes for cols. 6 to 10 ctd.

(i) Or 4 Kt×Kt, Q P×Kt; 5 P—Q 4 (5 Kt—B 3, Kt—B 3; 6 P—K Kt 3, B—Q B 4; 7 B—Kt 2, B—B 4; 8 O—O, O—O; 9 K—R 1, Q—Q 5! ∓. Réti—Torre, Marienbad, 1925), P × P *e.p.*; 6 Q × P, Q × Q; 7 P × Q, B—K B 4; 8 P—Q 4, O—O—O=. Tartakover—Alekhine, Warsaw, 1935.

(j) Better was 7 B—Kt 2, *e.g.* 7.., R—K 1; 8 P—Q 4, P × P *e.p.*; 9 Q × P, Kt—K 4; 10 Q—Q 2, etc. (Alekhine).

(k) Correct was 8.., K Kt—Kt 5 ! with a strong attack, *e.g.* (1) 9 Kt × P, Q × P; 10 B—K Kt 2 (10 P—B 3, Q × Kt !), B × P ch ; 11 K—B 1, Q—K B 4 etc. (2) 9 P—K 3, Q Kt—K 4; A. 10 P—Q 4 (or 10 B—K 2, Kt—Q 6 ch !; 11 B × Kt, P × B; etc.), Kt—B 6 ch ; 11 K—K 2, K Kt × R P !; 12 P × B, B—Kt 5, etc. B. 10 Kt × P, Q × P; 11 P—B 3, P—K B 4 !; 12 Kt × B, Kt × P ch ; 13 K—K 2, Q × Kt; etc. (3) 9 Kt—K 3, B × Kt; 10 B P × B, Q—B 3; 11 Q—B 2, Q—B 7 ch ; 12 K—Q 1, Q—B 4; 13 K—K 1 (13 Kt × P, Kt—Kt 5 followed by Q × Kt), Kt—Kt 5; etc. Analysis by Alekhine.

(l) Continued 13.., Q × Kt; 14 P—Q 3, Q R—Q 1; 15 P × P, B × P; 16 Q × Q. Drawn. Euwe—Alekhine, 18th match game, 1935.

(m) Rubinstein—Sämisch, Breslau, 1925.

Notes for cols. 11 to 15 ctd.

(l) 7 P—Q 4, P × P; 8 P × P, O—O; 9 O—O, Kt—B 4 (better is B—Kt 5; 10 P—K R 3, B × Kt ; 11 Kt × B, Kt—B 4; 12 P—Q 5, Q Kt—Q 5); 10 P—Q 5, Kt—K 4; 11 P—Kt 3, P—Q R 4; 12 B—Kt 2, Kt—Q 2; 13 P—Q R 3, Kt—B 4; 14 P—Q Kt 4, Kt—Q 2; 15 Q—Kt 3 +. Botvinnik—Reshevsky, Avro Tournament, 1938.

(m) Or 8 Kt—Q 5, Kt × Kt; 9 P × Kt, Kt—K 2; 10 P—Q 4, Kt—B 4; 11 P × P, P × P; 12 P—K 4, Kt—Q 3; 13 B—K 3, P—K B 4; 14 P × P, B × P; 15 Q—Kt 3, P—Kt 3; 16 Q R—B 1, Q—Q 2; 17 P—B 3, P—K R 4 ∓. Alexander—Reshevsky, Nottingham, 1936.

(n) Kan—Yudovitch, Tiflis, 1937.

Notes for cols. 21 to 25 ctd.

(i) If 11.., K—B 1; 12 B—B 3, B × B and Black has one tempo less than in the text.

(j) 13.., R—Q 1; 14 O—O, K—B 1; 15 R—K 1, Kt—Q 2; 16 Q—B6, P—K 4; 17 Q—K 4, K—Kt 1 (Alexander—Fine, Nottingham, 1936), and now 18 Q—Kt 4 ! is quite strong.

(k) Stronger is 6 Kt P × P, Kt P × P; 7 P—Q 4, P—K 3 (better 7.., B—B 4) ; 8 B—Q 3, R—Kt 1; 9 Q—B 3, P—K B 4; 10 Kt—K 2, P—Kt 3; 11 P—K R 3 !, B—Q Kt 2; 12 P—Kt 4, P × P; 13 P × P, P—K R 3; 14 B × P +. Kashdan—Simonson, 1st match game, New York, 1938.

(l) Flohr—Betbéder, Folkestone, 1933. White now played 13 P—Kt 4 ? upon which 13.., Q—K 2 (instead of the doubtful sacrifice 13.., Kt × P, which occurred in the game) ; 14 P—B 5, Q—B 3; 15 B × Kt, P × B ! would have given Black an overwhelming attack (Kashdan).

(m) 2.., P—B 4; 3 P—K Kt 3, P—Q 4; 4 P × P, Kt × P; 5 B—Kt 2, Kt × Kt; 6 Kt P × Kt, P—K Kt 3; 7 Kt—B 3, B—Kt 2; 8 Q—R 4 ch (Eliskases—Razinger, Linz, 1934), Kt—Q 2 =

(n) 13 B—B 3, Kt—K 1; 14 Q—Kt 2, P—K B 4. Maróczy—Yates, Hastings, 1924.

EVANS GAMBIT

DESPITE a prodigious amount of analysis, this offshoot of the Giuoco Piano still remains a problem child among the openings. About ten years ago Tartakover's investigations appeared to establish the correctness of the brilliant Pawn-sacrifice introduced over a century ago by Captain W. D. Evans; his conclusions have, however, since been questioned.

In the accepted form of the Gambit, the "Normal Position" (cols. 1 to 3) yields White adequate positional advantage for his Pawn; the "Compromised Defence" (col. 4), though possibly sound analytically, gives Black too difficult a game in actual play. In col. 5 White is able, though late, to Castle with advantage on the Queen's side; a rarity in this opening.

The variation in col. 6, based on Tartakover's analysis, avoids Lasker's Defence (col. 8), in which Black obtains a favourable end-game or else remains a Pawn ahead; but White's attack is not powerful enough to compensate for the material sacrificed. The line in note (d) may open new vistas for the first player. In col. 9, arising from 5..., B—B 4, in place of B—R 4, White does best by transposing into the Normal Position.

Many masters recommend Black to decline the Gambit, contending that White's 4th move is then a needless weakening of the Pawn-position in the Giuoco Piano variation arising therefrom. Nevertheless, Cordel's line (col. 1) has been adopted in some modern tournament games with favourable results for the first player, on account of his control of the open Queen's Rook's file. The enterprising variation based on 5 P—Kt 5 and 6 Kt × P is not quite sound for White, Black obtaining the superior game by 6..., Kt—R 3 and 8..., P × Kt (col. 3).

Black may effectively avoid the dangerous attacks in the Evans Gambit and the Giuoco Piano by the adoption of the Two Knights' Defence, in which it is difficult for White to retain the initiative.

1 P—K 4, P—K 4 ; 2 Kt—K B 3, Kt—Q B 3 ; 3 B—B 4, B—B 4
4 P—Q Kt 4.

4.., B×P ; 5 P—B 3, B—R 4 ; 6 P—Q 4.

	1	2	3	4	5
6	P×P..				B—Kt 3 (*i*)
7	O—O				P×P
	B—Kt 3........................			P×P (*f*)	P—K R 3 (*j*)
8	P×P			Q—Kt 3	Q—Q 5
	P—Q 3 (*a*)			Q—B 3	Q—K 2
9	Kt—B 3.....B—Kt 2.....	P—Q 5		P—K 5	B—R 3
	Kt—R 4	K Kt—K 2	Kt—R 4	Q—Kt 3	Q—K 3
10	B—KKt5 (*b*)	Kt—Kt 5 (*e*)	B—Kt 2	Kt×P	Q—Q 3
	P—K B 3	P—Q 4	Kt—K 2 !	KKt—K2(*g*)	Kt×P
11	B—K 3 ! (*c*)	P×P	B—Q 3	B—R 3	Kt×Kt
	Kt—K 2	Kt—R 4	O—O	B×Kt (*h*)	Q×Kt
12	P—K R 3	P—Q 6	Kt—B 3	Q×B	P—B 4
	B—Q 2	Kt×B	Kt—Kt 3	O—O	Q—K R 4
13	B—Kt 3	P×Kt	Kt—K 2	Q R—Q 1	Kt—Q 2
	Kt×B	Q—Q 4	P—Q B 4	R—K 1	P—Q 3
14	Q×Kt	Kt—Q B 3	Q—Q 2	K R—K 1	B—Kt 5 ch
	Q—B 1	Q×Kt !	P—B 3	R—Kt 1	B—Q 2
15	P—Q R 4	Q—R 4 ch	K—R 1	B—Q 3	B×B ch
	B—K 3	P—B 3	B—B 2	P—B 4	K×B
16	Q—R 3	Q×Kt	Q R—B 1	P×P *e.p.*	P—K 5
	P—Q R 4	B—R 6+	R—Kt 1	Q×P	R—K 1
17	KR—B1+ (*d*)		Kt—Kt 3	Q—Kt3 ch+	Kt—B 3+
			P—Kt 4 ∓		

(*a*) The Normal Position. If 8.., Kt—R 4 ; 9 B—K Kt 5, Kt—B 3 ; 10 P—K 5+.
(*b*) 10 R—K 1, Kt×B ; 11 Q—R 4 ch, P—B 3 ; 12 Q×Kt, Kt—K 2 ; 13 B—Kt 5, O—O ; 14 P—Q 5, P—B 3 ; 15 P×P ch, K—R 1 (P. Johner—Spielmann, Baden, 1914) ; 16 P×P=.
(*c*) 11 B—B 4, Kt—K 2 !; 12 R—K 1, P—B 3 ; 13 Q—Q 3, B—B 2 : 14 P- Q R 4, Kt×B ; 15 Q×Kt, Kt—Kt 3+. Motzko—Vidmar, correspondence, 1910.
(*d*) 17.., O—O ; 18 Kt—Q Kt 5, Q—Q 1 ; 19 P—Q 5.
(*e*) 10 P—Q 5, transposing to col. 3, is better.
(*f*) The Compromised Defence. Alternatives giving White an attack worth more than the Pawn are : (1) 7. , P—Q 3 ; 8 Q—Kt 3 (Waller's Attack), Q—B 3 ; 9 F—K 5, P×P ; 10 R—K 1, B—Q 2 ; 11 B—K Kt 5. (2) 7 ., K Kt—K 2 ; 8 P×P, P—Q 4, 9 P×P, K Kt×P (F. J. Wallis suggests 9 ., P—Q Kt 4 ; 10 B×P, Q×P ; 11 Q—R 4 B—Q 2 ; 12 B—R 3, P—Q R 3 !+) ; 10 B—R 3, B—K 3 ; 11 Q Kt—Q 2, B×Kt ; 12 Q×B. (3) 7.., P—Q 6 ; 8 Q—Kt 3, Q—B 3 ; 9 P—K 5. (4) 7. , Kt—B 3 ; 8 B—R 3, P—Q 3 ; 9 P—K 5, Kt—K Kt 5 ; 10 K P×P, B P×P ; 11 R—K 1 ch, K Kt—K 4 ; 12 Kt×Kt, P×Kt ; 13 Kt—Q 2.
(*g*) 10 ., B×Kt ; 11 Q×B, P—Q Kt 3 (or 11.., K Kt—K 2 ; 12 Kt—Kt 5, O—O ; 13 B—Q 3+); 12 P—K 6 !+. 10.., P—Kt 4 ; 11 Kt×P, R—Kt 1 ; 12 Kt—Kt 5 (12 Q—K 3, K Kt—K 2 ; 13 B—R 3, B—Kt 3 ; 14 Q—B 4. *Handbuch*), Kt—R 3 ; 13 P—B 4 (13 Q—K 3 !), O—O (P—R 3 !) ; 14 Q—Q 1, P—R 3 ; 15 B—Q 3, P—B 4 ; 16 P×P *e.p.*, Q×P ; 17 Q—B 2, Kt—B 4 ; 18 B—Kt 2, B—Kt 3 ch ; 19 K—R 1, Kt—Kt 6 ch ; 20 P×Kt, Q—R 3 ch ; 21 Kt—R 3, P×Kt ;. 22 K B×P=. C. H Alexander—E. Spencer, Worcester, 1931.
(*h*) 11 ., O—O ; 12 Q R—Q 1, P—Kt 4 (or 12 ., R—K 1 ; 13 B—Q 3, Q—R 4 ; 14 Kt—K 4+) ; 13 B—Q 3 !, Q—R 4 ; 14 Kt—K 4, P—Kt 5 ; 15 Kt—Kt 3, Q—Kt 5 ; 16 B—K 2+.
(*i*) 6.., P—Q Kt 4 (Leonhardt's Defence) is theoretically quite strong : 7 B—Q 5, P×P ; 8 Q—Kt 3, Q—B 3 ; 9 P—K 5, Q—Kt 3 ; 10 Kt—Kt R 3 ; 11 P—K 6, O—O ; 12 P×P ch, K×P ; 13 Kt×Kt, R×Kt ; 14 O—O, P×P+. If 6.., P×P ; 7 O—O, P—Q Kt 4 ; 8 B×P, P×P ; 9 B×Kt, P×B ; 10 Q—R 4, B—Kt 3 ; 11 Q×P ch, B—Q 2 ; 12 Q×P (B 3), Q—B 3 ; 13 P—K 5, Q—Kt 3=. Tartakover—P. Johner, Baden, 1914. 6.., Kt×P (Pierce's Defence) ; 7 Kt×P, Kt—K 3 ; 8 Kt×B P, Q—B 3 ; 9 B×Kt !, P×B ; 10 Kt×R+.
(*j*) 7 ., P—Q 3 and 7.., K Kt—K 2 are playable (Tartakover). The column is Tartakover—Chajes, Carlsbad, 1923.

1 P—K 4, P—K 4 ; 2 Kt—K B 3, Kt—Q B 3 ; 3 B—B 4, B—B 4
4 P—Q Kt 4.

	6	7	8	9	10
4	B×P (a)				
5	P—B 3 (b)				
	B—R 4			B—B 4	B—K 2 (n)
6	P—Q 4			P—Q 4	P—Q 4
	P—Q 3 (A)			P×P	Kt—R 4
7	Q—Kt 3.....	Q—R 4.....	O—O	O—O (k)	B—Q 3 (o)
	Q—Q 2 ! (c)	P×P	B—Kt 3 ! (i)	P—Q 6 (l)	P—Q 4
8	P—Q R 4 (d)	B—K Kt 5	B—R 3 (j)	Kt—Kt 5	Q P×P
	Kt—B 3 (e)	K Kt—K 2	P×P	Kt—R 3	P×P
9	O—O	Kt×P	P×P	Kt×B P	Q—R 4 ch
	O—O	Q—Q 2	B—Kt 5	Kt×Kt	P—B 3
10	P×P	B—Kt 5	B—Q Kt 5	B×Kt ch	Q×P
	K Kt×P	P—Q R 3	B×Kt	K×B	B—K 3
11	B—R 3	K B×Kt	B×Kt ch	Q—R 5 ch	=
	B—Kt 3	Kt×B	P×B	P—Kt 3	
12	Q—B 2 (f)	Kt—B 5	P×B	Q×B	
	Kt—B 4	P—B 3	Kt—K 2	P—Q 3	
13	R—Q 1	B—K 3	K—R 1	Q—Q 5 ch	
	Q—K 2	P-QKt4+ (h)	Kt—Kt 3	B—K 3	
14	P×P	R—Kt 1		Q×P (Q 3)	
	P×P+ (g)	O—O+		R—K 1 (m)	

(a) 4.., Kt×P, 5 Kt×P? (5 P—B 3, Kt—Q B 3; 6 P—Q 4, transposing to col. 9, is best), Q—B 3; 6 O—O, Q×Kt; 7 P—Q B 3, Kt—Q B 3; 8 P—Q 4, Kt×P+
(b) 5 O—O, Kt—B 3! (5. , P—Q 3; 6 P—Q 4, B—Q 2; 7 B—Kt 2 is suggested by Tartakover); 6 P—Q 4, P×P; 7 P—B 3, P×P; 8 P—K 5, P—Q 4; 9 B—QKt 5. Kt—Q 2!+. A. S. Pinkus—Marshall, New York, 1926.
(c) 7. , Q—K 2?; 8 P—Q 5, Kt—Q 5; 9 Kt×Kt, P×Kt; 10 Q—Kt 5 ch+ .
(d) 8 P×P, B—Kt 3 (8.., P×P?; 9 O—O, Kt—B 3?; 10 R—Q 1, Q—K 2; 11 B—R 3 ++); 9 Q Kt—Q 2, Kt—R 3; 10 O—O, O—O; 11 P×P, Q×P; 12 B—Q 5, Kt—R 4; 13 Q—Kt 4 ±. C. H. Alexander—T. H. Tylor, Hastings, 1935-36.
(e) Inferior for Black are (1) 8 (P—Q R 3; 9 P×P, B—Kt 3; 10 P—R 5! Kt×R P; 11 R×Kt, B×R; 12 P×P+. (2) 8 , B—Kt 3; 9 P—R 5!, Kt×R P; 10 R×Kt, B×R; 11 P×P. (3) 8.., Kt×P; 9 Kt×Kt, P×Kt; 10 O—O. P×P; 11 P—K 5+.
(f) So far Tartakover's analysis.
(g) 15 Q Kt—Q 2, B—Kt 5; 16 R—K 1, Q—Q 2; 17 B×Kt, B×B; 18 B—Q 3, P—K R 3+.
(h) Breyer—Réti, Baden, 1914.
(i) Lasker's Defence. The Sanders—Alapin Defence runs 7.., B—Q 2; 8 Q—Kt 3, Q—K 2; 9 P×P, P×P; 10 R—Q 1, R—Q 1; 11 R—Q 5 ±.
(j) Or 8P×P, P×P; 9B×P ch (both 9 Q—Kt 3. Q—B 3; 10 B—K Kt 5, Q—Kt 3; 11 B—Q 5, K Kt—K 2; 12 Q B×Kt, K×B; 13 B×Kt, Q×B; 14 Kt×P, Q—K 3 and 9 Q×Q ch, Kt×Q; 10 Kt×P, B—K 3; 11 B×B, Kt×B lead to endings in Black's favour, K×B; 10 Kt×P ch, K—K 1; 11 Q—R 5 ch, P—Kt 3; 12 Kt×P, Kt—B 3; 13 Q—R 6, R—K Kt 1; 14 Kt—B 4, Kt—K 4+ (S. Mlotkowski). If 8 Q—Kt 3, Q—B 3; or 8 P—Q R 4, Kt—B 3 and Black has a fairly easy defence with a Pawn ahead. The column is P. Johner—Fahrni, Baden, 1914.
(k) White's strongest line is 7 P×P, B—Kt 3 (if 7 ., B—Kt 5 ch; 8 K—B 1! Q—K 2; 9 Q—R 4+); 8 O—O, P—Q 3 transposing into the Normal Position, cols. 1 to 3.
(l) 7.., P—Q 3 transposes into the Normal Position.
(m) 15 P—K B 4, K—Kt 1; 16 B—Kt 2, P—Q 4; 17 P—B 4 ±. Dr. Dührssen—Kramer, Ebensee, 1930.
(n) 5. , B—Q 3; 6 P—Q 4, Kt—B 3; 7 O—O, O—O; 8 Q Kt—Q 2, Q—K 2; 9 B—Q 3 and Kt—B 4—K 3—Q 5 +. Or 5.., P—B 4 (Cordel); 6 P×B, P×P; 7 P—K 5!, Kt—R 4; 8 B×Kt, R×B; 9 O—O P×P+.
(o) If 7 Kt×P, Kt×B; 8 Kt×Kt, P—Q 4=.
(A) If 6 ., Q—B 3; 7 O—O, K Kt—K 2; 8 P—Q 5, Kt—Q 1; 9 Q—R 4, B—Kt 3; 10 B—K Kt 5, Q—Q 3; 11 Kt—R 3, P—Q B 3; 12 Q R—Q 1+. Tchigorin—Steinitz, 17th match game, 1889.

1 P—K 4, P—K 4; 2 Kt—K B 3, Kt—Q B 3; 3 B—B 4, B—B 4: 4 P—Q Kt 4, B—Kt 3 (a).

	1	2	3	4	5
5	B—Kt 2 (b) .. / P—Q 3	P—Q R 4.... / P—Q R 3	P—Kt 5 / Kt—R 4 (h)		
6	P—Q R 4 / P—Q R 3	O—O (g) / P—Q 3	Kt×P (i) / Kt—R 3...............		Q—Kt 4 (o)
7	P—Kt 5 / P×P (c)	P—R 5 / B—R 2	P—Q 4 / P—Q 3		B×P ch / K—B 1 (p)
8	P×P / R×R	P—Kt 5 / P×P	B×Kt / P×Kt !.....	P×B	B×Kt / Q×Kt
9	B×R / Kt—Q 5 (d)	B×P / Kt—K 2	B×P / R—K Kt 1	B×P ch (m) / K—K 2	B—Q 5 / P—B 3
10	B×Kt (e) / P×B	P—Q 4 / P×P	B×P ch / K×B	Q—B 3 (n) / B×P	Q—B 3 ch / K—K 1
11	O—O / Kt—B 3	Kt×P / B—Q 2	B×P / B—Kt 5 (j)	Kt—B 3 / P—B 3	Q—B 7 ch / K—Q 1
12	P—Q 3 / O—O	Kt×Kt / Kt×Kt	Q—Q 3 / P—B 4	P×P / B×Kt ch	P×P / Kt P×P
13	Q Kt—Q 2 / P—B 4	B×Kt / B×B	Kt—B 3 / P×P	Q×B / P×Kt	P—Q 4 / B×P
14	P×P e.p. / P×P	B—Kt 2 / O—O	Kt—Q 5 / Q—K 1	R—Q 1 / Q—B 2	B—K B 4 / Q—B 3
15	Q—R 1 / P—B 4	Q—Kt 4 / P—B 3=	Q—K Kt3 (k) / Kt—B 5	B—R 5 ! / B—K 3	Q×Q / B×Q
16	R—Kt 1 / B—R 4		Q—B 4 ch / K—K 3!+ (l)	Q—R 3 ch / K—B 3	P—K 5 / R—K 1
17	R—Kt 5 / B—B 2 (f)			Q—B 3 ch / K—K 2=	B—B 7 / R—K 2=

(a) 4.., P—Q 4; 5 P×P, Kt×P; 6 O—O (Maróczy recommends 6 B—R 3), Kt—K B 3; 7 Kt×P, Q Kt×Q P; 8 P—Q 4, B—Q 3; 9 B—K Kt 5, P—B 3; 10 Kt—Q 2 ±. Schiffers—Pillsbury, Nuremberg, 1896.

(b) 5 P—B 3, Kt—B 3; 6 Q—Kt 3, O—O; 7 P—Q 3, P—Q 3; 8 B—K Kt 5, Q—K 2=.

(c) 7.., Kt—R4; 8 B—K 2, Kt—K B 3; 9 Kt—B 3, B—Kt 5; 10 Kt—Q 5, Kt×Kt; 11 P×Kt ±. Tartakover—Fahrni, Baden, 1914.

(d) 9.., Kt—Kt 1; 10 P—Q 4, P×P; 11 B×P, B×B; 12 Q×B, Kt—K B 3 (Q—B 3!); 13 Kt—B 3, O—O; 14 O—O, Q Kt—Q 2; 15 P—R 3, R—K 1; 16 R—R 1, P—R 3; 17 Kt—K R 4, Kt—K 4; 18 R—R 8!+. Tartakover—Yates, Carlsbad, 1929.

(e) 10 Kt×Kt, P×Kt; 11 P—B 3, Kt—B 3; 12 O—O, O—O; 13 P—Q 3, P—Q 4. Tartakover—Rubinstein, The Hague, 1921.

(f) 18 Q—R 7 ±. P. Johner—Hromadka, Baden, 1914.

(g) Tartakover recommends 6 B—Kt 2, transposing into col. 1.

(h) 5.., Kt—Q 5; 6 Kt× Kt, B× Kt; 7 P—Q B 3, B—Kt 3; 8 P—Q 4, Q—B 3; 9 O—O, P—Q 3 (Spielmann—Nyholm, Baden, 1914); 10 B—K 3=.

(i) 6 B—K 2, P—Q 4; 7 P—Q 3, P×P; 8 P×P, Q×Q ch= is safest.

(j) 11.., Q—Kt 4; 12 Kt—B 3 (12 Kt—Q 2, Q×P; 13 Q—R 5 ch, Q—Kt 3; 14 Q×Q ch, R×Q+), Kt—B 5; 13 Kt—Q 3 (13 B—Kt 3, B—Kt 5; 14 Kt—K 2, B—R 4 ch!; 15 K—B 1, Q—R 4+. Réti—Perlis, Vienna, 1913), B—R 4 ch; 14 P—B 3, Kt×B; 15 P×Kt, P—B 3; 16 Q—B 3 ch, K—Kt 2; 17 P×P, P×P+. Analysis by S. Mlotkowski (B.C.M., 1917, p. 38).

(k) 15 B×P, B×B; 16 Q×B is better (Blümich).

(l) N. T. Whitaker—Sir G. A. Thomas, London—Washington cable match, 1930.

(m) 10 Kt×P, Q—B 3; 11 Kt×R, B×P +.

(n) 10 Kt—Q B 3, P×Kt; 11 Q—B 3, B—Kt 5!+. Dr. F. Deighton—J. H. Blake, Cambridge, 1894.

(o) 6..., Q—B 3; 7 B×P ch, K—B 1; 8 P—Q 4, P—Q 3; 9 B×Kt, P×Kt; 0 B—Q 5, P—B 3; 11 B—R 3 ch, K—K 1; 12 O—O.

(p) 7.., K—K 2; 8 B×Kt, R×B! (8.., Q×Kt; 9 B—Q 5, P—B 3; 10 P—Q 4, B×P; 11 P—K B 4 ∓).

FOUR KNIGHTS' GAME

THE Four Knights' is one of the soundest openings; indeed, its only weakness is that it is *too* sound. If he wish, the first player may draw against an opponent of equal strength more readily with this than with any other opening. But, on the other hand, the second player has various simplifying lines at his disposal, against which it is impossible for White to obtain an advantage.

Black has a choice of two main systems of defence. In the first place he may elect to follow White's development for a while; the attack based on the pinning of Black's King's Knight by B—K Kt 5, followed by the opening of the King's Bishop's file, having been shorn of many of its terrors.

The variations in cols. 1 to 15, in which Black exchanges Bishop for Knight on his 6th move, have in modern times had more vogue than the corresponding lines of play (cols. 16 to 21) in which such exchange is deferred or omitted altogether.

The key-move of the attack is B—K Kt 5 played on White's 8th move in cols. 1 to 12. Black has in reply a choice of :—

(i) 8..., Kt—K 2 (cols. 1 to 5), for a long time a very popular defence, until it was found that White retained an advantage by 9 Kt—R 4, reserving the choice of capturing Black's King's Knight.

(ii) 8..., B—Q 2 (col. 6 note (*a*)), a move of which the inferiority is not easily demonstrable.

(iii) 8..., Q—K 2 (cols. 6 to 10), an old defence attributed to E. Delmar in Philadelphia in 1875, though commonly called after J. Metger. It was disregarded for a period, but was revived very successfuly by Rubinstein. It leads to difficult position-play, in which the stronger player has the better chances. The line in col. 10 is a recent variation from master-play, with good opportunities for Black.

(iv) 8..., P—K R 3 (cols. 11 to 12), retaining the option of releasing the pin by P—K Kt 4 at a suitable moment. The line in col. 11, re-introduced by Lasker in 1914, equalises for Black; that exemplified in col. 12 is much weaker.

The Svenonius Variation (cols. 14 and 15) is theoretically insufficient.

Of the variations in which Black retains his King's Bishop (cols. 16 to 21), that in col. 18, recently revived by Dr. Lasker, appears satisfactorily to meet the embarrassing attack inaugurated by 8 Kt—K R 4. The possibility of a check at Q B 4 in some variations is an argument in favour of the retention of Black's King's Bishop. The symmetrical variations in col. 21 lead to extremely difficult play, in which the slightest error on Black's part is fatal.

The alternative 7 Kt—K 2 (cols. 22 and 23) limits Black's choice of replies, and in Maróczy's hands has produced some brilliant wins for the first player. The purely symmetrical variation in col. 23, played by Dr. Euwe in an important game, is not quite adequate.

The Nimzovitch Variation (cols. 24 and 25) gives White a very solid position, with the possibility of building up a dangerous King-side attack. Black may, however, readily draw by the simplifying line in col. 25, note (m).

In the old defence 4..., B—B 4 (cols. 31 to 35), Black appears to have no completely satisfactory reply after White's rejoinder 5 O—O. Cols. 34 and 35 show alternatives for White.

In the second place Black may elect to go in for an enterprising counter-attack with 4..., Kt—Q 5 (the Rubinstein Defence), a move which has been adopted by many of the strongest masters. Despite the fact that 4..., Kt—Q 5 violates an important opening principle, there is no way known in which the first player can obtain even a minimal superiority; on the contrary, he must always be careful not

to compromise his position. Most masters nowadays avoid
the Four Knights' Game solely because of the Rubinstein
Defence.

The six usual replies at White's disposal are :—

(i) 5 Kt × Kt (cols. 36 to 38), leading to fully equalised
positions and an early draw.

(ii) 5 O—O (cols. 39 and 40), approved by Schlechter
and analysed exhaustively by W. Henneberger. White is
better developed, and has the superior Pawn-position, but
Black's two Bishops are ample compensation for these
slight weaknesses.

(iii) 5 B—R 4 (cols. 41 and 42), yielding Black a very
strong attack at the expense of two Pawns.

(iv) 5 B—B 4 (cols. 43 and 44). The line given in col.
44 shows promise for the first player, and Black would do
best to adopt Schlechter's suggestion in note (k).

(v) 5 B—K 2 (col. 45), though favoured by Maróczy,
should occasion Black no anxiety.

(vi) 5 Kt × P (cols. 46 to 50), a popular line some years
ago. For a time the defence 5..., Q—K 2 fell into disrepute
owing to the line of play based on 6 P—B 4, devised by
Bogoljuboff (col. 46, note (b)). But the sacrificial variation
due to Teichmann has rehabilitated this defence, since
Tartakover's 12 P—K R 3 in note (d) has been refuted.
The alternative defence 5..., B—B 4, advocated by Tarrasch,
is hardly good enough against Schlechter's suggestion in
col. 49.

The reply 4..., P—Q R 3 (cols. 51 and 52), though
sometimes made, is theoretically unsound, but White's
advantage in col. 51, where Black's 13th move is an improvement due to Tarrasch, is inconsiderable.

Cols. 53 to 55 illustrate other 4th moves for White than
B—Kt 5. At the end of note (i) is an example of an old
move revived by Nimzovitch in the great Bled Tournament
of 1931.

1 P—K 4, P—K 4 ; 2 Kt—K B 3, Kt—Q B 3 ; 3 Kt—B 3, Kt—B 3.

4 B—Kt 5, B—Kt 5 ; 5 O—O, O—O ; 6 P—Q 3, B×Kt ; 7 P×B, P—Q 3 ; 8 B—Kt 5.

	1	2	3	4	5
8	Kt—K 2				
9	Kt—R 4 !			B×Kt	B—Q B 4
	Kt—Kt 3		P—B 3	P×B	Kt—Kt 3
10	Kt×Kt		B—Q B 4	Kt—R 4	Kt—R 4
	B P×Kt	R P×Kt	P—Q 4 (c)	P—B 3	Kt—B 5
11	B—B 4 ch	P—K B 4	B—Kt 3	B—B 4	B×Q Kt
	K—R 1	P—B 3	P×P	P—Q 4	P×B
12	P—B 4	B—B 4	P×P	B—Kt 3	Kt—B 3
	P—K R 3	Q—Kt 3 ch	Q×Q	Kt—Kt 3	B—Kt 5
13	P×P	K—R 1	Q R×Q	Kt×Kt	Q—Q 2
	P×P	Kt—Kt 5	Kt—Kt 3	R P×Kt	B×Kt
14	B—R 4	P×P (A)	Kt×Kt	P—K B 4	P×B
	P—K Kt 4	Kt×K P	P×Kt	K P×P (e)	Kt—R 4
15	B—K Kt 3	B—Kt 3	B×Kt	R×P	K—R 1
	Q—K 2	Q—B 2	P×B	K—Kt 2	K—R 1
16	P—Q 4+ (a)	P—Q 4	P-K B 4+ (d)	Q—B 3	R—K Kt 1
		Kt—Kt 5		B—K 3	Q—Q 2
17		Q—B 3		R-K B 1+ (f)	R—Kt 4
		Kt—R 3			Q R—K 1
18		Q—Kt 3			Q R—K Kt 1
		K—R 2 (b)			P—K B 4 ∓
					(g)

(a) Janowski—Spielmann, Nuremberg, 1906. 12.., Q—K 2 is better.

(b) 19 B×Kt+. Ed. Lasker—J. Raoux, Dartford, 1914.

(c) If 10.., Kt—K 1 ; 11 P—B 4 !, P—Q 4 ; 12 B—Kt 3, P—B 3 (Teichmann prefers P—K R 3) ; 13 B P×P, P×B ; 14 R×R ch, K×R ; 15 Q—B 3 ch, K—Kt 1 ; 16 R—K B 1, Kt—B 2 ; 17 Q—B 7 ch, K—R 1 ; 18 Q—B 8 ch (if P×P, B—K 3 !!, Q×Q ; 19 R×Q ch, Kt—Kt 1 ; 20 P×P, P×P ; 21 Kt—B 3+. Schlechter—Duras, San Sebastian, 1911.

(d) Note by Yates.

(e) 14. , Q P×P ? ; 15 Q P×P, Q×Q ; 16 Q R×Q, P×P ; 17 R×P, B—K 3 ; 18 B×B, P×B ; 19 P—K 5, P×P ; 20 R×R ch, R×R ; 21 R—Q 7, R—B 2 ; 22 R×R followed by P—K R 4, winning. A game won by Em. Lasker.

(f) Maróczy—O. S. Bernstein, Ostend, 1906.

(g) Janowski—Lasker, match, 1909.

(A) Even more forcible is 14 Q—B 3, Kt—K 6 ; 15 P—B 5, Kt×B (Kt×R ; 16 P×P+) ; 16 P—B 6+.

1 P—K 4, P—K 4 ;   2 Kt—K B 3, Kt—Q B 3 ;   3 Kt—B 3, Kt—B 3.

4 B—Kt 5, B—Kt 5 ;   5 O—O, O—O ;   6 P—Q 3, B×Kt ;   7 P×B, P—Q 3.

	6	7	8	9	10
8	(B—Kt 5) Q—K 2 (a)				
9	R—K 1 Kt—Q 1			....	P—Q R 3
10	P—Q 4 B—Kt 5	..... Kt—K 3			B—Q B 4 Kt—Q R 4
11	P—K R 3 B—R 4 (b)	B—Q B 1 P—B 4 (g)	...P—B 3	......R—Q 1	Kt—Q 2 P—R 3
12	P—Kt 4 B—Kt 3	P—Kt 3 Kt—B 2	B—B 1 Q—B 2	P—Kt 3 P—B 4 !	B—R 4 B—K 3
13	Kt—R 4 (c) P—K R 3	B—B 1 B—Kt 5	P—Kt 3 R—Q 1	P—Q 5 Kt—B 1 (h)	B—Q Kt 3 Kt×B
14	B—Q B 4 ! (d) Kt—K 3	P—K R 3 B—R 4	Kt—R 4 (i) P—Q 4	Kt—R 4 P—K R 3	R P×Kt P—K Kt 4
15	Kt×B P×Kt	B—K Kt 2 Q R—Q 1	P—K B 4 Kt×K P ! (j)	P—B 3 Q—B 2	B—Kt 3 Kt—K 1
16	P—K B 4 P×B (e)	P—Q 5 Q—Q 2	B P×P Kt×B P	B—B 1 Kt—Kt 3	P—Q 4 P—K B 3
17	P—B 5 Kt P×P	Q—Q 3 B—Kt 3 =	Q—Q 3 Kt—K 5+	Kt×Kt P×Kt (l)	Kt—B 1 Kt—Kt 2
18	Kt P×P (f)	(h)			(m)

(a) The Metger Variation. An alternative is 8.., B—Q 2 ; 9 Q—Q 2, P—K R 3 ; 10 B—K R 4, B—Kt 5 ! (Kt—K 2 ; 11 B×Kt, B×B ; 12 Kt—R 4 !+) ; 11 Q—K 3 (if 11 Kt—K 1, Kt×K P !+), B×Kt ; 12 Q×B, P—K Kt 4 ; 13 B—Kt 3, K—Kt 2=. Cp. col. 11.

(b) 11.., B×Kt ; 12 Q×B, P—K R 3 ; 13 B—K R 4, P—Kt 4 ; 14 B—Kt 3, P—B 3 ; 15 B—Q B 4, K—Kt 2 ; 16 P×P, P×P ; 17 Q—B 5+. Tarrasch—Kostich, Gothenburg, 1920.

(c) 13 P—Q 5, P—B 3 ; 14 B—K B 1 (or 14 B—Q 3, P×P ; 15 P×P ±), P×P ; 15 P×P, R—B 1 ; 16 P—B 4, P—Kt 3 ; 17 P—Q R 4 ±. Wolf—Cohen, Nuremberg, 1906. Or 13 B—Q 3, Kt—K 3 ; 14 B—Q B 1, Kt—Q 2 ; 15 R—Kt 1, P—Kt 3 ; 16 K—Kt 2, P—Q B 4 ; 17 P—Q 5, Kt—B 5 ch=. Bogoljuboff—Rubinstein, Hastings, 1922.

(d) Weak is 14 Kt×B, P×Kt ; 15 B—B 4 ch, K—R 2 ; 16 B—R 4, P—K Kt 4 ∓. Wolf—Rubinstein, Teplitz-Schönau, 1922.

(e) If 16 , K—R 1 ? ; 17 B×K Kt, Q×B ; 18 B×Kt, Q×B ; 19 P—Q 5, Q—B 3 ; 20 P—B 5+. Drewitt—Rubinstein, Hastings, 1922.

(f) 18. , P—K Kt 3= (Kmoch).

(g) More energetic than the usual P—B 3. If in reply 12 P×K P, P×P ; 13 Kt×P, Kt—B 2 wins a piece.

(h) Threatening Q Kt×P. Spielmann—Krejcik, Vienna, 1929.

(i) 14 B—K Kt 2, preventing 14.., P—Q 4, followed by 15 Kt—R 4 is stronger (Lasker).

(j) If 15.., P×B P ; 16 P—K 5 !, Kt—K 5 ; 17 P×P, P—K B 4 ; 18 P×P e.p. (18 Kt×P, Kt×K B P), Kt×P (B 3) ; 19 P—B 5+. Spielmann—Rubinstein Carlsbad, 1911. The continuation in column is suggested by *Deutsche Schachzeitung*.

(k) 13.., Kt—B 2 ; 14 B—B 1, P—Q Kt 4 (or 14.., Kt—K 1 ; 15 Kt—R 4, P—K Kt 3 ; 16 P—Q B 4, Kt—Kt 2 ; 17 B—K R 6. Spielmann—Löwy, Vienna, 1908) ; 15 Kt—R 4, P—Q Kt 4 ; 16 P—K R 3, B—Q 2 ; 17 B—K Kt 2, Q R—Kt 1 ; 18 P—K B 4, K Kt—K 1 ; 19 P—B 5. Perlis—Freyman, St. Petersburg, 1909. Lasker prefers 16.., K—R 1 followed by Kt—Kt 1, R—K 2, P—K Kt 3 and P—B 4.

(l) 18 B—K 3, R—B 1 ; 19 B—Kt 2, B—Q 2 followed by P—K Kt 4 and the doubling of Rooks on the K B file.

(m) Bogatyrchuk—Botvinnik, Moscow, 1935.

1 P—K 4, P—K 4; 2 Kt—K B 3, Kt—Q B 3; 3 Kt—B 3, Kt—B 3.

4 B—Kt 5, B—Kt 5; 5 O—O, O—O; 6 P—Q 3, B×Kt.

	11	12	13	14	15
7	(P×B)(P—Q 3)			P—Q 4 (g)	
8	(B—Kt 5)P—K R 3		R—K 1 / Q—K 2	B×Kt / P×B	P×P (k) / Q×P
9	B—K R 4 / B—Kt 5 (a)	..Q—K 2	Q—K 2 (e) / Kt—Q 1	Kt×P / Q—Q 3	K B—B 4 / Q—R 4
10	P—K R 3 / B×Kt	Q—Q 2 ! (c) / Kt—Q 1	P—Q 4 / P—B 4	B—B 4 / R—K 1	R—Kt 1 / P—Q R 3
11	Q×B / P—Kt 4	P—Q 4 / Kt—K 3	B—Q 3 / K—R 1	Q—B 3 (h) / P×P	R—K 1 / P—Q Kt 3
12	B—Kt 3 / Kt—Q 2 !	P×P / P×P	P—K R 3 / Kt—Kt 1	P×P / R×Kt	Q—K 2 / B—Kt 5 (l)
13	P—Q 4 / P—B 3	Kt×P / Kt—B 4	B—Kt 2 / Kt—K 3	Q R—Q 1 (i) / B—Kt 5	B—Kt 5 ±
14	Q—Kt 4 / K—R 1	Q—B 4 ! / P—Kt 4	P—Kt 3 / P—B 3	R×Q (j) / B×Q	
15	P—K R 4 / R—B 2	B×P / P×B	K—Kt 2 / B—Q 2	R×Kt / P×R	
16	P×P / R P×P	Q×P ch / K—R 2	P—Q 5 / Kt—Kt 4	B×R / P×B	
17	P—B 3 / Kt—B 1 = (b)	B—B 4 + (d)	Kt×Kt ± (f)	P×B / R—Kt 1 ⇌	

(a) If 9.., P—Kt 4?; 10 Kt×Kt P!, Kt×P (10 .., P×Kt; 11 B×P, Q—K 2; 12 Q—B 3+); 11 P—K B 4, P×P (Yates—Speyer, Hamburg, 1910); 12 P×Kt, P×Kt; 13 Q—R 5, P×B; 14 R×P+. 9.., K—R 1, followed by R—K Kt 1 and P—K Kt 4, leads to a position similar to that in col. 12, note (c).

(b) Capablanca—Lasker, St. Petersburg, 1914. Tarrasch maintained that White would have the better game by deferring the opening of the K R file (16 P⨯R) until he has tripled Queen and two Rooks on it.

(c) Better than either 10 R—K 1, B—Kt 5; 11 P—K R 3, B×Kt; 12 Q×B, P—Kt 4; 13 B—Kt 3, K—Kt 2; 14 P—Q 4, Kt—Q 2; 15 Q R—Q 1, Q R—Q 1; 16 R—K 3, P—R 3, 17 B—Q B 4. Q—B 3 = (Yates—R. H. V. Scott, Hastings, 1922); or 10 R—Kt 1, K—R 1; 11 Q—Q 2, R—K Kt 1; 12 B×K Kt (Black threatens P—Kt 4), Q×B; 13 B—R 4, Kt—K 2; 14 Kt—K 1, P—K Kt 4; 15 P—B 3, Kt—Kt 3; 16 P—Kt 3, R—Kt 2; 17 Kt—Kt 2, B—R 6; 18 R×P, Kt—R 5!+. J. A. J. Drewitt—Sir G. A. Thomas, Weston, 1924.

(d) 17.., B—K 3; 18 Kt—Kt 4!, B×Kt; 19 P—K 5, Kt—Kt 1; 20 Q×B + Tarrasch—Spielmann, Berlin, 1920.

(e) 9 P—Q 4, Kt—Q 1? (9., B—Kt 5 or 9.., Kt—Q 2 would have been better); 10 B—R 3, P—B 4; 11 Kt×P!!, Q—B 2; 12 Kt—B 4!, Kt—K 3 (12 ., P—Q R 3; 13 Kt×P!); 13 P—Q 5, Kt—B 5; 14 B—B 1, Kt—Kt 3; 15 Kt—Kt 2+. Simonson—Suesman, New York, 1938

(f) Tylor—Vidmar, Nottingham, 1936.

(g) The Svenonius Variation.

(h) 11 P×P, R×Kt; 12 P—Q 4, R—K 8!=.

(i) 13 K R—Q 1, B—Kt 5; 14 Q—Kt 3? (14 R×Q still draws), B×R; 15 B×R, Q—Q 7++. Capablanca—Tarrasch, St. Petersburg, 1914.

(j) 14 Q—Kt 3, Kt×P!; 15 Q×B, Q—K 3= (Tarrasch).

(k) 8 Q—K 2, P×P; 9 P×P, B—Kt 5; 10 P—K R 3, B×Kt; 11 Q×B, Q—Q 3; 12 R—Q 1, Q—B 4; 13 P—Q R 4, K R—Q 1; 14 R×R ch, R×R; 15 B—R 3, Q—Kt 3=. H. E. Price—B. Siegheim, Malvern, 1921.

(l) Lasker—Réti, Moscow, 1925. White's 13th move is suggested by Kmoch.

1 P—K4, P—K4 ; 2 Kt—KB3, Kt—QB3 ; 3 Kt—B3, Kt—B3

4 B—Kt5, B—Kt5 ; 5 O—O, O—O ; 6 P—Q3, P—Q3 ; 7 B—Kt5

	16	17	18	19	20
7	Kt—K2 (a)				
8	Kt—KR4			B×Kt	
	P—B3 (b)			P×B	
9	B—QB4			Kt—KR4	
	P—Q4......	Kt—Kt3 (e).K—R1		P—B3......	Kt—Kt3
10	B—Kt3	Kt×Kt	P—B4	B—B4	Kt×Kt
	Q—Q3 !	P×Kt	P×P	Kt—Kt3	R P×Kt
11	P—KR3 (c)	P—B4	B×Kt (g)	Kt×Kt	P—B4
	P—KR3	B—B4 ch	P×B	P×Kt	B—B4 ch
12	B×Kt	K—R1	R×P	P—B4	K—R1
	Q×B	B—K6	Kt—Kt3	K—Kt2	K—Kt2
13	Q—R5	Q—B3 !	Kt×Kt ch	Q—B3	P—B5
	P—Q5 (d)	B×P	R P×Kt	B—B4 ch (i)	P×P
14	Kt—K2	B×B	B—Kt3	K—R1	P×P
	K—R2	P×B	Q—K2	B—K3	R—R1
15	P—KB4	Q×P	Kt—K2	B—Kt3	Q—Kt4 ch
	B—Q3	Q—K2	B—R4	R—R1	K—B1 =(k)
16	P—B5 ±	Q—Kt3	P—B3	Kt—K2	
	B—K3 = (f)	B—Q2 ∓ (h)	Q—K2 (j)		

(a) For 7 ., B × Kt see cols. 1 to 15.   Tarrasch suggests 7.., B—K3 ; 8 P—Q 4, P × P ; 9 Kt × P, P—K R ; 3 10 B—K R 4, Kt—K 4 ; 11 P—B 4, B—Q B 4 (so far Tarrasch —Lasker, 16th match game, 1908) ;   12 K—R 1, Kt—Kt 3 ;   13 B × Kt, Q × B ; 14 K Kt—K 2=.

(b) If 8.., Kt—Kt 3 ; 9 Kt × Kt, R P × Kt ; 10 Kt—Q 5, B—B 4 ? ; 11 Kt × Kt ch, P × Kt ; 12 B—K R 6+.

(c) Or 11 P × P, B × Kt ; 12 P × B, Q Kt × P ; 13 Q—Q 2, B—Q 2 ; 14 Q R—K 1, Q R—K 1 ; 15 K—R 1, Kt—R 4 ; 16 P—Q 4, P—K 5.   H. E. Atkins—J. H. Blake, Glasgow, 1911.   11 Q—B 3 and 11 P—B 4 have also been played.

(d) Continuation in column suggested by Alekhine as "rather in favour of Black." Tarrasch—Yates, Hastings, 1922, continued 13.., B × Kt ; 14 P × B, K—R 2 ; 15 Kt—B3, Kt—Kt 3 ; 16 P × P+.

(e) 9 ., Kt—K 1 ;   10 Q—R 5, Kt—B 2 ; 11 Kt—B 5, Q B × Kt ; 12 P × B, P—Q 4 ; 13 P—B 6 !, P × P ; 14 Q B × P, Q—Q 2 ; 15 P—B 4 !+.   Spielmann—Forgacs, San Sebastian, 1912.   Or 9 ., B—K 3 ; 10 B × Kt, P × B ; 11 B × B, P × B ; 12 Q—Kt 4 ch, K—B 2 ; 13 P—B 4+.

(f) O. Buchmann—M. Marron, correspondence, 1930.

(g) If 11 R × P, B—B 4 ch ; 12 K—R 1, B—K 6+.   Best is 11 B × P (B 4).

(h) 17 Kt—Kt 3, B—B 2.   Tylor—Lasker, Nottingham, 1936.

(i) 13 ., R—R 1 ; 14 P × P ?, Q P × P ; 15 Q—Kt 3 (or Kt—K 2), B—B 4 ch ; 16 K—R 1, P—Q Kt 4 ; 17 B—Kt 3, R—R 4 ; 18 P—Q R 4, P—Kt 5 ∓.   G. E. Wainwright—Euwe, Weston, 1924.

(j) 17 P—B 5, B × B ; 18 R P × B, P—K Kt 4 ; 19 Kt—Kt 3 followed by Kt—R 5 ch and P—K Kt 4+.

(k) Krüger—Shories, Hamburg, 1921.

1 P—K 4, P—K 4 ; 2 Kt—K B 3, Kt—Q B 3 ; 3 Kt—B 3, Kt—B˙3.

4 B—Kt 5, B—Kt 5 ; 5 O—O, O—O.

	21	22	23	24	25
6	(P—Q 3)			B × Kt (h)	
	(P—Q 3) (a)			Q P × B (i)	
7	(B—Kt 5)...	Kt—K 2		P—Q 3 (j)	
	B—Kt 5	B—Q B 4..	Kt—K 2 (e)	Q—K 2.....	B—Kt 5 (l)
8	Kt—Q 5	P—B 3	P—B 3	Kt—K 2	P—K R 3
	Kt—Q 5	B—Kt 3	B—R 4	B—Kt 5	B—KR4(m)
9	P—B 3 (b)	Kt—Kt 3	Kt—Kt 3	Kt—Kt 3	B—Kt 5 (n)
	Kt × B	K—R 1	P—B 3	Q R—Q 1	Q—Q 3
10	Kt × B	B—K 3	B—R 4	P—K R 3	B × Kt
	P—B 3	Kt—K Kt 5	Kt—Kt 3	B—B 1	Q × B
11	Kt—B 2	B × B	P—Q 4	Q—K 2	P—Kt 4
	P—K R 3	R P × B	R—K 1 (f)	K R—K 1	B—Kt 3
12	B—R 4	P—Q 4	B—Kt 3	P—R 3	K—Kt 2
	P—Kt 4	P—B 3	P × P	B—Q 3	Q R—Q 1
13	B—Kt 3	P—K R 3	P × P	Kt—R 4	Q—K 2
	Kt—Q 2	Kt—R 3	B—K 3	K—R 1	B × Kt
14	Kt—K 3	B × Kt	Kt—Kt 5	Q Kt—B 5	P × B
	B—R 4	P × B ∓ (d)	B × B	Q—K 3	P—B 4
15	Kt—B 5		Q × B ± (g)	P—K Kt 4	Kt—Q 2
	Q—B 3 (c)			B—B 1 = (k)	Q—K 2 (o)

(a) 6. , P—Q 4 ? ; 7 Q Kt × P, Kt × Kt ; 8 P × Kt, Q × P ; 9 B—Q B 4, Q—Q 3 ; 10 P—B 3, B—Q B 4 ; 11 P—Q Kt 4, B—Kt 3 ; 12 P—Q R 4, P—Q R 4 ; 13 P—Kt 5, Kt—K 2 ; 14 Kt—Kt 5 +. Sterk—Marshall, Pistyan, 1912

(b) 9 B—Q B 4, Q—Q 2 ! (B—Q B 4 ; 10 Q—Q 2 !, P—B 3 ; 11 Kt × Kt ch, P × Kt ; 12 B—R 4, B × Kt ; 13 Q—R 6, Kt—K 7 ch ; 14 K—R 1, B × P ch ; 15 K × B, Kt—B 5 ch ; 16 K—R 1, Kt—Kt 3 ; 17 P—Q 4, B × P ; 18 P—Q B 3, followed by Q R—Q 1 and K R—Kt 1 +) ; 10 Kt × Kt ch, P × Kt ; 11 B × P, P—K R 3 ; 12 P—B 3, Kt × Kt ch ; 13 P × Kt, B—K R 4 ; 14 K—R 1, K—R 2 ; 15 R—K Kt 1, R—K Kt 1 ; 16 R—Kt 3, R—Kt 3. Analysis by Dr. B. and Ed. Lasker. 17 P × B, R × B ; 18 Q—K 2 ±.

(c) 16 P—K R 4 +. Chajes—Marshall, New York, 1915.

(d) Maróczy—Bogoljuboff, London, 1922.

(e) Or 7 ., B—Kt 5 ; 8 P—B 3, B—Q B 4 ; 9 B—K 3, B—Kt 2 ; 10 K—R 1, Kt—K 2 ; 11 Kt—Kt 3, Kt—R 4 ; 12 P—Q 4, K—R 1 ; 13 Kt × Kt, P × P ; 14 B × P, B × Q Kt ; 15 B—K 2, Kt—B 3 =. Maróczy—Tylor, Ramsgate, 1929.

(f) Simpler was 11.., P—Q 4 !

(g) 15.., Q—Q 2 ; 16 P—B 3, P—K R 3 ; 17 Kt—R 3. Alekhine—Euwe, Amsterdam, 1936.

(h) The Nimzovitch Variation.

(i) Or 6.., Kt P × B, Q—K 1 (if 7 ., R—K 1 ; 8 P—Q 4, B × Kt ; 9 P × B, Kt × P ; 10 Q—B 3 ±) ; 8 Kt—Q 3, B × Kt ; 9 Q P × B, Q × P , 10 R—K 1, Q—K R 5 ; 11 Q—B 3, B—R 3 ; 12 Kt—B 5, B—B 5 =.

(j) White can obtain an easily drawn position by 7 Kt × P, R—K 1 ; 8 Kt—Q 3, B × Kt ; 9 Q P × B, Kt × P ; 10 Q—B 3. Kt—Q 3 ; 11 B—B 4, Q—B 3.

(k) M. E. Goldstein—J. H. Blake, City of London Chess Championship, 1923.

(l) Or 7.., B—Q 3 ; 8 Kt—K 2 (Capablanca favours 8 P—K R 3), B—K Kt 5 ; 9 Kt—Kt 3, Kt—R 4 ; 10 Kt—B 5.

(m) 8.., Q B × Kt ; 9 Q × B, B × Kt ; 10 P × B, Kt—Q 2 gives Black complete equality.

(n) 9 P—Kt 4, Kt × Kt P ; 10 Kt × P !, Kt—B 3 ; 11 Kt—Kt 4 can be played

(o) 16 Kt—B 4 ±. Nimzovitch—Leonhardt, San Sebastian, 1911.

C

1 P—K4, P—K4; 2 Kt—KB3, Kt—QB3; 3 Kt—B3, Kt—B3.

	26	27	28	29	30
4	(B—Kt5)				
	(B—Kt5)				
5	(O—O)...........................			P—Q3......	Kt—Q5
	(O—O)......P—Q3?			Kt—Q5	Kt×Kt
6	Kt—Q5	Kt—Q5!		B—R4	P×Kt
	Kt×Kt	B—R4.....	B—QB4	O—O	P—K5
7	P×Kt	P—Q4	P—Q4	O—O	P×Kt
	P—K5	P—QR3	P×P	P—QB3	QP×P
8	P×Kt	B×Kt ch	Kt×QP	Kt×Kt	B—K2
	QP×P	P×B	B×Kt	P×Kt	P×Kt
9	B—K2	Kt×Kt ch	Q×B	Kt—K2	B×P
	P×Kt	P×Kt	O—O	P—Q4= (d)	=
10	B×P	Kt—R4+ (b)	Kt×Kt ch		
	P-KB4=(a)		Q×Kt (c)		

	31	32	33	34	35
4	B—B4				
5	O—O!...........................			Kt×P......	P—Q3
	P—Q3......O—O			Kt×Kt	P—Q3
6	P—Q4	Kt×P		P—Q4	P—KR3
	P×P	R—K1.....	B—Q5 (k)	B—Q3	P—KR3
7	Kt×P	Kt—B3!(h)	Kt—B3	P—KB4	O—O
	B—Q2	Kt×P	B×Kt	Kt—B3	P—KKt3
8	Kt—B5!(f)	P—Q4	QP×B	P—K5	P—Q4
	O—O	Kt×Kt	Kt×P	B—Kt5!	P×P
9	B—Kt5	P×Kt	R—K1	P—Q5	Kt×P
	B×Kt	B—K2 (i)	P—Q4	Kt—K5	B—Q2
10	P×B	P—Q5	P—B4!	Q—Q3	Kt×Kt
	Kt—Q5	Kt—Kt1	Kt—B3	Kt×Kt	P×Kt
11	B—Q3	B—KB4	B—Kt5+	KtP×Kt	B—QB4
	P—Q4 (g)	P—QR3 (j)		B—K2 (l)	Q—K2 (m)

(a) Walbrodt—Charousek, Nuremberg, 1896. 11 P—Q4.
(b) L. Savage—W. H. Watts, City of London Championship, 1915.
(c) 11 Q×Q, P×Q; 12 B—KR6, R—K1; 13 KR—K1, P—R3; 14 B—KB1+.
Tarrasch—Lasker, match, 1908. If 8 , B—Q2; 9 Kt—B5+.
(d) G. E. Wainwright—Yates, Malvern, 1921.
(e) Schiffers—Steinitz, Hastings, 1895.
(f) 8 B—K3, B—Kt3 (for O—O; 9 Kt×Kt, P×Kt; 10 B×B, P×KB see Ruy Lopez, Classical Defence); 9 P—KR3, O—O; 10 B×Kt, P×B; 11 B—Kt5, R—K1; 12 Q—Q3. A. Muffang—M. E. Goldstein, London, 1922.
(g) 12 B×Kt, P×B; 13 Kt—R4, Q—Q3; 14 Q—Kt4 ch ±.
(h) 7 Kt×Kt, QP×Kt; 8 B—B4, Kt—Kt5!; 9 P—KR3, Kt×P; 10 B×P ch, K—R1+ (Tattersall's Attack).
(i) 9. , B—B1; 10 B—Kt5!, B—K2; 11 B—KB4, B—B3; 12 Q—Q2, P—QR3; 13 B—Q3, P—Q3. Yates—A. R. B. Thomas, Edinburgh, 1926.
(j) 12 B—R4, B—B3; 13 P—Q6+. Maróczy—Pillsbury, Nuremberg, 1896.
(k) For 6.., Kt—Q5; 7 B—B4, see col. 49.
(l) 12 P×Kt, QP×P; 13 Q×Q ch=. Bardeleben's analysis.
(m) 12 K—R2, O—O—O; 13 Q—K2, QR—K1; 14 B—R6 ch, K—Kt1 (K—Q1!). Dr. W. Finn—Dr. O. S. Bernstein, Paris, 1929.

c *

1 P—K 4, P—K 4 ; 2 Kt—K B 3, Kt—Q B 3 ; 3 Kt—B 3, Kt—B 3.

RUBINSTEIN DEFENCE
4 B—Kt 5, Kt—Q 5.

	36	37	38	39	40
5	Kt × Kt............................			O—O (g)	
	P × Kt			Kt × B......	B—Kt 5 (h)
6	P—K 5.................		Kt—Q 5	Kt × Kt	B—R 4
	P × Kt		Kt × Kt	P—B 3	O—O
7	P × Kt		P × Kt	Kt—B 3	Kt × P
	Q × P (a)		Q—B 3 !	P—Q 3	P—Q 3
8	Q P × P		O—O	P—Q 4	Kt—Q 3
	Q—K 4 ch...	B—B 4	B—K 2	Q—B 2 (h)	B—R 4
9	Q—K 2 (b)	Q—K 2 ch (d)	P—K B 4	Kt—K 1 (i)	P—K 5
	Q × Q ch	Q—K 3	O—O	B—K 2	P × P
10	B × Q	B—Q B 4	Q—B 3	K—R 1	Kt × P ±
	P—Q 3	Q × Q ch	P—B 4	P—Q Kt 4	
11	B—K 3	K × Q	P—Q Kt 3	P—Q R 3	
	B—B 4	P—Q 3	P—Q 3	B—Kt 2	
12	B—Q 3	B—K 3	B—Kt 2	P—B 4	
	B × B	B × B	B—B 4	P × Q P	
13	P × B	K × B	Q R—Q B 1	Q × P	
	P—Q 4	B—K 3	B—Q 1 !	P—B 4	
14	P—Q 4	B × B	B—Q 3	Q—Q 3 (j)	
	K—Q 2 = (c)	P × B= (e)	B—R 4 ∓ (f)		

(a) If 7.., P × P ch ; 8 B × P, Q × P ; 9 O—O, B—K 2 ; 10 B—B 3, Q—Kt 4 ; 11 R—K 1, O—O (11..Q × B ?; 12 Q—Kt 4+ +); 12 R—K 5, P—K B 4 ; 13 Q—Q 5 ch, K—R 1 ; 14 Q R—K 1 + (Dr. Olland). With the opening of this game cp. Ruy Lopez, p. 242.

(b) 9 B—K 2, B—B 4 ; 10 O—O, O—O ; 11 B—Q 3, P—Q 4=.

(c) Maróczy—Kmoch, San Remo, 1930.

(d) 9 O—O, O—O ; 10 Q—R 5, P—Q 3 ; 11 B—Q 3, P—K R 3=.

(e) Kashdan—Alekhine, Bled, 1931.

(f) H. Wolf—Alekhine, Carlsbad, 1923.

(g) Good enough to equalise, but no more.

(h) Recommended by Tarrasch. If 8.., B—Kt 5 ; 9 P × P, B × Kt ; 10 Q × B, P × P ; 11 B—Kt 5, B—K 2 ; 12 Q R—Q 1, Q—B 2 ; 13 Q—B 5 ± (W. Henneberger),

(i) 9 P—K R 3 !, B—K 2 ; 10 B—K 3 (C. S. Howell), O—O=.

(j) 14 Kt × P ?, Q—B 3 !+ +. The column is Euwe—Bogoljuboff, 10th match game, 1929. Continued 14.., P—Q R 3 ; 15 Kt—B 3, R—Q 1 ; 16 B—Q 2, O—O ; 17 Q R—Q 1, K R—K 1 ; 18 Kt—Kt 5, P—R 3 ; 19 Kt—R 3, Q—B 3 ∓.

(k) 5.., P—B 3 ; 6 B—B 4, P—Q 4 ; 7 P × P, B—K Kt 5 ; 8 B—K 2 ! ±. The column is analysis by W. Henneberger.

1 P—K 4, P—K 4; 2 Kt—K B 3, Kt—Q B 3; 3 Kt—B 3, Kt—B ?

RUBINSTEIN DEFENCE
4 B—Kt 5, Kt—Q 5.

	41	42	43	44	45
5	B—R 4		B—B 4		B—K 2
	B—B 4		B—B 4		Kt × Kt ch
6	Kt×P (a)		Kt×P	P—Q 3	B×Kt
	O—O (b)		Q—K 2	P—Q 3	B—B 4
7	Kt—B 3 (c) ..	P—Q 3	Kt—B 3 (h)	Kt—Q R 4 !	O—O
	P—Q 4 !	P—Q 4	P—Q 4	P—Q Kt4 (k)	O—O
8	Kt×Kt	B—K Kt 5	B×P (i)	Kt×Kt	P—Q 3
	B×Kt	P—B 3	B—K Kt 5	P×B	P—Q 3
9	O—O	Q—Q 2	P—Q 3	Kt—K 2	B—K 3 (m)
	Kt×P (d)	R—K 1	P—B 3	P×P	B—K 3
10	Kt×Kt	P—B 4	B—Kt 3	Q×P	P—Q 4
	P×Kt	P—Kt 4	Kt—Q 2 (j)	B—Kt 3	B—Kt 3
11	P—Q 3	B—Kt 3	B—Kt 5	O—O	P—Q Kt 3
	P×P	P—K R 3	Kt×Kt ch	O—O	P×P
12	Q×P	B—K R 4	P×Kt	Kt—Kt 3 (l)	B×P
	B—K 3	Kt×KP! ∓	Q×B		Kt—Q 2
13	R—Q 1 (e)	(g)	P×B		B×B
	B—Kt 3		Kt—K 4		R P×B
14	B—Kt 3		P—K R 3		P—K 5 ! ±
	B×B (f)		Q—B 5 ∓		(n)

(a) Or 6 P—Q 3, O—O; 7 Kt×Kt, P×Kt; 8 Kt—K 2, P—Q 4; 9 P×P, Kt×P; 10 O—O. Or 6 O—O, Q—K 2; 7 P—Q 3, O—O; 8 Kt×Kt, B×Kt; 9 Kt—K 2, B—Kt 3; 10 B—K Kt 5, P—Q 3; 11 Q—Q 2, P—K R 3; 12 B—R 4 (better B—K 3). Allies—Grünfeld, Innsbruck, 1929.

(b) A gambit for a quick counter-attack.

(c) 7 Kt—Q 3, B—Kt 3; 8 P—K 5, Kt—K 1; 9 O—O, P—Q 3; 10 P×P, K Kt×P; 11 K—R 1 != (Dr. von Claparède). Here 9 Kt—Q 5, P—Q 3; 10 P—Q B 3, Q—R 5; 11 Kt—K 3, Q—K 5! is T. H. Tylor—P. S. Milner-Barry. Hastings, 1938-39.

(d) 9.., P×P! followed by B—Kt 5 (Becker).

(e) 13 B—Kt 3!, as Black could have replied to the text-move with 13.., B×P ch; 14 K×B, Q—R 5 ch+. Or with 13.., Q—R 5; 14 Q×B?, Q R—Q 1+ (Becker).

(f) 15 R P×B, Q×Q; 16 R×Q, Q R—Q 1; 17 R×R, R×R. Drawn. Havasi—Kmoch, Vienna, 1930.

(g) Tarrasch—Rubinstein, San Sebastian, 1912.

(h) 7 Kt—Q 3, P—Q 4; 8 B×P, Kt×B; 9 Kt×Kt, Q×P ch; 10 Kt—K 3, B—Q 3; 11 O—O, B—K 3; 12 Kt—K 1, O—O—O ∓. Nimzovitch—Alekhine, tie match, St. Petersburg, 1914.

(i) 8 Kt×P!, Q×P ch; 9 Kt—K 3, B—K Kt 5; 10 B—K 2, Kt×B; 11 Q×Kt B×Kt; 12 Q×B, Q×Q; 13 P×Q ± (Maróczy).

(j) O. S. Bernstein—Rubinstein, Vilna, 1912. The rest of the column is analysis by Tarrasch.

(k) 7 , B—Kt 3; 8 Kt×B, Kt×Kt ch; 9 Q×Kt (9 P×Kt, R P×Kt; 10 P—K B 4 is playable), R P×Kt; 10 B—Kt 5, B—K 3= (Schlechter).

(l) Post—Flamberg, Mannheim, 1914.

(m) 9 Kt—R 4, B—Kt 3=. Maróczy—Euwe, London, 1922.

(n) Alekhine—Van den Bosch, Nauheim, 1936. 9.., B×B would have been simpler.

1 P—K 4, P—K 4 ; 2 Kt—K B 3, Kt—Q B 3 ; 3 Kt—B 3, Kt—B 3.

RUBINSTEIN DEFENCE
4 B—Kt 5, Kt—Q 5.

	46	47	48	49	50
5	Kt×P Q—K 2	....	Kt×P	B—B 4	
6	P—B 4 Kt×B	Kt—B 3 (f) Kt×B (g)	Kt×Kt Kt×B	O—O ! (i) O—O	B—K 2 P—Q 4 (k)
7	Kt×Kt P—Q 3	Kt×Kt Q×P ch	Kt×B P ! Q—K 2	B—B 4 P—Q 3	Kt—Q 3 Kt×P
8	Kt—K B 3 Q×P ch (a)	Q—K 2 Q×Q ch	Kt×R Q×Kt ch	Kt—B 3 B—K Kt 5	Kt×Kt P×Kt
9	K—B 2 Kt—Kt 5 ch	K×Q Kt—Q 4	K—B 1 Kt—Q 5	B—K 2 ! + (j)	Kt×B Q—Kt 4
10	K—Kt 3 Q—Kt 3 (b)	R—K 1 P—Q 3 =	P—Q 3 Q—B 4		Kt—Kt 3 Q×P
11	Kt—R 4 (c) Q—R 4		P—K R 4 ! P—Q Kt 3		R—B 1 Kt—B 6 ch
12	Kt×P ch (d) K—Q 1		B—Kt 5 P—Kt 3		B×Kt P×B
13	Kt×R P—K Kt 4		Q—Q 2 B—K Kt 2		P—Q 4 B—R 6
14	P×P Q×P (e)		R—K 1 ch Kt—K 3 (h)		Q—Q 3 O—O (l)

(a) 8.., P—B 3; 9 Kt—B 3, Kt×P; 10 O—O, Kt×Kt; 11 Q P×Kt, Q—B 2; 12 R—K 1 ch (12 Kt—Q 4, B—K 2; 13 Q—K 2, B—Kt 5 (Rubinstein) is of doubtful value for Black.

(b) 10.., K—Q 1; 11 P—K R 3, Kt—R 3; 12 P—Q 4, B—K 2; 13 R—K 1, Q—Kt 3 ch; 14 K—R 2, R—K 1; 15 P—B 4, B—B 4; 16 B—Q 2 ±. Bogoljuboff—Rubinstein, match, 1920.

(c) Spielmann tried 11 Q—K 2 ch, K—Q 1; 12 P—K R 3, at Scheveningen, 1923. Teichmann suggests in reply 12 ., Kt—K 6 ch; 13 K—R 2, Kt×B P, with advantage to Black.

(d) If 12 P—K R 3, Kt—B 3; 13 Kt×P ch ? (13 Q×Q, Kt×Q ch; 14 K—B 2, K—Q 1 = is forced), K—Q 1; 14 Kt×R, Q×Kt ch!!; 15 K×Q, Kt—K 5; 16 Q—R 5, B—K 2 ch; 17 Q—Kt 5, B×Q ch; 18 P×B, P—K R 3!; 19 P—Kt 6, P×P; 20 R—B 1, B—K 3; 21 P—Q 3, P—Kt 4 ch; 22 K—R 5, Kt—Kt 6 ch; 23 K—Kt 6, Kt×R+ +.

(e) 15 Kt—B 3, Q—Kt 2+ +. Teichmann's analysis.

(f) If 6 Kt—Kt 4, Kt×Kt; 7 Q×Kt, Kt×P ch; 8 K—Q 1, Kt×R; 9 Kt—Q 5, Q—K 4!; 10 P—Q 4 (or 10 P—Q 3, P—K B 4; 11 Q—Kt 5, B—K 2), Q×P ch; 11 K—Q 2, B—B 4; 12 B—Q 2, O—O; 13 R—Q B 1, P—B 4+. Réti—Balla, Pistyan, 1922.

(g) 6. , K Kt×P?; 7 O—O, K Kt×Kt; 8 Q P×Kt, Kt×Kt ch (better Kt—K 3); 9 Q×Kt, Q—B 4; 10 R—K 1 ch, B—K 2; 11 B—Q 3+. Ed. Lasker—F. Englund, Scheveningen, 1913.

(h) 15 P—R 5+. Bogoljuboff—Rubinstein, match, 1920.

(i) Or 6 Kt—Q 3, B—Kt 3; 7 P—K 5, Kt×B; 8 Kt×Kt, Kt—Q 4; 9 O—O.

(j) Schlechter's Variation.

(k) Black's simplest means of equalising is 6.., O—O; 7 O—O, R—K 1; 8 Kt—B 3, Kt×P.

(l) 15 B—K 3, Q×P; 16 O—O—O, B×R; 17 R×B.

1 P—K 4, P—K 4 ; 2 Kt—K B 3, Kt—Q B 3 ; 3 Kt—B 3, Kt—B 3.

	51	52	53	54	55
4	(B—Kt 5)............ P—Q R 3 (a)		P—Q 4............ B—Kt 5 (f)		P—K Kt3 (i) P—Q 4
5	B × Kt (b) Q P × B		Kt × P K Kt × P....Q—K 2		P × P Kt × P
6	Kt × P Kt × P		Q—Kt 4 ! Kt × Kt	Q—Q 3 ! Kt × Kt	B—Kt 2 Kt × Kt
7	Kt × Kt Q—Q 5		Q × P R—B 1	P × Kt Q × P	Kt P × Kt B—Q 3
8	O—O Q × B Kt		P—Q R 3 B—R 4	B—Q 2 O—O	O—O O—O
9	R—K 1 B—K 3		Kt × Kt Q P × Kt	O—O—O B × Kt	P—Q 3 B—K Kt 5
10	P—Q 4 Q—K B 4	...Q—Q 4	Q—K 5 ch Q—K 2	B × B Q × K P	P—K R 3 B—Q 2
11	B—Kt 5 P—R 3 (c)	Kt—Kt 5 O—O—O	Q × Q ch K × Q	Q—Kt3 + (h)	R—Kt 1 R—Kt 1
12	Q—Q 3 K—Q 2	Kt × B P × Kt	B—Q 2 B—B 4		R—K 1 R—K 1 = (j)
13	B—R 4 Q—Q Kt 4 !	Q—Kt 4 Q × Q P (d)	B × Kt B × B ch		
14	Q—Q 2 R—K 1 =	Q × P ch Q—Q 2 (e)	P × B B × P (g)		

(a) For 4.., P—Q 3; 5 P—Q 4 and for 4.., B—K 2; 5 O—O, P—Q 3 see Ruy Lopez, Steinitz Defence.

(b) For 5 B—R 4 see Ruy Lopez, cols. 132-5.

(c) 11.., B—Q 3?; 12 P—K Kt 4, Q—Kt 3; 13 P—K B 4, P—K B 4; 14 Kt × B ch, P × Kt; 15 P—Q 5+. Znosko-Borovsky—Rubinstein, Ostend, 1907.

(d) 13.., R—K 1 (Bardeleben).

(e) 15 Q × Q ch, R × Q; 16 R—K 8 ch, R—Q 1; 17 R × R ch, followed by 18 P—Q Kt 3 and 19 B—Kt 2 with the better end-game position. Réti—Spielmann, Vienna, 1914. If 14., K—Kt 1?; 15 B—Kt 5, R—Q B 1; 16 Q ⸗ R ch !+.

(f) For 4.., P × P see Scotch Game, cols. 5-7.

(g) 15 K—Q 2 ±. Analysis by Krause.

(h) Spielmann—Bogoljuboff, Stockholm, 1919.

(i) For 4 B—B 4, B—B 4 see Giuoco Piano, and for 4 B—B 4, Kt × P see Two Knights' Defence. 4 P—Q R 3 (suggested originally by Gunsberg), P—Q 3; 5 B—B 4, Kt × P (giving back the tempo gained through White's 4th move); 6 Kt × Kt, P—Q 4; 7 B—Q 3, P × Kt; 8 B × P, B—Q 3; 9 P—Q 4, P × P; 10 B × Kt ch, P × B; 11 Q × P, O—O; 12 O—O is Nimzovitch—Kashdan, Bled, 1931.

(j) Nimzovitch—Grünfeld, Carlsbad, 1923.

FRENCH DEFENCE

OF the close defences to 1 P—K 4, the French is one of the best at the disposal of the second player, and therefore in modern master-practice it is still employed in almost every important contest, and by the majority of the leading experts. Of a solid character, it possesses great resources against premature attacks, which are apt to recoil on the first player. The efforts of analysts to demonstrate its weaknesses have always been met, eventually, by counter-analysis; and to-day it stands as high as ever it did. At the same time it is no good defence for those anxious to wrest the initiative early in the game.

The play divides into four main branches after the usual moves 1 P—K 4, P—K 3; 2 P—Q 4, P—Q 4. White has now the choice for his 3rd move of (i) P × P, (ii) Kt— Q B 3, (iii) Kt—Q 2, or (iv) P—K 5.

(i) 3 P × P, known as the Exchange Variation (cols. 1 to 5), frequently leads to an early draw after a dull game. The oldest and simplest line, it offers White little or no scope for combinative attack. Maróczy's line against the most plausible attempt, in col. 4, still holds its ground; and the Exchange Variation is rarely adopted, except with a view to draw.

(ii) 3 Kt—Q B 3, the normal or classical line, leads to an interesting struggle for the command of the centre. The simplifying defence by 3..., P × P (cols. 6 to 8) is of doubtful value, as White generally obtains a very strong attack. 3..., B—Kt 5 (cols. 9 to 18) for a long time held to be inferior, was revived mainly through the influence of Nimzovitch, and is now one of the most critical variations in the whole defence. Of the various possible replies.

4 P × P (col. 9) leads to an even position; 4 B—Q 2 (col. 10) is very tricky; 4 P—K 5 (cols. 11 to 15), in conjunction with either 5 P—Q R 3 (cols. 11 to 13), or 5 B—Q 2 (cols. 14 and 15) is by far the strongest—Lajos Steiner's line in col. 14 is particularly powerful; 4 Kt—K 2 (cols. 16 and 17) is very solid, but leads to nothing against best play; 4 P—Q R 3 (col. 18) is the most aggressive, but highly dangerous; 4 Q—Kt 4 and 4 B—Q 3 (col. 18, note (*f*)) are weak.

The deferred acceptance of the K P (cols. 19 to 22) is excellent for the second player. Cols. 23 to 34 present the normal line for both sides. In Alekhine's Attack (cols. 23 to 28) there have been some revolutionary changes since our last edition. It has been definitely shown that the only playable defence is 6..., P—K B 3! (cols. 27 and 28), for the other defences lead to cramped positions where Black has inadequate counterplay. The defence with 6..., P—K B 3, revived by the Russians Yudovitch and Belavenetz, gives Black at least equality. In the form of the opening with exchange of Bishops on the 6th move both 7 P—B 4 (as in col. 31) and 7 Q—Q 2 (col. 32) are in White's favour. The attack with 6 B × Kt (col. 34) is not easy to meet.

The McCutcheon Variation (cols. 35 to 38) has been rehabilitated and strengthened by the line in col. 37. This line was formerly thought to be the refutation of the McCutcheon, but after the improvement on Black's 13th move it is doubtful whether White can manage to draw.

The advance of P—K 5 on the 4th move (cols. 39 and 40), whereby White seeks a direct attack on the Castled King, has been revived by Spielmann, who avoids Maróczy's analysis, given in note (*k*). At present White appears to be able to obtain an advantage with the line in col. 39, but it is quite possible that the pendulum will soon swing in the other direction.

(iii) 3 Kt—Q 2 (cols. 41 to 43), recommended by Tarrasch, has often been seen since our last edition. In the most usual line, col. 41, the second player submits to an isolated Queen's Pawn, but finds sufficient compensation in the excellent placement of his minor pieces.

. (iv) 3 P—K 5 (cols. 44 to 46), favoured by Steinitz and later by Nimzovitch, has been revived by Keres and adopted by Alekhine, but has still failed to win general approval. With the immediate counter-attack against White's centre (P—Q B 4, and later P—K B 3) Black equalises the chances.

The remaining columns, 47 to 50, exemplify less common 2nd moves for White, all of which are kept alive by Tartakover's enterprising spirit. White can lay no claim to a theoretical advantage, but confronts the second player with unusual and difficult problems.

EXCHANGE VARIATION
1 P—K 4, P—K 3 ; 2 P—Q 4, P—Q 4 ; 3 P×P, P×P.

	1	2	3	4	5
4	Kt—K B 3.............		B—Q 3......	Kt—QB3 (a)	
	Kt—K B 3 ..B—Q 3		Kt—QB3 (i)	Kt—KB3 (l)	
5	B—Q 3	B—Q 3	Kt—K 2	B—KKt5 (m)	
	B—Q 3(a)	Kt—Q B 3	B—Q 3	B—K 2.....	Kt—B 3
6	O—O	P—B 3	P—Q B 3	B—Q 3	B—Kt 5 (p)
	O—O	K Kt—K 2	Q—R 5 ! (j)	O—O	B—K 2
7	Kt—B 3 (b)	O—O	Kt—Q 2	KKt—K2 (n)	K Kt—K 2
	P—B 3 (c)	B—K Kt 5	B—K Kt 5	Kt—B 3	O—O
8	B—K Kt 5	R—K 1	Q—B 2	O—O	O—O
	B—K Kt 5	Q—Q 2	O—O—O	Kt—K 1	P—Q R 3
9	P—K R 3	B—KKt5 (g)	Kt—K B 1	B×B	K B×Kt
	B—R 4 (d)	P—B 3	P—K Kt 3	Kt×B	P×B
10	P—K Kt 4	B—R 4	B—K 3	Q—Q 2	Kt—Kt 3
	B—Kt 3	P—K R 4	K Kt—K 2	P—Q B 3	P—R 3
11	Kt—K 5	Q Kt—Q 2	O—O—O	Q R—K 1	B×Kt
	Q—Kt 3 (e)	P—K Kt 4	B—K B 4	B—B 4	B×B
12	B×Kt	B—Kt 3	Kt(B1)—Kt3	Kt—B 4	Kt—R 4
	P×B	B×B	B×B	Kt—Q 3	Q—Q 3
13	Kt—B 3	B P×B	Q×B	P—Q Kt 3	P-QB3 ± (q)
	Q×Kt P	O—O—O ∓ (h)	P–KR3 ∓ (k)	Kt–Kt3 = (o)	
14	Kt—K 2+ (f)				

(a) 5 ., B—K 2 is safer. The pin on the K Kt becomes embarrassing.
(b) Better than 7 B—K Kt 5, B—K Kt 5 ; 8 Q Kt—Q 2, Q Kt—Q 2 ; 9 P—B 3, P—B 3 ; 10 Q—B 2, Q—B 2 ; 11 K R—K 1, K R—K 1 with a very drawish position.
(c) If 7.., Kt—B 3 ; 8 B—K Kt 5, B—K Kt 5 ; 9 K—R 1 ! ± (Maróczy).
(d) Preferable is 9 .,B×Kt ; 10 Q×B, Q Kt—Q 2=. (10 .., P—K R 3 ; 11 B—R 4, Q Kt—Q 2 ; 12 B—B 5, Q—B 2 ; 13 Q R—K 1 is Morphy–Löwenthal, 2nd match game, 1858 !).
(e) Or 11 , B—K 2 ; 12 P—B 4, B×B ; 13 Q×B, Q Kt—Q 2 ; 14 Q R—K 1 ±. Maróczy—Rubinstein, Prague, 1908.
(f) White's position is worth more than the Pawn. Maróczy—Réti, London, 1927.
(g) Weak. Correct is 9 Q Kt—Q 2, O—O—O ; 10 P—Q Kt 4, Kt—Kt 3 ; 11 Kt—Kt 3, Q R—K 1=. Maróczy—Spielmann, Sliac, 1932.
(h) Enoch—Nimzovitch, Berlin, 1927.
(i) A line similar to that in the text is 4 , B—Q 3 ; 5 Kt—K 2, Q—R 5 ! ; 6 Q Kt—B 3, P—QB3 ; 7 B—K 3, Kt—B 3 ; 8 Q—Q 2, Kt—Kt 5 ; 9 P—K R 3, Kt×B ; 10 Q×Kt ch, Q—K 2 ∓ (Maróczy—Nimzovitch, Carlsbad, 1929), while an alternative for Black is 4.., B—Q 3, 5 Kt—K 2, Kt—K 2 ; 6 P—Q B 3, O—O ; 7 Q—B 2, P—K R 3, 8 Kt—Q 2, P—Q Kt 3 ; 9 P—Q Kt 4, Kt—Q 2 ; 10 Q Kt—Kt 3, P—Q B 4 ; 11 Kt P×P, P×P ; 12 P×P=. Reshevsky—Fine, New York, 1936.
(j) Or 6. , K Kt—K 2 ; 7 Q—B 2, B—K Kt 5 ; 8 O—O, Q—Q 2 ; 9 R—K 1, O—O—O ; 10 P—Kt 4, B—K B 4 ; 11 P—Q R 4, Q R—K 1=. Berndtsson—Tartakover, Hamburg, 1930.
(k) Winter—Alekhine, Nottingham, 1936.
(h) 4 P—Q B 4, Kt—K B 3 ; 5 Kt—Q B 3, P—B 3=.
(l) The simplest reply is 4 , P—Q B 3 followed by 5 , B—Q 3 and 6 ., Kt—K 2.
(m) 5 B—Q 3, B—Q 3 ; 6 B—K Kt 5, P—B 3 ; 7 K Kt—K 2, O—O ; 8 Q—Q 2. B—K Kt 5 (8 , R—K 1 ; 9 P—K R 3, P—Kt 4 ; 10 O—O, Q Kt—Q 2 ; 11 Kt—Kt 3, Schlechter—Réti, Vienna, 1915), 9 O—O, Q Kt—Q 2 ; 10 Kt—Kt 3, Q—B 2 ; 11 P—K R 3, B×Kt, 12 B P×B, B—R 4 ; 13 Q—B 4 ±. Rubinstein—Danischevsky, Lodz, 1907.
(n) 7 Q—Q 2, P—B 3 ; 8 K Kt—K 2, Q R—K 1 ; 9 O—O, Q Kt—Q 2 ; 10 Kt—Kt 3, Kt—Kt 3 ; 11 Q R—K 1, Kt—B 5 ? ; 12 Q—B 1, B—Q 2 ; 13 R×B, R×R ; 14 Q B×Kt, P×B ; 15 Q—R 6, P—K B 4 ; 16 Kt—R 5, P—B 3 ; 17 Kt×P ch, K—R 1 ; 18 P—Q Kt 3, Kt—Q 3, 19 Kt×R P+. J. H. Blake—Maróczy, Liverpool, 1923.
(o) Teichmann—Maróczy, Carlsbad, 1923.
(p) 6 B×Kt, Q×B, 7 Q—K 2 ch, B—K 3 ; 8 Kt×P, Q—Q 1 ; 9 Kt—K 3, Q×P ; 10 P—Q B 3, Q—B 4, 11 P—K Kt 3, O—O—O=. Mieses—Bogoljuboff, Berlin, 1920.
(q) Spielmann—Tarrasch, Teplitz-Schönau, 1922.

1 P—K4, P—K3; 2 P—Q4, P—Q4; 3 Kt—QB3.

	6	7	8	9	10
3	P×P................................				B—Kt5
4	Kt×P / Kt—Q2................		Kt—KB3	P×P...... / P×P	B—Q2 / Kt—K2 (k)
5	Kt—KB3 / KKt—B3(a)		Kt×Kt ch / P×Kt	B—Q3 / Kt—QB3(i)	P×P / P×P
6	Kt×Kt ch / Kt×Kt		Kt—B3 / P—QKt3	K Kt—K2 / K Kt—K2	Q—B3? / Q Kt—B3
7	B—Q3(b) / B—K2.....P—B4		B—Kt5 ch / P—B3	O—O / B—KB4(j)	B—QKt5 / O—O
8	Q—K2 / P—QKt3(c)	P×P / B×P	B—Q3 / B—Kt2	B×B / Kt×B	K Kt—K2 / B—KB4
9	B—KKt5 / B—Kt2	O—O / O—O	B—K3 / Q—B2	Q—Q3 / Q—Q2	O—O—O / P—QR3!
10	O—O / O—O	B—KKt5 / P—QKt3(f)	Q—K2 / Kt—Q2	Kt—Q1 / O—O	B—Q3 / B×B
11	Q R—Q1 / P—Kt3(d)	Q—K2 / B—Kt2	B—QR6 / B×B	Kt—K3 / Kt×Kt	Q×B / Kt-R4! ∓ (l)
12	K R—K1 / Kt—R4	Q R—Q1 / Q—B2(g)	Q×B / B—Q3	B×Kt / K R—K1 ■	
13	B—KR6±(e)		O—O—O / P—Kt4= (h)		

(a) If 5. , B—K2; 6 B—QB4, K Kt—B3; 7 Kt×Kt ch, B×Kt; 8 Q—K2, O—O; 9 B—B4, P—B4; 10 O—O—O, P×P; 11 B—Q6, R—K1; 12 Kt×P, P—QR3; 13 Kt—B3 ±. Ragosin—Makagonoff, Leningrad, 1934.

(b) An energetic alternative is 7 Kt—K5!, B—Q3; 8 Q—B3, P—B3; 9 P—B3, O—O; 10 B—KKt5, B—K2; 11 B—Q3 ±. Capablanca—Blanco, Havana, 1913.

(c) Or 8.., O—O; 9 B—KKt5, P—KR3 (9.., P—QKt3! is now impossible because of 10 B×Kt, B×B; 11 Q—K4++); 10 B×Kt, B×B; 11 Q—K4, P—KKt3; 12 P—KR4+. Capablanca—Chajes, New York, 1918.

(d) If 11.., B×Kt; 12 Q×B, Q—Q4; 13 Q—K3 ±. Or 11.., P—KR3; 12 B—KB4, Q—Q4; 13 P—B4, Q—QR4; 14 B×B P+. Tarrasch—Mieses, match, 1916.

(e) Tarrasch—Mieses, 11th match game, 1916.

(f) 10.., B—K2; 11 Q—K2, Q—B2; 12 Q R—Q1, R—Q1; 13 P—B4, B—Q2; 14 B—Q2, Q R—B1; 15 B—B3, Black having a very cramped game. Maróczy—Rubinstein, Carlsbad, 1907. The column is analysis in Deutsche Schachzeitung, December, 1930, in examination of 10.., P—QKt3.

(g) The critical position. Deutsche Schachzeitung considers the variations (1) 13 B×Kt, P×B; 14 Kt—R4; (2) 13 Kt—R4; (3) 13 Kt—K5 and (4) 13 B×Kt, P×B; 14 B—K4, and concludes that in all Black has a playable game.

(h) Continued 14 B—Q2, Q—Kt3; 15 Q—R5, Q×Q=. L. Steiner—Kmoch, Niendorf, 1927.

(i) Or 5.., Kt—K2; 6 Kt—K2, B—KB4; 7 O—O, O—O; 8 Kt—Kt3, B—Kt3; 9 Q Kt—K4, Q—Q3; 10 B—K3, B—Q3; 11 Q—Q2, Q—Q2=. Marshall—Nimzovitch, New York, 1927.

(j) Or 7.., B—Kt5; 8 P—QR3, B—QR4; 9 P—QKt3, B—K3; 10 Kt—R4, B—Kt3; 11 P—QB3, Q—Q2; 12 R—K1, O—O; 13 Kt—B4, B—KB4. Marshall—Alekhine, New York, 1927. The column is Capablanca—Alekhine, 1st match game, 1927.

(k) Or 4.., P×P; 5 Q—Kt4! (5 Kt×P?, Q×P; 6 B—Q3, B×B ch; 7 Q×B (Alekhine—Flohr, Nottingham, 1936), and now, instead of the game continuation 7.. Q—Q1?; 8 O—O—O, Q—K2; 9 Kt—KB3, Kt—B3; 10 K R—K1 when White, is splendidly developed, 7.., Q×P should have been played—for two Pawns White's compensation is insufficient), B—B1 (if 5 , Q×P; 6 B—Q3 ... with a strong attack; 6 Q×KP, Kt—KB3; 7 Q—R4, B—K2; 8 O—O—O, P—QKt3; 9 Kt—B3, B—Kt2; 10 Kt—K5!, P—B3; 11 B—K2, Q Kt—Q2; 12 Q—Kt3 ±. Panoff—Ragosin, Tiflis, 1937.

(l) Speyer—Alekhine, Hamburg, 1910.

1 P—K4, P—K3; 2 P—Q4, P—Q4; 3 Kt—QB3, B—Kt5; 4 P—K5, P—QB4.

	11	12	13	14	15
5	P—QR3 (A)				B—Q2
	PxP		BxKt ch	Kt—K2	QKt-B3 (m)
6	PxB (a)		PxB	P—QR3!(j)	Kt—Kt5 (n)
	PxKt		Kt—K2 (f)	BxKt	BxB ch
7	Kt—B3 (b)..	Q—Kt4!(d)	Q—Kt4 (g)	PxB	QxB
	Q—B2	P—KKt3	Kt—B4 (h)	QKt—B3 (k)	KtxQ P!
8	Q—Q4	Kt—B3	B—Q3	Kt—B3	Ktx Kt
	KKt—K2	Q—B2	P—KR4	Q—B2	PxKt
9	B—Q3	B—Q3	Q—B4	P—KR4	Kt—B3
	Kt—Q2	Kt—QB3	PxP	Kt—B4?	Kt—K2
10	O—O	O—O	PxP	P—Kt4	KtxP
	Kt—QB3	KKt—K2	Q—R5!	KKt—K2	Kt—B3
11	QxBP	R—K1	Kt—B3	P—R5	KtxKt
	Q—Kt3	B—Q2	QxQ	P—KR3	PxKt
12	P—Kt5±(c)	PxP	BxQ	B—K3	B—Q3
		O—O—O	Kt—B3	P—B5	Q—Kt3
13		P—Kt5	P—B3	Kt—R4	QR—Kt1
		Kt—QKt1	B—Q2	B—Q2	O—O
14		Q—Kt4+ (e)	P—R3= (i)	P—B4 ± (l)	O—O= (o)

(A) A novel idea is 5 PxP, Kt—QB3; 6 Kt—B3, P—B3; 7 B—QKt5, BxP; 8 O—O, B—Q2; 9 R—K1, PxP?: 10 KtxKP, KtxKt; 11 RxKt, BxB; 12 KtxB+. Bogoljuboff—Alekhine, Bad Nauheim, 1937.

(a) If 6 QxP, PxB; 7 Q—KKt4, BxKt ch; 8 PxB, KtxP? (8..., K—B1 is essential); 9 QxKtP, Q—B3 (Kashdan—Tartakover, London, 1932) and now 10 B—KR6! would have won the Exchange.

(b) Rauser's improvement on the older 7 PxP, Q—B2; 8 Kt—B3, Kt—K2; 9 B—Q3, Kt—Kt3; 10 O—O, Kt—Q2; 11 R—K1, QxBP; 12 B—Q2, Q—B2; 13 Q—K2, O—O; 14 Q—K3, Kt—Kt3; 15 Q—Kt5, Kt—B5.∓ Dr. Em. Lasker—Maróczy, New York, 1924.

(c) Rauser—Alatorzeff, Russian Championship, 1933.

(d) Bogoljuboff's suggestion, which is also quite strong.

(e) Continued 14.., B—K1; 15 B—Kt5, R—Q2; 16 RxP, Q—Kt3; 17 R—R8, Q—Q1; 18 Kt—Q4, P—KR3; 19 B—B6, R—Kt1; 20 P—Kt6, Resigns. Bogoljuboff—Danielsson, Zoppot, 1935.

(f) 6 ., Q—B2; 7 Kt—B3, Kt—K2; 8 P—KR4!, P—QKt3; 9 P—R5, P—KR3; 10 P—R4!, B—R3; 11 B—Kt5 ch, BxB; 12 PxB, PxP; 13 PxP ± L. Steiner—Foltys, Lodz, 1938.

(g) If 7 Kt—B3, Kt—Kt3; 8 B—Q3, Q—B2; 9 O—O, P—B5; 10 B—K2, B—Q2; 11 Kt—R4, Kt—B4; 12 KtxKt, PxKt; 13 P—B4, K—B3; 14 P—QR4, P—KR3; 15 B—R3, Q—Q2=. Tylor—Flohr, Nottingham, 1936.

(h) Best. If 7.., Q—R4; 8 B—Q2, Q—R5; 9 QxKtP, R—Kt1; 10 QxRP, PxP; 11 Kt—K2!, QKt—B3; 12 KP—B4, R—Kt3; 13 P—R4, B—Q2; 14 P—R5, R—KKt1; 15 P—R6+. Bogatyrchuk—Alatorzeff, Russian Championship, 1934. And if 7 ., PxP; 8 QxKtP, R—Kt1; 9 QxRP, Q—B2; 10 Kt—K2!, QKt—B3; 11 P—KB4, B—Q2; 12 Q—Q3, PxP; 13 KtxP, P—QR3; 14 R—QKt1, R—QB1; 15 B—Q2+. Lilienthal—Lovenfisch, Moscow, 1936.

(i) Bogoljuboff—Flohr, Nottingham, 1936.

(j) Also strong is 6 Kt—Kt5, BxB ch; 7 QxB, O—O; 8 P—QB3 (8 PxP, Kt—Q2; 9 Q—B3, P—QR3; 10 Kt—Q6, Q—B2+), P—QKt3 (better Q—Kt3); 9 P—KB4, B—R3; 10 Kt—B3, Kt—Q2; 11 P—QR4, Kt—QB3; 12 P—QKt4 ±. Alekhine—Nimzovitch, San Remo, 1930.

(k) If 7.., P—B5?; 8 P—KR4, P—KR4; 9 B—K2, Kt—B4; 10 P—Kt3, P—KKt3; 11 B—Kt5, Q—R4; 12 Q—Q2 ±. L. Steiner—Nimzovitch, Berlin, 1928.

(l) L. Steiner—G. Koshnitzky, Perth, 1937.

(m) 5.., PxP; 6 Kt—Kt5, BxB ch; 7 QxB, Kt—QB3; 8 Kt—KB3, P—B3 9 Q—R4, Kt—R3; 10 Kt—Q6 ch, K—B1. Fine—Capablanca, Avro, 1938.

(n) Or 6 Q—Kt4, K—B1; 7 PxP, P—Q5; 8 Kt—K4, BxB ch; 9 KtxB, KtxP; 10 Q—Kt3, Kt—QB3; 11 O—O—O, KKt—K2. Kashdan—Simonson, match, 1938.

(o) Lasker—Bogatyrchuk, Moscow, 1935.'

1 P—K 4, P—K 3; 2 P—Q 4, P—Q 4; 3 Kt—Q B 3.

	16	17	18	19	20
3	(B—Kt 5)............................			Kt—K B 3	
4	Kt—K 2................		P—Q R 3 (f)	B—K Kt 5	
	P×P		B×Kt ch	P×P	
5	P—Q R 3		P×B	B×Kt......	Kt×P
	B—K 2.....	B×Kt ch	P×P	Q×B (i)	B—K 2
6	Kt×P	Kt×B	Q—Kt 4	Kt×P	B×Kt
	Kt—QB3!(a)	Kt—QB3(d)	Kt—K B 3	Q—Q 1	B×B
7	B—K 3 (b)	B—Q Kt 5	Q×Kt P	Kt—K B 3	Kt—KB3(k)
	Kt—B 3	K Kt—K 2	R—Kt 1	Kt—Q 2	Kt—Q 2
8	K Kt—B 3	O—O	Q—R 6	B—Q 3	P—B 3 (l)
	O—O	O—O	P—B 4	B—K 2	Q—K 2
9	Kt—Kt 3	B×Kt	Kt—K 2 (g)	Q—K 2	Q—B 2
	P—Q Kt 3	Kt×B	Q Kt—Q 2	P—Q B 4	P—B 4
10	B—K 2	P—Q 5	Kt—Kt 3	P×P	P×P
	B—Kt 2	P×P	R—Kt 3 ? (h)	B×P	Kt×P
11	O—O	Q×P	Q—K 3	Kt×B	B—Kt 5 ch
	Q—Q 2	Kt—Q 5 !	Kt—Q 4	Q—R 4 ch	B—Q 2
12	Q—Q 2	B—Kt 5	Q×P	P—B 3	B×B ch
	Q R—Q 1	Q×Q	Kt×P	Q×Kt	Kt×B
13	K R—Q 1	Kt×Q	Q—Q 3+	O—O	O-O-O±(m)
	Q—B 1= (c)	Kt—K 3 (e)		O—O= (j)	

(a) More accurate than 6.., Kt—K B 3; 7 K Kt—B 3, Q Kt—Q 2?; 8 B—K B 4, Kt×Kt (better Kt—Q 4); 9 Kt×Kt, Kt—B 3; 10 B—Q 3, O—O; 11 Kt×Kt ch, B×Kt; 12 P—Q B 3, Q—Q 4; 13 Q—K 2, P—B 3; 14 O—O ±. Lasker—Capablanca, Moscow, 1935.

(b) 7 P—K Kt 4 !? is best met by 7 .., P—K 4; 8 P—Q 5, Kt—Q 5; 9 K Kt—B 3 (not 9 Kt×Kt, Q×P; 10 Q—B 3, P×Kt !), P—K B 4; 10 P×P, B×B P; 11 B—K 3=; or 9.., P—K R 4; 10 P×P, P—K B 4; 11 Kt—Kt 3=. Weak is 7.., P—Q Kt 3; 8 Kt—B 2, B—Kt 2; 9 P—Q B 3, Kt—B 3; 10 K Kt—Kt 3, O—O?; 11 P—Kt 5, Kt×Kt; 12 Kt×Kt, K—R 1; 13 Q—R 5 ±. Alekhine—Euwe, 7th match game, 1935.

(c) Alekhine—Euwe, 5th match game, 1935.

(d) If 6.., P—K B 4: 7 P—B 3! gives White a powerful attack: 7 P—B 3 (weaker is 7 B—Q B 4, Kt—K B 3; 8 B—K Kt 5, O—O; 9 Q—Q 2, Kt—B 3; 10 O—O—O, K—R 1; 11 P—B 3, P×P; 12 P×P. Maróczy—Seitz, Györ, 1924), P×P; 8 Q×P, Q×P (better 8.., Q—R 5 ch); 9 Q—Kt 3!, Kt—K B 3? (preferable was 9 Kt—K 2; 10 Kt—Kt 5, Q—K 5 ch; 11 B—K 2, Q Kt×P ch, K—B 2 with a difficult position); 10 Q×Kt P, Q—K 4 ch; 11 B—K 2, R—Kt 1; 12 Q—R 6, R—Kt 3; 13 Q—R 4, B—Q 2; 14 B—K Kt 5+ +. Alekhine—Nimzovitch, Bied, 1931.

(e) 14 B—R 4=. Lasker—Kan, Moscow, 1936.

(f) Warmly recommended by Alekhine. Other possibilities are: (1) 4 Q—Kt 4, Kt—K B 3 (4.., K—B 1; 5 P—K 5, P—Q B 4; 6 P—Q R 3, Q—R 4; 7 Q—Q 2, P×P; 8 Q×P=); 5 Q×P, R—Kt 1; 6 Q—R 6, R—Kt 3; 7 Q—K 3, P—Q B 4! (better than 7 .., P—K 4; 8 B—Q 2, P×QP; 9 Q×P, P—Q B 4; 10 Q—K 5 ch+ or 7 ., Kt×P; 8 B—Q 3, P—K B 4; 9 Kt—K 2, P—B 4; 10 B×Kt+. Alekhine—Euwe, 9th match game, 1935); 8 B—Q 2, Kt—Kt 5; 9 Q—Q 3, Kt—Q B 3+ (Alekhine). (2) 4 B—Q 3, P×P; 5 B×P, P—Q B 4: 6 P—Q R 3, B×Kt ch; 7 P×B, Kt—K B 3; 8 B—Q 3, O—O; 9 Kt—B 3, Q—Kt 2; ₦ O—O, P×Kt 3; 11 Q—K 2, B—Kt 2; 12 Kt—K 5, R—Q B 1=. Tartakover—Przepiorka, Debreczin, 1925.

(g) Also strong is 9 B—Kt 2, Q Kt—Q 2; 10 O—O—O, Q—R 4; 11 P—B 3!, P—K B 3; 12 B P×P, P×P; 13 P×P+. A. Steiner—Böök, Kemeri, 1937.

(h) Necessary was 10.., Q—R 4; 11 B—Q 2, Q—R 5; 12 P×P, but Alekhine still prefers White's game. The column is Alekhine—Euwe, 3rd match game, 1935.

(i) Or 5.., P×B; 6 Kt×P, P—K B 4; 7 Kt—Q B 3, B—Kt 2; 8 Kt—B 3, O—O; 9 Q—Q 2, P—B 4; 10 P×P, Q—R 4; 11 Kt—Q Kt 5, Q×Q ch=. Alekhine—Tartakover, Vienna, 1922.

(j) Tartakover—Maróczy, Gothenburg, 1920.

(k) 7 P—Q B 3, Kt—Q 2; 8 P—K B 4!, Kt—B 3 (8.., B—K 2; 9 Q—Kt 3, P—Q Kt 3; 10 B—K 2, B—Kt 2; 11 B—B 3 ±); 9 Q—B 3, R—Q Kt 1; 10 B—Kt 5, B—Kt 2; 11 Kt—K 2, O—O; 12 O—O—O, B—K 2=. Alekhine—Landau, Amsterdam, 1936.

(l) 8 B—Q 3, P—B 4!; 9 P×P, Kt×P; 10 B—Kt 5 ch, K—K 2!; 11 Q×Q ch, R×Q; 12 Kt×Kt, R—Q 4; 13 Kt—K 6, B×P; 14 R—Q Kt 1, R×B; 15 Kt—B 7, B—R 6 ch; 16 K—K 2, R×R; 17 R×R, R—Kt 1; 18 Kt—R 6 draws.

(m) Alekhine—Petrov, Warsaw, 1935.

1 P—K4, P—K3; 2 P—Q4, P—Q4; 3 Kt—QB3, Kt—KB3; 4 B—KKt5.

	21	22	23	24	25
4	(P×P).................		B—K2		
5	(Kt×P)		P—K5		
	(B—K2)		KKt—Q2 (e)		
6	(B×Kt)		P—KR4 (f)		
	P×B		B×B......P—QB4		
7	Q—Q2	Kt—KB3	P×B	B×B (j)	
	P—KB4	P—QKt3 (b)	Q×P	K×B......Q×B	
8	Kt—QB3	B—Kt5 ch	Kt—R3	P—B4 (k)	Kt—Kt5
	P—QB3	P—B3	Q—K2 (g)	Kt—QB3 (l)	O—O
9	O—O—O	B—B4	Kt—B4	P×P	Kt—B7
	Kt—Q2	B—Kt2	P—QR3 (h)	Kt×BP	Kt×P (n)
10	P—KKt3	Q—K2	Q—Kt4	Q—Kt4 !	Kt×R
	P—Kt3	Q—B2	P—KKt3	K—B1	P×P
11	B—Kt2	O—O—O	O—O—O	O—O—O	Q×P
	B—Kt2	Kt—Q2 (c)	P—QB4	B—Q2	Q Kt—B3
12	Kt—R3	KR—K1	Q—Kt3	Kt—B3	Q—Q2
	Q—B2	O—O—O	Kt—Kt3	R—QB1	P—QKt3 (o)
13	Q—K2	K—Kt1	P×P	R—R3	B—K2
	Kt—B3	K—Kt1	Q×P	P—KR4	B—Kt2
14	KR—K1=(a)	B—Kt3=(d)	B—Q3+(i)	Q-Kt3±(m)	Kt-B3±(p)

(a) Euwe—Flohr, 2nd match game, 1932. Black now continued 14. , K—B1 ?; 15 Kt—K Kt 5, Q—Q3; 16 P—B4+. 14.., O—O—O would have made White's advantage negligible.

(b) 7 , P—KB4; 8 Kt—B3, P—QB3; 9 P—KKt3, Kt—Q2; 10 B—Kt2, Q—B2, 11 Q—K2, P—QKt3; 12 Kt—K5, B—Kt2; 13 O—O—O, Kt—Kt3; 14 Q—R5+. Bogoljuboff—Alekhine, 18th match game, 1929.

(c) Safer than 11 , P—QR3 (White's B was at Q3); 12 KR—K1, Kt—Q2; 13 K—Kt1, P—QB4; 14 P×P ±. Asztalos—Alekhine, Bled, 1931.

(d) L. Steiner—Flohr, Ujpest, 1934.

(e) If 5 , Kt—K5, 6 B×B (6 Kt×Kt, B×B; 7 Kt×B, Q×Kt; 8 Kt—B3, Q—K2; 9 P—B3, P—QB4; 10 B—Q3, Kt—B3=), Q×B; 7 Kt×B; P×Kt; 8 Q—K2, P—QKt3; 9 O—O—O, B—Kt2; 10 P—KKt3, P—QB4; 11 B—Kt2 ±. Flohr—Alekhine, Bled, 1931.

(f) Alekhine's Attack, sometimes also called Chatard's or Albin-Chatard's Attack.

(g) Or 8. , Q—R3; 9 P—KKt3, P—QB3; 10 B—Q3, P—KKt3; 11 P—B4, P—QKt3; 12 Q—K2, P—QR4; 13 O—O—O+.

(h) Or 9 , Kt—B1; 10 Q—Kt4, P—KB4; 11 P×P e.p., P×P; 12 O—O—O, P—B3; 13 R—K1, K—Q1; 14 R—R6+. Alekhine—Fahrni, Mannheim, 1914.

(i) 14 , Q—B1; 15 B—K4! A game won by Bogoljuboff.

(j) If 7 Kt—Kt5, P×P; 8 Kt—Q6 ch, K—B1; 9 B×B ch, Q×B; 10 Kt×B, Q—Kt5 ch, P×P; 12 Kt—Q1, Kt—QB3; 13 Kt—Q6, K Kt×P; 14 Kt—Kt5, R—B1+. Analysis by Breyer and Réti. On 7 Q—Kt4, Kt—QB3 is Black's best reply· 8 B×B, K×B; 9 Q—Kt5 ch, K—B1; 10 Q×Q ch, Kt×Q; 11 P—B4, Kt—QB3; 12 Kt—B3, B—Q2; 13 O—O—O, P—Q Kt4=. Lilienthal—Miss Menchik, Moscow, 1935.

(k) If 8 Q—Kt4, K—B1; 9 Kt—B3, P×P; 10 Q×QP, Q—Kt3; 11 Q×Q, P×Q= (but not 11 ., Kt×Q; 12 Kt—Q2, Kt—B 3, 13 P—B 4, B—Q 2; 14 O—O—O ±. Bogoljuboff—Spielmann, Baden-Baden, 1925).

(l) If 8 , P×P; 9 Q×P, Kt—QB3; 10 Q—Q2, Q—R4 (10 , Q—Kt3; 11 O—O—O, Kt—B4; 12 Kt—B3, B—Q2; 13 P—B5!+); 11 Kt—B3, R—Q1; 12 R—R3, K—B1, 13 B—(3, Kt—Kt3; 14 Kt—QKt5 ±. Lovenfisch—Miss Menchik, Moscow, 1935.

(m) Rumin—Stahlberg, Moscow, 1935.

(n) Or 9 , P×P, 10 Kt×R, P—B3, 11 Kt—B7, P×P; 12 Kt—Kt5, P—QR3; and now not 13 Kt×P, P×Kt; 14 Q×P, Kt—QB3; 15 Q—Q2, Kt—B3 ∓ (Gilg-Petrov, Mährisch-Ostrau, 1933), but 13 Kt—R7, Q—Kt5 ch; 14 Q—Q2+ (Kashdan).

(o) Better was Q—Q1 followed by B—Q2.

(p) 14 Kt×P was also strong. Rumin—Lilienthal, Moscow, 1935.

1 P—K 4, P—K 3; 2 P—Q 4, P—Q 4; 3 Kt—Q B 3, Kt—K B 3; 4 B—K Kt 5, B—K 2; 5 P—K 5, K Kt—Q 2.

	26	27	28	29	30
6	(P—K R 4).................,........P—K R 3 (A).P—K B 3 !		P—K B 3 !	B×B Q×B	
7	B—K 3 (a) P—Q B 4	B—Q 3 P—QB 4 !(d)	P×P (B) Kt×P	Kt—Kt 5....Kt—Kt 3	P—B 4 O—O
8	Q—Kt 4 K—B 1	Q—R 5 ch K—B 1	B—Q 3 P—B 4	P—Q B 3 (j) P—Q R 3	Q—Q 2 P—Q B 4
9	Kt—B 3 (b) Kt—Q B 3	Kt×P !? (e) P×B	P×P Kt—B 3	Kt—Q R 3 P—Q B 4	Kt—B 3 Kt—Q B 3
10	O—O—O P×P	R—R 3 P—Kt 5 !	Kt—R 3 Q—R 4	Kt—B 2 Kt—R 5	P—K Kt 3 P—B 3
11	B×Q P Q—R 4	Kt—B 4 Kt×P !	Q—Q 2 (h) Q×B P	R—Kt 1 P—Q Kt 4	P×K B P Kt×B P (m)
12	R—R 3 Kt—B 4	P×Kt P×R	O—O O—O	P—K B 4 Kt—B 3	B—Kt 2 P×P
13	R—Kt 3 P—K Kt 3	K B×P (f) R×B	Q R—K 1 P—K 4 !	Kt—B 3 B—Q 2	K Kt×P P—K 4 !
14	Q—B 4 ± (c)	Q×R P—R 7 ! (g)	B×Kt B×B= (i)	Q—Q 2 (k) R—Q B 1 =(l)	Kt×P K Kt×Kt∓ (n)

(A) Inferior alternatives are · (1) 6 ,P—Q R 3 ; 7 Q—Kt 4, B × B (better K—B 1) ; 8 P×B, P—K Kt 3 ; 9 B—Q 3, Q—K 2 ; 10 Kt—B 3, P—Q B 4 ; 12 O—O—O, Kt×B P ; 13 Q—K B P, Q—B 2 ; 14 R—R 6+. Bogoljuboff—Maróczy, San Remo, 1930. (2) 6 ., O—O : 7 B—Q 3, P—Q B 4 ; 8 Kt—R 3, R—K 1 ; 9 Kt—Kt 5, P—B 4 ; 10 Kt—Q 6+. Bogoljuboff—Spielmann, Vienna, 1922.

(B) On 7 Q—R 5 ch, K—B 1 ! (7 , P—Kt 3? ; 8 P×P!, P×Q ; 9 P×B+) ; 8 P×P, Kt×P ; 9 Q—B 3, P—B 4 ; 10 P×P, Q Kt—Q 2 ; 11 O—O—O, Kt×P ; 12 R—R 3, B—Q 2 ; 13 Q—K 3, R—B 1 Black has satisfactory counter-play. C. H. Alexander—T. H. Tylor, Brighton, 1938.

(a) An interesting possibility, recommended by the Russian analysts Belavenetz and Yudovitch, is 7 Q—R 5, e.g. 7. , P—Q R 3 ; 8 B—Q 3, P—B 4 ; 9 Kt×P !, B×B ! ; 10 P×B, P×Kt ; 11 P—K 6, Q—K 2 ; 12 O—O—O, Q×K P ; 13 Kt—B 3, with a strong attack.

(b) If 9 P—B 4, P×P ; 10 B×P, Kt—Q B 3 ; 11 Kt—B 3, Q—R 4 ; 12 R—R 3, P—R 4 ∓. Bogoljuboff—Maróczy, Bled, 1931.

(c) Dubinin—Rabinovitch, Leningrad, 1934.

(d) Alekhine gives 7.., P×B ; 8 Q—R 5 ch, K—B 1 ; 9 R—R 3, P×P ; 10 R—B 3 ch, Kt—B 3 ; 11 Kt—R 3, Q—K 1 ; 12 Q×P (R 4), K—Kt 1 ; 13 P×Kt, B×P, B×R, P×R ; 15 Q×B P with at least a draw.

(e) Best is 9 K P×P, Kt×P ; 10 B×Kt, B×B ; 11 P×P (Crakanthorp—Purdy, 1927), when Black's uncomfortable K position may still occasion him difficulties.

(f) There is no good continuation, e.g. 13 Kt—Kt 6 ch, P×Kt ; 14 Q×R ch, K—B 2 ; 15 Q—R 7, Q×B! ; 16 P×Q, P—R 7+ +.

(g) Continued 15 K—K 2, P—R 8=Q ; 16 Kt—Kt 6 ch, K—B 2 ; 17 Kt—R 8 ch, Q×Kt ; 18 Q×Q, Kt—B 3 ; 19 Q—R 5 ch, K—Kt 1 and Black won. Panoff—Yudovitch, Tiflis, 1937.

(h) Superior to 11 B—Q 2, Q×B P ; 12 Kt—B 4, O—O ; 13 Q—K 2, Kt—Q 5 ; 14 Q—B 1, B—Q 3 ∓. Yates—Maróczy, New York, 1924.

(i) Panoff—Belavenetz, Tiflis, 1937.

(j) 8 P—Q R 4, P—Q R 3 ; 9 P—R 5, P×Kt ; 10 P×Kt, R×R ; 11 Q×R, O—O ! ; 12 P×P, Q×P ; 13 B—Q 3, Kt—B 3 =.

(k) Not 14 Kt—K 3, P×P ; 15 P×P, Q R—B 1 ; 16 P—Q R 3, Kt—R 4 ∓. L. Steiner—Lilienthal, Ujpest, 1934.

(l) Lasker—Lilienthal, Moscow, 1936.

(m) 11 , Q×P ; 12 O—O—O, P—Q R 3 ; 13 B—Kt 2, Kt—Kt 3 ; 14 K R—K 1, Kt—B 5 ; 15 Q—B 2 ±. Rubinstein—Löwenfisch, Carlsbad, 1911.

(n) 15 B×Kt ch, K—R 1 ; 16 Kt—K 2, B—Kt 5 ; 17 O—O—O, Q R—Q 1 ; 18 P—B 4, Kt—Kt 5 ; 19 P—Q R 3, Kt×B. L. Steiner—Stahlberg, Ujpest, 1934.

1 P—K4, P—K3;   2 P—Q4, P—Q4;   3 Kt—QB3, Kt—KB3;   4 B—KKt5.

	31	32	33	34	35
4	(B—K2)				B—Kt5 (m)
5	(P—K5)			B×Kt	P×P
	(KKt—Q2)			B×B	Q×P
6	(B×B)			P—K5 (j)	B×Kt
	(Q×B)			B—K2	B×Ktch (n)
7	(P—B4)....	Q—Q2		Q—Kt4	P×B
	P—QR3	O—O		O—O	P×B
8	Kt—B3	P—B4......	Kt—Q1	B—Q3	Q—Q2 (o)
	P—QB4	P—QB4	P—QB4 (g)	P—QB4	Kt—Q2
9	P×P	Kt—B3	P—QB3	P×P	P—QB4
	Kt×P (a)	Kt—QB3	Kt—QB3	P—B4 (k)	Q—K5 ch
10	B—Q3 (b)	O—O—O (d)	P—KB4	Q—R3	Kt—K2
	Kt—QB3	P—B3	P—B3	Kt—Q2	Kt—Kt3
11	Q—Q2	KP×P	Kt—B3	P—B4	P—KB3
	B—Q2	Q×P (e)	P×QP	Kt×BP	Q—B3
12	O—O	P—KKt3	BP×P	O—O—O	P—B5
	P—KR3	P×P	P×P	B—Q2	Kt—Q4
13	QR—K1±(c)	KKt×P±	BP×P (h)	KKt—K2	P—QB4
		(f)	R×Kt!+ (i)	P—QKt4 (l)	Kt—K2 (p)

(a) Or 9 ,Q×P; 10 Q—Q4, Kt—QB3; 11 Q×Q, Kt×Q; 12 R—Q3, K—K2; 13 Kt—Q2, P—KKt3; 14 Kt—K2±. Konstantinopolsky—Lilienthal, Moscow, 1936.
Or 9 , Kt—QB3; 10 Kt—K2, Q×P; 11 Q—Q2, P—QKt4; 12 Q Kt—Q4, Kt×Kt; 13 Kt×Kt, Kt—Kt3; 14 P—QKt3, B—Q2; 15 Q—K3, R—QB1; 16 B—Q3, O—O; 17 O—O±. Eliskases—Stahlberg, Podebrady, 1936.
(b) Black's Kt is more valuable than White's B in this position.
(c) Kan—Lilienthal, Moscow, 1936.
(d) If instead 10 P×P, Kt×BP; 11 B—Q3, P—B3; 12 P×P, Q×P; 13 P—KKt3 (Capablanca—Réti, New York, 1924) and now 13 ., Kt×Bch; 14 P×Kt, P—K4; 15 O—O, B—R6; followed by QR—K1= (Alekhine).
(e) Better11.., Kt×BP; 12B—Q3, P×P; 13 Kt—QKt5, Q—Kt5; but after 14Q Kt×QP White retains the upper hand.
(f) 13 , Kt—B4; 14 B—Kt2, B—Q2; 15 KR—K1, QR—B1; 16 Kt×Kt, R×Kt; 17 B×P!. Stahlberg—Keres, Kemeri, 1937.
(g) Or 8. , P—KB3; 9 P×P, Kt×P; 10 B—Q3, Kt—B3; 11 Kt—KB3, P—K4; 12 P×P, Kt×P=. Lasker—Eliskases, Moscow, 1936.
(h) Correct is 13 QP×P, O—Kt5; 14 P—KKt3, Kt—B4; 15 Q×Q=. Sir G. A. Thomas—Lilienthal, Ujpest, 1934.
(i) First pointed out and played by Tarrasch. The best continuation is 14 P×R, Q—R5 ch; 15 Kt—B2, Kt×QP; 16 O—O—O, Kt×BP; 17 Q—K3, Q Kt×P; 18 Kt—Q3, Q—B3; 19 B—K2, Kt×Ktch; 20 B×Kt, Kt—K4, but Black should win.
(j) 6 Kt—B3?, O—O; 7 B—Q3, P—B4; 8 P—K5, B—K2; 9 P×P, Kt—Q2; 10 P—KR4, P—KB4; 11 P×P e.p., B×P (B3); 12 Q—Q2, Kt×P∓. Foltys—Keres, Prague, 1937.
(k) A sound alternative is 9. , P—KKt3; e.g. 10 Q—R3, Kt—B3; 11 P—B4, B×P, 12 Kt—B3, P—B3!; 13 Q—R6, R—B2; 14 P×P, Q×P; 15 P—KKt3, B—R6!+. Charousek—Maróczy, 1897.
(l) Richter—Stahlberg, Zoppot, 1935. White's attack was successful.
(m) The McCutcheon Variation.
(n) Simpler is 6 ,P×P; 7 Q—Q2, Q—QR4; 8 K Kt—K2, Kt—Q2; 9 Kt—B1, Kt—Kt3; 10 Kt—Kt3, Q—KKt4=. Capablanca—Bogoljuboff, New York, 1924.
(o) Or 8 Kt—B3, P—Kt3; 9 Q—Q2, B—Kt2; 10 B—K2, Kt—B2; 11 P—B4, Q—KB4; 12 O—O—O, O—O—O=. Capablanca—Znosko-Borovsky, 1913.
(p) Continued 14 Kt—B3, P—B4; 15 B—K2, R—KKt1; 16 O—O±. Capablanca—Alekhine, New York, 1924. Tarrasch suggests 10.., P—QKt3 followed by B—Kt2 and O—O—O.

1 P—K4, P—K3; 2 P—Q4, P—Q4; 3 Kt—QB3, Kt—KB3.

	36	37	38	39	40
4	(B—Kt5) (B—Kt5)			P—K5 K Kt—Q2	
5	P—K5 P—KR3		Kt—K2 PxP	QKt—K2(j) P—QB4	P—B4 P—QB4
6	PxKt PxB	B—Q2 BxKt(b)	P—QR3 B—K2	P—QB3 Kt—QB3	PxP Kt—QB3
7	PxP R—Kt1	PxB Kt—K5	BxKt PxB(g)	P—KB4 Q—Kt3	P—QR3 BxP(m)
8	P—KR4 PxP	Q—Kt4(A) P—KKt3(c)	KtxP P—Kt3(h)	Kt—B3 P—B3	Q—Kt4 O—O
9	Q—R5 Q—B3	B—Q3 KtxB	Q—Q2 B—Kt2	P—QR3(k) PxKP	B—Q3 P—B4
10	Kt—B3 Kt—B3	KxKt P—QB4(d)	K Kt—B3 P—KB4	BPxP PxP	Q—R3 BxKt
11	RxP QxKtP	P—KR4 Kt—B3	Kt—Kt3 P—KR4!	PxP B—K2	RxB Q—Kt3
12	O—O—O B—Q2	R—R3 PxP(e)	O—O—O P—R5	Kt—B4 O—O	Kt—K2 Kt—B4=
13	Q—R7 O—O—O	PxP Q-Kt3 ∓ (f)	Kt(Kt3)-K2 P—QB3=(i)	B—Q3 ± (l)	
14	QxQ= (a)				

(a) Rotlevy—Kostich, Carlsbad, 1911.
(b) If 6.., K Kt—Q2; 7 Q—Kt4, B—B1; 8 P—B4, P—QB4; 9 B—Q3, P—B5, 10 B—Kt6!, Kt—Kt3; 11 P—B5, Q—K2; 12 P—B6, PxP; 13 B—R5±. L. Steiner—Tartakover, Hastings, 1928.
(c) Best. If 8.., K—B1; 9 P—KR4, P—QB4; 10 R—R3, Kt—QB3; 11 B—Q3, KtxB; 12 KxKt, P—B5; 13 B—K2, Kt—K2; 14 Q—B4, B—Q2; 15 B—R5±. Yates—Znosko-Borovsky, Cheltenham, 1928.
(d) Inferior is 10 , Q—Kt4ch; 11 QxQ, PxQ; 12 P—KB4, PxP; 13 R—KB1±. Bogatyrchuk—Zubareff, Moscow, 1925.
(e) If 12.., Q—R4; 13 BxP+. Euwe—Bogoljuboff, Budapest, 1921. After the text-move 13 BxP is not playable because of 13 , KtxP.
(f) Lilienthal—Bondarevsky, Moscow, 1937. The older line is 13. , B—Q2; 14 P—QB3, Q—K2; 15 Q—Q1, Kt—R4=; or 14 R—B3, Q—Kt3; 15 Q—B4, Q—Kt5ch; 16 K—Q1, QxP; 17 QxPch, K—Q1; 18 R—QKt1, P—KB3; 19 R—B4, QxKP; 20 Kt—B3, Q—Q3 and Black is safe. Yates—Kinoch, Kecskemét, 1927. After the text-move White is at a loss for a good continuation, for if 14 BxP?, PxB; 15 QxKtPch, K—Q1; 16 Q—B6ch, K—B2; 17 QxR, QxPch++, while if 14 Kt—K2, Q—Kt5ch; 15 K—Q1, KtxKP+. There remains the game continuation: 14 Kt—B3, B—Q2; 15 Q—B4, O—O—O; 16 P—Kt4, Q—Kt5ch; 17 K—K2, P—B3!!+.
(g) Probably better for Black is 7.., BxB; 8 KtxP, O—O; 9 Q—Q3, P—K4; 10 P—Q5, B—K2; 11 O—O—O, P—KB4.
(h) 8.., P—KB4; 9 Q Kt—B3, B—Q2; 10 Q—Q2, B—Q3; 11 O—O—O, Q—K2; 12 Kt—Kt3±. Lasker—Réti, New York, 1924.
(i) Panoff—Lövenfisch, Tiflis, 1937.
(j) Preparing to support his QP. The Gledhill Attack, 5 Q—Kt4, P—QB4; 6 Kt—Kt5 is unsound. PxP; 7 Kt—KB3, Kt—QB3; 8 Kt—Q6ch, BxKt; 9 QxKtP, BxP; 10 KtxB, Q—B3; 11 QxQ, KtxQ; 12 B—QKt5, B—Q2; 13 Kt—B3, Kt—K5+. Bogoljuboff—Réti, Mährisch-Ostrau, 1923.
(k) Better than 9 P—KR3, PxP; 10 BPxP, PxP; 11 BPxP, B—Kt5ch; 12 K—B2, O—O; 13 B—K3, Kt(Q2)xP; 14 PxKt, RxKtch!++. Whitehead—Maróczy, London, 1923.
(l) Spielmann—Miss Menchik, Margate, 1938.
(m) Inferior is 7 , KtxBP; 8 P—QKt4, Kt—Q2; 9 B—Q3, P—QR4; 10 P—Kt5±. Pillsbury—Lasker, Nuremburg, 1896.
(A) After 8 B—Q3, KtxB; 9 QxKt, P—QB4; White's weak Pawn-position is a great handicap for the endgame.

1 P—K 4, P—K 3; 2 P—Q 4, P—Q 4.

	41	42	43	44	45
3	Kt—Q 2.................	....	.........P	P—K 5 (h)	
	P—Q B 4	...	Kt—K B 3	P—Q B 4	
4	K P × P.....	Q P × P	P—K 5	P—Q B 3....	Q—Kt 4
	K P × P (A)	B × P	K Kt—Q 2	Kt—Q B 3	Kt—Q B 3 (l)
5	B-Kt 5 ch (a)	B—Q 3	B—Q 3	Kt—K B 3	Kt—K B 3
	B—Q 2 (b)	Kt—Q B 3	P—Q B 4	Q—Kt 3	K Kt—K 2
6	Q—K 2 ch	P × P	P—Q B 3	B—Q 3	P—B 3
	Q—K 2	P × P (e)	Kt—Q B 3	P × P (i)	Kt—B 4
7	Q × Q ch (c)	Kt—Kt 3	Kt—K 2	P × P	B—Q 3
	B × Q	B—Kt 3	Q—Kt 3 (f)	B—Q 2	P × P!
8	B × B ch	Kt—B 3	Kt—B 3	B—K 2	O—O
	Kt × B	K Kt—K 2	P × P	K Kt—K 2	B—Q 2
9	P × P	O—O	P × P	P—Q Kt 3	R—K 1
	Kt × P	O—O	B—Kt 5 ch	Kt—B 4	P × P
10	Kt—Kt 3	P—B 3	B—Q 2 (B)	B—Kt 2	Kt × P
	Kt—R 5!	Q—Q 3	B × B ch	B—Kt 5 ch	P—K Kt 3
11	Kt—K 2	R—K 1	Q × B	K—B 1	B—K Kt 5
	B—B 3	Kt—Kt 3	Q—Kt 5	P—K R 4 (j)	B—K 2
12	P—Q B 3	B—K 3	R—Q B 1	P—Kt 3	Q—K B 4
	Kt—K 2	B × B	Q × Q ch	R—Q B 1	Q Kt-Q 5!
13	O—O	R × B=	K × Q	K—Kt 2	(m)
	O—O= (d)		Kt-Kt 3 = (g)	P—Kt 3 = (k)	

(A) 4.., Q × P! equalises more easily for Black.

(B) 10 K—B 1, B—K 2; 11 P—Q R 3, Kt—B 1 (better is P—Q R 4); 12 P—Q Kt 4! Alekhine—Capablanca, Avro, 1938.

(a) 5 K Kt—B 3, Kt—Q B 3; 6 B—Kt 5, Q—K 2 ch; 7 B—K 2, P × P; 8 O—O, Q—B 2, 9 Kt—Kt 3, B—Q 3; 10 Q Kt × P, P—Q R 3; 11 P—Q Kt 3, K Kt—K 2; 12 B—Kt 2, O—O; 13 Kt × Kt, P × Kt, 14 P—B 4 ± Keres—Capablanca, Avro, 1938.

(b) If 5 , Kt—B 3; 6 Q—K 2 ch, B—K 3; 7 K Kt—B 3 ±.

(c) More precise is 7 B × B ch, Kt × B; 8 P × P, Q × Q ch; 9 Kt × Q, for if 9.. B × P?; 10 Kt—Kt 3, B—Kt 3; 11 Q Kt—Q 4, K Kt—B 3; 12 B—Kt 5, O—O; 13 O—O—O, Kt—Kt 5; 14 B—R 4 ± (Kan—Bondarevsky, Tiflis, 1937), but Black should reply 9. , Kt × P and continue as in the text.

(d) Continued 14 R—Q 1, K R—Q 1; 15 R—Kt 1, Q R—B 1; 16 K—B 1, P—Q R 3, and the game was eventually drawn. Flohr—Botvinnik, 8th match game, 1933.

(e) Or 6 ., Q × P; 7 Kt—K 4, B—Kt 3; 8 P—Q B 4, Q—Q 1 followed by P—K 4 (Alekhine). The column is Spielmann—Alekhine, New York, 1927.

(f) 7 , P—B 3!?; 8 Kt—B 4, Q—K 2, 9 Kt—B 3, P × P and now not 10 Kt × P (K 5), K Kt × Kt; 11 P × Kt, P—K Kt 3; 12 O—O, Kt × P; 13 R—K 1, B—Kt 2 ∓ (Keres—Fine, Margate, 1937), but 10 Kt—Kt 6!, P × Kt; 11 B × P ch, K—Q 1; 12 B—Kt 5, Kt—B 3; 13 P × P ±.

(g) Yudovitch—Alatorzeff, Leningrad, 1934.

(h) 3 B—Q 3, P × P; 4 B × P, Kt—K B 3; 5 B—Q 3, P—B 4; 6 P × P, B × P; 7 Kt—K B 3, Kt—B 3, 8 O—O, Q—B 2=. Tartakover—Torre, Moscow, 1925.

(i) If 6 , B—Q 2?; 7 P × P, B × P; 8 O—O, P—B 3, 9 P—Q Kt 4, B—K 2; 10 B—K B 4, P × P; 11 Kt × P ±. Nimzovitch—Salwe, Carlsbad, 1911.

(j) If 11 , B—K 2; 12 P—Kt 3, P—Q R 4?; 13 P—Q R 4, R—Q B 1; 14 B—Kt 5 Kt × 5; 15 Kt—B 3, Kt—R 3; 16 K—Kt 1 ±. Nimzovitch—Tarrasch, San Sebastian, 1912.

(k) Nimzovitch—Rubinstein, Carlsbad, 1911.

(l) 4 , P × P is an equally good reply: 5 Kt—K B 3, Kt—Q B 3; 6 B—Q 3, Q—B 2! (Best, if instead (1) 6 , K Kt—K 2; 7 O—O, Kt—Kt 3; 8 R—K 1, Q—B 2; 9 Q—Kt 3, B—B 4, 10 P—K R 4, K—B 1; 11 P—R 5, K Kt—K 2; 12 P—R6+; Nimzovitch—Szekely, Kecskemét, 1927 (2) 6 ., K Kt—B 3; 7 P—K R 4, P—K R 4; 8 Q—Kt 3, K Kt—K 2; 9 O—O, Q—Kt 3; 10 P—R 4, Kt—K t 5; 11 B—K 5 ch, B—Q 2; 12 B × B ch. Batik-Duhrssen, correspondence, 1931); 7 Q—Kt 3 (or 7 B—K B 4, Kt—K t 5), P—B 3; 8 P × P (B—K B 4?; P—K Kt 4!; 9 B—Q 2, Kt × P; 10 Kt × Kt, Q × Kt ch+ Araiza—Fine, Syracuse, 1934). Q × P; 9 P—B 7 ch, K × P; 10 R P × Q, P—K 4! ∓

(m) Canepa—Alekhine, Montevideo, 1938

1 P—K 4, P—K 3.

	46	47	48	49	50
2	(P—Q 4)....	Q—K 2 (d)...	Kt—K 2....	P—K Kt3 (i).	P—Q Kt 3
	(P—Q 4)	P—Q B 4	P—Q 4	P—Q 4	P—Q 4 (k)
3	(P—K 5)	P—K B 4	P×P	Kt—Q B 3 (j)	B—Kt 2 !
	(P—Q B 4)	Kt—Q B 3	P×P	Kt—Q B 3	P×P
4	Kt—K B 3	Kt—K B 3	Kt—Kt 3	P×P	Kt—Q B 3
	Kt—QB3 (a)	K Kt—K 2	Kt—KB3 (g)	P×P	Kt—K B 3
5	B—Q 3	P—K Kt 3	P—Q 4	P—Q 4	Q—K 2
	P×P	P—K Kt3 (e)	B—Q 3	B—K B 4	B—Kt 5 (l)
6	O—O	P—Q 3	B—Q 3	P—Q R 3	O—O—O
	P—B 3 (b)	B—Kt 2	O—O	Q—Q 2	Q—K 2
7	B—Q Kt 5	Kt—B 3	O—O	B—Kt 2	Kt×P
	B—Q 2	Kt—Q 5	R—K 1	O—O—O	B—R 6
8	B×Kt	Kt×Kt	Kt—B 3	K Kt—K 2	Kt—K B 3
	P×B	P×Kt	Kt—B 3	Q Kt—K 2	B×B ch
9	Q×P	Kt—Q 1	Kt—B 5	Kt—B 4	K×B
	P×P	P—Kt 3	Kt—K 5 ?	Kt—K B 3	Q Kt—Q 2
10	Q×K P	B—Kt 2	Kt×B	P—K R 3	P—Q 4
	Kt—B 3	B—Kt 2	Q×Kt	P—K R 4	O—O
11	B—B 4	O—O	Kt—Kt 5	Kt—Q 3	Kt—K 5
	B—B 4	O—O	Q—Q 1	Kt—K 5	P—B 4
13	Kt—B 3	P—Kt 3	B—KB4 ± (h)	B—K 3	Kt×Kt ±
	O—O = (c)	Q—B 2 = (f)		Kt×Kt ∓	(m)

(a) Good alternatives for Black are: (1) 4.., P×P; 5 Q×P, Kt—Q B 3 (or 5.., Kt—K 2; 6 B—Q 3, K Kt—B 3; 7 Q—K B 4, Kt—Q 2; 8 O—O, P—B 3; 9 P×P, Q×P; 10 Kt—B 3, B—K 2=. Petrov—Opocensky, Podebrady, 1936), 6 Q—K B 4, P—B 4; 7 B—Q 3, K Kt—K 2; 8 O—O, Kt—Kt 3; 9 Q—Kt 3, B—K 2; 10 R—K 1, O—O; 11 P—Q R 3, Kt—Kt 1; 12 Q Kt—Q 2, P—Q R 4; 13 Kt—Kt 3, Kt—R 3 ∓. Keres—Euwe, Zandvoort, 1936. (2) 4.., Kt—K 2; 5 P×P, K Kt—B 3; 6 B—K B 4, Kt—Q 2; 7 P—Q R 3, Q—B 2; 8 P—Q Kt 4, P—Q R 4; 9 P—B 4, R P×P; 10 B P×P, K P×P; 11 Q×P, Kt×B P; 12 Kt—Q 4, Kt×Kt; 13 Q×Kt, Kt—K3; 14 Q—Q 2, B—B 4+. Keres—Stahlberg, Dresden, 1936.
(b) If 6 .., K Kt—K 2; 7 B—K B 4, Kt—Kt 3; 8 B—Kt 3, B—K 2; 9 R—K 1, Q—Kt 3; 10 Q Kt—Q 2, B—Q 2; 11 Kt—Kt 3, Q R—B 1; 12 P—Q R 3, P—Q B 3; 13 P—K R 4 ±. Keres—Hasenfuss, Kemeri, 1937.
(c) Alekhine—Euwe, Nottingham, 1936.
(d) Tchigorin's Attack. Alternatives are: (1) 2 P—Q B 4, P—Q B 4; 3 Kt—Q B 3, Kt—Q B 3; 4 P—K Kt 3, Kt—B 3; 5 B—Kt 2, B—K 2; 6 K Kt—K 2, P—Q R 3; 7 O—O, O—O; 8 P—Q 4. R. C. Griffith—E. Macdonald, 1923. (2) 2 P—Q 3, P—Q 4; 3 Kt—Q 2, P—Q B 4; 4 K Kt—B 3, Kt—Q B 3; 5 B—K 2, B—Q 3; 6 O—O, Q—B 2; 7 R—K 1, K Kt—K 2; 8 P—B 3, O—O; 9 P—Q R 3, P—B 4 ! ∓. Nimzovitch—Capablanca, San Sebastian, 1911.
(e) Inferior is 5.., Q—K 2; 6 P—Q 3, P—Q Kt 3; 7 B—Kt 2, P×P; 8 P×P, Kt—Kt 5; 9 Kt—R 3, B—R 3, 10 Kt—B 4, K Kt—B 3; 11 P—Q R 3!, Kt—Q 5; 12 Kt×Kt, Q×Kt; 13 P×K Kt, B×Kt; 14 Q—K 3 ±. Keres—Mikenas, Kemeri, 1937.
(f) Tartakover—Selesnieff, Pistyan, 1922.
(g) 4.., Q—R 5 was preferable.
(h) 12.., R—K 2; 13 P—K B 3, Kt—B 3; 14 R—K 1, Kt—K 1; 15 Q—Q 2. Tartakover—Fine, Kemeri, 1937.
(i) Tartakover's Attack. The column is J. S. Morrison—Nimzovitch, London, 1927.
(j) Or 3 B—Kt 2, P×P; 4 B×P (if 4 Kt—Q B 3, B—Q 2!; 5 Kt×P, B—B 3=), Kt—K B 3; 5 B—Kt 2, Kt—B 3; 6 Kt—K 2, B—Q 3; 7 Q Kt—B 3, O—O; 8 P—Q 3, P—K 4; 9 P—K R 3, Kt—Q 5=. Tartakover—Colle, Kecskemét, 1927.
(k) Better P—Q B 4 (Tartakover).
(l) 5.., B—K 2; 6 O—O—O, Q Kt—Q 2; 7 P—K Kt 4!, P—K R 3; 8 B—Kt 2, P—B 3; 9 P—K R 4 ±. Réti—Maróczy, Gothenburg, 1920.
(m) Spielmann—Grau, San Remo, 1930.

GIUOCO PIANO

In this classical opening, favoured by the early Italian players, the principles underlying correct development in the Open Game still find their best illustrations. Modern innovations have so extended its scope that it now ranges in fine gradations of style from the Pianissimo (col. 15) to the powerful Max Lange and impetuous Evans Gambit, which are treated as different openings on pp. 106 and 42 respectively. The variations arising from 4 P—B 3, followed by P—Q 4 (cols. 1 to 22), require to be met with considerable care, White obtaining an immediate and enduring attack owing to his great control of the centre. Black has three replies at his disposal :—

(i) 4..., Kt—B 3 (cols. 1 to 15). The sparkling Möller Attack (cols. 1 to 7) has received some recent tests, notably by Keres. His analysis confirms the opinion previously held that Black's defensive resources are adequate, and that the variation is a draw with best play. In the difficult line in col. 6 Black manages to keep the Pawn, but only at the cost of an exceedingly cramped position. Greco's original variation, dating back to 1619, has been modified by Dr. Bernstein's analysis· (col. 9, note (k)) and can be recommended as a simple equalising line for the second player. White need not necessarily sacrifice the Pawn, but, as cols. 11 and 12 show, this safer line leads to an early draw. The Cracow Variation has been little tested in master-play; in col. 13 Black shows to advantage. The Pianissimo (col. 15) promises little for White.

(ii) 4..., P—Q 3 (cols. 16 to 19) is inferior, since White's grip on the centre is too strong.

(iii) 4..., B—Kt 3, followed by 5..., Q—K 2 (cols. 20 to 22), an old defence reintroduced to tournament practice by Alekhine in 1923. Its object is to maintain Black's Pawn at K 4, but recent games indicate that the manœuvre costs too much time and that White can build up a powerful attacking position.

In the old Piano form (cols. 24 to 30) White has the choice of two varying systems of development. The posting of his Bishop at K 3 (cols. 25 and 26) leads to symmetrical positions, where Black's chances are superior. The alternative system is the Canal Variation (cols. 27 to 30), which is much stronger. Here White exchanges his Queen's Bishop for the Black King's Knight with a view to establishing a strong Pawn-centre. Capablanca's improvement in col. 28 is an important strengthening of the attack, and Black would do well to adopt one of the alternatives in note (f).

1 P—K4, P—K4; 2 Kt—KB3, Kt—QB3; 3 B—B4, B—B4.

4 P—B3, Kt—B3; 5 P—Q4, P×P; 6 P×P, B—Kt5 ch;
7 Kt—B3, Kt×KP; 8 O—O, B×Kt; 9 P—Q5! (a), B—B3;
10 R—K1, Kt—K2; 11 R×Kt.

	1	2	3	4	5
11	O—O......P—Q3				
12	P—Q6 (b)	B—Kt5................		P—KKt4 (j)	
	P×P	B×B.......	O—O	O—O......	P—KR3
13	Q×P (c)	Kt×B	B×B	P—Kt5	P—KR4
	Kt—B4	O—O	P×B	B—K4	Q—Q2
14	Q—Q5	Kt×RP! (e)	Q—Q2	Kt×B	Q—K2
	Kt—K2 (d)	K×Kt	Kt—Kt3	P×Kt	B—K4
15	Q—Q6	Q—R5 ch	QR—K1 (h)	R×P	Kt×B
	Kt—B4	K—Kt1	P—KB4 (i)	Kt—Kt3	P×Kt (l)
16	Q—Q5	R—R4	Q—R6	R—K1	B—K3
	Kt—K2=	P—KB4	Q—B3	Q—Q3	O—O
17		R—R3! (f)	R—K7!+	P—QKt3±	P—Kt5
		P—B5! (g)		(h)	

(a) The Möller Attack.

(b) 11 12 B—KKt5, Kt—Kt3! (better than 12 ., P—Q3, transposing into col. 3). White should transpose into col. 4 by 12 P—KKt4, P—Q3; 13 P—Kt5.

(c) If 13 B—B4, P—Q4!; 14 B×P, Kt×B; 15 Q×Kt, P—Q3; 16 B×P, B—K3 ∓. 13 ., P—Q4 is also a satisfactory reply to 13 B—KKt5.

(d) 14.., P—Q3?, 15 Kt—Kt5, B×Kt; 16 B×B, Q—B2; 17 Q—Q3, B—Q2; 18 P—KKt4!, P—KR3; 19 B—B4+. Rydberg—Jensen, Gothenburg, 1910.

(e) The Therkatz Variation.

(f) This position has received a great deal of attention from analysts, but no conclusive win for either side has as yet been established. The text is a recent innovation, due to Keres. The best lines in the alternative variations, including some traps which must be avoided, are · (1) 17 B—K2, R—K1; 18 R—K1, K—B1; 19 B—Kt5, P—B3; 20 R—K6, P×B; 21 R—B6 ch, P×R; 22 Q—R6 ch, K—B2; 23 Q—R7 ch draw by perpetual check. (2) 17 Q—R7 ch, K—B2; 18 R—R6, R—KKt1; 19 R—R7, Q—B1; 20 B—Kt5, R—R1; 21 Q×R, P×R; 22 Q—R7 ch, K—B3; 23 R×Kt, Q×R; 24 Q×RP ch, K—K4; 25 Q×Kt ch, K—B3; 26 Q—R6 ch, draw by perpetual check. (3) 17 R—K1, Kt—Kt3; 18 R—R3, R—B3!; 19 Q—R7 ch, K—B2; 20 R—K6, B×R (20 , P—B3?; 21 R(R3)—K3, B—Q2; 22 R×R ch, K×R; 23 R—KKt3, B—K1; 24 Q—R5, K—K2; 25 Q×P, P×P; 26 B×P, Q—B1; 27 Q—Kt5 ch+. Keres—Sachsenmaier, correspondence, 1934—35); 21 B×Bch, R×P; 22 B×Rch, K×B; 23 Q×Kt ch, Q—B3 with a likely draw. (4) 17 P—KKt3?, Q—K1 (but not 17 ., R—K1?; 18 R—K1, K—B1; 19 R—K6!, P—B3; 20 R—B6 ch!, P×R; 21 Q—R6 ch, K—B2; 22 Q—R7 ch, K—B1; 23 R—R6, Kt—Kt1, 24 R—KKt6, R—K8 ch; 25 K—Kt2, R—B3; 26 R—Kt7, Resigns. B. Ohls—A. Wagner, correspondence, 1929—31); 18 Q—R7 ch, K—B2; 19 R—K1, B—Q2; 20 B—K2, Kt—Kt3; 21 B—R5, Q×R ch; 22 K—Kt2, Q—K2!!; 23 Q×Kt ch, K—Kt1; 24 R—R3, Q—B3++.

(g) The only defence, but a sufficient one. If e.g. 17.., B—Q2; 18 R—K1, R—B3; 19 Q—R7 ch, K—B1; 20 R—KKt3, P—KKt3; 21 P—KR4!, P—B5; 22 R—Kt5, B—B4; 23 P—R5, Kt—Kt1; 24 P×P, Q—Q2; 25 P×KtP ch, K—B2; 26 Q—R5 ch, B—Kt3; 27 R×B, R×R; 28 R—K6, Q×R; 29 P×Q ch++. After 17 ., P—B5; 18 P—KKt4, P×P e.p.!; 19 Q—R7 ch, K—B2 White must take the draw by perpetual check. Analysis by Keres. If here 20 Q—R5 ch, Kt—Kt3?; 21 R×P, Q—B3; 22 R—KB3, and wins, while if 20 ., P—Kt3; 21 Q—R7 ch, K—K1; 22 R×P with a winning attack.

(h) 15 Q—R6, K—R1; 16 Kt—R4, R—KKt1; 17 QR—K1, B—Q2; 18 Kt—K7, K—R2; 19 Kt×Kt ch, R×Kt; 20 Q—R4 is also strong.

(i) Or 15 , B—B4; 16 KR—K3, Kt—K4; 17 B—Kt3±. The column is Spielmann—Duras, Carlsbad, 1907.

(j) Schlechter's "Bayonet Attack."

(k) 17.., B—B4; 18 Q—Q4, P—B4; 19 B—R3 (A. Ritzen, 1924).

(l) Leonhardt's analysis ends here as in Black's favour, but White retains a strong attack.

1 P—K 4, P—K 4 ; 2 Kt—K B 3, Kt—Q B 3 ; 3 B—B 4, B—B 4.

4 P—B 3, Kt—B 3 ; 5 P—Q 4, P×P ; 6 P×P, B—Kt 5 ch ;
7 Kt—B 3.

	6	7	8	9	10
7	(Kt×K P)..				P—Q 4
8	(O—O)				P×P
	(B×Kt).............................			Kt×Kt	K Kt×P
9	(P—Q 5)................		P×B	P×Kt	O—O
	Kt—K 4....B—R 4 (e)		P—Q 4	B×P (j)	B×Kt
10	P×B (a)	P×Kt	B—R 3 (g)	Q—Kt 3	P×B
	Kt×B	Kt P×P (f)	P×B	P—Q 4 (k)	O—O
11	Q—Q 4	Kt—K 5	R—K 1	B×P (l)	R—K 1
	P—K B.4 (b)	Kt—Q 3	B—K 3 (h)	O—O	B—K 3 ?
12	Q×Kt (c)	Q—Kt 4	R×Kt	B×P ch	Kt—Kt 5
	P—Q 3	Q—B 3	Q—Q 4	K—R 1	R—K 1
13	Kt—Q 4	P—Kt 4	Q—K 2	Q×B (m)	Q—R 5
	O—O	B×P	O—O—O	R×B	Kt—B 3
14	R—Kt 1	B—Kt 2	Kt—K 5	Kt—K 5	B×B
	P—Q Kt 3	Kt×B	K R—K 1	Kt×Kt	Kt×Q
15	R—K 1	Kt×Kt	Kt×Kt	P×Kt	B×Pch+ +
	B—Q 2 (d)	Q—Kt 3	Q×Kt	B—K 3	
16		KR—K1ch!+	Q R—K 1	B—K 3 = (n)	
			R—Kt 1 + (i)		

(a) If 10 Q—K 2, Kt×Kt ch ; 11 P×Kt, B—B 3 ; 12 P×Kt, P—Q 3 ; 13 P—B 4, O—O ∓ is best for Black. If (10 Q—K 2), O—O ; 11 P×B, Kt×B (11 ., Kt×Kt ch ; 12 Q×Kt, Q—R 5 ; 13 R—K 1, Kt×K B P ; 14 B—B 4, Kt—Kt 5 ; 15 P—Q 6, P—Q B 3 ; 16 B—K Kt 3, Q—R 4 ; 17 R—K 5 ! + Znosko-Borovsky—Freymann, 1907) ; 12 Q×Q Kt, Kt—Q 3 ; 13 Q—Q 4, Kt—K 1 ; 14 B—Kt 5, P—K B 3 ; 15 B—B 4, P—Q 3 ; 16 Q R—Kt 1 ±.
(b) 11.., Q Kt—Q 3 ? ; 12 Q×Kt P, Q—B 3 ; 13 Q×Q, Kt×Q ; 14 R—K 1 ch, K—B 1 ; 15 B—R 6 ch, K—Kt 1 ; 16 R—K 5, K Kt—K 5 (16 , Q Kt—K 5 ; 17 Kt—Q 2, P—Q 3 ; 18 Kt×Kt+) ; 17 R—K 1, P—K B 3 ; 18 R—K 7, P—Kt 3 ; 19 Kt—R 4+.
(c) 12 Q×Kt P ? ?, R—B 1 ; 13 B—Kt 5, Kt×B ; 14 Kt×Kt, Q—B 3 ; 15 R—K 1 ch, K—Q 1 + +. Schlechter—Lasker, London, 1899.
(d) Black's position is quite solid.
(e) 9 ., Kt—R 4 ; 10 B—Q 3, P—K B 4 ; 11 P×B, O—O ; 12 Q—R 4+.
(f) 10 ., O—O ; 11 Q—Q 5, Kt—Q 3 ; 12 B—Q 3, B—Kt 3 ; 13 B×P ch+ +, or 10. , Q P×P ; 11 Q—R 4, B—Kt 3 ; 12 B×P ch, K×B ; 13 Q×Kt, Q—Q 4 ; 14 Kt—Kt 5 ch+ +.
(g) Steinitz's Variation. If 10 B—Q 3, O—O ; 11 B×Kt, P×B ; 12 Kt—Kt 5, Q—Q 4+.
(h) 11 ., P—B 4 ; 12 Kt—Q 2, K—B 2 ; 13 Kt×Kt, P×Kt ; 14 R×P, Q—B 3 !. Steinitz—Lasker, 1st match game, 1896. The text is simpler, however.
(i) Steinitz—Lasker, 3rd match game, 1896.
(j) 9.., P—Q 4 ; 10 P×B, P×B ; 11 P—Kt 5, Kt—K 2 ; 12 B—R 3, B—K 3 ? (Correct was 12.., O—O ; 13 Q—K 2, R—K 1 ; 14 K R—K 1, B—K 3 ; 15 Kt—Kt 5, Kt—Q 4) ; 13 B—K 1, Kt—Q 4 ; 14 Kt—K 5, Q—Q R 3 ; 15 P—Kt 6 ', P×P ; 16 Kt×Q B P, Q—Q 2 ; 17 Q—Kt 4+. Fähndrich and Neumann—Alapin and Hamlisch, consultation, 1900.
(k) Dr. O. S. Bernstein's Variation. 10.., B×R is fatal : 11 B×P ch, K—B 1 ; 12 B—K Kt 5, Kt—K 2 ; 13 R—K 1.
(l) Or 11 Q×B, P×B ; 12 P—Q 5, Kt—K 2 ; 13 R—K 1, O—O ; 14 B—R 3, Kt×P ; 15 Q×P, Kt—Kt 3 ; 16 Q—K 2, P—Q B 3=. Analysis by Bernstein, 1922.
(m) 13 B—R 3 ?, B×R ; 14 B×R, Kt×P ! ; 15 Kt×Kt, B×Kt ; 16 R—K 1, Q—B 3+ +. Spielmann—Eliskases, 1st match game, 1936-37.
(n) Analysis by Tartakover in *Die Hypermoderne Schachpartie.*

1 P—K 4, P—K 4; 2 Kt—K B 3, Kt—Q B 3; 3 B—B 4, B—B 4.

4 P—B 3, Kt—B 3.

	11	12	13	14	15
5	(P—Q 4) (P×P)	....			P—Q 3 (l) P—Q 3
6	(P×P) (B—Kt 5 ch)	....		P—K 5 P—Q 4	B—K 3 B—Kt 3
7	B—Q 2 B×B ch (a)	....	K—B 1 (f) K Kt×P (g)	B—K 2 (j) Kt—K 5	Q Kt—Q 2 Kt—K 2
8	Q Kt×B P—Q 4		P—Q 5 Kt—K 2	P×P B—Kt 3	P—Q 4 (m) Kt—Kt 3
9	P×P K Kt×P		Q—Q 4 Kt—K B 3	O—O O—O	P—K R 4! Q—K 2
10	Q—Kt 3 Q Kt—K 2	O—O O—O	B—K Kt 5 P—B 4!	Kt—B 3 P—B 4	P—R 5 Kt—B 5
11	O—O O—O	R—K 1 Q Kt—K 2	Q—K 3 Kt—Kt 5 (h)	P×P e.p. Kt×P (B 3)	B×Kt P×B
12	K R—K 1 P—Q B 3	Kt—K 5 P—Q B 3	Q—K 4 P—Q 3	B—K 3 = (k)	Q—K 2 Kt—Kt 5
13	Kt—K 4 (b) Kt-Q Kt3 (c)	Kt—K 4 B—B 4	B—Kt 5 ch K—B 1		O—O—O O—O
14	Kt—B 5 Kt×B	Kt—B 5 Q—B 2	P—K R 3 Kt—K B 3		P—R 6 P—Kt 3
15	Q×Kt P—QKt3 = (d)	Q—Kt 3 QR—QKt1 (e)	B×Kt P×B (i)		Kt—R 4 P—B 4 (n)

(a) 7.., K Kt×P; 8 B×B, Kt×B; 9 Q—Kt 3, P—Q 4; 10 Q×Kt, P×B
11 O—O, Q—Q 4; 12 Kt—R 3=.

(b) 13 P—Q R 4, Q—Kt 3; 14 Q—R 3, B—K 3; 15 P—R 5. Q—B 2; 16 Kt—K 4, Q R—Q 1; 17 Kt—B 5, B—B 1 (Tarrasch—Capablanca, San Sebastian, 1911); 18 Kt—K 5!

(c) Tarrasch—Rubinstein, Berlin, 1918.

(d) 16 Kt—Q 3, B—Kt 2 (if 16 , B—K 3?; 17 R×B!+. Tartakover).

(e) 16 Q R—B 1, K R—Q 1; 17 Q—K B 3, B—Kt 3=. P. Johner—Opocensky, Baden, 1914.

(f) The Cracow Variation.

(g) 7.., P—Q 4; 8 P×P, K Kt×P; 9 Kt—B 3, B—K 3; 10 Q—K 2 Now 10.., O—O is safe and sound, while if 10.., B×Kt; 11 P×B, Kt×B P; 12 Q—K 1, Kt—Q 4; 13 B—R 3, P—Q R 3; 14 R—B 1, Q—Q 2; 15 Q—K 2, White has a lasting attack.

(h) 11.., P—Q 3; 12 B×Kt, P×B; 13 Q Kt—Q 2, O—O; 14 Kt—K 4, Kt—Kt 3; 15 Q—R 6, R—K 1; 16 Kt—Kt 3, K—R 1; 17 P—K R 4. Dr. Hatschek—Martin, correspondence.

(i) 16 P—R 3, P—B 4; 17 Q—R 4, B—R 4; 18 Kt—B 3, Kt—Kt 3; 19 Q—R 6 ch, K—Kt 1. J. Mihalek—v. Feilitzsch, correspondence, 1928. 20 K—Kt 1 is now best.

(j) 7 B—Q Kt 5, Kt—K 5; 8 Kt×P (if 8 P×P, B—Kt 5 ch!), O—O; 9 B×Kt, P×B, 10 O—O, P—B 3; 11 B×B, B—Q 2 (or 11 , Q—K 1) ∓.

(k) Analysis by Tartakover in Die Hypermoderne Schachpartie.

(l) The Giuoco Pianissimo.

(m) 8 Kt—B 1 (the old continuation), P—B 3; 9 Q—B 2, Kt—Kt 3; 10 O—O—O, O—O; 11 P—Q 4, Q—K 2. Blackburne—Zukertort, London, 1883.

(n) 16 Kt—Kt 3, P—R 3; 17 P—Kt 3, P×Kt P; 18 B P×P=. Alekhine, Znosko-Borovsky, etc.—Bogoljuboff, Kmoch, etc., Wiesbaden, 1925.

1 P—K 4, P—K 4 ; 2 Kt—K B 3, Kt—Q B 3 ; 3 B—B 4, B—B 4.

	16	17	18	19	20
4	(P—B 3) P—Q 3 (a) .... B—Kt 3				
5	P—Q 4 P×P				P—Q 4 (j) Q—K 2
6	P×P B—Kt 3			B—Kt 5 ch	O—O P—Q 3
7	Kt—B 3 B—Kt 5	..... Kt—B 3		K—B 1 (g) B—Kt 5 (h)	P—Q R 4 P—Q R 3
8	B—Q Kt 5 (b) B×Kt	Q—Q 3 (d) B—Kt 5	...O—O B—K Kt 5	Q—R 4 P—Q R 3	P—Q Kt 4 Kt—B 3
9	P×B Q—R 5	B—K 3 O—O	B—K 3 O—O	Kt—Kt 5 Q—B 3	B—R 3 B—Kt 5
10	O—O ! O—O—O	P—Q R 3 R—K 1	B—Kt 3 R—K 1	B—K 3 B—Q 2	P—Kt 5 B×Kt
11	B×Kt P×B	B—R 2 Q—Q 2	Q—Q 3 B—K R 4	P—K 5 P×P	Q×B Kt—Q R 4
12	P—R 4 P—Q R 4	Kt—Q 2 R—K 2	Kt—Q 2 B—Kt 3 (f)	B×P ch K—Q 1	Kt—Q 2 O—O
13	R—Kt 1 (c)	O—O Q R—K 1	P—Q 5 Kt—K 4	P×P Q—B 4	Q R-K 1 ± (k)
14		P—B 3 B—K R 4 (e)	Q—K 2 ±	Q—Kt 3+ (i)	

(a) 4.., Q—K 2 ; 5 P—Q 4, B—Kt 3 ! transposes into cols. 21 and 22.

(b) 8 B—K 3, Kt—B 3 ; 9 B—Kt 3, Q—K 2 ; 10 Q—Q 3, O—O—O ; 11 P—Q R 3, K R—K 1 ; 12 Kt—Q 2, B—K R 4 ; 13 P—B 3, P—Q 4 !+ Maróczy—Perlis, Vienna, 1908.

(c) *Handbuch*, 1913.

(d) 8 P—Q 5, Kt—K 2 ; 9 B—Kt 5, Kt—Kt 3 ; 10 P—K 5, P×P ; 11 Kt—K 4, or 8 B—Q Kt 5, B—Q 2 ; 9 B×Kt B×B ; 10 Q—Q 3, O—O ; 11 O—O, R—K 1 ; 12 K—K 1, Q—K 2 ; 13 P—Q 5 (or 13 Kt—Q 2), B—Q 2 ; 14 B—Kt 5.

(e) 15 Kt—B 4, B—Kt 3 (M. E. Goldstein—J. G. Rennie, City of London Championship, 1922) ; 16 Q—Q 2±.

(f) 12.., Kt—K Kt 5 ; 13 Kt—B 3 !, Kt×B ; 14 P×Kt ±. Becker—Mattison, Carlsbad, 1929.

(g) 7 Kt—B 3, Kt—B 3 (if 7.., B—Kt 5 ; 8 B—K 3, Kt—B 3 ; 9 Q—Q 3, Q—K 2 ; 10 Kt—Q 2+) ; 8 O—O, B×Kt ; 9 P×B, P—K R 3 ; 10 P—K 5, P×P ; 11 B—R 3, B—K 3 ; 12 B×B, P×B ; 13 Kt—Kt 3, Q—B 1 ; 14 Q R—K 1+. Lovenborg—Nilsson, 1917. The column is the "Miss-in-Baulk."

(h) 7.., Q—Q 2 ; 8 Q—R 4, B—R 4 ; 9 P—Q 5, Kt—K 4 ; 10 B—Q Kt 5 P—Q B 3 ; 11 Kt×Kt, P×B ; 12 Q×B, P×Kt ; 13 Kt—B 3, P—Q R 3 ; 14 P—Q R 4 !+.

(i) Analysis by W. T. Pierce.

(j) If 5 P—Q 3, it is no longer necessary for Black to post his Queen at K 2, and he can transpose into col. 15 by 5.., P—Q 3.

(k) *Handbuch*, 1913.

1 P—K 4, P—K 4 ; 2 Kt—K B 3, Kt—Q B 3 ; 3 B—B 4, B—B 4.

	21	22	23	24	25
4	(P—B 3)...............		O—O (e)....	P—Q 3	
	(B—Kt 3)		P—Q 3	Kt—B 3 (i)	
5	(P—Q 4)		P—B 3	Kt—B 3 (j)	
	(Q—K 2)		B—K Kt 5 !	P—Q 3	
6	(O—O) (a)		P—Q 4	O—O......	B—K 3 (m)
	Kt—B 3 !		P×P	B—K Kt 5	B×B (n)
7	R—K 1.....	P—Q 5	Q—Kt 3 !	Kt—QR4 (k)	P×B
	P—Q 3	Kt—Q Kt 1	Q—Q 2 (f)	Kt—Q 5	Kt—Q R 4
8	P—Q R 4	B—Q 3	B×P ch	Kt×B	B—Kt 3
	P—Q R 3	P—Q 3	Q×B	P×Kt	Kt×B
9	P—R 3	Q Kt—Q 2	Q×P	B×P ch	R P×Kt
	O—O	P—Q R 3	K—Q 2	K—K 2 !	Kt—Kt 5
10	P—Q Kt 4 (b)	Kt—B 4	Q×R	B—Kt 3	Q—Q 2
	P—K R 3	B—R 2	B×Kt	Q—K 1	P—K B 4
11	B—R 3	P—Q R 4	P×B	P—B 3	P×P
	Kt—Q 2	O—O	Kt—K 4 (g)	Kt×Kt ch	B×P
12	P—Kt 5	P—Q Kt 4	Kt—Q 2	P×Kt	O—O
	Kt—Q 1 (c)	Kt—K 1 (d)	Kt×P ch (h)	Q—R 4+ (l)	O—O (o)

(a) 6 P—Q 5, Kt—Kt 1 ; 7 P—Q 6 ?, Q×P ; 8 Q×Q, P×Q ; 9 Kt—R 3, K Kt—B 3 ; 10 B—Q 5, Kt×B ; 11 P×Kt, P—B 3 ; 12 Kt—Q 2, K—K 2 ∓. Van den Bosch—Ahues, Bad Nauheim, 1936.

(b) 10 B—K Kt 5, P—R 3 ; 11 B—K 3, Q—Q 1 ! ; 12 B—Q 3, R—K 1 ; 13 Q Kt—Q 2, B—R 2 ! (forestalling Kt—B 4) ∓. Tarrasch—Alekhine, Baden-Baden 1925.

(c) 13 Q Kt—Q 2, Q—B 3 ; 14 Kt—B 1, Kt—K 3 ; 15 Kt—K 3, Kt—Kt 4 ; 16 Kt×Kt ±. Spielmann—Eliskases, 5th match game, 1936–37.

(d) 13 Q—B 2, P—K Kt 3 ; 14 B—R 6 ±. Eliskases—Grünfeld, Mährisch-Ostrau, 1933.

(e) 4 P—Q 4, P×P transposes into the Scotch Gambit.

(f) 7 , B×Kt ; 8 B×P ch, K—B 1 ; 9 P×B !, Kt—B 3 ! ; 10 B—K B 4, P×P ; 11 P×P, Kt—Q R 4 ; 12 Q—K 6, Q—K 2=. Von Feilitzsch—A. Ritzen, correspondence.

(g) 11 , Q×B P ; 12 Kt—Q 2, Q—R 6 ; 13 Q—K B 8 (13 P—K 5, Q P×P ; 14 P—Kt 4, Kt—B 3 !+ A. Strautmanis—L. Palau, The Hague, 1928), K Kt—K 2 ! ; 14 Q×R (14 Q—B 3, Q—K 3 with Kt—K 4 to follow), P×P ; 15 P×P, Kt—K 4 ; 16 Q—K B 8, P—Kt 4 ; 17 R—Kt 1, Kt—Kt 5 ; 18 Kt—B 3, and Black's attack is at an end. If Kt×R P ; 19 Kt×Kt, P—Kt 5 ; 20 B—Kt 5 !+ +.

(h) 13 Kt×Kt, Q×Kt secures Black a draw by perpetual check ; but after 14 Q—Q 5 he has nothing better.

(i) 4.., P—Q 3 transposes into other columns.

(j) 5 B—K 3, B—Kt 3 (5.., P—Q 3 ? ; 6 B×B, P×B ; 7 B—Kt 5, Q—Q 3 ; 8 B×Kt ch+) ; 6 Q Kt—Q 2, P—Q 4 ; 7 P×P, Kt×P ; 8 Q—K 2, B—K 3 9 O—O=. Tartakover—Réti, Pistyan, 1922. Or 5 B—K Kt 5, P—Q 3 ; 6 Q Kt—Q 2, B—K 3 ; 7 P—B 3, P—K R 3 ; 8 B—R 4, Q—K 2=. Sjoberg—E. Cohn, Stockholm, 1912.

(k) 7 B—K 3, B—Kt 3 ; 8 K—R 1, Kt—K 2 ; 9 P—K R 3 is much better

(l) 13 Q—Q 2, B×P ; 14 Q—Kt 5, Q×Q ; 15 B×Q, B—K 7. H. Jacobs—Sir G. A. Thomas, City of London Championship, 1924.

(m) 6 P—K R 3, Kt—Q R 4 ; 7 B—Kt 3, P—B 3 ; 8 P—Q 4, P×P=.

(n) 6 ., O—O ; 7 P—K R 3, Q—K 2 ; 8 O—O, B—K 3 ; 9 B—Kt 3, Q R—Q 1. Schlechter—Tarrasch, Berlin, 1918.

(o) 13 P—K R 3 ±. Schlechter—Salwe, Carlsbad, 1907.

1 P—K 4, P—K 4 ; 2 Kt—K B 3, Kt—Q B 3 ; 3 B—B 4, B—B 4.

4 P—Q 3, Kt—B 3 ; 5 Kt—B 3, P—Q 3.

	26	27	28	29	30
6	(B—K 3).... B—Kt 3	B—KKt5 (e) P—K R 3 (f)			
7	Q—Q 2 (a) B—KKt5 (b)	B×Kt ! Q×B			
8	Kt—K Kt 5 O—O (c)	Kt—Q 5 Q—Q 1			
9	P—B 3 B—Q 2 !	P—B 3 Kt—K 2................O—O.......Kt—R 4			
10	P—K Kt 4 B×B	P—Q 4 (g) P×P (h)	...Kt—K 3 B—K 3 (l)	P—Q R 4 P—Q R 4	P—Q Kt 4 Kt×B
11	Q×B Kt—Q 5	K Kt×P (i) Kt×Kt	B×B P×B	O—O Kt—K 2	P×B Kt—R 4
12	O—O—O P—Kt 4 !	B×Kt O—O	Q—Kt 3 Q—B 1	P—Q 4 P×P	P×P Q×P
13	B—Kt 3 P—Q R 4	Q—Q 3 B×Kt (j)	P—Q 4 P×P	Kt×P Kt×Kt	P—Q 4 Kt—B 3
14	P—Q R 4 Kt×B ch ∓ (d)	P×B P—B 3 = (k)	Kt×P! ±(m)	B×Kt Q—B 3 =(n)	P×P Kt×P= (o)

(a) Alternatives are: (1) 7 O—O, B—K 3 ; 8 B—Kt 3, P—K R 3, 9 Q—Q 2=.
(2) 7 P—K R 3, B—K 3 ; 8 B—Kt 3, Q B×B ; 9 R P×B, B×B ; 10 P×B, P—Q 4 ;
11 P×P, Kt×P ; 12 Kt×Kt, Q×Kt =   (3) 7 P—K R 3, Kt—K 2 ; 8 P—Q 4, P×P ;
9 Q B×P, Kt—Kt 3. Tarrasch—Yates, Baden-Baden, 1925.

(b) 7..,O—O ; 8O—O—O,B—K 3 ; 9 Kt—Q 5,B×Kt ; 10 P×B,B×B ; 11 P×B,
Kt—K 2 ; 12 P—K 4=. Kostich—Capablanca, match, 1919.

(c) 8.., B—K R 4 ; 9 P—B 3, P—K R 3 ; 10 Kt—R 3, Q—Q 2 ; 11 P—K Kt 4,
Kt—Q 5 ; 12 B×Kt, B×B ; 13 Kt—K Kt 1 !, B—K Kt 3 ; 14 K Kt—K 2, B—Kt 3 ;
15 O—O—O ±. Tartakover—Rubinstein, Gothenburg, 1920.

(d) 15 P×Kt, P—B 4. Prokes—Ahues, Hamburg, 1930.

(e) The Canal Variation.

(f) 6 ., Kt—Q R 4 ; 7 B—Kt 3, P—B 3= (Bogoljuboff). Or 6.., B—K 3 ;
7 Kt—Q 5, B×Kt ; 8 P×B, Kt—Q R 4=.

(g) 10 Kt×Kt, Q×Kt ; 11 Q—K 2, B—K Kt 5 ; 12 P—K R 3, B×Kt ; 13 Q×B.
Draw agreed. Spielmann—Vidmar, San Remo, 1930.

(h) 10. , Kt×Kt ; 11 P×B, Kt—B 5 ; 12 B—Kt 5 ch, B—Q 2 ; 13 B×B ch,
Q×B ; 14 P--K Kt 3, Kt—K 3 ; 15 P×P, Q×P=. Tartakover—Fine, Hastings,
1935-36.

(i) 11 P×P, B—Kt 3 ; 12 Kt×B (12 O—O, Kt×Kt; 13 B×Kt, O—O ;
14 P—K R 3, P—Q B 3=. H. Golombek—R. P. Michell, Hastings, 1935-36), R P×Kt ;
13 Q—Kt 3, O—O ; 14 O—O, Kt—B 3 ; 15 Q—B 3, Kt—R 4 ?, 16 B—Q 3, P—Q 4 ? ;
17 P×P+. Grob—Fine, Ostend, 1937.

(j) 13.., Q—B 3 ; 14 B—Kt 3, R—K 1 ; 15 O—O, B—K 3 (or 15 , B—Q 2 ;
16 B—B 2, P—K Kt 3 ; 17 P—B 4 ±. Foltys—Eliskases, Mahrisch-Ostrau, 1933) ;
16 B—B 2, P—K Kt 3 ; 17 K—R 1, Q R—Q 1 ; 18 P—K B 4 ±. Canal—P. Johner,
Carlsbad, 1929—a game which won a brilliancy prize.

(k) 15 B—Kt 3, Q—R 4 ch with a quick draw. Tartakover—Rubinstein, Budapest,
1929.

(l) Weak. Best is 10.., O—O (Capablanca).

(m) Capablanca—Eliskases, Moscow, 1936.

(n) Canal--Capablanca, Carlsbad, 1929.

(o) Tartakover—Araiza, Nice, 1930.

IRREGULAR AND UNUSUAL OPENINGS

THE term "irregular openings" is difficult to define. Openings which in the past would without hesitation have been relegated to such a category have now become favourite weapons of the routine-player—witness the countless variations arising from 1 P—Q 4—and must to-day be called eminently regular. On the other hand, openings which formerly dominated the tournament repertory have now disappeared almost completely. Where there may be a doubt as to the propriety of calling the lines given here irregular, their unusualness is a matter of statistics.

We have attempted to surmount the difficulty of classification by dividing the lines given in this section into three sub-sections: (1) Fianchetto Defences; (2) King's Knight's Openings; (2) other unusual lines of play, to which we have left the plain heading of Irregular Openings.

FIANCHETTO DEFENCES.

In the King's Fianchetto Defence (cols. 1 to 3), so frequently adopted by Amos Burn and his school, it cannot be said that a clear advantage can be demonstrated for White; at best the first player remains in control of more terrain. The Queen's Fianchetto Defence (col. 4) and Double Fianchetto (col. 5) are definitely inferior.

KING'S KNIGHT'S OPENING.

The irregular variations of these fall under two general heads, according as the development is on steady or on gambit lines. In the former case the Hungarian Defence (cols. 1 to 3) is quite playable for Black, who remains with a cramped but solid position. Both the Inverted Hanham (col. 4) and Alapin's Opening (col. 5) are indifferent continuations for White.

In the latter case Greco's Counter-Gambit has been given a new lease of life by the researches of Latvian analysts (particularly K. Behting), who maintain that the gambit is perfectly sound. Their analysis seems to be quite correct, but in practical play by Black usually loses. 7 B—B 4, brought into prominence by Sir G. A. Thomas's victory with it over Tartakover at Spa, 1926 (col. 6), still holds the field as White's best resource.

The Queen's Pawn Counter-Gambit (col. 10) is inadequate for Black.

IRREGULAR OPENINGS.

Under this heading Nimzovitch's Defence (cols. 1 to 7) is by far the most important. Black's strategical object is to lock the centre and undertake an attack against White's King's side. However, White's counter-attack against Black's Queen's side is much easier to play and much stronger than Black's King-side manœuvres. In col. 2, which is one of the pioneer games in this variation, this is demonstrated clearly. In col. 4 Black plays a French Defence without an early P—Q B4. Nimzovitch handled this line with great virtuosity, but since his death the line is no longer seen.

Cols. 8 and 9 show variations beginning with 1 Kt—K B 3, which do not properly come under Réti's Opening. The Tenison Gambit (col. 8) is unsound.

The Queen's Knight's Opening (col. 10) has been transferred to the irregular openings because only two examples of its adoption have occurred in the past six years. Cols. 11 to 15 and note (m) show unusual first moves for White. The Saragossa Opening is the strongest of these and has received the enthusiastic support of the Spanish analyst Señor Jose Juncosa. It transposes frequently into various opening lines, some with the colours reversed.

FIANCHETTO DEFENCES

	1	2	3	4	5
1	P—K4				
	P—K Kt3	. . . .		P—Q Kt3 (g)	
2	P—Q4			P—Q4	
	B—Kt2	. . . .	P—Q3	B—Kt2 (h)	
3	P—K B4 (a) .	Kt—K B3	B—Q B4	B—Q3	
	P—Q3	P—Q3	B—Kt2	P—K3	
4	P—B3	Kt—B3	Kt—K B3	P—Q B4. . . .	B—K3
	Kt—K B3	Kt—KB3 (A)	Kt—K B3	Kt—K B3	P—Kt3 (i)
5	B—Q3	B—Q B4 (b)	Q—K2 (e)	Kt—Q B3	Kt—Q2
	O—O	O—O	Kt—B3	B—Kt5	B—Kt2
6	P—K5	O—O (c)	P—K R3	Q—K2	K Kt—B3
	K Kt—Q2	Kt—B3	O—O	Kt—B3	Kt—K2
7	Kt—B3	P—K R3	Kt—B3	Kt—B3	Q—K2
	P—Q B4	Kt—Q2	P—K4	P—Q3	P—Q3
8	O—O	B—K3	PxP	P—K5	P—K R4 (j)
	Q—Kt3	P—K R3	PxP	PxP	P—K R4
9	K—R1	Q—Q2	B—K3	PxP	Kt—Kt5
	Kt—Q B3	K—R2	Q—K2	Kt—Q2	Kt—Q2
10	Kt—R3 ±	Kt—R2	O—O—O	B—K4	O—O—O
		P—K4	B—K3	Kt—B4	P—K4
11		PxP	Kt—K Kt5	B—Kt5 ±	B—Q B4
		K KtxP	BxB		R—K B1
12		B—K2	QxB		Q—B3+ (k)
		B—K3 (d)	K R—Q1 (f)		

(a) 3 P—Q B3, P—Q4; 4 PxP, QxP; 5 Kt—B3, B—Kt5; 6 Q Kt—Q2, Kt—QB3; 7 B—B4, Q—K B4; 8 Q—Kt3, Kt—Q1 ±. Zander—Carls, Hamburg, 1921.

(b) 5 P—K R3, O—O; 6 B—K3, P—B3 (6 ., Kt—B3, on the lines of col. 3 is preferable); 7 Q—Q2, R—K1; 8 B—Q3, P—Q Kt4; 9 O—O, B—Kt2; 10 K R—Q1+. Rubinstein—Selesnieff, Triberg, 1921.

(c) 6 Q—K2, P—B3; 7 O—O, B—Kt5; 8 P—K R3, BxKt; 9 QxB, P—K4; 10 PxP, PxP; 11 B—K Kt5, Q Kt—Q2; 12 Q R—Q1, Q—B2=. M. A. Shapiro—V. Buerger, Anglo-American Universities cable match, 1924.

(d) 13 P—Q Kt3, P—B4. Olland—Yates, Scheveningen, 1923.

(e) 5 Kt—B3?, KtxP!.

(f) 13 B—B5, Q—K1; 14 Kt—Kt5!, RxR ch; 15 RxR, R—B1; 16 BxP, P—Kt3; 17 K—Kt1, Kt—Q R4; 18 QxP ch!, QxQ; 19 KtxQ, KxKt; 20 BxP!, R—Q Kt1; 21 BxKt, RxKt; 22 BxP, with three passed Pawns for a Knight, +. Alekhine—Allies, Montreal, 1923.

(g) For 1 ., P—Q Kt4 (Polish Defence); 2 P—Q4, B—Kt2 see Queen's Pawn Game, p. 210, col. 166.

(h) 2 ., P—K3; 3 Kt—K B3, B—Kt2; 4 B—Q3, P—Q B4; 5 P—B3, P—Q3; 6 O—O, Kt—Q2; 7 R—K1, Kt—K2; 8 B—K Kt5, Q—B2; 9 Kt—R3, Kt—Kt3; 10 P—K R4+. Mattison—Tartakover, Carlsbad, 1929.

(i) Double Fianchetto Defence.

(j) This advance is more effective after Black has played O—O.

(k) Janowski—Delmar, Cambridge Spr ngs, 1904.

(A)-Quite weak is 4 ., Kt—Q2; 5 B—Q B4, P—K3; 6 O—O, Kt—K2; 7 P—Q R4, O—O; 8 B—K3, P—K R3; 9 Q—Q2, K—R2; 10 P—R3, P—Q B3; 11 B—B4, P—Q4; 12 B—Q3, P—R3; 13 B—Q6+. Alekhine—Mikenas, Folkestone, 1935.

KING'S KNIGHT'S OPENING

	1	2	3	4	5
1	P—K4				
	P—K4				
2	Kt—KB3....................................				Kt—K2 (k)
	Kt—QB3				Kt—KB3(l)
3	B—B4............................			B—K2	P—KB4
	B—K2 (a)			Kt—B3	Kt×P (m)
4	P—Q4................	O—O	P—Q3	P—Q3	
	P—Q3 (b)	P—Q3	P—Q4	Kt—B4	
5	P—KR3....P—Q5	P—B3	QKt—Q2(i)	P×P	
	Kt—B3	Kt—Kt1	Kt—B3	P—KKt3(j)	P—Q4
6	Kt—B3	B—Q3	R—K1	P—B3	P—Q4
	O—O	Kt—Q2 (f)	O—O	B—Kt2	Kt—K3
7	O—O (c)	P—B4	P—Q3	Q—B2	Kt—B4
	P×P (d)	K Kt—B3	B—Q2	O—O	P—QB4
8	Kt×P	Kt—B3	B—Kt3	Kt—B1	Kt—B3
	Kt×Kt	Kt—B1 (g)	P—KR3	P—Kt3	P×P
9	Q×Kt	P—KR3	Q Kt—Q2	Kt—Kt3	Q Kt×P
	B—K3!=(e)	P—KR3	R—K1	B—Kt2	Kt—B3
10		Kt—R2	Kt—B1	P—KR4	B—Kt5
		P—KKt4	B—B1	P—KR4	Kt×Kt
11		Kt—Kt4	Kt—Kt3	B—Kt5	B×Kt ch
		Kt—Kt3	P—KKt3	Q—Q3 ∓	P×B
12		P—KKt3	B—K3		Kt×Kt
			Q—K2 (h)		B—Kt5ch=

(a) The Hungarian Defence, which may be reached also from the Four Knights' Game by 3 Kt—B 3, Kt—B 3; 4 B—B 4, B—K 2 An alternative is 3 , P—Q 3; 4 P—B 3, B—K 3; 5 B×B, P×B; 6 Q—Kt 3, Q—B 1; 7 Kt—Kt 5?, Kt—Q 1; 8 P—Q 4, Kt—K B 3; 9 P×P, P×P; 10 O—O, P—K R 3; 11 Kt—B 3, B—Q 3 ∓. Grob—Alekhine, Zürich, 1934.

(b) 4. , P×P; 5 P—B 3 (5 Kt×P, Kt—B 3 transposes into the Two Knights' Defence), Kt—B 3! and if 6 P—K 5, Kt—K 5 (Tartakover). 5 , P—Q 6; 6 Q—Kt 3, Kt—R 4; 7 B×P ch, K—B 1; 8 Q—R 4, K×B; 9 Q×Kt, P—Q 3; 10 Q—Q 5 ch, B—K 3; 11 Q×P (Q 3)+ is Kostich—A. J Maas, Nice, 1930.

(c) 7 B—K 3, P×P; 8 Kt×P, Kt×P; 9 Q Kt×Kt, P—Q 4; 10 Kt×Kt, Kt P×Kt; 11 B—Q 3, P×Kt; 12 K B×P+. Tartakover—Davidson, The Hague, 1921.

(d) 7.., P—K R 3?; 8 B—K 3, Kt—R 2? (better R—K 1); 9 P×P, Kt×P; 10 Kt×Kt, P×Kt; 11 Q—R 5+. L. Steiner—Vadja, Kecskemét, 1927.

(e) If 10 B×B?, P×B; 11 P—K 5, Kt—Q 2! White's advantage is infinitesimal.

(f) 6 , Kt—KB 3; 7 P—B 4, O—O; 8 Kt—B 3, R—K 1; 9 P—K R 3, B—B 1; 10 B—K 3, P—K Kt 3; 11 P—K Kt 4 ±.

(g) 8 , O—O; 9 P—K R 3, Kt—B 4; 10 B—B 2, P—Q R 4; 11 B—K 3, P—Q Kt 3; 12 P—K Kt 4+. Leonhardt—Hromadka, Pistyan, 1912.

(h) 13 P—Q 4, Kt—Q R 4 Evenssohn—Nimzovitch, St. Petersburg, 1914.

(i) Inverted Hanham Opening. The column is Tartakover—Bogoljuboff, London, 1922.

(j) 5.., B—Q 3 or 5 , B—K Kt 5 can also be played. The column should be compared with Philidor's Defence, p. 117, col. 3.

(k) Alapin's Opening. If 2 P—Q B 3, a good reply is 2.., P—Q 4.

(l) 2 . , B—B 4; 3 P—Q 4, P×P; 4 Kt×P transposes into the Centre Game, cols. 1—5, note (a).

(m) 3.., P×P; 4 Kt×P, P—Q 4 or Q—K 2 is Black's simplest line.

KING'S KNIGHT'S OPENING
1 P—K 4, P—K 4 ; 2 Kt—K B 3.

	6	7	8	9	10
2	P—K B 4 (a)	....			P—Q 4 (n)
3	Kt×P ! (b)	....		P—Q 4	P×P (o)
	Q—B 3			B P×P	P—K 5 (p)
4	P—Q 4			Kt × P	Q—K 2
	P—Q 3			Kt—K B 3	Q—K 2 (q)
5	Kt—B 4 (c)			B—Q B 4 (l)	Kt—Q 4
	P×P			P—Q 4	Kt—K B 3
6	Kt—B 3 (d)			B—Kt 3	Kt—Q B 3
	Q—Kt 3 (e)			B—K 3	Q—K 4
7	B—B 4	......P—B 3......	...P—Q 5 (j)	O—O	Kt—B 3
	Kt—K B 3	P×P	Kt—K B 3	B—K 2	Q—K 2
8	Kt—K 3	Q×P	B—K 3	B—Kt 5	Kt—K Kt 5
	B—K 2	Kt—Q B 3	B—K 2	O—O	B—B 4
9	B—B 4	B—Q 3	Q—Q 4	Kt—Q 2	Q—Kt5ch +
	P—B 3	Q—Kt 5 (g)	O—O	Kt—B 3 !	
10	P—Q 5	Q—K 3 ch	Kt—Q 2	Kt×Kt	
	P—Kt 4	B—K 2	P—B 4	P×Kt	
11	B—K 2	O—O (h)	P×P e.p.	P—Q B 4	
	P—Kt 5	Kt—B 3	Kt×P	R—Kt 1	
12	Kt—R 4	P—Q 5	Q—B 4 ch	R—B 1	
	B—Q 2 (f)	Kt—Kt 5 (i)	K—R 1 (k)	P—Q R 4 ∓ (m)	

(a) The Greco Counter-Gambit. If 2 , P—K B 3 (Damiano's Defence) ; 3 Kt × P,
Q—K 2 ; 4 Kt—K B 3, P—Q 4 ; 5 P—Q 3, P × P ; 6 P × P+.
  (b) Mlotkowski recommends 3 Kt—B 3, P—Q 3 ; 4 P × P, P—B 4 ; 5 B—Kt 5 ch.
If 3 P × P, Q—B 3 !. If 3 B—B 4, P × P ; 4 Kt × P, Q—Kt 4 ; 5 Kt—B 7, Q × Kt P ;
6 R—B 1, P—Q 4 ; 7 Kt × R, Kt—K B 3 ; 8 B × P, B—K R 6 ; 9 B—B 7 ch, K—K 2 ;
10 B—B 4, Kt—B 3 ; 11 P—Q 4, R—Q 1 ; 12 B—K 3, Kt—K 4 ∓.
  (c) 5 Kt—K B 3 !, P × P ; 6 Kt—Kt 5, P—Q 4 ; 7 P—Q B 4, P—K R 3 ;
8 Kt—K R 3, B × Kt ; 9 P × B, Kt—B 3 ; 10 B—K 3, O—O—O ; 11 P × P+.
A. Steiner—Apscheneek, Kemeri, 1937.
  (d) Nimzovitch maintained that 6 Kt—K 3 is best, but considered only 6 .., P—B 3
a feasible reply. However, a correspondence game Stockholm—Riga went 6 . , Kt—B 3 ;
7 Kt—Q 5, Q—B 2 ; 8 Q Kt—B 3, B—K 3 ; 9 Kt × B P ch, Q × Kt ; 10 P—Q 5,
Kt—B 3 ! ; 11 P × B, P—Q 4 ! ; 12 B—Q Kt 5, O—O—O ; 13 B—Kt 5, P—Q 5 ! +.
  (e) 6 .., P—B 3 ; 7 Kt × K P, Q—K 3 ; 8 Q—K 2, P—Q 4 ; 9 Kt (K 4)—Q 6 ch,
K—Q 2 ; 10 Kt—B 7 !, P × Kt ; 11 Q × Q ch, K × Q ; 12 B × P ch, K—K 2 ; 13 Kt × R,
B—K 3 ; 14 B—Q 3 + (Lärobok).
  (f) 13 P—Q R 3 !, Kt P × P ; 14 R × P+. Sir G. A. Thomas—Tartakover, Spa, 1926.
  (g) 9 .., Q—K 3 ch ; 10 B—K 3, Q—Kt 5 ; 11 Q—B 2, Kt—B 3 ; 12 O—O, B—K 2.
L. Steiner—Tartakover, Berlin, 1928.
  (h) 11 Kt—Kt 5, Q × Kt P, 12 R—K Kt 1, Q × R P ; 13 P—B 3 !, K—Q 1 ;
14 R × P, P—K R 4 ! ∓. Ilyin-Zhenevsky—Behting, correspondence, 1921-25.
  (i) 13 R—B 4, Q—Q 2 ; 14 Kt—Kt 6, R P × Kt ; 15 R × Q R (Nimzovitch).
The game is about level.
  (j) 7 Kt—K 3, Kt—K B 3 ; 8 K Kt—Q 5, Kt × Kt ; 9 Kt × Kt, Q—B 2 ;
10 B—Q B 4, P—B 3 ; 11 Kt—K 3, P—Q 4 ; 12 B—Kt 3, B—K 3 ; 13 O—O, B—Q 3 ;
14 P—K B 4+. A. Steiner—Apscheneek, Hamburg, 1929.
  (k) 13 O—O—O, B—Kt 5 ; 14 P—B 3, P—Q 4 ; 15 Kt × Q P, Kt × Kt ;
16 Q × K Kt, P × P ; 17 P × P, Q R—B 1 ?. Spielmann—Tartakover, Semmering, 1926.
Alekhine suggests 17 . , Kt—K 5 ; 18 Q—K 3, P—Q R 4 (or Q R—B 1—Vidmar).
  (l) Or 5 B—K Kt 5, P—Q 3 ; 6 Kt—B 4, B—K 2 ; 7 B—K 2, O—O ; 8 O—O =.
S. R. Wolf—Apscheneek, Hamburg, 1930.
  (m) Stockholm—Riga, correspondence. (n) The Queen's Pawn Counter-Gambit.
  (o) Another possibility is 3 Kt × P, P × P ; 4 B—B 4, Q—Kt 4 ; 5 B × P ch, K—K 2 ;
6 P—Q 4, Q × P ; 7 R—B 1, B—R 6 ; 8 B—Q 5, Kt—K B 3 ; 9 B—B 4, Q Kt—Q 2 ;
10 Q—Q 2 ±. Von Feilitzsch—Keres, correspondence, 1934-35.
  (p) 3 .., Q × P ; 4 Kt—B 3, Q—K 3 ; 5 B—Kt 5 ch, B—Q 2 ; 6 O—O+.
  (q) 4 ., Kt—K B 3 ; 5 P—Q 3, B—K 2 ; 6 P × P, O—O ; 7 Q—B 4. F. Gutmayer
—F. Becker, correspondence, 1920-21.

NIMZOVITCH'S DEFENCE
1 P—K 4, Kt—Q B 3.

	1	2	3	4	5
2	P—Q 4 / P—Q 4				P—K 4 (j)
3	P—K 5 / P—B 3	......B—B 4	P×P / Q×P	Kt—Q B 3 / P—K 3 (g)	P×P / Kt×P
4	Kt—K B 3 / B—Kt 5	P—Q B 3 / P—B 3 (c)	Kt—K B 3 / P—K 4 !	P—K 5 (h) / K Kt—K 2	P—K B 4 (k) / Kt—Kt 3
5	B—K 2 / P—K 3	P—K B 4 / P—K 3	P×P (f) / Q×Q ch	Kt—B 3 / P—Q Kt 3	Kt-KB3? (l) / B—B 4
6	P×P / Kt×B P	Kt—B 3 (d) / Q—Q 2	K×Q / B—Q B 4	Kt—K 2 / B—R 3 !	B—B 4 / P—Q 3
7	P—B 3 / B—Q 3	B—Q 3 / B—K 5	K—K 1 / B—B 4	P—B 3 / Q—Q 2	Kt—Kt 5 / Kt—R 3
8	B—K Kt 5 / Q—Q 2	Q—K 2 / P—B 4	P—B 3 / O—O—O	Kt—Kt 3 / B×B	Kt—Q B 3 / O—O
9	Q Kt—Q 2 / P—K R 3 (a)	B—K 3 / Kt—R 3	B—K 2 / P—B 3	Kt×B / P—K R 4	Kt—R 4 / Q—B 3 !
10	B—R 4 / P—K Kt 4	Q Kt—Q 2 / B—K 2	B—K B 4 / P×P	B—Kt 5 / Kt—R4 ∓ (i)	Q—Q 2 (m) / Q—Q 5
11	B—Kt 3 / O—O—O ± (b)	P—K R 3 / O—O ± (e)	Kt×P / Kt×Kt+		B—Kt 3 / B—Q Kt 5 ∓

(a) 9.., O—O, followed by Kt—K 2, seems safer (Tartakover).

(b) Treybal—Spielmann, Carlsbad, 1923.

(c) 4.., P—K 3; 5 Kt—K 2, K Kt—K 2; 6 Kt—Kt 3, B—Kt 3; 7 B—Q 3, Q—Q 2; 8 Q—B 3, P—Kt 3; 9 Kt—Q 2, Kt—R 4; 10 P—K R 4, B×B; 11 Q×B, P—Q B 4; 12 P—Kt 4! ±. Kashdan—Flohr, Hamburg, 1930.

(d) Better than either 6 Kt—K 2, Kt—R 3; 7 Kt—Kt 3, P×P; 8 B P×P, Q—R 5; 9 Q—R 5 ch, Q×Q; 10 Kt×Q, P—K Kt 3= (Asztalos—Kostich, Bled, 1931) or 6 Kt—Q 2, Kt—R 3, 7 P—K Kt 3, B—K 2; 8 B—R 3, B P×P=. Balla—Breyer, 1919.

(e) 12 Kt—Kt 3, Kt—B 2; 13 P—Kt 4! Duras—Nimzovitch, Ostend, 1907.

(f) 5 Kt—B 3, B—Q Kt 5; 6 B—Q 2 is sounder. The column is Lövenborg—Nimzovitch, Copenhagen, 1924.

(g) Or 3.., P×P; 4 P—Q 5, Kt—K 4; 5 Q—Q 4±.

(h) Better 4 Kt—B 3, B—Kt 5; 5 P—K 5, B×Kt ch; 6 P×B, Kt—R 4; 7 P—Q R 4, Kt—K 2; 8 B—Q 3, P—Q Kt 3; 9 Kt—Q 2, P—Q B 4; 10 Q—Kt 4 with a strong attack. Becker—Nimzovitch, Breslau, 1925.

(i) Vadja—Nimzovitch, Kecskemét, 1927.

(j) Or 2.., P—Q 3; 3 Kt—K B 3, B—Kt 5; 4 B—Q Kt 5, P—Q R 3; 5 B—R 4, P—Q Kt 4; 6 B—Kt 3, Kt—B 3; 7 P—B 3, P—K 3; 8 Q—K 2, B—K 2, 9 O - O, O—O; 10 Q Kt—Q 2, B—R 4; 11 P—Q R 4 ±. Fine—Mikenas, Hastings, 1937-38.

(k) 4 Kt—Q B 3, Kt—K B 3 transposes into Euwe—Breyer, Vienna, 1921, which continued 5 P—B 4, Kt—B 3; 6 P—K 5, Kt—K Kt 1; 7 B—B 4, P—Q 3; 8 Kt—B 3, B—Kt 5; 9 O—O, Q—Q 2; 10 Q—K 1, O—O—O; 11 Kt—K Kt 5, P×P! ∓.

(l) Much stronger is 5 B—K 3, e.g. B—Kt 5 ch; 6 Kt—Q 2, Kt—B 3; 7 P—B 3, B—R 4; 8 B—Q 3, Q—Q 3 ± (not 9 Kt×B, Kt—B 3, Kt—Kt 5; or 9 Kt—R 3, B—Kt 3; 10 Kt×B, R P×Kt and now if 11 Q—B 3, Kt—K 5!; 12 Q—R 3, Kt×K P; or 11 Q—B 2, Kt—Kt 5!++. Analysis by S Bernstein.

(m) Forced, for if 10 Kt×B, Kt×P!; 11 Kt—Q 3, Kt×P ch+; or 10 Q—B 3, B—Kt 5; 11 Q—B 1, B—Kt 5 ch; 12 P—B 3, B—Q R 4 ∓. The column is A. Steiner—Mikenas, Kemeri, 1937.

D

	6	7	8	9	10
1	(P—K 4)................ (Kt—Q B 3)		Kt—KB3(f) P—Q 4	.... P—Q Kt 3	Kt—Q B3 (m) P—Q 4 (n)
2	Kt—Q B 3... P—K 3 (a)	Kt—K B 3 P—K 3 (d)	P—K 4 (g) P×P	P—K 3 B—Kt 2	P—K 4 (o) P—Q 5
3	P—Q 4 B—Kt 5	P—Q 4 P—Q 4	Kt—Kt 5 P—K 4 (h)	P—Q Kt 3 P—K B 4	Q Kt—K 2 P—K 4
4	Kt—K 2 (b) P—Q 4	P—K 5 P—Q Kt 3	P—K R 4 Kt—QB3 (i)	B—Kt 2 P—K 3	Kt—Kt 3 B—K 3
5	P—K 5 P—K R 4	P—B 3 Q Kt—K 2	B—B 4 Kt—K R 3	Kt—K 5 (k) Kt—K B 3	P—Q 3 Kt—Q B 3
6	Kt—B 4 P—K Kt 3	B—Q 3 P—Q R 4	Kt—Q B 3 B—K Kt 5	P—K B 4 P—Kt 3	P—Q R 3 P—K Kt 3
7	B—K 3 B×Kt ch	Q—K 2 Kt—B 4	P—B 3 P×P	P—B 4 B—Kt 2	P—K B 4 P×P
8	P×B Kt—R 4	P—K R 4 P—K R 4	P×P (j) B—K B 4	Kt—B 3 O—O	B×P B—Q 3
9	B—Q 3 Kt—K 2	Kt—Kt 5 P—Kt 3	P—Q 3 B—B 4	Q—K 2 P—Q 3+ (l)	Q—Q 2 Q—K 2
10	Kt—R 3 P—Q B 4	Kt—Q 2 ! K Kt—K 2	Q Kt—K 4 B—Q Kt 3+		Kt—B 3 O—O—O
11	B—Kt5 ± (c)	Kt—B 1+ (e)			Kt—Kt 5 P—KR4 = (p)

(a) P—K 4 leads to the Vienna Game, P—K Kt 3 to the King's Fianchetto Defence.

(b) Superior to 4 Kt—B 3, P—Q 3; 5 B—K B 4, K Kt—K 2; 6 B—K 2, B×Kt ch; 7 P×B, O—O; 8 O—O, Kt—Kt3; 9 B—K 3, Q—K2; 10 R—K 1, B—Q 2=. Maróczy—Nimzovitch, San Remo, 1930.

(c) Kmoch—Nimzovitch, Niendorf, 1927.

(d) Black may lead into the ordinary forms of the King's Knight's Opening by 2 ., P—K 4 or into the King's Fianchetto Defence by 2 ., P—K Kt 3. The reply 2 ., P—Q 4, recommended by Nimzovitch, is doubtful, as after 3 P×P, Q×P; 4 Kt—B 3, Q—Q R 4, 5 B—Kt 5 a variation of the Centre Counter unfavourable for Black (col. 4) results.

(e) Spielmann—Nimzovitch, New York, 1927.

(f) Zukertort's Opening. See also Réti Opening, p. 219.

(g) The Tenison (also called Lemberg) Gambit.

(h) P—K B 4, as in N. T. Miniati—H. Jones, Manchester, 1891 (Cook's Compendium, p. 288), is inferior.

(i) 4.., B—K 2; 5 Kt—Q B 3, Kt—K B 3; 6 B—B 4, O—O; 7 QKt×P, Kt—B 3; 8Kt×Kt ch, B×Kt, 9 Q—R 5, B×Kt; 10 P×B, B—B 4; 11 P—Q 3. S. Goravsky—A. Z. Sarazevsky, correspondence, 1925.

(j) Analysis by V. Geier, Wiener Schachzeitung, 1926.

(k) Better 5 P—B 4, followed by Kt—B 3 (Nimzovitch).

(l) Ahues—Nimzovitch, Kecskemét, 1928.

(m) The Queen's Knight's Opening.

(n) 1 ., P—K 4; 2 P—Q 4, P×P; 3 Q×P, Kt—Q B 3; 4 Q—Q R 4, Kt—B 3; 5 B—Kt 5, B—K 2; 6 P—K 4, P—K R 3; 7 B—R 4, P—Q 3; 8 O—O—O, B—Q 2; 9 B—K 2, O—O ±. C. G. Steele—G. E. Wainwright, Southsea, 1923.

(o) For 2 P—Q 4 see Queen's Pawn Game, cols. 24-7.

(p) Petrov—Ragosin, Semmering-Baden, 1937.

D *

	11	12	13	14	15
1	P—Q B3 (a)	P—Q Kt 3 ...	P—Q Kt4 (j) .	P—K 3 (m)
	P—Q B 4	P—K B 4 (d)	P—K 4	P—K 4	P—K 4 (n)
2	P—Q 4	P—Q 4	B—Kt 2	B—Kt 2	Kt—Q B 3
	P—K 3	P—Q Kt3 (e)	P—K B 3	P—K B 3	P—Q 4
3	P—K 4	Kt—B 3	P—K 4 (h)	P—K 4 (k)	P—Q 4
	Kt—K B3 (b)	B—Kt 2	B—B 4	B×P	P×P
4	P—K 5	P—K Kt3	B—B 4	B—B 4	Q×P
	Kt—Q 4	P—Q 3 (f)	Kt—K 2	Kt—K 2	Kt—K B 3
5	Kt—B 3	B—Kt 2	Q—R 5 ch	P—B 4	P—K 4
	P—Q 3	Kt—Q 2	P—K Kt 3	P—Q 4	Kt—QB3(o)
6	K P×P	Q—Kt 3 !	Q—B 3	P×Q P	B—Q Kt 5
	B×P	P—Q 4	Q Kt—B 3	P×P	B—Q 2
7	P×P	Kt—Kt 5	Kt—K 2	Q—B 3	B×Kt
	B×P	Q Kt—B 3	R—B 1	B—Q 3	B×B
8	B—Kt 5 ch	B—B 4	P—K Kt 4	Kt—K 2	P—K 5
	B—Q 2	Q—Q 2	P—B 4	Kt—Kt 3	Kt—K 5
9	B×B ch	Kt—Q R 3	Kt P×P	P—Q 4	Kt×Kt
	Kt×B	P—K R 3	P—Q 4	Q—K 2	P×Kt
10	O—O	Kt—B 3	P×Q P	B—B 1	Kt—K 2
	O—O	P—K Kt 4	R×P	B—K B 4	B—K 2
11	Q Kt—Q 2	Kt—K 5	Q—K 4	B—Q 3	B—K 3
	Q—B 2	Q—K 3	Kt—Kt 5	B×B	Q×Q
12	Kt—K 4	B—K 3	Q Kt—B 3	Q×B	Kt×Q
	B—K 2 = (c)	Kt—Q 2 (g)	B×P ch (i)	O—O = (l)	B—Q 2 = (p).

(a) The Saragossa Opening.
(b) P—Q 4 is a good alternative.
(c) Tartakover—Réti, Baden-Baden, 1925.
(d) 1 .., P—K 4; 2 P—Q 4, P×P; 3 Q×P gives White a Centre Counter with a move in hand. 1 .., P—Q 4; 2 P—Q 4, Kt—K B 3 may transpose into the Queen's Pawn Game, with the Colle system for White (p. 177). Another line is 1 , Kt—K B 3; 2 P—Q 4, P—Q Kt 3; 3 B—Kt 5, B—Kt 2; 4 Kt—Q 2, P—Q 4 (Mieses—Leonhardt, Mannheim, 1922).
(e) Or 2 , P—K 3; 3 P—K Kt 3, B—K 2 with a Dutch Defence formation. Here 3 .., P—Q 4 is Tarrasch—Leonhardt, Mannheim, 1922.
(f) Much better was 4 , P—K 3, with the possible continuation 5 B—Kt 2, B—K 2; 6 O—O, Kt—K B 3; 7 B—Kt 5, Kt—K 5.
(g) 13 Kt—Kt 5! +. Tarrasch—Mieses, Mannheim, 1922.
(h) Or 3 P—K 3, P—Q 4; 4 Kt—K B 3, B—Q 3 (if 4 , P—K 5; 5 Kt—Q 4, P—Q B 4; 6 Kt—Kt 5, P—Q R 3; 7 Q—R 5 ch, P—K Kt 3; 8 Q×Q P, P×Kt; 9 B×P ch with three Pawns against a piece (Tartakover).
(i) 13 K—Q 1, P—B 3 ∓. Nimzovitch—Winter, London, 1927.
(j) The Polish Opening.
(k) An interesting gambit, favoured by Tartakover. 3 P—Q R 3 is quite safe.
(l) Tartakover—Colle, Bartfield, 1926.
(m) Van 't Kruys Opening. Other first moves seldom encountered are: (1) 1 P—Q R 3 (Anderssen's Opening), best met by P—Q 4, if P—K 4, 2 P—Q B 4 leads into the English Opening; (2) 1 P—K Kt 3 (King's Fianchetto Opening); (3) 1 P—K Kt 4 (the "Spike"). 1 , P—Q 4; 2 B—Kt 2, B×P; 3 P—Q B 4, P—Q B 3; 4 P×P, Kt—B 3; 5 Kt—Q B 3, P—K 4; 6 P×P e.p., B×P (K 3); 7 P—Q 4, Q Kt—Q 2; 8 P—K 4, Kt—Kt 3; 9 K Kt—K 2 ±. Keres—Niemann, correspondence, 1934-35.
(n) 1 .., Kt—K B 3; 2 P—Q B 4, P—Q 3; 3 Kt—K B 3, P—Q 3; 4 P—Q 4, Q Kt—Q 2. Sokolsky—Panoff, Moscow, 1936.
(o) 5 .., P×P; 6 Q×Q ch, K×Q; 7 B—K Kt 5 (or B—Q B 4), B—K B 4; 8 O—O—O ch, Kt—Q 2; 9 Kt—K 2 (note by Nimzovitch and Tartakover). Cp. Nimzovitch's Defence.
(p) Nimzovitch—Tarrasch, Kissingen, 1928.

KING'S GAMBIT

In the group of openings arising from 1 P—K 4, P—K 4;
2 P—K B 4, P × P, White speculates on an attack on Black's
K B 2, with the help of the open King's Bishop's file. On
his 3rd move White's main choice lies between B—B 4, the
Bishop's Gambit, or Kt—K B 3, the King's Knight's Gambit.
These gambits, once very popular, are still occasionally
practised by masters such as Spielmann, Tartakover, and
Stoltz, and by a few leading amateurs.

Since the Abbazia Gambit Tournament of 1912 it has
been recognised that by an immediate counter-attack in the
centre, without attempting to maintain his gain in material,
Black obtains at least an equal, if not the superior, game, ·
and is exposed to none of the traps in the classical attacks
springing from the Bishop's and Knight's Gambits.

This does not lead to such complicated positions as the
Knight's Gambit, but has the merit of greater soundness.
One of the strongest defences, based upon the counter-
sacrifice of Black's Queen's Pawn, is shown in cols. 1 to 3.
The line in col. 1 may be recommended, together with that
in col. 5, as the safest equalising defences. The reply 3...,
Kt—K B 3, favoured by Morphy, has been somewhat
discredited by modern tournament play; Bogoljuboff's
Defence being demolished by Tartakover's analysis in col. 7
and note (f).

In the Lesser Bishop's Gambit (col. 8) White seeks to
recover the Gambit Pawn without exposing his minor pieces
to the counter-attacks available to Black in the Bishop's and
Knight's Gambits. It was adopted by Tartakover at the
New York Tournament, 1924, with a considerable measure
of success, and may be the soundest form of the King's
Gambits.

KING'S KNIGHT'S GAMBIT.

The strongest defence to this is shown in cols. 1 to 5, Black obtaining an advantage in development, and retaining the Pawn on B 5. Consequently, the Knight's Gambit is now but little played, the possibilities of the Bishop's Gambit offering more attractions.

The classical reply 3..., P—K Kt 4, retaining the Gambit Pawn, is not now encountered in serious play, White's attacking chances, under the influence of the time-limit, far outweighing that theoretical superiority which Black finds so difficult to demonstrate in practice. White has the choice of two systems of attack, according as he plays to break up Black's Pawns by the immediate advance 4 P—K R 4 (cols. 11 to 25), or contents himself with rapid development by 4 B—B 4 (cols. 26 to 40), inviting the reply 4..., P—Kt 5.

In the former case, the Allgaier Gambit (cols. 11 to 15) gives White an exceedingly strong attack, equalling the Muzio Gambit in vigour. Black's defence in the usual lines (cols. 11 to 14) is extraordinarily difficult, despite the advantage of a piece. The Kieseritzky Gambit (cols. 16 to 25) has been advocated by Rubinstein, who maintains that White recovers the Gambit Pawn with the superior game, an ambitious claim not supported by the evidence of practical play.

In the latter case, Black maintains his Pawn in the Berlin Defence (cols. 26 to 29), but his task is by no means easy in an over-the-board game.

Black has the alternative P—Kt 5 on his 4th move, compelling the sacrifice of a piece, since the natural reply 5 Kt—K 5, the Salvio Gambit, exposes White to the overwhelming attack in col. 30. The brilliant Muzio Gambit (cols. 31 to 40) appears to yield White full compensation for the material sacrificed. Col. 33 deserves special notice.

The old defence 6..., Q—K 2 (col. 34), favoured by From, offers Black his best chance. Brentano's Defence (cols. 35 to 37) has proved inadequate, Black losing so many Pawns that, even though he be successful in staving off the attack, he is left at a serious disadvantage in the resulting endgame.

The two gambits in cols. 9 and 10, although rarely seen, are worthy of mention. Breyer's Gambit (col. 9) resembles the Vienna Game, and is at least as good for White as most variations of the King's Knight's Gambit. The Keres Gambit (col. 10) is an old line, which has been played by Keres in recent correspondence games, after being well tested by his fellow-Estonian, the late Martin Willemson. It leads to unusual positions, where White has much scope for his imagination.

BISHOP'S GAMBIT
1 P—K4, P—K4; 2 P—KB4, PxP; 3 B—B4.

	1	2	3	4	5
3	P—Q4			Kt—QB3	P—KB4 (j)
4	BxP		PxP	P—Q4 (g)	Q—K2
	Kt—KB3	Q—R5 ch	Kt—KB3	Kt—B3	Q—R5 ch
5	Kt—QB3	K—B1	Kt—QB3	P—K5 (h)	K—Q1
	B—QKt5	P—KKt4 (a)	B—Q3	P—Q4	PxP
6	Kt—B3	Kt—QB3 (b)	Q—K2 ch	B—Kt3	QxP ch (k)
	BxKt	Kt—KB3 (c)	Q—K2	Kt—K5	B—K2
7	QPxB	P—Q4	QxQ ch	QBxP (i)	P—Q4
	P—B3	P—B3	KxQ	Q—R5 ch	Kt—KB3
8	B—B4	B—Kt3	KKt—K2	P—Kt3	QxBP
	QxQ ch	B—Kt2	P—QR3	KtxKtP	QxQ
9	KxQ	Kt—B3	P—Q3	BxKt	BxQ
	O—O	Q—R4	P—QKt4 (e)	Q—K5 ch	P—Q4
10	BxP	P—KR4	B—Kt3	K—B2	B—Q3
	KtxP	B—Kt5 (d)	P—Kt5	QxR	B—Kt5 ch
11	R—K1 =	P—K5	Kt—R4	Kt—QB3	Kt—K2
		BxKt	Kt—R4	Kt—K2	Kt—B3=
12		QxB	O—O	Q—K2	
		QxQ ch	P—Kt4	P—KR4	
13		PxQ	B—Q2 (f)	R—K1	
		Kt—R4		P—R5	
14		Kt—K4+		B—KB4	
				Kt—Kt3+	

(a) 5.., Kt—KB3; 6 Kt—QB3, B—QKt5; 7 B—Kt3, Kt—B3; 8 Kt—B3, Q—R4; 9 P—K5, BxKt. Spielmann—Jacobson, Copenhagen, 1923. If 5 , Kt—K2; 6 Kt—QB3, P—KKt4; 7 Kt—B3, Q—R4; 8 P—KR4, P—KR3; 9 BxP ch, QxB; 10 Kt—K5, Q—Kt2; 11 Q—R5 ch+ (Sanders Attack).

(b) Or 6 Q—B3, P—QB3; 7 P—KKt3, B—R6 ch; 8 K—K1, Q—Kt5; 9 QxQ, BxQ; 10 B—Kt3, PxP; 11 PxP. If 6 P—Q4, B—Kt2; 7 Kt—KB3, Q—R4; 8 P—KR4, P—KR3; 9 Kt—B3, Kt—K2; 10 Q—Q3, O—O; 11 B—Kt3, Q Kt—B3; 12 Kt—K2, B—Kt5; 13 P—B3, Q R—Q1; 14 Q Kt—Kt1, Kt—Kt3+. Nenarokoff—Sosin, Russian National Tournament, 1926.

(c) Or 6.., B—Kt2; 7 P—Q4, Kt—K2; 8 Kt—B3, Q—R4; 9 P—KR4, P—KR3; 10 Q—Q3, Q Kt—B3; 11 Kt—Kt5, O—O; 12 P—B3+.

(d) If 10 ., P—KR3; 11 K—Kt1+. The column is Spielmann—Lovenfisch, Moscow, 1925.

(e) 8 , Kt—R4 (8.., P—KKt4; 9 P—KR4); 9 P—KR3; 10 Kt—K4, P—KKt4; 11 P—KR4, P—KB3; 12 PxP, RPxP; 13 KtxP (B4), PxKt; 14 B—K2+ (Sosin).

(f) Bogoljuboff—Sosin, Moscow, 1924. Black should now continue 13. , R—K1, 14 P—B4, PxP e.p.: 15 PxP, B—KB4 (Sosin).

(g) For 4 Kt—KB3 see King's Knight's Gambit.

(h) Or 5 Kt—QB3, B—Kt5; 6 Q—Q3, Kt—B3, 7 PxP, K KtxP; 8 Kt—B3, O—O; 9 O—O, BxKt; 10 PxB, R—K1; 11 BxKt, QxB ∓. Spielmann—Réti, Baden, 1914.

(i) 7 Kt—KB3 is better. The column is analysis by Kmoch.

(j) The Lopez Counter-Gambit. Or 3 , Q—R5 ch; 4 K—B1, P—KKt4 (the Classical Defence); 5 Kt—QB3, B—Kt5; 6 PxP, K Kt—K2; 7 P—K4, Kt 3 (MacDonnell's Attack), PxP; 8 K—Kt2, Q—R3; 9 PxP, Q—Kt3; 10 Kt—B3, P—KR3; 11 Kt—Q5+.

(k) 6 Kt—QB3, K—Q1; 7 KtxP (7 BxKt, RxB; 8 QxP, B—Q3), P—B3; 8 Kt—KB3, Q—K2; 9 BxKt, RxB; 10 P—Q3, P—Q4; 11 BxP, P—KR3=.

BISHOP'S GAMBIT ; BREYER GAMBIT ; KERES GAMBIT
1 P—K 4, P—K 4 ; 2 P—K B 4, P×P.

	6	7	8	9	10
3	(B—B 4)................		B—K 2 (h)	...Q—B 3 (m)	..Kt—Q B 3 (q)
	Kt—K B 3		P—Q 4 (i)	Kt—Q B 3	Q—R 5 ch
4	Kt—Q B 3		P×P	P—B 3 (n)	K—K 2
	Kt—B 3.....P—B 3 (d)		Kt—K B 3	Kt—B 3 (o)	P—Q 3
5	Kt—B 3	Q—B 3 (e)	P—B 4	P—Q 4	Kt—Q 5
	B—Kt 5	P—Q 4 (f)	P—B 3	P—Q 4	B—Kt 5 ch
6	Kt—Q 5 (a)	P×P	P—Q 4	P—K 5	Kt—B 3
	O—O (b)	B—Q 3	B—Kt 5 ch	Kt—K 5	B×Kt ch
7	O—O	P—Q 3	K—B 1 (j)	B×P	P×B
	Kt×Kt	B—K Kt 5	P×P	P—B 3	K—Q 1
8	P×Kt	Q—B 2	B×P (k)	B—Q Kt 5	P—Q 3
	Kt—K 2	O—O	P×P	B—K 2	P—K Kt 4
9	P—Q 4	B×P	B×Kt	P×P	B—Q 2
	Kt—Kt 3	R—K 1 ch	Kt—Q 4 !	B×P	B—Kt 2
10	Kt—K 5 (c)	K—B 1	K—B 2	Kt—K 2	B—K 1
	B—Q 3	P—Q Kt 4	R×B	O—O	Q—R 4
11	Kt×Kt	B—Kt 3	B×P	O—O	P—K R 4 (r)
	B P×Kt	P—Kt 5	O—O	P—Kt 4	P—Q B 3
12	Q—Kt 4+	Q Kt—K 2	Kt—K B 3	B×Kt	Kt—B 3
		Kt×P (g)	Kt—B 3+ (l)	QKtP×B(p)	Kt—K 2

(a) 6 O—O (or 6 P—K 5, P—Q 4), O—O ; 7 P—Q 3, B×Kt ; 8 P×B, P—Q 4⹀.
(b) 6 ., Kt×P ; 7 O—O, O—O ; 8 P—Q 4, B—B 3 ; 9 Kt×B, Kt×Kt ;
10 B×P ± Spielmann—Bogoljuboff, Triberg, 1921. Or 8 , B—K 2 ; 9 B×P, P—Q 3 ;
10 Q—Q 3 ±. Spielmann—Grunfeld, Innsbruck, 1922.
(c) Inferior is 10 P—K R 4, B—Q 3 ; 11 P—R 5, Kt—R 5 ; 12 Q—K 1, Kt×Kt ch ;
13 R×Kt, Q—Kt 4 ; 14 R—K R 3, P—Kt 4+. Loman—Yates, Scheveningen, 1923.
(d) Bogoljuboff's Defence. If 4 ., B—Kt 5 ; 5 P—K 5, P—Q 4 ; 6 B—Kt 5 ch,
P—B 3 ; 7 P×Kt, P×B ; 8 Q—K 2 ch+.
(e) 5 B—Kt 3, P—Q 4, 6 P×P, P×P ; 7 P—Q 4, B—Q 3 ; 8 K Kt—K 2, O—O ;
9 O—O, P—K Kt 4+. Spielmann—Bogoljuboff, Mährisch-Ostrau, 1923. Or 5 P—Q 4,
B—Kt 5 ; 6 Q—B 3, P—Q 4 ; 7 P×P, O—O ; 8 K Kt—K 2, P×P+. Spielmann—
Bogoljuboff, Carlsbad, 1923.
(f) 5 , Q—K 2 ; 6 K Kt—K 2, P—Q Kt 4 ; 7 B×P, P×B ; 8 P—K 5+.
Tartakover.
(g) 13 B×Kt, P×B ; 14 Q—Kt 3, B×B ; 15 Kt×B+ (Tartakover). The column
to Black's ninth move is Shanghai—Chefoo, correspondence.
(h) The Lesser Bishop's Gambit.
(i) 3 , Kt—K 2, 4 P—Q 4, P—Q 4 ; 5 P×P, Kt×P ; 6 Kt—K B 3, B—Kt 5 ch ;
7 P—B 3, B—K 2 ; 8 O—O, O—O ; 9 P—B 4, Kt—K 6 ! ; 10 B×Kt, P×B, 11 Q—Q 3,
B—B 3 ; 12 Kt—B 3 (if 12 Q×P, P—B 4 !), Kt—B 3 ; 13 Kt—Q 5, B—Kt 5 (better
R—K 1) ; 14 Kt×B ch, Q×Kt ; 15 P—Q 5. Tartakover—Alekhine, New York, 1924
(j) 7 B—Q 2, B×B ch ; 8 Q×B was better (Tartakover).
(k) 8 P—B 5 should have been played (Tartakover).
(l) Tartakover—Capablanca, New York, 1924.
(m) The Breyer Gambit.
(n) Tartakover recommends 4 Q×P, Kt—B 3 ; 5 Kt—Q B 3, Kt—Q Kt 5 .
4 Kt—K 2 is met by 4 ., P—Q 4.
(o) 4 , P—Q 4 ; 5 P×P, Kt—K 4 ; 6 Q—K 4, Q—K 2 ; 7 P—Q 4, Kt—Kt 3
8 Q×Q ch, B×Q ; 9 B—Q 3, Kt—B 3. C. H. Alexander—T. H. Tylor, Chester, 1934.
(p) Spielmann—Tarrasch, Gothenburg, 1920.
(q) The Keres, Willemson, or Pernau Gambit.
(r) Keres—Kunerth, correspondence, 1935

1 P—K 4, P—K 4 ; 2 P—K B 4, P×P ; 3 Kt—K B 3.

	1	2	3	4	5
3	P—Q 4				
4	P×P (a)				
	Kt—K B 3				
5	Kt—B 3...				B—Kt 5 ch
	Kt×P				P—B 3
6	B—Kt 5 ch..	B—K 2.....	Kt×Kt		P×P
	P—B 3	Kt×Kt	Q×Kt		P×P
7	Q—K 2 ch	Kt P×Kt	P—Q 4	..B—Q 3	B—B 4
	B—K 3	B—Q 3	B—K 2 (d)..		B—Q 3
8	B—B 4	P—Q 4	B—Q 3	P—B 4	Q—K 2 ch
	B—K 2	O—O	P—K Kt 4	Q—K 3 ch	Q—K 2
9	Kt×Kt	O—O	Q—K 2	K—B 2	Q×Q ch
	P×Kt	Kt—B 3	B—K B 4	P—Q B 4	K×Q
10	B—Kt 5 ch	P—B 4	B×B	B—Q 3	P—Q 4
	Kt—B 3	P—Q Kt 3	Q×B	Q—R 3	B—K B 4
11	P—Q 4	P—B 3	P—K Kt 4	R—K 1 ch	Kt—K 5
	Q—B 2	B—K Kt 5	Q—Q 2+ (e)	K—B 1	B×Kt
12	B×Kt ch	Kt—K 1		Q—K 2	P×B
	P×B (b)	B×B (c)		B—Q 2 (f)	Kt—Q 4 (g)

	6	7	8	9	10
3	Kt—K B 3..............................			B—K 2 (l)...	P—K Kt 4
4	Kt—B 3.....	P—K 5		B—B 4	Kt—B 3 (n)
	P—Q 4	Kt—R 4		B—R 5 ch	P—Kt 5
5	P—K 5 (h)	P—Q 4		K—B 1 (m)	Kt—K 5
	Kt—K 5	P—Q 4		P—Q 4	Q—R 5 ch
6	B—K 2	P—B 4......	B—Q 3 (j)	B×P	P—Kt 3
	P—K Kt 4	Kt—Q B 3	Kt—Q B 3	Kt—K B 3	P×P
7	O—O	P×P	O—O	Kt—B 3	Q×P
	Kt—Q B 3	Q×P	P—K Kt 3	O—O	Q×Q (o)
8	B—Kt 5	Kt—B 3	Kt—B 3	P—Q 4	Kt×Q
	P—Q R 3	B—Q Kt 5	B—R 3	P—B 3	P—Q 4
9	B×Kt ch	K—B 2	Kt—K 2	B—Kt 3	B—R 3
	P×B	B×Kt	O—O	B—Kt 5	Q P×P
10	P—Q 3	P×B	P—K Kt 3	B×P	Kt—B 6 ch
	B—B 4 ch	B—Kt 5	B—R 6	Kt—R 4	K—Q 1
11	P—Q 4	B—K 2	R—B 2	Q—Q 2	B×B
	B—K 2+	O—O (i)	P—K Kt 4+	B×Kt	K×B
			(k)		

(a) 4 P—K 5, P—K Kt 4 ; 5 P—K R 3, Kt—K R 3 ; 6 P—Q 4, Kt—B 4+.
(b) 13 O—O, O—O ; 14 Kt—K 5, Q—Kt 3 ; 15 P—B 3. Rubinstein—Tarrasch, Meran, 1924.
(c) Spielmann—Nyholm, Abbazia, 1912.
(d) If 7. , Kt—B 3? ; 8 B×P, B—Kt 5, 9 B×P, K—Q 2 ; 10 B—Kt 3, R—K 1 ch ; 11 K—B 2+. Spielmann—Eliskases, 3rd match game, 1937.
(e) Rubinstein—Yates, Hastings, 1922.
(f) 13 P—Q Kt 4, P—Q Kt 3 ; 14 B—K 4. Réti—Nyholm, Baden, 1914.
(g) 13 B×Kt+. Nimzovitch—Schweinburg, 1934.
(h) 5 P×P is best, transposing into cols. 1—4. The column is Spielmann—Bogoljuboff, Berlin, 1919.

Notes ctd. on p. 99

ALLGAIER GAMBIT

1 P—K4, P—K4; 2 P—KB4, PxP; 3 Kt—KB3, P—KKt4;
4 P—KR4, P—Kt5; 5 Kt—Kt5.

	11	12	13	14	15
5	P—KR3				Kt—KB3 (*i*)
6	KtxP			P—K5	
	KxKt			Q—K2	
7	P—Q4 (*a*)		.........P—B6	B—B4 ch (*e*)	Q—K2 (*j*)
	P—Q4			P—Q4	Kt—R4
8	BxP		B—B4 ch	BxP ch	Kt—QB3
	Kt—KB3 (*b*)		P—Q4	K—K1 (*f*)	Kt—Kt6
9	Kt—B3		BxP ch	P—Q4	Q—B4
	B—Kt5 .....PxP		K—Kt2 (*d*)	Kt—KB3 (*g*)	QxP ch (*k*)
10	B—K2	B—B4 ch	PxP	Kt—B3	B—K2
	BxKt ch (*c*)	K—Kt3	Kt—KB3	B—Kt5	KtxR
11	PxB	P—R5 ch	Kt—B3	BxBP	QxP ch
	PxP	K—R2	B—Kt5	KtxB	K—Q1
12	Q—Q2	Q—K2	B—QB4	PxKt	P—Q4
	K—Kt3	B—Kt2	PxP	QxP	Q—Kt2
13	O—O	O—O—O	R—Kt1 ch	O—O	BxBP
	B—K3	R—B1	Kt—Kt5	BxKt	QxQ
14	P—B4	B—K5	QxP	PxB	KtxQ ch
	P—B3	Kt—B3	QxP ch	Kt—B3	K—K1
15	QR—Kt1	KR—B1	R—Kt3	Q—Q2	KtxR
	P—Kt3	Q—K2	R—B1	B—K3	P—B3
16	R—B2	Kt—Q5	B—B4	QR—K1	BxP+
	QKt—Q2	KtxKt	B—K2	K—Q2	
17	B—Q6	QxP ch		B—K5 (*h*)	

(*a*) The Allgaier-Thorold Attack. If 7 QxP, Kt—KB3; 8 QxP, B—Q3; 9 Q—B3, Kt—B3; 10 P—B3, Kt—K4+.

(*b*) 8 , PxP; 9 B—B4 ch, K—Kt2; 10 B—K5 ch, Kt—B3; 11 O—O, B—K2; 12 Kt—B3 or 8.., B—K3; 9 B—Q3, Kt—KB3; 10 Kt—B3, B—K2; 11 Kt—Kt5, Kt—R3; 12 B—K5.

(*c*) Dr. A. von Claparède considers that Black obtains the better game by 10.., Kt—B3. The column is Fähndrich and Schlechter—Fleissig and Marco, 1903.

(*d*) 9.., K—K1; 10 PxP, P—Kt6 (10 , Kt—KB3; 11 Kt—B3, B—Kt5; 12 O—O, BxKt; 13 PxB, KtxB; 14 PxKt, QxRP; 15 B—B4, R—Kt1; 16 Q—K1 ch, QxQ; 17 QRxQ ch); 11 B—K3, B—K2; 12 Kt—B3, BxP; 13 K—Q2. Fleissig and Marco—Fähndrich and Schlechter, 1903.

(*e*) The Ourousoff Attack.

(*f*) 8.., K—Kt2; 9 P—Q4, P—B6; 10 PxP, Kt—KB3 transposes into col. 13.

(*g*) 9.., P—B6; 10 PxP transposes into col. 13, note (*d*).

(*h*) If 17 P—B4 (Mieses—Pillsbury, Vienna, 1903), QxQ P ch.

(*i*) 5.., P—Q4; 6 PxP, P—KR3 (or 6 ., B—K2; 7 B—Kt5 ch, P—B3; 8 PxP, PxP; 9 B—B4); 7 Kt—K4, B—K2; 8 Q—K2, BxP ch; 9 Kt—B2 ch, B—K2; 10 KtxP. S. Mlotkowski—E. R. Perry, 1920

(*j*) Or 7 P—Q4, P—Q4 (better 7.., P—KR3; 8 KtxP, R—R2); 8 B—K2, Kt—R4, 9 KBxP, Kt—Kt6; 10 Kt—QB3, B—K3; 11 R—R3+. Dus-Chotimirsky—Rabinovitch, Moscow, 1925.

(*k*) 9 ., KtxR; 10 P—Q4, P—QB3; 11 BxP, P—Q3 (or 11 , P—Q4; 12 KtxQP+); 12 Kt—K4, PxP; 13 BxP+. The note and column are from *Lärobok*, 1921.

KIESERITZKY GAMBIT

1 P—K4, P—K4; 2 P—KB4, P×P; 3 Kt—KB3, P—KKt4; 4 P—KR4, P—Kt5; 5 Kt—K5.

	16	17	18	19	20
5	B—Kt2 (a)	....	Kt—KB3	....	P—Q3
6	Kt×KtP	...P—Q4	P—Q4	...B—B4	Kt×KtP
	P—Q4	Kt—KB3	P—Q3	P—Q4	P—KR4
7	P—Q4	B—B4 (c)	Kt—Q3	P×P	Kt—B2
	P×P	P—Q4	Kt×P	B—Q3 (g)	Kt—KB3
8	B×P	P×P	B×P	O—O (h)	P—Q4
	Q×P	Kt—R4	Q—K2	B×Kt	B—R3
9	Q×Q	Kt—QB3	Q—K2	R—K1	Kt—B3
	B×Q	O—O	B—Kt2	Q—K2	Kt—Kt5
10	P—B3	Kt—K4 (d)	P—B3	P—B3	Q—B3
	B×Kt	Kt—Q2	P—KR4	Kt—R4	Kt—K6
11	P×B	Kt×BP	Kt—Q2	P—Q4	B×Kt
	Kt—QB3	Q—K1	Kt×Kt	Kt—Q2	P×B
12	B—QKt5	Kt(B7)—Kt5	K×Kt	P×B	K Kt—Q1
	O—O—O	Kt—Kt6	Q×Q ch	Kt×P	B—Kt5
13	B×Kt	Kt—K6	B×Q	P—QKt3	Q—Kt3
	P×B (b)	Kt—Kt3 (e)	B—B4 (f)	O—O (i)	Q—B3 (j)

	21	22	23	24	25
5	P—Q4 (k)	...Kt—QB3 (n).	Q—K2	..... B—K2	..... P—KR4
6	P—Q4	P—Q4	P—Q4	B—B4	B—B4
	Kt—KB3	Kt×Kt	P—Q3	B×P ch	R—R2
7	B×P	P×Kt	Kt×KtP	K—B1	P—Q4
	Kt×P	P—Q3	P—KB4	P—Q4	P—B6 (o)
8	Kt—Q2	B×P	Kt—B2	B×P	P×P
	Kt×Kt	Q—K2	Kt—KB3	Kt—KR3	P—Q3
9	Q×Kt	P×P	B×P	P—Q4	Kt—Q3
	B—Q3	Q×KP ch	Kt×P	B—Kt4	B—K2
10	O—O—O	Q—K2	Q—R5 ch	P—KKt3	B—K3
	B—K3	Q×Q ch	K—Q1	Q—B3	B×P ch
11	B—Q3	B×Q	B—K2	P×P	K—Q2
	Kt—Q2 (l)	B×P	Kt—KB3	B×P	B—Kt4
12	Q R—K1	B×B	Q—B3	K—Kt2	P—B4
	Kt×Kt	P×B	Kt—B3	P—B3	B—R3
13	B×Kt	Kt—B3	P—B3+	B×B	Kt—B3
	B×B			Q×B	B—Kt2
14	R×B (m)			Q—Q2 +	P—B5+

(a) Paulsen's Defence.

(b) 14 O—O, P—KR4; 15 Kt—B3 (if 15 B—Kt5, P—B3; 16 R×P, Kt×R; 17 B×Kt, K R—K1. Schlechter), P—KB4; 16 Q R—B1, R—Q2; 17 P—Q5, P×P; 18 Kt—Kt5 ± (Lärobok, 1921).

(c) 7 Kt—QB3, P—Q3; 8 Kt—Q3, O—O; 9 Kt×P, Kt×P; 10 Kt×Kt, R—K1; 11 K—B2, R×Kt; 12 P—B3, Q—B3; 13 P—K Kt3.

(d) 10 Kt—K2, P—QB4; 11 P—B3, P×P; 12 P×P, Kt—Q2; 13 Kt×Kt, B×Kt+. Steinitz—Zukertort, Vienna, 1882.

(e) 14 B—Kt3, Kt×F; 15 B×Kt, B×Kt+. Analysis by Cordel and Schlechter.

(f) Stoltz—Sämisch, Swinemünde, 1932. White won.

Notes ctd n p. 99.

KING'S KNIGHT'S GAMBIT
1 P—K 4, P—K 4 ; 2 P—K B 4, P×P ; 3 Kt—K B 3, P—K Kt 4 ;
4 B—B 4.

	26	27	28	29	30
4	B—Kt 2				P—Kt 5
5	O—O			P—K R 4 (f)	Kt—K 5 (i)
	P—Q 3			P—K R 3	Q—R 5 ch
6	P—Q 4			P—Q 4	K—B 1
	P—K R 3			P—Q 3	Kt—Q B 3
7	P—B 3 (a)			Kt—B 3 (g)	B×P ch (j)
	Kt—Q B 3		Kt—K 2	Kt—Q B 3	K—K 2
8	P—K Kt 3		P—K Kt 3	Kt—K 2	Kt×Kt ch
	B—R 6	P—Kt 5	P—Kt 5	Q—K 2	Q P×Kt
9	P×P	Kt—R 4	Kt—R 4	Q—Q 3	B×Kt
	B×R	P—B 6	P—B 6	B—Q 2	R×B
10	Q×B	Q—Kt 3 (c)	Kt×P (e)	B—Q 2	Q—K 1
	P×P	Q—K 2	P×Kt	O—O—O	P—Kt 6
11	B×P	Kt—B 5	Q×P	B—B 3	P—Q 4
	Q—B 3	B×Kt	O—O	R—K 1	P—B 6
12	B—K Kt 3	P×B	B×P ch	P—Q 5	P—K R 3
	O—O—O	Kt—Q 1 (d)	K—R 1	Kt—K 4	B—Kt 5
13	Q Kt—Q 2	B—B 4	Q—R 5	Kt×Kt	Q—K 3
	K Kt—K 2	Kt—K B 3	Kt—Kt 1	P×Kt	R-Kt 3+ (k)
14	Q—R 3 ch	Kt—Q 2	P—K 5	O—O—O	
	K—Kt 1	O—O	P×P+	Kt—B 3+ (h)	
15	R—K B 1	P—K R 3			
	Q—Kt 3	P—K R 4			
16	Kt—R 4	B—Q 3			
	Q—Kt 4 (b)				

(a) If 7 Kt—B 3, Schlechter advises 7 . ., B—K 3 followed eventually by O—O—O. If 7 P—K Kt 3, P—Kt 5 ; 8 Kt—R 4, P—B 6 ; 9 P—B 3, B—B 3 ; 10 Kt×P, P×Kt ; 11 Q×P, Q—K 2+.

(b) Spielmann—Grünfeld, Carlsbad, 1923. The chances are even.

(c) 10 Kt—Q 2, B—B 3 ; 11 Q Kt×P, P×Kt ; 12 Q×P (Spielmann—Grünfeld, Teplitz-Schonau, 1922), B—R 6+.

(d) With 12 . ., O—O—O! ; 13 B×P, Q—K 7! Black can force a draw by 14 R—B 2, Q—K 8 ch ; 15 R—B 1, Q—K 7 ; for if 14 Q—K 6 ch?, R—Q 2! ; 15 R—B 2, Q—Q 8 ch+ (Nimzovitch) The column is Spielmann—Grünfeld, Vienna, 1922.

(e) 10 Kt—R 3, O—O ; 11 B—B 4, P—Q 4 (11 . ., P—R 3) ; 12 Kt—Kt 5 +. Réti—E. Cohn, Abbazia, 1912.

(f) The Calabrese-Philidor Gambit.

(g) Alternatives are 7 P×P, P×P ; 8 R×R, B×R ; 9 Kt—R 2. Or 7 P—B 3, P—Kt 5 ; 8 B×P, P×Kt ; 9 Q×P, B—K 3 ; 10 B×B, P×B ; 11 Q—R 5 ch, K—Q 2 ; 12 Q—Kt 4, Q—K 2+. Or 7 Q—Q 3, P—Kt 5 ; 8 Kt—Kt 1, Q—B 3 ; 9 P—B 3, P—K R 4 ; 10 Kt—Q R 3, Kt—K 2 ; 11 Kt—K 2. Marshall—Pillsbury, Vienna, 1903. 11 . ., B—R 3.

(h) Anderssen—Neumann, 1866.

(i) The Salvio Gambit.

(j) 7 Kt×B P, B—B 4 ; 8 Q—K 1, P—Kt 6 ; 9 Kt×R, B—B 7 ; 10 Q—Q 1, Kt—B 3+. Or 7 P—Q 4, Kt×Kt ; 8 P×Kt, B—B 4 ; 9 Q—K 1, P—Kt 6 ; 10 Kt—B3, P—Q 3 ; 11 P×Q P, P—B 6+.

(k) Dublin—Cambridge, correspondence, 1892.

MUZIO GAMBIT

1 P—K4, P—K4; 2 P—KB4, P×P; 3 Kt—KB3, P—KKt4; 4 B—B4, P—Kt5.

	31	32	33	34	35
5	O—O P×Kt				P—Q4 (k)
6	Q×P Q—B3			Q—K2	P×P P×Kt
7	P—K5 (a) Q×P			P—Q4 (i) Kt—QB3	Q×P B—Q3
8	P—Q3 (b) B—R3			Kt—B3 Kt×P	P—Q3 Kt—K2 (l)
9	Kt—B3 Kt—K2			Q—Q3 Kt—K3	B×P B×B
10	B—Q2 QKt—B3		P—QB3	Kt—Q5 Q—B4 ch	Q×B O—O
11	QR—K1 Q—B4	Q—B4 ch	QR—K1 Q—B4 ch	K—R1 P—Kt4	Kt—B3 Kt—Kt3
12	Kt—Q5 K—Q1	K—R1 K—Q1 (f)	K—R1 P—Q4	B—Kt3 B—KR3	Q—Kt3 Kt—Q2
13	Q—K2 (c) Q—K3	QB×P Kt—Q5	Q—R5 Q—Q3	B—Q2 Q—B1 (j)	QR—K1 K—Kt2 (m)
14	Q—B2 (d) Q—B4 (e)	Q—B2 B×B	B×QP P×B	Q—QB3	Kt—Kt5 P—QB3
15	Q—K2 Q—K3	Q×B Kt—K3	Kt—Kt5 Q—QKt3		Kt—B7 R—QKt1
16		Q—B6 R—K1 (g)	B—Kt4 Kt—B3		P×P P×P
17		Kt—Q5+	Kt—Q6 ch K—Q2 (h)		R×P ch+

(a) 7 P—Q3, B—R3; 8 Kt—B3, Kt—K2; 9 B×P, B×B; 10 Q×B, Q×Q, 11 R×Q, P—KB4; 12 P×P, P—B3. F. Edmonds suggests 7 P—B3, P—Q3; 8 P—Q4, B—R3; 9 Kt—R3, Kt—K2; 10 B—Q3, O—O.

(b) 8 B×P ch, K×B; 9 P—Q4, Q×P ch; 10 B—K3, Q—Kt2+ (Rev. T. Hamilton).

(c) Lean's Attack. If 13..., Kt×Kt; 14 B×Kt, Q×B; 15 B—B3+.

(d) 14 Kt×Kt, Q×Q; 15 Kt×Kt ch, Kt P×Kt; 16 R×Q ±. If 14..., Q×Kt; 15 Q—R5. Q—Kt4; 16 Q×P, R—B1; 17 Q×R ch+. Analysis by Tchigorin and W. T. Pierce.

(e) 14.., Q—Kt5; 15 P—KR3, Q--Kt3; 16 B×P+ (Znosko-Borovsky).

(f) 12.., O—O; 13 B×P, B—Kt2; 14 B—K3, Kt—Q5; 15 B×P ch, K—R1; 16 Q—K4, K Kt—B3; 17 Kt—Q5, Q—R4; 18 P—B3, Kt—K3; 19 R—B5+ (Lärobok).

(g) Maróczy and Meergrün—Tartakover and Frankl, consultation, 1920.

(h) 18 B—R3!, B—Kt2; 19 Q—Kt4 ch, K—B2; 20 Q×P, B—Kt4; 21 R×B, Kt×R; 22 Q×Kt, Kt—Kt3; 23 Q—Kt3+ (better still 23 Kt—Kt5 ch, Nimzovitch). Sämisch and others—Gunter and others, Hanover, 1926. At move 15 in the column Kt×P was previously considered White's best line.

(i) 7 Q×P, Q—B4 ch; 8 P—Q4, Q×P ch; 9 B—K3, Q×B; 10 Q—K5 ch, Q—K3; 11 Q×R, Q—K Kt3+. F. Edmonds suggests 7 P—QKt3, B—Kt2; 8 Kt—B3.

(j) Steinitz—Anderssen, London, 1862.

(k) Brentano's Defence. The column and notes are from the Handbuch.

(l) Alternatives are (1) 8.., B—KB4; 9 B×P, B—Kt3; 10 Kt—B3, Kt—K2; 11 QR—K1, B×B; 12 Q×B, O—O, 13 Kt—K4. (2) 8.., Q—Kt4; 9 Kt—B3, B—KKt5; 10 Q—K4 ch, Q—K2; 11 B×P+.

(m) 13..., Kt—Kt3; 14 B—Kt3, Q—Q3 (if 14.., B—Q2; 15 Kt—K4); 15 Q×Q, P×Q; 16 Kt—Kt5, R—Q1; 17 Kt—B7, R—Kt1; 18 R—K8 ch+.

MUZIO GAMBIT

1 P—K 4, P—K 4 ; 2 P—K B 4, P×P ; 3 Kt—K B 3, P—K Kt 4;
4 B—B 4, P—Kt 5.

	36	37	38	39	40
5	(O—O)	....	Kt—B 3 (d)..	P—Q 4 (h)...	B×P ch (k)
	(P—Q 4)		P×Kt	P×Kt	K×B
6	B×P		Q×P	Q×P (i)	Kt-K 5 ch (l)
	P×Kt......	P—Q B 3	P—Q 3 (e)	P—Q 4	K—K 1
7	Q×P	B×K B P ch	P—Q 4 (f)	B×Q P	Q×P
	P—Q B 3 (a)	K×B	B—K 3	Kt—K B 3	Kt—K B 3
8	Q×P	Kt—K 5 ch	Kt—Q 5	O—O	Q×P
	Kt—B 3	K—K 1	P—Q B 3	P—B 3	P—Q 3
9	Kt—B 3	P—Q 4	O—O	Kt—B 3	Kt—K B 3
	B—K 2	P—B 6	P×Kt	P×B	R—Kt 1
10	P—K 5	P×P	P×P	P×P	O—O
	P×B	B—Kt 2	B—B 4	B—Kt 2	R—Kt 5
11	P×Kt	P—K B 4	B×P	B×P	Q—K 3
	B—Q 3	Kt—K 2	B—Kt 3	O—O	R×P+ (m)
12	R—K 1 ch	P—B 3	B—Kt 5 ch	B—Kt 5	
	B—K 3	Kt—Kt 3	Kt—Q 2	Q—Kt 3	
13	Q—Kt 5	Kt×Kt P	Q R—K 1 ch	B×Kt	
	B—B 4 ch	Q—R 5	B—K 2	B×B	
14	K—R 1	P—B 5+ (c)	B×P	Q×B	
	Kt –Q 2		Q—Kt 3	Q×Q+ (j)	
	Kt×P+ (b)		Q—Q R 3 (g)		

(a) 7 ., Kt—K B 3, 8 Q×P, B—K 2 ; 9 Kt—B 3, O—O ; 10 P—Q 3. Aurbach—Spielmann, Abbazia, 1912.

(b) Analysis by F. Edmonds.

(c) Analysis by Marco.

(d) MacDonell's attack.

(e) 6.., P—Q 4 ; 7 Kt×P, Kt—Q B 3 ; 8 O—O, B—B 3, 9 P—Q 4, Kt×P ;
10 Q—R 5, B—K 3 ; 11 B×P, B×B ; 12 Kt×B, B×B ; 13 Q—K 5 ch. Charousek
and Fähndrich—Halprin and Marco, consultation, 1897

(f) 7 O—O, B—K 3 ; 8 Kt—Q 5, P—Q B 3 ; 9 Q—B 3, P×Kt ; 10 Q×R, P×B ;
11 Q×Kt, Q—Kt 3 ch (J. Malchin, 1912).

(g) 15.., Q×P ch ; 16 K—R 1, B—K 5 ; 17 Q—R 3, P—B 4 (Maróczy).

(h) Ghulam Kassim's Attack.

(i) 6 B×P, P—Q 4 ; 7 B×Q P, Kt—K B 3. If 6.., P×P ; 7 B×P ch, K×B ;
8 Q—R 5 ch, K—K 2 ; 9 Kt—B 3, P×R=Q ch. 12 K—B 2+.

(j) Handbuch, 1913.

(k) The " Wild Muzio."

(l) 6 O—O, P×Kt ; 7 Q×P (the Double Muzio), P—Q 3 ; 8 Q×P ch, Kt—B 3 ;
9 P—Q 4, Kt—B 3 ; 10 Kt—B 3, B—Kt 2+.

(m) Analysis by Dr. E. von Schmidt.

Notes for cols. 1 to 10 ctd.

(i) Réti—Nyholm, Abbazia, 1912.

(j) If 6 P×P *e.p.*, B×P; 7 P—B 4, P—Q B 4; 8 P—Q 5, B—Kt 5; 9 B—K 2
B×Kt; 10 B×B, Q—R 5 ch+. Grob—Naegeli, match, 1933–34.

(k) Gumzsrich—Rellstab, Berlin, 1933.

(l) The Cunningham Gambit.

(m) If 5 P—K Kt 3, P×P; 6 O—O, P—Q 4; 7 B×P, Kt—K B 3; 8 B×P ch,
K×B; 9 P—K 5, B—R 6; 10 P×Kt, B×R+.

(n) The Quaade Gambit. An alternative is 4 P—Q 4 (Rosentreter Gambit),
P—Kt 5; 5 Kt—K 5, Q—R 5 ch; 6 P—Kt 3, P×P; 7 Q×P, Q×Q. In both gambits,
4.., B—Kt 2 leads to the Berlin Defence.

(o) If 7.., P—Kt 7 dis ch; 8 Q×Q, P×R=Q; 9 Q—R 5+.

Notes for cols. 16 to 25 ctd.

(g) 7.., B—Kt 2; 8 P—Q 4, Kt—R 4, transposing into col. 17, is safest for Black.

(h) The Rice Gambit.

(i) 14 B—R 3, Kt—B 6 ch; 15 P×Kt, Q×P; 16 R—K 5, B—B 4; 17 Kt—Q 2,
Q—Kt 6 ch; 18 K—B 1, Q—R 7; 19 B×R, P—Kt 6; 20 B—B 5, P—Kt 7 ch.
Analysis by Capablanca, Burn, and Ed. Lasker.

(j) 14 P—K 5, P×P; 15 Kt—Q 5, Q—B 5!; 16 Kt×Q, K B×Kt; 17 Q×P,
B×Q; 18 Kt×B+. *Larobok*, 1921.

(k) Brentano's Defence.

(l) 11.., P—K B 3; 12 Q R—K 1, B×Kt; 13 B×B, K—Q 2; 14 B×K B P+

(m) 14.., Q—Q 2; 15 B—B 5, O—O—O; 16 B×B, P×B (Schlechter); 17 Q—K 2,
P—K R 4; 18 K R—B 1 (Rubinstein).

(n) Neumann's Defence. The column is from *Lärobok*, 1921.

(o) 7.., B—K 2; 8 B×P, B×P ch; 9 P—Kt 3, B—Kt 4; 10 R×P, R×R;
11 B×P ch, K—B 1; 12 B×R, B×B; 13 Kt—Kt 6 ch+.

KING'S GAMBIT DECLINED

THE customary method of declining the King's Gambit gives rise to positions of great complexity, frequently reacting to the detriment of the second player, who, under the stress of match-play, would be well advised to select instead one of the excellent lines at his disposal in the Gambit Accepted. But the number of times that, in modern master-play, Black is called upon to make a choice of how to defend is strictly limited by the fact that he hardly ever has the Gambit offered to him.

The usual defence 2..., B—B 4 (cols. 1 to 10) gives White chances of a successful attack on the King's Bishop's file after neutralising the restraining influence of Black's King's Bishop. The interesting variations in cols. 1 to 4, which have given rise to some of the most brilliant games on record, are now very seldom encountered. The line in col. 2, beginning with 7..., Kt—Q 5, is the best for Black; but he would be well advised to avoid these variations by the earlier 6..., B—K 3 (col. 5), recommended first by Tarrasch and then by Alekhine.

The most promising continuation for the attack, however, is that which begins 4 P—B 3 (cols. 8 and 9), a favourite in Morphy's days and with that great master himself, and now again in favour with the experts. Col. 10 shows what appears to be Black's strongest defence.

The Falkbeer Counter-Gambit, 2...,P—Q 4 (cols. 11 to 20), had a strenuous advocate in Tarrasch, whose sensational victory with it over Spielmann in 1923 (see col. 11, note (b)) caused the latter to write—prematurely, it is true—of the demolition of the King's Gambit. Since our last edition White's attack has been strengthened by the totally new variations in cols. 12 and 13, due to Keres, where White always obtains a clear superiority.

In addition, Keres and Stoltz have shown that the line in col. 15, which had been considered unfavourable for White since the celebrated game Leonhardt—Marshall, San Sebastian, 1911, is with best play as good as won for the first player.

Since Black's other defences have long been refuted, some considerable improvements will have to be found before the Falkbeer Counter-Gambit can again be considered playable.

Attention may be drawn to the interesting line in col. 20, introduced by P. S. Milner-Barry.

1 P—K 4, P—K 4; 2 P—K B 4, B—B 4, 3 Kt—K B 3, P—Q 3; 4 Kt—B 3, Kt—K B 3; 5 B—B 4, Kt—B 3; 6 P—Q 3.

	1	2	3	4	5
6	B—K Kt 5				B—K 3 !
7	Kt—Q R 4................		P—K R 3		B—Kt 5 (j)
	B×Kt......	Kt—Q 5	B×Kt		P—Q R 3
8	Q×B	Kt×B	Q×B		B×Kt ch
	Kt—Q 5	P×Kt	Kt—Q 5 (f)		P×B
9	Q—Kt 3 (a)	P×P (d)	Q—Kt 3		Q—K 2 (k)
	Kt×P ch	Kt—Q 2	Kt×P ch....	Q—K 2	P×P
10	K—Q 1	B—B 4	K—Q 1	P×P	B×P
	Kt×R	Q—K 2	Kt×R	P×P	Q—Kt 1 !
11	Q×P	O—O	Q×P	K—Q 1	Kt—Q 1
	R—K B 1	O—O—O	R—K B 1	P—B 3	O—O
12	Kt×B	Q—Q 2	P×P	P—Q R 4	P—B 3
	P×Kt	B×Kt	P×P	R—K Kt 1 (h)	R—K 1
13	P×P	P×B	B—Kt 5	R—B 1	B—K 3
	Kt×P (b)	P—K Kt 4	B—K 2	P—K R 3	B×B
14	B—K R 6	B—Kt 3	R—B 1	Kt—K 2	Kt×B
	Q—K 2	P—K R 4	P—B 3	O—O—O	Kt—Kt 5
15	R—B 1	P—B 3	R×Kt	Kt×Kt	O—O
	O—O—O	P—R 5	B×R	B×Kt	Q—Kt 3
16	Q—Kt 4 ch	P×Kt	B×B+ (g)	P—B 3	Kt—Q 4
	K—Kt 1	P×B		B—Kt 3	Kt×Kt
17	B×R	R P×P		P—R 5+ (i)	Q×Kt
	Q×P (c)	P×P (e)			P—Q B 4 ⇒

(a) 9 Q—Q 1, P—Q Kt 4; 10 Kt×B, P×B; 11 B P×P, P×Kt; 12 P×Kt, Q×P+. Spielmann—Leonhardt, match, 1910.

(b) If 13.., Q—Q 2; 14 Q×Kt threatening B—K Kt 5 is decisive.

(c) 18 B—Kt 7, Q—K 2; 19 K—B 1+. The column from White's 15th move is analysis by H. B. Uber.

(d) Or 9 P—B 3!, Kt×Kt ch; 10 P×Kt, B—R 4; 11 Q—K 2, Q—Q 3; 12 P—B 5, P—K Kt 3. Spielmann—Bogatyrchuk, Moscow, 1925. Better 12 P×P, Q×K P; 13 P—K B 4, Q—K 2; 14 Q—Kt 2.

(e) Continued 18 Q—R 5, K—Kt 1; 19 P—K 6, P×P+. Spielmann—Rabinovitch, Moscow, 1925.

(f) 8.., P×P; 9 B×P (or 9 Q×P, Kt—K 4; 10 B—Kt 3, Kt—R 4; Rubinstein recommends 9 B—Kt 5!=), Kt—Q 5; 10 Q—Kt 3, Kt—R 4; 11 Q—Kt 4, Kt×B; 12 Q×Kt, Kt×P ch; 13 K—Q 1, Kt—K 6 ch followed by Kt×B+ (Svenonius).

(g) If 16.., Q—Q 3; 17 Kt—K 5+. Or 16.., Q—Q 5; 17 B×P ch+. Or 16.., Q—Q 2; 17 Q—Kt 5+. The analysis from White's 15th move is due to J. H. Blake.

(h) Better is 12.., O—O—O and if 13 Q×Kt P, K R—Kt 1; 14 Q×B P, Q×Q; 15 B×Q, R×P ∓. White plays best 13 R—B 1, with about equal chances.

(i) Rubinstein—Hromadka, Mahrisch-Ostrau, 1923.

(j) 7 Kt—Q 5, B×Kt; 8 P×B, Kt—Q 5; 9 P×P, P×P is favourable to Black (Kmoch). The column down to Black's 14th move is Spielmann—Tarrasch, Pistyan, 1922.

(k) 9 P—B 5?, B—B 1; 10 B—Kt 5, B—Kt 2; 11 Kt—K 2, Q—K 2; 12 Q—Q 2, P—Q 4; 13 P—B 3, O—O—O+. E. M. Jellie—M. E. Goldstein, 1923.

1 P—K 4, P—K 4; 2 P—KB 4, B—B 4; 3 Kt—KB 3, P—Q 3.

	6	7	8	9	10
4	(Kt—B 3)...Kt—B 3 (c)..P—B 3 (A)				
	(Kt—K B 3)	Kt—Q B 3	Kt—K B 3..B—K Kt 5..P—K B 4		
5	(B—B 4)	B—Kt 5 (d)	P×P	P×P	P×K P
	(Kt—B 3)	Kt—K 2	P×P	P×P	Q P×P
6	(P—Q 3)	P×P	P—Q 4 (f)	Q—R 4 ch! (h)	P—Q 4
	P—Q R 3 (a)	P×P	P×P	B—Q 2 (i)	K P×P
7	P×P	P—Q 3 (e)	P×P	Q—B 2	B—Q B 4
	P×P	O—O	B—Kt 5 ch	Kt—Q B 3 (j)	Kt-K B 3 (k)
8	B—K Kt 5	B—Kt 5	B—Q 2	P—Q Kt 4	P—K 5
	Q—Q 3	Q—Q 3	B×B ch	B—Q 3	Kt—K 5
9	B×Kt	Q—Q 2	Q Kt×B	B—B 4	P×P
	Q×B	Kt—Q 5	O—O	Kt—B 3	B—Kt5ch(l)
10	Kt—Q 5	B—Q B 4	B—Q 3	P—Q 3	K—K 2
	Q—Q 3	P—B 3=	P—B 4	Kt—K 2	P—B 3
11	Q—Q 2		P—Q 5	O—O	Q—Kt 3
	P—K R 3		B—Kt 5	Kt—Kt 3	Q—K 2
12	K R—B 1		O—O	P—Q R 4	Kt—B 3
	B—K 3= (b)		Q Kt—Q 2 (g)		B×Kt= (m)

(a) 6 , Kt—Q 5; 7 P×P, Kt—Kt 5; 8 Kt×Kt, B×Kt; 9 P—K 6, Q—R 5 ch;
10 P—Kt 3, B—B 7 ch; 11 K—K 2, Q—R 4; 12 P—K R 3, Kt—K 6 ch; 13 P—Kt 4+.
P. S. Milner-Barry—Sir G. A. Thomas, Hastings, 1933-34.

(b) Spielmann—Yates, Moscow, 1925.

(c) 4 P×P (the Soldatenkoff Attack), P×P; 5 P—B 3, Kt—Q B 3; 6 P—Q Kt 4,
B—Kt 3; 7 B—Kt 5, Kt—B 3; 8 Kt×P, O—O; 9 Kt×Kt, P×Kt; 10 B×P,
Kt×P+. Tartakover—Burn, Carlsbad, 1911.

(d) 5 B—B 4, B—K Kt 5; 6 P—K R 3, B×Kt; 7 Q×B, Q—R 5 ch (or 7.., P×P;
8 Q×P, Q—B 3); 8 P—Kt 3, Kt—Q 5; 9 Q—Kt 2, Q—R 4.

(e) If 7 Kt×P, O—O gives Black a strong attack.

(f) 6 Kt×P, Q—K 2; 7 P—Q 4, B—Q 3; 8 Kt—B 3, Kt×P; 9 B—K 2, O—O;
10 O—O, P—Q B 4; 11 Q Kt—Q 2, Kt×Kt ∓. Charousek—Janowski, Berlin, 1897.

(g) 13 Q—B 2 ±. Spielmann—Van Scheltinga, Amsterdam, 1938.

(h) Marshall's Variation. The column to Black's 11th move is Spielmann—
Tarrasch, 1923.

(i) If 6.., Kt—B 3; 7 Kt×P, Q—R 5 ch; 8 P—Kt 3, B—B 7 ch; 9 K×B,
Q—B 3 ch; 10 K—Kt 1, Q×Kt; 11 B—Kt 2+ (Spielmann).

(j) 7.., Q—K 2; 8 P—Q 4, P×P; 9 P×P, B—Kt 5 ch; 10 Kt—B 3, B—B 3;
11 B—Q 3, B×Kt ch; 12 P×B, B×P; 13 B×B, P—K B 4; 14 O—O, P×B;
15 Q—Kt 3 ch+. Euwe—Maróczy, match, 1921.

(k) If 7.., B P×P; 8 Kt—K 5, Kt—K B 3; 9 Kt—B 7, Q—K 2; 10 Kt×R,
P—Q 6; 11 B—Kt 5, B—B 7 ch; 12 K×B, Q—B 4 ch; 13 B—K 3, Q×B;
14 P—K R 3, B—K 3; 15 Kt—Q 2+. Stoltz—Spielmann, match, 1932.

(l) 9 ., B—Kt 3; 10 Kt—B 3, Kt—Q B 3; 11 B—K 3, Kt—R 4; 12 B—Q 3+.
Réti—Hromadka, Pistyan, 1922.

(m) Stoltz—Flohr, match, 1931.

(A) 4 P—Q Kt 4 (Heath's Variation), B—Kt 3; 5 P—B 4, B—Q 5; 6 Kt×B,
P×Kt; 7 P—Q 3, P—Q B 4; 8 P×P, P×P; 9 B—K 2, Q—R 5 ch=. C. B. Heath—
Dr. R Macdonald, Glasgow, 1923.

FALKBEER COUNTER GAMBIT

1 P—K4, P—K4; 2 P—KB4, P—Q4; 3 KP×P, P—K5;
4 P—Q3 (A).

	11	12	13	14	15
4	Kt—KB3			Q×P	P×P
5	P×P	Kt—Q2! (c)		Q—K2	Q×P (h)
	Kt×KP	B—KB4 (d)	.P—K6	Kt—KB3	Kt—KB3
6	Kt—KB3	P×P	Kt—B4	Kt—QB3	Kt—QB3
	B—QB4	Kt×KP	Kt×P (i)	B—QKt5	B—QB4 (l)
7	Q—K2	KKt—B3 (e)	Kt×P	B—Q2	B—Q2
	B—B4 (a)	P—QB3? (f)	Kt×P	B×Kt	O—O
8	Kt—B3! (b)	Kt—Q4	P—KKt3	B×B	O—O—O
	Q—K2	B—Kt3 (g)	Kt—Kt3	B—Kt5	QKt—Q2
9	B—K3	Q—K2	B—Kt2	P×P	P—KKt3!
	B×B	B—Kt5	B—Q3	Q×KP	Kt—Kt3
10	Q×B	P—B3	Kt—B3	Q×Q ch	B—Kt2
	Kt×Kt	O—O	O—O	Kt×Q	B—KKt5
11	Q×Q ch	Kt×Kt	O—O	B×P	Kt—B3
	K×Q	B×Kt	Kt—B3	R—Kt1	QKt×P
12	P×Kt	P×B	K—R1	B—K5	P—KR3
	B×P	R—K1	P—B4	Kt—QB3	Kt×Kt
13	Kt—Q4	B—K3	Kt—B4!	B—Q3	Q×Kt
	B—K5	Kt—R3	P—B5	Kt×B	B×Kt
14	Kt—Kt5	Q—Q2	Kt×B	B×Kt	B×B
	Kt—R3	B×QP	P×Kt	Kt—B5 (j)	Q—Q3
15	P—B4=	B×Kt+ (h)	B×P ±	B×KtP+	Q-Kt3+ (m)

(a) If 7. , B—B7ch; 8 K—Q1, Q×Pch; 9 KKt—Q2 (Alapin's Variation), P—KB4; 10 Kt—B3, Q—Q5; 11 Kt×Kt, P×Kt; 12 P—B3, Q—K6; 13 Q—R5ch, K—B1; 14 O—QB4+. Réti—Breyer, Budapest, 1921. 7.., P—B4 is also bad.

(b) 8 P—KKt4, O—O; 9 P×B, R—K1; 10 B—Kt2, Kt—B7; 11 Kt—K5, Kt×R; 12 B×Kt, Kt—Q2; 13 Kt—QB3, P—KB3+. Spielmann—Tarrasch, Mährisch-Ostrau, 1923.

(c) The Keres Variation.

(d) Recommended by Keres as best. If 5.., P×P; 6 B×P, Kt×P; 7 Kt—K4!, B—K2; 8 Kt—KB3, Kt—Q2; 9 O—O, P—QB3; 10 K—R1, QKt—B3; 11 Kt—K5+. Keres—Malmgren, correspondence, 1934. Or 5.., Q×P?; 6 P×P, Kt×P; 7 B—B4, Q—QB4; 8 Q—K2, P—B4; 9 Kt×Kt, P×Kt; 10 Q×Pch, B—K2; 11 Kt—B3+. Ketting—Van Nuss, Rotterdam, 1936.

(e) 7Q—K2, Q—K2; 8 KKt—B3, Kt—Q2; 9 Kt—Kt3, O—O—O; 10 B—K3. Q—Kt5ch; 11 B—Q2, Kt×B ∓.

(f) B—QKt5 is a sufficient defence (Dr. von Claparède). See also B.C.M., 1937, p. 466.

(g) 8 ., Kt×Kt; 9 Kt×B, Kt—K5; 10 B—B4, B—B4; 11 Kt—K3 would leave White with only a minimal advantage (Keres).

(h) Keres—Zirker, correspondence, 1935.

(i) 6 ., P—QKt4; 7 Kt×P, B—Q3; 8 Q—B3, O—O; 9 B—Q2, B—QB4; 10 B—K2+. Ketting—V d Vaart, correspondence, 1938. The column is Keres—Stalda, correspondence, 1933-34.

(j) Réti—Tarrasch, Gothenburg, 1920.

(k) 5 B×P, Q×P?; 6 Kt—QB3, Q—K3ch; 7 KKt—K2, Kt—KB3; 8 O—O, Q×Kt3ch; 9 K—R1, B—K2; 10 Q—K1, Kt—B3; 11 P—QR3, O—O; 12 P—QKt4+. Keres—Vidmar, correspondence, 1936.

(l) 6 , B—QKt5; 7 B—Q2, O—O; 8 O—O—O, QKt—Q2; 9 B—K2 (9 P—KKt3!, as in the text), Kt—Kt3; 10 B—B3, B—Kt5 ∓. Leonhardt—Marshall, San Sebastian, 1911.

(m) Stoltz—Marshall, Folkestone, 1933.

(A) Tartakover discusses the alternatives : (1) Kt—QB3; (2) P—Q4; (3) Q—K2, (4) P—KKt3 in Die Hypermoderne Schachpartie, 1924.

FALKBEER COUNTER GAMBIT
1 P—K 4, P—K 4 ; 2 P—K B 4, P—Q 4.

	16	17	18	19	20
3	(K P×P)................		Kt—K B 3..	P—Q 4......	Kt—QB3 (j)
	(P—K 5).....	P—QB3 (c)	Q P×P	P×Q P	P—Q 5
4	B—Kt 5 ch	Kt—QB3 (d)	Kt×P	Q×P	Q Kt—K 2
	P—B 3	K P×P (e)	Kt—Q 2 (g)	Kt—KB3 (h)	B—K Kt 5
5	P×P	Kt—B 3	P—Q 4	P×P	P—Q 3
	Kt×P (a)	Kt—B 3	P×P e.p.	Q×P	B—Q 3
6	P—Q 3	P—Q 4	Kt×Q P	Kt—K B 3	P×P
	Kt—B 3	Kt×P	K Kt—B 3	Kt—B 3	B×P
7	Kt—Q B 3	Kt×Kt	Q—B 3	Q—K 3 ch	Q—Q 2
	B—Q Kt 5	Q×Kt	B—K 2	Q—K 5	Kt—Q B 3
8	B—Q 2	B×P	B—K 3	Kt—B 3	Kt—K B 3
	B—Kt 5	Q—K 5 ch	O—O	B—Q Kt 5	B×Kt
9	K Kt—K 2	Q—K 2	Kt—B 3	B—Q 3	P×B
	O—O !	Q×Q ch	Kt—Kt 3	Q×Q ch	Q—R 5 ch
10	P×P	B×Q	Kt—K 5	B×Q	K—Q 1
	B×Q Kt	B—K 2	B—K B 4	Kt—Q 4	P—K B 4 (k)
11	B×B	O—O	B—Q 3	B—Q 2	Q—Kt 5
	Kt×P	B—K 3	B×B	Kt×Kt ∓ (i)	Q×Q
12	Q×Q	P—B 4	O—O—O+		B×Q
	Q R×Q (b)	O—O (f)			P-KR3 ∓ (l)

(a) 5.., P×P; 6 B—B 4, Kt—B 3; 7 P—Q 3 (7 P—Q 4, B—Q 3; 8 Kt—K 2, O—O; 9 O—O, P—B 4; 10 P—Q 5, Q Kt—Q 2; 11 B—Kt 3, P—B 5; 12 B×P, B—B 4 ch+. Tchigorin—Pillsbury, Vienna, 1898), B—Q B 4; 8 Kt—K 2, B—K Kt 5; 9 Q Kt—B 3, P×P; 10 Q×P, Q—Kt 3; 11 B—Q 2, B—B 7 ch; 12 K—B 1, P—Q R 4; 13 Kt—R 4, Q—R 2; 14 B—B 3+ (L. Godai).

(b) 13 B×Kt, P×B; 14 B—Kt 4, P—B 4 ∓. Analysis by L. Godai, *Wiener Schachzeitung*, 1930.

(c) Nimzovitch's Variation. If 3. , P×P; 4 Q—B 3, Kt—K B 3; 5 B—Kt 5 ch, B—Q 2; 6 Kt—B 3, B—Q Kt 5; 7 K Kt—K 2, O—O; 8 B×B, Q Kt×B; 9 O—O, Kt—Kt 3; 10 Kt×P+. Réti—Rubinstein, Stockholm, 1919.

(d) 4 P×B P, Kt×P; 5 P—Q 3, B—Q B 4!; 6 Kt—Q B 3, Kt—B 3; 7 Kt—B 3 O—O; 8 P×P, Kt×P!+. F. Lazard—Tartakover, Paris, 1929.

(e) If 4.., B—Q Kt 5; 5 Kt—B 3, B×Kt; 6 Q P×B, P—K 5; 7 Kt—K 5, P×P; 8 B—Kt 5 ch, K—B 1; 9 B—K 3 (Rubinstein). Or 4.., B P×P; 5 P×P, P—Q 5; 6 Kt—K 4, Q—Q 4; 7 B—Q 3, Kt—Q B 3; 8 Q—K 2, Kt—R 3; 9 B—B 4, Q—R 4; 10 Kt—K B 3, B—K Kt 5; 11 Kt—Q 6 ch+. Opocensky—P. Johner, Baden, 1914.

(f) 13 Kt—Kt 5! ±. Stoltz—Brinckmann, Swinemünde, 1932.

(g) The following alternatives are inferior: (1) 4.., Kt—K B 3 ; 5 B—B 4, B—Q B 4; 6 B×P ch, K—K 2 ; 7 B—Kt 3, R—K 1 ; 8 Q—K 2, K—B 1 ; 9 Q—B 4+. (2) 4 ., Kt—Q B 3; 5 B—Kt 5, Kt—B 3 ; 6 Q—K 2+. Tartakover—T. Gruber, Vienna, 1919. 4.., B—Q 3 is playable, for if 5 Q—K 2, Q—K 2 ; 6 Q×P, P—K B 3. The column is analysis by Tartakover.

(h) 4.., Kt—Q B 3 ; 5 Q×Q P, Q×Q; 6 P×Q, Kt—Kt 5 ; 7 Kt—R 3, Kt×Q P , 8 Kt—B 4, B—K B 4 ; 9 P—B 3, O—O—O ∓. Dr. von Claparède.

(i) Tartakover—Grunfeld, Vienna ,1923.

(j) Milner-Barry's Variation.

(k) 10.., O—O—O; 11 Q—Kt 5, Q×Q; 12 B—R 3 ch, K—Kt 1 ; 13 B×Q P—K B 3; 14 B—R 4 ±. Milner-Barry—Alexander, Margate, 1937.

(l) Milner-Barry—Keres, Margate, 1937.

MAX LANGE

THIS exceedingly complicated offshoot of the Giuoco Piano, named after the great German analyst of the last century, offers the first player limitless possibilities of brilliant combinations at the expense of a Pawn. So difficult is Black's game that no master was found willing to defend the position after Marshall's games against Tarrasch in 1910 and Leonhardt in 1911. But the well-known correspondence-player, M. Seibold, in the *Deutsche Schachzeitung* for 1935 advanced strong arguments against the soundness of White's attack. See col. 1, notes (*e*) and (*f*).

The characteristic position after Black's 7th move, shown in cols. 1 to 11, is generally reached by transposition from the Bishop's Opening, Centre Game, Scotch Gambit, or Two Knights' Defence. In the most usual form of the opening (cols. 1 to 9), Black has the choice on his 9th move of two replies :—

(i) 9..., Q—Q 4 (cols. 1 to 6), which was considered to give Black the better game until the strength of Marshall's innovation, 15 B—R 6! (col. 1), was realised. After the usual moves, 10 Kt—Q B 3, Q—B 4; 11 Q Kt—K 4, Black's position is certainly very difficult. A plausible suggestion for the defence is 11..., B—K B 1 (cols. 3 to 5), but analysis is in favour of the first player, who recovers his Pawn and retains a powerful attack.

(ii) 9..., P—K Kt 3 (cols. 7 to 9), suggested by R. J. Loman, but untenable against either 10 Kt—Q 2 or 10 Q—B 3.

It seems doubtful whether Schlechter's simplifying variation, based on 9 P × P, is satisfactory against the best defence (col. 10). The variations based on 5..., B × P (cols. 14 and 15) spring from the Giuoco Piano, and yield White an indifferent game, as he loses a Pawn with little compensation.

1 P—K 4, P—K 4 ; 2 Kt—K B 3, Kt—Q B 3 ; 3 B—B 4, B—B 4;
    4 O—O, Kt—B 3 ; 5 P—Q 4.

5.., P×P ; 6 P—K 5, P—Q 4 ; 7 P×Kt, P×B ; 8 R—K 1 ch,
B—K 3 ; 9 Kt—Kt 5, Q—Q 4 ; 10 Kt—Q B 3, Q—B 4;
    11 Q Kt—K 4 (a).

	1	2	3	4	5
11	O—O—O		B—K B 1 (g)		
12	K Kt×B....P—K Kt 4		Kt×B P !		.......P—K Kt 4
	P×Kt	Q—K 4	K×Kt		Q×P ch !
13	P—K Kt 4	Kt—K B 3	Kt—Kt 5 ch		Q×Q
	Q—K 4	Q—Q 4	K—Kt 1 ....K—Kt 3		B×Q
14	P×P	P×P	P—K Kt 4	P×P	P×P
	K R—Kt 1	B×P !	Q—Q 4 (h)	B×P	B×P
15	B—R 6 !	P×R=Q	Kt×B (A)	R×B ch	Kt—B 6 ch
	P—Q 6 (b)	R×Q	R—B 1	B—B 3	K—B 1
16	P—Q B 3	Kt—B 6	Kt—B 4	P—K Kt 4	K Kt×P ch
	P—Q 7 (c)	Q×Kt	Q—B 2 (i)	Q—Q 4	R×Kt [(l)
17	R—K 2	Kt×B	P×P	Kt—R 3 !	Kt×R ch
	R—Q 6 ! (d)	Q×Q	B×P	K—Kt 2	K—Kt 1
18	Q—K B 1 (e)	R×Q	Kt—R 5	Kt—B 4	Kt—Kt 5
	B—Kt 3	R—Kt 1	P—K R 3	Q—Q 2	Kt—Kt 5
19	R—Q 1	P—K R 3	P—B 4	Kt—R5ch+	R—K 7
	Kt—Q 1	P—K R 4 =	K—R 2	(k)	Kt×B P
20	P—Kt 5		Q—B 3		R—Kt 1
	Kt—B 2		K R—K 1		B—R 4
21	Kt—Kt 3 !		B—Q 2 + (j)		R×Q B P
	Q—Q 4 (f)				P—Kt 4 (m)

(a) 11 P—K Kt 4, Q—Kt 3 , 12 Q Kt—K 4, B—Kt 3 ; 13 P—B 4, O—O—O ;
14 P—B 5, B×P ; 15 P×B, Q×P (B 4). Blackburne—Teichmann, Nuremberg, 1896.
(b) If 15.., B—K 2 ; 16 Q—B 3, with a continuation similar to note (c), looks
good, or 16 Kt—Kt 5, Q—Q 4 ; 17 Kt×K P, Kt—K 4 ; 18 R×Kt, Q×R ; 19 Kt×R
(J. H. Blake).
(c) 16.., B—Q 3 ?; 17 P—B 4, Q—Q 4 ; 18 Q—B 3, B—K 2 ; 19 P—Kt 5,
Q—K B 4 (Q R—K 1, or R—Q 2, so as to allow Kt—Q 1 may be better) ; 20 Kt—Kt 3,
Q—B 2 (Q—R 6, Alapin ; or Q—Kt 4, *Deutsche Schachblatter*) ; 21 Q—Kt 4 !+.
Marshall—Tarrasch, Hamburg, 1910. If 16.., B—K 2 , 17 Q—B 3 !, Q—Q 4 ; 18 Q—B 3,
where M. Seibold gives the continuation B—R 5 ; 19 Q R—Q 1, Kt—K 4 ; 20 Q—B 4,
Kt—Kt 3 ; 21 Q—B 7, Kt—K 4, etc.
(d) 17 , B—Kt 3 ; 18 Q—K B 1, R—Q 6 ; 19 R—Q 1, Kt—Q 1 ; 20 P—Kt 5,
Kt—B 2 ; 21 Q—Kt 2 (Marshall—Leonhardt, 1st match game, 1911). 21 Kt—Kt 3, as
in the column, is a later improvement.
(e) 18 Kt×B, Q×Kt ; 19 R×P (Q 2)!, Kt—K 4 ; 20 R×R, P×R ; 21 Q—R 4!,
Q—Q 4 ; 22 Q—K B 4, Kt—B 6 ch ; 23 K—B 1, R—Q 1 ; 24 Q—B 8, P—Q 7 ;
25 R—Q 1, Kt×P ch + (Seibold's analysis).
(f) 22 Q—R 3 (22 Q—Kt 2, Kt×P ; 23 Q×Q, Kt—R 6 ch, etc.), Kt—K 4, with the
better prospects (Seibold).
(g) Rubinstein's Defence.
(h) If 14.., Q—Kt 3 ; 15 P×P, K B×P ; 16 R×B, B—B 3 ; 17 Kt—K 4,
R—K B 1; 18 P—Kt 5+ (Tarrasch).
(i) 16 , Q—Q 2 ; 17 Q—K 2, P—Q Kt 4 ; 18 P—Q R 4, P—Q R 3 ; 19 R P×P,
R P×P ; 20 P—Kt 3+.
(j) Notes and column are from analysis by Tartakover in *Wiener Schachzeitung*, 1924.
(k) Analysis by V. Vukovitch.
(l) 16 Kt×B, P—K R 4 ! +.
(m) 22 B—Q 2 (or P—B 4), B—Kt 3+. Analysis in Kagan's *Neueste Schachnach-richten*, 1922.
(A) 15 R×B !, P×P ; 16 R×P+. White has the important souare K B 5 for his
R and threatens Kt—B 7 (Tarrasch).

1 P—K 4, P—K 4;   2 Kt—K B 3, Kt—Q B 3;   3 B—B 4, B—B 4 ;   4 O—O, Kt—B 3;   5 P—Q 4.

5.., P×P;   6 P—K 5, P—Q 4;   7 P×Kt, P×B,   8 R—K 1 ch, B—K 3 (a).

	6	7	8	9	10
9	(Kt—Kt 5)......................				P×P (h)
	(Q—Q 4)	....P—K Kt3 (d)			R—K Kt 1
10	(Kt—Q B 3)	Kt—Q 2.....	Q—B 3 (g)		B—Kt 5
	(Q—B 4)	Q—Q 4	O—O		B—K 2
11	(Q Kt—K 4)	Q Kt—K 4	R×B		B×B
	B—Kt 3 (b)	O—O—O (e)	P×R		Q×B ! (l)
12	P×P (c)	Kt×Q B	P—B 7 ch		P—B 3 (m)
	R—K Kt 1	P×Kt	K—R 1		O—O—O
13	P—K Kt 4	Kt×B	Kt×K P		P×P
	Q—Kt 3	Q×Kt	Q—K 2		R×Kt P
14	Kt×B	B—R 6	B—Kt 5		Kt—B 3 (n)
	P×Kt	Q—B 4	Q×P.......	R×P	
15	B—Kt 5	Q—B 3 !	Kt×B	B×Q	
	R×P	P—K 4	QR—K1 (h)	R×Q	
16	Q—B 3	P—B 7	Kt—Q 2	B×B	
	K—Q 2	Q×Q	K—Kt 2	R—B 3	
17	Kt—B 6 ch	P×Q	K Kt—K 4	Kt×B P	
	K—B 1	K—Q 2	Q×Q	R—Q B 1	
18	R×P+	P—B 4	P×Q	Kt—Kt 5	
		P×P (f)	P—K R3 (i)	R—B 4 (j)	

(a) If 8 , K—B 1?; 9 B—Kt5, P×P; 10 B—R 6 ch, K—Kt 1; 11 Kt—B 3, B—K Kt 5; 12 Kt—K 4+.

(b) 11.., B—Q 3; 12 Kt×B P, O—O; 13 K Kt×B, P×Kt; 14 P×P, K×P; 15 Q—Q 2, Q R—Q 1; 16 Q—R 6 ch, K—R 1; 17 B—Kt 5, R—Q 2; 18 P—B 4, Q—B 2; 19 Kt—B 6, R—K 2; 20 Kt×P+.

(c) If 12 Kt—Kt 3, Q—Kt 3; 13 Kt×B, P×Kt; 14 R×P ch, K×P; 15 Kt—R 5 !, K R—K 1!; 16 Kt—B 4, Q—B 2; 17 Q—B 3, Q R—Q 1; 18 B—Q 2, P×P; 19 Q R—K 1 (Tchigorin—Charousek, Budapest, 1896). 19.., Kt—K 4!; 20 Q—Q 5 ch, K—B 1; 21 R×R, Q×R+.

(d) The Loman Defence.

(e) If 11.., K—Q 2; 12 Kt×Q B, P×Kt; 13 P—B 7+ ; or 11.., O—O; 12 K×Q B, P×Kt; 13 B—R 6+.

(f) 19 R—K 4, P—K Kt 4; 20 R—Q 1, Q R—K B 1; 21 B—Kt 7+. A. Olson—Spielmann, Stockholm, 1910.

(g) If 10 Q—Kt 4, Q—Q 4; 11 Kt—Q 2, K—Q 2; 12 Kt×B, P×Kt; 13 Kt—K 4, B—Q 3; 14 Kt×B, P×Kt; 15 B—R 6, Kt—K 4; 16 Q—Kt 5, K R—K 1; 17 R×Kt, Q×R; 18 P—B 7, R—K B 1; 19 Q×Q, P×Q, 20 B×R, R×B+ + Handbuch, 1913. 10 Kt×B, P×Kt; 11 R×P ch, K—B 2; 12 R—K 4, Q—Q 2; 13 Kt—B 3, Q R—K 1; 14 B—R 6, R—K 3; 15 R×R, Q×R; 16 Kt—R 4, B—Q 3+. E. W. Osler—P. W. Sergeant, 1922. If 10 R×B ch, P×R; 11 P—B 7 ch, K—Q 2; 12 Kt—K 4, B—K 2; 13 B—R 6, Kt—K 4; 14 B—Kt 7, Kt×P; 15 Q×P ch, K—K 1; 16 B×R, Q×Q, R—Q 1.

(h) Or 15.., Q×Q; 16 P×Q, R—B 4; 17 Kt—K 4, R—K 1 (if 17.., K—Kt 2; 18 Q Kt—Q 2, Kt—K 4; 19 P—B 4+); 18 Q Kt—Q 2, P—B 6 (or Kt—Kt 5); 19 P×P, P×P; 20 B—B 6 ch+.

(i) 19 B—R 4, Kt—K 4; 20 B—Kt 3, Kt×P ch; 21 Kt×Kt, Q R×Kt; 22 Kt×P!+. Von Feilitzsch—Dr. Vecsey, correspondence, 1920.

(j) 19 B×P ch+. Analysis by W. T. Pierce and N. J. Roughton.

(k) Schlechter's Variation Compare col. 11.

(l) 11.., K×B; 12 R—K 4!, P—B 4 (or 12 , P—Q 6; 13 Kt—B 3, P×P; 14 Q×P, R×P; 15 R—Q 1, Q—Q B 1; 16 Kt—Q 5 ch+. Therkatz); 13 R—R 4, K—B 2; 14 R×R P, R×P; 15 R×R ch, K×R; 16 Q Kt—Q 2, Q—B 3; 17 Q—K 2+. Fahrni—Tartakover, Baden, 1914.

(m) If 12 Kt×P, R—Q 1; 13 P—Q B 3, R×P; 14 Q—R 4, K—B 1!+ (Em. Lasker).

(n) Analysis by Tartakover in Die Hypermoderne Schachpartie.

1 P—K 4, P—K 4; 2 Kt—K B 3, Kt—Q B 3; 3 B—B 4, B—B 4;
4 O—O, Kt—B 3; 5 P—Q 4.

	11	12	13	14	15
5	(P×P).............................				B×P
6	(P—K 5)			Kt×B	
	(P—Q 4)..............Kt—K Kt 5			Kt×Kt (i)	
7	(P×Kt).....B—Q Kt 5		P—B 3 (f)	P—B 4 (j)	
	(P×B)	Kt—K 5	P—Q 4	P—Q 3	
8	P×P	Kt×P	P×P e.p. (g)	P×P	
	R—K Kt 1	B—Q 2 (c)	B×P (h)	P×P	
9	B—Kt 5	Kt—Kt 3 (d)	R—K 1 ch	B—K Kt 5	
	P—B 3 (a)	Kt—K 2	Kt—K 2	Q—K 2 (k)	
10	R—K 1 ch	B—Q 3	P—K R 3	Kt—R 3....Kt—B 3	
	K—B 2	B—Kt 3	Kt—B 3	B—K 3	P—B 3 (m)
11	Kt—K 5 ch	B×Kt	B—Kt 5	P—B 3	Kt—K 2
	Kt×Kt	P×B	Kt—Q 2	B×B	B—Kt 5
12	R×Kt	Kt—B 3	Kt×P	Kt×B	P—B 3
	B—K 2	B—B 3	Kt—Q Kt 3	Kt—K 3	Kt×Kt ch
13	Q—R 5 ch	Q—K 2	B—Kt5ch+	B×Kt	B×Kt
	K×P	Kt—Kt 3		P×B	B×B
14	Q—R 6 ch	R—Q 1		Q—R 4 ch	Q×B
	K—B 2	Q—B 1		P—B 3	O—O—O+
15	Q×R P ch	Kt×K P		Kt—K 3	
	R—Kt 2 (b)	Q—B 4 (e)		Q—B 4 (l)	

(a) If 9 ., B—K 2; 10 B×B, K×B (10.., Q×B?; 11 Kt×P, R×P; 12 R—K 1, B—K 3; 13 Kt—B 5+); 11 R—K 1 ch, B—K 3; 12 R—K 4! transposes into col. 10, note (l).

(b) 16 Q—R 5 ch and draws.

(c) Or 8 , O—O; 9 B×Kt, P×B; 10 Kt×P, Q—R 5; 11 B—K 3, B×B; 12 P×B, B—Kt 5; 13 Q—Q 3 (Lärobok).

(d) 9 B×Kt, P×B; 10 B—K 3 (Mason—Loman, Dresden, 1892). 10.., B—Kt3.

(e) 16 Kt—Kt 3, Q×K P; 17 Q×Q ch, Kt×Q; 18 R—K 1, P—B 3; 19 B—B 4, O—O ∓. The column is a suggestion by Em. Lasker.

(f) Dr. Krause's Variation. If 7 B—B 4, O—O; 8 P—K R 3, Kt—K 3; 9 B—K Kt 5, B—K 2; 10 B×Kt, P×B; 11 R—K 1, P—Q 3 (Bardeleben). Or 7 B—K Kt 5, B—K 2; 8 B—B 4, P—Q 3; 9 P×P, B×P; 10 R—K 1 ch, B—K 2; 11 B—Q Kt 5.

(g) If 8 B—Q Kt 5, P×P; 9 Kt×P, B—K 3.

(h) 8.., O—O; 9 B P×P, B×P (Q 3); 10 P—K R 3, Kt—B 3; 11 B—K Kt 5= The column is Burghold—Nestman, Leipzig, 1923.

(i) If 6.., P×Kt; 7 P—K 5, P—Q 4; 8 P×Kt, P×B; 9 P×P, R—K Kt 1; 10 R—K 1 ch, B—K 3; 11 Q—R 5, Q—B 3; 12 B—Kt 5, Q—Kt 3; 13 Q×Q, R P×Q, 14 B—B 6+ (Handbuch).

(j) Tartakover recommends 7 B—K Kt 5, P—K R 3; 8 B—R 4, Q—K 2; 9 P—B 4, P—Q 3.

(k) 9 ., B—K 3; 10 B×B (10 Kt—R 3, Q—K 2 transposes into the column), Kt×B; 11 Q×Q ch=.

(l) 16 Q R—K O—O—O; 17 K—R 1, K—Kt 1.

(m) If 10 , Q—B 4?; 11 B×P ch! (v. Holzhausen's Attack), K×B; 12 Q—R 5 ch, K—K 3; 13 B×Kt, P×B; 14 Kt—Q 5, K—Q 3!; 15 P—Q Kt 4+. Black can play 10.., B—K 3; 11 B—Q 3, O—O—O

NIMZOVITCH'S ATTACK

OF this opening, which he prefers to call the Queen's Indian Attack (on analogy with the Queen's Indian Defence in the Queen's Pawn Game), Hans Kmoch, in the book of the Kecskemét Tournament, 1927, gives the characteristic moves for White as Kt—K B 3, P—Q Kt 3, B—Kt 2, P—K 3, Kt—K 5, P—K B 4. It is hardly possible to limit the selection of the variations which follow strictly to those which exhibit this plan of campaign for White, owing to the fact that White always has an adversary with a large choice of moves! In fact, only once (in col. 6) have we found White's plan carried out in its entirety.

Roughly, however, we have taken Kmoch's definition as a guide in choosing the illustrations of this ultra-modern opening, which has been adopted after Nimzovitch's death by some of the younger Russian players.

It is obvious, that the opening moves 1 Kt—K B 3, ⁓ ; 2 P—Q Kt 3 or 1 P—Q Kt 3, ⁓; 2 B—Kt 2, ⁓ ; 3 Kt—K B 3 are in no sense Nimzovitch's copyright. We have only to refer to the Réti Opening and the Queen's Fianchetto Opening (p. 87, col. 13); and for White's general plan of campaign compare the well-known game Bird—Janowski, Hastings, 1895, in Bird's Opening.

In the defence Black must be careful not to give White absolute control of White's K 5; he can do this, either by the fianchetto development of his King's Bishop (cols. 1 and 4), or by pinning White's King's Knight (cols. 3, 5 and 8), or even by seizing the square by P—K B 3 and P—K 4 (col. 7).

1 Kt—K B 3, Kt—K B 3; 2 P—Q Kt 3

	1	2	3	4	5
2	P—K Kt 3	...P—Q 4 (b)			
3	B—Kt 2 / B—Kt 2	B—Kt 2 / P—K 3	.....B—Kt 5	....P—B 4	
4	P—B 4 / P—B 4	P—K 3 (A) / Q Kt—Q 2	P—B 4 / P—K 3	P—K 3 / Kt—B 3	.....B—Kt 5
5	P—K 3 / O—O	P—B 4 / B—Q 3 (c)	P—K 3 / Q Kt—Q 2	B—Kt 5 / Q—Kt 3	B—K 2 (h) / Kt—B 3
6	B—K 2 / P—Kt 3	Kt—B 3 / O—O	B—K 2 / P—B 3	B×Kt ch / Q×B	O—O / P—K 3
7	P—Q 4 / P×P	Q—B 2 / P—B 3	Kt—Q 4 / B×B	P—Q 3 / P—K Kt 3	P—Q 4 (i) / B—Q 3
8	Kt×P / B—Kt 2	R—B 1 / Q—K 2	Q×B / B—Q 3	Q Kt—Q 2 / B—Kt 2	Q Kt—Q ∷ / P×P
9	B—K B 3 / Kt—B 3	Kt—Q 4 / B—R 6 (d)	P—B 4 / O—O	Q—K 2 / O—O	P×P / O—O
10	Kt—B 3 / Q—Kt 1	B×B / Q×B	O—O / R—K 1	P—Q R 4 / R—Q 1	P—Q R 3 (j) / R—B 1
11	Kt×Kt / P×Kt	P×P / K P×P (e)	Q Kt—B 3 / Kt—K 5	O—O / P—Kt 3=(g)	P—B 4 / Q—B 2
12	O—O / R—Q 1 (a)	Kt—R 4 ±	P×P / B P×P= (f)		P—B 5 / B—B 5

(a) Nimzovitch—Alekhine, Carlsbad, 1923.

(b) Or 2 ., P—Q 3; 3 P—Kt 3, P—K 4; 4 P—B 4, P—K 5 (P—K Kt 3 seems better); 5 Kt—R 4, P—Q 4; 6 P×P, Q×P; 7 Kt—Q B 3, Q—B 3; 8 P—K 3, P—Q R 3; 9 B—Q Kt 2, B—K Kt 5; 10 B—K 2, B×B, 11 Kt×B, Q Kt—Q 2. Nimzovitch—Alekhine, New York, 1927. Or 2.., P—B 4; 3 P—B 4, P—Q 4; 4 P×P, Kt×P; 5 B—Kt 2, Kt—Q B 3; 6 P—K 3, B—K 5; 7 B—K 2, B×Kt!; 8 B×B, Kt—Q 5; 9 B—Kt 2, P—K 3; 10 O—O, Q—Kt 3=. M. E. Goldstein—W. S. Viner, Sydney, 1932.

(c) 5.., B—K 2; 6 Kt—B 3, O—O; 7 Q—B 2, P—B 3; 8 B—K 2, P×P?; 9 P×P, P—B 4; 10 O—O, P—Q Kt 3; 11 P—Q 4, P×P; 12 P×P, B—Kt 2; 13 Q R—Q 1, Q—B 1; 14 Kt—K 5 ±. Lisitzin—Lilienthal, Moscow, 1935.

(d) Kmoch suggests 9 , R—K 1, preparing for Kt—B 1.

(e) Better was Kt×P. The column is Nimzovitch—Maróczy, Bled, 1931.

(f) Rabinovitch—Rauser, Russian Championship, 1934.

(g) Nimzovitch—Kashdan, Frankfurt, 1930.

(h) 5 P—K R 3, B—R 4; 6 B—Kt 5 ch, Q Kt—Q 2; 7 O—O, P—Q R 3, 8 B—K 2, P—Q 5. A. H. Privonitz—W. P. Hergenrother, correspondence, 1929.

(i) White is defending the Queen's Gambit Declined, with a move in hand.

(j) 10 P—B 4 or 10 Kt—K 5 would be more commendable (J. H. Blake). The column is Vilner—Rokhlin, Russia, 1928.

(A) For 4 P—K Kt 3 see the Réti Opening.

	6	7	8	9	10
1	Kt—K B 3 . . . . P—Q Kt 3				
	P—Q 4 (a)				Kt—K B 3
2	P—Q Kt 3				B—Kt 2
	P—Q B 4	Kt—K B 3			P—B 4 (m)
3	B—Kt 2		P—K 3	B—Kt 2	Kt—K B 3
	Kt—Q B 3		B—Kt 5	Q Kt—Q 2	Kt—B 3
4	P—K 3		B—Kt 2	P—K 3	P—K 3
	Kt—B 3 (b) . . Q—B 2		Q Kt—Q 2	P—K 3	P—K 3
5	B—Kt 5 (c)	B—Kt 5	P—K R 3	P—B 4	B—Kt 5
	B—Q 2	P—Q R 3	B—R 4	B—Q 3	B—K 2
6	O—O	B × Kt ch	P—Q 3 (g)	Kt—B 3	O—O
	P—K 3	Q × B	P—K R 3	P—B 3	O—O
7	P—Q 3	P—Q 3	Q Kt—Q 2	Q—B 2	K B × Kt
	B—K 2 (d)	P—B 3	P—K 3	O—O ! (j)	Kt P × B
8	Q Kt—Q 2	Q—K 2	Q—K 2	B—K 2	Kt—K 5
	O—O	P—K 4	B—Q Kt 5	P—Q R 3	Q—Kt 3
9	K B × Kt	P—B 4	P—Kt 4	P—K 4 (h)	Q—B 3
	B × B	Kt—K 2	B—Kt 3	Kt × P	B—R 3
10	Kt—K 5	O—O	Kt—K 5	Kt × Kt	P—Q 3
	R—B 1	B—Kt 5	Kt × Kt	P × Kt	Q R—Q 1
11	P—K B 4	R—K 1	B × Kt	Q × P	Kt—Q 2
	Kt—Q 2	O—O—O	B—Q 3 (h)	P—K 4	Kt—K 1
12	Q—Kt 4	P—K 4	Kt—B 3	Q—B 2	Q—R 3
	Kt × Kt (e)	P × K P (f)	Q—K 2 (i)	Q—K 2 (l)	P—Q 4 (n)

(a) 1.., P—Q B 4; 2 P—Q Kt 3, Kt—Q B 3; 3 B—Kt 2, Kt—B 3; 4 Kt—B 3, P—Q 4; 5 P—K 3, P—K 3; 6 P—Q 4 (producing a kind of Queen's Pawn Game), Q—R 4; 7 B—Kt 5 !, Kt—K 5; 8 B × Kt ch, P × B; 9 O—O, Kt × Kt, 10 Q—Q 2, P × P; 11 Kt × P, Kt—K 7 ch; 12 Q × Kt, B—R 3; 13 P—Q B 4. Krejcik—Beutum, Vienna, 1929.

(b) Or 4.., B—Kt 5; 5 P—K R 3, B × Kt; 6 Q × B, P—K 4; 7 B—Kt 5, Q—Q 3; 3 P—K 4, P—Q 5; 9 Kt—R 3 followed by Kt—B 4. Nimzovitch—Rosselli, Baden-Baden, 1925.

(c) 5 Kt—B 3, P—K 3; 6 P—Q 4 transposes into note (a).

(d) If 7.., B—Q 3 White can play 8 P—K 4, P × P; 9 P × P, Kt × P ? ; 10 R—K 1 + (Alekhine).

(e) 13 B × Kt, B—B 3; 14 R—B 3±. Nimzovitch—Spielmann, New York, 1927

(f) 13 P × P, Kt—Kt 3=. Dr. Weil—Fine, exhibition game, Vienna, 1937.

(g) On 6 B—K 2, P—K 3; 7 Kt—K 5, B × B; 8 Q × B, B—Q 3; 9 Kt × Kt, Q × Kt; 10 P—Q B 4, P—B 3. Nimzovitch—Vidmar, New York, 1927.

(h) Loss of time. 11 ., Q—K 2 followed by O—O—O was better (Alekhine).

(i) 13 B—K Kt 2, O—O—O; 14 O—O—O. Nimzovitch—Marshall, New York, 1927. Alekhine suggests the continuation 14. , B—R 6 ch; 15 K—Kt 1, Kt--K 1 followed by P—K B 3.

(j) 7.., Q—K 2; 8 Kt—Q 4 !, P—Q R 3? (P—B 4!; 9 K Kt—Kt 5, B --Kt 1. J. H. Blake) ; 9 B—K 2, O—O; 10 O—O, P—B 4 ; 11 Kt—B 3 +. Nimzovitch—Ahues, Frankfurt, 1930.

(k) Much better was 9 P—Q 4.

(l) 13 O—O—O (13 P—Q 3 !. Blumich), P—K 5. Tartakover—Sultan Khan, 12th match game, 1931.

(m) Or 2 , P—K Kt 3; 3 P—K 3, B—Kt 2; 4 P—K B 4, P—Q 3; 5 Q—B 1 (better 5 Kt—K B 3), O—O; 6 Kt—K B 3, B—Kt 5; 7 B—K 2, Kt—B 3; 8 O—O, P—K 4. Nimzovitch—Euwe, Carlsbad, 1929.

(n) 13 Q R—Q 1 B—B 1 ; 14 P—B 4, Kt—Q 3. Nimzovitch—Yates, Kissingen, 1928.

PETROFF'S DEFENCE

THIS variation of the King's Knight's Game, though often adopted in order to avoid having to defend the Ruy Lopez, has also been used by Marshall (following his countryman Pillsbury) as a weapon of counter-attack. It is generally held that the opening is slightly in White's favour; but no decisive advantage has been established by analysis.

The variations commencing with 3 P—Q 4 (cols. 1 and 2), recommended by Steinitz as White's strongest continuation, may give rise to very complicated play on both sides. In the more usual form of the opening, after 3 Kt × P, P—Q 3 ; 4 Kt—K B 3, Kt × P, White has the choice of three moves :—

(i) 5 Kt—B 3 (col. 3), leading to no more than an equal game with best play.

(ii) 5 Q—K 2 (cols. 4 to 6), reintroduced by Lasker at St. Petersburg, 1914, by which White gains a slight positional advantage, which is, however, insufficient against careful defensive play.

(iii) 5 P—Q 4 (cols. 7 to 10), giving rise to brilliant attacking possibilities for Black, who is a move ahead in his development. Marshall's favourite variation, best illustrated in col. 8, has been refuted by C. H. Alexander's very marked improvement in note (h).

Early variations by White, 3 Kt—B 3 and 3 B—B 4, are not considered in this section, but under the Three Knights' and Bishop's Openings.

1 P—K4, P—K4; 2 Kt—KB3, Kt—KB3.

	1	2	3	4	5
3	P—Q4		Kt×P		
	Kt×P (a)	...P×P (e)	P—Q3		
4	B—Q3	P—K5	Kt—KB3		
	P—Q4	Kt—K5	Kt×P		
5	Kt×P	Q×P (f)	Kt—B3.....		Q—K2
	B—Q3 (b)	P—Q4	Kt×Kt (k)	Q—K2	
6	O—O	P×P e.p.	QP×Kt	P—Q3	
	O—O	Kt×QP	B—K2	Kt—KB3	
7	P—QB4	B—Kt5 (g)	B—Q3	B—Kt5	
	Kt—QB3! (c)	Kt—B3 (h)	Kt—B3	Q×Q ch	
8	P×P	Q—B3 (i)	B—KB4	B×Q	
	Kt×QP	P—B3	B—K3	B—K2	
9	B×Kt	B—KB4	O—O	Kt—B3	
	B×Kt	Q—K2 ch	Q—Q2	B—Q2 (l)	
10	P—B4	B—K2	Q—Q2	O—O.......	O—O—O
	B—B3	B—K3	B—B4	O—O	P—KR3 (n)
11	Kt—B3	QKt—Q2	KR—K1	KR—K1	B—R4
	B—B4	O—O—O	O—O=	Kt—B3	Kt—B3
12	Q—Q3	O—O= (j)		P—Q4	P—Q4
	B×B (d)			KR—K1 (m)	O—O—O (o)

(a) 3 ., P—Q3 transposes into Philidor's Defence.

(b) 5 , B—K2; 6 O—O, O—O; 7 P—QB4, P—QB3; 8 Q—Kt3, Q—Kt3, is a playable alternative.

(c) More aggressive than 7.., P—QB3; 8 Q—B2, Kt—B3; 9 B—Kt5, P—KR3; 10 B—R4=.

(d) Alekhine—C. H. Alexander, Hastings, 1933-34. Continued 13 Kt×B (safer 13 Q×B) Q×P; 14 Kt×B ch, P×Kt; 15 K—R1, Q—Q Kt4'+.

(e) 3 ., P—Q4; 4 P×QP, P×P; 5 B—Kt5 ch, P—B3; 6 P×P, P×P; 7 B—Q4, Q—K2 ch; 8 B—K2, P—B4; 9 P—B3, P×P; 10 Kt×P+.

(f) 5 Q—K2, B—Kt5 ch; 6 K—Q1, P—Q4; 7 P×P e.p., P—KB4; 8 P×P, Q×P; 9 Kt×P, Kt—B3. Steinitz—Pillsbury, 1895.

(g) 7 B—Q3, Kt—B3; 8 Q—KB4, B—K2; 9 O—O, B—K3, 10 Kt—B3. O—O; 11 P—QKt3, B—B3; 12 B—Kt2, Q—B1; 13 QR—Q1+. Paris—Berne, correspondence, 1922.

(h) 7 , P—B3; 8 B—KB4, Kt—B3; 9 Q—K3 ch, Q—K2; 10 Q×Q ch, B×Q; 11 Kt—B3, B—B4=. Zubareff—Marshall, Moscow, 1925.

(i) 8 Q—K3 ch, B—K2; 9 B×B, Q×B; 10 Q×Q ch, Kt×Q=. Kostich—Kashdan, Bled, 1931.

(j) Bogoljuboff and others—Romanovsky and others, Leningrad, 1924.

(k) 5 ., P—Q4; 6 Q—K2, B—K2; 7 Kt×Kt, P×Kt; 8 Q×P, O—O; 9 B—B4+. Leonhardt—Schlechter, Barmen, 1905.

(l) If 9 ', Kt—B3; 10 Kt—Kt5, K—Q1; 11 O—O, P—QR3; 12 Q Kt—Q4, Kt×Kt; 13 Kt×Kt, P—B4; 14 Kt—B3, B—K3; 15 B—Q2, P—R3; 16 P—QKt3 ±. Kashdan—Mikenas, Folkestone, 1933.

(m) Capablanca—Kostich, match, 1919.

(n) 10.., Kt—B3; 11 P—KR3, P—KR3; 12 B—K3, O—O—O; 13 P—Q4, P—Q4; 14 Kt—K5, B—K1; 15 P—QR3 ±. Eliskases—C. H. Alexander, Hastings, 1933-34.

(o) 13 KR—K1, QR—K1; 14 B—B4, Kt—Q1=. Fine—Kashdan, New York 1934.

1 P—K 4, P—K 4; 2 Kt—K B 3, Kt—K B 3; 3 Kt×P, P—Q 3; 4 Kt—K B 3, Kt×P.

	6	7	8	9	10
5	(Q—K 2).... (Q—K 2)	P—Q 4 (b) P—Q 4			
6	(P—Q 3) (Kt—K B 3)	B—Q 3 B—Q 3............................			B—K 2 (h)
7	(B—Kt 5) B—K 3	O—O.................... O—O.......B—K Kt 5		P—B 4 B—Kt 5 ch	O—O Kt—Q B 3
8	Kt—B 3 Q Kt—Q 2	Kt—B 3 Kt×Kt	P—B 4 (e) O—O	Q Kt—Q 2 B×Kt ch	R—K 1 (l) B—K Kt 5
9	O—O—O P—K R 3	P×Kt B—K Kt5 (c)	P×P P—K B 4	B×B O—O	P—B 3 (m) P—B 4
10	B—R 4 P—K Kt 4	R—Kt 1 P—Q Kt 3	Kt—B 3 (f) Kt—Q 2	O—O B—Kt 5	P—B 4 (n) B×Kt
11	B—Kt 3 Kt—R 4	P—B 4 P—Q B 3	P—K R 3 (g) B—R 4	B—B 4 Kt—Q B 3	P×B Kt—B 3
12	P—Q 4 Kt×B	R—K 1 Kt—Q 2	Kt×Kt P×Kt	R—K 1 Kt×Q P (i)	B×P P×P
13	R P×Kt P—Kt 5 (a)	P×P P×P (d)	B×P Kt—B 3 (h)	B×Kt P×B (j)	B—K 3 Q—Q 4

(a) 14 Kt—K R 4+. Em. Lasker—Marshall, St. Petersburg, 1914.

(b) 5 P—B 4 is Kaufmann's Variation, now rarely played. See P. W. Sergeant's Charousek's Games, p. 185.

(c) Kmoch suggests 9. , P—Q B 4; 10 P—B 4, P×B P; 11 B×B P, P×P.

(d) Yates—Marshall, London, 1927.

(e) By 8 R—K 1, P—K B 4; 9 Kt—B 3, O—O; 10 P—K R 3, as advised by Tarrasch, White can get an easier game, but no appreciable advantage.

(f) Not 10 R—K 1, B×P ch; 11 K×B, Kt×P; 12 Q—K 2, Kt×B; 13 Q×Kt, B×Kt followed by Q—R 5 ch (the Marshall Trap).

(g) Here 11 R—K 1 is playable. If 11 , B×P ch; 12 K×B, Kt×P; 13 B—K Kt 5+. List—Kostich, Berlin, 1928.

(h) 14 B—B 5, K—R 1; 15 P—K Kt 4! (if 15 Q—Kt 3, Kt×P ! Black can draw. O.S.Bernstein—Marshall,San Sebastian,1911),Kt×Q P(if15 ,B—B 2, 16 B—K 6+); 16 B—K 6!, B—B 2, 17 Kt—Kt 5!, B×B; 18 Kt×B, Q—R 5; 19 Q—Kt 3!+. C. H. Alexander—H. V. Mallison, Brighton, 1938.

(i) If 12 , B×Kt; 13 Q×B, Kt×Q P; 14 Q—K 3, Kt—K B 4; 15 Q—R 3+ (Tarrasch).

(j) Continued 14 Q×Kt, P×Kt; 15 Q×Q, K R×Q; 16 B×P, R—Q 7=. Tarrasch—Marshall, St. Petersburg, 1914.

(k) If 6 , B—Kt 5?; 7 O—O, P—K B 4; 8 P—B 4, Kt—Q B 3; 9 Kt—B 3, B×Kt; 10 P×B, Kt×Q P; 11 P×Kt, Q P×P; 12 B×P!+. Sir G. A. Thomas— A. R. B. Thomas, Hastings, 1937-38.

(l) 8 P—B 4, Kt—B 3; 9 B—K 3, P×P; 10 B×P, B—K Kt 5; 11 B—K 2, Q—Q 2; 12 Kt—B 3, O—O. Here 8 , Kt—Kt 5; 9 P×P, Kt×B; 10 Q×Kt, Q×P; 11 R—K 1, B—K B 4; 12 Kt—B 3, Kt×Kt; 13 Q×Kt, P—Q B 3; 14 B—Q 2, P—K R 3; 15 R—K 5, Q—Q 2; 16 Q R—K 1, B—K 3 is Yates—Kashdan, Hastings, 1931.

(m) 9 P—B 4, Kt—B 3; 10 P×P, K Kt×P; 11 Kt—B 3, O—O; 12 B—K 4, B—K 3.

(n) 10 Q Kt—Q 2, O—O; 11 Q—Kt 3, K—R 1; 12 Kt—B 1. Capablanca— Kostich, match, 1919.

PHILIDOR'S DEFENCE

THIS old opening is an attempt to evade the stereotyped attacks in the King's Knight's Opening without giving up the centre; but White by developing normally can assure himself of the freer game. Alekhine occasionally adopts the Defence.

Nimzovitch's modification of the Hanham Variation, followed by advance of the Queen-side Pawns, for some time seemed to give Black a playable game, but after preventing this advance by P—Q R 4 (col. 1) the simple exchange of centre Pawns at the right moment leaves Black with a cramped and lifeless game. The consensus of opinion concerning the difficult variation arising from 6 Kt—K Kt 5, illustrated in col. 2, is that it is in Black's favour. The mode of attack arising from 4 B—Q B 4 is met most simply by the line of defence in col. 4, note (h).

Of the less commonly adopted lines of play, 3..., Q Kt—Q 2 (cols. 6 and 7), the Hanham Variation, leads to difficult positions, where Black must constantly be on guard against an early assault on his King; 3..., P × P (cols. 8 and 9) cedes the centre to the adversary prematurely; and 3..., P—K B 4 (col. 10) involves too great a weakening of Black's defensive position on the King's wing.

1 P—K 4, P—K 4 ; 2 Kt—K B 3, P—Q 3.

	1	2	3	4	5
3	P—'⌐4 Kt—K B 3				
4	Kt—B 3............................ Q Kt—Q 2			B—Q B 4.... P×P (h)	P×P (i) Kt×P
5	B—Q B 4............... B—K 2 (a)	P—K Kt 3 B—K 2	Kt—Kt 5 B—K 3	Q—Q 5 Kt—B 4	
6	O—O....... O—O	Kt-KKt5(e) O—O	B—Kt 2 O—O	Kt×B P×Kt	B-K Kt5 (j) Q—Q 2 (k)
7	Q—K 2 (b) P—B 3 (c)	B×P ch R×B	O—O P—B 3	B—Kt 5 P—Q 4	Kt—B 3 P×P
8	P—Q R 4 P—K R 3	Kt—K 6 Q—K 1	P—Kt 3 R—K 1	B×Kt Q×B	B—Kt 5 P—Q B 3
9	B—Kt 3 Q—B 2	Kt×B P Q—Q 1	B—Kt 2 B—B 1	P×P P×P	Q×K P ch Kt—K 3 (l)
10	P—R 3 K—R 2	Kt×R P—Q Kt 3 (f)	Q—Q 2 Q—B 2	B×P B—Kt 5 ch	R—Q 1 P—B 3
11	B--K 3 P--K Kt 3	P×P P×P	Q R—Q 1 P—Q Kt 4	Kt—Q 2 Q—K 4 ch	Q—K 2 Q—K B 2
12	Q R—Q 1 (d)	Kt×P Q×Kt	B—R 3 P—Q R 4	Q—K 2 B×Kt ch	B—Q B 4 +
13		O—O B—R 3	P×P (g) P—Kt 5		

(a) 5 ., P—K R 3 : 6 P×P, P×P ; 7 Q—K 2, P—B 3 ; 8 P—Q R 4, Q—B 2 ;
● O -C ±. Tylor—Tartakover, Nottingham, 1936.

(b) Tartakover gives 7 B—K 3, P—B 3 ; 8 B—Kt 3 !, Q—B 2 ; 9 Q—K 2+.

(c) 7.., P×P ; 8 Kt×P, R—K 1 ? (Kt—K 4 or Kt—Kt 3 is correct) ; 9 B×P ch,
K×B : 10 Kt—K 6, K×Kt ; 11 Q—B 4 ch, P—Q 4 ; 12 P×P ch, K—B 2 ; 13 P—Q 6 ch,
Kt—Q 4 ; 14 P×B++. T. H. Tylor—Koltanowski, Hastings, 1930.

(d) Alekhine—Marco, Stockholm. 1912.

(e) If 6 B×P ch, K×B ; 7 Kt—Kt 5 ch, K—Kt 1 ; 8 Kt—K 6, Q—K 1 ;
9 Kt×B P, Q—Kt 3 ; 10 Kt×R, Q×P ; 11 R—B 1, P×P ; 12 Q×P, Kt—K 4+
(Mlotkowski).

(f) 10.., P—Q Kt 4 ; 11 Kt×P, Q—R 4 ch ; 12 Kt—B 3, Kt×P ; 13 O—O,
Kt×Kt (Lärobok, 1921).

(g) Tartakover—Kostich, Teplitz-Schönau, 1922. Black's 13th move is due to
Grünfeld.

(h) A simple equalising line is 4.., Kt×P ; 5 O—O (or 5 P×P, P—Q B 3), B—K 2 ;
6 P×P, O—O.

(i) 4 Kt—Kt 5, P—K R 3 ; 5 Kt×B P (the Locock Gambit), K×Kt ; 6 P×P,
Kt—Kt 5 ; 7 B—B 4 ch, K—K 1 ; 8 P—K 6, K Kt—B 3 ; 9 Kt—B 3, Q—K 2. White's
attack does not appear sufficient.

(j) 6 Kt—Kt 5, B—K 3 ; 7 Kt×B, P×Kt ; 8 Q—B 3, Q Kt—Q 2 ; 9 P×P,
B×P ; 10 Kt—B 3, Q—R 5 ; 11 P—K Kt 3, Kt—K 4 ! ; 12 Q—K 2, Q—B 3 ; 13 P—B 4,
Kt—B 3+. L. Steiner—Alekhine, Podebrady, 1936

(k) Better is 6.., B—K 2 ; 7 P×P, Q×P ; 8 Kt—B 3, O—O. 6.., P—K B 3 ;
7 P×B P, P×P ; 8 B—K 3, B—K 3 ; 9 Q—R 5 ch, B—B 2 ; 10 Q—R 4, Q Kt—Q 2 ;
11 Kt—B 3, P—B 3 ; 12 O—O—O + is Maróczy—Bogoljuboff, Bled, 1931. The column
is L. Rellstab—T. H. Tylor, Hastings, 1930.

(l) If 9.., Q—K 3 ; 10 O—O—O.

E

1 P—K 4, P—K 4; 2 Kt—K B 3, P—Q 3.

	6	7	8	9	10
3	(P—Q 4) Kt—Q 2 (a)	....	P×P (f)	....	P—K B 4
4	B—Q B 4 P—Q B 3		Kt×P Kt—K B 3	Q×P Kt—Q B 3	Kt—B 3 (j) Kt—K B 3
5	P—Q R 4.... B—K 2	Kt—B 3 (d) B—K 2	Kt—Q B 3 B—K 2	B—Q Kt 5 B—Q 2	P×K P Kt×P
6	Kt—B 3 Kt—K B 3	O—O P—K R 3	B—K 2 (g) O—O	B×Kt B×B	Kt×Kt P×Kt
7	O—O P—K R 3	P×P P×P	O—O Kt—B 3	Kt—B 3 (i) Kt—B 3	Kt—Kt 5 P—Q 4
8	P—Q Kt 3 Q—B 2	Q—K 2 Q—B 2	Kt×Kt P×Kt	B—K 3 P—K Kt 3	P—K 6 B—B 4
9	B—Kt 2 Kt—B 1 ? (b)	B—K 3 P—Q Kt 4	P—Q Kt 3 P—Q 4	Kt—Q 5 B—Kt 2	Kt×K P B—K 2
10	P×P P×P	B—Kt 3 K Kt—B 3	P—K 5 Kt—K 1	B—Kt 5 B×Kt	Q—R 5 ch P—Kt 3
11	Kt×P Q×Kt	P—Q R 3 Kt—B 4	P—B 4 P—K B 4	P×B O—O	Q—K 5 R—B 1
12	Kt—Q 5+ (c)	B—R 2 Kt—K 3 (e)	B—K 3+ (h)	O—O ±	Kt—Kt 5 +

(a) The Hanham Variation.

(b) 9 , O—O was necessary, but White has still the better game (Kmoch).

(c) Continued 12.., Q—Q 3; 13 B—R 3, P—B 4; 14 P—K 5, Q×P; 15 R—K 1+ +. Nimzovitch—Marco, Gothenburg, 1920. If 12.., Q—Kt 1; 13 Kt×B, K×Kt; 14 B—R 3 ch, K—K 1; 15 B—Q 6+ +.

(d) If 5 Kt—Kt 5, Kt—K R 3; 6 O—O, Black should play 6.., Kt—Kt 3 or 6 , P×P; not 6 ., B—K 2 on account of 7 Kt—K 6, P×Kt; 8 B×Kt, Kt—Kt 3; 9 B×Kt P, Kt×B; 10 B×R, K—B 2; 11 P—Q Kt 3, Kt—Kt 3; 12 P—K B 4, Q×B; 13 Q—R 5 ch+ (Kmoch). 5 O—O, B—K 2; 6 P×P, P×P; 7 Kt—Kt 5, B×Kt; 8 Q—R 5, P—K Kt 3; 9 Q×B, Q×Q; 10 B×Q, P—B 3; 11 B—K 3, with a minimal advantage.

(e) Sir G. A. Thomas—Alekhine, Hastings, 1933–34.

(f) This early abandonment of the centre is not advisable.

(g) 6 B—K B 4, O—O; 7 Q—Q 2, R—K 1; 8 O—O—O, B—B 1; 9 P—B 3, Q Kt—Q 2; 10 P—K Kt 4+. Kashdan—Koltanowski, *Referee* Tournament, London, 1932. Alternatives are 6 B—Q B 4, O—O; 7 O—O, Kt—B 3; and 6 B—Q 3, O—O; 7 O—O, B—Q 2; 8 P—B 4, Kt—B 3; 9 K Kt—K 2.

(h) Leonhardt—Nimzovitch, San Sebastian, 1912.

(i) 7 B—Kt 5 is also good, Kt—B 3 being the best reply. The column and notes are by Mlotkowski.

(j) Or 4 B—Q B 4, K P×P; 5 Kt—Kt 5, Kt—K R 3; 6 O—O, Q—B 3; 7 P×P, B×P; 8 R—K 1 ch. Alapin has shown that Black obtains a playable game after 4 Q P×P, B P×P; 5 Kt—Kt 5, P—Q 4; 6 P—K 6, Kt—K R 3; 7 Kt—Q B 3, P—B 3; 8 K Kt×K P, Kt—B 4; 9 Kt—K Kt 5, Q—B 3; 10 B—Q 3, P—K R 3. The column is Philidor's Counter-attack.

E *

PONZIANI'S OPENING

THE Ponziani, or English Knight's Opening, is scarcely satisfactory for White, Black being left with a variety of adequate replies. The move 3 P—Q B 3 lies open to the twofold objection that it takes away the best square from White's Queen's Knight and that it leaves him behind in his development, so that Black can effectively adopt several strong sacrificial counter-attacks.

The three customary replies are :—

(i) 3..., P—Q 4 (cols. 1 to 8), anticipating White's intention to form a centre, at once the commonest and the most natural continuation for the second player. After 4 Q—R 4 Black can advantageously offer one or more Pawns for the sake of rapid development (cols. 1 and 2). The Steinitz Defence (cols. 3 to 5) is hardly sufficient, White obtaining too strong an attack after O—O—O, which is represented in cols. 3 and 4. Caro's Defence (col. 6), recommended by the *Lärobok,* has much to be said for it.

(ii) 3..., P—B 4 (cols. 9 and 10), a fighting defence, which gives Black a free hand at the cost of some insecurity of position. The *Lärobok's* line against it (col. 9) was held to upset it; but the suggestions in notes (*k*), (*l*), and (*m*) make this at least doubtful.

(iii) 3..., Kt—B 3 (cols. 11 to 15), a comparatively safe defence, less fertile of resource than 3..., P—Q 4. White obtains a promising attack in the usual lines shown in cols. 11 and 12. Black may adopt the variation in col. 14 if he wishes to be certain of the draw.

1 P—K 4, P—K 4 ; 2 Kt—K B 3, Kt—Q B 3 ; 3 P—B 3, P—Q 4 ; 4 Q—R 4.

1	2	3	4	5
4 Kt—B 3 (a)		P—B 3 (f)		
5 Kt×P B—Q 3		B—Kt 5 Kt—K 2		
6 Kt×Kt P×Kt	P×P B×Kt (e)	P×P Q×P		
7 P—Q 3 (b) O—O	P×Kt O—O	P—Q 4 B—Q 2 (g)	 B—Kt 5	O—O B—Q 2 (l)
8 B—K Kt 5 (c) P—K R 3	B—K 2 R—K 1	B—K 3 P×P	P—B 4 Q—K 5 ch	P—Q 4 P×P
9 B×Kt Q×B	P—Q 4 B—Q 3	P×P Kt—K 4 (h)	B—K 3 B×Kt	P×P Kt—K 4
10 Kt—Q 2 (d) R—Kt 1	B—Kt 5 P×P	Kt—B 3 Kt×Kt ch	Kt—Q 2 Q—Kt 3	Kt—B 3 Kt×Kt ch
11 Q—B 2 Q—Kt 3	Kt—Q 2 Q—K 2	P×Kt Q—K B 4	P×B P×P	P×Kt Q—K B 4
12 O—O—O	Q—B 4 P—Q R 4	O—O—O P—Q R 3 (i)	B×P P—Q R 3	P—Q 5 P—Q R 3
13	Q—Q 3 B—K B 4 +	P—Q 5 O—O—O (j)	O—O—O R—Q 1 (k)	B×B ch Q×B (m)

(a) Leonhardt's Defence.

(b) 7 P—Q 4, P×P; 8 B—Q R 6, B—Q 2; 9 B—Kt 7, P—B 4; 10 B—B 6, P×P; 11 B×B ch, Q×B; 12 Q×Q P= (Tartakover).

(c) 8 B—K 2, Kt—Kt 5; 9 B×Kt (If 9 P—K R 3, Q—R 5), B×B; 10 O—O, B—K 7 +.

(d) Or 10 B—K 2, Q—Kt 4; 11 Kt—Q 2, Q×P; 12 B—B 3, Q—R 6; 13 O—O—O, Kt—B 5 +. Berne—Paris, correspondence, 1921.

(e) Or 6.., Q—K 2. The column is Rabinovitch—Alekhine, Moscow, 1915.

(f) Steinitz's Defence.

(g) 7 , P—K 5; 8 P—B 4, Q—Q 1; 9 K Kt—Q 2, Q×P; 10 Kt—Kt 3, Q—Q 3; 11 B—K 3 +. Von Popiel—Burn, Cologne, 1898.

(h) Tchigorin's Variation; compare col. 5.

(i) 12. , P—B 3; 13 B—Q 3, Q×P; 14 K R—K 1, K—Q 1; 15 B—K 4, Q—R 4 (Rev. F. E. Hamond—Rev. W. E. Evill, correspondence, 1915); 16 Q—Kt 3 +.

(j) 14 B×B ch, R×B; 15 P—Q 6, P×P; 16 P—Kt 4, K—Kt 1; 17 K—Kt 2, Kt—B 1; 18 P—Kt 5, P×P; 19 Kt×P + +. Rev. F. E. Hamond—Rev. A. Baker, correspondence, 1914.

(k) 14 B×Kt ch, Kt×B; 15 K R—K 1 ch +.

(l) 7 , P—K 5; 8 B×Kt ch, Kt×B; 9 R—K 1, P—B 4; 10 P—B 4, Q—Q 1; 11 P—Q 3 +.

(m) 14 Q—Kt 3, P—Q Kt 3; 15 R—K 1 +.

1 P—K4, P—K4; 2 Kt—KB3, Kt—QB3; 3 P—B3.

	6	7	8	9	10
3	(P—Q4)		....	P—B4 (i)	
4	(Q—R4)		B—Kt5	P—Q4 (j)	
	B—Q2 (a)...PxP		PxP	P—Q3 (k)	
5	PxP	KtxP	KtxP	KPxP.....	P—Q5 (o)
	Kt—Q5	Q—Q4	Q—Q4	BxP (l)	PxP (p)
6	Q—Q1	KtxKt (d)	Q—R4	B—QKt5	Kt—Kt5
	KtxKt ch	PxKt	Kt—K2	PxP	Kt—Kt1
7	QxKt	B—B4	P—KB4	KtxP	KtxKP
	P—KB4	Q—Q2	PxP e.p. (h)	B—Q2	Kt—KB3
8	P—Q4 (b)	O—O	KtxP (B3)	BxKt	B—Q3
	P—K5	B—Q3	P—QR3	PxB	B—K2
9	Q—Q1 (c)	R—K1 (e)	B—K2	O—O	B—Kt5
	B—Q3	Kt—B3	Kt—Kt3	Kt—B3 (m)	KtxKt
10	P—QB4	P—Q3	O—O	R—K1 ch	BxB
	P—QKt3	O—O		B—K2	QxB
11	P—QR3	PxP		Q—K2	BxKt
	P—QR4	Q—Kt5 (f)		P—Q4	Kt—Q2 ▪
12	Kt—B3	P—K5		Kt—B3+ (n)	
	Kt—B3	R—K1 (g)			

(a) Caro's Defence. If 4.., Q—Q3; 5 B—Kt5, B—Q2; 6 PxP, QxP; 7 O—O.

(b) Tartakover suggests 8 B—B4, B—Q3; 9 P—Q3.

(c) 9 Q—Kt3, Kt—B3; 10 P—QB4, B—Q3; 11 Q—QB3, P—QKt3; 12 B—Kt5, O—O; 13 Kt—Q2, R—K1; 14 O—O—O, KtxP+. Analysis in *Deutsche Schachzeitung*.

(d) For 6 B—Kt5, Kt—K2 see col. 8.

(e) 9 B—Kt5?, Kt—K2; 10 QxKP, P—KB4; 11 Q—B3, PxB; 12 QxR, P—B3; 13 P—QR4, P—Kt5, 14 PxP, O—O; 15 P—Kt5, P—B5+ (Mlotkowski).

(f) Or 11.., Kt—Kt5; 12 P—KR3+. The text-move threatens BxP ch.

(g) 13 B—B4, Kt—R4; 14 B—KKt3, KtxB; 15 RPxKt, RxP; 16 RxR, BxR; 17 QxBP+.

(h) 7.., B—Q2; 8 KtxB, KxKt; 9 O—O, Kt—B4; 10 P—QKt4, B—Q3; 11 Kt—R3 (Tartakover).

(i) 3.., B—B4; 4 P—QKt4 (for 4 B—Kt5 see Ruy Lopez, Classical Defence), B—Kt3; 5 P—Kt5, Kt—R4, 6 KtxP, Q—K2; 7 P—Q4!, P—Q3; 8 B—R3, PxB3; 9 Kt—B3+. Cols. 9 and 10 are Ponziani's Counter-attack.

(j) If 4 PxP, Q—B3.

(k) Alternatives for Black are: (1) 4 .., KPxP; 5 KPxP, P—Q4; 6 KtxP, Kt—B3. (2) 4 , BPxP; 5 KtxP, Q—B3!.

(l) Better is 5 ., PxP; 6 KtxP, KtxKt; 7 QxKt, BxP; with Kt—B3 to follow.

(m) Q—B3 is worth consideration.

(n) *Lärobok*, 1921. If now 12.., P—KR3; 13 Kt—R4, etc.

(o) 5 B—QKt5, BPxP, 6 KtxP, PxKt; 7 BxKt, PxB; 8 Q—R5ch, K—Q2; 9 Q—B5 ch, K—K2 and draws. 5 QPxP is met by 5.., BPxP; 6 Kt—Kt5, KtxP; 7 KtxKP, P—Q4; 8 Kt—Kt3, Kt—KB3+ (Burn).

(p) 5.., QKt—K2; 6 B—Kt5 ch, B—Q2 or P—B3 is also good for Black.

1 P—K4, P—K4;   2 Kt—KB3, Kt—QB3;   3 P—B3, Kt—B3;   4 P—Q4.

	11	12	13	14	15
4	KtxKP	....	....	P—Q4	P—Q3 (i)
5	P—Q5			B—QKt5 (g)	B—K3
	Kt—Kt1	.... Kt—K2	.... B—B4	KPxP	B—K2
6	B—Q3 (a)	KtxP	PxKt (d)	KtxP	P—Q5
	Kt—B4 (b)	Kt—Kt3	BxP ch (e)	B—Q2	Kt—QKt1
7	KtxP	KtxKt	K—K2	PxP	QKt—Q2
	KtxB ch	RPxKt	KtPxP	KtxKt	O—O
8	KtxKt	B—Q3	Q—R4	BxB ch	P—KR3
	P—Q3	Kt—B3	P—KB4	QxB	KtxKP
9	O—O (c)	Q—B3	QKt—Q2	QxKt	KtxKt
	B—K2	P—Q3	O—O	QxP	P—KB4
10	P—KB4	P—KR3	KtxKt	Q—K3 ch	B—Q3
	O—O	Q—K2 ch	PxKt	B—K2	PxKt
11	P—B5	B—K3	QxKP	O—O	BxKP
	Kt—Q2	B—Q2	B—Kt3	Q—Q2	Kt—Q2 =
12	B—K3	Kt—Q2	B—Kt5	Q—B3	
	B—B3	O—O—O	Q—K1	O—O—O	
13	Kt—Q2+	O—O—O+	R—K1	B—K3	
			P—Q3 (f)	Q—Kt5 = (h)	

(a) 6 KtxP, B—B4; 7 Q—Kt4, O—O; 8 QxKt, P—Q3, 9 B—Q3, P—B4; 10 Q—QB4, P—QKt4, 11 QxP, Q—K2, 12 O—O, PxKt, 13 B—QB4, K—R1; 14 B—K3, B—Q3+. Spiess—Hauser, correspondence, 1912.

(b) 6.., Kt—B3; 7 KtxP, B—B4; 8 O—O, O—O; 9 B—B5 ± (Tartakover).

(c) Or 9 Q—B3, B—K2; 10 O—O, O—O; 11 B—K3, Kt—Q2; 12 B—Q4, P—QKt3; 13 Kt—Q2+. Heilmann—Lowy, Nuremburg, 1906.

(d) 6 B—K3, BxB; 7 PxB, Kt—Kt1; 8 B—Q3, Kt—B4; 9 KtxP, Q—Kt4+. J. H. White—R. C. Griffith, 1910.

(e) 6.., KtxKBP, 7 Q—Q5, B—Kt3; 8 QxKP ch, Q—K2; 9 QxQ ch, KxQ; 10 R—Kt1 followed by Kt—Q4+ (Sir G. A. Thomas).

(f) Black has fair drawing chances (Maróczy). If 13 ., P—Q4; 14 QxKP, Q—Kt2, 15 K—Q2, B—KB4; 16 B—K2, P—KR3; 17 B—K7, R—B2; 18 Kt—R4+.

(g) 5 KPxP, QxP; 6 B—K2 (better than 6 P—B4), P—K5 (for PxP; 7 PxP, see Danish Gambit); 7 KKt—Q2, P—K6!, 8 PxP, QxKtP; 9 B—B3, Q—R6; 10 Q—K2, Kt—KKt5, 11 Kt—K4, Q—R5 ch, 12 K—Q1 (not 12 Kt—Kt3, B—Q3; 13 Q—Kt2, KtxRP+), B—Q2; 13 B—Q2, O—O—O+. Tartakover—Bogoljuboff, 1927.

(h) Tartakover—Bogoljuboff, 1928.

(i) Or 4.., PxP?; 5 P—K5, Kt—Q4; 6 PxP, P—Q3; 7 B—QKt5, B—Q2; 8 Q—Kt3+. If 5.., Kt—K5; 6 Q—K2, Kt—B4; 7 PxP, Kt—K3; 8 P—Q5, QKt—Q5; 9 KtxKt, KtxKt; 10 Q—K4+.

QUEEN'S GAMBIT

Queen's Gambit Accepted.

Since in almost all variations of the Queen's Gambit Black sooner or later captures the gambit Pawn, many masters recommend the immediate capture on the 2nd move. This gives Black more freedom of action than the regular variations of the Gambit Declined, but often exposes him to a powerful attack.

After the moves 1 P—Q 4, P—Q 4; 2 P—Q B 4, P × P White must play 3 Kt—K B 3 to prevent the equalising P—K 4.

In the most regular variations (cols. 1 to 12) both sides proceed to develop as quickly as possible; Black concentrates on the Queen's side and White on the King's. In cols. 1 to 4 White omits the development of his Queen's Knight in the hope of profiting from Black's cramped King's position. For a while this line enjoyed a considerable vogue, but master-practice has shown that the advance of his Pawn to B 5, as in col. 1, assures Black at least an even game. Consequently theory at present recommends the lines·in cols. 5 and 6 where White exchanges at Q B 5 and thereby obtains a terrific lead in development. In col. 7 White exchanges Pawns at an earlier stage and his position still remains preferable. The best line for Black is shown in col. 8. Here the second player postpones the development of his Queen's Knight and King's Bishop, thereby avoiding the loss of time of the other columns. It is not advisable for White to prevent Black's Q Kt 4 (col. 9).

In col. 10 White exchanges Pawns too early. Cols. 11 and 12 show the variations where Black isolates White's Queen's Pawn. This gives rise to positions where White generally obtains a powerful attack.

Bogoljuboff's 4 Q—R 4 ch (cols. 13 to 16) may be recommended for those who wish to avoid the drawing possibilities of the earlier columns, for it is not easy to see how Black can obtain complete equality against this line. In cols. 17 to 19 are shown some unusual 3rd moves for Black. Col. 17 has been played and recommended by Alekhine, but is nevertheless not quite sufficient. In col. 20 White tries the Bogoljuboff Variation (Q—R 4 ch) on his 3rd move with good results.

QUEEN'S GAMBIT DECLINED.

This, together with the Queen's Pawn Game, is the typical form of the close game. The majority of modern players use one of these two openings and prefer them to any other. A study of the chess magazines and columns all over the world easily proves this.

In the Orthodox Defence (cols. 1 to 85), Black must content himself with a very cramped game, but avoids the organic weaknesses which the other defences involve. In the main variation White has three main lines on his 7th move :—(i) 7 R—B 1 (cols. 1 to 20); (ii) 7 Q—B 2 (cols. 21 to 28); (iii) 7 B—Q 3 (cols. 30 to 33).

(i) 7 R—B 1 has been analysed almost to exhaustion and the trend now is away from this line. In the main variation (cols. 1 to 7), where Black adopts Capablanca's freeing manœuvre, beginning with 8..., P × P, theory at present can suggest no continuation for White which avoids easy equality. Perhaps the line in col. 5 (13 B—Kt 3), which has attracted a good deal of attention of late, may be the solution.

Alekhine's attack by 11 Kt—K 4 (cols. 6 and 7) has also been shorn of its terrors. In cols. 8 and 9 Black attempts a more enterprising defensive manœuvre, postponing early exchanges. With best play White can maintain a slight pull. In col. 10 White avoids the exchange of pieces.

The older continuation against the Orthodox Defence, 8 Q—B 2, is shown in cols. 11 to 15. This line has practically disappeared from master-practice because of the strength of the reply 8..., Kt—K 5. In general, if Black can play Kt—K 5 with impunity he has solved his opening difficulties.

The Queen's Fianchetto defence for Black (cols. 18 to 20), which was popular when Pillsbury introduced White's attack about 40 years ago, is now a rarity, for White's position remains clearly superior.

(ii) 7 Q—B 2 (cols. 21 to 28) is favoured by many of the younger players, particularly Flohr, Reshevsky, and Lilienthal. Against the best reply 7..., P—B 4 White can either maintain the tension with R—Q 1 (col. 21), when it is difficult for Black to find a good square for his Queen and Queen's Bishop, or play to give Black an isolated Pawn (cols. 23 and 24). White's slight superiority is a dangerous weapon in the hands of Flohr; Black can, however, avoid the isolated Pawn by the line given in col. 25. Col. 26, where the second player attempts to maintain both Pawns in the centre, is unfavourable for him. Alternatives to 7 P—B 4 are unsatisfactory (cols. 27 and 28).

(iii) 7 B—Q 3 (cols. 30 to 33) is played occasionally, but should occasion Black no anxiety.

The Cambridge Springs Defence (cols. 36 to 50) has seen a number of innovations for both sides since our last edition. After Black's 6th move the main variations for White are : 7 Kt—Q 2, 7 B × Kt, and 7 P × P. 7 Kt—Q 2 (cols. 36 to 43) is the older line. Both the counter-attack 7..., B—Kt 5 and the immediate exchange 7..., P × P are sufficient for equality. 7 B × Kt (col. 44) likewise occasions Black no difficulties. 7 P × P (cols. 45 to 50) is the modern line. Black must recapture with the Kt on Q 4, when the position generally becomes very complicated. On his 8th move White then has the choice of 8 Q—Kt 3 (cols. 45 to

47) and 8 Q—Q 2 (cols. 48 and 49). Q—Kt 3 is the stronger of the two and, in conjunction with Landau's B—Q B 4 (col. 47), leaves White a very slight positional advantage.

Variations where White attempts to avoid the Cambridge Springs Defence are shown in cols. 51 to 54. If Black attempts Q—R 4 at all costs he will remain with the inferior position; he can, however, develop normally and transpose into orthodox variations.

The Manhattan Variation (cols. 55 to 59) has not been played much since our last edition. It is occasionally tried by the more enterprising of the masters, but is theoretically inadequate.

The Exchange Variation (cols. 60 to 65) is one of the strongest weapons at White's disposal, since Black can no longer play Capablanca's freeing manœuvre. White can develop his King's Knight either at K 2 (cols. 60 and 61), when he should Castle on the Queen's wing and play for a King-side attack, or at B 3, when Castling on the Queen's wing is unfavourable for him. In the latter case he can Castle on the King's side (col. 63) and proceed with the minority-attack on the other wing, an attack which most experts prefer to avoid with Black. It is advisable for Black to defer Castling until White's intentions are clear (col. 64). To prevent the minority-attack the second player can recapture with B P at Q 4, but this has disadvantages (col. 65).

Lasker's Defence (cols. 66 to 69) is by far the simplest method for Black to draw. The immediate excursion 5..., Kt—K 5 is unfavourable (col. 67), but deferred for one or two moves practically forces a level ending. Tartakover's line, shown in col. 70, is unfavourable for Black.

The development of White's Queen's Bishop at K B 4 instead of Kt 5 has only the element of variety to recommend it. In the line where White plays both Knights out before

developing his Queen's Bishop, Black can reply either 4....
B—Kt 5 (cols. 76 to 79), which leads to lively positions
with chances for both sides, or 4..., P—B 4 (cols. 80 to 85).
In this latter variation the second player obtains the majority
of Pawns on the Queen's side, but must often submit to a
dangerous attack. The immediate exchange of the centre
Pawns is theoretically bad for White, but practice has
shown that the weakness of White's Queen's side is of
little consequence (cols. 80 to 82). Against Pillsbury's old
move, 5 B—Kt 5, Black should adopt the suggestion in col.
84, note (*i*).

The Tarrasch Defence (cols. 86 to 105) is an attempt by
Black to obtain a free game for his pieces at the expense
of an insecure Pawn-position.

The Rubinstein Variation (cols. 86 to 100) is, however,
so strong that most masters prefer to avoid the defence
altogether. The so-called " Folkestone Variation " (cols.
97 to 100) is an interesting method of avoiding the main
line of the Rubinstein Variation. It has been played by
the Swedish players with a good deal of success, but the
lines in cols. 99 and 100 practically refute Black's strategy
In cols. 101 to 105 are seen some less usual lines. The
Von Hennig-Schara Variation (cols. 100 to 102) is now
definitely unsound. Against what Tarrasch called " the
normal variation " (cols. 104 and 105), Black can obtain
at least an equal game by breaking the symmetry.

Cols. 106 to 115 show some unusual defences to the
Gambit. Janowski's Defence, 3..., P—Q R 3 (cols. 106 and
107), costs an important tempo; the same is true of 3...,
P—Q Kt 3 (cols. 108 and 109). Col. 111 is an interesting
attempt by Alekhine to avoid the routine lines.

In all the variations discussed up to now White develops
his Queen's Knight at Q B 3. He can, however, postpone
the development of this Kt, as in cols. 116 to 123, and
develop his King's Knight first. Against this the Vienna

Variation (cols. 116 to 118), which should really be called
Grünfeld's Variation, was very popular for a while and,
although its reputation has fallen a good deal, it is still an
important resource for the second player. In the extremely
complicated line in col. 116 White shows to advantage, but
various theoreticians do not consider the analysis definitive.
Where White, as in cols. 121 to 123, develops his Knight
at Q 2 (one of Capablanca's favourite lines) an early P—
Q B 4 equalises for the second player. In cols. 124 and 125
White omits the development of his Queen's Bishop
altogether ; Black does best to exchange at B 5, transposing
to the Queen's Gambit Accepted.

The Slav Defence (cols. 126 to 165) is now considered by
many the best defence for Black. It has the great advantage
over the other defences that it does not shut in Black's
Queen's Bishop. In the variation where Black captures the
gambit Pawn on his 4th move, now considered the most
important line, White must choose among three possible
systems on his 6th move. 6 P—K 3 (cols. 126 to 130) is
the strongest. Euwe had a great deal of success with it
in his return match with Alekhine; nevertheless, it cannot
be shown that White obtains a clear theoretical advantage.
Against 6 Kt—K 5 (cols. 131 to 134) the older move
6 Q Kt—Q 2 has been refuted by the line in col. 131, but
Bogoljuboff's 6..., P—K 3 (cols. 133 to 143) assures Black
complete equality. 6 Kt—K R 4 (col. 135) has no independent value, for after B—B 1 White's Knight must return
to B 3.

Since the move 5 P—Q R 4, by which the first player
prevents Black's P—Q Kt 4, leads to little or no advantage,
some masters, notably Reshevsky and Stahlberg, prefer to
omit this attempt altogether. This variation has not been
analysed very much, and is consequently a welcome alternative to the routine lines.

The Meran Variation (cols. 141 to 145) has practically
disappeared from tournament practice, and will not re-

appear until an adequate reply to Reshevsky's improvement in the Stahlberg Attack (col. 141) is found.

Some players prefer to avoid the Meran Variation, contenting themselves with a quiet but solid development. Posting his King's Bishop at Q 3 (cols. 146 and 147) is better for Black than at K 2 (cols. 148 and 149), but in both variations Black's position remains cramped, and if White does not break too early in the centre he will retain a clear advantage.

The variations where White defers the development of his Queen's Knight are shown in cols. 153 to 159. By developing his Queen's Bishop as soon as is feasible Black overcomes all opening difficulties. The Landau Variation (col. 154, note (*l*)) was thought to be a refutation of this line, but this opinion is no longer held by any prominent master

In cols. 157 to 159 Black shuts in his Queen's Bishop and White develops his Kt at Q 2. This development of the Queen's Knight, sometimes known as the " Semmering system," is not to be feared.

The Semi-Slav Defence (col. 160) gives rise to interesting complications, which are, however, in White's favour. The immediate development of White's Queen's Knight (cols. 161 to 163) is recommended by Alekhine, who scored a notable success with it against Euwe. The complications shown in col. 161 are certainly favourable for White, but Black can obtain an even position by adopting the variation in note (*c*). It would be interesting to see Winawer's Counter-Gambit (col. 163) adopted in tournament play, since no theoretical refutation is known. The Exchange Variation (cols. 164 and 165), long one of Marshall's pet lines, is no more considered dangerous for Black.

Albin's Counter-Gambit (cols. 166 to 170) is sometimes adopted to avoid the difficulties of the close defences. In the main line (cols. 166 to 168) Black can only regain the gambit Pawn at the cost of a disrupted position.

1 P—Q 4, P—Q 4 ;   2 P—Q B 4, P×P ;   3 Kt—K B 3 (A), Kt—K B 3 ; 4 P—K 3, P—K 3 ;   5 B×P, P—B 4 ;   6 O—O, P—Q R 3 ;   7 Q—K 2, Kt—B 3.

	1	2	3	4	5
8	R—Q 1				Kt—B 3
	P—Q Kt 4				P—Q Kt 4
9	B—Kt 3		P×P		B—Kt 3 !
	P—B 5	Q—Kt 3	Q—B 2		B—K 2 (i)
10	B—B 2	P—Q R 4	B—Q 3		P×P
	Kt—Q Kt 5	B—Kt 2	Kt—Q Kt 5 .. B×P		B×P
11	Kt—B 3	R P×P	P—Q R 3	P—Q R 4	P—K 4
	Kt×B	R P×P	Kt×B	P×P ! (g)	P—Kt 5 (j)
12	Q×Kt	R×R ch	Q×Kt	R×P	P—K 5 !
	B—Kt 2 (a)	B×R	B×P	Kt—Q Kt 5	P×Kt
13	P—Q 5 !	Kt—B 3	P—Q Kt 4	B—Kt 5 ch	P×Kt
	Q—B 2 ! (b)	P—B 5	B—K 2	B—Q 2	Kt P×P
14	P—K 4	B—B 2	B—Kt 2	B×B ch	Q—B 4
	P—K 4	B—Kt 5 ! (d)	B—Kt 2	Kt×B	Q—Kt 3
15	B—Kt 5	P—K 4	B—K 5	B—Q 2	Q×B P
	Kt—Q 2	Kt–K 2 ! = (e)	Q—B 3	P—Q R 4	Kt—Q 5
16	B—K 3		Q Kt—Q 2	R—Q B 1	Kt×Kt
	B—B 4		R–Q B 1 ∓ (f)	Q—Kt 2	B×Kt
17	B×B			B—B 3 = (h)	B—R 4 ch +
	Q×B= (c)				(k)

(A) 3 Kt—Q B 3, P—K 4 ! ; 4 P—K 3, P×P ; 5 P×P, Kt—Q B 3=. Marshall--Janowski, New York, 1924. If 3 P—K 4, P—K 4 ; 4 P—Q 5, Kt—K B 3 ; 5 Kt—Q B 3, B—Q B 4 ; 6 B×P, Kt—Kt 5 +. Steinitz—Blackburne, London, 1899. If 3 P—K 3, equally P—K 4 !.

(a) 12.., Kt—Q 4 is a good alternative, e.g. 13 P—K 4, Kt—Kt 5 ; 14 Q—K 2, Kt—Q 6 ; 15 P—Q Kt 3, B—Kt 5 ; 16 B—Q 2, O—O ; 17 P×P, P×P ; 18 Kt—K 1 (18 Q—K 3, P—B 4 ! ∓. Landau—A. Reynolds, Ostend, 1937), Q×P ; 19 Kt—B 2=. Schmidt—Turn, Reval, 1936.

(b) 13.., P×P ; 14 P—K 4, B—K 2 ; 15 P—K 5 !, Kt—Q 2 ; 16 Q—B 5, O—O ; 17 Kt×P+. Euwe—Grunfeld, Zandvoort, 1936.

(c) Reshevsky—Flohr, Nottingham, 1936.

(d) 14.., B—K 2 ; 15 P—K 4, Kt—Q Kt 5 ; 16 B—Kt 1, O—O ; 17 P—K 5, K Kt—Q 4 ; 18 Kt—Kt 5 ±. Lilienthal—Belavenetz, match, Moscow, 1935.

(e) Grünfeld—Opocensky, Marienbad, 1925.

(f) Goglidse—Lasker, Moscow, 1935.

(g) 11 , P—Kt 5 ? ; 12 Q Kt—Q 2, Kt—Q R 4 (or 12 , O—O ; 13 Kt—Kt 3, B—K 2 ; 14 P—K 4 ±. Alekhine—Flohr, Bled, 1931) ; 13 P—Q Kt 3, Kt—Q 4, (O—O !) ; 14 B—Kt 2, Kt—B 6 ; 15 B×Kt, P×B ; 16 Kt—K 4, Kt×P ; 17 Q R—Kt 1, Kt—R 4 ; 18 K R—Q B 1 ! +. Euwe—Flohr, 8th match game, 1932.

(h) Botvinnik—Flohr, 3rd match game, 1933.

(i) 9. , P—Kt 5 ; 10 P—Q 5 !, Kt—Q R 4 ; 11 B—R 4 ch, B—Q 2 ; 12 P×P !, P×P ; 13 R—Q 1 ! !, P×Kt ; 14 R×B ! !, Kt×R ; 15 Kt—K 5, R—R 2 ; 16 P×P ! ! + +. Alekhine—Book, Margate, 1938.

(j) Preferable is 11 , Kt—Q 2 ; 12 P—K 5, O—O ; 13 Kt—K 4, P—R 3 (13.., Kt—Q 5 ? ; 14 Kt×Kt, B×Kt ; 15 Kt—Kt 5 !+) ; 14 R—Q 1, Q—K 2 ±.

(k) 17.., K—K 2 ; 18 B—K 3 ! ! and White won quickly. Euwe—Alekhine, 5th match game, 1937.

1 P—Q 4, P—Q 4 ; 2 P—Q B 4, P×P ; 3 Kt—K B 3, Kt—K B 3 ;
4 P—K 3, P—K 3 ; 5 B×P, P—B 4 ; 6 O—O.

	6	7	8	9	10
6	(P—Q R 3)				Kt—B 3
7	(Q—K 2)			P—Q R 4	Kt—B 3
	(Kt—B 3)		P—Q Kt 4	Kt—B 3	B—K 2
8	(Kt—B 3)...P×P		B—Kt 3	Q—K 2 (g)	P×P
	(P—Q Kt 4)	B×P	B—Kt 2	B—K 2	Q×Q
9	(B—Kt 3)	P—Q R 3	R—Q 1 (e)	R—Q 1 (h)	R×Q
	B—Kt 2	P—Q Kt 4	Q Kt—Q 2	Q—B 2	B×P
10	R—Q 1	B—R 2	P—Q R 4	Kt—B 3	P—Q R 3
	Q—Kt 3	B—Kt 2	P—Kt 5	O—O	K—K 2 (k)
11	P—Q 5 !	P—Q Kt 4	Q Kt—Q 2	P—R 3	P—Q Kt 4
	P×P	B—K 2 (c)	Q—B 2	R—Q 1 (i)	B—Kt 3
12	P—K 4 (a)	B—Kt 2	Kt—B 4	P—Q 5	B—Kt 2
	P×P ? (b)	O—O	B—K 2	P×P	R—Q 1
13	Kt×K P .	Q Kt—Q 2	K Kt—K 5	B×P !	R×R
	Kt×Kt	Q—Kt 3	O—O	Kt—Q Kt 5	B×R
14	Q×Kt ch	Kt—Kt 3	B—Q 2	P—K 4	P—K 4
	B—K 2	K R—Q 1	Q R—B 1	K Kt×B	B—Q 2
15	B—Q 5 ! +	QR-B1 ± (d)	Q R—B 1	P×Kt	B—Q 3
			K R—Q 1 = (f)	B—B 4 = (j)	P-KR3 = (l)

(a) If 12 B×P, P—Kt 5; 13 B×P ch¹? (13 Kt—K Kt 5, O—O—O! is the alternative), K×B; 14 Q—B 4 ch, K—K 2! (14 .., K—K 1?; 15 Q—K 6 ch, B—K 2; 16 Kt—K 5!, R—K B 1; 17 Kt—Q 5!, Q—Q 1; 18 K Kt×Kt, B×Kt; 19 Q×B ch + Stahlberg—Böök, Kemeri, 1937); 15 Kt—Q 5 ch, Kt×Kt; 16 Q×Kt, R—Q 1; 17 Q—K 4 ch, K—B 3; 18 Q—B 4 ch, K—K 2 with a draw by perpetual check. Analysis by Fred Reinfeld.

(b) The only playable move is 13 .., O—O—O! (Reshevsky). The column is Reshevsky—Vidmar, Nottingham, 1936.

(c) 11 .., B—Kt 3 is preferable.

(d) Eliskases—Muffang, Warsaw, 1935.

(e) 9 P—Q R 4, Q Kt—Q 2!; 10 R—Q 1, B—K 2 (10 .., P—Kt 5 transposes back into the column); 11 Q P×P, O—O; 12 B—B 2 (better 12 P—B 6. Euwe), B×P; 13 Kt—K 5, P—Kt 5; 14 Kt×Kt, Kt×Kt; 15 Kt—Q 2, P—B 4!=. Euwe—Alekhine, Bad Nauheim, 1937.

(f) Keres—Reshevsky, Semmering-Baden, 1937.

(g) 8 Kt—B 3, B—K 2; 9 P×P (for 9 Q—K 2 see note (h)), B×P!; 10 Q×Q ch, K×Q; 11 P—K 4, Kt—K Kt 5; 12 B—B 4, P—B 3; 13 P—R 3, K Kt—K 4; 14 K R—Q 1 ch, K—K 2 ∓. Flohr—Rubinstein, Prague, 1931.

(h) If 9 Kt—B 3, P×P; 10 R—Q 1, P—K 4; 11 P×P, P×P; 12 Kt×P, Kt×Kt; 13 Q—K 5, Q—Q 3¹=.

(i) 11 .., P—Q Kt 3?; 12 P—Q 5!, P×P; 13 B×Q P, B—Kt 2; 14 P—K 4, Q R—Q 1; 15 B—K 3, Kt—Q 2; 16 R—Q 2, B—B 3; 17 Q R—Q 1+. Eliskases—Reshevsky, Semmering-Baden, 1937.

(j) 16 B—B 4!, Q×B; 17 Q×B and now 17 .., B×P (17 .., P—Q Kt 3?; 18 P—R 5, R—K 1; 19 Q—R 4, Q×Q; 20 Kt×Q, B—B 7; 21 R—Q 2, P×P; 22 R×P ±. Reshevsky—Fine, Semmering-Baden, 1937), 18 Kt—K 2, Q—Kt 5; 19 Kt—Kt 3, Kt×P; 20 Q×Kt P, Q—B 1; 21 Q×Q, B×Q; 22 Kt—K 4, P—B 5.

(k) 10 .., P—Q R 3?; 11 P—Q Kt 4, B—K 2; 12 B—Kt 2, O—O is playable, but not 12 .., P—Q Kt 4?; 13 Kt×P!, P×Kt; 14 B×Kt P, B—Q 2; 15 R×B!++, Bogoljuboff—Flohr, Bled, 1931.

(l) Bogoljuboff—Alekhine, 5th match game, 1934.

1 P—Q 4, P—Q 4; 2 P—Q B 4, P×P; 3 Kt—K B 3, Kt—K B 3 (a).

	11	12	13	14	15
4	(P—K 3)		Q—R 4 ch		
	(P—K 3)		Q—Q 2	B—Q 2	P—B 3
5	(B×P)		Q×B P	Q×B P	Q×B P
	(P—B 4)		Q—B 3	P—K 3	B—B 4
6	(O—O)		Kt—Q R 3 !	Kt—B 3	Kt—B 3
	P×P		Q×Q	Kt—R 3	Q Kt—Q 2
7	P×P		Kt×Q	P—K 4	P—K Kt 3
	P—Q R 3	B—K 2	P—K 3	P—B 4	P—K 3 (h)
8	Q—K 2 (b)	Q—K 2	P—Q R 3	B—K 2	B—Kt 2
	P—Q Kt 4	Kt—B 3	P—B 4	P×P	B—B 7 !? (i)
9	B—Q 3	R—Q 1	B—B 4 !	Kt×P	P—K 3
	B—Kt 2	P—Q R 3	Kt—B 3	R—B 1	B—K 2
10	P—Q R 4 ! (c)	Kt—B 3	P×P	Q—Q 3	O—O
	P—Kt 5	Kt—Q Kt 5	B×P	Kt—Q Kt 5	O—O
11	Q Kt—Q 2	B—K Kt 5	P—Q Kt 4	Q—Kt 1	P—Q R 3
	B—K 2	O—O	B—K 2	P—K 4	P—Q R 4
12	Kt—B 4	Kt—K 5	P—Kt 5	Kt—B 3	Q—K 2
	P—Q R 4	Q Kt—Q 4	Kt—Q Kt 1	B—Q B 4	B—Kt 3
13	B—B 4	Q R—B 1	Kt—Q 6 ch	O—O	P—K 4
	O—O	R—K 1	B×Kt	Kt—B 3	Q—Kt 3
14	KR—Q1 ± (d)	B—Q 3	B×B ± (f)	B-KKt5±(g)	P—R 3 ±(j)
		P—R 3 (e)			

(a) If 3 .., B—Kt 5 ?; 4 Kt—K 5, B—R 4; 5 Kt—Q B 3, P—K 3; 6 P—K Kt 4, B—Kt 3; 7 P—K R 4, P—K B 3; 8 Q—R 4 ch, P—B 3; 9 Kt×B, P×Kt; 10 Q×P (B 4)+. Alekhine—Grunfeld, Semmering, 1926.

(b) 8 P—Q R 3, Kt—B 3; 9 Kt—B 3, B—K 2; 10 B—K 3, O—O; 11 B—Q 3, P—Q Kt 4; 12 B—B 2, B—Kt 2; 13 Q—K 2, R—B 1; 14 Q R—B 1, Kt—Q R 4; 15 Kt—K 5 ±. Bogoljuboff—Fine, Zandvoort, 1936.

(c) 10 Kt—B 3, B—K 2; 11 B—Kt 5, O—O; 12 Q R—Q 1, Q Kt—Q 2; 13 Kt—K 5, Kt—Q 4; 14 B—B 1, K Kt×Kt; 15 P×Kt, Kt—B 3∓. Lasker—Reshevsky, Nottingham, 1936.

(d) Landau—Reshevsky, Kemeri, 1937.

(e) 15 B—R 4, B—Q 2; 16 B—Kt 1. White has attacking chances, Black a better Pawn position. The position is slightly in White's favour. The column is Colle—Maróczy, Hastings, 1924

(f) Alekhine—Fine, Kemeri, 1937.

(g) Tartakover—Book, Kemeri, 1937.

(h) 7 .., Kt—K 5; 8 B—Kt 2, Kt×Kt! (8 .., Kt—Q 3; 9 Q—R 4, Kt—Kt 3; 10 Q—Q 1, Q—B 1, 11 O—O, B—R 6; 12 P—K 4, B×B; 13 K×B, P—K 3; 14 P—Q 5!+. Botvinnik—Lövenfisch, Moscow, 1935); 9 P×Kt, Kt—Kt 3; 10 Q—Kt 3, B—K 5; 11 Kt—K 5, B—Q 4!, 12 B×B, Q×B; 13 P—B 3=.

(i) Threatening .., Kt—Kt 3, winning White's Queen.

(j) Bogoljuboff—Alekhine, 23rd match game, 1934.

1 P—Q 4, P—Q 4; 2 P—Q B 4, P×P.

	16	17	18	19	20
3	(Kt—K B 3).................................				Q—R 4 ch
	(Kt—K B 3).P—Q R 3	....P—K 3	.....P—Q B 4		Q—Q 2
4	(Q—R 4 ch)	P—K 3 (g)	P—K 4	P—Q 5	Q×B P
	Q Kt—Q 2	B—Kt 5	P—Q B 4	P—K 3	Q—B 3
5	Kt—B 3 (a)	B×P	B×P	P—K 4	P—K 3
	P—K 3	P—K 3	P×P	P×P	P—K 3
6	P—K 4	P—K R 3 (h)	Kt×P	P×P	Kt—Q B 3
	P—B 4 ! (b)	B—R 4	Kt—KB3(j)	Kt—K B 3	Q×Q
7	P—Q 5 (c)	Kt—B 3	Kt—Q B 3	B×P	B×Q
	P×P	Kt—K B 3	B—B 4	B—Q 3	Kt—KB3(n)
8	P—K 5	O—O	B—K 3	O—O	Kt—Kt 5
	P—QKt4!(d)	Kt—B 3	QKt—Q2(k)	O—O	Kt—R 3
9	Q×Kt P (e)	P—R 3	B×P	B—K Kt 5	P—Q R 3
	K—Q Kt 1	B—Q 3	P×B	B—Kt 5	P—Q Kt 3
10	Q—R 4	B—K 2	Kt×P	Kt—B 3	Kt—K 2
	P—Q 5	O—O	Q—R 4	Q Kt—Q 2	B—Kt 2
11	P×Kt	Kt—Q 2	O—O	Kt—K 4 (m)	P—B 3
	P×Kt	B×B	B×B	B—K 4 =	B—K 2
12	B×P	Q×B	P×B		P—K 4
	R-Kt5! ∓ (f)	P—K 4	K—B 2		P—B 3
13		P×P= (i)	Q—Kt 3+ (l)		QKt—B3±

(a) P—K Kt 3, here or on the next move, transposes to the Catalan System, p. 228.

(b) If 6. , B—K 2; 7 B×P, O—O; 8 Q—B 2, P—B 4; 9 P×P, B×P; 10 O—O ±. H. Muller—Grünfeld, Vienna, 1934.

(c) 7 B×P is safer.

(d) If 8.., P—Q 5; 9 P×Kt, P×Kt; 10 B×P+.

(e) If 9 Kt×Kt P?, Kt—K 5; 10 B—B 4, B—K 2; 11 P—K 6, O—O!; 12 P×Kt, B×P; 13 Q—R 6, B—B 3; 14 R—Q Kt 1, P—Kt 4!; 15 Kt—B 7, P×B, 16 Kt×R, Q×Kt+. Raud—Schmidt, 1936-37. A possible alternative is 9 Q—B 2, Kt—K 5; 10 Kt×Q P, P—B 4 with an unclear position.

(f) 12 , B P×P?; 13 B×P ch!, K×B; 14 Q—B 4 ch, K—K 1; 15 P—B 7 ch!, K—K 2; 16 B×P, R×B; 17 O—O with a winning attack. The column and notes are due to Keres.

(g) 4 Kt—B 3, Kt—K B 3; 5 P—K 4?, P—Q Kt 4; 6 P—K 5, Kt—Q 4; 7 Kt—Kt 5, P—K 3; 8 Q—B 3, Q—Q 2; 9 Kt×Kt, P×Kt; 10 P—Q R 3, Kt—B 3 + Bogoljuboff—Alekhine, 17th match game, 1934 If 4 P—Q R 4, Kt—K B 3; 5 P—K 3 B—Kt 5; 6 B×P, Kt—B 3; 7 Kt—B 3, Kt—B 3; 8 B—K 2, B—Kt 5; 9 O—O O—O; 10 Kt—Q 2, B×B ∓. Ahues—Alekhine, Bad Nauheim, 1936.

(h) A stronger line is 6 Q—Kt 3, B×Kt; 7 P×B, P—Q Kt 4; 8 B—K 2, Kt—K B 3, 9 P—Q R 4, P—Kt 5; 10 Q—B 4! ± (but not 10 P—R 5?, P—B 4; 11 P×P, B×P: 12 Q—B 4, Q—K 2 ∓. Euwe—Reshevsky, Stockholm, 1937)

(i) Bogoljuboff—Alekhine, 3rd match game, 1934.

(j) Or 6. , P—Q R 3; 7 Kt—Q B 3, B—Q 2, 8 O—O, Kt—Q B 3, 9 Kt—B 3, Q—B 2; 10 Q—K 2, B—Q 3; 11 R—Q 1, K Kt—K 2; 12 B—K 3, Kt—K 4. 13 Kt×Kt ±. Spielmann—Grünfeld, Carlsbad, 1929.

(k) 8 , O—O is necessary, but Black remains cramped

(l) Capablanca—Bogoljuboff, Moscow, 1925

(m) Capablanca—Zubareff, Moscow, 1925

(n) 7 ., P—Q R 3 is better   The column is Reshevsky—Dake, New York, 1936.

1 P—Q4, P—Q4; 2 P—QB4, P—K3; 3 Kt—QB3, Kt—KB3; 4 B—Kt5, QKt—Q2.

5 P—K3, B—K2; 6 Kt—B3, O—O; 7 R—B1, P—B3; 8 B—Q3, P×P; 9 B×P, Kt—Q4; 10 B×B, Q×B; 11 O—O, Kt×Kt; 12 R×Kt, P—K4 (a).

	1	2	3	4	5
13	P×P Kt×P		Q—B2 P×P	......P—K5	B—Kt3 P—K5
14	Kt×Kt Q×Kt		P×P Kt—B3 (k)	Kt—Q2 Kt—B3	Kt—Q2 K—R1
15	P—B4 Q—B3 (b)	...Q—K5	R—K1 Q—Q3	R—B1 B—B4 (m)	Q—B2 Kt—B3 (o)
16	P—B5 (c) P—QKt4 (d)	B—Kt3 B—B4 (g)	Kt—Kt5 B—Kt5 !	P—B4 QR—Q1	P—KR3 B—K3
17	B—Q3 B—Kt2 (e)	Q—R5 P—KKt3 (h)	Q—Kt3 B—R4	P—QR3 P—KR4	B×B Q×B
18	Q—B3 QR—Q1	Q—R4 (i) QR—Q1	Q×P QR—Kt1	P—QKt4 P—KKt3	R—Kt3 Q—K2
19	B×P R—Q7	B—B2 Q—Q4	Q×RP R×P= (l)	Q—Kt3 R—Q2= (n)	R—B1 KR—K1
20	R—Kt3 (f) R×P	R—Q1 Q—R4			Q—B5 P—QR4 ?
21	B—B4 R×R	R×R Q×R			R—R3 Q×Q
22	P×R ±	Q×Q R×Q= (j)			P×Q+

(a) If 12 , P—QKt3; 13 Q—B2, P—QB4; 14 P×P, Kt×P; 15 P—QKt4, Kt—R3; 16 P—QR3, B—Kt2; 17 B—Q3, P—Kt3; 18 KR—B1+. Capablanca—H. Steiner, Budapest, 1928.

(b) If 15.., Q—K2 (played in the exhibition game Rubinstein—Lasker, 1924, where this variation first appeared); 16 P—B5, P—QKt4; 17 B—Kt3, P—Kt5; 18 P—B6!, P×P; 19 QR×P, Q×Pch; 20 K—R1, B—Kt2; 21 QR×P++. Euwe—Sir G. A. Thomas, Hastings, 1934-35.

(c) 16 P—K4, B—K3; 17 P—K5, Q—K2; 18 B×B, P×B! leads to a very drawish position.

(d) If 16.., R—Q1; not 17 Q—R5?, P—QKt4; 18 B—Kt3, P—Kt5; 19 R—QB2, B—R3; 20 R—K1, B—Q6 ∓; but 17 R—Q3!, R×R; 18 Q×R+, for if 18 , P—QKt4?; 19 B×P!, P×B; 20 Q—K4 and wins.

(e) Tartakover recommends 17.., P—Kt5; 18 R—B2, R—Q1; 19 Q—K2, P—QR4; 20 KR—B1, B×P =.

(f) Suggested by Grünfeld. If instead 20 B×P, R×P; 21 QR—B1, B—R3; 22 KR—K1, R×P; 23 B—Q5, R—Q7; 24 P—K4, B—B1 ∓. Grünfeld—Becker, Vienna, 1934.

(g) 16.., B—K3?; 17 B—B2, Q—QKt5; 18 P—B5, Q×P; 19 Q—K1!, B×RP; 20 P—B6, P—KKt3; 21 Q—R4!, K—R1; 22 Q—R6, R—KKt1; 23 R—KB4++.

(h) 17.., B—Kt3?; 18 Q—R3!+.

(i) If 18 Q—R6, QR—Q1; 19 B—B2, Q—Q4; 20 P—K4, B×P; 21 R—KR3 (21 B×B?, Q×B; 22 R—KR3, Q—Q5ch; 23 K—R1, Q—Kt2+), Q—B4ch!; 22 R—B2 (22 K—R1?, B×Pch; 23 K×B, Q×Pch++), KR—K1; 23 Q×RPch, K—B1; 24 R—QB3, Q—Q5; 25 P—KR3, B×B+.

(j) Analysis by Lövenfisch.

(k) 14.., Kt—Kt3; 15 R—K1, Q—B3; 16 B—Kt3, B—B4; 17 Q—K2, QR—Q1; 18 Q—K7, R—Q2; 19 Q—Q3!±.

(l) Black's attack is worth the Pawn (Alekhine).

(m) 15.., B—Kt5?; 16 P—Kt4!, P—QR3; 17 Q—Kt1, QR—Q1; 18 P—QR4, R—Q3; 19 P—Kt5+. Vidmar—Fine, Warsaw, 1935.

(n) Winter—Vidmar, Nottingham, 1936.

(o) If 15.., P—KB4; 16 P—B3, Kt—B3; 17 P×P, P×P; 18 QR—B5 ±, but not 18 Kt×P?, B—B4!!; 19 R×B, Kt×Kt+. Stahlberg—Grob, Ostend, 1936. The column is Stahlberg—Fine, 8th match game, 1937.

1 P—Q 4, P—Q 4 ; 2 P—Q B 4, P—K 3 ; 3 Kt—Q B 3, Kt—K B 3 ; 4 B—Kt 5, Q Kt—Q 2.

5 P—K 3, B—K 2 ; 6 Kt—B 3, O—O ; 7 R—B 1, P—B 3 ; 8 B—Q 3.

	6	7	8	9	10
8	(P×P)			P—K R 3	
9	(B×P)		B—R 4		B—B 4
	(Kt—Q 4)		P×P		Kt—R 4
10	(B×B) (o)		B×P .		B—K 5
	(Q×B)		P—Q Kt 4		Kt×B
11	Kt—K 4		B—Q 3		P×Kt
	K Kt—B 3 ..P—K 4 (c)		P—Q R 3		P-K Kt3 (m)
12	Kt—Kt 3	P×P	P—Q R 4 (g)..	O—O	O—O
	P—K 4 (a)	Q Kt×P	P×P	P—B 4	B—Q 2
13	O—O	B×Kt (d)	Kt×P	P—Q R 4	Q—Q 2
	P×P	P×B	Q—R 4 ch	P—B 5	P×P
14	Kt—B 5	Q×P (e)	Kt—Q 2 (h)	B—Kt 1	B×P
	Q—Q 1	Kt×Kt ch	B—Kt 5	Kt—Q 4	Q—B 2
15	K Kt×P	P×Kt	Kt—B 3	B×B (k)	Kt—K 4
	Kt—K 4	B—K 3	P—B 4	Q×B	Q R—Q 1
16	B—Kt 3	Q—Q R 5 (f)	Kt—B 4	P—Q Kt3 !	Q—B 3
	B×Kt	P—Q Kt 3	Q—Q 1 ! (i)	Q Kt—Kt 3	B—B 1 = (n)
17	Kt×B	Q—R 4	Kt—K 5	P×B P ± (l)	
	P—KKt3 !=	P—K B 4	P×P != (j)		
		(b)			

(a) 12.., Q—Kt 5 ch; 13 Q—Q 2, Q×Q ch; 14 K×Q, R—Q 1; 15 K R—Q 1, P—Q Kt 3; 16 P—K 4, B—Kt 2; 17 P—K 5, Kt—K 1 (Alekhine—Capablanca, 22nd match game, 1927) is inferior for Black.

(b) Euwe—Flohr, Nottingham, 1936. If here 17. , Q—Kt 3?; 18 Q—Q 6, Q Kt—Q 2; 19 K R—Q 1, Q R—Q 1; 20 Q—Kt 3+. Alekhine—Lasker, Zurich, 1934.

(c) 11.., Q—Kt 5 ch; 12 Q—Q 2, Q×Q ch; 13 K×Q, R—Q 1, Kt (Q 2)—B 3; 15 Kt×Kt ch, Kt×Kt; 16 B—Kt 3, K—B 1; 17 K—K 2 ±. Alekhine—Capablanca, 6th match game, 1927.

(d) If 13 Kt×Kt, Q×Kt; 14 B×Kt, P×B; 15 Kt—B 3, R—Q 1 followed by P—Q 5. V. Buerger—R. P. Michell, 1926.

(e) If 14 Kt—B 3, B—Kt 5; 15 Kt×P, Q—Q 3; 16 O—O?, Q R—Q 1+ +. R. P. Michell—A. R. B. Thomas, Edinburgh, 1926.

(f) The alternative is 16 Q—K 5, Q—Kt 5 ch; 17 Q—B 3, Q R—B 1; 18 Q×Q, R×R ch with a difficult ending. Black now obtains a strong attack. The column is Winter—R. P. Michell, London, 1928.

(g) 12 P—K 4?, Kt×P!; 13 B×Kt, B×B; 14 B×P, R—R 2; 15 O—O, Kt—Kt 3; 16 Kt—K 4, B—K 2; 17 Kt—K 5, R—B 2; 18 Q—Q 3, Kt—B 5!; 19 Kt×Kt, R×B; 20 Kt—K 5, R×R ∓ Euwe—Alekhine, 28th match game, 1935.

(h) 13 Kt—B 3, Kt—R 1; 14 R—R 1, Q—Kt 5; 15 O—O, B—Kt 2; 16 Q—K 2, P×P; 17 P×P, B×Kt =. Vidmar—Lasker, Nottingham, 1936.

(i) 16.., Q—B 2; 17 B—Kt 3, Q—Kt 2; 18 O—O, P×P; 19 ♙×P, R—Q 1; 20 Kt—R 4, Kt—Q 4; 21 K—R 4 ±. Fine—Belavenetz, Moscow, 1937.

(j) 18 P×P, B—Kt 2!; 19 Kt×Kt, Q×Kt; 20 B×Kt, P×B.

(k) 15 Q—B 2, P—Kt 3!; 16 B×B, Q×B; 17 P—K 4, Kt×Kt; 18 Q×Kt, B—Kt 2; 19 Q—R 5, K R—B 1; 20 P—Q Kt 3, Kt—B 3!=. Ragosin—Eliskases, Semmering-Baden, 1937.

(l) Alatorzeff—Ragosin, Russian Championship, 1938.

(m) 11.., P×P?; 12 B×P, Q×Q ch; 73 R×Q, P—K Kt 3; 14 P—K Kt 4, Kt—Kt 2; 15 Kt—K 4+. Fine—Maroczy, Zandvoort, 1936.

(n) Sir G. A. Thomas—Lasker, Nottingham, 1936.

(o) 10 B—B 4, Kt×B; 11 P×Kt, Kt—K 3!; 12 B—Kt 3, Kt—Q 4; 13 P—Kt 3, Kt×Kt; 14 P×Kt, P—Q B 4 =. Or 10 P—K R 4, Kt×Kt (10.., P—B 3; 11 B—B 4, Kt×B; 12 P×Kt, Kt—Kt 3, as in Janowski—Capablanca, New York, 1924, is weaker); 11 R×Kt, P—Q Kt 3; 13 B—Kt 3, B—Kt 2 =.

1 P—Q 4, P—Q 4 ; 2 P—Q B 4, P—K 3 ; 3 Kt—Q B 3, Kt—K B 3 ; 4 B—Kt 5, Q Kt—Q 2.

5 P—K 3, B—K 2 ; 6 Kt—B 3, O—O ; 7 R—B 1, P—B 3 ; 8 Q—B 2.

	11	12	13	14	15
8	Kt—K 5 !...P×P	....	P—Q R 3	....	P—K R 3 (*k*)
9	B×B	B×P	P—Q R 3....P×P	B—R 4
	Q×B	Kt—Q 4	R—K 1	K P×P	P—R 3
10	Kt×Kt (*a*)	B×B (*d*)	P—K R 3	B—Q 3	P—Q R 3
	P×Kt	Q×B	P—K R 3	P—R 3	P—Q Kt 4
11	Q×P	O—O	B—R 4 (*f*)	B—R 4	P—B 5 (*l*)
	Q—Kt 5 ch	Kt×Kt	P×P	Kt—K 1	P—K 4
12	Kt—Q 2	Q×Kt	B×P	B—Kt 3	P×P
	Q×Kt P	P—Q Kt 3	P—Q Kt 4	B—Q 3	Kt—K 1
13	R—Q Kt 1	Q—Q 3	B—R 2	O—O	B×B
	Q—R 6 (*b*)	R—Q 1	P—B 4	B×B	Q×B
14	Q—B 2	Q—K 2	P×P (*g*)	R P×B	Kt—K 2
	P—K 4	B—Kt 2 (*e*)	Kt×P (*h*)	Kt—Q 3	Kt×K P
15	B—Q 3	B—R 6	B—Kt 1 (*i*)	Kt—Q R 4	Kt×Kt
	P×P	B×B	Q Kt—Q 2 !	R—K 1	Q×Kt
16	B×P ch	Q×B	O—O	K R—K 1	Kt—Q 4
	K—R 1	P—Q B 4	Kt—B 1	Kt—B 3	B—Q 2
17	O—O	K R—Q 1	K R—Q 1	Kt—K 5	B—Q 3
	Q—Q 3 = (*c*)	P—K 4 =	Q—Kt 3 =	Kt(B)—K 5 =	Kt—B 2 =
				(*j*)	(*m*)

(*a*) 10 B—Q 3, P—K B 4 ; 11 Kt—K 5 (or 11 O—O, R—B 3 ; 12 Kt—K 1, R—R 3 ; 13 P—B 3 ?, Q—R 5 ; 14 P×Kt, Q×P ch ; 15 K—B 2, B P×P ; 16 B×P, P×B ; 17 Kt×P, Kt—B 3 +. Bogoljuboff—Przepiorka, Munich, 1926 ; here 13 P—B 4, Q Kt—B 3 = is correct), Kt×Kt, 12 P×Kt, P—Q Kt 3 ; 13 O—O, Kt×Kt ; 14 Q×Kt, P—B 4 ; 15 P—B 4, B—Kt 2 =. Gereben—Znosko-Borovsky, 1935.
(*b*) 13.., Q×R P, 14 B—Q 3, Kt—B 3 ; 15 Q—R 4 with a strong attack.
(*c*) 18 B—B 5, Kt—B 4. Alekhine—Van den Bosch, Amsterdam, 1936.
(*d*) 10 Kt—K 4, Q—R 4 ch ; 11 K—K 2, P—B 3 ; 12 B—R 4, Q Kt—Kt 3 with at least an even game, for if 13 B—Q Kt 3, Kt—Kt 5 ∓ (Alekhine).
(*e*) 14. , P—Q R 3 ? ; 15 B—Q 3, B—Kt 2 ; 16 B—K 4, Q R—B 1 ; 17 Kt—Q 2, P—K 4 ; 18 Kt—B 4 ±. Alekhine and others—Bogoljuboff and others, Budapest, 1921.
(*f*) 11 B—B 4, P×P ; 12 B×B P, P—Q Kt 4 ; 13 B—Q 2, P—B 4 ; 14 P—Q 5, P×P, 15 Kt×Q P, R—R 2 !; 16 Kt×B ch, Q×Kt =. Flohr—Fine, Warsaw 1935.
(*g*) 14 R—Q 1, P×P ; 15 Kt×Q P, Q—Kt 3 ; 16 B—Kt 1, B—Kt 2 !; 17 O—O, Q R—B 1 ∓. Grünfeld—Alekhine, Carlsbad, 1923.
(*h*) 14. , B×P ? ; 15 O—O, B—Kt 2 ; 16 K R—Q 1, Q—Kt 3 ; 17 B—Kt 1, B—Q 3 ; 18 R×B !, Q×R ; 19 R—Q 1, Q—B 2 ; 20 R×Kt !++. Pirc—H. Steiner, Prague, 1931.
(*i*) If 15 O—O, Q—Q 6 =. But not 15 ., B—Kt 2 ? ; 16 K R—Q 1, Q—Kt 3 ; 17 B×Kt !, B×B ; 18 P—Q Kt 4, B×K Kt ; 19 P×B+. Pirc—Tylor, Hastings, 1932-33.
(*j*) Capablanca—Alekhine, 27th match game, 1927.
(*k*) If 8..., P—B 4 ? ; 9 B P×P, K P×P ; 10 B×Kt, Kt×B ; 11 P×P, Q—R 4 ; 12 B—Q 3, Q×B P ; 13 O—O, B—Q 2, 14 Kt—Q 4, K R—B 1 ; 15 B—B 5, R—B 2 ; 16 B×B ±. Réti—Yates, Carlsbad, 1923.
(*l*) 12 P×Q P, B P×P ; 13 B—Q 3, B—Kt 2 ; 14 O—O, R—Q B 1 ; 15 Q—Kt 1 ? Q—R 4 ; 16 Kt—K 2, Kt—Kt 3 ; 17 Kt— K 5, Kt—B 5 ∓. Alekhine—Capablanca, 12th match game, 1927.
(*m*) Eliskases—Ragosin, Semmering-Baden, 1937.

1 P—Q4, P—Q4; 2 P—QB4, P—K3; 3 Kt—QB3, Kt—KB3; 4 B—Kt5, QKt—Q2.

5 P—K3, B—K2; 6 Kt—B3, O—O; 7 R—B1.

	16	17	18	19	20
7	(P—B3)....	P—QR3....	P—QKt3 (e)		
8	P—QR3 / Kt—K5 (a)	P—QR3 (c) / P—R3	PxP / PxP		
9	BxB / QxB	B—R4 / PxP	B—Q3...... / B—Kt2	B—Kt5..... / B—Kt2	Q—R4 / P—B4
10	Q—B2 / KtxKt	BxP / P—QKt4	O—O / P—B4	O—O / P—B4 (h)	Q—B6 (j) / R—Kt1
11	QxKt / R—K1	B—K2 / B—Kt2	Q—K2 / P—B5 (f)	Q—R4 / P—QR3	KtxP / KtxKt (k)
12	R—Q1 / PxP	O—O / P—B4	B—Kt1 / P—QR3	BxQKt / KtxB	QxKKt / B—Kt2
13	BxP / P—QKt3	PxP / KtxP	Kt—K5 / P—Kt4	BxB / QxB	BxB· / QxB
14	O—O / B—Kt2	Kt—Q4 (d) / R—B1	P—B4 / Kt—K5	PxP / PxP	Q—Kt5 / QxQ
15	P—K4 / P—B4= (b)	P—QKt4 / QKt—Q2	BxKt / PxB	Q—KB4 / QR—B1	KtxQ / PxP
16		B—Kt3 / Kt—Kt3 =	KtxKt ± (g)	KR—Q1 ± (i)	PxP / Kt—B3 =

(a) 8.., R—K1; 9 B—B4, P—KR3; 10 B—Q3, PxP; 11 BxBP, P—QKt4; 12 B—R2, P—R3; 13 P—K4, B—Kt2; 14 P—K5, Kt—Q4; 15 KtxKt ± Botvinnik—Kan, Leningrad, 1934.

(b) Fine—Stahlberg, Stockholm, 1937.

(c) 8 PxP, KPxP; 9 Q—B2 transposes into col. 14. If 8 P—B5, P—B3; 9 P—QKt4, P—QR4; 10 P—QR3, PxP; 11 PxP, P—QKt3; 12 B—Q3 (12 B—KB4, PxP; 13 KtPxP, R—R6; 14 B—Q3, Q—R4; 15 Q—Q2, B—R3 ∓. Alekhine—Henneberger, Berne, 1925), PxP; 13 KtPxP, P—K4!; 14 KtxKP KtxK; 15 PxKt, Kt—Q2 ∓. Gibaud—Chéron, Biarritz, 1926.

(d) If 14 BxKt, BxB; 15 KtxP, QxQ; 16 KRxQ, Kt—Kt6!; 17 R—B7, BxKt; 18 BxB, PxKt; 19 BxR, RxB+. The column is Capablanca—Alekhine, 21st match game, 1927.

(e) If 7.., P—B4?; 8 PxBP (8 PxQP, KtxP; 9 BxB, KtxB; 10 B—Q3, PxP; 11 KtxP, P—K4; 12 Kt—B3, Kt—QB4!=. Grunfeld—Landau, Amsterdam, 1936), PxP (8.., KtxP?; 9 PxP, PxP; 10 KtxP, KtxKt; 11 RxKt+), 9 P—B6, Kt—Kt3; 10 QxQ, RxQ; 11 Kt—K5+.

(f) 11. , Kt—K5; 12 B—KB4, KtxKt; 13 PxKt, P—B5; 14 B—B5, P—Kt3; 15 B—Kt1, P—B4; 16 Kt—K5 is also in White's favour.

(g) Continued 16.., QxKt; 17 BxB, QxB; 18 P—B5, P—B3; 19 R—B4. Vidmar—Yates, London, 1922.

(h) Or 10.., P—QR3; 11 B—QR4, P—B4; 12 PxP, KtxP; 13 Q—K2, R—B1; 14 KR—Q1, KtxB; 15 KtxKt, BxQKt. Capablanca—Teichmann, 1913. If 12.., PxP; 13 BxQKt, QxB; 14 Kt—QR4!, Q—Kt4; 15 BxKt, PxB; 16 P—QKt4!, P—B5; 17 Kt—Q4+ (Alekhine).

(i) Réti—E. G. Sergeant, Tunbridge Wells, 1927.

(j) Or 10 B—Kt5, B—Kt2; 11 B—B6, BxB; 12 QxB, R—B1 (Q—B1!), 13 Q—R4, PxP; 14 PxP ±. Winter—J. A. J. Drewitt, Tunbridge Wells, 1927.

(k) 11.., B—Kt2; 12 KtxB ch, QxKt; 13 Q—R4, QR—B1; 14 Q—R3 Capablanca—Lasker, 5th match game, 1921. The rest of the column is analysis.

1 P—Q 4, P—Q 4 ; 2 P—Q B 4, P—K 3 ; 3 Kt—Q B 3, Kt—K B 3 ;
4 B—Kt 5, Q Kt—Q 2.

5 P—K 3, B—K 2 ; 6 Kt—B 3, O—O ; 7 Q—B 2.

	21	22	23	24	25
7	P—B 4 !				
8	R—Q 1	O—O—O	B P×P		
	P—K R 3	Q—R 4	B P×P		Kt×P
9	B—R 4	B P×P	Kt×P (g)		Kt×Kt
	Q—R 4	K P×P	Kt×P		P×Kt (k)
10	B—Q 3	P×P	B×B		B×B
	B P×P (a)	Kt×P	Q×B	Kt×B	Q×B
11	K P×P	Kt—Q 4 (e)	Kt×Kt	B—Q 3	B—Q 3
	P×P	B—K 3	P×Kt	K Kt–Kt3 (j)	P—K Kt 3
12	B×P	K—Kt 1	B—Q 3	R—Q 1	P×P
	Kt—Kt 3	Q R—B 1	Q—Kt 5 ch	Q—K 2	Kt×P
13	B—Kt 3	B—Q 3	Q—Q 2	P—K R 4	O—O (l)
	B—Q 2	P—K R 3	Kt—B 4 (h)	R—Q 1	B—Kt 5
14	O—O	B×Kt	B—Kt 5 !	B×Kt	Kt—Q 4
	Q R—B 1 (b)	B×B	Q×Q ch	R P×B	Q R—B 1
15	Kt—K 5 (c)	B—B 5	K×Q	P—R 5	Q—Q 2
	B—Kt 4	K R—Q 1	P—Q R 3	P×P	P—Q R 3
16	K R—K 1	B×B	B—Q 3	R×P	B—B 2
	B—B 5 (d)	P×B+ (f)	B—K 3 (i)	Kt—B 3 =	Q-Kt4=(m)

(a) Or 10.., Q P×P; 11 B×P, P—R 3 (Bogoljuboff suggests 11.., Kt—Kt 3 followed by .., P×P and Q Kt—Q 4); 12 P×P?, Kt×P; 13 O—O, P—Q Kt4; 14 B—Q Kt 3, B—Kt 2; 15 Kt—Q 4, Q R—B 1; 16 Q—K 2, Kt×B ∓. Davidson—Teichmann, match, 1922. Or 10.., Kt—Kt 3; 11 P×Q P, B P×P?; 12 P—Q 6!, B×P; 13 B×Kt, P×B; 14 Kt×P ±. Alekhine—Foltys, Podebrady, 1936.

(b) 14.., B—B 3?; 15 Kt—K 5, B—Q 4?; 16 Kt×B, Q Kt×Kt; 17 Q—K 2, Q R—Q 1; 18 P—B 4+. Stahlberg—Capablanca, Moscow, 1935.

(c) 15 Q—K 2 (Burn's suggestion) is a strong alternative.

(d) Continued 17 B×B, Kt×B; 18 B×Kt, B×B; 19 Kt—Q 7, K R—Q 1; 20 Kt×B ch, P×Kt; 21 R—Q 3 ±. Euwe—Landau, Noordwijk, 1938. Here 16. , Q Kt—Q 4 is Lasker—Capablanca, 10th match game, 1921. Subsequently Breyer demonstrated that 17 Q B×Kt !, B×B; 18 B×Kt, P×B; 19 Q—B 5 ± should have been played.

(e) If 11 B×Kt, B×B; 12 Kt×P, B—K 3; 13 K—Kt 1, Q R—B 1+ or 11 Kt×P, Kt×Kt; 12 R×Kt, B—K 3+.

(f) 17 Q—Kt 6, R—Q 3. Rotlevy—Teichmann, Carlsbad, 1911.

(g) Not 9 P×K P, P×Kt; 10 P×Kt, P×Kt P+.

(h) Or 13.., Kt—K 4; 14 B—K 2, Q×Q ch; 15 K×Q B—Q 2; 16 Q R—B 1, K R—B 1. Alekhine—Capablanca, 8th match game, 1927.

(i) Flohr—Capablanca, Moscow, 1935. White has a slight pull, but should not win against best play.

(j) 11.., Kt—K B 3 is more precise, since 12 O—O—O would now have given White a strong attack. The column is Lilienthal—Goglidse, Moscow, 1935.

(k) 9.., B×B; and if 10 P—K R 4, B—K 2 is quite satisfactory for Black.

(l) If 13 Q R—B 1, Kt×B ch; 14 Q×Kt, B—B 4 !; 15 Q—Q 4 (15 Q×P, K R—Q 1; 16 Q—K 5, Q×Q; 17 Kt×Q, Q R—B 1; 18 O—O, R×R; 19 R×R, R—Q 7+), B—K 5; 16 O—O, B×Kt with a quick draw. Alekhine—Capablanca, 10th match game 1927.

(m) Flohr—Vidmar, Nottingham, 1936. Black must still play carefully.

1 P—Q 4, P—Q 4 ; 2 P—Q B 4, P—K 3 ; 3 Kt—Q B 3, Kt—K B 3 ;
    4 B—Kt 5, Q Kt—Q 2.

5 P—K 3, B—K 2 ; 6 Kt—B 3, O—O.

	26	27	28	29	30
7	(Q—B 2)............................P—Q R 3....B—Q 3				
	(P—B 4)....P—Q Kt 3...P—B 3			P × P	P—B 4
8	(B P × P)	P × P	P—Q R 3	B × P	O—O
	K P × P	P × P	R—K 1	P—B 4	B P × P (*m*)
9	B—Q 3 (*a*)	B—Q 3	R—Q 1	O—O	K P × P
	P—B 5	B—Kt 2	P—Q R 3 (*g*)	P—Q R 3	P × P
10	B—B 5	O—O—O (A)	B—Q 3 (*h*)	P × P	B × P
	R—K 1	P—B 4 (*d*)	P × P (*i*)	Kt × P	Kt—Kt 3
11	O—O	P—K R 4	B × P	P—Q Kt 4	B—Kt 3 !
	P—K Kt 3 (*b*)	P—B 5 (*e*)	Kt—Q 4	Q Kt—K 5	B—Q 2
12	B—R 3	B—B 5	B × B	Kt × Kt	Q—Q 3
	Kt—B 1	R—K 1	Q × B	Kt × Kt	Q Kt—Q 4
13	B × B	B × K Kt	Kt—K 4 (*j*)	B × B	Kt—K 5
	R × B	Kt × B	K Kt—B 3	Q × B	B—B 3
14	B × Kt	P—K Kt 4	B—Q 3 !	Q—Q 4	Q R—Q 1
	B × B	B—Q 3	Kt × Kt	Kt—Q 3 !	Kt—Q Kt 5
15	P—Q Kt 3 (*c*)	P—Kt 5	B × Kt	B—K 2	Q—R 3
	Q—Q 2 !	Kt—K 5	P—R 3	P—Q Kt 4	B—Q 4
16	P—Q Kt 4	P—R 5 ± (*f*)	O—O ± (*k*)	K R—Q 1	Kt × B ±
	P—K R 4 !＝			K R—Q 1 ＝ (*l*)	

(*a*) If 9 P × P, Kt × P ; 10 R—Q 1, Q—R 4 ! ; 11 B—Q 3, Q Kt—K 5 ; 12 K B × Kt, P × B ; 13 B × Kt, B × B ; 14 Kt—Q 4, B—Kt 5 ＝. Kostich—Teichmann, Carlsbad, 1911. If 11 B × Kt, B × B ; 12 R × P, B—K 3 +. A strong line for White here is 9 R—Q 1 ! P—B 5 ; 10 Kt—K 5, P—Q R 3 ; 11 P—Q R 3, Q—R 4 ; 12 B—K 2, P—R 3 ; 13 B—R 4, P—K Kt 4 ? ; 14 B—Kt 3, Kt—K 5 ? ; 15 B × P, P × B ; 16 Q × Kt, B × P ; 17 Q—B 2 +. Eliskases—Tartakover, Noordwijk, 1938. 9 B—K 2, P—B 5 ; 10 Kt—K 5, Kt × Kt ; 11 P × Kt, Kt—K 5 ; 12 B × B, Q × B ; 13 R—Q 1, Q × P ; 14 R × P, Q—B 2 ; 15 R—Q 4, Kt—K 4 ; 16 P—B 4, Kt—B 3 ; 17 R × P, B—K 3 (Euwe—Tartakover, Noordwijk, 1938) gives Black some attack for the Pawn.
(*b*) 11 , Kt—B 1 ? ; 12 B × B, R × B ; 13 B × Kt, B × B ; 14 Q—B 5 + +.
(*c*) Reshevsky—Capablanca, Margate, 1935. Capablanca now played 15. ., Q—R 4 ? whereupon followed 16 P—Q Kt 4 !, Q—Q 1 ; 17 Q—R 4, P—Q R 3 ; 18 P—Kt 5, R—K 3 ; 19 Q R—Kt 1 +. The continuation in the column is due to Kashdan.
(*d*) 10. ., Kt—K 5 ; 11 P—K R 4, P—K B 4 ; 12 K—Kt 1, P—B 4 ; 13 P × P, P × P ; 14 Kt × Kt, B P × Kt ; 15 B × P, P × B ; 16 Q—Kt 3 ch +. Rubinstein—Znosko-Borovsky, St. Petersburg, 1909.
(*e*) 11. , R—B 1 ; 12 K—Kt 1, R—K 1 ; 13 P × P, R × P ; 14 Kt—Q 4. Rubinstein—Teichmann, Carlsbad, 1907.
(*f*) Rubinstein—Teichmann, match, 1908.
(*g*) 9. ., P × P ? ; 10 B × P, Kt—Q 4 ; 11 B × B, Q × B ; 12 O—O, Kt × Kt ; 13 Q × Kt, P—Q B 4 ; 14 P—Q 5, P × P ; 15 R × P ±. Flohr—Fine, Hastings, 1935-36.
(*h*) 10 P—B 5 ?, P—K 4 ; 11 B × B, Q × B ; 12 Kt—Q 2, Kt—R 4 ; 13 B × B, Q × B ; 14 Kt—K 2, P—K Kt 3 ∓. Landau—Fine, Amsterdam, 1936.
(*i*) If 10. ., P—K R 3 ; 11 B—R 4, P—Q Kt 4 ; 12 P—B 5, P—K 4 ? ; 13 P × P, Kt—Kt 5 ; 14 B—Kt 3, P × P ; 15 Kt—K 2 !, Q—K 2 ; 16 O—O, K Kt × P (K 5) ; 17 Kt × Kt, Kt × Kt ; 18 B × Kt !, R × B ; 19 R—BB 1 +. Flohr—Eliskases, Podebrady, 1936.
(*j*) An improvement on 13 O—O, Kt × Kt ; 14 Q × Kt, P—Q B 4 ; 15 P × P (if now 15 P—Q 5, P × P ; 16 R × P, P—Q Kt 4 ; 17 B—R 2, B—Kt 2 ∓), Kt × P ＝.
(*k*) 16. ., P—Q B 4 ; 17 Kt—K 5. Eliskases—Landau, Noordwijk, 1938.
(*l*) Capablanca—Goglidse, Moscow, 1935.
(*m*) If 8. ., P—Q R 3 ; 9 P × Q P, Kt × P ; 10 B × B, Q × B ; 11 Kt × Kt, P × Kt ; 12 Q—B 2, P—K Kt 3 ; 13 P × P, Kt × P ; 14 R—Q B 1 ±. Euwe—Fine, Amsterdam, 1936. The column is Botvinnik—Vidmar, Nottingham, 1936.
(A) 10 O—O, P—K R 3 ; 11 B—K B 4, P—R 3 ; 12 K R—Q 1, Kt—K 1 ; 13 Q R—B 1 ±. Keres—Smysloff, Moscow 1939.

1 P—Q 4, P—Q 4 ; 2 P—Q B 4, P—K 3 ; 3 Kt—Q B 3, Kt—K B 3 ;
4 B—Kt 5, Q Kt—Q 2.

5 P—K 3, B—K 2 ; 6 Kt—B 3.

	31	32	33	34	35
6	(O—O)................................P—B 3......P×P (*l*)
7	(B—Q 3) (*a*)			B—Q 3 (*i*)	B×P
	P×P...................P—Q Kt 3		P×P	P—Q R 3
8	B×P		P×P	B×B P	O—O
	P—B 4......P—Q Kt 3		P×P	Kt—Q 4	P—Kt 4
9	O—O	O—O	O—O (*f*)	B×B	B—Q 3
	P—Q R 3	B—Kt 2	B—Kt 2	Q×B	P—B 4
10	P—Q R 4 (*b*)	Q—K 2	Q—K 2 (*g*)	Q—B 2	Q—K 2
	P—Q Kt 3	Kt—Q 4 (*d*)	P—B 4	Kt×Kt	B—Kt 2
11	Q—K 2	B—B 4	P×P	Q×Kt	K R—Q 1
	B—Kt 2	Kt×B	Kt×P	O—O	Q—Kt 3
12	K R—Q 1	P×Kt	K R—Q 1	O—O	Q R—B 1
	Q—B 2	Kt—B 3	K Kt—Q 2	P—Q Kt 3	O—O
13	B—B 4	Q R—Q 1	B—K B 4	Q—Q 3	Kt—K 5
	B—Q 3 (*c*)	B—Kt 5	Kt—K 3	R—Q 1	K R-Kt 1 ? (*m*)
14	B×B	P—K Kt 3	B—Q R 6	Q—K 2	P×P
	Q×B	K B×Kt	Kt×B	P—Q B 4 (*j*)	Kt×P
15	Q R—B 1	P×B	P×Kt	Q R—Q 1	B×Kt
	Q—K 2 =	Kt—Q 4 = (*e*)	B×B = (*h*)	B—Kt 2 (*k*)	B×B (*n*)

(*a*) For 7 P×P see the Exchange Variation, cols. 60–65.

(*b*) Or 10 P×P, Kt×P; 11 Q×Q, R×Q; 12 P—Q Kt 4, Q Kt—Q 2; 13 P—Kt 5, Kt—B 4; 14 K R—Q 1, B—Q 2; 15 P×P, P×P; 16 Kt—K 5 =. Sir G. A. Thomas—Rubinstein, Carlsbad, 1929.

(*c*) P. Rubinstein, Berlin, 1926.

(*d*) Or 10 ., Kt—K 5; 11 Kt×Kt, B×Kt; 12 B—B 4, B—Q 3; 13 B—Kt 3 =. P. Johner—Treybal, Carlsbad, 1929.

(*e*) Euwe—Becker, Zandvoort, 1936.

(*f*) Stronger is 9 Q—B 2, B—Kt 2; 10 O—O—O, transposing into col. 27.

(*g*) Or 10 Kt—K 5, Kt×Kt; 11 P×Kt, Kt—K 5; 12 B—B 4, Kt×Kt; 13 P×Kt, Q—Q 2; 14 Q—B 3, P—Q B 4 with a satisfactory game for Black. Yates—Davidson, Scheveningen, 1924.

(*h*) Tarrasch—P. Johner, Teplitz-Schonau, 1922.

(*i*) Alternatives are (1) 7 R—B 1, Kt—K 5; 8 B×B, Q×B; 9 Q—B 2, P—K B 4; 10 B—Q 3, O—O transposes into col. 11, note (*a*). (2) 7 Q—B 2, Kt—K 5 ! (for 7.., O—O, 8 R—Q 1 see col. 28); 8 B×B, Q×B; 9 Kt×Kt, P×Kt; 10 Q×P, Q—Kt 5 ch; 11 Kt—Q 2, Q×Kt P; 12 Q—Kt 1 (12 R—Kt 1 ?, Q×R P; 13 B—Q 3, Q—R 6; 14 K—K 2, Kt—B 3; 15 Q—B 4, Q—K 2; 16 Kt—B 3, P—K R 3+ +. Znosko-Borovsky—Tartakover, Nice, 1930), Q—B 6; 13 Q—B 1, Q—R 4; 14 P—B 5, P—K 4 ∓. Reshevsky—Tylor, Nottingham, 1936.

(*j*) 14 , P—K 4 is superior. With this column cp Lasker's Defence, col. 69.

(*k*) 16 B—R 6 ±. Samisch—Selesnieff, Pistyan, 1922.

(*l*) 6.., P—Q Kt 3 ?; 7 P×P, Kt×P (7 , P×P loses a Pawn by 8 B—Kt 5, B—Kt 2; 9 Kt—K 5, O—O, 10 B—B 6, B×B; 11 Kt×B, Q –K 1; 12 Kt×B ch, Q×Kt; 13 Kt×P; if now Q—K 5; 14 Kt×Kt ch, P×Kt, 15 B—R 6, Q×Kt P; 16 Q—B 3!+ +—the Pittsburgh Variation); 8 B×B, Kt×B; 9 B—Q 3, B—Kt 2; 10 O—O, O—O; 11 R—B 1, P—Q R 3; 12 Kt—K 4, P—R 3; 13 B—Kt 1, R—B 1; 14 Q—K 2 ±. Salwe—Marco, Ostend, 1907.

(*m*) Q R—K 1 is necessary, as Schlechter pointed out in a note to the brilliancy prize game Janowski—Chajes, New York, 1916, where the same position occurred.

(*n*) 16 B×P ch, K×B; 17 Q—R 5 ch, K—Kt 1; 18 Q×P ch, K—R 2 ? ? (K—R 1 left White with nothing better than a draw by perpetual check); 19 Q—R 5 ch ?, K—Kt 1; 20 Q—B 7 ch and drew by perpetual check. Mikenas—Kashdan, Prague, 1931. Mikenas could have won, as Janowski did in the game cited, by 19 Kt—Q 7 !, Kt×Kt; 20 R×Kt, B—B 3 .; 21 Kt—K 4 !, B×P; 22 Kt—Kt 5 ch, etc.

CAMBRIDGE SPRINGS DEFENCE

1 P—Q4, P—Q4; 2 P—QB4, P—K3; 3 Kt—QB3, Kt—KB3; 4 B—Kt5, QKt—Q2; 5 P—K3, P—B3; 6 Kt—B3, Q—R4; 7 Kt—Q2, B—Kt5.

	36	37	38	39	40
8	Q—B2 O--O..				P×P
9	B×Kt...... Kt×B	B—K2............ P—K4 (d)		B—R4 P—K4 (h)	B×Kt Kt×B
10	B—Q3 R—K1	O—O....... KP×P	QP×P (f) Kt—K5	QP×P Kt—K5	Kt×P B×Kt ch (l)
11	O—O (a) P—K4	Kt—Kt3 Q—B2	K Kt×Kt P×Kt	K Kt×Kt P×Kt	Q×B Q×Q ch
12	Q P×P R×P	K Kt×P P×P	O—O B×Kt	P—K6 Kt—K4	P×Q K—K2
13	P×P B×Kt (b)	B×P B×Kt	P×B Kt×P	P×P ch (i) R×P	P—B3 B—Q2
14	Kt—B4 Q×QP	P×B Kt—K4	Q×P Kt—Kt3 (g)	O—O—O (j) B×Kt	Q R—Kt1 P—QKt3
15	Q×B R—KKt4	B—K2 Q—K2	B—B4 Kt×B	Q×B Q×Q ch	Kt—K5 KR—QB1
16	P—B3 B—K3 = (c)	QR—Q1 ± (e)	Q×Kt Q×BP ∓	P×Q B—B4 (k)	B—R6 R-B2 = (m)

(a) If 11 P—B4, P—B4 (Kt—Kt5; 12 K—K2); 12 O—O, BP×P; 13 KP×P, P×P; 14 Kt×P, Q—Q1; 15 Kt—K2, P—QKt3 ∓.

(b) If 13.., P×P; 14 Kt—Kt3, Q—Q1; 15 P—QR3, B—B1; 16 Kt—Q4, B—Q2; 17 Q—Kt3 ±. Euwe—Grunfeld, Carlsbad, 1929.

(c) 17 QR—Q1, Q—QB4. Euwe—Bogoljuboff, match, 1928.

(d) If 9 ., P×P; 10 B×Kt, Kt×B; 11 Kt×P, B×Kt ch; 12 Q×B, Q×Q ch; 13 P×Q, B—Q2; 14 B—B3, KR—Q1; 15 P—QR4, QR—B1; 16 K—Q2 ±. Alekhine—Bogoljuboff, 9th match game, 1929. Compare col. 40.

(e) Analysis by Bogoljuboff.

(f) Or 10 B×Kt, Kt×B; 11 QP×P, Kt—K5; 12 KKt×Kt, P×Kt; 13 O—O B×Kt; 14 Q×B, Q×Q; 15 P×Q, R—K1; 16 KR—Q1, K—B1 ∓.

(g) Or 14.., P—B3; 15 B—R4 (15 B—B4?, B—B4!; 16 Q—Q4, QR—Q1+), B—K3 = (Euwe).

(h) Best. Alternatives are: (1) 9. , Kt—K5; 10 KKt×Kt, P×Kt; 11 B—K2, P—K4; 12 O—O, P×P (if 12. , P—KB4; 13 P—B5 followed by B—B4 ch. Kashdan); 13 Kt×P, P—KB4; 14 P—QR3, P×Kt; 15 P×B, Q×P; 16 Q×P (16 P×P is sufficient for an advantage. Kashdan), Kt—B4; 17 B—K7 +. Kashdan—Marshall, New York League match, 1932. (2) 9 ., P—B4; 10 Kt—Kt3, Q—R5; 11 B×Kt, Kt×B; 12 QP×P, Kt—K5; 13 P×P, B×Kt ch; 14 P×B, Kt×P (B4); 15 R—Q1+. Capablanca—Alekhine, 7th match game, 1927.

(i) 13 P—K7, R—K1; 14 O—O—O (14 P—QR3, Kt—Kt3, etc.), Kt—Kt3; 15 R—Q8, B—KB4; 16 R×QR, R×R; 17 B—Kt3, B×Kt; 18 P×B, Kt×P ∓.

(j) If instead 14 B—K2, Kt—Q6ch; 15 B×Kt, P×B; 16 Q×P, B—KB4; 17 Q—Q2, R—Q2; 18 Q—B1, B—Q6+. The continuation in the column is recommended by Euwe.

(k) Black should draw (Euwe).

(l) Or 10 ., Q—Q4; 11 Kt—Q2, B×Kt; 12 P×B, P—K4; 13 P—K4, Q—K3; 14 B—B4, Q—K2; 15 O—O+. Grunfeld—Becker, Carlsbad, 1929. Here 11 O—O—O, B×Kt; 12 P×B? (12 Q×B! and if O—O, then 13 K—Kt1), O—O is Sämisch—Pirc, Rogaska-Slatina, 1929.

(m) Alekhine—Bogoljuboff, 10th match game, 1934.

CAMBRIDGE SPRINGS DEFENCE

1 P—Q4, P—Q4; 2 P—QB4, P—K3; 3 Kt—QB3, Kt—KB3;
4 B—Kt5, QKt—Q2; 5 P—K3, P—B3; 6 Kt—B3, Q—R4.

	41	42	43	44	45
7	(Kt—Q2)..........................			B×Kt......	P×P
	(B—Kt5)...P×P			Kt×B	Kt×P (f)
8	(Q—B2)	B×Kt		B—Q3	Q—Kt3
	(P×P)	Kt×B		B—Kt5	B—Kt5
9	(B×Kt)	Kt×P		Q—Kt3	R—B1
	(Kt×B)	Q—B2		P×P	P—K4!
10	(Kt×P)	R—B1......	B—Q3	B×BP	Kt×P (g)
	Q—B2	Kt—Q4!	B—K2	O—O	Kt×Kt
11	P—QR3 (a)	B—Q3	O—O	O—O	P×Kt
	B—K2	Kt×Kt	O—O	B×Kt	B—K3 (h)
12	P—KKt3	P×Kt	R—B1	P×B	P—QR3
	O—O	B—K2	R—Q1	P—QKt3	Kt×Kt (i)
13	B—Kt2	O—O	Q—K2	Kt—K5	P×B
	B—Q2	O—O	B—Q2	B—Kt2	Q×KP
14	P—QKt4	P—B4	Kt—K5	B—K2	B—KB4
	P—QKt3	P—KKt3	B—K1	P—B4	B×Q
15	O—O	Kt—K5 (c)	P—B4	Kt—B4	B×Q
	P—QR4 = (b)	P—QB4 =	P—B4! (d)	Q—R3 = (e)	Kt-R7+ (j)

(a) Or 11 B—K2, O—O, 12 O—O, R—Q1; 13 P—QR3 (13 QR—Q1, Kt—Q4; 14 Kt—K4, B—K2; 15 P—QR3, P—QKt3; Bogoljuboff—Alekhine, 10th match game, 1929), B—K2; 14 P—QKt4, P—QKt3; 15 KR—Q1, Kt—Q4; 16 Kt—K5, Kt×Kt; 17 Q×Kt, B—Kt2 =. Mikenas—Alekhine, Prague, 1931.

(b) Continued 16 Kt—K5, P×P; 17 P×P, R×R. Capablanca—Alekhine, 29th match game, 1927.

(c) Lasker—Bogoljuboff, Nottingham, 1936.

(d) Continued 16 P×P, Q×P!; 17 Kt—K4, Q—R4; 18 Kt—Kt5, QR—B1 ∓. Alekhine—Kashdan, Bled, 1931.

(e) Capablanca—Ed. Lasker, New York, 1924.

(f) Best. Alternatives are: (1) 7.., BP×P; 8 B—Q3, Kt—K5; 9 Q—Kt3, Kt×B; 10 Kt×Kt ±. (2) 7. , KP×P; 8 B—Q3, Kt—K5; 9 O—O! (9 Q—B2, Kt×B; 10 Kt×Kt, P—KR3; 11 Kt—B3 is also good), Kt×B (9. , Kt×Kt; 10 P×Kt, Q×BP; 11 P—K4 gives White a powerful attack, while if 9.., QKt—B3; 10 QB×Kt, Kt×Kt; 11 P×Kt, P×B; 12 Q—B2, B—Q3; 13 B—B5, B—K3; 14 QR—Kt1, Q—B2; 15 B×B, P×B; 16 P—K4, O—O—O; 17 P—B4 ++. Capablanca—Ed. Lasker, Lake Hopatcong, 1926); 10 Kt×Kt, Kt—B3; 11 P—B4 ±. See also col. 50.

(g) If 10 P×P, Kt—B4 followed by Kt—R5 +.

(h) 11.., Kt×Kt; 12 P×Kt, B—QR6; 13 R—QKt1, B—K3 ∓ is also good (Euwe).

(i) If 12.., B×Ktch; 13 P×B, O—O; 14 Q—Kt2 (14 B—QB4?, P—KR3; 15 B—R4, Kt×KP!; 16 P×Kt, Q—B4; 17 B×B, Q×P ch and wins), KR—K1; 15 B—K2, Kt—Kt3; 16 B—KB4, Kt—B5; 17 B×Kt, B×B; 18 P—B3, P—KKt4 (analysis by Asztalos and Vukovitch); 19 B—Kt3. White's position is still tenable.

(j) Analysis by Canal.

CAMBRIDGE SPRINGS DEFENCE

1 P—Q 4, P—Q 4 ; 2 P—Q B 4, P—K 3 ; 3 Kt—Q B 3, Kt—K B 3 ;
4 B—Kt 5, Q Kt—Q 2 ; 5 P—K 3, P—B 3 ; 6 Kt—B 3, Q—R 4 ;
7 P×P.

	46	47	48	49	50
7	(Kt×P)........				........Kt—K 5
8	(Q—Kt 3)........		Q—Q 2		P×K P (j)
	(B—Kt 5)		B—Kt 5.....	Q Kt—Kt 3	P×P
9	(R—B 1)		R—B 1	R—Q B 1	Q—R 4 (k)
	(P—K 4)		P—B 3 (e)	Kt×Kt	Q×Q
10	P—Q R 3 (a)	. B—Q B 4 !	B—R 4	P×Kt	Kt×Q
	B×Kt ch	P×P (c)	O—O	Kt—Q 4	B—Kt 5 ch
11	P×B	B×Kt	B—B 4	B—Q 3 (g)	K—K 2
	P×P	P×B	Q Kt—Kt 3	Kt×B P	P—Q Kt 4
12	K P×P	P×P	B—Q Kt 3	O—O	P—Q R 3 (l)
	O—O	O—O	Kt×Kt	B—Kt 5	Kt×B
13	B—Q 3 (b)	O—O	P×Kt	P—Q R 3	Kt×Kt
	R—K 1 ch	Kt—Kt 3	B—R 6	Q×P	B—K 2
14	K—Q 1	P—Q R 3	R—B 2	R—R 1	Kt×K P
	Kt—B 1	B×Kt	P—Q B 4	Q—Kt 6	P×Kt
15	B—Q 2	R×B	Q—Q 3	Kt—K 5 ! (h)	Kt—B 7 ch
	Q—B 2 ∓	B—Q 2 (d)	P—B 5 ! ∓ (f)	O—O ! (i)	K—Q 1 (m)

(a) Or 10 B—Q 3, P—K R 3 ; 11 B—R 4, P×P ; 12 P×P, Kt—B 5 ∓ (Asztalos).

(b) If 13 B—K 2, R—K 1 ; 14 R—B 2, Kt—B 1 +, for if 15 O—O ?, Kt×P. The column is Rabinovitch—Tartakover, Moscow, 1925.

(c) The alternative is 10 ., Kt (Q 2)—Kt 3 ; 11 B×Kt, Kt×B ; 12 Kt×P, B—K 3 ; 13 Kt—B 4! (if instead 13 P—Q R 3? then not 13 , B×Kt ch?; 14 P×B, Kt—Kt 3 ; 15 Q—Q 1 ±. Landau—Bogoljuboff, Zandvoort, 1936; but 13 , Kt×Kt; 14 P×B, B×Q; 15 P×Q, Kt—R 7+), Kt×Kt; 14 Kt×Q, Kt×P ch; 15 Q×B, Kt×Q.

(d) 16 R—B 5, Q—R 3 =. Flohr—Winter, Hastings, 1935—36.

(e) 9 .., O—O; 10 P—K 4, Kt×Kt; 11 P×Kt, B—R 6; 12 R—Q Kt 1, P—K 4; 13 B—Q 3, R—K 1! (13.., B—Q 3; 14 O—O, P—B 3; 15 B—K 3, R—Q 1; 16 K R—Q 1 ±. Spielmann—Pirc, Moscow, 1935); 14 O—O, P—Q Kt 3; 15 K R—K 1, B—R 3 =. Grünfeld—Vajda, London, 1927.

(f) Continued 16 K B×P, Kt×B; 17 Q×Kt, B—Q 2; 18 O—O, Q R—B 1; 19 Q—Kt 3, Q—R 3!. Stahlberg—Spielmann, Moscow, 1935.

(g) 11 K—Q 1, B—R 6; 12 R—B 2, P—B 3 ∓. Lövenfisch—Euwe, Leningrad, 1934. If 11 B—Q B 4, B—R 6! (not 11.., Kt×B P; 12 O—O, B—Q R 3; 13 P—Q R 3, Q×P; 14 R—R 1, Kt—K 5; 15 Q×K 2, Q—B 6; 16 K R—B 1, Kt×B; 17 Kt×Kt!+. Stahlberg—Rellstab, Zoppot, 1935); 12 R—Q Kt 1, Kt×B P; 13 R—Kt 3, P—Kt 4!; 14 B—Q 3, P—Kt 5 ∓.

(h) Weaker is 15 B—B 2, Q—Q 4; 16 P—K 4, Kt×P; 17 Q×B, Kt×B+. Alekhine—Euwe, 25th match game, 1935.

(i) If instead 15.., Kt—K 5; 16 Q—K 2, Kt×B; 17 Q—R 5+. The best continuation after 15.., O—O is 16 B—Q B 4, Kt—K 5; e.g., 17 Q—K 2, Q—B 6; 18 Q R—B 1, Q—Q 7; 19 Q—Kt 4, Kt×B; 20 Q R—Q 1, Q—B 6. White can now force a draw, but has nothing better.

(j) 8 P×B P, P×P; 9 Q—R 4, Q×Q; 10 Kt×Q, B—Kt 5 ch; 11 K—K 2, B—R 3 ch; 12 K—Q 1, B—Kt 4!+. G. S. A. Wheatcroft—M. E. Goldstein, London, 1926. The column is analysis by Grünfeld, Asztalos and Vukovitch.

(k) Euwe recommends 10 B—R 4, Kt×Kt; 11 P×Kt, Q×P ch; 12 Kt—Q 2 ±.

(l) 12 Kt—B 3, Kt×Kt ch; 13 P×Kt, B×P; 14 R—B 1, P—Kt 5; 15K—Q 1. P—K 4!±. Rubinstein—Réti, Berlin, 1928.

(m) 16 Kt×R, B—Kt 2; 17 P—K 4±.

1 P—Q 4, P—Q 4 ; 2 P—Q B 4, P—K 3 ; 3 Kt—Q B 3, Kt—K B 3 ; 4 B—Kt 5, Q Kt—Q 2.

	51	52	53	54	55
5	(P—K 3) / (P—B 3)			Kt—B 3 / P—B 3	/ B—Kt 5 (j)
6	P—Q R 3.... / B—K 2	Q—B 2 / Q—R 4 (b)	......B—Q 3 / Q—R 4	P—K 4 / P×K P	P×P / P×P
7	Kt—B 3 / O—O	B—R 4 (c) / P—B 4	B—R 4 / P×P	Kt×P / B—K 2 (g)	P—K 3 (k) / P—B 4
8	B—Q 3 / P×P	Kt—B 3 / P—Q R 3	B×B P / P—Q Kt 4	Kt—B 3 / O—O	B—Q 3 / P—B 5 (l)
9	B×P / Kt—Q 4	B—K 2 / Q P×P	B—Q Kt 3 / B—Kt 2	Q—B 2 / P—K 4 (h)	B—B 2 / Q—R 4
10	B×B / Q×B	O—O / Q—B 2	Kt—B 3 / P—B 4 (e)	O—O—O / P×P	O—O / B×Kt
11	Kt—K 4 ! / Kt(Q4)—B3	K R—Q 1 / P×P	P×P / B×P	Kt×P / Q—R 4	P×B / Q×B P (m)
12	Kt—Kt 3 / P—B 4	P×P / B—Q 3	O—O / O—O	B—K 3 / Kt—B 4 (i)	Q—Kt 1 / O—O
13	O—O / Kt—Kt 3 (a)	P—Q 5 ! / P—K 4	Kt—Q 4 / P—Q R 3		P—K 4 / P×P
14	B—R 2 / P×P	P—Q R 4 / O—O	Q—K 2 (f)		B—Q 2 / Q—R 6
15	Kt×P ±	Kt—Q2 ± (d)			B—Kt 4 (n)

(a) 13 , P—Q Kt 3, followed by B—Kt 2, seems preferable. The column is Alekhine—Capablanca, 34th match game, 1927.

(b) 6. , B—K 2 ; 7 Kt—B 3 transposes into col. 34, note (i).

(c) 7 P×P, Kt×P ; 8 P—K 4, Kt×Kt ; 9 B—Q 2, Q—R 5 ; 10 Q×Kt, P—Q R 4 ; 11 Kt—B 3, B—Kt 5 ; 12 Q—B 1, O—O ; 13 P—Q R 3, B×B ch ; 14 Q×B, P—K 4 ! ; 15 R—B 1 !, P×P ; 16 R—B 4, Q—Kt 4 ; 17 R×Q P, Q—Q B 4. Capablanca—Alekhine, 9th match game, 1927. White cannot continue 18 R×Kt, B×R ; 19 Q×B because of 19 , Q R—Q 1 ; 20 Q moves, Q—B 7 and wins.

(d); Ragosin—Fine, Semmering-Baden, 1937.

(e) 10 , B—Kt 5, 11 R—Q B 1, Kt—K 5 ; 12 O—O, Kt×Kt ; 13 P×Kt, B×P ; 14 B×K P, P×B ; 15 Q—Kt 3+.

(f) If 14 Kt×K P, P×Kt ; 15 B×P ch, K—R 1 ; 16 K B×Kt, Q R—Q 1+. The column is Capablanca—Alekhine, 31st match game, 1927.

(g) 7. , Q—Kt 3 ; 8 Kt×Kt ch (8 B—Q 3 ! gives White a dangerous attack), P×Kt ; 9 B—B 1, P—K 4 ; 10 B—Q 3, P×P ; 11 O—O, B—K 2, 12 R—K 1, Kt—B 1 ; 13 Kt—R 4, B—K 3 ; 14 Kt—B 5, B—Kt 5 ; 15 Kt—Kt 7 ch. Alekhine—Bogoljuboff, 11th match game, 1929.

(h) 9 , P—Q Kt 3 ; 10 O—O—O, B—Kt 2 ; 11 P—K R 4, Q—B 2 ; 12 B—Q 3 ± Alekhine—Bogoljuboff, 19th Match Game, 1929.

(i) Alekhine—Lundin, Orebro, 1935. White stands better.

(j) The Manhattan Variation.

(k) If 7 Q—Kt 3, P—B 4 ; 8 P—Q R 3, B×Kt ch ; 9 Q×B, P—B 5 ; 10 Q—K 3 ch, Q—K 2 ; 11 Q×Q ch, K×Q =. Capablanca—Spielmann, New York, 1927.

(l) If 8 , O—O ; 9 O—O, B×Kt ; 10 P×B, P—B 5 ; 11 B—B 2, Q—R 4 ; 12 Kt—K 5 !, Q×B P ; 13 Kt×Kt, Kt×Kt ; 14 Q—Kt 1 ! ±. Alekhine—Vidmar, New York, 1927.

(m) 11 , Kt—K 5 ; 12 B—K R 4 ?, Q Kt—B 3 ; 13 Kt—K 5, B—K 3 ; 14 P—Q R 3, P—K Kt 4 ; 15 B—K Kt 3, O—O—O ; 16 Kt—Kt 1, P—K R 4 =. Foltys—Milner-Barry, Margate, 1937. Here 12 Q—K 1 ! is best, e.g., 12.., Kt×Q B P ? ; 13 P—K 4+, or 12 , Q×B P ; 13 B×Kt, Q×Q ; 14 K R×Q, P×B ; 15 Kt—Q 2 regaining the Pawn with a fine game. If 12 ., O—O ; 13 B—K 7, R—K 1 ; 14 B—Kt 4 ± or 12. , Q Kt—B 3 ; 13 B×Kt, Kt×B ; 14 P—K 4 ± (Euwe).

(n) 15 , Q—R 3 ; 16 B×R, P×Kt ; 17 B—Kt 4 (17 B—K 7 ? ?, Q—K 3 !) 18 Resigns. Maróczy—Tenner, New York, 1926). Both Alekhine and Bogoljuboff prefer White, but Black has excellent counter chances.

1 P—Q 4, P—Q 4; 2 P—Q B 4, P—K 3; 3 Kt—Q B 3, Kt—K B 3;
4 B—Kt 5, Q Kt—Q 2.

MANHATTAN VARIATION (A)

	56	57	58	59	60
5	(Kt—B 3)	...P—K 3			P×P (h)
	(B—Kt 5)	B—Kt 5			P×P
6	(P×P)	P×P			P—K 3
	(P×P)	P×P			P—B 3
7	Q—R 4	B—Q 3			B—Q 3
	B×Kt ch (a)	P—B 4			B—K 2 (l)
8	P×B	Kt—K 2	Kt—B 3		KKt-K2 (m)
	O—O	P×P (d)	Q—R 4		O—O (n)
9	P—K 3	P×P (e)	Q—B 2 (g)	P—K R 3	Kt—Kt 3
	P—B 4	O—O	P—B 5		Kt—K 1
10	B—Q 3	O—O	B—B 5	B—R 4	P—K R 4
	P—B 5	Kt—Kt 3	O—O	O—O	Kt (Q 2)-B 3
11	B—B 2	R—B 1	O—O	O—O	Q—B 2
	Q—K 2 (b)	P—K R.3	R—K 1	P—B 5	B—K 3 [(o)
12	O—O	B×Kt	P—Q R 3	B—B 5	Kt—B 5
	P—Q R 3	Q×B= (f)	B×Kt	R—K 1	B×Kt
13	K R—K 1		Q×B	Q R—Kt 1	B×B
	Q—K 3		Q×Q	B×Kt	Kt—Q 3
14	Kt—Q 2		P×Q	P×B	B—Q 3
	P—Q Kt 4		Kt—Kt 3 (h)	Kt—K 5	P—K R 3
15	Q—R 5+ (c)		B×B ± (i)	B×Kt ± (j)	B—K B 4 ± (p)

(A) See also col. 55.
(a) Euwe recommends 7.., Q—K 2.
(b) If 11.., P—Q R 3; 12 Kt—K 5, P—Kt 4; 13 Q—R 3 ±.
(c) 15.., Kt—K 5; 16 Kt×Kt, P×Kt; 17 P—Q R 4!, Q×Q 4?; 18 P×P!+.
Capablanca—Spielmann, New York, 1927.
(d) 8 ., P—B 5; 9 B—B 2, P—K R 3; 10 B—K R 4, O—O; 11 O—O, B—K 2;
12 P—B 3 ±. Kmoch—Fine, Amsterdam, 1936.
(e) Or 9 Kt×P, P—K R 3; 10 B—R 4, O—O; 11 O—O, B×Kt; 12 P×B,
Kt—B 4; 13 B—B 2, R—K 1; 14 R—B 1, P—Q Kt 3 =. Pleci—Marshall, Liège,
1930.
(f) Sámisch—Marshall, Brünn, 1928.
(g) 9 O—O, B×Kt; 10 P×B, Q×B P? (10. , P—B 5, transposing into col. 55,
is necessary); 11 R—B 1, Q—R 4; 12 B×Kt, P×B; 13 P×P, Kt×P; 14 B—Kt 1,
B—K 3; 15 Q—Q 4 ±. Analysis by Bogoljuboff.
(h) 14. , Kt—K 5; 15 B×K Kt, P×B; 16 Kt—Q 2 ±.
(i) Continued 15 , Kt×B; 16 B×Kt, P×B; 17 Kt—Q 2. Bogoljuboff—
Spielmann, Dortmund, 1928.
(j) Becker—Spielmann, Vienna, 1936.
(k) The Exchange Variation.
(l) Or 7.., B—Q 3; 8 K Kt—K 2, Kt—B 1; 9 Q—B 2, P—K R 3; 10 B—R 4,
Q—K 2, 11 P—Q R 3, B—Q 2; 12 P—K 4!, P—K Kt 4; 13 B—Kt 3, P×P;
14 Kt×P, Kt×Kt; 15 B×Kt, B×B; 16 R P×B, Q—Q 3; 17 O—O—O ±.
Spielmann—Capablanca, Carlsbad, 1929.
(m) For 8 Kt—B 3 see cols. 62-64.
(n) Better is 8 ., Kt—K 5, 9 B×B, Kt×Kt; 10 P×Kt, Q×B; 11 Q—B 2,
P—K R 3; 12 Kt—Kt 3, Kt—B 3 (Tartakover).
(o) Not 10 , B×B; 11 B×P ch, K×B; 12 P×B dis ch, K—Kt 1; 13 Q—R 5
and wins The column is Alekhine—Capablanca, 32nd match game, 1927.
(p) 15. , R—B 1; 16 P—K Kt 4

EXCHANGE VARIATION (A)

1 P—Q 4, P—Q 4; 2 P—Q B 4, P—K 3; 3 Kt—Q B 3, Kt—K B 3; 4 B—Kt 5, Q Kt—Q 2; 5 P—K 3, P—B 3; 6 P×P.

	61	62	63	64	65
6	K P×P				B P×P
7	B—Q 3 B—K 2 (a)				Kt—B 3 B—K 2
8	Q—B 2 O—O (b)			Kt—B 1	B—Q 3 O—O
9	K Kt—K 2 R—K 1	Kt—B 3 R—K 1		Kt—B 3 Kt—K 3	O—O P—Q R 3
10	P—K R 3 (c) Kt—B 1 (d)	O—O—O Kt—B 1	O—O (g) Kt—B 1	B—R 4 P—K Kt 3	R—B 1 P—Q Kt 4
11	O—O—O P—Q Kt 4	B—K B 4 Kt—Kt 3	Kt—K 5 Kt—Kt 5	O—O—O O—O	Kt—K 5 B—Kt 2 (k)
12	P—K Kt P—Q R 4	B—Kt 3 B—Q 3	B×B Q×B	K—Kt 1 (i) Kt—Kt 2	P—B 4 P—R 3
13	Kt—Kt 3 P—R 5	B×B Q×B	Kt×Kt B×Kt	P—K R 3 B—K B 4	B—R 4 Kt×Kt
14	K—Kt 1 Q—R 4	P—K R 3 B—Q 2	Kt—K 2 Q—R 5	B×Kt K B×B	B P×Kt (l) Kt—K 5
15	Q Kt—K 2! ± (e) K R—Q B 1 (f)	P—K Kt 4	Kt-Kt 3 ± (h)	P—K Kt 4 = (j)	B×B ± (m)

(A) No attention has been paid to transpositions on this page, so that for the purpose of these variations White may have played P×P on any one of his 3rd, 4th 5th or 6th moves.

(a) 7.., B—Q 3?; 8 Kt—B 3, O—O; 9 O—O, P—K R 3; 10 B—R 4, R—K 1; 11 Q—B 2, Kt—B 1; 12 P—K 4?, P×P; 13 Kt×P, B—K 2; 14 B×Kt, B×B; 15 K R—K 1, B—Kt 5 ∓. Marshall—Lasker, Moscow, 1925.

(b) 8.., P—K R 3?; 9 B—K B 4, O—O; 10 O—O—O, P—Q Kt 4; 11 Kt—B 3, P—Q R 4; 12 P—K Kt 4 ±. Fine—Thorvaldson, Folkestone, 1933.

(c) On 10 O—O—O, Kt—K 5?; 11 B×Kt, P×B; 12 P—K R 4!, P—K B 4 {12.., B×B; 13 P×B, Q×P; 14 Kt×P, Q—Kt 3; 15 P—B 3+. Nimzovitch—Spielmann, Bad Kissingen, 1928); 13 Q—Kt 3 ch, K—R 1; 14 Kt—B 4, Kt—B 1; 15 Q—B 7+ (Spielmann—Sir G. A. Thomas, Carlsbad, 1929), or 14 ., Kt—B 3; 15 P—R 5, P—K R 3; 16 Q—B 7!, Kt—Kt 1; 17 Kt—Kt 6 ch, K—R 2; 18 Kt×B+ Alekhine—Kashdan, Pasadena, 1932.

(d) 10 ., Kt—K 5; 11 B×B, Q×B; 12 B×Kt, P×B; 13 P—K Kt 4, Kt—B 3; 14 Kt—Kt 3, P—K R 3; 15 O—O—O, P—Q Kt 4; 16 K—Kt 1 ±. Dake—Kashdan, Milwaukee, 1935.

(e) Flohr—Asgeirsson, Folkestoné, 1933.

(f) 16 K—Kt 1, P—Q Kt 4 =. Reshevsky—Monticelli, Syracuse, 1934.

(g) 10 B—K B 4, Kt—B 1; 11 P—K R 3, B—Q 3; 12 B×B, Q×B; 13 O—O, P—K Kt 3; 14 Q R—Kt 1, Kt—R 4; 15 P—Q Kt 4, P—Q R 3; 16 Kt—Q R 4 ±. Reshevsky—Flohr, Stockholm, 1937.

(h) Flohr—Keres, Semmering-Baden, 1937. The advance of White's Q-side Pawns is difficult for Black to meet.

(i) This allows Black to simplify. 12 P—K R 3 was stronger.

(j) Reshevsky—Stahlberg, Kemeri, 1937.

(k) An alternative is 11.., Kt×Kt; 12 P×Kt, Kt—Q 2; 13 B—K B 4, B—Kt 2; 14 Kt—K 2, Q—Kt 1; 15 Kt—Q 4 ±. Euwe—Bogoljuboff, match, 1928.

(l) Weaker is 14 Q P×Kt, Kt—K 5; 15 B×B, Q×B =. Eliskases—Fine, Semmering-Baden, 1927.

(m) Continued 15. , Q×B; 16 B×Kt, P×B; 17 Q—Kt 4, Q—Kt 4; 18 Q×Q, P×Q (Lovenfisch—Fine, Leningrad, 1937); and now 19 R—Q B 2!+.

1 P—Q 4, P—Q 4; 2 P—Q B 4, P—K 3; 3 Kt—Q B 3, Kt—K B 3;
4 B—Kt 5, B—K 2; 5 P—K 3.

LASKER'S DEFENCE

	66	67	68	69	70
5	Q Kt—Q 2	...Kt—K 5	....O—O		
6	Kt—B 3 / P—K R 3 (a)	B×B / Q×B	Kt—B 3 / Kt—K 5.....P—K R 3		
7	B—R 4 / Kt—K 5	P×P / Kt×Kt	B×B / Q×B	B—R 4 / Kt—K 5.....P—Q Kt 3 (m)	
8	B×B / Q×B	P×Kt / P×P	P×P / Kt×Kt	B×B / Q×B	P×P / P×P
9	R—B 1 / P—Q B 3	Q—Kt 3 / P—Q B 3	P×Kt / P×P	Q—B 2 / Kt×Kt (j)	B—Q 3 / B—K 3
10	Kt×Kt (b) / P×Kt	Kt—B 3 / O—O	Q—Kt 3 / R—Q 1 (e)	Q×Kt / P—Q B 3	O—O / P—QB4? (n)
11	Kt—Q 2 / P—K B 4	P—B 4 / R—Q 1	P—B 4 (f) / Kt—B 3	B—Q 3 / Kt—Q 2	Kt—K 5 ! / K Kt—Q 2
12	P—B 5 / O—O	B—Q 3 / B—K 3 (d)	P×P (g) / Q—Kt 5 ch (h)	O—O (h) / P×P	B×B / Q×B
13	Kt—B 4 / P—K 4 !	P—B 5 / P—Q Kt 3	Kt—Q 2 / Q×Q	B×P / P—Q Kt 3	P—B 4 / P×P
14	Kt—Q 6 / P×P (c)	R—Q B 1 ±	Kt×Q / Kt—Kt 5 (i)	Q—Q 3 / R—Q 1 = (l)	P×P ±

(a) An advisable in-between move when Black intends playing Lasker's Defence.
6.., Kt—K 5; 7 B×B, Q×B; 8 R—B 1, P—Q B 3; 9 B—Q 3, P—K B 4; 10 Kt—K 5,
Q—B 3; 11 Kt×Kt, B×Kt; 12 Q—Kt 3, P—Q Kt 3; 13 B×Kt, B P×B; 14 P×P,
B P×P; 15 Kt×Q P!, P×Kt; 16 Q×P, R—Q B 1! = is Euwe—Tartakover, Carlsbad,
1929.
(b) 10 Q—B 2, P—K B 4 transposes into col. 11, note (a).
(c) 15 B—B 4 ch, K—R 2 =. Capablanca—Rubinstein, Budapest, 1929.
(d) Or 12.., Kt—Q 2; 13 O—O, P×P; 14 B×P. Janowski—Kostich, 1916.
The column is Marshall—Vidmar, San Sebastian, 1911.
(e) 10.., Q—Q 3 (Bernstein's Variation) is an excellent alternative. Euwe—
Eliskases, Noordwijk, 1938, continued 12 P—B 4, P×P! (5.., P—K R 3; 6 B—R 4
had been interpolated); 13 B×P, Kt—B 3!; 14 Q—B 3, B—Kt 5; 15 O—O, B×Kt;
16 P×B, Q R—Q 1; 17 K—R 1, Q—B 3; 18 B—K 2, K R—K 1; 19 Q R—K 1,
R—Q 2; 20 R—K Kt 1, Kt—K 2=. The older continuation 10.., P—Q B 3; 11 P—B 4,
B—K 3; 12 R—Q Kt 1, Q—Q Kt 3; 13 B—Q 3 ± is inferior.
(f) 11 B—Q 3, P—Q B 4; 12 Q—R 3, P—Q Kt 3; 13 O—O, Kt—B 3; 14 B—Kt 5,
P—B 5; 15 Q×Q, Kt×Q =. Marshall—Treybal, Folkestone, 1933.
(g) 12 P—B 5, B—Kt 5 (if 12.., P—Q Kt 3; 13 B—Kt 5, B—Q 2; 14 B×Kt,
B×B; 15 O—O, P×P; 16 Q—R 3+. Fine—Böök, Kemeri, 1937); 13 Q×Kt P,
B×Kt; 14 Q×Kt, B—K 5; 15 Q—R 4, Q R—Kt 1 gives Black a strong attack.
(h) 12.., Kt—R 4; 13 Q—B 3, R×P; 14 B—Q 3, P—Q Kt 3; 15 O—O, R—R 4;
16 Q R—B 1 ±. Eliskases—Spielmann, match, 1932.
(i) 15 R—B 1, Kt×Q P; 16 P—K 4, R—K 1; 17 P—B 3, P—K B 4 (17..,
P—Q B 3, tried in the match Bogoljuboff—Spielmann, 1932, is weaker); 18 B—B 4,
P—B 3; 19 B×Kt ch, P×B; 20 P—K 5, P—Q Kt 3 =.
(j) Or 9.., Kt—K B 3!; 10 B—Q 3, P×P, P—B 4; 12 O—O, Kt—B 3;
13 K R—Q 1, B—Q 2 =. Stahlberg—Lasker, Moscow, 1935.
(k) 12 P×P, K P×P; 13 O—O, Kt—B 3; 14 Q—R 4, B—Kt 5; 15 Kt—K 5,
B—R 4; 16 Q—B 5. Flohr—Böök, Warsaw, 1935. The ending is tenable for Black.
(l) Continued 15 Q—K 2!, P—K 4; 16 Q—B 2!, Q—B 3!; 17 Q—K 4, R—K 1;
18 K R—Q 1. Flohr—Bernstein, Zürich, 1934.
(m) Tartakover's Variation. See also next column.
(n) 10.., Q Kt—Q 2 was better, e.g., 11 Kt—K 5, Kt×Kt; 12 P×Kt, Kt—Q 2;
13 B×B, Q×B; 14 P—B 4, P—K B 4 with a good game. The column is Flohr—
Capablanca, Moscow, 1936

1 P—Q 4, P—Q 4; 2 P—Q B 4, P—K 3; 3 Kt—Q B 3, Kt—K B 3; 4 Kt—B 3.

	71	72	73	74	75
4	(B—K 2)...............		Q Kt—Q 2...............		Kt—K 5
5	(B—Kt 5)...	B—B 4	B—B 4......	P×P	Q—Kt 3
	(O—O)	O—O (d)	P×P	P×P	P—Q B 3
6	(P—K 3)	P—K 3	P—K 3	B—B 4 (i)	P—K 3 (m)
	(P—K R 3)	P—B 4! (e)	Kt—Q 4 (g)	P—B 3	Kt—Q 2
7	(B—R 4)	P×B P	K B×P	P—K 3 (j)	P×P
	(P—Q Kt 3)	B×P	Kt×B	B—K 2 (k)	K P×P
8	(P×P) (a)	P×P	P×Kt	B—Q 3	Kt×Kt
	Kt×P	Kt×P	B—Q 3	O—O	P×Kt
9	B×B	Kt×Kt	P—K Kt 3	P—K R 3	B—B 4
	Q×B (b)	P×Kt	Kt—B 3	R—K 1	Q—B 3
10	Kt×Kt	B—Q 3	O—O	O—O	Kt—Q 2
	P×Kt	B—Q 3 (f)	O—O	Kt—B 1	Q—Kt 3
11	R—Q B 1	B×B	Q—K 2	Kt—K 5	O—O
	B—K 3	Q×B	P—Q Kt 3	B—Q 3	Kt—B 3
12	Q—R 4	O—O	K R—Q 1	B—R 2	P—B 3
	P—Q B 4	Kt—B 3	B—Kt 2	K Kt—Q 2	P—Kt 4
13	Q—R 3	R—B 1	Q R—B 1	P—B 4	B—K 2
	R—Q B 1	P—K Kt 3	P—Q R 3	P—B 3	B—K 3
14	B—K 2	Q—Kt 3	B—Q3 ± (h)	Kt—Kt 4	Q—B 2
	Kt—Q 2 (c)	R—Kt 1 =		P—K R 4 (l)	B—Q 4 (n)

(a) 8 Q—B 2, B—Kt 2; 9 R—Q 1, Q Kt—Q 2; 10 P×P, P×P; 11 B—Q 3, Kt—R 4; 12 B—Kt 3, P—Q B 4; 13 B—B 5, P—B 5 =. Alekhine—Tartakover, Folkestone, 1933.

(b) If 9.., Kt×B; 10 B—K 2, B—Kt 2; 11 O—O, Kt—Q 2; 12 Q—R 4, P—Q R 3; 13 K R—Q 1, Kt—Q 4; 14 Q R—B 1 ±. Flohr—Capablanca, Nottingham, 1936.

(c) 15 O—O, P—Q R 3 =. Eliskases—Spielmann, match, 1936.

(d) 5.., P—Q R 3?; 6 P—B 5!, O—O; 7 P—K R 3, Kt—B 3; 8 P—K 3, P—Q Kt 3; 9 P×P, P×P; 10 R—B 1 ±. Bogoljuboff—Spielmann, Triberg, 1921.

(e) 6.., P×P; 7 K B×P, Kt—Q 4; 8 O—O, Kt×B; 9 P×Kt, Kt—Q 2; 10 Q—K 2, Kt—Kt 3; 11 B—Kt 3, B—B 3; 12 Kt—K 4, Kt—Q 4; 13 P—K Kt 3 ±. Flohr—Milner-Barry, Margate, 1936.

(f) Or 10 , B—Kt 5 ch; 11 Kt—Q 2, P—Q 5 !; 12 P—K 4, Q—B 3; 13 B—Kt 3, Kt—Q 2; 14 O—O, Kt—B 4 = (Bogoljuboff). 10 , Kt—B 3; 11 O—O, P—Q 5 is also good. The column is Bogoljuboff—Maróczy, Carlsbad, 1929.

(g) 6 , Kt—Kt 3; 7 K B×P, Kt×B; 8 Q—R 4 ch, P—B 3; 9 Q×Kt, Kt—Q 4 = is much better for Black.

(h) Capablanca—Becker, Carlsbad, 1929.

(i) Sämisch's Variation.

(j) 7 P—K R 3, B—K 2; 8 P—K 3, Kt—K 5; 9 Q—B 2, P—K B 4; 10 B—Q 3, O—O; 11 O—O, B—Q 3, 12 B×B, Kt×B; 13 Q R—Q 1, Q—B 3. Sämisch—H. Wolf, Teplitz-Schonau, 1922.

(k) If 7 , Kt—R 4; 8 B—K 5, P—B 3; 9 B—Kt 3 is good for White, but not 8 B—Q 3, Kt×B; 9 P×Kt, B—Q 3; 10 P—K Kt 3, O—O; 11 O—O, R—K 1 ∓. Alekhine—Em. Lasker, New York, 1924.

(l) Continued 15 Kt—K 5 !, P×Kt; 16 B P×Kt, B×P!; 17 P×B, Kt×P; 18 R×Kt ch!!, K×R; 19 Q×P, Kt×B; 20 R—B 1 ch, K—Kt 1; 21 Q—B 7 ch. Drawn by perpetual check. Alekhine—Vidmar, New York, 1927.

(m) Bogoljuboff suggests 6 B—B 4.

(n) Brinckmann—Réti Kiel, 1921

1 P—Q 4, P—Q 4; 2 P—Q B 4, P—K 3; 3 Kt—Q B 3, Kt—K B 3; 4 Kt—B 3.

	76	77	78	79	80
4	B—Kt 5 (a)				P—B 4 (n)
5	Q—R 4 ch			P—K 3 (k)	B P×P
	Kt—B 3	•		O—O (l)	Kt×P (o)
6	Kt—K 5	P—K 3	P×P (i)	B—Q 3	P—K 4 (p)
	B—Q 2	O—O	Kt×P ·	Kt—B 3	Kt×Kt
7	Kt×B (b)	B—Q 2	B—Q 2	O—O	P×Kt
	Q×Kt	P—Q R 3 (g)	Kt—Kt 3	Q—K 2	P×P
8	P—K 3 (c)	Q—B 2	Q—Kt 5	P—Q R 3	P×P
	P—K 4	P×P	P—Q R 3	P×P	B-Kt5ch (q)
9	Q P×P (d)	B×P	Q—Q 3	B×P	B—Q 2
	P—Q 5 !	B—Q 3	B—K 2	B×Kt ?	Q—R 4
10	P—Q R 3 !	P—Q R 3	R—Q 1	P×B	R—QKt1(r)
	B×Kt ch	P—K 4	P—K 4 !	P—K 4	B×B ch
11	P×B	P—Q 5	P×P	P—Q R 4 !	Q×B
	P×K P !	Kt—K 2	Q×Q	R—Q 1	Q×Q ch
12	B×P (e)	P—R 3	P×Q	B—R 3	K×Q
	Kt—K K Kt 5	P—Q Kt 4	B—K Kt 5	Q—K 1	O—O
13	B—Q 4	B—R 2	B—K 2	Kt—Kt 5 ±	B—Kt 5 ! (s)
	K Kt×P	Q—Q 2 !	O—O—O	(m)	P—Q R 3
14	P—B 4	P—K 4	B—B 4		B—Q3 ± (t)
	Kt×B = (f)	P-QR4=(h)	B—Kt 5 ! ∓ (j)		

(a) Known in Russia as the Ragosin System.

(b) If 7 Kt×Kt, B×Kt ch; 8 P×B, B×Kt; 9 Q—Kt 3, P×P; 10 Q×B P, Kt—K 5 ∓. Freymann—Ragosin, Leningrad, 1934. If now 11 B—B 4, Q—B 3; 12 P—K 3, P—K Kt 4.

(c) Better is 8 P—Q R 3, B×Kt ch; 9 P×B, P—K 4; 10 P—K 3 ± (Alekhine).

(d) 9 P—Q R 3, K P×P; 10 P×B, P×Kt; 11 Kt P×P, O—O; 12 B—K 2, P×P ∓ Colle—Alekhine, Hastings, 1926.

(e) If 12 P×Kt?, P×P ch; 13 K×P, Q—B 4 ch; 14 K—K 1 (14 K—Kt 3, P×P), O—O—O, with a winning attack.

(f) 15 Q×Q ch, K×Q. Spielmann—Fine, Zandvoort, 1936.

(g) Or 7 , B—Q 2; 8 Q—B 2, R—K 1; 9 R—Q 1, B—Q 3; 10 B—B 1, P—Q R 4; 11 P—Q R 3, P—R 5?; 12 P—B 5 ±. Eliskases—Ragosin, Moscow, 1936.

(h) Reshevsky—Ragosin, Semmering-Baden, 1937.

(i) If 6 B—Kt 5?, P×P (this position can also arise in the Vienna Variation, see col. 116 and notes) ; 7 P—K 3, Q—Q 4; 8 B×Kt, P×B; 9 Kt—Q 2, B×Kt; 10 P×B, P—Kt 4 +. Rabinovitch—Ragosin, Moscow, 1935.

(j) Romanovsky—Ragosin, Leningrad, 1934.

(k) 5 B—Kt 5, P—B 3 (5 , P×P transposes into the Vienna Variation, col. 116) ; 6 P×P, K P×P; 7 Q—Kt 3, B—K 2; 8 P—K 3, Q×Q; 9 Kt×Kt, P—Q R 4 =. Van Scheltinga—Fine, Amsterdam, 1936. 5 Q—B 2, Kt—B 3; 6 P—K 3, O—O; 7 P—Q R 3, B×Kt ch; 8 Q×B, B—Q 2; 9 P—Q Kt 4, P—Q R 4; 10 P—Kt 5, Kt—R 2; 11 P—Q R 4, P—Q B 3!; 12 B—R 3, R—K 1 ∓. Rumin—Ragosin, Leningrad, 1934.

(l) For other replies see Nimzovitch's Defence (Queen's Pawn Game), with 4 P—K 3.

(m) Dubinin—Ragosin, Leningrad, 1934.

(n) Although this position can also arise from the Tarrasch Defence, it more frequently comes from the Queen's Gambit Declined.

(o) If 5 .. K P×P; 6 B—Kt 5, B—K 3; 7 P—K 4 ±. 5 , B P×P; 6 Q×P, P×P; 7 B—Kt 5, B—K 2; 8 P—K 3, Kt—B 3; 9 B—Kt 5, O—O; 10 Q—Q 2, B—K 3; 11 O—O, Q—Kt 3; 12 K R—Q 1, K R—Q 1 =. Euwe—Milner-Barry, Hastings, 1938-39.

(p) 6 P—K 3, Kt—Q B 3; 7 B—B 4, P×P; 8 P×P, B—K 2; 9 O—O, O—O; 10 R—K 1, P—Q Kt 3? (Kt—Kt 3!; 10 B—Kt 3, B—B 3. Euwe); 11 Kt×Kt, P×Kt; 12 B—Q Kt 5 ±. Botvinnik—Alekhine, Avro, 1938.

(q) 8 , B—K 2; 9 B—K 2, O—O; 10 O—O, P—Q Kt 3; 11 Q—Q 2 !, B—Kt 2; 12 Q—K 3, Kt—Q 2; 13 B—Kt 2, R—B 1; 14 Q R—B 1 ±. Lilienthal—Flohr, Moscow, 1935.

(r) 10 B—K 2, Kt—B 3; 11 R—Q Kt 1, B×B ch, 12 Q×B, O—O; 13 B—Kt 5, Q×Q ch; 14 K×Q, Kt—R 4; 15 K R—B 1 ±. Stahlberg—Lasker, Zurich, 1934.

(s) Best. If 13 B—K 2, P—Q Kt 3, 14 K R—Q B 1, B—Kt 2; 15 K—K 3, Kt—B 3; 16 R—B 3, Q R—B 1 =. Keres—Landau, Ostend, 1937.

(t) 14 ., R—Q 1; 15 K R—Q B 1, P—Q Kt 4; 16 R—B 7, Kt—Q 2; 17 K—K 3, Kt—B 3; 18 Kt—K 5 and Black's position is very uncomfortable. Rubinstein—Schlechter, San Sebastian, 1912.

1 P—Q 4, P—Q 4 ; 2 P—Q B 4, P—K 3 ; 3 Kt—Q B 3, Kt—K B 3 ;
4 Kt—B 3, P—B 4.

	81	82	83	84	85
5	(B P × P)			B—Kt 5	
	(Kt × P)			B P × P	
6	(P—K 4)		P—K Kt 3	K Kt × P (g)	
	(Kt × Kt)		Kt—Q B 3	P—K 4 (h)	
7	(P × Kt)		B—Kt 2	Kt—O	..... K Kt—Kt 5
	(P × P)		Kt × P (e)	P—Q 5	P—Q R 3 ! (k)
8	(P × P)		K Kt × Kt	Kt—Q 5	Q—R 4 ! (l)
	(B—Kt 5 ch)		Kt × Kt	Kt—B 3 (i)	B—Q 2
9	(B—Q 2)		P × Kt	P—K 4	P—K 4 ! (m)
	B × B ch		P × Kt	B—K 2	P × B P
10	Q × B		Q × P	B × Kt	B × P
	O—O		Q × Q	B × B	P × Kt
11	B—B 4	...... B—K 2 (o)	P × Q	P—Q Kt 4 !	B × P ch
	Kt—B 3 (a)	P—Q Kt 3	B—Q 3	O—O	K × B
12	O—O	O—O	P—Q R 4 (f)	B—Q 3	Q × R
	P—Q Kt 3	B—Kt 2	R—Q Kt 1	P—Q R 4	B—B 3
13	K R—Q 1	Q—B 4	B—R 3	P—Q R 3	O—O
	B—Kt 2	Kt—B 3 (c)	K—K 2	B—K 3	Q—B 2
14	Q—B 4	K R—Q 1	B × B ch	R—Q Kt 1 ±	O—R 7
	R—B 1 (b)	Kt—K 2 (d)	K × B		(j) Q Kt—Q 2 (n)

(a) If 11 .., P—Q Kt 3 ; 12 P—Q 5+. Possible is 11.., Kt—Q 2 ; 12 O—O, P—Q Kt 3 ; 13 Q R—Q 1, B—Kt 2 ; 14 K R—K 1, R—B 1 ; 15 B—Kt 3, Kt—B 3 ; 16 Q—B 4, Q—B 2, 17 Q—R 4, K R—Q 1 ; 18 R—K 3, P—Q Kt 4 =. Keres—Fine Ostend, 1937.
(b) Or 14.., Q—B 3 ; 15 Q—K 3, K R—Q 1 ; 16 P—K 5, Q—R 3 ! ; 17 Q R—B 1, Q × Q =. Reshevsky—Fine, Hastings, 1937–38. The column is Alekhine—Euwe, 18th match game, 1937, which continued 15 P—Q 5, P × P ; 16 B × P, Q—K 2 ; 17 Kt—Kt 5 !, Kt—K 4 ; 18 B × B, Kt—Kt 3 =.
(c) Or 13 , Kt—Q 2 ; 14 Q R—B 1, Kt—B 3 ; 15 B—Q 3, R—B 1 ; 16 R × R, B × R ; 17 R—B 1, B—Kt 2. Alekhine—Grünfeld, Prague, 1931.
(d) 15 Q R—B 1, Kt—Kt 3 ∓. Fairhurst—Alekhine, Folkestone, 1933.
(e) Or 7 , Q—R 4 ! ; 8 Q—Q 2, Kt × Kt ; 9 P × Kt, P × P ; 10 Kt × P, Kt × Kt ; 11 Q × Kt, P—K 4 ; 12 Q—K 3, B—K 2 ; 13 O—O =. Reinfeld—Reshevsky, New York, 1938. The column is Alekhine—Euwe, 30th match game, 1937.
(f) Simpler is 12 B—B 4, B × B ; 13 P × B, R—Q Kt 1 =. Rubinstein—Tartakover, Carlsbad, 1929.
(g) If 6 Q × P, not 6.., Kt—B 3 ? ; 7 B × Kt, P × B ; 8 Q—R 4, P × P ; 9 R—Q 1, B—Q 2 ; 10 P—K 3, Kt—K 4 ; 11 Kt × Kt, P × Kt ; 12 Q × B P+ (Pillsbury—Lasker, Cambridge Springs, 1904), but 6.., B—K 2 ; 7 P × P (7 O—O—O ?, Kt—B 3 ; 8 Q—R 4, Q—R 4 ; 9 P—K 3, B—Q 2 ; 10 K—Kt 1, P—K R 3 ∓. Pillsbury—Lasker, St. Petersburg, 1895–96), P × P ; 8 P—K 3, Kt—B 3 ; 9 B—Kt 5 !, O—O ; 10 Q—R 4 B—Q 2 =. Dake—Fine, New York, 1936.
(h) 6.., P × P ; 7 P—K 3, Q—Kt 3 ; 8 B × Kt, P × B ; 9 B × P, B—Q 2 ; 10 O—O, Kt—B 3 ; 11 B—Kt 3 ∓. Bogoljuboff—Alekhine, 1st match game, 1934.
(i) 8.., B—K 2 is better.
(j) Euwe—Alekhine, 29th match gane, 1937.
(k) 7 , P—Q 5 ; 8 Kt—Q 5, Kt—R 3 ; 9 Q—R 4, B—Q 2 ; 10 B × Kt, P × B ; 11 P—Q Kt 4 ±.
(l) 8 Kt × P ? ?, P × Kt ; 9 Kt × Kt ch, Q × Kt ! ! ; 10 B × Q, B—Kt 5 ch ; 11 Q—Q 2, B × Q ch + +. Yudovitch—Fine, Moscow, 1937. The text continuation was suggested in analysis after the game by Dr. Lasker.
(m) If 9 P × P, Q—Kt 3 ; 10 B × Kt, P × B ; 11 P—K 4, R—R 2 ! +. Or 9 Kt × P, B × Kt +.
(n) White has R + P for two pieces and the freer game.
(o) Alternatives are : (1) 11 B—Kt 5 (Kmoch's suggestion), P—Q Kt 3 ; 12 R—Q B 1, B—Kt 2, 13 Q—K 3, Kt—Q 2, 14 O—O, Kt—B 3 ; 15 B—Q 3, Q—K 2 ; 16 Kt—K 5, K R—B 1 ; 17 Kt—B 4, R—B 2 ; 18 P—K 5, Kt—K 1 =. Reshevsky—Horowitz, New York, 1935. (2) 11 B—Q 3, Kt—B 3 ; 12 Q—K 3 (12 P—K 5, Q—R 4 =), P—Q Kt 3, 13 O—O, Q—K 2 =. Horowitz—S. Bernstein, New York, 1936.

F *

TARRASCH DEFENCE
1 P—Q4, P—Q4; 2 P—QB4, P—K3; 3 Kt—QB3, P—QB4.

RUBINSTEIN VARIATION
4 BP×P, K P×P; 5 Kt—B3 (a), Kt—QB3; 6 P—K Kt3, Kt—B3;
7 B--Kt2, B—K2; 8 O—O, O—O (b).

	86	87	88	89	90
9	P×P B×P			P—Q5	
10	Kt—QR4 (c) B—K2		B—Kt5 P—Q5! (h)	Kt—QR4 (k) B—B4	
11	B—K3 Kt—K5		Kt—K4 B—K2	Kt—R4 (l).. 	B—B4! Kt—K5
12	R—B1 Q—R4	Kt—Q4 Kt—K4 (f)	Kt×Kt ch B×Kt	P—B3 B—Q4	P—Q Kt4! Kt×Kt P
13	Kt—Q4 Kt×Kt (d)	R—B1 Q—R4	B×B (i) Q×B	P—K4 B—B5	Kt×P B—Kt3
14	Q B×Kt B—K3	B—B4! Kt—Kt3	Q—R4 B—K3	R—B2 Kt—Q2 (m)	R—Kt1 P—Q R4
15	P—B3 Kt—B3	B—B7 Q—R3	Q—Kt5 QR-Kt1 = (j)	Kt—B5 Kt×P	P—Q R3 (n) Kt—Q B3
16	Kt—B5 Q×P'	P—Q R3 B—Q2		Q—B2 Kt×Kt ·	Kt×Kt P×Kt
17	Kt×B ± (e)	Kt-QB3+ (g)		Q×B ±	R—Kt7+

(a) If instead 5 P×P, P—Q5; 6 Kt—Q R4, P—Q Kt4!; 7 P×P e.p., P×P;
8 P—Q Kt3, K Kt—B3; 9 P—K3, B--Q2!; 10 Q×P (or 10 P×P, B—Kt5 ch;
11 B—Q2, Q—K2 ch; 12 B—K2, Kt—K5+); 10 ., Kt—B3; 11 Q×P, B—Kt5 ch,
12 B—Q2, B×B ch; 13 K×B, Q—K2+ (Bogoljuboff).

(b) The "normal position" in the Tarrasch Defence (Tartakover). If 8.., B—K3;
9 P×P, B×P; 10 Kt—K Kt5!+; or 8 , Kt—K5; 9 P×P, Kt×Kt; 10 P×Kt,
B×P; 11 Kt—K1 followed by Kt—Q3 and B4 (Bogoljuboff).

(c) The Réti Variation.

(d) Lövenfisch recommends 13.., B—Q2 followed by .., Q R—Q1. If 13..,
B—Q2; 14 B×Kt, P×B; 15 Kt—Kt3, Q×Kt; 16 Q×B, Q×P; 17 Q×P, Q R—Kt1;
18 Q×Kt, Q×Kt; 19 B×P, R—Kt5 =.

(e) 17.., P×Kt; 18 B—R3, Q—R3; 19 Q—Q3, Q—Q3; 20 Q—K3!, K—B2;
21 Q B—B5+. Alekhine—Euwe, match, 1927.

(f) 12 ., Kt×Kt; 13 Q B×Kt, B—K3; 14 Kt—B3, Kt×Kt; 15 B×Kt ±.
Analysis by Bogoljuboff.

(g) Capablanca—Znosko-Borovsky, Paris, 1938.

(h) 10.., B—K2; 11 Kt—Q4, Kt×Kt; 12 Q×Kt+ transposes into col. 93.

(i) 13 Q—Q2, B—Kt5; 14 P—K R3? (better 14 Q—B4), B×B; 15 Kt×B,
B×K P; 16 Kt×B P, Q—K2; 17 K R—K1, P—Q6. Capablanca—Euwe, 5th
match game, 1931.

(j) Capablanca—Lasker, 9th match game, 1921.

(k) 10 Kt—Q Kt5, B×P; 11 B—Kt5, B—Kt3; 12 Kt—Q2, P—K R3;
13 Q B×Kt, Q×B; 14 Kt—B4, B—Q B4 =. Colle—Alekhine, Bled, 1931.

(l) If 11 P—Q R3, Kt—K5; 12 P—Q Kt4, Kt—B6; 13 Kt×Kt, P×Kt;
14 Q×Q, Q R×Q; 15 B—Kt5, B×B; 16 Kt×B, Kt—Q5+.

(m) 14.., P—K Kt3 is better. The column is Bogoljuboff—Maróczy, Bad Sliac,
1932.

(n) 15 R—K· 2, Q—K1; 16 P—Q R3, Kt—Q4; 17 B—B1, R—Q1; 18 P—K3,
Kt×Q B P =. Alatorzeff—Fine, Moscow, 1937.

TARRASCH DEFENCE

1 P—Q4, P—Q4; 2 P—QB4, P—K3; 3 Kt—QB3, P—QB4.

RUBINSTEIN VARIATION

4 BPxP, KPxP; 5 Kt—B3, Kt—QB3; 6 P—KKt3.

	91	92	93	94	95
6	(Kt—B3)				
7	(B—Kt2)				B—Kt5 (k)
	(B—K2)	....		PxP	
8	(O—O)			KKtxP	B—K3
	(O—O)			B—QB4	BxKt (l)
9	B—Kt5 (a)			Kt—Kt3!(g)	BxB
	B—K3	....	PxP	B—Kt3 (h)	Q—Q2
10	PxP (b)	R—B1	KKtxP	O—O (i)	O—O
	BxP	Kt—K5 (d)	KtxKt	B—K3	R—Q1
11	R—B1	BxB	QxKt	B—Kt5	R—B1
	B—Kt3!	QxB	B—K3	O—O	B—K2
12	P—Kt3	PxP	QR—B1	Kt—R4	Kt—R4
	R—K1	QR—Q1	Q—R4	P—KR3	Kt—KKt5
13	P—K3	Kt—Q4!	P—QR3	KtxB	KtxP
	Kt—QKt5	KtxQBP	KR—Q1	PxKt	KtxB
14	Kt—Q4	KtxKt	Q—Q3!	B—K3	PxKt
	P—KR3	PxKt	P—Q5	QKt—R4	BxKt
15	BxKt	Q—Q4+(e)	Kt—K4+(f)	Kt—Q4±(j)	RxB+(m)
	QxB = (c)				

(a) 9 B—K3, Kt—KKt5; 10 B—B4, B—K3; 11 PxP, BxP; 12 Kt—K1, B—Q5!; 13 Kt—Q3, Kt—B3; 14 R—B1, P—KR3 =. Flohr—Lasker, Moscow, 1935.
(b) Other possibilities are: (1) 10 P—QR3, Kt—K5 =. (2) 10 BxKt, BxB; 11 PxP, BxKt (the sacrifice 11.., P—Q5; 12 Kt—QR4 is not quite sound); 12 PxB, Q—R4 = (Euwe)
(c) 16 P—QR3, Kt—B3; 17 KtxP, BxKt; 18 BxB, KtxKt; 19 PxKt, QR—Q1. Rubinstein—Lasker, Berlin, 1918.
(d) 10 , P—B5; 11 Kt—K5, Q—Kt3 is Black's best line (Bogoljuboff). 12 P—K3, QxKtP; 13 P—B4 gives White a strong attack, however.
(e) Analysis by Bogoljuboff.
(f) Flohr—Euwe, 11th match game, 1932.
(g) Alternatives are: 9 KtxKt, PxKt, 10 O—O, O—O; 11 B—Kt5, R—Kt1; 12 R—B1, P—KR3. Grunfeld—Spielmann, Mahrisch-Ostrau, 1923. Or 9 B—K3, Q—Kt3; 10 O—O, BxKt; 11 Kt—R4, BxB! (if 11 , Q—Kt5; 12 P—QR3, Q—B5!; 13 R—B1+); 12 KtxQ, BxKt; 13 BxP, KtxB; 14 QxKt, O—O = (Grünfeld).
(h) 9.., B—QKt5; 10 O—O, BxKt; 11 PxB, O—O; 12 B—Kt5, B—K3; 13 Kt—B5, Q—K2; 14 KtxB, PxKt; 15 P—QB4!+. Rubinstein—Marshall, Breslau, 1912.
(i) If 10 KtxP, KtxKt; 11 QxKt, QxQ; 12 BxQ, Kt—Kt5 with sufficient compensation for the Pawn.
(j) Takacs—Spielmann, Meran, 1924. Grunfeld suggests 15 B—Q4, Kt—B5; 16 Kt—Q2.
(k) The Wagner Variation. See also col. 96.
(l) 8 , P—B5; 9 O—O, BxKt, 10 BxB, P—KR3; 11 Q—B2, Q—Q2; 12 P—Kt3+. Gilg—P. Johner, Carlsbad, 1929.
(m) 15 , Kt—K2; 16 Q—B1!, O—O; 17 R—B7. Post—Wagner, Oeynhausen, 1922

TARRASCH DEFENCE

1 P—Q 4, P—Q 4 ; 2 P—Q B 4, P—K 3 ; 3 Kt—Q B 3 (n), P—Q B 4.

RUBINSTEIN VARIATION

4 B P×P, K P×P ; 5 Kt—B 3, Kt—Q B 3 ; 6 P—K Kt 3.

	96	97	98	99	100
6	(Kt—B 3)	...P—B 5 (d)			
7	(B—Kt 2)	B—Kt 2..........................			P—K 4 !
	(B—Kt 5)	B—Q Kt 5			P×P
8	Kt—K 5 ! (a)	O—O			Kt—K Kt 5
	P×P (b)	K Kt—K 2			Q×P (k)
9	Kt×B	Kt—K 5....	B—B 4.....	P—K 4	B—B 4 !
	P×Kt	O—O	O—O	P×P (h)	P—K R 3 (l)
10	Kt×Kt ch	Kt×Kt	R—B 1	Kt×P	K Kt×K P
	Q×Kt	P×Kt	Q—R 4	B—K B 4	Q×Q ch
11	P×P	P—K 4	P—Q R 3	Kt—K 5	R×Q
	Q×Q B P ch	B—K 3	B×Kt	Kt×Kt (i)	B—K 3
12	B—Q 2	B—Kt 5 (e)	R×B	P×Kt	Kt—Kt 5
	Q—B 3	P—B 3	P—Q Kt 4	Kt—B 3	B—Kt 5 ch
13	O—O !	B—Q 2	B—Q 6	B—Kt 5	K—K 2
	R—Q 1	R—Kt 1	R—Q 1	Q×Q	R—Q 1
14	Q—Kt 3	R—K 1	B—B 5	K R×Q	KKt—Q6ch
	P—Q Kt 3	B—B 2	Q—B 2	P—K R 3	K—K 2
15	B—Q B 3 + (c)	P—Q R 3 (f)	R—K 1	B—B 4 ± (j)	B—Kt 2 !+
			P—Q R 4 = (g)		(m)

(a) Nimzovitch analyses 8 B—Kt 5, B—K 2; 9 P×P, O—O; 10 O—O, P—Q 5; 11 B×Kt, B×B; 12 Kt—K 4, B—K 2; 13 Q—Kt 3, Q R—Kt 1; 14 Q R—Q 1, K—R 1; 15 Q—R 4, in White's favour.

(b) 8 , B—K 3; 9 Kt×Kt, P×Kt; 10 P—K 4, B P×P; 11 P×P, P×P; 12 Q×P, B—K 2; 13 O—O ±. Brinckmann—Wagner, Hamburg, 1921.

(c) Euwe—Stoltz, Hastings, 1932.

(d) The Folkestone (or Swedish) Variation, popularised by the Swedish team at Folkestone, 1933.

(e) Weaker is 12 B—K 3, R—Kt 1; 13 Q—B 2, P—K B 4!, 14 P×Q P, Kt×P!; 15 Kt×Kt, B×Kt, 16 B—B 4, B—Q 3 ∓. Fine—Lundin, Folkestone, 1933.

(f) 15 , B—Q R 4; 16 P×P, P×P? (16 ., Kt×P was necessary); [17] R×Kt ! +. Grünfeld—Stahlberg, Folkestone, 1933.

(g) Sultan Khan—Stahlberg, Folkestone, 1933.

(h) 9 , O—O?; 10 Kt×P, Kt×Kt, 11 P×Kt, Q×P; 12 P—Q R 3!+, e.g. 12 .., B—R 4, 13 Kt—K 5, Q×P; 14 Kt×Kt, Q×Q; 15 Kt—K 7 ch and wins.

(i) 11 , Q×P; 12 Q×Q, Kt×Q, 13 P—Q R 3!, B×Kt; 14 B×B, B—B 4; 15 B×Kt P, R—Q Kt 1; 16 B—R 6+. Nimzovitch—Stoltz, match, 1933.

(j) Analysis by Euwe.

(k) Or 8 ., Kt×P; 9 B×P, Kt—K 3; 10 B—Kt 5 ch, B—Q 2; 11 Kt×Kt +; or 8 , P—K R 3; 9 K Kt×K P, B—K B 4; 10 P×P, Q×P; 11 Q—Kt 3, B×Kt; 12 B×P ch, K—Q 1; 13 B—K 3, Q—K 4; 14 O—O—O ch +.

(l) 9 . , Q×Q ch; 10 R×Q, B—K Kt 5; 11 B×P!, B×R; 12 B×P ch, K—Q 1; 13 K×B, Kt—R 3; 14 K—B 1, with a powerful attack.

(m) 15 ., Kt—B 3; 16 Kt×Kt P, B—Kt 5 ch; 17 P—B 3, R×R; 18 R×R, B—K B 4; 19 P—Q R 3, B—Q 6 ch; 20 K—B 2, etc. Rey—Johannson, correspondence, 1935.

(n) 3 Kt—K B 3, P—Q B 4; 4 P×Q P, K P×P; 5 P—K Kt 3, Q Kt—B 3; 6 B—Kt 2, Kt—B 3; 7 O—O, B—K 2; 8 P×P, B×P; 9 Q Kt—Q 2, P—Q 5? (9.., Kt—K 5; 10 Kt—Kt 3, B—Kt 3; 11 K Kt—Q 4, Q—B 3 = Kashdan—Horowitz, New York, 1938); 10 Kt—Kt 3, B—Kt 3; 11 Q—Q 3, B—K 3; 12 R—Q 1, B×Kt; 13 Q×B, Q—K 2; 14 B—Q 2, O—O; 15 P—Q R 4 ±. Lasker—Tarrasch, St. Petersburg, 1914.

TARRASCH DEFENCE

1 P—Q 4, P—Q 4; 2 P—Q B 4, P—K 3; 3 Kt—Q B 3, P—Q B 4.

	101	102	103	104	105
4	(B P×P)			P—K 3 (j)	
	B P×P (a)		K P×P	Kt—K B 3	
5	Q×P	Q—R 4 ch	P—K 4 (h)	Kt—B 3	
	Kt—Q B 3	B—Q 2 (f)	Q P×P	Kt—B 3	
6	Q—Q 1	Q×Q P	P—Q 5	P—Q R 3....	B—Q 3
	P×P	P×P	P—B 4	B—Q 3 (k)	B—Q 3 (m)
7	Q×P	Q×Q P	B—Kt 5 ch	Q P×P	O—O
	B—K 3	Kt—K B 3	B—Q 2	B×B P	O—O
8	Q×Q ch	Q—Kt 3	Kt—R 3	P—Q Kt 4	Q—K 2
	R×Q	Kt—B 3	B×B	B—Q 3	Q—K 2
9	P—K 3! (b)	P—K 3	Kt×B	B—Kt 2	P×B P
	Kt—Kt 5	B—Q Kt 5	Q—R 4 ch	P—Q R 4	B×P
10	B—Kt 5 ch	B—Q 2	Kt—B 3	P—Kt 5	P—K 4!
	K—K 2	O—O	Kt—Q R 3	Kt—K 4	P×B P (n)
11	B—R 4	Kt—B 3	P—B 3	P×P	B×P
	P—Q Kt 4	Q—K 2	Kt—B 3	P×P	P—K 4
12	Kt×P! (c)	B—K 2	O—O	B—K 2	B—K Kt 5
	B—B 5	B—K 3	B—K 2	B—K 3	B—K 3
13	Kt—R 3! (d)	Q—B 2	Kt—K Kt 5	Kt—Q 4	Kt—Q 5
	B—R 3	Q R—B 1	O—O+ (i)	R—Q B 1 =(l)	B×Kt
14	Kt—K 2!+ (e)	O—O+ (g)			B×B (o)

(a) The von Hennig—Schara (or Duisburg) Gambit.

(b) 9 P—B 3, Kt—Kt 5; 10 K—B 2, Kt—B 7; 11 R—Kt 1, B—B 4 ch; 12 P—K 3, Kt—R 3; 13 B—Kt 5 ch, K—K 2; 14 P—K Kt 4, P—B 4; 15 P—Kt 5, P—B 5!?; 16 P×Kt, P×P ch; 17 K—B 1, P×P with a strong attack. Kashdan—Tartakover, Bled, 1931. Another good line for White is 9 P—K 4, Kt—Kt 5; 10 B—Kt 5 ch, K—K 2, 11 K—B 1.

(c) 12 B—Q 1?, Kt—Q 6 ch!; 13 K—B 1, P—Kt 5; 14 Kt—K 4, P—B 4; 15 Kt—Kt 3, Kt×B P; 16 K×Kt, R×B ∓. Makarczyk—Betbéder, Prague, 1931.

(d) Cheriogolovko—Kiseff, 1938. If now 13 ., Kt—Q 6 ch; 14 K—B 1, Kt×Kt P ch; 15 Kt×B, Kt×B; 16 B—R 3 ch+.

(e) 14. , Kt—Q 6 ch; 15 K—B 1, Kt×B; 16 R×Kt, R—Q 7; 17 Kt—B 4 B×Kt; 18 R×B.

(f) 5.., Q—Q 2; 6 Kt—Kt 5, Kt—Q R 3; 7 P—Q 6, K—Q 1 (7. , Q—B 3 is better); 8 B—B 4, P—B 3; 9 Kt—K B 3, P—K 4; 10 B×P, P×B; 11 Kt×K P, Q—K 3; 12 Q×P, B—Q 2; 13 P—K 4, R—B 1; 14 Kt×P, B×P; 15 Kt×B+. Havasi—Tartakover, Budapest, 1929.

(g) Dake—Makarczyk, Folkestone, 1933.

(h) Marshall's Variation.

(i) Oskam—Euwe, 1920.

(j) The Normal Variation, which had the enthusiastic support of Tarrasch. But it has not found favour with the other masters.

(k) 6 ., Kt—K 5 (recommended by Alekhine); 7 Q—B 2, Q—R 4; 8 P×P, B×P; 9 P×P, P×P; 10 B—Q 3, Kt×Kt; 11 P×Kt, P—K R 3; 12 O—O, O—O =. Foltys—Fine, Stockholm, 1937.

(l) Rosselli—Alekhine, Folkestone, 1933.

(m) 6 , Q P×P; 7 B×P, P—Q R 3, transposing to the Queen's Gambit Accepted, is Black's best course.

(n) If 10 , P×K P; 11 Kt×P, Kt×Kt; 12 B×Kt, B—Q 2; 13 P—Q R 3, Q R—K 1; 14 P—Q Kt 4, B—Q 3; 15 B—Kt 2 ±. The column and notes are analysis by Lövenfisch.

(o) 14.., Kt—Q 5; 15 Kt×Kt, B×Kt; 16 Q R—B 1 ±.

1 P—Q 4, P—Q 4 ; 2 P—Q B 4.

	106	107	108	109	110
2	P—K 3				P--Q B 4
3	Kt—Q B 3				B P × P (k)
	P—Q R 3 (a)		P—Q Kt 3 (f)		Q × P
4	P × P		Kt—B 3	P × P	Kt—KB3(l)
	P × P		B—Kt 2	P × P	P × P
5	B—B 4 (b)	...Kt—B 3	P × P	Q—R 4 ch (i)	Kt—B 3
	Kt—K B 3	Kt—K B 3	P × P	P—B 3	Q—Q R 4
6	P--K 3	B—Kt 5	B—B 4	Kt—B 3	Kt × P
	B—Q 3	B—K 2	B—Q 3	B—Q 3	Kt—K B 3
7	B × B	P—K 3	B × B	P—K 4	Kt—Kt 3
	Q × B	Q Kt—Q 2	Q × B	P × P	Q—B 2
8	B—Q 3	Q—B 2	P—K 3	Kt × P	P—Kt 3
	Kt—B 3	O—O	K Kt—B 3	Q—K 2	P—K 4
9	K Kt—K 2	B—Q 3	Kt—K 5 (g)	Kt—K 5	B—Kt 2
	O—O	R—K 1 (d)	O—O	B × Kt	Kt—B 3
10	P—Q R 3	P—K R 3	B—Q 3	P × B	O—O + (m)
	Kt—K 2	P—B 3	P—B 4 !	Q × P	
11	Q—B 2	O—O—O	O—O	B—K 3	
	P-Q Kt 3 ? (c)	Kt—B 1	Kt—B 3 !	Kt—B 3	
12	P—Q Kt4 ±	B × Kt ± (e)	P—B 4	Kt × Kt ch	
			P × P = (h)	Q × Kt (j)	

(a) Janowski's Defence. For 3 ., P—B 3 see Slav Defence.

(b) 5 Kt—B 3, P—Q B 3 ; 6 Q—Kt 3 (Bogoljuboff suggests 6 Q—B 2, B—Q 3 ; 7 P—K Kt 3, Kt—K 2 ; 8 B—Kt 2), B—Q 3 ; 7 B—Kt 5, Kt—K 2 ; 8 P—K 4, P × P ; 9 Kt × P, O—O ; 10 B—Q B 4 ±. Grünfeld—Bogoljuboff, Baden-Baden, 1925.

(c) This should have lost a Pawn by 12 P—K 4. But White's reply also suffices for an advantage. The column is Euwe—Alekhine, Zürich, 1934.

(d) 9.., P—B 3 ? ; 10 P—K Kt 4 !, Kt × P ; 11 B × P ch, K—R 1 ; 12 B—B 4, Q Kt—B 3 ; 13 B—Q 3, Kt—R 4 ; 14 P—K R 3, K Kt—B 3 ; 15 B—K 5 +. Botvinnik —Alatorzeff, Leningrad, 1934.

(e) 12 , B × Kt ; 13 P—K Kt4, B—Q 2 ; 14 Q R—Kt 1 with a strong attack. Stahlberg—Bogatyrchuk, Moscow, 1935.

(f) Occasionally played by Tartakover.

(g) 9 Q—R 4 ch ?, P—B 3 ; 10 B—Q 3, O—O ; 11 O—O, P—Q B 4 ; 12 P × P, P × P ; 13 K R—Q 1, Q Kt—Q 2 ∓. R. P. Michell—Tartakover, Hastings, 1935–36. The column is Flohr—Tartakover, Hastings, 1935–36.

(h) Continued 13 P × P, Kt × P ; 14 B × P ch, K × B ; 15 Q × Kt, Q—B 4 ; 16 Q R—Q 1, Q R—Q 1 ; 17 K R—K 1, K—Kt 1 !

(i) 5 P—K Kt 3, Kt—K B 3 ; 6 B—Kt 2, B—Kt 2 ; 7 Kt—R 3, B—K 2 ; 8 O—O, O—O ; 9 Kt—B 4, Kt—K 5 ? (9 , P—B 3 is necessary) ; 10 K Kt × P, Kt × Kt ; 11 Kt × Kt +. Reshevsky—Tartakover, Nottingham, 1936.

(j) 13 O—O—O ±. Euwe—Tartakover, Zandvoort, 1936.

(k) 3 Kt—Q B 3, Kt—K B 3 ; 4 Kt—B 3, P × Q P ; 5 K Kt × P ? (Q Kt × P), P—K 4 ; 6 Kt—B 3, P—Q 5 ∓. V. Buerger—E. Spencer, Tenby, 1938.

(l) Or 4 P—K 3, P × P ; 5 Kt—Q B 3, Q—Q R 4 ; 6 P × P, Kt—K B 3 ; 7 B—Q B 4, Kt—B 3 ; 8 Q—Kt 3, P—K 3 ; 9 Kt—B 3, Q—Kt 5 ; 10 O—O, B—Q 2 ; 11 P—Q 5 ± Alapin—Duras, Carlsbad, 1911.

(m) Przepiorka—Seitz, Hastings, 1924–25.

1 P—Q 4, P—Q 4; 2 P—Q B 4.

111	112	113	114	115
2 P—K Kt 3	...Kt—QB3(b)	....	Kt—K B 3	...B—B 4
3 P×P / Q×P	Kt—K B 3... / B—Kt 5	Kt—Q B 3 / P—K 4 (d)	P×P / Kt×P (f)	Kt-K B 3 (i) / P—K 3
4 Kt—Q B 3 / Q—Q R 4	Q—R 4 / B×Kt	P×Q P / Kt×P	Kt—KB3 (g) / B—B 4	Q—Kt 3 / Kt—Q B 3
5 Kt—B 3 / B—Kt 2	K P×B / P—K 3	P—K 3 / Kt—B 4	P—K 3 / Kt—Q B 3	P—B 5 / R—Kt 1
6 B—Q 2 / P—Q B 3	Kt—B 3 / B—Kt 5	P—K 4 / Kt—Q 3	Q Kt—Q 2 ! / Kt—Kt 3	B—B 4 / B—K 2
7 P—K 4 / Q—Kt 3	P—Q R 3 / B×Kt ch	Kt—B 3 / B—Kt 5	P—K 4 / B—Kt 3	Kt—B 3 / Kt—B 3 (j)
8 B—Q B 4 ! / B×P	P×B / Kt—K 2	Q—R 4 ch / B—Q 2	P—Q 5 / Kt—Kt 1	P—K 3 / O—O
9 Kt×B / Q×Kt	R—Q Kt 1 / R—Q Kt 1	Q—Kt 3 / P—K B 3	P—Q R 4 / P—Q R 4	B—Q Kt 5 / Kt—K 5
10 Q—Kt 3 / Q—Kt 2	B—Q 3 / P×P	B—K 3 / Kt—K 2	Kt—K 5 / Q Kt—Q 2	O—O / Kt×Kt
11 O—O / Kt—Q 2 ,	B×P / O—O	R—B 1 / K Kt—B 1	B—Q Kt 5 / Q—B 1	Q×Kt / B—B 3
12 K R—K 1 / Kt—K 4 (a)	O—O ± (c)	B—Q 3 ± (e)	Q Kt—B4+ (h)	P—Q Kt 4+

(a) 13 P—B 4, Kt×B; 14 Q×Kt, Kt—R 3; 15 Q—B 5! ±. Stahlberg—Alekhine, Kemeri, 1937.

(b) Tchigorin's Defence. If in reply 3 P×P, Q×P; 4 Kt—K B 3, B—Kt 5; 5 Kt—B 3, Q—Q R 4; 6 P—K 3, O—O—O; 7 B—Q 2, P—K 4+. Landau—Colle, match, 1928.

(c) Alekhine—Colle, Baden-Baden, 1925.

(d) Or 3 ., P×P; 4 Kt—B 3 (4 P—Q 5, Kt—R 4; 5 Q—R 4 ch, P—B 3; 6 P—Q Kt 4, P—Q Kt 4!; 7 Q×Kt, Q×Q; 8 P×Q, P—Kt 5; 9 Kt—Q 1, P×P =. Vienna—St. Petersburg, correspondence, 1897-99), Kt—B 3; 5 P—K 4, B—Kt 5; 6 B—K 3, B×Kt; 7 P×B, P—K 4; 8 P—Q 5, Kt—K 2; 9 Q—R 4 ch ±. Analysis by Euwe.

(e) 12 ., B—K 2; 13 O—O, O—O; 14 Kt—Q Kt 5, B×Kt; 15 B×B. Euwe—Tartakover, Nottingham, 1936.

(f) 3 , Q×P; 4 Kt—Q B 3, Q—Q R 4; 5 Kt—B 3, P—B 3 (5.., Kt—B 3; 6 B—Q 2, B—Kt 5; 7 P—K 4, B×Kt; 8 P×B, Q—R 4; 9 P—K 5, Kt—Q 2; 10 Kt—Q 5 ±); 6 P—K 3 ±.

(g) 4 P—K 4, Kt—K B 3; 5 B—Q 3, P—K 4; 6 P×P, Kt—Kt 5; 7 Kt—K B 3, Kt—Q B 3; 8 B—K Kt 5, B—K 2; 9 B×B (9 B—K B 4??, Kt—Kt 5 and wins), Q×B; 10 Kt—B 3, Q Kt×P; 11 Kt×Kt, Kt×Kt (11.., Q×Kt?; 12 P—K R 3, Kt—B 3; 13 Q—Q 2, B—Q 2; 14 Q—K 3, B—B 3; 15 O—O—O, O—O; 16 P—B 4 ±. Alekhine—Marshall, Baden-Baden, 1925); 12 B—K 2, P—Q B 3 =. Grünfeld—Becker, Breslau, 1925.

(h) Takacs—Havasi, Budapest, 1926.

(i) 3 Q—Kt 3, P—K 4!; 4 Q×Kt P, Kt—Q 2; 5 Kt—K B 3, R—Kt 1; 6 Q—R 6, B—Kt 5 ch; 7 Kt—B 3, Kt—K B 3; 8 P—K 3, O—O; 9 P—Q R 3, B—Q 3 with a strong attack, for if 10 P—B 5?, B×P!; 11 P×B, Kt×P; 12 Q×P, Kt—Kt 6+. If here 4 Q P×P, Kt—Q B 3; 5 P×P? (5 Kt—K B 3, P—Q 5), B—Kt 5 ch!; 6 Kt—B 3, Kt—Q 5++.

(j) 7.., P—K Kt 4?; 8 B—Kt 3, P—Kt 5; 9 Kt—K 5, B—B 3; 10 Q—R 4, Kt—K 2; 11 Kt×Kt, P×Kt; 12 P—Kt 3+. Fine—Grau, Stockholm, 1937

1 P—Q 4, P—Q 4 ; 2 P—Q B 4, P—K 3 ; 3 Kt—K B 3, Kt—K B 3.

	116	117	118	119	120
4	B—Kt 5 B—Kt 5 ch (a)			P—K R 3	
5	Kt—B 3 P×P			B×Kt (k) Q×B	
6	P—K 4 P—B 4	P—K R 3 !	Q—R 4 ch (h) Kt—B 3	Kt—B 3 (A) P—B 3 (l)	
7	P—K 5 P×P	B×Kt Q×B	P—K 4 B—Q 2	Q—Kt 3 Kt—Q 2 (m).B—Q 3	
8	Q—R 4 ch (b) Kt—B 3	B×P P—B 4	Q—B 2 P—K R 3	P—K 3 B—Q 3	P—K 4 P×K P
9	O—O—O B—Q 2 (c)	O—O (f) P×P	B—Q 2 Kt—QR4! (i)	B—K 2 Q—K 2	Kt×P Q—K 2
10	Kt—K 4 ! B—K 2	Q—R 4 ch Kt—B 3	P—K 5 Kt—Kt 1 !	Kt—Q 2 O—O	Kt×B ch Q×Kt
11	P×Kt P×P	B—Kt 5 O—O	B—K 2 Kt—K 2	O—O—O Kt—B 3	B—Q 3 Kt—Q 2
12	B—R 4 Kt—Kt 5 (d)	B×Kt P×B	Kt—K 4 B×B ch	B—B 3 ? P—Q Kt 4 !	O—O O—O
13	Q×Kt ! B×Q	Q×B P×Kt (g)	Q Kt×B P-QKt4+ (j)	P—B 5 B—B 2	Q R—Q 1 P—Q Kt 3
14	Kt×P ch+ (e) Q×Q =	Q×P		P—K 4 ? P×P ‡	B-Kt1 ± (n)

(a) The Vienna Variation, first played and analysed by the great theoretician Grünfeld.

(b) 8 P×Kt, P×P; 9 Q—R 4 ch, Kt—B 3; 10 O—O—O, P×B; 11 Kt×P, B×Kt!; 12 P×B, B—Q 2; 13 Kt×Kt, Q—B 2; 14 B×P, B×Kt =. Hönlinger and Wolf—Grunfeld and Kaufmann, Vienna, 1933. Here 10 ., B×Kt; 11 B—R 4 ? (11 P×B is necessary), P—Q Kt 4 ! !; 12 Q×Kt P, R—Q Kt 1 !; 13 Q×Kt ch, B—Q 2; 14 Q×P, B×P ch; 15 K—B 2, Q—R 4+ + is Apscheneek—Grünfeld, Folkestone, 1933.

(c) If 9 .., P—K R 3; 10 P×Kt, P×B; 11 P×P, R—K Kt 1, 12 Kt×P, B—Q 2; 13 Kt—K 4, Q—K 2; 14 Kt—B 2 ! ±. Vidmar—Bogoljuboff, Nottingham, 1936.

(d) This loses, as was first shown in the game Gereben—De Groot, Munich, 1936. Possible alternatives which merit consideration are 12 , Kt—R 4; 13 Q—B 2, P—K 4; 14 Kt×Q P;-P×Kt; 15 R×P, Q—Kt 3; 16 R—Q 6! and 12 ., R—Q B 1; 13 K—Kt 1, Kt—R 4; 14 Q—B 2, P—K 4; 15 Kt×Q P, P×Kt; 16 R×P, Q—Kt 3 ∓. Fine—Euwe, Avro, 1938.

(e) 14. , K—B 1; 15 R×P, Q—R 4; 16 Kt×B ch, K—K 1; 17 Kt—B 6 ch, K—B 1; 18 B×P, R—B 1; 19 K—Kt 1. Fine—Grünfeld, Amsterdam, 1936.

(f) More aggressive is 9 P—K 5, Q—K 2; 10 O—O, B×Kt; 11 P×B, P×P; 12 Q×P, Kt—B 3; 13 Q—Kt 4 with attacking possibilities.

(g) Goglidse—Alatorzeff, Leningrad, 1936.

(h) If 6 P—K 3, P—Q Kt 4; 7 P—Q R 4, P—B 3; 8 B—K 2, B—Kt 2; 9 O—O, P—Q R 3+.

(i) 9. , B×Kt; 10 B×B gives White a strong attack.

(j) Grunfeld and Kaufmann—Kmoch and Wolf, Vienna, 1933.

(k) 5 B—R 4, P×P; 6 P—K 3, P—Q Kt 4; 7 P—Q R 4, P—B 3; 8 Kt—B 3, Q—Kt 3; 9 B—K 2, Q Kt—Q 2; 10 O—O, B—Kt 5; 11 Q—B 2, B—Kt 2+. Janowski—Tartakover, New York, 1924. Or 5 B—R 4, B—Kt 5 ch; 6 Q Kt—Q 2, P—B 4; 7 P—K 3, P—K Kt 4; 8 B—Kt 3, P—Kt 5; 9 P—Q R 3, B—R 4; 10 Kt—K 5, B×Kt ch; 11 Q×B, Kt—K 5; 12 Q—B 2, Q—R 4 ch ∓. Ed. Lasker—Marshall, match, 1923.

(l) Or 6 ., B—Kt 5; 7 Q—Kt 3, P—B 4; 8 P×B P, Kt—B 3; 9 P×P, P×P; 10 P—Q R 3, B×Kt ch; 11 P×B + (Alekhine).

(m) 7 , P×P; 8 Q×B P, Kt -Q 2; 9 P—K 4, P—K 4; 10 P—Q 5, Kt—Kt 3 =. Petrov—Stahlberg, Kemeri, 1937. The column is Vidmar—Capablanca, Nottingham, 1936.

(n) Winter—Perkins, cable match, 1926.

(A) 6 Q—Kt 3, P—B 3; 7 Q Kt- Q 2, Kt—Q 2; 8 P—K 4, P×K P; 9 Kt×P, Q—B 5; 10 B—Q 3, P—K 4; 11 O—O, B—K 2; 12 K R—K 1±. Euwe—Fine, Avro, 1938.

1 P—Q4, P—Q4; 2 P—QB4, P—K3; 3 Kt—KB3, Kt—KB3.

	121	122	123	124	125
4	(B—Kt5)	....		Kt—B3	
	QKt—Q2	...P—B3	......B—K2	B—K2	
5	P—K3	P—K3 (b)	P—K3	P—K3	
	P—B3	B—Kt5 ch	O—O	O—O (f)	
6	QKt—Q2	QKt—Q2	QKt—Q2	P—QKt3	
	B—Q3 (a)	P—KR3	P—QKt3	P—B4 (g)	
7	B—Q3	B×Kt	B—Q3	B—Q3	
	O—O	Q×B	B—Kt2	P—QKt3	
8	O—O	P—QR3	Q—B2	O—O	
	P—K4	B—R4 (c)	QKt—Q2	B—Kt2	
9	BP×P	B—Q3	O—O	B—Kt2	
	BP×P	Kt—Q2	P—B4	QKt—Q2...Kt—B3	
10	P×P	O—O	QR—Q1	Q—K2	R—B1
	Kt×P	O—O	P—KR3	QP×P (h)	R—B1
11	Kt×Kt	P—K4	B—R4	KtP×P	P×BP (j)
	B×Kt	P×KP	BP×P	P×P	KtP×P
12	Kt—B3 =	Kt×P	KP×P	P×P	Q—K2
		Q—K2	P×P	R—B1	P—Q5
13		Q—K2	B×P	Kt—K5	P×P
		B—B2	R—B1	P—QR3	P×P
14		KR—K1 ±	Q—Q3	QR—Q1 ±	Kt—K4 ±
		(d)	Kt—Q4 = (e)	(i)	

(a) Or 6 , B—K2; 7 B—Q3, O—O; 8 O—O, P—B4. The column is Vidmar—Marshall, Carlsbad, 1929.

(b) For 5 Kt—B3, P—B3; 6 P—Q4 see col. 54.

(c) If 8.., B—Q3; 9 P—K4 ±.

(d) Continued 14.., P—QKt3; 15 P—QKt4, R—Q1; 16 P—B5. Bogoljuboff—Réti, Berlin, 1926.

(e) Alekhine—Yates, Hastings, 1922.

(f) Black's best course is to accept the gambit Pawn now.

(g) 6.., B—Kt5; 7 B—Q2, Q—K2; 8 B—Q3, P—QKt3; 9 O—O, B—Kt2; 10 Q—B2, P×P; 11 P×P, P—B4 =. Konstantinopolsky—Rauser, Leningrad, 1936.

(h) 10 ., Kt—K5; 11 QR—Q1, Q—B2; 12 Kt—QKt5, Q—Kt1; 13 P×QP, B×P; 14 Kt—K5, Kt×Kt? (R—Q1); 15 P×Kt, P—B4; 16 P×P e.p.+. Fine—Landau, Zandvoort, 1936.

(i) Reshevsky—Feigin, Kemeri, 1937.

(j) 11 Q—K2?, P×QP (but not 11... Q—B2; 12 P×QP, KP×P; 13 Kt—QKt5, Q—Kt1; 14 P×P, P×P; 15 B×Kt+. Fine—Tartakover, Zandvoort, 1936); 12 KP×P, P×P; 13 P×P, Kt—QKt5 ± (but not 13 , Kt×P?; 14 Kt×Kt, Q×Kt; 15 Kt—Q5, Q—B4; 16 B×Kt, P×B; 17 Q—Kt4 ch, K—R1; 18 Q—R4, P—B4; 19 Kt×B+).

SLAV DEFENCE

1 P—Q4, P—Q4; 2 P—QB4, P—QB3; 3 Kt—KB3, Kt—B3;
4 Kt—B3, PxP; 5 P—QR4, B—B4; 6 P—K3, P—K3 (a).

	126	127	128	129	130
7	BxP B—Q Kt5				Q Kt—Q2
8	O—O O—O				Q—K2 (l) B—Q Kt5
9	Q—K2 (b) B—Kt5 (c)	..Kt—K5		Q—Kt3 Q—K2	O—O B—Kt3! (m)
10	R—Q1 Q Kt—Q2	B—Q3! BxKt	KtxKt (h) BxKt	P—R5 (j) P—B4	B—Q3 BxB
11	P—R3 B—KR4	PxB (f) KtxQBP	R—Q1 Kt—Q2	Kt—K5 PxP (k)	QxB O—O
12	P—K4 Q—K2	Q—B2 BxB	B—Q3 BxB	PxP Kt—B3 ·	R—Q1 Q—K2
13	P—K5 Kt—Q4	QxB Kt—Q4	QxB Q—R4	KtxKt PxKt =	P—K4 P—K4
14	Kt—K4 P—KR3! (d)	B—R3 R—K1	B—Q2 BxB		B—Kt5 P—KR3
15	Kt—Kt3 B—Kt3 = (e)	QR—Kt1 P—QKt3 (g)	KtxB KR—Q1 = (i)		BxKt QxB = (n)

(a) 6.., Kt—R3?; 7 BxP, Kt—QKt5; 8 O—O, P—K3; 9 Q—K2, B—K2; 10 R—Q1, O—O; 11 P—K4, B—Kt5; 12 B—Kt3!, Q—R4; 13 P—R3 ±.

(b) If 9 Kt—K5, P—B4 (9.., Q—K2 and then P—B4 is also good); 10 Kt—R2 B—R4; 11 PxP, QxQ; 12 RxQ, B—B7; 13 R—Q4, B—B2; 14 Kt—KB3, Kt—B3 ∓. Capablanca—Euwe, Nottingham, 1936.

(c) Now 9.., P—B4? is a mistake: 10 Kt—R2, B—R4; 11 PxP, Kt—B3; 12 R—Q1, Q—K2; 13 Kt—Q4, KR—Q1; 14 P—QKt4!!, B—B2 (14 ., KtxP; 15 B—Q2); 15 P—R3+. Ragosin—Flohr, Moscow, 1936.

(d) 14.., P—B3; 15 PxP, PxP; 16 Kt—Kt3, B—B2; 17 B—R6, KR—K1; 18 Kt—K1! ±. Capablanca—Fine, Semmering-Baden, 1937.

(e) Flohr—Reshevsky, Semmering-Baden, 1937.

(f) 11 BxKt, B—QKt5; 12 B—Q2, Q—R4 =. Schmidt—Euwe, Noordwijk, 1938.

(g) 16 KR—B1, KR—B3!; 17 P—K4, P—K4!; 18 R—Q1, PxP; 19 P—K5, P—B4 =. If here 16.., P—QR4?; 17 Kt—K5, Kt—Kt5; 18 BxKt, PxB; 19 KtxQBP+. Euwe—Alekhine, 17th match game, 1937.

(h) 10 P—Kt4 (Sämisch's continuation), B—Kt3; 11 Kt—K5, KtxKt (11.., BxKt; 12 PxB, Kt—Q2; 13 KtxB ±. Sämisch—Alekhine, German Quadrangular Tournament, 1937); 12 PxKt, BxP; 13 KtxB, RPxKt; 14 R—Kt1, Q—K2; 15 P—B4, P—QB4; 16 PxP, Kt—B3 =. Alekhine—Euwe, 26th match game, 1937. Or 10 Kt—R2, B—K2; 11 B—Q3, Kt—Kt4; 12 Kt—K1, BxB; 13 KtxB, Kt—R3; 14 Kt—B3. Flohr—Capablanca, Avro, 1938.

(i) Reshevsky—Flohr, Semmering-Baden, 1937.

(j) On other moves P—B4 is likewise best. E.g., 10 Kt—K5, P—B4; 11 Kt—R2, B—R4; 12 Q—Kt5?, P—QKt3; 14 P—K4?, B—Kt3+. Ragosin—Capablanca, Semmering-Baden, 1937. Or 10 B—Q2, QKt—Q2?; 11 KR—K1, P—KR3; 12 P—K4, B—R2; 13 P—K5, Kt—K1; 14 P—R5 ±. Kashdan—Fine, New York, 1933.

(k) 11 ., Kt—B3?; 12 P—R6!.

(l) 8 O—O, B—Q3? (B—QKt5); 9 Q—K2, Kt—K5; 10 KtxKt, BxKt; 11 Kt—Q2, B—Kt3; 12 P—K4, O—O (B—B2; 13 P—Q5); 13 P—B4, B—B2; 14 P—B5, PxP; 15 PxP, R—K1; 16 Kt—K4!+. Reinfeld—Collins, New York, 1938. If 16.., BxP; 17 K—R1!.

(m) 9.., Kt—K5; 10 B—Q3!, BxKt; 11 BxKt!, B—QKt5; 12 BxB, PxB; 13 P—Q5!, PxP; 14 Q—Kt5+. Euwe—Alekhine, 13th match game, 1937.

(n) Euwe—Alekhine, 15th match game, 1937.

SLAV DEFENCE

1 P—Q4, P—Q4; 2 P—QB4, P—QB3; 3 Kt—KB3, Kt—B3;
4 Kt—B3, PxP; 5 P—QR4, B—B4.

	131	132	133	134	135
6	Kt—K5				Kt—R4
	QKt—Q2		P—K3 (f)		B—B1 (l)
7	KtxP (B4)		P—B3		P—K3
	Q—B2		B—QKt5 (g)		P—K4!
8	P—KKt3 (a)		B—Kt5.....	KtxP (B4)	PxP
	P—K4		P—KR3!(h)	O—O [(j)]	QxQ ch
9	PxP		BxKt	B—Kt5	KtxQ
	KtxP		PxB	P—B4	B—Kt5 ch
10	B—B4		KtxP (B4)	PxP	B—Q2
	KKt—Q2		P—QB4	QxQ ch	BxB ch
11	B—Kt2		PxP	KxQ	KxB
	P—B3 (b)		QxQ ch	BxP	Kt—K5 ch
12	O—O		RxQ	P—K4	K—K1
	R—Q1		B—B7	B—Kt3	B—K3
13	Q—B1		R—B1	Kt—K5	P—B4
	B—K3 (c)		B—Kt6	KKt—Q2	Kt—R3
14	Kt—K4!...KtxKt		Kt—Q2	KtxB	Kt—B2
	B—QKt5 KtxKt		BxKt	RPxKt	KtxKt
15	P—R5+(d)	P—R5 = (e)	RxB	K—B2	KxKt
			BxP = (i)	Kt—QB3 (k)	O—O—O+
					(m)

(a) 8 Q—Kt3?, P—K4!; 9 PxP, Kt—B4; 10 Q—R2, Kt—R3; 11 P—K4, KtxP; 12 KtxKt, BxKt; 13 Kt—Q6ch, BxKt +. Petrov—Capablanca. Semmering-Baden, 1937.

(b) 11 , B—K3; 12 KtxKt, KtxKt; 13 O—O, B—K2; 14 Q—B2, R—Q1; 15 KR—Q1, O—O; 16 Kt—Kt5+. Alekhine—Euwe, 1st match game, 1935

(c) 13.., Q—Kt1, 14 Kt—K4, B—K2, 15 Q—B3, O—O; 16 QR—Q1, B—K3; 17 KtxKt, KtxKt; 18 Kt—Kt5!+. Euwe—Alekhine, 20th match game, 1935.

(d) Euwe—Alekhine, 1st match game, 1937. 15 ., O—O; 16 KtxKt (16 P—R6, played in the game, is weaker), KtxKt; 17 Kt—B5, BxKt; 18 QxB+.

(e) 15 ., P—QR3; 16 Kt—K4, B—QKt5; 17 Kt—B5 (or 17 B—Q2, BxB; 18 KtxB =), B—B1; 18 Kt—Q3 (18 BxKt?, PxB; 19 P—B4, B—Q7+. Alekhine—Euwe, 21st match game, 1935), KtxKt; 19 BxQ, KtxQ; 20 QRxKt, R—Q2 =.

(f) Bogoljuboff's continuation, now considered best.

(g) 7 , P—B4; 8 PxP, QxQch; 9 KxQ, BxP; 10 P—K4, B—KKt3; 11 BxP, Kt—B3!; 12 KtxKt, PxKt; 13 B—B4, Kt—R4, 14 B—Q2, R—QKt1; 15 K—B2 ±. Alekhine—Bogoljuboff, 3rd match game, 1929.

(h) If 8 , P—B4; 9 PxP, QxQ4; 10 QxQ, PxQ; 11 P—K4!, PxP; 12 KtxP(B4), O—O;. 13 BxKt, PxB; 13 O—O—O (Alekhine—Euwe, 4th match game, 1937), the ensuing complications are in White's favour.

(i) Euwe—Alekhine, 11th match game, 1937.

(j) If 8 P—K4, BxP!; 9 PxB, KtxP; 10 Q—B3, QxP; 11 QxPch, K—Q1; 12 B—Kt5ch (12 QxKKtP??, BxKtch, 13 PxB, Q—B7ch, 14 K—Q1, KxP mate), K—B1, 13 BxP, KtxB; 14 QxKtP, Q—K6ch; 15 K—Q1, R—Q1ch+. Vidmar—Mikenas, Prague, 1931. If here 13 QxKPch, Kt—Q2!; 14 QxKtch, QxQ, 15 KtxQ, KtxKt; 16 BxP, Kt—B5ch+.

(k) Flohr—Mikenas, Prague, 1931. White stands slightly better.

(l) 6 , P—K3; 7 KtxB, PxKt; 8 P—K3, QKt—Q2; 9 BxP, Kt—Kt3; 10 KtxB3, B—Q3, 11 Q—B3, Q—Q2; 12 P—R3, Kt—B1; 13 P—R5 ±. Alekhine—Stoltz, Bled, 1931. After 6 , B—B1 White has nothing better than 7 Kt—B3, when 7 , B—B4 can be played again.

(m) Alekhine—Euwe, 15th match game, 1935.

SLAV DEFENCE
1 P—Q 4, P—Q 4; 2 P—Q B 4, P—Q B 3; 3 Kt—K B 3. Kt—B 3;
4 Kt—B 3.

	136	137	138	139	140
4	(P×P)...			B—B 4......	Q—Kt 3 (n)
5	(P—Q R 4)..P—K 3	P—K 3		P×P	P—B 5
	P—K 3	P—Q Kt 4 (d)		P×P (?)	Q—B 2
6	P—K 4 !	P—Q R 4		Q—Kt 3	P—K Kt 3
	B—Kt 5	P—Kt 5		Q—Kt 3	Kt—R 4
7	P—K 5	Kt—R 2.....Kt—Kt 1		Kt×P	P—K 4
	Kt—K 5 (a)	P—K 3	B—R 3	Kt×Kt (m)	P×P
8	Q—B 2	B×P	B—K 2 (i)	Q×Kt	Kt—K 5
	Q—Q 4	Q Kt—Q 2 (e)	P—K 3	P—K 3	P—K Kt 3
9	B—K 2	O—O	Kt—K 5	Q—Kt 3	B—Q B 4
	P—Q B 4	B—Kt 2	B—K 2	Q×Q	P—K 3
10	O—O	Q—K 2	O—O	P×Q	Kt×K P
	Kt×Kt	P—B 4	O—O	B—B 7	Kt—Q 2
11	P×Kt	R—Q 1	Kt×P (B 4)	B—Q 2	P—B 4
	P×P	Q—Kt 3 (f)	P—B 4 (j)	B×P	B—K 2
12	P×P (b)	P—K 4 ! ! (g)	P×P	P—K 4	Kt×K B P
	P—B 6	P×P	Q Kt—Q 2	P—B 3	K×Kt
13	B—Q 2	Kt×Q P	P—B 6	B—B 3	P—K Kt 4+
	Kt—B 3 (c)	B—B 4	Kt—B 4	B—B 7	(o)
14	B×P+	Kt—Kt 3 ±	Q Kt—Q 2	Kt—Q 2+	
		(h)	Q—B 2 ∓ (k)		

(a) 7. ., Kt—Q 4; 8 B—Q 2, B×Kt; 9 P×B, P—Q Kt 4; 10 Kt—Kt 5 !, P—B 3;
11 P×P, Kt×P; 12 B—K 2+. Alekhine—Bogoljuboff, 1st match game, 1929.
(b) 12 Kt×P, B—B 4; 13 Kt—B 3, Kt—Q 2, 14 R—Q 1, Q—B 3, 15 B×P,
O—O; 16 Kt—Kt5, P—K Kt 3 ∓. Alekhine—Bogoljuboff, Nottingham, 1936
(c) If 13 , Q—R 4; 14 B×P !, B×B; 15 R—R 3+, for if 15. , B—Q 2;
16 R×B, B×P; 17 B—Kt 5 ch ! ! and wins (Alekhine). The column is Alekhine—
Euwe, 19th match game, 1935.
(d) 5 , B—B 4; 6 B×P, P—K 3; 7 O—O, Q Kt—Q 2; 8 P—K R 3, B—Q 3;
9 Q—K 2, Kt—K 5 =. Reshevsky—Simonson, New York, 1938.
(e) Black must be prepared to play P—B 4 as soon as White threatens P—K 4.
If 8. ., B—K 2; 9 O—O, O—O; 10 Q—K 2, Q Kt—Q 2; 11 R—Q 1, B—Kt 2;
12 P—K 4, P—Q R 4; 13 B—K Kt 5 ±. Alekhine—Tarrasch, Hastings, 1922.
(f) 11.., Q—B 2; 12 P—K 4 !, P×P, 13 Kt×P, B—B 4; 14 B—K 3 ±
(g) If now 12 ., B×P (12 ., Kt×P; 13 P—Q 5+); 13 Kt—K 5, B—Kt 2;
14 P—R 5, Q—Q 3; 15 B—B 4+ (W. A. Fairhurst).
(h) 14.. , O—O; 15 Kt×B, Kt×Kt; 16 B—K 3, K R—Q 1; 17 P—B 3.
Fairhurst—Reshevsky, Hastings, 1937-38.
(i) Or 8 Q—B 2, Q—Q 4 (8 , P—K 3; 9 B×P, B×B; 10 Q×B, Q—Q 4;
11 Q Kt—Q 2, Q Kt—Q 2; 12 Q—K 2, Kt—K 5; 13 Kt×Kt, Q×Kt =. Stahlberg—
Euwe, Stockholm, 1937); 9 K Kt—Q 2, Kt—B 2; 10 Kt×P, B—K 2; 11 Q Kt—Q 2,
O—O; 12 Kt—B 3, P—B 4, 13 B—K 2, P×P; 14 Kt×P, Kt—B 3 ∓. Grunfeld—
Tarrasch, Mährisch-Ostrau, 1923.
(j) Alekhine recommends 11 Kt—Q 2, for if then 11.., P—B 6 ? ; 12 B×B, P×Kt ;
13 B—Kt 7, P×B=Q; 14 R×Q+.
(k) Alekhine—Euwe, 23rd match game, 1935.
(l) If 5 , Kt×P; 6 Q—Kt 3, Q—Kt 3 : 7 Kt×Kt, Q×Q; 8 Kt—B 7 ch, K—Q 2 ;
9 P×Q, K×Kt; 10 B—B 4 ch+ (Bogoljuboff).
(m) Or 7.., Q×Q; 8 Kt×K t ch, K P×Kt; 9 P×Q, B—B 7; 10 Kt—Q 2,
B—Kt 5; 11 R—R 4, B×Kt ch; 12 B×B, B×P; 13 R—R 3+ (Bogoljuboff). The
column is Torre—Gotthilf, Moscow, 1925.
(n) Süchting's Variation.
(o) Kostich—Balogh, Gyula, 1921.

SLAV DEFENCE
1 P—Q 4, P—Q 4; 2 P—Q B 4, P—Q B 3; 3 Kt—K B 3, Kt—B 3.

MERAN VARIATION
4 P—K 3, P—K 3; 5 Kt—B 3, Q Kt—Q 2; 6 B—Q 3, P×P;
7 B×B P, P—Q Kt 4; 8 B—Q 3.

	141	142	143	144	145
8	P—Q R 3..				P—Kt 5
9	P—K 4...............................			O—O	Kt—K 4
	P—B 4.................		P—Kt 5	P—B 4	B—K 2 (o)
10	P—K 5		Kt—Q R 4	P—Q R 4	Kt × Kt ch
	P×P		P—B 4	P—Kt 5	Kt × Kt
11	Kt × KtP! (a)		P—K 5 (l)	Kt—K 4	P—K 4 !
	Kt × KP! (b)		Kt—Q 4	B—Kt 2	B—Kt 2
12	Kt × Kt		O—O	Kt × P (m)	B—Kt 5
	P × Kt		P×P	Kt × Kt	O—O
13	Q—B 3 !.....O—O (h)		R—K 1	P × Kt	R—Q B 1 ±
	B—Kt 5 ch (c)	Q—Q 4	Kt—B 4	B × P	(p)
14	K—K 2	Q—K 2	B—Kt 5 !	Q—K 2	
	R—Q Kt 1 (d)	B—R 3 (i)	Q—R 4	Q—K 2	
15	Q—Kt 3 (e)	B—Kt 5	Kt × Kt	P—K 4	
	Q—Q 3 (f)	B—K 2	B × Kt	P—R 3 !	
16	Kt—B 3 ! (g)	P—B 4 (j)	R—Q B 1	P—Q Kt 3	
	Q×Q	O—O	P—K R 3	O—O	
17	R P×Q ±	R—B 3	B—R 4 ±	B—Kt 2	
		P—R 3! ∓ (k)		K R-Q 1 = (n)	

(a) Blumenfeld's continuation. On Freymann's suggestion. 11 Kt—K 4. Bogoljuboff gives 11 ., Kt—Q 4; 12 O—O, B—K 2; 13 P—Q R 4, P—Kt 5; 14 R—K 1, P—R 3; 15 K B—B 4, B—Kt 2; 16 Q × P, Q—Kt 3 =.

(b) This is undoubtedly best. Alternatives are· (1) 11.., P × Kt; 12 P × Kt, P—K 4; 13 P × Kt P, B × P; 14 Q—K 2, Q—K 2; 15 O—O, B—Kt 2; 16 R—K 1, Q—Q 3; 17 Kt—R 4+. Bogoljuboff—Sir G. A. Thomas, Baden-Baden, 1925. (2) 11.., Kt—Kt 5; 12 Q Kt × P, K Kt × K P; 13 B—K 4, B—Kt 5 ch; 14 B—Q 2, R—Q Kt 1; 15 O—O, B × B; 16 Q × B ±. Eliskases—Spielmann, Noordwijk, 1938. (3) 11.., Kt—K Kt 1; 12 Q Kt × P, Kt × P; 13 B—K 4, Kt × Kt ch; 14 B × Kt, B—Kt 5 ch; 15 B—Q 2, B × B ch; 16 Q × B, R—Kt 1; 17 R—Q 1, Kt—K 2; 18 B—B 6 ch, B—Q 2; 19 Kt × P !+. Eliskases—W. Michel, Bad Elster, 1938.

(c) Or 13 ., R—R 4; 14 O—O, P—K 5; 15 B—K B 4, B—K 2; 16 K R—B 1, O—O; 17 Q—R 3+. Capablanca—Lövenfisch, Moscow, 1935.

(d) Or (1) 14.., Q—Q 4; 15 Q × Q, Kt × Q; 16 B × P ch, K—B 1; 17 Kt—B 6 ±. (2) 14.., B—Q 2; 15 B—Kt 5, R—Q Kt 1; 16 Kt × B, Q × Kt; 17 B × Kt, P × B; 18 Q × P+. Stahlberg—Spielmann, match, 1935.

(e) Reshevsky's move. If 15 Kt—B 6, B—Kt 2; 16 B × P, Q—Kt 3 ∓.

(f) 15 ., Q—Q 4; 16 Kt—B 3, P—K 4; 17 Q × P ch (17 Q × Kt P, P—K 5 !), Q × Q; 18 Kt × Q, R—Kt 3; 19 B—Q 2, B × B; 20 K × B ±. Landau—Schmidt, Stockholm, 1937.

(g) 16 Kt—B 6 !, Q × Kt!; 17 Q × R, O—O; 18 P—B 3, B—Kt 2 gives Black excellent attacking chances. Reshevsky—Petrov, Kemeri, 1937.

(h) 13 B × P ch, B—Q 2; 14 Kt × B, Q—R 4 ch =.

(i) 14 ., R—Kt 1; 15 B—Kt 5, B—Q 3 (15.., Kt—Q 2; 16 B—K B 4, Kt × Kt; 17 Q × Kt+); 16 P—B 4, B × Kt; 17 P × B, Kt—Q 2; 18 R × P !!++. Vajda—Rosselli, Nice, 1930.

(j) 16 P—Q R 4, O—O; 17 P × P, B—Kt 2; 18 P—B 4, P—R 3 ∓. Alekhine—Bogoljuboff, 12th match game, 1934.

(k) 18 R—R 3, B—Kt 2; 19 R—K B 1, K R—B 1; 20 B × Kt, B × B; 21 Kt—Kt 4, K—B 1 !. Polland—Kashdan, Boston, 1938.

(l) 11 P × P, B × P; 12 O—O, B—Kt 2; 13 Q—K 2, B—K 2; 14 K R—Q 1, Q—R 4; 15 P—Q Kt 3, O—O =. Fine—Vidmar, Nottingham, 1936. The column is Ragosin—Lövenfisch, Moscow, 1935.

(m) 12 Q Kt—Q 2, B—K 2; 13 Q—K 2 (13 P—R 5, O—O; 14 Kt—B 4, Q—B 2; 15 O—K 2. Alekhine—Bogoljuboff, 2nd match game, 1934. 15.., B—K 5 ! =), O—O; 14 R—Q 1, P—Q R 4 ∓. Grünfeld—Rubinstein, Meran, 1924.

(n) Flohr—Vidmar, Bad Sliac, 1932.

(o) If 9.., P—B 4; 10 Q—R 4, P×P; 11 Kt × Kt ch, P × Kt; 12 B—K 4, R—Q Kt 1; 13 Kt × P+.

(p) Botvinnik—Lisitzin, Leningrad, 1933.

SLAV DEFENCE

1 P—Q 4, P—Q 4 ; 2 P—Q B 4, P—Q B 3 ; 3 Kt—K B 3, Kt—B 3 ;
4 Kt—B 3, P—K 3 ; 5 P—K 3, Q Kt—Q 2.

	146	147	148	149	150
6	(B—Q 3)..				Kt—K 5 (k)
	B—Q 3..................		B—K 2 (f)		B—K 2 (l)
7	O—O (a)		O—O		B—Q 3
	O—O		O—O		O—O
8	P—K 4		P—K 4.....P—Q Kt 3 !		P—B 4
	P×B P.....P×K P		P×K P	P—Q Kt 3	P—B 4 !
9	B×P	Kt×P	Kt×P	B—Kt 2	B P×P
	P—K 4	Kt×Kt	P—Q Kt 3	B—Kt 2	Kt×P
10	B—K Kt5 (b)	B×Kt	Q—K 2	Q—K 2	Kt×Kt
	P—K R 3	P—Q B 4	B—Kt 2	P—B 4 (i)	P×Kt
11	B—R 4	B—B 2	R—Q 1 (g)	Q R—Q 1	O—O
	P×P	Q—B 2	Q—B 2	Kt—K 5	Kt—B 3
12	Q×P	Q—Q 3	B—Kt 5	P×B P	B—Q 2
	B—B 4	P—B 4	P—B 4	Kt×Kt	P×P
13	Q—Q 3	R—Q 1	P×P	B×Kt	P×P
	Kt—Kt 3 (c)	P×P	P×P	Kt P×P	Kt—K5 ⇌
14	P—K 5 !	Q×P	Kt×Kt ch	P×P	(m)
	Q×Q	B—B 4	Kt×Kt	P×P	
15	B×Q	Q—R 4	Kt-K 5 ± (h)	B—R 6+ (j)	
	K Kt-Q 4 (d)	Kt—B 3 = (e)			

(a) If 7 P—K 4, P×K P (7 .., P×B P; 8 B×P, P—K 4?; 9 P×P, Q Kt×P;
10 Kt×Kt, B×Kt; 11 Q×Q ch, K×Q; 12 B×P, B×Kt ch; 13 P×B, Kt×P;
14 O—O, Kt×Q B P?; 15 B—Kt 2+. Grunfeld); 8 Kt×P, Kt×Kt; 9 B×Kt,
Kt—B 3; 10 B—B 2, B—Kt 5 ch; 11 B—Q 2, B×B ch and Black drew easily.
Grünfeld—Tartakover, Kecskémet, 1927.

(b) Or 10 P—Q 5, Kt—Kt 3; 11 B—Kt 3, B—K Kt 5 =.

(c) Johner—Capablanca, 1911.

(d) 16 Kt—K 4, B—K 2 =.

(e) Grünfeld—Bogoljuboff, Berlin, 1926. White's advantage is dissipated, and he
would therefore have done better to proceed as in col. 149.

(f) 6 ., B—Kt5; 7 O—O, O—O; 8 P—Q R 3, B×Kt; 9 P×B, Q—B 2;
10 Kt—Q 2, P—K 4; 11 B—Kt 2, P—K 5; 12 B—K 2, P—Q Kt 4; 13 P×Kt P,
P×P; 14 P—Q R 4 ! ±. Euwe—Alekhine, 3rd match game, 1937.

(g) 11 B—B 4, P—B 4; 12 P×P, Kt×Kt; 13 B×Kt, B×B; 14 Q×B, Kt×P;
15 Q—K 3, Q—Q 6 =. Alekhine—Bogoljuboff, 21st match game, 1929.

(h) 15..., Q R—Q 1; 16 B—Q 2. Alatorzeff—Lövenfisch, 1934. Cp. French
Defence, cols. 6 and 7.

(i) Or 10.., Q—B 2; 11 K R—Q 1, Q R—Q 1; 12 Q R—B 1, Q—Kt 1;
13 P—K R 3, B—Q 3?; 14 P—K 4, P×P; 15 Kt×P ±. Botvinnik—Rabinovitch,
1934.

(j) Euwe—Winter, Nottingham, 1936.

(k) Rubinstein's Anti-Meran System.

(l) 6.., Kt×Kt; 7 P×Kt, Kt—Q 2; 8 P—B 4, B—Kt 5 (8.., B—B 4, followed
by Q—K 2, is better); 9 B—Q 2, Q—Kt 3; 10 B—K 2, O—O; 11 O—O, B×Kt;
12 P×B ±. Rubinstein—Vidmar, San Remo, 1930.

(m) Spielmann—Euwe, match, 1932.

164 QUEEN'S GAMBIT DECLINED

SLAV DEFENCE
1 P—Q 4, P—Q 4; 2 P—Q B 4, P—Q B 3; 3 Kt—K B 3, Kt—B 3.

	151	152	153	154	155
4	(Kt—B 3) .... (P—K 3)		P—K 3 B—B 4		
5	(P—K 3) .... P—Q R 3 (a)	B—Kt 5 P×P (e)	P×P .... P×P (i)		Kt—B 3 P—K 3
6	P—B 5 ! (b) P—Q Kt 3 (c)	P—K 4 P—Q Kt 4	Kt—B 3 ..... P—K 3	Q—Kt 3 Q—B 2 ! (l)	Kt—K R 4 B—Kt 5 (n)
7	P×P Q Kt—Q 2	P—K 5 P—K R 3	Kt—K 5 K Kt—Q 2 ! (j)	Kt—R 3 Kt—B 3	Q—Kt 3 Q—Kt 3
8	Kt—Q R 4 Kt×P	B—R 4 P—K Kt 4	Q—Kt 3 Q—B 1	B—Q 2 P—K 3	P—K R 3 B—R 4
9	B—Q 2 Kt×Kt	Kt×K Kt P P×Kt ! (f)	B—Q 2 Kt—Q B 3	R—B 1 Kt—K 5 !	P—Kt 4 B—Kt 3
10	Q×Kt Q—Kt 3	B×Kt P Q Kt—Q 2 !	R—B 1 K Kt×Kt	B—Kt 5 Kt×B	Kt×B R P×Kt
11	R—B 1 B—Q 2	P×Kt B—Q Kt 2 ! (g)	P×Kt B—K 2	Kt×Kt R—B 1	B—Kt 2 B—Kt 5
12	Kt—K 5 Q×Kt P	B—K 2 Kt×P	B—K 2 O—O	O—O P—Q R 3	B—Q 2 Q Kt—Q 2
13	Kt×B Kt×Kt	P—Q R 4 B—K 2 !	Kt—Kt 5 Q—Q 2	B×Kt ch P×B	O—O—O B×Kt
14	B—Q 3+ (d)	P×P P×P ∓ (h)	O—O (k) K R—B 1 =	R—B 3 B—Q 3 ∓ (m)	B×B Q×Q = (o)

(a) To avoid the main line (Blumenfeld's, col. 141) of the Meran Variation.
(b) 6 P×P, K P×P; 7 B—Q 3, B—Q 3; 8 O—O, O—O is inferior. If 6 Kt—K 5, P—B 4; 7 P×Q P, Kt×P; 8 B—K 2, Kt—Q B 3; 9 Kt×Kt, P×Kt; 10 O—O F×P; 11 Q×P, P—Q B 4; 12 Q—K Kt 4, Q—B 2; 13 B—B 3, B—Q 3 =. Bogoljuboff—Alekhine, Berne, 1932.
(c) 6 .., Q Kt—Q 2; 7 P—Q Kt 4, P—Q R 4; 8 P—Kt 5, Kt—K 5; 9 Kt×Kt, P×Kt; 10 Kt—Q 2, P—B 4; 11 P—B 3, Q—R 5 ch; 12 P—Kt 3, Q—R 3; 13 Q—K 2+. Euwe—Alekhine, 10th match game, 1935.
(d) Euwe—Alekhine, 8th match game, 1935.
(e) For 5 .., P—K R 3 see col. 118.
(f) Or 9 ., Kt—Q 4 ?, 10 Kt—B 3 (10 Kt×B P is also good for White), Q—R 4; 11 Q—Q 2, P—Kt 5, 12 Kt×Kt, B P×Kt; 13 B—K 2, P—B 6; 14 P×P+. Flohr—Stahlberg, Zürich, 1934.
(g) If 11 , Kt×P ?; 12 Q—B 3+.
(h) 15 B—B 3, Kt—Q 4; 16 B×Kt, Q B×B; 17 B×B, K×B !. Van Scheltinga—Grunfeld, Amsterdam, 1936. Better for White is 15 Kt×P, Q—Kt 3; 16 B×P, P—Q R 3; 17 Kt—B 3, B×P =.
(i) 5. , Kt×P; 6 B—B 4, P—K 3; 7 O—O, Kt—Q 2; 8 Q—K 2, B—K Kt 5; 9 P—K R 3, B—R 4; 10 Kt—Q 2, P—K 4 ±. Euwe—Alekhine, 6th match game, 1935.
(j) If 7 , Q Kt—Q 2 ?; 8 P—K Kt 4 !, B—Kt 3; 9 P—K R 4, P—K R 3; 10 Kt×B, P×Kt; 11 B—Q 3+. Bogoljuboff—Gothilf, Moscow, 1925.
(k) Alekhine—Euwe, 11th match game, 1935.
(l) The most precise. If 6. , Q—B 1; 7 B—Q 2, P—K 3; 8 Kt—R 3 ! (Landau's Variation), Kt—B 3; 9 R—B 1, only 9. , Kt—Q 2 ! suffices; 10 B—Kt 5, B—K 2; 11 Q—R 4, O—O; 12 B×Kt, P×B; 13 Q×B P, Q×Q; 14 R×Q, Q R—Kt 1, 15 B—B 1, B×Kt =. If here 9 , Kt—K 5; 10 Kt—K 5, Kt×B; 11 K×Kt B—Kt 5 ch; 12 K—Q 1, B—K 2; 13 B—R 6!+.
(m) Reshevsky—Capablanca, Semmering-Baden, 1937.
(n) 6 , B—K 5; 7 P—B 3, B—Kt 3; 8 Q—Kt 3, Q—B 2; 9 B—Q 2, B—K 2; 10 Kt×B, R P×Kt; 11 O—O, Q—Q 2; 12 B—K 2, P×P; 13 B×P, Kt—Kt 3; 14 P—Kt 3 ±. Fine—P. Schmidt, Stockholm, 1937.
(o) 15 P×Q, Kt—Kt 3 !. Fine—Reinfeld, New York, 1938.

SLAV DEFENCE
1 P—Q 4, P—Q 4 ; 2 P—Q B 4, P—Q B 3.

	156	157	158	159	160
3	(Kt—K B 3) / (Kt—B 3)				P—K 3 (k)
4	(P—K 3) / (B—B 4)....	P—K 3			Kt—B 3 / P×P
5	B—Q 3 / P—K 3	Q Kt—Q 2 (c) / Q Kt—Q 2...	P—Q B 4 (e)..	Kt—K 5 (g)	P—Q R 4 (l) / B—Kt 5
6	Kt—B 3 / B×B	B—Q 3 / B—K 2	B—K 2 / Kt—B 3	B—Q 3 (h) / P—K B 4	P—K 3 / P—Q Kt 4
7	Q×B / Q Kt—Q 2	O—O / O—O	O—O / B—Q 3	Kt—K 5 / Q—R 5	B—Q 2 / P—Q R 4
8	O—O / B—Kt 5 (a)	P—Q Kt 3 / P—Q Kt 3	P—Q R 3 / P×Q P	O—O / B—Q 3.	P×P / B×Kt
9	Kt—Q 2 / O—O	B—Kt 2 / B—Kt 2	K P×P / P—Q R 4	P—K B 4 / O—O (i)	B×B / P×P
10	P—K 4 / P×B P	Q—K 2 / P—Q R 4	B—Q 3 / O—O	Q Kt—B 3 / Q—R 3	P—Q Kt 3 / B—Kt 2
11	Q×P / Q—K 2	P—Q R 4 / B—Kt 5	R—K 1 / P—Q Kt 3	B—Q 2 / Kt—Q 2	P×P / P—Kt 5
12	P—Q R 3 / B—R 4	P—K 4 / P×K P	P—Q Kt 3 / B—Kt 2	B—K 1 / Q Kt—B 3	B—Kt 2 / Kt—K B 3
13	P—B 4 / B—Kt 3 = (b)	Kt×P ± (d)	B—Kt 2 / Kt—K 2 = (f)	Q—K 2 / B—Q 2 = (j)	B—Q 3 / B—K 5 ! (m)

(a) 8 , P×P; 9 Q×B P, B—K 2; 10 P—K 4, O—O; 11 B—Kt 5, P—K R 3; 12 B—R 4, Kt—Kt3; 13 Q—K 2 ±. Petrov—Reshevsky, Semmering-Baden, 1937.

(b) 14 P—K 5, Kt—Q 4. Petrov—Flohr, Semmering-Baden, 1937.

(c) For 5 Kt—B 3 see cols. 136—147.

(d) Alekhine—Bogoljuboff, 6th match game, 1934.

(e) Or 5.., P—K Kt3; 6 P—Q Kt 3 (threatening B—R 3), Q—R 4; 7 B—Q 3, B—Kt 2; 8 O—O, O—O; 9 Q—B 2, Q Kt—Q 2; 10 B—Kt 2, R—Q 1; 11 P—Q R 3 ±. Rubinstein--Spielmann, Semmering, 1926.

(f) Alekhine—Vidmar, Semmering, 1926.

(g) The Stonewall Variation.

(h) If 6 Kt×Kt, P×Kt; 7 Kt—Q 2, P—K B 4; 8 Q—Kt 3, B—Q 3; 9 P—B 5, B—B 2; 10 Kt—B 4, Kt—Q 2; 11 B—Q 2, Kt—B 3; 12 P—B 3, O—O; 13 O—O—O, P—Q Kt 3 ∓. Bogoljuboff—Maróczy, New York, 1924.

(i) Or 9 , Kt—Q 2; 10 R—B 3, Q—K 2; 11 R—R 3, Q Kt×Kt; 12 B P×Kt B—B 2; 13 Q—R 5 ch, Q—B 2; 14 Q×Q ch, K×Q; 15 Kt—Kt 3 =. Rabinovitch—Tarrasch. Baden-Baden, 1925.

(j) 14 Kt×B, Kt×Kt. Alekhine—Euwe, 8th match game, 1927.

(k) The Semi-Slav Defence. The column is the Noteboom Variation.

(l) 5 P—K 4, P—Q Kt 4; 6 P—K 5, B—Kt 2; 7 B—K 2, Kt—K 2; 8 Kt—K 4, Kt—Q 4; 9 O—O, Kt—Q 2; 10 K Kt—Kt 5, B—K 2; 11 P—B 4, P—Kt 3 ∓. Spielmann—Eliskases, 7th match game, 1932.

(m) 14 B×B, Kt×B; 15 Q—B 2, P—B 4; 16 P—Q 5, P×P! with a complicated position (Euwe). If here 13 , Q Kt—Q 2?, 14 O—O, R—R 2; 15 R—K 1, Q—R 1: 16 P—K 4!, B×P, 17 B×B, Kt×B; 18 P—Q 5!+. Pirc—Winter, Prague, 1931.

SLAV DEFENCE
1 P—Q4, P—Q4; 2 P—QB4, P—QB3.

	161	162	163	164	165
3	Kt—QB3 (a)			P×P (i)	
	P×P	Kt—B3	P—K4 (g)	P×P	
4	P—K4! (b)	P—K3	P×KP (h)	Kt—KB3	
	P—K4 (c)	B—B4	P—Q5	Kt—KB3	
5	B×P!	P×P	Kt—K4	Kt—B3	
	P×P	Kt×P (e)	Q—R4 ch	Kt—B3	
6	Kt—B3!	B—B4	Kt—Q2	B—B4	
	P×Kt (d)	Kt×Kt	Kt—Q2	B—B4	P—K3
7	B×P ch	P×Kt	Kt—B3	P—K3 (j)	P—K3
	K—K2	P—K3	Kt×P	P—QR3 (k)	B—K2 (m)
8	Q—Kt3!	Kt—K2	Kt×P	R—B1 (l)	B—Q3
	Kt—B3	B—Q3	Kt×P	R—B1	O—O
9	B—K3	Kt—Kt3	Kt—Kt3	B—K2	O—O (n)
	Q—R4	B—Kt3	Q—R5	P—K3	Kt—KR4
10	O—O—O	P—B4	Kt×Kt	O—O	B—K5
	Q Kt—Q2	Q—R4	Q×Kt	B—K2	P—B4
11	P—K5	B—Q2	P—K3	Kt—K5	R—B1
	Kt—Q4	P—R4	B—Kt5 ch	O—O	Kt—B3
12	B×Kt+	Q—Kt3	B—Q2	P—QR3	B×Kt
		P—R5 (f)	B×B ch =	Kt×Kt =	P×B = (o)

(a) On 3 P—K3, B—B4; 4 Q—Kt3 Black should play 4.., Q—B1 but not
4.., Q—Kt3; 5 P×P, B×P (Q×Q?; 6 P×Q, B×Kt; 7 P×P!, B—K5;
8 R×P!!++. Schlechter—Perlis, Carlsbad, 1911); 6 R×B, Q×Q; 7 P×Q ±.
(b) Alekhine's brilliant innovation. If 4 P—QR4 (or 4 P—K3, P—QKt4;
5 Kt×P?, P×Kt; 6 Q—B3, Q—B2; 7 Q×R, B—Kt2; 8 Q×P, P—K4!+),
P—K4; 5 P×P, Q×Q ch; 6 K×Q, Kt—QR3; 7 P—K3, B—K5; 8 Kt—B3,
O—O—O ch ∓. Fine—Euwe, Zandvoort, 1936.
(c) The safest line is 4.., P—QKt4; 5 P—QR4, P—Kt5; 6 Kt—Kt1,
Kt—B3 =.
(d) 6.., P—QKt4?; 7 Kt×Kt P! wins at once for White. Alekhine—Euwe, 6th
match game, 1937. 6.., B—QB4 is probably best. Strongest then is 7 Kt—K5, P×Kt!
(but not 7.., Q—B3; 8 Kt×KBP, P×Kt; 9 O—O, B—K3; 10 B—KKt5, Q×B;
11 Kt×Q+. Kashdan—Polland, New York, 1938); 8 B×P ch, K—K2; 9 Q—R5
P×P; 10 B—Kt5 ch, Kt—B3; 11 R—Q1 with a winning attack.
(e) If 5., P×P?; 6 Q—Kt3, B—B1 (best); 7 Kt—B3 followed by Kt—K5+.
Zukertort—Steinitz, match game, 1886.
(f) 13 Kt—K2 ±. Spielmann—Jacobson, Copenhagen, 1923.
(g) Winawer's Counter-Gambit, a clear refutation of which has not yet been found.
(h) 4 P×QP, BP×Kt; 5 Kt—B3, P—K5; 6 Kt—K5, Q—R4; 7 B—Q2,
P—B3!+.
(i) The Exchange Variation.
(j) If 7 Q—Kt3, Kt—QR4; 8 Q—R4 ch, B—Q2; 9 Q—B2, R—B1;
10 P—K3, P—QKt4! ∓. Kan—Lasker, Moscow, 1935.
(k) If 7.., Q—Kt3; 8 B—Q3, B×B; 9 Q×B, P—K3; 10 O—O ±. Or
8 Q—Kt3!,Q×Q; 9 P×Q, R—B1?(P—K3; 10B—QKt5, Kt—Q2; 11 K—K2 ±);
10 Kt—K5!, P—QR3; 11 Kt×Kt, R×Kt; 12 P—QKt4!, P—QKt4; 13 R×P!+
(Purdy).
(l) An original idea is 8 Kt—K5!, R—B1; 9 P—KKt4!, B—Q2 (better 9..,
Kt×Kt); 10 B—Kt2, B×Kt; 11 O—O, P—R3; 12 B—Kt3, P—KR4; 13 Kt×B,
Kt×Kt; 14 P×P+. Alekhine—Euwe, Avro Tournament, 1938.
(m) Or 7.., B—Q3; 8 B×B (8 B—Kt3, O—O; 9 B—Q3, P—QKt3; 10 R—B1,
Q—K2 =), Q×B; 9 B—K2, O—O; 10 O—O, P—QR3, 11 Q—Kt3, P—QKt4;
12 KR—B1, B—Q2; 13 Q—Q1, KR—B1 =. Keres—Spielmann, Zandvoort,
1936.
(n) 9 R—QB1, Kt—KR4; 10 B—K5, P—B3; 11 B—Kt3, Kt×B; 12 RP×Kt,
P—KKt3; 13 P—QR3, B—Q2; 14 Kt—Q2, R—B2 ∓. Pirc—Fine, Stockholm,
1937.
(o) 13 Kt—KR4, K—R1. Capablanca—Lasker, New York, 1924.

ALBIN COUNTER GAMBIT

1 P—Q4, P—Q4; 2 P—QB4, P—K4; 3 QP×P (a). P—Q5.

	166	167	168	169	17O
4	Kt—KB3(b) Kt—QB3	....	....	....	P—QB4
5	Q Kt—Q2 B—KKt5	...P—B3 (e)	...B—K3	P—QR3 B—KKt5 (i)	P—K3 Kt—QB3
6	P—KR3 B×Kt	P×P Q×P (f)	P—KKt3 (g) Q—Q2	Q Kt—Q2 Q—K2	P×P P×P
7	Kt×B B—B4 (c)	P—KKt3 B—KB4	P—QR3 KKt—K2	P—R3 B×Kt	B—Q3 B—Kt5
8	P—QR3 P—QR4	P—QR3 O—O—O	Q—R4 Kt—Kt3	Kt×B O—O—O	O—O Q—B2
9	P—KKt3 KKt—K2	B—Kt2 P—Q6	B—Kt2 B—K2	Q—Q3 P—KR3 (j)	P—KR3 B×Kt
10	B—Kt2 Kt—Kt3	P—K3 P—KKt4	O—O O—O	P—KKt3 P—KKt3	Q×B Kt×P
11	O—O QR—Kt1	R—R2 P—KR4	P—QKt4 QR—Q1	B—Kt2 B—Kt2	R—K1 B—Q3
12	Q—B2 Q—K2 (d)	P—QKt4 B—Kt2	B—Kt2 P—Kt3	O—O Kt×P	B—KB4 Kt—K2
13	B—Q2 ±	B—Kt2 Q—K2	QR—B1 P—QR4	Kt×Kt B×Kt	B×Kt B×B
14		P—Kt5+	P—Kt5+ (h)	P—QKt4+ (k)	Kt—R3+ (l)

(a) 3 P—K3, KP×P; 4 KP×P transposes to the French Defence, Exchange Variation, col. 4, note (A).

(b) Not 4 P—K3?, B—Kt5 ch; 5 B—Q2, P×P; 6 P×P (6 B×B?, P×P ch; 7 K—K2, P×Kt=Kt ch+ +. Or 6 Q—R4 ch, Kt—B3; 7 B×B, P×P ch; 8 K×P, Q—R5 ch+ +), Q—R5 ch; 7 P—Kt3, Q—K5; 8 Kt—KB3, Q×P ch ∓. If 4 P—QR3, Kt—QB3; 5 P—K3, B—KB4; 6 Kt—KB3, P×P; 7 Q×Q ch, R×Q; 8 B×P, KKt—K2; 9 Kt—B3, Kt—Kt3 =. W. Cohn—H. Wolf, Munich, 1900.

(c) Or 7.., B—Kt5 ch; 8 B—Q2, B—B4; 9 P—R3, P—QR4; 10 P—KKt3, KKt—K2; 11 B—Kt2, Kt—Kt3; 12 Q—R4+.

(d) If 12 , KKt×P; 13 Kt×Kt, Kt×Kt; 14 B×P, R×B; 15 Q—K4+. The column is analysis from *Lärobok*.

(e) If 5.., B—QKt5; 6 P—QR3, B×Kt ch; 7 B×B, B—KKt5; 8 Q—Kt3, KKt—K2; 9 P—KKt3, O—O; 10 B—Kt2, B×Kt; 11 P×B, Kt×P; 12 P—B4, Q Kt—B3; 13 Q—Q3+ (Grunfeld). The column is Post—Spielmann, Berlin, 1907.

(f) Or 6.., Kt×P; 7 P—QR3, B—KKt5; 8 P—R3, B×Kt; 9 Kt×B+.

(g) 6 Kt—Kt3 is inferior: B—Kt5 ch; 7 B—Q2, Q—K2; 8 Q Kt×P, Kt×Kt; 9 Kt×Kt, O—O—O; 10 Kt—B3, B×BP; 11 Q—R4, B×B ch; 12 Kt×B, B—R3; 13 P—K3, B×B; 14 R×B, Q×P; 15 O—O—O, Q—B4 ch; 16 Q—B4, Q×Q; 17 Kt×Q, Kt—K2 =. Analysis by Dr. Krause.

(h) Spielmann—Kostich, Bled, 1931.

(i) 5 , B—K3; 6 P—K3? (6 Q Kt—Q2 is still best), P×P; 7 Q×Q ch, R×Q; 8 B×P, KKt—K2; 9 B—Kt3, P—KR4 ∓. Simonson—Opocensky, Folkestone, 1933.

(j) If 9.., Kt×P; 10 Q—B5 ch, Kt—Q2; 11 Kt×P+.

(k) Lasker—Alekhine, St. Petersburg, 1914.

(l) Grünfeld—Tartakover, Carlsbad, 1923.

QUEEN'S PAWN GAME

THIS opening comprises all lines of play arising from 1 P—Q 4 other than the Queen's Gambit. It divides into three main groups, according as Black answers P—Q 4 (cols. 1 to 30), Kt—K B 3 (cols. 31 to 169), or makes any other reply (cols. 170 to 195).

In the first group P—Q B 4 at an early stage would transpose into the Queen's Gambit. The most important variation in this group is the Colle System (cols. 1 to 7), where White is really playing a variation of the Queen's Gambit Declined with colours reversed. In the hands of an attacking player it can be a formidable line. The development of Black's Knight at Q B 3 (cols. 1 and 2) is inferior, but the development at Q 2 generally results in advantage for Black. The King's fianchetto development (cols. 5 and 6) is certainly Black's best defensive line. White's attack is broken, and the first player often has a good deal of trouble in preserving equality. In col. 7 Black, in his attempt to avoid the loss of a tempo by P—K 3 and P—K 4 at a later stage, leaves his position too open.

The lines in cols. 8 to 10 are interesting deviations from routine. Black can avoid the dangers of Colle's System by adopting one of the alternatives in cols. 11 to 13. In col. 11 the loss of time involved is serious; in cols. 12 and 13 Black develops his Queen's Bishop immediately, thereby banishing all opening difficulties. In cols. 14 and 15 White plays P—Q B 4 on his 3rd move, but Black's replies cannot possibly transpose into any variation of the Queen's Gambit Declined. Both cols. 14 and 15 are quite good, but are very rarely seen.

White may play his Queen's Bishop to B 4 on the 3rd or even the 2nd move (cols. 16 to 18); against this Black's best line is the advance of his Queen's Bishop's Pawn, attacking White's centre. The omission of P—Q B 4 on White's part leaves the position rather sterile, and Black should have no trouble in equalising.

The development of White's Bishop at K Kt 5, adopted by Tartakover in some recent tournaments, is not so simple for Black to meet. White's strategical plan is to play his Knight to K 5, followed by P—K B 4 and R—B 3, with a strong attacking position. In col. 19 Black is successful in preventing the execution of this plan, but in col. 20 he plays for a counter-attack and drifts into an indefensible position.

Col. 21 has historical interest as one of the first examples of the Catalan Opening, which in a slightly revised form is now one of the most popular débuts.

In cols. 24 to 27 White develops his Queen's Knight at B 3 on his 2nd move, with the object of forcing an early P—K 4. Black can, however, equalise in various ways, and often obtains an advantage against colourless play.

The Stonewall Variation has the same strategical basis as the Colle System. White wishes to solidify the centre and then undertake an attack on the King's side. In col. 28 he is able to carry out his plan because Black does not take advantage of the opportunity to develop his Queen's Bishop. In col. 29 the second player does take care of this "problem child" of the Queen's Pawn Opening and achieves an easy equality.

THE INDIAN DEFENCES.

The Indian Defences are those where Black plays Kt—K B 3 on the first move and does not continue with P—Q 4. They are essentially hypermodern and flourished right after the war, when the hypermodern school was at its zenith.

(A) Nimzo-Indian* Defence (cols. 31 to 69). The move 3..., B—Kt 5, although known before Nimzovitch's days, only became popular after it had been played and analysed by the great Russo-Danish master. After the opening moves 1 P—Q 4, Kt—Q B 3; 2 P—Q B 4, P—K 3; 3 Kt—Q B 3, B—Kt 5, White has a number of possible replies :—

---

* This term is a contraction of Nimzovitch-Indian; and its brevity is the excuse for its employment.

(i) 4 Q—B 2 (cols. 31 to 47) is the most usual, and probably the strongest. Here again Black can branch off into four lines. 4..., P—Q 4 (cols. 31 to 38) has received a good deal of attention since our last edition. If White exchanges Pawns at Q 5 Black should recapture with the Queen, when his chances are at least as good as White's. Col. 31 shows the best line for both sides. In cols. 33 and 34 White attempts to vary, but without success. The recapture with the Pawn at Q 5 (cols. 35 and 36) is less favourable for Black. White can also force the exchange of the Black King's Bishop by 5 P—Q R 3 (cols. 37 and 38). The wild continuation in col. 37, where White first sacrifices the Exchange and then Black a piece, has been analysed exhaustively, and the first player should win. Black need not, however, go in for these complications, but can adopt the simple line in col. 38. 4..., P—B 4 (cols. 39 to 41) has fallen into disrepute; Black can at best obtain a difficult equality. 4..., B × Kt ch is a critical variation which has received little attention. Nimzovitch loved such positions and played them with virtuosity, but they are not to every-one's taste. 4..., Kt—B 3 (the Zürich or Milner-Barry Variation (cols. 43 to 47)) is considered by Euwe and others the most crucial line in Nimzovitch's Defence. Here Black omits the counter-attack on White's centre by P—Q B 4 in order to prepare the advance of his King's Pawn. This line is more dangerous for Black, but also more enterprising. The most recent tests have all been in Black's favour (col. 45, for example).

(ii) 4 Q—Kt 3 (cols. 48 to 55). Now Black's Bishop is attacked, so that he has less choice than after 4 Q—B 2. Nevertheless the Queen is not well placed at Kt 3, and the move has not been seen much of late. In the usual varia-tion Black plays P—Q B 4, followed by Kt—Q B 3, Kt—K 5, Kt × Q B P, etc. This plan which is due in large measure to Nimzovitch, has been discredited, since the loss of time has almost fatal consequences (cols. 48 to 52). Far better for Black is the immediate recapture of the Bishop's Pawn (col. 53). Botvinnik's 6 B—Kt 5 (col. 54) is an interesting departure from routine. 4..., Kt—B 3 generally transposes into a Zürich variation; col. 55 is an important exception.

(iii) 4 P—K 3 (cols. 56 to 60) was one of Rubinstein's favourite lines. The idea is to develop the King's side quietly and to play for an attack. Black has various defences at his disposal. The immediate counter-attack in the centre (cols. 56 and 59) is not as good as was formerly thought to be the case, while the dilatory 4..., O—O (col. 58) is decidedly inferior. The best defence is the advance of the Queen's Pawn only, coupled with the fianchetto of Black's Queen's Bishop (col. 57 and note (h)).

(iv) 4 P—Q R 3 (cols. 61 to 64) was introduced by Sämisch, and has often been adopted by Lilienthal and Euwe. White forces Black to saddle him with doubled Pawns, in order to be able to build up a strong Pawn-centre. Black must not underestimate the seriousness of White's threat; his best line is an immediate counter-attack against the White centre (col. 61).

(v) 4 P—Kt 3 (col. 65) has gained importance by its adoption by Alekhine in a recent game.

(vi) 4 Kt—B 3 (cols. 66 to 68) is a difficult variation for both sides. Here too White is prepared to accept the doubled-Pawns, but it is not so easy for him to build up a strong centre. Sämisch's line (col. 66) shows the ideal set-up for White; simpler for Black is a quiet development, as in col. 68.

(vii) 4 B—Q 3 and 4 B—Kt 5 (cols. 69 and note (i)) have no theoretical value, since Black equalises immediately.

(B) Queen's Indian Defence (cols. 71 to 90 and 96 to 105) is another of the excellent Indian defences. The characteristic move is the fianchetto of the Black Queen's Bishop (just as the characteristic move in the King's Indian

Defence is the fianchetto of his King's Bishop). The strategical object of this fianchetto is control of Black's K 5, and the central importance of this square conditions the play on both sides.

The fianchetto is rarely played at once, the usual order of moves being 1 P—Q 4, Kt—K B 3; 2 P—Q B 4, P—K 3; 3 Kt—K B 3, P—Q Kt 3. The strongest continuation for White now is P—K Kt 3, to oppose Black's Queen's Bishop and thereby challenge Black's control of the long diagonal. On Black's 5th move he has a choice of five continuations : (*i*) 5..., B—K 2 (cols. 71 to 75) is the simplest way for the second player to equalise. (*ii*) 5..., B—Kt 5 ch (cols. 75 to 80) exchanges Black's important King's Bishop and leaves White with a lasting initiative. The recapture with the Queen on White's 7th move, as in cols. 76 and 77, is superior to the recapture with the Knight. (*iii*) 5..., P—B 4 (cols. 81 and 82) is a weak continuation, White maintaining a strong Pawn at Q 5, which seriously cripples Black's game. (*iv*) 5..., P—Q 4 (col. 83) is good only in conjunction with the recapture at Q 4 with the Pawn. (*v*) 5..., Q—B 1 (col. 84) is played with the object of defending the Queen's Bishop, thereby making an early P—Q B 4 possible. If White wishes to avoid an early draw he must adopt the complicated sacrificial line in note (*g*).

In the variations where White omits the fianchetto of his King's Bishop, Black's task is simpler. However, 4 Kt—B 3 (cols. 85 to 88) can lead to great complications. Cols. 86 and 88 are a combination of the Queen's Indian and Nimzo-Indian Defences.

It has already been mentioned that one rarely sees Black fianchetto on his 2nd move. There is, however, no good reason for this, so that it can be ascribed to the dictates of fashion. In cols. 96 to 105 are shown the lines where Black does fianchetto on the 2nd move and White continues irregularly. The line in col. 96 is of particular importance.

3 B—B 4 (col. 97), 3 B—Kt 5 (col. 98), and 3 P—K 3 followed by the Colle set-up for White (cols. 99 and 100) are inferior continuations for the first player. In cols. 104 and 105 Black tries the immediate fianchetto against 2 P— Q—B 4. Here too there is no way known in which White can obtain an advantage.

(C) Bogoljuboff's Variation (cols. 91 to 95), is closely allied to the Queen's Indian Defence. In col. 94 White can obtain an advantage by the fianchetto of his King's Bishop, transposing into the Queen's Indian Defence; in col. 93 Black obtains an inferior position because he avoids the transposition.

(D) King's Indian Defence (cols. 106 to 150). In this defence Black has a choice of two main systems. In the first place he can play P—Q 3, followed by an eventual P—K 4 or P—Q B 4; in the second place he can play P— Q 4 either before or after the development of his King's Bishop.

The first system (P—Q 3 and P—K 4) is the older line, developed chiefly by Réti and Euwe just after the War, but has since practically disappeared from master-play. This is by no means accidental, but is due to the strength of the King's Fianchetto for White, shown in cols. 115 to 118. In the lines where White does not fianchetto his King's Bishop Black is also unsuccessful in achieving complete equality, but always secures a dangerous counter-attack. When White does not so fianchetto, the most customary continuation is 6 B—K 2 (cols 106 to 109, when it is difficult to decide whether White's advance on the Queen's side is more effective than Black's on the King's. Recent master-play consistently prefers White. The Four Pawns' Attack (cols. 113 and 114) is unsound. As has been mentioned, the best line for White is the fianchetto of his King's Bishop, coupled with an early P—K 4. This leaves him in full command of the centre, and Black's game in this variation is almost lost after the opening. White should be careful to play first Kt—Q B 3 and P—K 4 and then P—K Kt 3 (col. 116), for against the immediate 3 P—K Kt 3 Black can secure adequate counterplay by P—B 3, preparing P— Q 4. The attack with 3 P—B 3 has been played with success by Alekhine, Nimzovitch, and Bogoljuboff. In both cols. 124 and 125 White shows to advantage, but in col. 126 the original 3..., P—B 4, which has attracted the attention of Russian analysts, equalises. Some unusual variations for White are shown in cols. 127 to 130; because of the omission of P—Q B 4 White can not hope for even a slight superiority.

In the second system, where Black plays P—Q 4 at an early stage, he generally obtains adequate counterplay. The most important branch here is the Grünfeld Defence (cols. 131 to 150), where White must play with considerable care to maintain the advantage of the move. After 3 Kt—Q B 3, P—Q 4 White has no less than six possible continuations :—

(i) 4 P × P (cols. 131 to 133) is the oldest line, formerly thought to be unfavourable for White, an opinion which is no longer tenable. Black obtains the majority of Pawns on the Queen's side, but finds it difficult to consolidate the action of his heavy pieces. Recent tests indicate that White cannot hope for much advantage, but that Black in turn must play carefully to equalise.

(ii) 4 B—Kt 5 (cols. 134 and 135) stirred a sensation some years ago when Lundin won a match-game with it against Spielmann. His analysis has, however, since been demolished, and the move is now considered weak for White.

(iii) 4 B—B 4 (cols. 136 to 139) has been analysed much of late. It has the advantage that White's Bishop is not shut in, but allows Black to win an important tempo at a later stage. In the main variation (col. 136) it is played in conjunction with Q—Kt 3. Black can exchange Pawns and force a practically even ending; yet, as the line in col. 139 demonstrates, White cannot afford to omit Q—Kt 3.

(iv) 4 P—K 3 (cols. 140 to 145) is at present considered best, but White's advantage is often ephemeral. There are two main lines, according as White plays Q—Kt 3 or continues with simple development of his King's side. Against Q—Kt 3 (cols. 140 to 142) the Queen's fianchetto for Black solves his opening difficulties. In the Schlechter Variation (cols. 144 and 145), where White omits Q—Kt 3, Black often obtains the upper hand.

(v) 4 Q—Kt 3 (cols. 146 to 148) was introduced by Botvinnik. The object of the move is to force an early liquidation of Black's Queen's Pawn, in the hope that White will then be able to set up a powerful Pawn-centre. Black does best to accept White's challenge; in col. 146 he obtains a great superiority in development. The interesting line in col. 148, due to Reshevsky, deserves further analysis.

(vi) 4 Kt—B 3 is essentially a move of transposition played as an independent variation as in cols. 149 and 150, it is weak.

(E) Tchigorin's Defence (cols. 151 to 155). This defence has little to recommend it. Black can develop his Queen's Bishop, but his King's Bishop is a problem. By preparing the advance of his King's Pawn White secures an enormously superior position.

(F) The Budapest Defence (cols. 156 to 160). This is an attempt by Black to wrest the initiative from White at the temporary expense of a Pawn; but White, by returning the Pawn, is left with an advantage in development which frequently proves decisive.

(G) Cols. 161 to 165 exemplify some defences which do not fit into any of the more regular lines. The Blumenfeld Counter-Gambit (cols. 161 to 163) is not quite sound. The lines in cols. 164 and 165 leave Black with a hopelessly cramped position.

The Benoni Counter-Gambit (cols. 171 to 175) is played with a view to setting up a solid centre and continuing with an attack on the King's side. It has been played by Alekhine, but is theoretically bad.

The Dutch Defence (cols. 176 to 195) is the most important in this group. It is adopted by the more enterprising of the masters, notably Alekhine and Botvinnik. One of the objectives of the defence is an attack against White's King; consequently, the best line for White is a King's fianchetto (cols. 176 to 189).

Where White develops Kt—K B 3 Black has a choice of two main systems of defence, depending on whether he plays P—Q 3 or Q 4. In the former variation, played by Alekhine for a while, White, by preparing the advance of his King's Pawn, obtains a clear superiority (cols. 176 and 177). The other system, P—Q 4, known as the Stonewall Defence, gives rise to an exceedingly complicated and difficult position where the better player generally wins.

The development of White's Knight at K R 3 is recommended by some authorities. Here the situation is reversed; P—Q 4 is decidedly weak, while P—Q 3 leaves White's Knight misplaced.

If White plays P—Q B 4 on his 2nd, 3rd, or 4th move, the second player can obtain adequate counterplay by checking at Kt 5 with his Bishop. If the first player then plays B—Q 2, Black can banish all his opening difficulties by B x B ch and P—Q 4 (col. 186). The lines in cols. 188 and 189, where White avoids this exchange of Bishops, deserve more attention in practical play.

The Staunton Gambit fell out of favour some time ago and still remains so, although it offers White considerable attacking chances.

COLLE SYSTEM

1 P—Q 4, P—Q 4 ;   2 Kt—K B 3, Kt—K B 3 ;   3 P—K 3, P—B 4 ;
4 P—B 3.

	1	2	3	4	5
4	P—K 3 (a)				P—K Kt 3
5	Q Kt—Q 2				Q Kt—Q 2
	Kt—B 3		Q Kt—Q 2		Q Kt—Q 2
6	B—Q 3		B—Q 3		B—Q 3 (o)
	B—Q 3 (b)		B—Q 3		B—Kt 2
7	O—O		O—O		O—O
	O—O (c)		O—O		O—O
8	P×P (d)		P—K 4......	R—K 1	P—Q Kt 4 !
	B×P		B P×P	Q—B 2 (m)	P×Kt P
9	P—K 4		B P×P	P—K 4	P×P
	Q—B 2......	P—K 4 (h)	P×P	B P×P	Kt—K 1
10	Q—K 2 (e)	P×P	Kt×P	B P×P	B—Kt 2
	B—Q 3	Q×P (i)	Kt×Kt	P×P	Kt—Q 3
11	R—K 1	Q—K 2	B×Kt	Kt×P	Q—Kt 3
	Kt—K Kt 5	B—K Kt 5	Q—Kt 3 (k)	Kt×Kt	Kt—Kt 3
12	P—K R 3	Kt—K 4	B—B 2	R×Kt	P—Q R 4
	K Kt—K 4	K R—Q 1	Kt—B 3	R—K 1	B—B 4 !
13	Kt×Kt ! (f)	Kt×Kt ch	Q—Q 3	R—R 4 !	B×B
	Kt×Kt	P×Kt	B—Q 2	Kt—B 1	P×B
14	P×P ± (g)	B—K 4 ± (j)	Kt—K 5 ?	Kt—Kt 5	P—Kt 5
			B—Kt 4 ∓ (l)	P—K R 3 (n)	Q Kt—B 5 ▬
					(p)

(a) 4.., Kt—B 3 ; 5 B—Q 3, B—Kt 5 ; 6 P—K R 3 (simpler is 6 Q Kt—Q 2,
P—K 3 ; 7 Q—R 4, as in Apscheneek—Alekhine, Kemeri, 1937, transposing to
Cambridge Springs Defence with colours reversed), B×Kt ; 7 Q×B. P—B 5 !? ;
8 B—B 2, P—K 4 ; 9 P×P, Kt×P ; 10 B—R 4 ch, K—K 2, 11 Q—Q 1, Kt—Q 6 ch ∓.
Araiza—Alekhine, Pasadena, 1932.
(b) 6. , B—K 2 ; 7 O—O, O—O ; 8 Q—K 2, R—K 1 ; 9 P×P, B×P ; 10 P—K 4,
Kt—Q 2 !, 11 R—K 1, K Kt—K 4 ! ; 12 Kt×Kt, Kt×Kt ; 13 B—B 2, B—Q 2 ▬
Rumin—Lasker, Moscow, 1936.
(c) If 7 ., P×P ?, 8 K P×P, Q—B 2 ; 9 R—K 1, O—O ; 10 Q—K 2, R—K1 ;
11 Kt—K 5, B×Kt ; 12 P×B, Kt—Q 2 ; 13 Kt—B 3, P—B 4 ; 14 P×P e.p. ±.
Przepiorka—Stoltz, Hamburg, 1930.
(d) This manœuvre is often postponed one move in order to avoid the exchange
of Queens. 8 Q—K 2 is then played, and in that case Black's best reply is again
8.., Q—B 2.
(e) 10 P×P, P×P ; 11 Kt—Kt 3, B—Kt 3 (11 ., ▭—Q 3 ? ; 12 P—K R 3,
R—K 1 ; 13 Q Kt—Q 4 ±. Colle—Yates, Budapest, 1926), 12 Q—B 2, R—K 1 ;
13 B—K Kt 5, Kt—K 5, 14 Q R—K 1, B—K B 4 =. Colle—Kashdan, Bled, 1931.
(f) 13 B—B 2, P—K R 3 ; 14 Kt×Kt, Kt×Kt ; 15 Kt—B 3, Kt×Kt ch=. Gilg—
Alekhine, Kecskemét, 1927.
(g) Continued 14 , P×P ; 15 Kt—B 3 !, Kt×B ; 16 Q×Kt, Q—B 5 ; 17 R—Q 1.
Koltanowski—Soultanbeieff, Brussels, 1935.
(h) If 9 , P×P ; 10 Kt×P, Kt×Kt, 11 B×Kt, Q×Q, 12 R×Q ±, since Black's
development is backward.
(i) Better is 10 , Kt×P ; 11 Kt—K 4, B—K 2 ; 12 Kt—Kt 3, P—B 4 , 13 B—Q B 4,
B—K 3 ; 14 R—K 1, P—K 5 =. Colle—Euwe, 2nd match game, 1928.
(j) Colle—Sir G. A. Thomas, Ghent, 1926.
(k) If 11.., Kt—B 3 ; 12 B—Q 3 ! (an improvement on 12 B—B 2, P—K R 3 ;
13 Q—K 2, P—Q Kt 3 ; 14 Kt—K 5, B—Kt 2, 15 K R—Q 1, B—B 1 ∓. Rumin—
Capablanca, Moscow, 1936), P—K R 3 ; 13 Kt—K 5, Q—K 2 (P—Q Kt 3 ? ;
14 Q—B 3 !), 14 Q—B 3, R—Kt 1 ; 15 Q—Kt 3 ±. Prins—Grünfeld, Zandvoort,
1936.
(l) 15 Q—K R 3, Q×P. Colle—Bogoljuboff, 1925.

Notes ctd on p. 216

1 P—Q 4, P—Q 4; 2 Kt—K B 3, Kt—K B 3, 3 P—K 3, P—B 4 (a)

COLLE SYSTEM

	6	7	8	9	10
4	(P—B 3)		Q Kt—Q 2		P—Q Kt 3
	(P—KKt3)	..Q Kt—Q 2	Q Kt—Q 2 (h)		P—K 3
5	(Q Kt—Q 2)	Q Kt—Q 2	P—Q R 3		B—Kt 2
	(Q Kt—Q 2)	Q—B 2	Q—B 2	P—K 3	Kt—B 3
6	(B—Q 3)	Q—R 4 !	P—B 4	P×P	B—Q 3
	(B—Kt 2)	P—KKt3 (e)	P—K Kt 3	B×P	B—Q 3
7	(O—O)	P—B 4	P×Q P	P—Q Kt 4	O—O
	(O—O)	B—Kt 2	Kt×P	B—K 2	O—O
8	P—K 4	B P×P	Q—Kt 3	B—Kt 2	Q Kt—Q 2 (k)
	Q P×P (b)	Kt×P	K Kt—Kt 3	O—O	Q—K 2
9	Kt×P	P—K 4 (f)	P—Q R 4	P—B 4	Kt—K 5 (l)
	P×P	Kt—Kt 3	P×P	P—Q Kt 3	P×P
10	Kt×P	Q—B 2	P×P	B—Q 3	P×P
	Kt—K 4 (c)	Q—Q 3	Kt—B 3	P×P	B—R 6
11	Kt×Kt ch	P—Q R 4 !	B—Kt 5 ch	Kt×P	B×B ? (m)
	B×Kt	P—Q R 4	Kt(Kt3)—Q2	B—Kt 2	Q×B
12	B—K 2	P—Q 5	Kt—K 5	O—O	Q Kt—B 3
	B—Q 2	O—O	P—K 3	R—B 1	B—Q 2
13	B—R 6	B—Q 3 ± (g)	Q Kt—B 3 ±	Q—K 2 ± (j)	Kt×Kt
	R—K1 ∓ (d)		(i)		B×Kt ∓ (n)

(a) 3 , P—K 3; 4 B—Q 3, B—Q 3 (for 4. , P—B 4 see cols. 1—4); 5 Q Kt—Q 2, O—O; 6 O—O, P—Q Kt 3; 7 P—Q Kt 3, B—Kt 2; 8 B—Kt 2, Q Kt—Q 2, 9 P—B 4, Q—K 2; 10 R—B 1, K R—Q 1; 11 Kt—K 5 ±. Colle—Yates, Carlsbad, 1929.

(b) If 8.., B P×P; 9 P—K 5 (but not 9 Kt×P ?, Kt—B 4+), Kt—K 1; 10 P×P ±.

(c) 10.., Kt×Kt is weaker: 11 B×Kt, Kt—B 3 (11 , Kt—B 4; 12 B—B 3, P—K 4; 13 Kt—Kt 3, Kt—K 3; 14 B—K 3, Q—B 2 is playable. P. W. Sergeant—R. Schadle, Premier Reserves, London, 1932); 12 B—B 3, P—K 4; 13 Kt—Kt 5, Q—Kt 3; 14 P—Q R 4, R—Q 1; 15 Q—K 1 ±. Colle—Monticelli, San Remo, 1930.

(d) 14 Q—Kt 3, Q—B 1; 15 Q R—Q 1, R—Q 1; 16 K R—K 1, P—Q R 3. Colle—Grunfeld, Carlsbad, 1929.

(e) 6 .,P—K 3; 7 B—Q 3, B—Q 3; 8 P×P, B×B P; 9 O—O, O—O; 10 Q—R 4, B—K 2?; 11 B×P ch, Kt×B; 12 Q×B, K Kt—B 3; 13 Q—Kt 4 +. Colle—Spielmann, Bled, 1931.

(f) 9 Q—Kt 3, K Kt—Kt 3; 10 P—Q R 4, P×P; 11 P×P, P—Q R 4; 12 B—Kt 5, O—O; 13 O—O, Kt—B 3; 14 R—K 1, B—B 4 ∓. Alekhine—Reshevsky, Nottingham, 1936.

(g) 13.., Kt—Kt 1; 14 O—O, Kt—R 3; 15 B×Kt, R×B; 16 Kt—Kt 3. Colle—Rubinstein, Rotterdam, 1931.

(h) 4.., Kt—B 3; 5 P—Q R 3, P×P?; 6 P×P, P—K 3; 7 B—Q 3, B—Q 3; 8 O—O, O—O; 9 R—K 1, R—K 1; 10 P—R 3, P—K R 3; 11 P—B 3, P—Q R 4; 12 Kt—K 5 ±. Rubinstein—Sultan Khan, Hamburg, 1930.

(i) Tartakover—Keres, Noordwijk, 1938.

(j) Rubinstein—Monticelli, Budapest, 1929.

(k) Or 8 Kt—K 5, Kt—K 2; 9 Kt—Q 2, P—Q Kt 3; 10 P—K B 4, B—Kt 2; 11 Q—B 3, R—B 1; 12 Kt—Kt 4, Kt×Kt; 13 Q×Kt, Kt—Kt 3; 14 Kt—B 3, P—B 4; 15 Q—R 5, B—K 2 =. Maroczy—Bogoljuboff, New York, 1924. Bogoljuboff recommends 8 P—Q R 3, Q—K 2 (8 , P—Q Kt 3 is preferable); 9 Kt—K 5.

(l) If 9 P—Q R 3, P—K 4.

(m) 11 Q—B 1, with complete equality.

(n) Bogoljuboff—Capablanca, New York, 1924.

1 P—Q 4, P—Q 4 ; 2 Kt—K B 3, Kt—K B 3.

	11	12	13	14	15
3	(P—K 3)............................			P—B 4	
	P—B 3......B—B 4......B—Kt 5			P—B 4......B—B 4	
4	Q Kt—Q 2	B—Q 3	P—B 4	B P×P	P×P (l)
	B—B 4	P—K 3	P—K 3	B P×P	Kt×P
5	B—Q 3	B×B	Q—Kt 3 (e)	Q×P (h)	Q Kt—Q 2
	B×B	P×B	Q—B 1	Q×P	Kt—K B 3
6	P×B	Q—Q 3 (b)	Kt—K 5	Kt—Q B 3	Q—Kt 3
	P—K 3	Q—B 1	B—K B 4	Q×Q	Q—B 1
7	O—O	P—Q Kt3 (c)	Kt—Q B 3	Kt×Q	P—K 3
	B—K 2	Kt—R 3	P—B 3	P—Q R 3 (i)	P—K 3
8	R—K 1	O—O	P×P	P—K Kt3 (j)	B—Q 3
	O—O	B—K 2	K P×P	P—K 4	B×B
9	P—K 4	P—B 4	B—Q 2	Kt—B 2	Q×B
	Kt—R 3	O—O	B—Q 3	B—Q 2	Q Kt—Q 2
10	P—K 5	Kt—B 3	R—B 1	B—Kt 2	O—O
	Kt—Q 2	P—B 3	O—O	B—B 3	P—B 4
11	Kt—B 1	B—Kt 2	Kt—Kt 5	O—O	P—Q Kt 3
	P—Q B 4	Kt—K 5	B—K 2	B×B	P×P
12	P×P	K R—B 1	B—Q 3 (f)	K×B	Kt×P
	Kt(Q2)×BP	K R—Q 1	B×B	Kt—B 3 (k)	B—K 2
13	P—Q R 3 ±	Q—K 2	Q×B	B—Kt 5	B—Kt 2
	(a)	Q—K 3 = (d)	Kt—R3 = (g)	B—K 2=	O—O = (m)

(a) Colle—Bogoljuboff, San Remo, 1930.

(b) 6 O—O, Q Kt—Q 2; 7 P—B 4, P×P; 8 Q—R 4, B—Q 3; 9 Q Kt—Q 2, O—O; 10 Kt×P, Kt—Kt 3; 11 Kt×Kt, R P×Kt; 12 Q—B 2, Q—Q 2 ∓. Colle—Alekhine, San Remo, 1930.

(c) Or 7 O—O, B—Q 3; 8 P—Q Kt3, O—O; 9 P—B 4, P—B 3; 10 Kt—B 3, P—Q Kt3; 11 P×P, Kt×P; 12 Kt×Kt, P×Kt; 13 B—Kt 2, P—Kt 3; 14 K R—B 1, Q—R 3. Alekhine—Kostich, Bled, 1931.

(d) 14 P—Q R 3, Kt—B 2. Alekhine—Euwe, 17th match game, 1935.

(e) 5 Q Kt—Q 2, followed by B—Q 3, O—O and P—Q Kt3 was a good alternative.

(f) 12 B—Kt 4 was superior (Kmoch).

(g) Colle—P. Johner, Berlin, 1926.

(h) For 5 Kt×P, Kt×P ; 6 P—K 4, Kt—Kt 5 see English Opening, col. 18.

(i) If 7.., P—K 4; 8 K Kt—Kt 5, Kt—R 3 ; 9 B—Kt 5 ±.

(j) Znosko-Borovsky suggests 8 B—Kt 5, P—K 4 ? ; 9 B×Kt, P×B; 10 Kt—Q 5, P×Kt; 11 Kt—B 7 ch, K—Q 1 ; 12 Kt×R, B—Kt 5 ch ; 13 K—Q 1 +. Black could play, however, 8. , B—Q 2, 9 B×Kt, K P×B; 10 Kt—Q 5, B—Q 3 with a good position. See analysis in L'Echiquier, November, 1928.

(k) Tartakover suggests 12. , P—K R 3. The column is P. Johner—Seitz, Debreczin, 1925.

(l) Or 4 Kt—B 3, P—K 3 ; 5 B—Kt 5, P—B 3 ; 6 Q—Kt 3, Q—Kt 3 ; 7 P—B 5, Q—B 2; 8 P—K 3, Q Kt—Q 2; 9 B—K B 4, Q—B 1; 10 P—K R 3, B—K 2; 11 R—B 1 =. Marshall—Torre, Moscow, 1925.

(m) Gilg—Marshall, Carlsbad, 1929

1 P—Q 4, P—Q 4 ;   2 Kt—K B 3, Kt—K B 3.

	16	17	18	19	20
3	B—B 4............................		............B—Kt 5		
	P—B 4.................		P—K 3 (e)	P—K 3	
4	P—K 3		P—K 3	P—K 3	
	Kt—B 3		B—Q 3 (f)	P—B 4	
5	P—B 3		B—Q 3	P—B 3	
	B—Kt 5.....	Q—Kt 3	O—O	B—K 2 (h)	
6	Q Kt—Q 2	Q—B 1 (b)	Q Kt—Q 2	B—Q 3	
	P—K 3	B—B 4	B×B	Q Kt—Q 2...	Kt—B 3
7	Q—R 4	P×P (c)	P×B	Q Kt—Q 2	Q Kt—Q 2
	B×Kt	Q×B P	P—B 4	O—O	P—K R 3
8	Kt×B	Q Kt—Q 2	P×P	O—O	B—R 4
	Q—Kt 3	R—B 1	Q—B 2	Q—B 2	O—O
9	Q R—Kt 1	Kt—Kt 3	P—K Kt 3	Q—K 2	O—O
	B—K 2	Q—Kt 3	Q×Q B P	P—Q Kt 3	P—Q Kt 3
10	B—Q 3	Q—Q 2	O—O	P—K 4	Kt—K 5
	O—O	P—K 3	Kt—B 3	Q P×P	Kt×Kt
11	O—O	B—Q 3	P—B 3	Kt×P	P×Kt
	K R—Q 1	B—K 5	P—Q Kt 4	B—Kt 2	Kt—Q 2
12	B—Kt 3	Q—K 2	Q—K 2	P×P	B—Kt 3
	Q R—B 1	B—K 2	R—Kt 1	Kt×P	B—R 5 (j)
13	Kt—K 5	O—O	P—Q Kt 4 (g)	Kt×Kt	B×B
	Kt—K R 4 =	O—O (d)	Q—Kt 3	Q×Kt = (i)	Q×B (k)
	(a)				

(a) Keres—Reshevsky, Kemeri, 1937.

(b) 6 Q—Kt 3, P—B 5 ? ;   7 Q×Q, P×Q ;   8 Kt—R 3, P—K 4 ;   9 Kt—Q Kt 5, R—R 4 ;   10 Kt—B 7 ch, K—Q 2 ;   11 P×P, Kt—R 4 ;   12 Kt×P, R×Kt ;   13 B×P, R—R 4 ;   14 B×P+ (Maróczy).

c) Alternatives are· (1) 7 B—K 2, P—K 3 ;   8 O—O, B—K 2 ;   9 Q Kt—Q 2, O—O ;   10 Kt—Kt 3, Kt—K 5 ;   11 K Kt—Q 2, Q R—B 1 ;   12 Kt×Kt. Selesnieff—Teichmann, match, 1921   (2) 7 Kt—R 4, B—K 5 ;   8 Kt—Q 2, P—K 3 ;   9 P—B 3, B—Kt 3 ;   10 Kt×B, R P×Kt ;   11 Kt—Kt 3, P—B 5 ;   12 Kt—Q 2, Kt—K R 4 ∓. C. G. Watson—Capablanca, London, 1922.

(d) Capablanca—Maróczy, New York, 1924.

(e) 3. , P—B 3 ;   4 P—K 3, Q—Kt 3 ;   5 B—Q 3, Q×Kt P ;   6 Q Kt—Q 2, Q—Kt 3 ;   7 O—O, P—K 3 ;   8 P—K 4 with positional compensation for the Pawn. Torre—Grunfeld, Marienbad, 1925.

(f) Or 4 ', P—B 4 ;   5 P—B 3, Kt—B 3 ;   6 B—Q 3, Q—Kt 3 ;   7 Q—B 1, B—Q 2 ;   8 Q Kt—Q 2, R—B 1 ;   9 Q—Kt 1, B—K 2 ;   10 P—K R 3, O—O ;   11 Kt—K 5, K R—Q 1 ;   12 B—R 2, B—K 1. Samisch—Rubinstein, Dresden, 1926.

(g) 13 Kt—Kt 3 (Grünfeld). The column is Rubinstein—Capablanca, London, 1922, up to move 12.

(h) 5. , Q Kt—Q 2 ;   6 Q Kt—Q 2, Q—Kt 3 ;   7 Q—B 2, B—Q 3 ;   8 B—Q 3, P—K R 3 ;   9 B—R 4, O—O ;   10 O—O, Q—B 2 ;   11 B—Kt 3, P—Q R 3 ;   12 Q R—Q 1, P—Q Kt 4 ;   13 P×P ?, B×B ;   14 R P×B, Kt×P ∓. Tartakover—Fine, Nottingham, 1936.

(i) Tartakover—Capablanca, Nottingham, 1936.

(j) Keres recommends 12 , B—Kt 2, since in reply to the text White could have played 13 B—K B 4, P—K Kt 4 ;   14 Q—R 5 !, K—Kt 2 ;   15 P—K Kt 3, P×B ;   16 P×B, with a strong attack.

(k) 14 P—K B 4, B—Kt 2 ;   15 R—B 3 ±. Tartakover—Keres, Kemeri, 1937.

1 P—Q 4, P—Q 4.

	21	22	23	24	25
2	(Kt—K B 3)			Kt—Q B 3 (*i*)	
	(Kt—K B 3) . . P—Q B 4	Kt—Q B 3		Kt—K B 3	
3	P—K Kt 3	P×P (*c*)	B—B 4 (*f*)	B—Kt 5	
	P—B 3 (*a*)	P—K 3 (*d*)	B—Kt 5	B—B 4	
4	B—Kt 2	P—K 4	P—K 3	P—K 3 (*j*) . . . P—B 3	
	B—B 4	B×P	P—K 3	P—B 3	Q Kt—Q 2
5	Kt—R 4	P×P	B—K 2 (*g*)	B—Q 3	Kt×P (*l*)
	B—Kt 3	P×P	B×Kt	B—Kt 3	Kt×Kt
6	O—O	B—Kt 5 ch	B×B	Kt—B 3	P—K 4
	P—K 3	Kt—Q B 3	B—Q 3	Q Kt—Q 2	P—K R 3
7	Kt—Q 2	O—O	B—Kt 3	O—O	B—R 4
	B—K 2	Kt—K 2	Kt—B 3	P—K 3	Kt—K 6
8	Kt×B	Q Kt—Q 2	O—O	Kt—K 5	Q—K 2
	R P×Kt	O—O	O—O	Q—Kt 3	B×P
9	P—Q B 4	Kt—Kt 3	P—B 4	Kt×Kt	P×B
	Q Kt—Q 2	B—Kt 3	B×B	Kt×Kt	Kt×B
10	Q—Kt 3	R—K 1 (*e*)	R P×B	R—Kt 1	O—O—O
	Q—Kt 3	B—Kt 5	Kt—K 2	B—Q 3	P—K Kt 4
11	Q×Q	B—Q 3	Kt—B 3	B—R 4	B—B 2
	P×Q	Kt—Kt 3	P—B 3	Q—B 2	Kt×P
12	R—Q 1	P—K R 3	P—B 5	B—Kt 3	R×Kt
	B—Kt 5 (*b*)	B×Kt =	P—K 4 (*h*)	B×B ∓ (*k*)	B—Kt 2 (*m*)

(*a*) For 3.., P—K 3; 4 B—Kt 2, P—B 4 see Réti Opening, cols. 26-29 and 41.

(*b*) Tartakover—Sultan Khan, 4th match game, 1931.

(*c*) 3 P—B 4, P—K 3 transposes into the Queen's Gambit Declined, Tarrasch Defence.

(*d*) Or 3.., Kt—K B 3; 4 P—B 4, P—K 3; 5 P—Q R 3 (Tartakover). 3.., Q—R 4 ch is also good.

(*e*) Preferable is 10 P—K R 3, to hinder the development of Black's Q B. The column is Capablanca—Rubinstein, Berlin, 1928.

(*f*) For 3 P—B 4, see Queen's Gambit Declined, col. 112.

(*g*) 5 P—B 4, B—Kt 5 ch; 6 Kt—B 3, K Kt—K 2; 7 R—B 1, O—O; 8 P—K R 3, B×K Kt; 9 Q×B, Kt—Kt 3. Miss Menchik—Colle, Carlsbad, 1929.

(*h*) 13 P×P, Kt—Q 2; 14 P—K 4, P×P; 15 Kt×P, Kt×K P; 16 Kt—Q 6 ±. Gilg—Colle, Carlsbad, 1929.

(*i*) 2 B—B 4, P—Q B 4; 3 P—K 3, Q—Kt 3; 4 Kt—Q B 3, P—K 3; 5 Kt—Kt 5, Kt—Q R 3; 6 P—Q B 3, P—B 5; 7 P—Q R 4, B—Q 2; 8 P—Q Kt 3, B×Kt; 9 P×B, Q×Kt P; 10 P×P, P×P; 11 Q—R 4+. Analysis from *Lärobok*, 1921.

(*j*) 4 B×Kt, K P×B; 5 P—K 3, P—B 3 (or 5 , Kt—B 3; 6 B—Q 3, Q—Q 2; 7 K Kt—K 2, Kt—Kt 5; 8 B×B, Q×B; 9 O—O, B—Q 3; 10 P—Q R 3, Kt—R 3; 1923); 6 B—Q 3, Q—B 1; 7 K Kt—K 2, B—Q 3; 8 P—K 4, P×P; 9 Kt×P, B×Kt; 10 B×B, Q—B 2; 11 Q—Q 3, Kt—Q 2; 12 O—O—O, P—K Kt 3; 13 P—K Kt 3, P—K B 4 =. Tartakover—Réti, Vienna, 1922.

(*k*) 13 B P×B, P—K 4; 14 B—B 5, O—O. Rellstab—Keres, Kemeri, 1937.

(*l*) If 5 Q—Q 2, P—B 3; 6 P—K 4, P×P; 7 Q—B 4, Q—R 4; 8 O—O—O, P—K 3; 9 B×Kt, Kt×B; 10 P×P, B—Kt 3; 11 B—Q 3, B—Kt 5, 12 K Kt—K 2, O—O—O+. Spielmann—Bogoljuboff, Moscow, 1925.

(*m*) Breyer and Réti—Marco and Spielmann, Gothenburg, 1920. **White has** sufficient compensation for the lost material.

1 P—Q 4, P—Q 4.

	26	27	28	29	30
			STONEWALL VARIATION		
2	(Kt—QB3) / (Kt—K B 3)	....	P—K 3 (e) / Kt—K B 3		
3	(B—Kt 5) / (B—B 4)	....P—B 3 (c)	B—Q 3 / P—B 4	....	Kt—B 3
4	(P—B 3) / P—B 3	P—B 3 / Q—Kt 3	P—Q B 3 / P—K 3	....Kt—B 3	P—K B 4 / Kt—Q Kt 5
5	P—K 4 (a) / P×P	Q—Q 2 / Q×Kt P	P—K B 4 / Q Kt—Q 2 (f)	P—K B 4 / B—Kt 5	Kt—K B 3 / Kt×B ch
6	B×Kt / K P×B	R—Kt 1 / Q—R 6	Kt—B 3 / B—Q 3	Kt—B 3 / P—K 3	P×Kt / P—K Kt 3 (j)
7	P×P / B—Kt 3	P—K 4 / P—K 3	Q Kt—Q 2 / P—Q Kt 3	Q Kt—Q 2 / B—Q 3	Kt—B 3 / B—Kt 2
8	Kt—B 3 / Kt—Q 2	B×Kt / P×B	Kt—K 5 / B—Kt 2	P—K R 3 (i) / B—R 4	O—O / O—O
9	B—Q 3 / B—Q 3	P×P / K P×P	Q—B 3 / P—K R 4	P—Q Kt 3 / P×P	Kt—K 2 / P—Kt 3
10	Q—Q 2 / Q—B 2	R—Kt 3 / Q—K 2 ch	Q—Kt 3 / K—B 1 (g)	B P×P / R—Q B 1	B—Q 2 / P—B 4
11	O—O / O—O	K—B 2 / B—Kt 2	O—O / P—R 5	O—O / B—Kt 3	R—B 1 / B—Q R 3
12	Q R—K 1 / K R—K 1 =	P—B 4 / O—O+ (d)	Q—R 3 / R—B 1 (h)	B×B / R P×B =	Kt—K 5 / Kt—Q 2 =
		(b)			(k)

(a) Weaker is 5 Q—Q 2, Q—B 2; 6 B—B 4, Q—Q 1?; 7 B—Kt 5?, Q Kt—Q 2; 8 Q—B 4? (8 O—O—O !). Vilner—Marsky, 1932.

(b) Sämisch—Tarrasch, Baden-Baden, 1925.

(c) Alternatives leading to equality are: (1) 3.., P—K Kt 3; 4 B×Kt, P×B; 5 P—K 4, P×P; 6 Kt×P, B—Kt 2; 7 Kt—K B 3, O—O; 8 B—K 2, P—K B 4; 9 Kt—B 5, P—Q Kt 3; 10 Kt—Kt 3, B—Kt 2. Tartakover—Kostich, Bad Niendorf, 1927. (2) 3.., Q Kt—Q 2; 4 P—B 3, P—B 3; 5 P—K 4, P×P; 6 P×P, Q—R 4; 7 Q—Q 2, P—K 4; 8 Kt—B 3, B—B 3; 9 B—Q B 3, B—K 2; 9 B—Q B 4, P×P; 10 Q×P, Q—R 3, Tartakover—Sir G. A. Thomas, Carlsbad, 1923. (3) 3 , Kt—K 5; 4 Kt×Kt, P×Kt; 5 Q—Q 2, P—K R 3; 6 B—B 4, B—B 4; 7 P—K 3, P—Q B 4; 8 P—Q B 4, Kt—Q 2; 9 Kt—K 2, P—K Kt 4. Hampstead—Brighton, correspondence, 1917.

(d) Stoltz—Bogoljuboff, Berlin, 1928.

(e) 2 P—K 4? (the Blackmar Gambit), P×P; 3 P—K B 3, P—K 4; 4 Q P×P (or 4 B—K 3, P×Q P; 5 B×P, Kt—Q B 3; 6 B—Kt 5, B—Q 2; 7 Kt—B 3, Q—Kt 4; 8 B×Kt, B×B; 9 Q×Q, P—O—O+), Q×Q ch; 5 K×Q, B—Q B 3; 6 B—Q B 4, K Kt—K 2; 7 B—Q Kt 5, Kt—Kt 3; 8 B—Kt 3, B—K B 4; 9 B×Kt ch, P×B+.

(f) Or 5 ., Kt—B 3; 6 Kt—Q 2, B—Q 3; 7 Q—B 2, B—Q 2; 8 Kt—R 3, Q—Kt 3; 9 Kt—B 2, O—O; 10 O—O, Kt—K 1; 11 P—K 4, Q P×P; 12 K Kt×Kt, Kt×Kt; 13 Kt×Kt, B—K 2; 14 P×P, B×P ch; 15 Kt×B ±. Marshall—Rubinstein, Vienna, 1908.

(g) If 10 , Q—K 2; 11 Q×P, R—K Kt 1; 12 Q—R 6, R×P; 13 B—Kt 5 !.

(h) Continued 13 Q Kt—B 3, Kt—K 5; 14 B—Q 2, Kt×B; 15 Q Kt×Kt, Kt—B 3; 16 Q Kt—B 3 ±. Sultan Khan—Rubinstein, Prague, 1931.

(i) Or 8 O—O, O—O; 9 Q—K 1. The column is Gunsberg—Teichmann, Monte Carlo, 1902.

(j) 6 , P—K 3; 7 Kt—B 3, B—K 2; 8 O—O, O—O; 9 B—Q 2, P—Q Kt 3; 10 Kt—K 5, B—Kt 2; 11 R—B 3, P—B 4; 12 R—R 3, R—B 1; 13 Q—B 3, P—Q R 3; 14 P—K Kt 4 with a good attack. Marshall—Teichmann, Vienna, 1908.

(k) Yates—Schlechter, Pistyan, 1912.

G *

NIMZO-INDIAN DEFENCE

1 P—Q 4, Kt—K B 3 ; 2 P—Q B 4, P—K 3 ; 3 Kt—Q B 3, B—Kt 5 ;
4 Q—B 2, P—Q 4.

	31	32	33	34	35
5	P × P (a)				
	Q × P				P × P
6	P—K 3 (b)			Kt—B 3	B—Kt 5 (o)
	P—B 4			P—B 4	Q—Q 3
7	P—Q R 3		B—Q 2	B—Q 2	P—K 3 (p)
	B × Kt ch		B × Kt	B × Kt	Kt—K 5
8	P × B (c)		P × B	B × B	B—K B 4
	O—O	Q Kt—Q 2 (f)	O—O	P × P (m)	Q—K 2 (q)
9	Kt—B 3	Kt—B 3 (g)	Kt—B 3	Kt × P	B—Q 3
	P × P	P—Q Kt 3	Kt—B 3	P—K 4	P—K B 4
10	B P × P	P—B 4	B—Q 3 (k)	Kt—B 3 (n)	Kt—K 2
	P—Q Kt 3 (d)	Q—Q 3	P—B 5 !	Kt—B 3	O—O
11	B—B 4	B—Kt 2	B—K 2	R—Q 1	O—O
	Q—B 3	B—Kt 2	P—K 4 !	Q—B 4	P—B 3
12	B—Q 3	B—K 2	P × P	P—K 3	P—B 3
	Q × Q	R—Q B 1 (h)	Kt × P	O—O	Kt × Kt
13	B × Q	O—O (i)	Kt × Kt	B—K 2	P × Kt
	B—R 3	B—K 5	Q × Kt	B—Kt 5	B—Q 3
14	Kt—K 5	Q—B 3	O—O	O—O	B × B ±
	Q Kt—Q 2 =	P × P ! (j)	B—B4 ! ∓ (l)	Q R—B 1 =	
	(e)				

(a) Or 5 P—K 3, O—O ; 6 Kt—B 3, P—Q Kt 3 ; 7 P—Q R 3, B × Kt ch ; 8 P × B,
P—B 4 ; 9 B P × P, K P × P =. Nimzovitch—Marshall, London, 1927. If 5 B—Kt 5,
P × P ; 6 Kt—B 3, P—Q Kt 4 ; 7 P—Q R 4, P—B 3 ; 8 B × Kt, P × B, 9 P—K Kt 3,
P—Q R 3 +, since Black can hold the Pawn. Capablanca—Nimzovitch, Kissingen
1928.
(b) 6 P—Q R 3, B × Kt ch ; 7 Q × B, Kt—B 3, 8 Kt—B 3, Kt—K 5 ; 9 Q—Q 3,
P—K 4 ; 10 P × P, Q—R 4 ch =. Rubinstein—Colle, Budapest, 1929.
(c) 8 Q × B, Q Kt—Q 2 ; 9 Kt—B 3, P × P ; 10 Q × P, Kt—B 4 ; 11 B—B 4, Q × Q ;
12 Kt × Q, B—Q 2 ; 13 B—Q 2, K Kt—K 5 with a level ending. Euwe—Grünfeld,
Amsterdam, 1936.
(d) Somewhat better than 10 ., B—Q 2 ; 11 B—Q B 4, Q—K R 4 ; 12 O—O,
R—B 1 ; 13 Q—Q 3, Kt—B 3 ; 14 B—R 2, Kt—R 4 ; 15 Kt—K 5, Kt—Kt 5. Euwe—
Alekhine, match, 1926-27.
(e) Alekhine—Euwe, 12th match game, 1937.
(f) 8 , Kt—B 3 ; 9 Kt—B 3, O—O ; 10 P—B 4, Q—Q 3 ; 11 B—Kt 2, P × P ;
12 P × P, P—Q Kt 3 , 13 B—Q 3, B—Kt 2 (Alekhine—Euwe, 10th match game, 1937)
leads to a two-edged position.
(g) 9 P—B 3, P × P ; 10 B P × P, Kt—Kt 3 , 11 Kt—K 2, B—Q 2 ; 12 Kt—B 4,
Q—Q 3 ; 13 B—Q 2, R—B 1 =. Alekhine—Euwe, 8th match game, 1937.
(h) Or 12.., P × P ; 13 P × P, O—O ; 14 O—O, Kt—Kt 5, 15 P—R 3, B × Kt =.
Lövenfisch—Botvinnik, 3rd match game, 1937.
(i) 13 Q—Kt 3, O—O ; 14 R—Q 1, P × P ; 15 P × P, Q—B 2 ; 16 O—O,
Kt—Kt 5 ! =. Kinoch—Grünfeld, Amsterdam, 1936.
(j) 15 Kt × P, Kt—B 4 ; 16 Kt—Kt 5, Q—Kt 1 ; 17 K R—Q 1, O—O ; 18 Kt—Q 6,
Kt—R 5 ! =. Analysis by Grunfeld. If here 14 , O—O, 15 Q R—Q 1, K R—Q 1 ;
16 P—Q 5 !, Q—B 1 ; 17 P × P ±. Euwe—Botvinnik, Nottingham, 1936.
(k) 10 P—B 4, Q—Q 3 ; 11 P × P ?, Q × B P ; 12 R—Q Kt 1, P—K 4 ; 13 Kt—Kt 5,
P—K R 3 ; 14 Kt—K 4, Kt × Kt ; 15 Q × Kt, R—Q 1 ∓. Alekhine—Euwe, 20th match
game, 1937.
(l) Flohr—Colle, Bled, 1931.
(m) 8 , Kt—B 3 ; 9 R—Q 1 ! (better than 9 P—K 3, P × P ; 10 Kt × P, Kt × Kt ;
11 B × Kt, O—O ; 12 B × Kt, P × B, 13 B—Q 3, Q—R 4 ch ; 14 Q—Q 2 ±. Nimzovitch—
Canal, Carlsbad, 1929), O—O ; 10 P—K 3, P—Q Kt 3 , 11 P—Q R 3, B—Kt 2 ; 12 P × P,
Q × P ; 13 P—Q Kt 4, Q—K R 4 ; 14 B × Kt ±. Capablanca—Fine, Avro, 1938.

Notes ctd. on p. 216

NIMZO-INDIAN DEFENCE

1 P—Q 4, Kt—K B 3 ; 2 P—Q B 4, P—K 3 ; 3 Kt—Q B 3, B—Kt 5 ;
4 Q—B 2.

	36	37	38	39	40
4	(P—Q 4)................................P—B 4				
5	(P×P)......P—Q R 3			P×P (j)	
	(P×P)......B×Kt ch			Kt—B 3.....B×P	
6	(B—Kt 5)	Q×B		Kt—B 3	Kt—B 3
	P—B 3 (a)	Kt—K 5 (c)		B×P	P—Q 4 !
7	P—K 3	Q—B 2		B—Kt 5	P—K 3
	B—Kt 5	Kt—QB3 (d).P—Q B 4 !		P—Q Kt3 (k)	O—O
8	Kt—K 2	P—K 3 (e)	Q P×P	P—K 3	B—K 2
	Q Kt—Q 2	P—K 4	Kt—Q B 3	B—Kt 2	P×P
9	Kt—Kt 3	B P×P	P—K 3	B—K 2	B×P
	P—K R 3	Q×P	Q—R 4 ch	B—K 2	Q Kt—Q 2
10	B—K B 4	B—B 4	B—Q 2	O—O	O—O
	P—K Kt 4	Q—R 4 ch	Kt×B (g)	R—Q B 1	P—Q R 3
11	B—K 5	P—Q Kt 4	Q×Kt	Q R—Q 1 (l)	P—Q R 3
	Kt×B	Kt×Kt P	P×P !	P—Q 3	P—Q Kt 4
12	P×Kt	Q×Kt	Q×Q (h)	R—Q 2	B—K 2
	Kt—Q 2	Kt—B7dblch	Kt×Q	P—Q R 3	B—Kt 2
13	P—K R 3	K—K 2 !	R—B 1	K R—Q 1	P—Q Kt 4
	B—K 3	Q—K 8 ch	P—Q Kt4 !	O—O (m)	B—Kt 3
14	O—O—O	K—B 3	P×P e.p.	B—B 4	B—Kt 2
	Q—R 4 ! (b)	Kt×R (f)	B—Kt2 = (i)	Kt—K 1 (n)	R—B 1 = (o)

(a) If 6.., B—Kt 5; 7 Q—Kt 3 !, Kt—B 3; 8 P—K 3, O—O; 9 P—Q R 3,
B×Kt ch; 10 Q×B ±. Flohr—Naegeli, Berne, 1932.
(b) 15 P—B 4, P×P; 16 P×P, O—O—O with chances for both sides. Alekhine—
Naegeli, Berne, 1932.
(c) 6.., P×P; 7 Q×P, O—O; 8 B—Kt 5 P—B 3; 9 Kt—B 3, Q Kt—Q 2;
10 P—K 3, Q—R 4 ch; 11 P—Q Kt 4, Q—Q 4; 12 Q—B 2, P—K R 3; 13 B—Q B 4,
Q—Q 3; 14 B×Kt ±. Euwe—Capablanca, Carlsbad, 1929.
(d) 7..O—O; 8 P—K 3, P—Q K 3 ! is quite good for Black: 9 B—Q 3, B—R 3 !;
10 Kt—K 2, Kt—Q 2; 11 O—O, P—Q B 4; 12 P—Q Kt3, P×Q P, 13 Kt×P,
Q Kt—B 4 ∓. Bogoljuboff—Euwe, 3rd match game 1928. If, however, 8 ., Kt—Q 2;
9 B—Q 3, P—K B 4; 10 Kt—K 2, P—B 3; 11 O—O, Kt—Q 3; 12 P—B 5, Kt—K 5;
13 P—Q Kt 4 ±. Fine—Danielsson, Stockholm, 1937.
(e) If instead 8 Kt—B 3, P—K 4; 9 P—K 3, B—B 4; 10 Q—Kt 3 (10 Q—R 4,
O—O; 11 P×Q P, Q×P; 12 Q—Kt 5, Q×Q; 13 B×Q, Kt—R 4; 14 B—R 4, P×P;
15 Kt×P, Kt—B 4 ! =), Kt—R 4 ! (O—O?; 11 P×Q P, Kt—R 4; 12 Q—R 2,
P—Q B 3; 13 P—Q Kt 4, Kt—B 6; 14 Q—Q 2 +. Fine—Stahlberg, 1st match game,
1937), 11 Q—R 4 ch, P—B 3; 12 P×Q P, Q×P; 13 P—Q Kt 4, Q—Kt 6 =.
(f) 15 B—Kt 2, B—R 3 (or 15.., O—O; 16 K—Kt 3, B—Q 2; 17 Kt—B 3, Q×R;
18 Kt—Kt 5, P—K Kt 3; 19 Q×K P, Q R—K 1; 20 Q—B 6, R×P ch; 21 P×R,
Q—K 8 ch; 22 Q—B 2) ; 16 P—Q 5, O—O—O; 17 P×B, P×P; 18 P—Kt 3
(if 18 K—Kt 4?, Q×B P); 19 B×Kt, P—R 4 ch; 20 K—R 3, P—K Kt 4+. Feigin—
Fine, Hastings, 1936-37, while if 18 K—Kt 3, K R—B 1; 19 B×P ch, K—Kt 1;
20 B×P, Q R—K 1 with excellent counter-chances. Not, however, 20 ., R×P?;
21 K—R 3, R—B 8; 22 B—Kt 4+. Winter—A. Reynolds, Birmingham, 1937),
K R—B 1 ch; 19 K—Kt 4 !+.
(g) 10 ., Q×B P; 11 P—Q Kt 4, Q—K 2; 12 B—B 1 !, P—Q R 4; 13 P—Kt 5,
Kt—K 4; 14 B—Kt 2+. Rumin—Capablanca, Moscow, 1935.
(h) Or 12 B×P, Q×B P; 13 R—B 1, Q—K Kt 4; 14 P—B 4, Q—R 5 ch;
15 Q—B 2 (Euwe—Petrov, Stockholm, 1937), Q×Q ch =.
(i) 15 Kt—B 3, K—K 2 ! (if 15 , O—O; 16 P×P, R×P; 17 Kt—Q 2 B—R 3;
18 R—B 3!+); 16 P×P, R×P; 17 Kt—Q 2, B—R 3; 18 R—B 3, R—Q Kt 1.

Notes ctd on p. 216

NIMZO-INDIAN DEFENCE

1 P—Q 4, Kt—K B 3 ; 2 P—Q B 4, P—K 3 ; 3 Kt—Q B 3, B—Kt 5 ;
4 Q—B 2.

	41	42	43	44	45
4	(P—B 4).....	B × Kt ch....	Kt—B 3 (f)		
5	(P×P)	P×B (d)	P—K 3	Kt—B 3	
	Kt—R 3 (a)	P—Q 3	P—K 4	P—Q 3	
6	P—Q R 3 !	Kt—K B 3	P—Q 5	P—Q R 3	
	B × Kt ch	Q—K 2	Kt—K 2	B × Kt ch	
7	Q×B	P—K Kt 3	Kt—B 3	Q×B	
	Kt×P	P—Q Kt 3	B × Kt ch	O—O	
8	P—B 3 !	B—Kt 2	Q×B	P—Q Kt 4	
	P—Q 3 (b)	B—Kt 2	P—Q 3	P—K 4......R—K 1 ! (j)	
9	P—K 4	O—O	B—K 2	P×P	P—Kt 5 ? (k)
	P—K 4	Q Kt—Q 2	O—O	Kt—K 5 (h)	Kt—Kt 1
10	B—K 3	P—Q R 4	O—O	Q—Kt 2 (i)	P—Kt 3
	Q—B 2	B—K 5	Kt—K 5	P×P	Q Kt—Q 2
11	Kt—K 2	Q—Kt 3	Q—B 2	Kt×P	B—K Kt 2
	B—K 3	P—Q R 4	P—B 4	Kt×Kt	P—Q R 3
12	Q—B 2	B—K R 3	Kt—Q 2	Q×Kt	P—Q R 4
	O—O	O—O	Kt×Kt	R—K 1	P×P
13	Kt—B 3	Kt—Q 2	B×Kt	Q—Kt 2	R P×P
	K R—B 1	B—Kt 2	P²—B 5	Q—R 5	Kt—K 5
14	B—K 2+(c)	P—B 3	P×P	P—Kt 3 ±	Q—Kt 2
		P—K 4 = (e)	P×P ∓ (g)		R×R ∓ (l)

(a) 5. , B×Kt ch; 6 P×B!, Q—B 2; 7 Kt—B 3, Kt—R 3; 8 Kt—Q 4 !, O—O;
9 P—B 6, Kt P×P; 10 B—Kt 5, Kt—B 4; 11 B×Kt ±. Stahlberg—A. Steiner,
Kemeri, 1937.
(b) Or 8 ., P—Q R 4; 9 P—K 4, O—O; 10 B—B 4, Q—Kt 3; 11 R—Q 1, Kt—K 1;
12 Kt—K 2+. Bogoljuboff—Alekhine, 4th match game, 1929.
(c) Flohr—Botvinnik, 6th match game, 1933.
(d) Or 5 Q×B, Kt—K 5; 6 Q—B 2, P—Q 4; 7 P—K 3, P—Q B 4; 8 P×B P
(8 B P×P, K P×P; 9 B—Q 3, Q—R 4 ch; 10 K—B 1, O—O; 11 P×P, Kt—Q B 3
is more difficult for Black to meet. Tartakover—Nimzovitch, Kissingen, 1928), Q—R 4 ch;
9 B—Q 2, Q×B P; 10 R—B 1, Kt—Q B 3; 11 Kt—B 3, Kt×B; 12 Q×Kt, P×P;
13 B×P, Q—K 2 =. Note by Tartakover and Nimzovitch.
(e) Bogoljuboff—Nimzovitch, Kissingen, 1928 Cf. col. 67.
(f) The Zurich Variation (also known as the Milner-Barry Variation). Continuations
rarely seen are: (1) 4 ., P—Q 3; 5 B—Kt 5, Q Kt—Q 2; 6 P—K 3, P—Q Kt 3;
7 B—Q 3, B—Kt 2; 8 P—B 3, B×Kt ch; 9 Q×B, P—B 4; 10 Kt—R 3, P—K R 3;
11 B—B 4 ±. Alekhine—Nimzovitch, New York, 1927. (2) 4 ., P—Q B 4; 5 P×P,
B×Kt ch; 6 P×B, P—Q 3; 7 P—B 4, P—K 4; 8 B—Q 3, Q—K 2; 9 Kt—B 3,
Kt—B 3; 10 O—O, B—Kt 2; 11 R—Q Kt 1, O—O—O; 12 P—B 5!+. Noteboom—
Flohr, Hastings, 1929—30. 4 ., O—O transposes after 5 P—Q R 3, B×Kt ch; 6 Q×B,
Kt—B 3 into cols. 44 and 45, after 6 , P—Q 4 into col. 37.
(g) Keres—Alekhine, Dresden, 1936.
(h) Or 9 ., Kt×P; 10 Kt×Kt, P×Kt; 11 Q×P, R—K 1; 12 Q—Kt 2, Q—Q 6
(12.., Kt—K 5; 13 B—B 4, B—B 4; 14 P—B 3, P—K Kt 4; 15 B—B 1+. Flohr—
Milner-Barry, London, 1932), 13 P—K 3! (13 B—Kt 5, Kt—Kt 5; 14 P—K 3, Q—B 4;
15 B—R 4, Q—K 5; 16 O—O—O, P—Q B 4 =. Fine—Van den Bosch, Amsterdam,
1936), Q—Kt 3; 14 P—B 3, B—B 4; 15 K—B 2, B—Q 6; 16 B—K 2!+.
(i) 10 Q—K 3 is also good. P—B 4; 11 B—Kt 2, Kt×K P; 12 Kt×Kt, P×Kt;
13 P—Kt 3 (but not 13 B×P?, Q—K 2; 14 P—B 4, B—K 3; 15 P—Kt 3, B×P+.
Winter—C. H. Alexander, Hastings, 1935—36), B—K 3; 14 P—B 3, Kt—Q 3;
15 Q×K P, Q—K 2; 16 P—K 3 ±. Fine—Alexander, Margate, 1937.
(j) If 8 , Q—K 2; 9 B—Kt 2, R—K 1; 10 P—K 3 (or 10 P—Kt 5, Kt—Kt 1;
11 P—K t 3, P—Q Kt 3; 12 B—Kt 2, B—Kt 2; 13 O—O, Q Kt—Q 2; 14 P—Q R 4,
P—Q R 3; 15 B—Q R 3, R—R 2; 16 Kt—K 5+. Fine—Becker, Zandvoort, 1936),
P—K 4; 11 P×P, Kt×P; 12 Kt×Kt, P×Kt; 13 B—Q 3, B—Q 2; 14 O—O,
Q R—Q 1; 15 B—B 2 ±. Flohr—Nimzovitch, Bled, 1931.
(k) Now this is premature. 9 P—K 3, P—K 4; 10 P×P should have been played.
(l) 15 Q×R, Kt—Kt 3; 16 Q—R 2, P—Q 4!; 17 P—B 5, Kt—B 5. Lilienthal—
Rovner, 1938.

NIMZO-INDIAN DEFENCE
1 P—Q 4, Kt—K B 3 ; 2 P—Q B 4, P—K 3 ; 3 Kt—Q B 3, B—Kt 5.

	46	47	48	49	50
4	(Q—B 2) / (Kt—B 3)	....	Q—Kt 3 / P—B 4		
5	(Kt—B 3) / (P—Q 3)		P×P / Kt—B 3 (e)		
6	(P—Q R 3) / (B×Kt ch)	...B—Q 2 / O—O	Kt—B 3 (f) / Kt—K 5		
7	(Q×B) / P—Q R 4	P—Q R 3 / B×Kt	B—Q 2 / Kt×B	....	/ Kt×Q B P
8	P—KKt3 (a) / Kt—K 5	B×B / Q—K 2 (c)	Kt×Kt / P—B 4	...... B×P	Q—B 2 / P—B 4
9	Q—B 2 / P—B 4	P—K 3 / P—K 4	P—K 3 / B×P	P—K 3 (h) / P—Q Kt 3	P—K Kt 3 / O—O [(m)
10	B—Kt 2 / O—O	P—Q 5 / Kt—Kt 1	B—K 2 / O—O	O—O—O / B—Kt 2	B—Kt 2 / P—Q 3 (n)
11	O—O / P—K 4	B—Q 3 / Q Kt—Q 2	O—O—O (g) / P—Q Kt3 (h)	K Kt—K 4 / B—K 2	R—Q 1 / P—K 4
12	B—K 3 / Q—K 2	Kt—Kt 5 / P—K Kt 3 !	Kt—B 3 / B—Kt 2 (i)	Kt—Q 6 ch / B×Kt	P—Q R 3 / B×Kt
13	P×P / P×P (b)	Kt—K 4 / Kt×Kt = (d)	R—Q 2 ± (j)	R×B / Q—K 2 = (l)	B×B ± (o)

(a) 8 B—Kt 5, P—K R 3 ; 9 B× Kt, Q× B, 10 P—K 3, O—O; 11 B—K 2, P—K 4 ;
12 P×P, P×P ; 13 O—O, B—Kt 5 ; 14 P—R 3, B—R 4 ; 15 K R—Q 1, K R—K 1 =.
Lasker—Alekhine, Nottingham, 1936.

(b) 14 Kt—Q 2, Kt—B 3 ; 15 Kt—Kt 3, P—R 5 ; 16 Kt—B 1, Kt—K Kt 5 ;
17 B× Kt, P×B ; 18 P—Q Kt 4, P—B 5 !+. Becker—Glass, Vienna, 1937.

(c) Or 8.., R—K 1 ; 9 R—Q 1, Q—K 2 ; 10 P—K 3, P—K 4 ; 11 P—Q 5, Kt—Kt 1 ;
12 Kt—Q 2?, Q Kt—Q 2 ; 13 P—K 4?, Kt—R 4 ! ; 14 P—K Kt 3, P—B 4 !, 15 P×P,
P—K 5 ∓. Fine—A. Reynolds, Ostend, 1937.

(d) Euwe—Alekhine, 22nd match game, 1935.

(e) 5 , Kt—R 3 ; 6 P—Q R 3, B×P (B×Kt ch ; 7 Q×B transposes into col. 41) ;
7 Kt—B 3, P—Q Kt 3 ; 8 B—Kt 5, B—Kt 2 ; 9 P—K 3, B—K 2 =. Eliskases—
Botvinnik, Moscow, 1936.

(f) 6 B—Q 2, B×P ; 7 P—K 3, O—O ; 8 Kt—B 3, P—Q 4 ; 9 O—O—O, P×P ;
10 Q×P, Q—K 2 ; 11 B—Q 3, Kt—Q Kt 5 ; 12 B—Kt 1, P—Q Kt 3 ∓. E. Rabinovitch
—Romanovsky, Moscow, 1925.

(g) Stronger than 11 O—O, e.g., P—Q Kt 3 ; 12 Kt—B 3, B—Kt 2 ; 13 K R—Q 1,
R—B 1 ; 14 Kt—Q Kt 5?, Q—K 2 ; 15 P—Q R 3, P—Q R 3 ; 16 Kt—B 3, P—B 5 ∓.
Naegeli—Kashdan, Prague, 1931.

(h) 11.., Q—K 2 ; 12 Kt—B 3, P—Q R 3 ; 13 K—Kt 1, P—Q 3 ; 14 Kt—Q R 4,
B—R 2 ? (Q—Q B 2 is better) ; 15 Kt—Kt 6 ±. Fine—R. P Michell, Hastings, 1936-37

(i) Or 12.., B—R 3 ; 13 R—Q 2, Q—K 2 ; 14 K R—Q 1, Q R—Q 1 ; 15 P—Q R 3,
P—B 5 ; 16 Kt—K 4+. Spielmann—Colle, Carlsbad, 1929.

(j) Spielmann—P. Johner, Carlsbad, 1929.

(k) A good alternative is 9 P—K Kt 3, P—B 4 ; 10 B—Kt 2, O—O ; 11 O—O,
P—Q Kt 3 ; 12 Q—R 4, B—Kt 2 ; 13 Kt—Kt 3 ±. Spielmann—Najdorf, Warsaw,
1935.

(l) Since White cannot maintain his R at Q 6, his advantage will disappear. The
column is Euwe—Nimzovitch, Zürich, 1934.

(m) 9 P—Q R 3 (col. 51) is also good, but 9 P—K 3 is weaker : 9.., O—O ;
10 P—Q R 3 (or 10 B—K 2, P—Q Kt 3 ; 11 O—O—O, P—Q R 4 ; 12 P—Q R 3?,
P—R 5 !+. Bogoljuboff—Nimzovitch, San Remo, 1930), B×Kt ; 11 B×B, P—Q Kt 3 ;
12 P—Q Kt 4, Kt—K 5 ; 13 B—Kt 2 (if 13 B—Q 3, Kt×B ; 14 Q×Kt, B—Kt 2 ;
15 O—O, Kt—K 2 ; 16 B—K 2, Q—K 1, 17 K R—Q 1, R—Q 1 ; 18 P—Q R 4,
P—B 5 ∓. Stahlberg—Alekhine, Hamburg, 1930), B—Kt 2 ; 14 B—K 2, R—B 1 ;
15 O—O, Kt—K 2 ; 16 Q R—Q 1, Q—K 1 =. Dake—H. Steiner, Mexico City, 1934-35.

(n) Or 10 , P—Q 4 ; 11 P×P, P×P ; 12 P—Q R 3, P—Q 5 ; 13 P×B, Kt×P ;
14 Q—Q 1, B—K 3 ; 15 O—O, B—Kt 6? ; 16 Q—B 1, P×Kt ; 17 Q×P+. R. P.
Michell—Colle, Hastings, 1931.

(o) Winter—Sultan Khan, Hastings, 1931.

NIMZO-INDIAN DEFENCE
1 P—Q4, Kt—KB3; 2 P—QB4, P—K3; 3 Kt—QB3, B—Kt5.

	51	52	53	54	55
4	(Q—Kt3) (P—B4)				.....Kt—B3 (m)
5	(P×P) (Kt—B3)				Kt—B3 (n) P—QR4 (o)
6	(Kt—B3) (Kt—K5)		B×P (f)	B—Kt5 (i) P—KR3 (j)	P—QR3 P—R5
7	(B—Q2) (Kt×QBP)		B—Kt5 (g) P—KR3	B—R4 Kt—Q5 (k)	Q—B2 B×Kt ch
8	(Q—B2) (P—B4)	O—O	B×Kt Q×B	Q—R4! B×Kt ch	Q×B P—R3
9	P—QR3 B×Kt	P—QR3 (c) B×Kt	P—K3 P—QKt3	P×B Kt—B4	P—Q5 P×P
10	B×B O—O	B×B P—QR4	B—K2 B—Kt2	B×Kt Q×B	P×P Kt—QR4
11	P—QKt4 Kt—K5	P—KKt3 Q—K2 (d)	Kt—K4 Q—K2	R—B1 Q—Kt4	P—Q6 P×P
12	B—Kt2 P—QKt3	B—Kt2 P—K4	O—O O—O	Q—R3 P—QKt3?	B—B4 O—O
13	P—Kt3 (a) B—Kt2	O—O P—K5	QR—Q1 KR—Q1	Kt—B3! Q—K2	R—Q1 R—K1
14	R—B1 ± (b)	Kt—Q2 ± (e)	P—QR3 QR-B1 = (h)	P-KKt4!+ (l)	P—K3 Kt-K5 = (p)

(a) On 13 P—KKt4!, Kt×BP! is the only good defence but forces White to take a draw by 14 K×Kt, P×P; 15 R—KKt1, Q—R5 ch; 16 K—K3, Q—R3 ch; 17 K--B2, Q—R5 ch; 18 K—K3, etc. If, however, 17 K—Q3, P—Q4; 18 Q—Q2! Q—Kt3 ch; 19 K—B3, Q—K5; 20 Q—Q3, P×Kt, 21 P×QP, KP×P; 22 Q×Q, P×Q; 23 K—Q2, P—Kt3+. Eglı—Stalda, correspondence, 1933.

(b) Euwe—Mulder, Amsterdam, 1933.

(c) If at once 9 P—KKt3?, P—Q4!; 10 P×P, P×P; 11 P—QR3, P—Q5!; 12 P×B, Kt×P; 13 Q—Q1, Q—K2!+. Reinfeld—H. Steiner, Minneapolis, 1932.

(d) Or 11.., P—R5; 12 B—Kt2, P—QKt3; 13 O—O, B—Kt2; 14 QR—Q1, Kt—R4, 15 B—Kt4, B—K5; 16 Q—B3 ±. Stahlberg—Nimzovitch, 5th match game, 1934.

(e) 14 ., P—Q3; 15 P—QKt4!. Stahlberg—Nimzovitch, 3rd match game, 1934.

(f) Alternatives are · (1) 6. , Q—R4; 7 B—Q2, Q×BP; 8 P—QR3 (8 R—B1?, Kt—QR4; 9 Q—B2, Q×P!; 10 Kt—QR4, Kt×B'!; 11 Kt×Q, Kt—K5 dis.ch; 12 Kt—Q2, B×Kt ch; 13 K—Q1, B×R; 14 Kt×Kt, Kt×Kt; 15 Q×Kt, B×P ∓. Rojahn—Takacs, correspondence, 1931), B×Kt; 9 B×B, Kt—QR4, 10 B×Kt, Q×B ch; 11 Q—Kt4, Q—B2 ∓. Aguilera—Capablanca, Barcelona, 1929. (2) 6. O—O; 7 B—Kt5, P—KR3; 8 B—R4 (8 B×Kt, Q×B; 9 P—K3, P—QR4; 10 Q—B2, P—R5; 11 P—QR3, B×Kt ch=. Bogoljuboff—Förder, Swinemünde, 1931), P—KKt4; 9 B—Kt3, Kt—K5, 10 P—K3, Q—R4; 11 R—B1, P—B4, with a complicated position. Winter—Capablanca, 1930.

(g) 7 P—K3, O—O, 8 B—Q2, P—QKt3; 9 O—O, B—Kt2; 10 P—QR3, Q—K2; 11 R—Q1, K R—Q1; 12 B—Q2, P—Q4 ∓. Kashdan—Fine, New York, 1936.

(h) Bogoljuboff—Alekhine, 2nd match game, 1929.

(i) Botvinnik's line.

(j) If 6. , Q—R4; 7 B×Kt, P×B; 8 Kt—B3, Q×BP; 9 P—QR3, B—R4; 10 P—K4, Botvinnik—Miassoyedoff, Leningrad, 1932. On 6., B×Kt ch; 7 Q×B (7 P×B, as in col. 41, note (a) is also playable), Kt—K5!; 8 Q×P is bad, as A. F. Mackenzie's analysis in B.C.M., May, 1938, shows : Q×B; e.g., 9 Q×R ch K—K2; 10 Kt—B3, Q×BP; 11 P—K3, Q—Kt5 ch; 12 K—K2, Q×BP ch; K—Q1, Q—Q4 ch; 14 K—B1, Q—B4 ch; 15 K—Kt1, Kt—Kt5; 16 B—Q3, Kt×B++. However, 8 B×Q, Kt×Q; 9 B—R4 (or even 9 P×Kt), Kt—K5; 10 O—O—O gives White a minimum advantage.

Notes ctd. on p. 216

NIMZO-INDIAN DEFENCE

1 P—Q4, Kt—KB3; 2 P—QB4, P—K3; 3 Kt—QB3, B—Kt5.

	56	57	58	59	60
4	P—K3 (a)				
	P—Q4	P—Q Kt3	O—O	P—B4	B×Kt ch
5	B—Q3 (b)	Kt—K2 (h)	Kt—K2 (k)	Kt—K2 (p)	P×B
	O—O	O—O	P—Q4	P×P	P—Q3
6	Kt—K2 (c)	P—Q R3	P—Q R3	P×P	B—Q3
	P—B4 (d)	B—K2	B—K2	P—Q4 (q)	O—O
7	O—O	Kt—B4 (i)	P×P (l)	P—B5 (r)	P—K4
	Kt—B3 (e)	B—Kt2	P×P (m)	O—O	P—K4
8	P×QP! (f)	B—K2	Kt—Kt3	P—Q R3	Kt—K2
	KP×P	P—Q3	P—B4	B×Kt ch	R—K1
9	P×P	B—B3	B—Q3 (n)	Kt×B	P—B3
	B×P	P—B3	Kt—B3	P—Q Kt3	P—Q Kt3
10	P—Q R3	O—O	O—O	P—Q Kt4	O—O
	B—K3	P—Q4	P—K Kt3?	P×P	Kt—B3
11	P Q Kt4	P—Q Kt3	P×P	Q P×P	B—K3
	B Kt3	Q Kt—Q2	B×P	P—K4	B—R3
12	Kt—R4	B—Kt2	P—Kt4	B—K Kt5	Kt—Kt3
	B—B2	R—B1	B—Q3	B—Kt2	Kt—Q R4
13	Kt—B5	R—B1	P—Kt5	Kt—Kt5	Q—K2
	P—Q Kt3	B—Q3	Kt—K4	P—Q5	P—B4
14	Kt×B ± (g)	P×P	B—K2 ± (o)	Kt-Q6 ± (s)	P—Q5 ± (t)
		BP×P = (j)			

(a) The Rubinstein Variation.

(b) If 5 Kt—K2?, P×P!; 6 P—Q R3, B—R4 ; 7 Q—R4 ch, P—B3, 8 Q×P, O—O; 9 Kt—Kt3, Q Kt—Q2; 10 P—B4, Kt—Kt3; 11 Q—Q3, P—B4! ∓. Euwe—Capablanca, 4th match game, 1931. 5 P—Q R3, B×Kt ch; 6 P×B, P—B4; 7 P×QP, KP×P; 8 B—Q3, O—O; 9 Kt—K2, P—Q Kt3; 10 O—O, B—R3; 11 B×B. Botvinnik—Capablanca, Avro, 1938.

(c) If 6 Kt—B3, P×P!; 7 B×P, P—B4, 8 O—O, Kt—B3; 9 P—Q R3, B—R4!; 10 Q—Q3, P—Q R3; 11 Kt—K4, P—Q Kt4 ∓. Landau—A. Steiner, Kemeri, 1937. 6 ., P—B4 is also possible here; after 7 O—O, P×QP; 8 KP×P, P×P; 9 B×P the position is almost the same as that in the Queen's Gambit Accepted, col. 12.

(d) Or 6 ., P×P; 7 B×P, P—K4!. Bogoljuboff—Colle, Bled, 1931. Continued 8 O—O, P×P; 9 Kt×P, P—Q R3; 10 Q—B2, P—Q Kt4?; 11 B—K2, P—B4 =.

(e) Stronger is 7 ., P×QP; 8 KP×P, etc. Cp next note.

(f) 8 P—Q R3, P×QP!; 9 KP×P, P×P; 10 B×P, B—Q3· 11 P—K R3, P—K R3!; 12 Q—Q3, P—R3; 13 B—Kt3, Q—B2 ∓. Reshevsky—Tartakover Kemeri, 1937.

(g) Landau—Kmoch, Amsterdam, 1936.

(h) 5 B—Q3, B—Kt2; 6 P—B3 (6 Kt—K2?, B×P; 7 R—K Kt1, B—K5!; 8 B×B, Kt×B; 9 R×P, Kt×P!+), P—B4; 7 Kt—K2, Kt—B3; 8 O—O, P×P; 9 P×P, P—Q4; 10 P×P, Kt×P =. Capablanca—Kan, Moscow, 1936.

(i) 7 P—Q5, P—Q Kt4?, 8 Q P×P, B P×P; 9 Kt×P, B—Kt2; 10 Kt—Kt2; P—Q R3; 11 Kt—Q4, Kt—B3; 12 Kt—B3+. Landau—List, Ostend, 1937.

(j) Eliskases—Lilienthal, Moscow, 1936.

(k) 5 Kt—B3, P—Q Kt3, 6 B—Q3, B—Kt2; 7 O—O, B×Q Kt; 8 P×B, B—K5 ; 9 B×B, Kt×B; 10 Q—B2, P—K B4. Reshevsky—Alekhine, Avro, 1938. Or 5 B—Q3, P—Q3; 6 K Kt—K2, P—K4; 7 O—O, R—K1; 8 Kt—Kt3, B—B4; 9 P×B, P—B4; 10 Q—B2, P—K R3; 11 P—Q5. Reshevsky—Keres in a later round.

(l) Or 7 Kt—B4, P—B3; 8 P×P, KP×P (8 ., Kt×P?; 9 B—Q3, Kt—Q2, 10 O—O, Kt×K Kt; 11 P×Kt, Kt—B3; 12 B—K3, Q—B2; 13 Q—B3 ± Petrov—Eliskases,Semmering-Baden,1937); 9 B—Q3,R—K1; 10 O—O, Q Kt—Q2= Rubinstein—Yates, Kissingen, 1928.

Notes ctd. on p. 217

NIMZO-INDIAN DEFENCE

1 P—Q 4, Kt—K B 3; 2 P—Q B 4, P—K 3; 3 Kt—Q B 3, B—Kt 5.

	61	62	63	64	65
4	P—Q R 3 (a)				P—K Kt 3
	B × Kt ch				P—Q 4 (q)
5	P × B				B—Kt 2
	P—B 4 !	P—Q Kt 3	P—Q 3	O—O (n)	O—O
6	P—B 3 (b)	P—B 3	P—B 3 (k)	P—K 3 (o)	Kt—B 3
	P—Q 4	P—Q 4	P—B 4 (l)	P—Q 4	P—B 4
7	P—K 3	B—Kt 5	P—K 4	B—Q 3	B P × P
	O—O (c)	B—R 3 (g)	Kt—B 3	P—B 4	Kt × P
8	B P × P (d)	P—K 4 !	B—K 3	P × Q P	B—Q 2
	Kt × P ! (e)	P—K R 3	P—Q Kt 3	Q × P !	Kt—Q B 3
9	B—Q 2	B—R 4	B—Q 3	Q—B 3	P—Q R 3
	Kt—Q B 3	B × P (h)	P—K 4	Q—Q 1 !	Kt × Kt
10	B—Q 3	B × B	Kt—K 2	Q—K 2	P × Kt
	P × P	P × B	Kt—Q R 4	Q—B 2 !	B—R 4
11	B P × P	Q—R 4 ch	B—Kt 5	B—Kt 2	O—O
	P—K 4 !	Q—Q 2	P—K R 3	P—K 4	P × P
12	P × P	Q × B P	B—R 4	P × K P	P × P
	Q Kt × P	Q—B 3 (i)	P—K Kt 4	Q × P	B × B
13	B—K 4	Q—Q 3 + (j)	B—B 2	P—Q B 4	Q × B
	Kt—QB 5 ∓ (f)		Kt-R 4 = (m)	Q—K 2 = (p)	Q—K 2 (r)

(a) The Sämisch Variation.
(b) 6 Q—B 2, Kt—B 3; 7 Kt—B 3, P—Q 4?; 8 P—K 3, O—O; 9 B P × P, K P × P; 10 P × P, Q—R 4; 11 B—Q 3, Kt—K 5; 12 O—O, Q × P (B 4); 13 P—Q R 4± Alekhine and Monosson—Flohr and Reilly, Nice, 1931. 6 P—K 3, O—O; 7 B—Q 3, Kt—B 3; 8 Kt—K 2, P—Q 3; 9 Kt—Kt 3, P—Q Kt 3; 10 B—K 2, B—R 3; 11 P—K 4, R—B 1; 12 R—Q B 1, P × P (perhaps P—K 4 is stronger). Botvinnik—Keres, Avro, 1938.
(c) 7.., Kt—B 3; 8 P × Q P, K P × P, 9 B—Q 3, Kt—K 2; 10 Kt—K 2, B—B 4; 11 O—O, O—O; 12 B × B, Kt × B; 13 P—K 4 ! ±. Euwe—Bogoljuboff, Zurich, 1934.
(d) Necessary, for if 8 B—Q 3, Q—B 2 !; 9 P × Q P, B P × P !; 10 Q—B 2, P × K P; 11 P × P, B × P; 12 B × K P, B—B 5 !+. Fine—L. Steiner, Lodz, 1935.
(e) 8 , K P × P is much weaker: 9 B—Q 3, Kt—B 3 (or 9 ., P—Q Kt 3; 10 Kt—K 2, B—R 3; 11 O—O, B × B; 12 Q × B, Kt—B 3; 13 P—K 4 ! ±. Euwe—Van den Bosch, 3rd match game, 1934); 10 Kt—K 2, R—K 1; 11 O—O, P—Q R 3 (11 , B—Q 2; 12 Kt—Kt 3, Q—B 1; 13 B—Q 2, K—R 1; 14 R—B 1, Kt—Q R 4; 15 P—K 4 !+. Lilienthal—Eliskases, Ujpest, 1934); 12 Q—K 1 ! ±. Lilienthal—Ragosin, Moscow, 1935.
(f) Lilienthal—Botvinnik, Moscow, 1935.
(g) 7.., B—Kt 2; 8 P—K 3, Q Kt—Q 2; 9 B—Q 3, P—K R 3; 10 B—R 4, P—B 4; 11 Kt—K 2, R—Q B 1; 12 B P × P, K P × P; 13 O—O+. Euwe—Kan, Leningrad, 1934.
(h) 9.., P × K P; 10 P × P, P—K Kt 4; 11 B—Kt 3, Kt × P; 12 B—K 5 gives White an excellent attack, but it is doubtful whether Black's position is then any worse than in the column continuation.
(i) Or 12 , Kt—B 3; 13 Kt—K 2, Kt—Q R 4; 14 Q—Q 3, Q—B 3; 15 O—O, O—O—O (Alekhine—Eliskases, Hastings, 1933–34); 16 P—K 5 !+.
(j) Lilienthal—Capablanca, Hastings, 1934–35.
(k) 6 Q—B 2, O—O, 7 P—K 4, P—K 4; 8 B—Q 3, P—B 4; 9 Kt—K 2, Kt—B 3; 10 P—Q 5, Kt—K 2?; 11 P—B 3 ±. Capablanca—Ragosin, Moscow, 1935.
(l) 6 , O—O; 7 P—K 4, P—K 4; 8 B—Q 3, Kt—B 3; 9 Kt—K 2, Kt—Q 2; 10 O—O, P—Q Kt 3; 11 B—K 3, B—R 3; 12 Kt—Kt 3, Kt—Q R 4, 13 Q—K 2 ±. Samisch—Grunfeld, Carlsbad, 1929.
(m) Euwe—Van Scheltinga, Amsterdam, 1936.

Notes ctd. on p. 217

1 P—Q4, Kt—KB3; 2 P—QB4, P—K3; 3 Kt—QB3.

NIMZO-INDIAN DEFENCE

	66	67	68	69	70
3	B—Kt5				P—Q Kt 3
4	Kt—B 3			B—Q 2 (*i*)	P—K 4
	B × Kt ch		P—Q Kt3 (*e*)	O—O	P—B 4 (*m*)
5	P × B		B—Kt 5 (*f*)	P—K 3 (*j*)	P—Q 5
	P—Q Kt3 (*a*)		P—K R 3 (*g*)	P—Q 4 (*k*)	P—Q 3
6	B—Kt 5	P—Kt 3	B × Kt	Kt—B 3	B—Q 3
	B—Kt 2	B—Kt 2	B × Kt ch	P—B 4	Q Kt—Q 2
7	Kt—Q 2	B—Kt 2	P × B	P—Q R 3	P—B 4
	P—Q 3	O—O	Q × B	B × Kt	P × P
8	P—B 3	O—O	P—K 4	B × B	B P × P
	P—K 4	R—K 1	B—Kt 2	Kt—K 5	P—Q R 3
9	P—K 4	R—K 1	B—Q 3	R—B 1	Kt—B 3
	Kt—B 3	P—Q 3	P—Q 3	Kt × B	Q—B 2
10	Kt—Kt 3	Q—B 2	O—O	R × Kt	O—O
	P—K R 3	B—K 5	P—K 4	P × Q P	B—Kt 2
11	B—K 3	Q—Kt 3	P—B 5	K P × P	Q—K 2
	Kt—K 2 (*b*)	Kt—B 3	O—O	Kt—B 3	B—K 2
12	B—Q 3	B—B 1	R—Kt 1	B—K 2	B—Q 2
	Kt—R 4	P—K 4	R—Q 1	P × P	P—Q Kt 4
13	Q—Q 2	P × P	Q—B 2	B × P	Q R—Q 1
	Kt—Kt 3	Kt × P	Kt—Q 2	Q—B 3	Kt—Kt 3
14	P—Kt3 ± (*c*)	Kt × Kt	P × Q P	O—O	K—R 1 ± (*n*)
		R × Kt ∓ (*d*)	P × P = (*h*)	R—Q 1 = (*l*)	

(*a*) 5 ., P—Q 3; 6 Q—B 2, Q—K 2; 7 B—R 3, P—B 4; 8 P—Kt 3, P—Q Kt 3; 9 B—Kt 2, B—Kt 2; 10 O—O, O—O; 11 Kt—R 4, B × B; 12 K × B?, Q—Kt 2 ch+. Mattison—Nimzovitch, Carlsbad, 1929. Nimzovitch recommended 7 P—K 4 here.

(*b*) Or 11 , O—O; 12 B—Q 3, Q—K 2, 13 O—O, Kt—Q 1; 14 Q—Q 2, Kt—K 3. Winter—Fine, Lodz, 1935. 15 P—Kt 3 is now best.

(*c*) Samisch—Stahlberg, Helsingfors, 1935.

(*d*) Bogoljuboff—Nimzovitch, Carlsbad, 1929.

(*e*) If 4 , Kt—K 5?; 5 Q—B 2, P—Q 4; 6 P—K 3, P—Q B 4; 7 B—Q 3, Kt—K B 3 (7.., Q—R 4; 8 O—O!, B × Kt; 9 P × B, Kt—K B 3; 10 R—Kt 1, Q Kt—Q 2; 11 Kt—K 5+. Keres—List, Ostend, 1937); 8 P × Q P, K P × P, 9 P × P, B × P; 10 O—O, Kt—B 3; 11 P—K 4!, B—K 2!; 12 P—K 5, Kt—K Kt 5; 13 R—K 1+. Euwe—Alekhine, 19th match game, 1937. A playable alternative is 4 ., P—B 4; 5 P—K Kt 3, Kt—K 5; 6 B—Q 2, B × Kt; 7 Q × Kt, Q—R 4, 8 B—Kt 2, O—O; 9 O—O, P × P; 10 Kt × P, Kt—B 3; 11 K R—B 1, Q—B 4 =. Rubinstein—Maróczy, London, 1922.

(*f*) Or 5 P—K 3, O—O; 6 B—Q 3, P—Q 4; 7 O—O, B—Kt 2; 8 ṙ × P, P × P; 9 P—Q R 3, B—K 2; 10 P—Q Kt 4, Q Kt—Q 2; 11 R—Kt 1, P—Q R 3; 12 Kt—K 5, Kt × Kt; 13 P × Kt, Kt—Q 2; 14 P—B 4, R—K 1. Bogoljuboff—Euwe, match, 1929.

(*g*) 5 , B × Kt ch, 6 P × B, B—Kt 2; 7 P—K 3, P—Q 3, 8 B—Q 3, Q Kt—Q 2; 9 O—O, Q—K 2 = If now 10 Kt—Q 2, P—K R 3; 11 B—R 4, P—K Kt 4; 12 B—Kt 3, O—O—O ∓. Bogoljuboff—Monticelli, San Remo, 1930.

(*h*) Euwe—Alekhine, 27th match game, 1937.

(*i*) 4 B—Kt 5, P—K R 3; 5 B—R 4 (5 B × Kt, B × Kt ch; 6 P × B, Q × B is best), P—B 4; 6 P—K 3, Q—R 4; 7 Q—Kt 3, Kt—K 5; 8 R—B 1, P × P; 9 P × P, Kt—Q B 3 ∓. Réti—Marshall, Brunn, 1928.

(*j*) Or 5 Kt—B 3, P—Q Kt 3; 6 P—K 3, B × Kt (if 6.., B—Kt 2; 7 B—Q 3, B × Q Kt; 8 B × B, Kt—K 5; 9 B × Kt, B × B; 10 Kt—Q 2, B × P?; 11 R—K Kt 1+. Nimzovitch); 7 B × B, Kt—K 5, 8 Q—B 2, B—Kt 2; 9 O—O—O P—K B 4; 10 Kt—K 5, B × Kt, Q × Kt, P—Q 3; 13 Kt—Q 3, Kt—Q 2, 14 K—Kt 1, Q R—Q 1 ∓. Ahues—Nimzovitch, Berlin, 1927.

(*k*) If 5 , P—Q Kt 3?; 6 Q—B 3, P—Q 4; 7 B—Q 3, B—Kt 2; 8 Kt—R 3 ±.

(*l*) Alekhine—Kmoch, San Remo, 1930.

Notes ctd. on p. 217

QUEEN'S INDIAN DEFENCE

1 P—Q 4, Kt—K B 3 , 2 P—Q B 4, P—K 3 ; 3 Kt—K B 3, P—Q Kt 3 ;
4 P—K Kt 3, B—Kt 2 ; 5 B—Kt 2, B—K 2 ; 6 O—O, O—O.

	71	72	73	74	75
7	Kt—B 3	......	......	Q—B 2	P—Kt 3 (m)
	Kt—K 5	P—Q 4		P—B 4 (j)	P—Q 4 (n)
8	Q—B 2 (a)	Kt—K 5	....P×P	P×P	Kt—K 5
	Kt×Kt (b)	P—B 3 (e)	P×P	P×P ! (k)	P—B 4
9	Q×Kt (c)	P—K 4 (f)	Q—B 2	Kt—B 3	P×B P
	B—K 5	P×B P	Q Kt—Q 2	Kt—B 3	Kt P×P
10	R—Q 1	Kt×P (B 4)	R—Q 1	R—Q 1	P×P
	P—Q 3	B—R 3	R—K 1	Q—Kt 1	P×P
11	Kt—K 1	P—Kt 3	B—B 4	P—Kt 3	Kt—B 3
	B×B	P—Q Kt 4	P—B 3	P—Q 3	Q Kt—Q 2
12	Kt×B	Kt—K 5	Q R—B 1	B—Kt 2	Kt—Q 3
	Kt—Q 2	P—Kt 5	Kt—B 1	P—K R 3	Kt—Kt 3
13	P—Kt 3	Kt—K 2	B—R 3	P—K 3	P—Q R 4
	P—Q B 3	K Kt—Q 2 (g)	Kt—Kt 3	K R—Q 1	P—Q R 4
14	P—K 4	Kt—Q B 4	B—Kt 5	Q R—B 1	B—R 3
	Kt—B 3	Kt—Kt 3	P—K R 3	P—Q R 3	R—B 1
15	Q—B 2	Q—B 2 ± (h)	B—K 3	Q—K 2	Kt—Kt 5
	P—Q 4 (d)		B—Q 3 = (i)	Q—B 2 = (l)	Kt-K5 = (o)

(a) The older line 8 Kt×Kt, B×Kt; 9 B—B 4, P—Q 3; 10 Q—Q 2, Kt—Q 2, 11 K R—Q 1, P—Q R 4?; 12 Q R—B 1, Q—K 1; 13 Kt—K 1, B×B; 14 Kt×B, P—K B 4 (Rubinstein—Samisch, Marienbad, 1925) may be better.

(b) 8 ., P—Q 4; 9 P×P, Kt×Kt; 10 P×Kt, P×P; 11 Kt—K 5, Q—B 1; 12 P—Q B 4, P×P; 13 B×B, Q×B; 14 Q×P, P—Q B 4 =. Tartakover—Alekhine, Baden-Baden, 1925.

(c) 9 P×Kt!, Q—B 1 (9 , P—Q 3, 10 P—K 4, Kt—Q 2; 11 B—K 3, P—K B 4; 12 P—Q 5 ! ±. Pirc—Romanovsky, Moscow, 1935); 10 P—K 4, Kt—B 3; 11 Kt—Q 2, P—K 4!; 12 Kt—Kt 3, B—R 3; 13 Q—K 2, R—Kt 1 =. Pirc—Kan, Moscow, 1935.

(d) Reshevsky—Eliskases, Semmering-Baden, 1937. White controls more space but Black's position is quite solid.

(e) Or 8.., Q Kt—Q 2; 9 P×P, Kt×Kt?; 10 P—Q 6!, B×B; 11 P×B, Q×K P; 12 P×Kt, B×R; 13 P×Kt, Q×P; 14 Q×B +. Bogoljuboff—Nimzovitch, Carlsbad, 1923. Or here 9 , P×P; 10 Q—R 4, Kt—Kt 1 ±. Clausen—Alekhine, 1935. 9.., Kt×P is the only playable reply.

(f) Best. Alternatives are: (1) 9 P×P, B P×P; 10 B—B 4, P—Q R 3; 11 R—B 1, P—Q Kt 4; 12 Q—Kt 3, Kt—B 3; 13 Kt×Kt, B×Kt; 14 P—K R 3, Q—Q 2; 15 K—R 2, Kt—R 4; 16 B—Q 2, P—B 4 ∓. Sámisch—Nimzovitch, Carlsbad, 1923 (the immortal Zugzwang game). (2) 9 P—Kt 3, Q Kt—Q 2; 10 B—Kt 2, R—B 1, 11 P—K 4, Kt×Kt, 12 P×Kt, Kt×P; 13 Kt×Kt, P×Kt, 14 B×P, Q×Q; 15 R×Q, R—B 2 =. Vajda—Grunfeld, Kecskemét, 1927.

(g) 13 ., B×Kt; 14 Q×B, Q×P; 15 B—Kt 2 gives White a strong attack.

(h) Kmoch—Romanovsky, Leningrad, 1934.

(i) Samychovsky—Botvinnik, Moscow, 1931.

(j) Another satisfactory line is 7 ., Kt—B 3; 8 Kt—B 3, P—Q 4; 9 P×P, Kt—Q Kt 5; 10 Q—Kt 3, Q Kt×Q P; 11 R—Q 1, Q—B 1; 12 B—Kt 5, Kt×Kt; 13 Q×Kt, P—B 4; 14 Q—R 3, Kt—K 1. Sámisch—Grünfeld, Berlin, 1926.

(k) Better than 8.., B×P; 9 Kt—B 3, B—K 2; 10 P—K 4, P—Q 3; 11 P—Kt 3, P—Q R 3; 12 B—Kt 2, Q—B 2; 13 Q R—B 1, Q Kt—Q 2; 14 K R—K 1, Q R—B 1; 15 Q—K 2 +. Vidmar—Kmoch, San Remo, 1930.

(l) Grünfeld—Eliskases, Vienna, 1935.

(m) 7 R—K 1, P—Q 4; 8 Kt—B 3, Q Kt—Q 2; 9 Kt—K 5, Kt—K 5; 10 P×P, Kt×Q Kt; 11 P×Kt, Kt×Kt; 12 P—Q 6!, B×B; 13 P×B, Q×P; 14 K×B, Kt—B3=. Keres—Botvinnik, Avro, 1938.

(n) Weaker is 7 ., Q—B 1; 8 Kt—B 3, P—Q 4; 9 P×P, Kt×Kt; 10 B—Kt 2, P—Q B 4; 11 R—B 1, Kt×Kt?; 12 B×Kt, R—Q 1; 13 Q—Q 2, B—Q 4?; 14 Q—B 4!, Q—Kt 2; 15 P×P +. Alekhine and Monosson—Stoltz and Reilly, Nice, 1931. However, 7.., P—B 4 is excellent: 8 B—Kt 2 (if 8 P—Q 5, P×P, 9 Kt—R 4, Kt—K 5! ∓ ⋅ ⋅⋅ P, 9 Kt×P, B×B; 10 K×B, P—Q 4! =. Kmoch—Van Scheltinga, Amsterdam, 1936.

(, ...e— ..lekhine, 23rd match game, 1937.

QUEEN'S INDIAN DEFENCE

1 P—Q 4, Kt—K B 3 ; 2 P—Q B 4, P—K 3 ; 3 Kt—K B 3, P—Q Kt 3 ;
4 P—K Kt 3, B—Kt 2 ; 5 B—Kt 2, B—Kt 5 ch.

	76	77	78	79	80
0	B—Q 2............			........Q Kt—Q 2	
	B × B ch (a)............			Q—K 2	O—O (n)
7	Q × B............		Q Kt × B	O—O	P—Q R 3 (o)
	O—O (b)		O—O (i)	B × B	B—K 2
8	Kt—B 3 (c)		Q—B 2	Q × B	O—O
	Kt—K 5....P—Q 3		P—Q 3 (j)	O—O (l)	P—Q 4
9	Q—B 2	Q—B 2	O—O	R—K 1	P—Q Kt 4
	Kt × Kt (d)	Q—K 2 (f)	P—B 4	P—Q 4	P—B 4 (p)
10	Kt—Kt 5	O—O	K R—Q 1	Kt—K 5	Kt P × P
	Kt—K 5	P—B 4 (g)	Q—B 2	Kt—K 5	Kt P × P
11	B × Kt	Q R—Q 1	P—Q R 3	Q—B 2	Q P × P
	B × B	P × P	Kt—B 3	P—K B 3	B × P
12	Q × B	Kt × P	Q—B 3	P × P	B—Kt 2
	Q × Kt	B × B	Q R—Q 1	P × P	Q Kt—Q 2
13	Q × R	K × B	Q R—B 1	Kt—Q 3	Kt—K 5
	Kt—B 3	R—B 1	P—Q R 4	Kt—Q B 3	Kt × Kt
14	Q—Kt 7+ (e)	Q—Q 3 ± (h)	P—K 3	Q—R 4 ± (m)	B × Kt
			K R—K 1 = (k)		Kt—Kt 5 ∓
					(q)

(a) 6 ., B—K 2; 7 Kt—B 3 Kt—K 5; 8 O—O, O—O; 9 P—Q 5, Kt × B (Euwe—Alekhine, 21st match game, 1937); and here 10 Kt × Kt, Q—B 1; 11 P—K 4, P—Q 3; 12 P—B 4, Kt—Q 2; 13 B—R 3 ± was possible.

(b) 7 , P—Q 3; 8 Kt—B 3, Kt—K 5?; 9 Q—B 4!, Kt × Kt (Kt—K B 3); 10 Kt—Kt 5!, P—K B 3; 11 B × B, P × Kt; 12 Q—K 3, Kt—Q 2; 13 Q × P ch, K—B 1; 14 B × R, Q × B; 15 P—B 3, Resigns. Becker—Fuss, Vienna, 1933.

(c) 8 O—O, P—Q 3; 9 Kt—B 3, Kt—K 5; 10 Q—B 2, Kt × Kt; 11 Q × Kt (if now 11 Kt—Kt 5 ?, Kt × P ch +), Kt—Q 2; 12 Q R—Q 1, Q—K 2; 13 K R—K 1, P—K B 4; 14 Kt—R 4, B × B =. Vidmar—Alekhine, New York, 1927.

(d) A risky venture. But if 9 , P—K B 4; 10 Kt—K 5!, P—Q 4; 11 P × P, P × P, 12 O—O, Kt—Q 2; 13 P—B 4, Q Kt—B 3; 14 Q R—B 1 +. Euwe—Flohr, 2nd match game, 1932.

(e) 14 , Kt × P; 15 O—O! (15 R—Q 1, P—Q B 4!—better than 15.., Q—K 4— 16 P—K 3, Kt—B 7 ch; 1⁷ K—Q 2, Q—B 4; 18 Q—Kt 2, Kt—Kt 5; 19 P—K 4, Q—B 3 =. Euwe—Capablanca, 10th match game, 1932), Kt × P ch; 16 K—Kt 2, P—K B 4; 17 P—B 4, and White should win.

(f) 9 , Q Kt—Q 2; 10 O—O, Q—B 1; 11 P—K 4, P—Q R 3; 12 K R—K 1, P—K R 3; 13 P—Kt 3, Kt R 2; 14 Q R—Q 1, R—Kt 1; 15 Kt—K R 4, Q—Q 1; 16 P—B 4 +. Reshevsky—Sir G. A. Thomas, Hastings, 1937-38.

(g) After 10 , Q Kt—Q 2; 11 P—K 4, Q R—B 1, 12 K R—K 1, P—K 4; 13 O R—Q 1, P—B 3; 14 Q—R 4, R—B 2; 15 Q—R 3, R—K 1; 16 P—Kt 3, P—Kt 3 (Reshevsky—Keres. Semmering-Baden, 1937) Black's position, though cramped, is by no means devoid of counter-chances.

(h) Euwe—Reshevsky, Nottingham, 1936.

(i) Or 7 , P—B 4; 8 P × P, P × P; 9 O—O, Q—B 2; 10 Q—B 2, O—O; 11 Q R—Q 1, P—K R 3; 12 P—Q R 3, Kt—B 3. Bogoljuboff—Nimzovitch, Berlin, 1927.

(j) 8. , P—B 4; 9 P—K 4, P—Q 3; 10 O—O, Kt—B 3; 11 P—Q 5, Kt—Q 5; 12 Kt × Kt, P × Kt; 13 P—K R 3, P—K 4; 14 P—B 4. Sacconi—Colle, Meran, 1926. White has the same line of play at his disposal on the next move.

(k) Colle—Vidmar, Hastings, 1926.

(l) 8 , P—Q 3; 9 Q—B 2, B—K 5; 10 Q—Kt 3, B—Kt 2; 11 Kt—B 3, Q Kt—Q 2; 12 Q—B 2, R—Q B 1; 13 P—K 4 ±. Fine—Sir G. A. Thomas, Nottingham, 1936.

(m) Euwe—Spielmann, match, 1932.

(n) 6.., Kt—K 5; 7 O—O, Kt × Kt; 8 B × Kt, B × B; 9 Q × B, P—Q 3; 10 K R—Q 1 ±. Réti—Capablanca, Kissingen, 1928.

(o) 7 O—O, K B × Kt ?, 8 Q × B, P—Q 3; 9 P—Kt 3, Q Kt—Q 2; 10 B—Kt 2, R—Kt 1; 11 Q R—Q 1 ±. Alekhine—Alexander, Nottingham, 1936.

(p) Best. After 9 ., P—Q R 4; 10 P—Kt 5 Black has a cramped game. Alekhine—Colle, Scarborough, 1926.

(q) Rubinstein—Alekhine, Semmering, 1926.

QUEEN'S INDIAN DEFENCE
1 P—Q 4, Kt—K B 3 ; 2 P—Q B 4, P—K 3 ; 3 Kt—K B 3, P—Q Kt 3.

	81	82	83	84	85
4	(P—K Kt 3) (B—Kt 2)				Kt—B 3 B—Kt 2
5	(B—Kt 2) P—B 4		P—Q 4	Q—B 1 (j)	P—Q R 3 B—K 2
6	P—Q 5 (a) P×P		P×P Kt×P (g)	O—O P—B 4	B—B 4 O—O
7	Kt—R 4 (b) Q—B 2	P—Kt 3 (d)	O—O Kt—Q 2	P—Kt 3 (k) P×P	Q—B 2 Kt—R 4 (m)
8	P×P P—Q 3	Kt—Q B 3 B—Kt 2	P—K 4 (h) K Kt—B 3	B—Kt 2 B—K 2	B—Q 2 P—K B 4
9	O—O Q Kt—Q 2	O—O O—O	P—K 5 Kt—Q 4	Kt×P B×B	P—K 3 P—Q 3
10	Kt—Q B 3 P—Q R 3	B—Kt 5 Kt—B 3 (e)	Kt—Kt 5 ! B—K 2	K×B P—Q 4	B—Q 3 P—Kt 3
11	P—K 4 P—Kt 3	Kt×Q P P—K R 3	Q—R 5 P—Kt 3	P×P Kt×P	P—K 4 Q Kt—Q 2
12	P—B 4 O—O—O	Kt×Kt ch B×Kt	Q—R 6 B—K B 1	P—K 4 Kt—K B 3	O—O- O Q Kt—B 3
13	B—K 3 B—Kt 2 (c)	B×B ± (f)	Q—R 3 ± (i)	Kt—Q 2 = (l)	P×P ± (n)

(a) 6 O—O is also a promising line : 6. , P×P; 7 Kt×P, B×B; 8 K×B, P—Q 4; 9 Q—R 4 ch, Q—Q 2; 10 Kt—Kt 5, Kt—B 3; 11 P×P, P×P; 12 B—B 4 ±. Capablanca—Alekhine, 3rd match game, 1927. Or here 8.., B—K 2; 9 Kt—Q B 3, O—O; 10 P—K 4, Q—B 1; 11 P—Kt 3, Q—Kt 2; 12 P—B 3 ±. Capablanca—Vidmar, New York, 1927. 6 P×P is a weaker alternative : 6.., P×P (or 6 , B×P; 7 Kt—B 3, Kt—K 5! =); 7 O—O, Q—B 2; 8 Kt—B 3, P—Q R 3; 9 R—K 1, Kt—K 5; 10 Kt×Kt, B×Kt; 11 P—Kt 3, B—K 2; 12 B—Kt 2, O—O ∓. Ruben—Sultan Khan, Hamburg, 1930.

(b) Or 7 Kt—Kt 5, B—K 2 (if 7.., Kt—K 5; 8 P—K R 4, P—K R 3; 9 Kt×Kt, P×Kt; 10 Kt—B 3, P—B 4 Black holds his Pawn, but has a compromised position—Tartakover); 8 Kt—Q B 3, O—O; 9 O—O, Kt—R 3; 10 Kt—R 3, Q—B 1; 11 P×P, P—Q 3; 12 P—K 4, P—B 5; 13 P—B 4, Kt—B 4; 14 Kt—B 2 ±. V. Buerger—Colle, Tunbridge Wells, 1927.

(c) Continued 14 K—R 1, K R—K 1. Vidmar—Alexander, Nottingham, 1936. 15 B—Kt 1 now gives White a minimal advantage.

(d) Col. 81 is best for Black. If (1) 7.., Q—B 1; 8 P×P, P—Q 3; 9 Kt—Q B 3, B—K 2; 10 P—K 4, O—O; 11 Kt—B 5 ±. (2) 7 , Kt—R 3; 8 Kt—Q B 3, Kt—B 2; 9 P×P, P—Q 3; 10 P—K 4, B—K 2; 11 Kt—B 5, O—O; 12 O—O, K—K 1; 13 P—B 4 +. Yudovitch—Alatorzeff, Moscow, 1937.

(e) If 10.., P—K R 3; 11 Kt×Q P (or 11 B×Kt, B×B?—Q×B must be played— 12 Kt×KtP!! wins), B×Kt; 12 B×Kt, Q×B; 13 Q×B, Kt—B 3; 14 Q×Q P +. Capablanca—Marshall, Carlsbad, 1929.

(f) Sámisch—Réti, Bad Homburg, 1927. Black has some positional compensation for his Pawn.

(g) 6 , P×P, transposing into col. 73, is best.

(h) Weaker is 8 R—K 1, K Kt—B 3; 9 Kt—B 3, B—Kt 5; 10 Q—Kt 3, P—B 4; 11 P—Q R 3, B×Kt; 12 P×B, O—O =. Rubinstein—Nimzovitch, Baden-Baden, 1925.

(i) Bogoljuboff—Alexander, Nottingham, 1936.

(j) 5.., B—K 2, 6 O—O, O—O; 7 Kt—B 3, Kt—K 5; 8 Q—B 2, Kt×Kt; 9 Q×Kt, P—K B 4; 10 B—K B 3, B—K B 3; 11 Q—Q 2, P—Q 3; 12 P—Q 5. Alekhine—Botvinnik, Avro, 1938. Capablanca played 7 Q—B 2, and Alekhine answered B—K 5 with a slight advantage, in an earlier round.

(k) An interesting sacrificial line here is 7 P—Q 5!?, P×P; 8 P×P, e.g., B×P; 9 Kt—B 3, B—B 3; 10 P—K 4, B—K 2; 11 P—K 5, Kt—Kt 1; 12 R—K 1, Q—Kt 2; 13 Q—Q 3 with a winning attack. Fine—Landau, Ostend, 1937. 8.., Kt×P; 9 P—K 4, Kt—B 2; 10 Kt—B 3, B—K 2 is a better defence.

(l) Grünfeld—Keres, Zandvoort, 1936.

(m) This loses too much time. 7 , P—B 4 was simple and good

(n) Alekhine—L. Steiner, Warsaw, 1935.

QUEEN'S INDIAN DEFENCE
1 P—Q 4, Kt—K B 3; 2 P—Q B 4, P—K 3; 3 Kt—K B 3, P—Q Kt 3.

	86	87	88	89	90
4	(Kt—B 3)	....	....	B—Kt 5	P—K 3
	(B—Kt 2)			B—Kt 2	B—Kt 5 ch
5	B—Kt 5	....	Q—B 2	P—K 3	Q Kt—Q 2 (l)
	B—Kt 5	P—K R 3	B—Kt 5 (g)	B—K 2 (i)	B—Kt 2
6	Q—B 2 (a)	B—R 4	P—Q R 3	B—Q 3	B—Q 3
	P—K R 3	B—K 2	B×Kt ch	P—B 4	Kt—K 5
7	B—R 4	Q—B 2 (e)	Q×B	Kt—B 3 (j)	O—O
	O—O (b)	P—Q 4	Kt—K 5	Kt—B 3	P—K B 4
8	P—K 3	P—K 3	Q—B 2	O—O	Q—B 2
	P—Q 3	O—O	O—O	P—Q 3	B×Kt
9	B—Q 3	R—Q 1	P—K Kt 3	Q—K 2	Kt×B
	Q Kt—Q 2	Q Kt—Q 2	P—K B 4	P—K R 3	Q—R 5
10	O—O (c)	P×P	B—Kt 2	B×Kt	Kt—B 3 (m)
	K B×Kt	Kt×P	Kt—K B 3 !	B×B	Q—K 2
11	P×B	B—Kt 3	P—Q Kt 4	P—Q 5	Q—K 2
	P—K Kt 4	Q Kt—B 3	B—K 5	Kt—K 2	O—O
12	B—Kt 3	B—Q B 4	Q—B 3	P×P	Kt—Q 2
	Kt—R 4	Kt×Kt	P—Q R 4	P×P	P—Q 3
13	Kt—Q 2	Q×Kt	P—Kt 5	Kt—KR4 ±	P—Q Kt 3 ±
	P—B 4 (d)	Kt—K 5 = (f)	P—Q 3 = (h)	(k)	(n)

(a) Or 6 Q—Kt 3, B×Kt ch; 7 Q×B, P—K R 3; 8 B—R 4, P—Q 3; 9 P—K 3, Q Kt—Q 2; 10 B—Q 3, Q—K 2 =. Janowski—Grunfeld, Marienbad, 1925.

(b) Safer, but less aggressive, is 7.., Kt—B 3; 8 P—K 3, O—O; 9 B—Q 3, B—K 2; 10 P—Q R 3, Kt—K R 4; 11 B×B, Kt×B; 12 Q—K B 4, 13 O—O, Kt—Kt 3; 14 Q R—Q 1, Q—K 1; 15 Kt—Q Kt 5, Q—Q 1. Drawn. Tarrasch—Marshall, Kissingen, 1928.

(c) After 10 O—O, P—B 4; 11 P—Q 5?, B×Kt; 12 P×B, P×P; 13 P×P, Q—B 2; 14 P—K 4, P—B 5; 15 B—B 1, K R—K 1 the chances are about even. Flohr—Eliskases, Moscow, 1936.

(d) 14 P—B 4, Q Kt—B 3. Flohr—Botvinnik, Moscow, 1936. 15 P—Q 5 is now difficult for Black to meet.

(e) Or 7 P—K 3, Kt—K 5; 8 B×B, Q×B; 9 Kt×Kt, B×Kt; 10 B—K 2, O—O; 11 O—O, P—Q 3; 12 Kt—Q 2, B—Kt 2, 13 B—B 3, B×B, 14 Q×B, Kt—Q 2 =. Lasker—Sämisch, Moscow, 1925.

(f) Alekhine—Gilg, Kecskemét, 1927.

(g) Best. If (1) 5 , P—B 4; 6 P—K 4, P×P; 7 Kt×P, P—Q 3; 8 B—K 2, B—K 2; 9 B—K 3, O—O; 10 O—O, Q Kt—Q 2; 11 K R—Q 1, P—Q R 3; 12 P—B 3, Q R—B 1; 13 Q—Q 2, Kt—K 4; 14 P—Q Kt 3 ±. Monticelli—Réti, Budapest, 1926 (2) 5.., P—Q 3; 6 P—K 4, Q Kt—Q 2; 7 P—K R 3, P—K 4; 8 B—K 3, P×P; 9 B×P, Q—K 2; 10 O—O—O, O—O—O; 11 Kt—Q 5+. Tartakover—Flohr, London. 1932.

(h) Lisitzin—Kan, Moscow, 1935.

(i) A trap to be avoided is 5 , P—K R 3; 6 B—R 4, B—Kt 5 ch; 7 Q Kt—Q 2 ? ? (7 K Kt—Q 2 or 7 Kt—B 3), P—K Kt 4!; 8 B—Kt 3 followed by P—Kt 5 and Kt—K 5 and Black wins a piece. Tarrasch—Bogoljuboff, Gothenburg, 1920.

(j) On 7 Q Kt—Q 2, P—Q 3, 8 O—O, Q Kt—Q 2; 9 Q—K 2, P—K R 3; 10 B×Kt, is necessary, for if 10 B—R 4, P—K Kt 4!; 11 B—Kt 3, P—K R 4; 12 Kt×P, P—R 5; 13 B—B 4, P—K 4+. Grob—Canal, Meran, 1926.

(k) Vidmar—Yates, Semmering, 1926.

(l) Or 5 P—Q 3, B×B ch; 6 Q Kt×B, P—Q 3; 7 B—Q 3, B—Kt 2; 8 O—O, Q Kt—Q 2; 9 Q—B 2, Q—K 2; 10 K R—Q 1, O—O =. Miss Menchik—Alekhine London, 1932.

(m) 10 P—K Kt 3, Kt—Kt 4 ! exposes White to a dangerous attack.

(n) Flohr—Rabinovitch, Moscow, 1935.

BOGOLJUBOFF VARIATION
1 P—Q 4, Kt—K B 3 ; 2 P—Q B 4, P—K 3 ; 3 Kt—K B 3, B—Kt 5 ch.

	91	92	93	94	95
4	B—Q 2				Q Kt—Q 2
	B × B ch...............	Q—K 2			O—O
5	Q × B.......	Q Kt × B	P—K Kt 3 ...Kt—B 3 (m)		P—Q R 3
	P—Q 4 (a)	P—Q 3 (e)	O—O (h)	O—O (n)	B × Kt ch
6	P—K 3	P—K 3 (f)	B—Kt 2	P—K 3	Q × B
	O—O (b)	O—O	B × B ch (i)	P—Q 3	P—Q Kt 3
7	Kt—B 3	B—Q 3	Q × B (j)	B—K 2	Q—B 2
	Q Kt—Q 2	Kt—B 3	P—Q 3	P—Q Kt 3	B—Kt 2
8	B—Q 3	O—O	Kt—B 3	O—O	B—Kt 5
	P—Q B 3	P—K 4	Kt—B 3	B—Kt 2	P—Q 3
9	O—O	P—Q R 3	O—O	Q—B 2	P—K 3
	P × P	B—Kt 5	P—K 4	Q Kt—Q 2	B—K 5
10	B × B P	Q—B 2	Kt—Q 5 !	Q R—Q 1	Q—B 3
	P—K 4	R—K 1	Q—Q 1 (k)	K B × Kt	Q Kt—Q 2
11	B—Kt 3 (c)	P—Q 5	Q R—Q 1	B × B	B—K 2
	P × P (d)	Kt—K 2	B—Kt 5	Kt—K 5	Q—K 2
12	Q × P	Kt—Kt 5	P × P	B—K 1	O—O
	Q—Kt 3	Kt—Kt 3	P × P	P—K B 4	P—K R 3
13	Q—K B 4	P—B 3	Q—K 3 ± (l)	Q—Kt 3	B—R 4
	Kt—B 4 =	B—Q 2 = (g)		P—B 4 = (o)	P-K Kt 4 (p)

(a) If 5 , P—Q Kt 3 White plays best 6 P—K Kt 3, transposing into cols 76—80.
On 6 P—K Kt 3, B—R 3 (A. Steiner's Variation) ; 7 Kt—R 3 is an excellent reply :
7.., O—O ; 8 B—Kt 2, P—Q 4 ; 9 O—O, Kt—K 5, 10 Q—B 2, Kt—Q 3, 11 P × P,
P × P ; 12 Kt—K 5, B—Kt 2 ; 13 Q R—B 1 ±. Grunfeld—A. Steiner, Ujpest. 1934.
Inferior is the attempt to force P—K 4 by 6 Kt—B 3, B—Kt 2 ; 7 Q—B 2, B × Kt ;
8 Kt P × B, Kt—B 3 ; 9 P—K 3, Q—K 2 ∓. Sämisch—Spielmann, Moscow, 1925.
(b) The Stonewall formation is weak here : 6 , P—B 3 ; 7 Kt—B 3, Kt—K 5 ;
8 Q—B 2, P—K B 4 ; 9 P—K Kt 4+. Freymann—Bogatyrchuk, Moscow, 1927.
(c) If 11 P × P, Kt × P ; 12 Q × Q, Kt × Kt ch ; 13 P × Kt, R × Q ∓.
(d) Better than 11. , Q—K 2 ; 12 P—K 4, P × P ; 13 Kt × P, Kt—B 4 ; 14 B—B 2,
R—Q 1 ; 15 Q R—Q 1 ±. Alekhine—Bogoljuboff, Budapest, 1921.
(e) If 5.., P—Q 4 ; 6 P—K 3 (6 P—K Kt 3, O—O ; 7 B—Kt 2, Q Kt—Q 2 ;
8 O—O, Q—K 2 ; 9 Q—B 2, P—Q Kt 3 ; 10 P × P, Kt × P ; 11 P—K 4 ±. Capablanca—
Marshall, New York, 1927), O—O ; 7 Q—B 2, Q Kt—Q 2 ; 8 B—Q 3, P—K R 3 ;
9 O—O, P—B 4 ; 10 P × Q P ±. Vidmar—Marshall, New York, 1927.
(f) Alternatives are : (1) 6 P—K 4, O—O ; 7 B—Q 3 (7 Q—B 2 ?, Kt—B 3 ; 8 R—Q 1,
Q—K 2 ; 9 B—K 2, P—K 4 ∓. Pokorny—Lasker, Mahrisch-Ostrau, 1923), Q—K 2
(better is 7.., Kt—B 3) ; 8 P—Q R 3 ?, P—K 4 ; 9 P—Q 5, Kt—R 4 ; 10 P—K Kt 3,
P—K Kt 3 ; 11 Kt—Q 2, Kt—K 2 =. Nimzovitch—Tarrasch, Semmering, 1926
(2) 6 P—K Kt 3, O—O ; 7 B—Kt 2, Kt—B 3 ; 8 O—O, P—K 4 ; 9 P—Q 5, Kt—K 2 ;
10 P—K 4, Kt—Q 2 ; 11 Kt—R 4, P—Q R 4 =. Grünfeld—Zimmermann, Zürich, 1929.
(g) Vajda—Prokes, Budapest, 1926.
(h) 5. , Kt—B 3 ; 6 B—Kt 2, B × B ch ; 7 Q Kt × B, P—Q 3 ; 8 O—O, O—O ,
9 P—K 4, P—K 4 ; 10 P—Q 5 was played by Euwe—Flohr, Avro, 1938.
(i) 6 , P—Q 4 ; 7 Q—B 2, Kt—K 5 ; 8 O—O, Kt × B ; 9 Q Kt × Kt, P—Q B 3 ;
10 P—K 4, B × Kt ; 11 Kt × B, P × K P ; 12 Kt × P ±. Reshevsky—Treysman, New
York, 1938. See also Catalan System, p. 229.
(j) If 7 Q Kt × B, P—Q 3, 8 O—O, P—K 4 ; 9 Q—B 2, Kt—B 3 ; 10 P—K 3,
B—Q 2 ; 11 P—Q R 3, K R—K 1 ; 12 P—Q 5, Kt—Q 1 =. Vidmar—Alekhine, New
York, 1927.
(k) Or 10.., Kt × Kt ; 11 P × Kt, Kt × P ; 12 Kt × Kt, P × Kt ; 13 K R—K 1,
B—Kt 5 ; 14 Q × P, Q—Q 2 ; 15 Q R—B 1 ±. Becker—Konig, Vienna, 1926.
(l) Euwe—Henneberger, Berne, 1932.
(m) An alternative is 5 P—Q R 3, B × B ch ; 6 Q Kt × B, P—Q 3 ; 7 Q—B 2. P—K 4 ;
8 P—K 4, B—Kt 5 ; 9 P—Q 5, O—O. P. Johner—Grunfeld, Berlin, 1926.
(n) Better than 5 , P—Q Kt 3 ; 6 P—K 3, B—Kt 2 ; 7 B—Q 3, K B × Kt ;
8 B × B, Kt—K 5 ; 9 B × Kt (9 R—B 1, O—O ; 10 O—O, P—Q 3 ; 11 Kt—Q 2 leads
only to equality), B × B ; 10 O—O, O—O ; 11 Kt—Q 2, B—Kt 2 ; 12 P—K 4 ±.
Marshall—Kashdan, New York, 1927.
(o) Vidmar—Nimzovitch, New York, 1927.
(p) Grunfeld—List, 1926. The chances are even.

QUEEN'S INDIAN DEFENCE
1 P—Q 4, Kt—K B 3 ; 2 Kt—K B 3, P—Q Kt 3.

	96	97	98	99	100
3	P—K Kt 3 ... B—Kt 2	B—B 4 ...... B—Kt 2	B—Kt 5 (f) Kt—K 5 (g)	..P—K 3 (i) B—Kt 2	
4	B—Kt 2 P—B 4	P—K 3 P—K 3 (d)	B—R 4 B—Kt 2	Q Kt—Q 2 P—K 3	
5	O—O (a) P×P	Q Kt—Q 2 Kt—R 4	P—K 3 P—K R 3	B—Q 3 P—B 4	
6	Kt×P B×B	B—Kt 3 P—Q 3	Q Kt—Q 2 P—K Kt 4	O—O (j) Kt—B 3	
7	K×B P—Kt 3	B—Q 3 Kt—Q 2	B—Kt 3 Kt×B	P—B 3 (k) B—K 2 (l)	...Q—B 2
8	P—Q B 4 (b) B—Kt 2	Q—K 2 B—K 2	R P×Kt P—K 3	P—K 4 (m) P×P	Q—K 2 B—K 2
9	Kt—Q B 3 Q—B 1	P—B 3 P—Q B 4	P—B 3 P—Q 3	Kt×P O—O	P—K 4 P×P
10	P—Kt 3 Q—Kt 2 ch	Kt—K 4 Kt×B	Q—R 4 ch P—B 3	Q—K 2 Kt—K 4	Kt×P Kt—K 4 (o)
11	P—B 3 P—Q 4	R P×Kt P—K R 3(e)	Kt—K 4 P—Kt 5	B—B 2 Q—B 1	B—B 2 Q—B 1
12	P×P Kt×P = (c)		Kt—R 4 Kt—Q 2 = (h)	P—K B 4 B—R 3 ∓ (n)	P—Q R 3 Kt—B 3 (p)

(a) A novel continuation is 5 P—B 4 !, P×P ; 6 Q×P, P—Kt 3 ; 7 O—O, B—Kt 2 , 8 Kt—B 3, Kt—B 3 ; 9 Q—Q 1, Kt—Q R 4 ; 10 Kt—Q 2, B×B ; 11 K×B, Q—B 1 (P—Q 4 equalises) ; 12 Q—R 4, O—O ; 13 Q R—Kt 1, Q—Kt 2 ch ; 14 K—Kt 1. T. Berg—Alekhine, Kemeri, 1937.

(b) Or 8 P—Kt 3, B—Kt 2 ; 9 B—Kt 2, O—O ; 10 P—Q B 4, P—Q 4 ; 11 P×P Kt×P ; 12 P—K 4, Kt—Kt 5 =. Winter—Capablanca, Nottingham, 1936.

(c) Capablanca—Botvinnik, Nottingham, 1936.

(d) Or 4 , Kt—R 4 ; 5 B—Q 3, Kt×B ; 6 P×Kt, P—Kt 3 ; 7 Q Kt—Q 2, B—Kt 2 ; 8 P—B 5, P—B 4 ; 9 P×B P, Q Kt P×P ; 10 P×P, R P×P ; 11 P—B 3, Q—Kt 3 ; 12 Q—K 2, P—Q 4 =. Colle—Kostich, Meran, 1926.

(e) Romih—Capablanca, Paris, 1938.

(f) 3 Kt—B 3, B—Kt 2 ; 4 B—Kt 5, P—Q 4 ; 5 Kt—K 5, P—K 3 ; 6 P—K 4, P×P ; 7 B—Kt 5 ch, P—B 3 ; 8 B—Q B 4, Q Kt—Q 2. Euwe—Kmoch, Amsterdam, 1936. White has sufficient compensation for the Pawn.

(g) Or 3 , B—Kt 2 ; 4 Q Kt—Q 2, P—B 4 (equally good is 4 , P—K 3 ; 5 P—K 4, P—K R 3 ; 6 B×Kt, Q×B ; 7 B—Q 3, P—Q 3, 8 Q—K 2, Q—Q 1 ; 9 O—O, B—K 2. Marshall—Alekhine, New York, 1927) ; 5 P—B 3, Kt—B 3 ; 6 P—K 3, P—K 3 ; 7 B—Q 3, B×Kt 2 ; 8 Q—K 2, Kt—Q 4 ; 9 B×B, Q×B ; 10 O—O, O—O ; 11 B—R 6, B×B ; 12 Q×B, Kt—B 2 ; 13 Q—K 2, P—Q 4 ; 14 P—K 4, P×Q P =. Marshall—Capablanca, Kissingen, 1928.

(h) Bogoljuboff—Alekhine, 13th match game, 1934.

(i) In this and the next column White chooses a Colle System formation.

(j) 6 P—B 3, B—K 2 ; 7 Q—K 2, Kt—Q 4 ; 8 P×P, P×P ; 9 Kt—B 1, Q—B 2 ; 10 Kt—Kt 3, Kt—Q B 3 ; 11 B—Q 2, P—K Kt 4; 12 P—B 4, K Kt—Kt 5 ∓. Ahues—Alekhine, San Remo, 1930.

(k) If 7 P—Q Kt 3, B—K 2 ; 8 P×P, P×P ; 9 B—Kt 2, O—O ; 10 P—B 4, Q—B 2 ; 11 P—K R 3, Kt—K 1 ; 12 P—R 3, P—B 4 ∓. Rubinstein—Geiger, Rogaska-Slatina, 1929.

(l) Or 7 .., R—Q B 1 ; 8 Q—K 2, B—K 2 ; 9 P×P, P×P ; 10 P—K 4. Tartakover—Nimzovitch, London, 1927.

(m) 8 P×P, P×P ; 9 P—K 4, Q—B 2 ; 10 Q—K 2, P—Q 3 ; 11 Kt—B 4, O—O ; 12 P—K 5, P×P ; 13 Q Kt×P, Kt×Kt =. Colle—Pirc, Frankfurt, 1930.

(n) Colle—Capablanca, Carlsbad, 1929.

(o) 10 , P—Q 4 ; 11 Kt×Kt, B×Kt? ; 12 P—K 5 !, Kt—Q 2 ; 13 Kt—B 3, Kt—B 4 ; 14 B—B 2, B—Kt 2 ; 15 R—K 1 ±. Spielmann—Alatorzeff, Moscow, 1935.

(p) 13 Q Kt—B 3, Kt×Kt ; 14 Kt×Kt, P—Q 3 ∓. Spielmann—Eliskases, 9th match game, 1936.

QUEEN'S INDIAN DEFENCE
1 P—Q 4, Kt—K B 3.

	2 Kt—K B 3, P—Q Kt 3.			2 P—Q B 4, P—Q Kt 3.	
	101	102	103	104	105
3	(P—K 3) (B—Kt 2)			Kt—QB3 (e) B—Kt 2	
4	(B—Q 3) (P—K 3)...............		P—B 4	Q—B 2.....P—B 3 P—Q 4 (f)	P—Q 4
5	(Q Kt—Q 2) (P—B 4)....	P—Q 4	Q Kt—Q 2 P—Kt 3	P×P Kt×P	P×P Kt×P
6	(O—O) (Kt—B 3)	Kt—K 5 B—Q 3	P—B 3 B—Kt 2	P—K 4 Kt×Kt	Kt×Kt (i) Q×Kt
7	P—B 4 B—K 2	P—K B 4 Q Kt—Q 2 (b)	P—K 4 P—Q 3	P×Kt P—K 3 (g)	P—K 4 Q—Q 2
8	P—Q Kt 3 P×P	Q—B 3 P—B 4	O—O O—O	Kt—B 3 B—K 2	B—Q B 4 P—K 3
9	P×P P—Q 4	P—B 3 Q—B 2	Q—K 2 P×P	B—Q 3 Kt—Q 2	Kt—K 2 B—Kt 5 ch
10	B—Kt 2 Kt—Q Kt 5	P—K Kt 4 P×P	P×P Kt—B 3	O—O P—Q B 4	B—Q 2 B×B ch
11	B—Kt 1 O—O	K P×P B×Kt !?	P—Q R 3 Kt—Q 2	B—K B 4 O—O	Q×B (j)
12	R—K 1 R—B 1	B P×B Q Kt×P	Kt—Kt 3 P—Q R 4	Q R—Q 1 P×P	
13	Kt—K 5 Kt—B3 = (a)	P×Kt + (c)	P—QR4 ± (d)	P×P R—B 1 ∓ (h)	

(a) Tartakover and Turover—Alekhine and Cukiermann, Paris, 1931.

(b) If 7.., O—O; 8 Q—B 3, K Kt—Q 2 (P—B 4!); 9 Q—R 3, P—K B 4; 10 Q Kt—B 3, Kt—K B 3; 11 B—Q 2, B—R 3?; 12 R—K B 1, B×B; 13 P×B, Q—K 1; 14 K—B 2 +. Sultan Khan—Mattison, Prague, 1931.

(c) 13.., P—Q 5; 14 Q—K 2, B×R; 15 P×Kt, Q P×P; 16 Kt—K 4!. Tartakover—Winter, London, 1932.

(d) Continued 13.., Kt—Kt 5; 14 B—Q Kt 5, Kt—K B 3; 15 P—Q 5, P—K 4; 16 P×P e.p., Kt×P; 17 Kt—Kt 5!+. Koltanowski—Alekhine, Hastings, 1936-37.

(e) 3 P—B 3, B—Kt 2; 4 P—K 4, P—K 4 ? (4 , P—Q 3 is necessary, but White retains the superior position); 5 P×P, Kt×P; 6 P×Kt, Q—R 5 ch; 7 K—Q 2, Q—B 5 ch; 8 K—B 2, B×P ch; 9 B—Q 3, B×B ch, 10 Q×B, Q—B 7 ch; 11 Kt—Q 2 + +. Fine—Petrov, Semmering-Baden, 1937.

(f) Best. If 4 , P—K 3; 5 P—K 4, B—Kt 5; 6 B—Q 3, Kt—B 3; 7 Kt—K 2, P—K 4; 8 P—Q 5, Kt—Q Kt 1; 9 P—Q R 3+. Grunfeld—Kostich, Trentschin-Teplitz, 1928. Or here 5.., P—Q 4, 6 B P×P, P×P; 7 P—K 5, Kt—K 5, 8 B—Kt 5 ch, P—B 3; 9 B—Q 3, P—K B 4 (Spielmann—Berndtsson, Gothenburg, 1933); 10 P×P e.p.+.

(g) Better than 7 , P—K 4; 8 Kt—B 3! (8 P×P, Q—R 5 as in Euwe—Alekhine, Budapest, 1921, gives Black an excellent attack), P×P; 9 B—Kt 5 ch, P—B 3; 10 B—Q 4, P—Q Kt 4; 11 Q×P, Kt—Q 2; 12 Q×P, Kt—Q 2; 14 B—Kt 2, Kt—B 4; 15 Q—B 2! ±. Spielmann—Chekhover, Moscow, 1935.

(h) 14 Q—R 4, P—Q R 3. Moritz—Grünfeld, Breslau, 1925. Black's Queen's side majority gives him the advantage.

(i) Or 6 P—K 4, Kt×Kt; 7 P×Kt, P—K 3; 8 Q—R 4 ch, P—B 3; 9 B—K B 4 Kt—Q 2; 10 Kt—R 3, B—K 2; 11 B—K 2, O—O; 12 O—O, K—R 1 ⇌. Van Doesburgh—Bogoljuboff, Zandvoort, 1936.

(j) Euwe—Tartakover, Stockholm, 1937. White's advantage is negligible.

KING'S INDIAN DEFENCE

1 P—Q 4, Kt—K B 3 ; 2 P—Q B 4, P—K Kt 3 ; 3 Kt—Q B 3, B—Kt 2;
4 P—K 4, P—Q 3 ; 5 Kt—B 3, O—O.

	106	107	108	109	110
6	B—K 2				P—K R 3
	Q Kt—Q 2				P—B 4
7	O—O				B—K 3 (h)
	P—K 4				P×P
8	P—Q 5 (a)			P×P (f)	Kt×P
	Kt—B 4		P—Q R 4	P×P	P—Q Kt 3
9	Kt—Q 2		Q—B 2	Q—B 2	B—K 2 (i)
	P—Q R 4		Kt—R 4 (d)	P—B 3	B—Kt 2
10	Q—B 2		P—K Kt 3	P—Q Kt 3	Q—B 2
	K Kt—Q 2	B—Kt 5	Kt—B 4	Q—R 4	Kt—B 3
11	Kt—Kt 3	Kt—Kt 3	Kt—K 1	B—Kt 2	Kt×Kt
	P—B 4	B×B	B—R 6	Kt—R 4	B×Kt
12	P×P	Q×B	Kt—Kt 2	Q R—Q 1	O—O
	R×P	Q Kt—Q 2	Kt—B 3	Kt—B 5	Q—B 1
13	B—Kt 4	B—K 3	R—K 1 ?	K R—K 1	K R—Q 1
	R—B 1	P—K R 3	K Kt—Q 2	R—K 1	Q—Kt 2
14	B—K 3	Kt—B 1	B—K 3	B—B 1	B—Q 3
	P—Kt 3	Kt—R 2	P—B 4	Kt—B 1 ∓ (g)	Kt—Q 2
15	Kt×Kt+ (b)	Kt—Q 3 ± (c)	P—B 3		P—B 3 ± (j)
			P—B 5 ∓ (e)		

(a) In a match game against Euwe, 1928, Bogoljuboff played 8 B—Kt 5, P—K R 3; 9 B—R 4, R—K 1, 10 P×P, P×P; 11 Q—B 2, P—B 3; 12 Kt—Q 2, Kt—B 4; 13 Kt—Kt 3, Kt—K 3; 14 K R—Q 1, Q—K 2; 15 B—B 1, P—K Kt 4 with a satisfactory game for Black.

(b) Bogoljuboff—Euwe, 5th match game, 1929.

(c) Flohr—Bogoljuboff, Bad Sliac, 1932.

(d) Or 9.., Kt—B 4; 10 B—K 3 (10 P—Q Kt 3?, Kt—R 4; 11 R—K 1, P—B 4!; 12 Kt—Q 2, Kt—B 3; 13 P—B 3, Kt—R 4 ! ∓. Stähelin—Eliskases, Zürich, 1935), P—Kt 3; 11 Kt—Q 2, Kt—B 3; 13 P—B 3, P—B 5; 14 B—B 2, Kt—R 3; 15 Q R—Kt 1, Q—Kt 4? (P—K Kt 4 followed by a general advance on the K-side was in order) ; 16 K R—B 1, P—K R 4; 17 K—R 1, Q—R 3, 18 P—Q Kt 4 ±. Lilienthal—Kan, Moscow, 1935.

(e) R. P. Michell—Flohr, Hastings, 1934–35.

(f) Unusual but strong is 8 R—K 1, e.g. 8.., R—K 1; 9 B—B 1, P×P; 10 Kt×P, Kt—B 4; 11 P—B 3, Kt—K 3; 12 B—K 3, Kt—R 4; 13 K Kt—K 2, P—Q R 3; 14 Q—Q 2, B—Q 2; 15 K R—Q 1 ±. Antze—Carls, 1932.

(g) Colle—Landau, match, 1928.

(h) Stronger than 7 P—Q 5, P—K 3; 8 P×P, P×P; 9 P—K 5, P×P; 10 Q×Q, R×Q; 11 Kt×P, Kt—Q 4. Grünfeld—Réti, Vienna, 1923.

(i) Better than 9 Q—Q 2, B—Kt 2; 10 P—B 3, Kt—R 4 (Koltanowski—Euwe, London, 1927), when Black has some counterplay.

(j) Continued 15 ., Kt—B 4; 16 B—K 2, P—Q R 4; 17 Q—Q 2, P—B 4; 18 P×P. Grünfeld—Sämisch, Baden-Baden, 1925.

KING'S INDIAN DEFENCE

1 P—Q 4, Kt—K B 3 ; 2 P—Q B 4, P—K Kt 3 ; 3 Kt—Q B 3, B—Kt 2;
4 P—K 4, P—Q 3.

	111	112	113	114	115
5	(Kt—B 3)..............		P—B 4..................		P—K Kt 3
	(O—O)		O—O		O—O
6	(P—K R 3)..B—Q 3 (c)		Kt—B 3 (g)		B—Kt 2
	(P—K 4)	B—Kt 5 (d)	P—B 4 (h)		Q Kt—Q 2 (l)
7	P—Q 5	P—K R 3	P—Q 5......	P × P	K Kt—K 2
	P—K R 3	B × Kt	P—K 3	Q—R 4	P—K 4
8	B—K 3	Q × B	B—Q 3	B—Q 2	P—Q 5 (m)
	K—R 2	Q Kt—Q 2 (e)	P × P	Q × B P	P—Q R 4
9	P—K Kt 4	B—K 3	B P × P	Q—K 2 (k)	P—Q R 3
	Kt—Kt 1	P—B 4	Q—Kt 3	Kt—B 3	Kt—B 4
10	Q—Q 2 (a)	P—Q 5	Kt—Q 2 (i)	O—O—O	O—O
	P—Kt 3	Kt—K 4	Kt—Kt 5	B—Kt 5	Kt—K 1 (n)
11	O—O—O	Q—K 2	Kt—B 4	Q—K 3	B—K 3
	Kt—R 3	Kt × B ch	Q—Q 1	Kt—Q 2	P—B 4
12	B—K 2	Q × Kt	B—K 2	Kt—Q R 4	P × P
	Kt—B 4	Kt—Q 2	P—K R 4	Q × Q	P × P
13	P–K R 4 ± (b)	O—O	B × Kt (j)	B × Q	P—B 4
		Q—R 4	B × B	B × Kt ∓	P—Kt 3
14		B—Q 2	Q—B 2		P–R 3 ! ± (o)
		P–Q R 3 = (f)	Q—R 5 ch +		

(a) Or 10 B—K 2, P—K B 4?, 11 Kt P × P, P × P, 12 P × P, B × P; 13 Q—Q 2, Kt—Q 2; 14 P—K R 4 +. Sämisch—Réti, Teplitz-Schönau, 1922.

(b) Grunfeld—Euwe, Mährisch-Ostrau, 1923.

(c) Or 6 B—K 3, Q Kt—Q 2, 7 Kt—Q 2, P—K 4; 8 P—Q 5, Kt—K 1; 9 B—K 2, P—K B 4; 10 P—B 3 (the object of his 7th move), P—B 5 =. Sultan Khan—Flohr, Prague, 1931. If 6 P—K Kt 3, B—Kt 5; 7 B—Kt 2, Kt—B 3; 8 O—O, P—K 4; 9 P—Q 5, Kt—Q 5 =. On 6 B—B 4, Kt—B 3 is best for Black : 7 Q—Q 2, B—Kt 5; 8 P—Q 5, P—K 4; 9 P × Kt, P × B; 10 P × P, R—K 1 with sufficient compensation for the Pawn. If, however, 6 ., P—K R 3 (after 6 B—B 4); 7 Q—Q 2, K—R 2; 8 P—K R 3, Q Kt—Q 2; 9 O—O—O, P—Kt 3; 10 P—K 5, Kt—K Kt 1; 11 B—Q 3 +. Bogoljuboff—Tarrasch, Carlsbad, 1923.

(d) If 6 ., Q Kt—Q 2; 7 O—O, P—K 4; 8 P—Q 5, Kt—B 4; 9 B—B 2, P—Q R 4; 10 Kt—Q 2, Kt—K 1; 11 Kt—Kt 3, P—B 4; 12 P × P, P × P; 13 P—B 4, P—K 5; 14 B—K 3 +. Kashdan—Flohr, Prague, 1931.

(e) Or 8.., Kt—B 3; 9 B—K 3, K Kt—Q 2; 10 Kt—K 2??, Kt—K 4! and wins. G. M. Norman—Vidmar, Hastings, 1926. 10 P—Q 5 is necessary; there can then follow 10.., Q Kt—K 4; 11 Q—K 2, Kt × B ch ∓.

(f) Marshall—Réti, New York, 1924.

(g) Or 6 B—K 2, P—Q 5, 7 P—Q 5, P—K 3; 8 P × P, P × P; 9 B—B 3, Kt—B 3; 10 K Kt—K 2, P—K 4; 11 O—O, Kt—Q 5 ∓. Rabinovitch—Torre, Baden-Baden, 1925.

(h) Best. If instead (1) 6 , B—Kt 5; 7 B—K 2, Kt—B 3; 8 P—Q 5, Kt—K 1; 9 O—O, Kt—Q 2; 10 Kt—K Kt 5, B × B; 11 Q × B, P—K R 3; 12 Kt—B 3, P—K 3; 13 P—K 5, P × K P; 14 B P × P, Kt—Kt 5; 15 B—B 4 ±. Alekhine—Marshall, New York, 1924. (2) 6 ., P—K 4!?; 7 B P × P, P × P; 8 P—Q 5, Q Kt—Q 2; 9 B—Q 3, Kt—B 4; 10 B—B 2 ±. Alekhine—Ed. Lasker, New York, 1924.

(i) Or 10 B—B 2, P—B 5!, 11 Q—K 2, R—K 1; 12 B—R 4, B—Q 2; 13 B × B, Q Kt × B; 14 Kt—Q 2, Kt × K P!+. Colle—Euwe, Antwerp, 1926.

(j) Sämisch—Euwe, Wiesbaden, 1925. Continued 13 Kt—Kt 5, P—Q R 3; 14 Q Kt × P, P—Q Kt 4; 15 Kt × B, P × Kt+ +. The continuation in the column is due to Kmoch.

(k) Or 9 B—Q 3, Kt—B 3; 10 Kt—Q R 4, Q—K R 4 ∓. The column is V. L. Wahltuch—Vidmar, Hastings, 1926.

(l) Or 6 ., Kt—B 3; 7 P—Q 5, Kt—Kt 1; 8 K Kt—K 2, P—K 4; 9 P—K R 3, Q Kt—Q 2, 10 B—K 3, Kt—B 4; 11 P—R 3, P—Q R 4; 12 O—O ±. Winter—Bogoljuboff, Nottingham, 1936.

(m) 8 O—O is also strong, e.g., 8 , R—K 1; 9 R—K 1, P × P?; 10 Kt × P, Kt—B 4; 11 P—Kt 3, B—Kt 5; 12 P—B 3, B—Q 2; 13 B—Kt 2 ±.

(n) On 10.., P—K Kt 3; 11 P—R 3, Q—K 2; 12 B—K 3, Kt—R 4; 13 P—Q Kt 4, P × P; 14 P × P, R × R; 15 Q × R, Kt—R 3; 16 P—Kt 5, Kt—B 4; 17 Q—R 7 ±. Capablanca—Bogoljuboff, Carlsbad, 1929.

(o) Winter—Tartakover, Warsaw, 1935.

KING'S INDIAN DEFENCE
1 P—Q4, Kt—KB3; 2 P—QB4, P—KKt3.

	116	117	118	119	120
3	(Kt—QB3) / (B—Kt2) (a)	..P—KKt3 / B—Kt2	....	P—Q4	
4	(P—K4) / (P—Q3)	B—Kt2 / O—O		B—Kt2 / B—Kt2	
5	(P—KKt3) / (O—O)	Kt—QB3 / P—Q3		P×P / Kt×P	
6	(B—Kt2) / (QKt—Q2)	Kt—B3 / QKt—Q2	...Kt—B3	P—K4...... / Kt—Kt5 (k)	Kt—KB3 / O—O
7	Kt—B3 / P—K4	O—O / P—K4	P—Q5 (g) / Kt—Kt1	P—QR3 (l) / KKt—B3	O—O / P—QB4!
8	O—O / R—K1 (b)	P—Kt3 (d) / R—K1 (e)	O—O (h) / P—QR4	P—Q5 / Kt—Q5	P—K4 (n) / Kt—KB3
9	P—Q5 / Kt—B4	Q—B2 / Kt—Kt5	P—KR3 / Kt—R3	Kt—K2 / B—Kt5	P—K5 / Kt—Q4
10	Kt—K1 / P—QR4	P×P / KKt×P	B—K3 (i) / P—Kt3	QKt—B3 / P—K4	P×P / Kt—R3
11	P—Kt3 / B—Q2	Kt×Kt / Kt×Kt	Kt—Q4 / B—Q2	O—O / Q—B3	P—QR3 / Kt×P
12	P—KR3 / R—KB1	B—Kt2 / P—KR4	P—R3 / Q—K1	P—B3 / B—Q2	P—QKt4 / Kt—K3
13	B—K3 ± (c)	QR-Q1 ± (f)	P—Kt3+ (j)	B—K3± (m)	B—Kt2 / P-QR4 ∓ (o)

(a) For 3.., P—Q4 (the Grunfeld Defence) see cols 131—150.

(b) Or 8 ,Q—K2; 9 P—Kt3,P×P?; 10 Kt×P, Kt—B4; 11 R—K1,B—Q2; 12 B—Kt2, KR—K1; 13 Q—Q2, Q—K4; 14 P—Qht4, Kt—R3; 15 P—B4+. Keres—Becker, Zandvoort, 1936. After the text both 9 P—Kt3 and 9 R—K1 are also strong.

(c) Continued 13. , Kt—K1; 14 R—B1, P—Kt3; 15 Q—Q2, P—B4; 16 P×P, B×P; 17 P—KKt4!. Flohr—Lilienthal, Moscow, 1936.

(d) Best. If instead 8 Q—B2, P×P; 9 Kt×P, Kt—Kt3, 10 Q—Q3, P—Q4; 11 P×P, KKt×P; 12 Kt×Kt, Kt×Kt=. Alekhine—Réti, Pistyan, 1922. Or 8 P×P, P×P, 9 Q—B2 (or 9 P—KR3, P—B3; 10 B—K3, Q—K2; 11 Q—Kt3, P—KR3; 12 KR—Q1, K—R2; 13 P—B5, Kt—R4 =. Spielmann—Bogoljuboff, Kissingen, 1928), P—B3; 10 R—Q1, Q—K2; 11 Kt—QR4?, R—K1; 12 P—KR3, Kt—R4, 13 P—B5?, P—K5; 14 Kt—Q4, P—K6!+. Goglidse—Flohr, Moscow, 1935.

(e) If now 8 ., P×P?; 9 Kt×P, Kt—B4; 10 B—Kt2, R—K1; 11 Q—B2, Kt—K3; 12 QR—Q1, Q—K2; 13 KR—K1+. Alekhine—Sämisch, Berlin, 1921.

(f) Alekhine—Bogoljuboff, 26th match game, 1934.

(g) This advance must occur immediately, for if 7 O—O, P—K4; 8 P—Q5 (if 8 P—K4, P×P, 9 Kt×P, Kt×P!; 10 KKt×Kt, Kt×Kt; 11 Kt×Q, Kt×Q; 12 Kt×KtP, B×Kt!; 13 R×Kt, QR—Kt1=), Kt—K2; 9 P—K4, Kt—Q2; 10 Kt—KR4, P—KB4; 11 B—Kt5, Kt—B6; 12 Q—Q2, P×P; 13 Kt×KP, Kt×Kt=. Abramavicius—Simonson, Folkestone, 1933.

(h) If 8 P—K4, QKt—Q2; 9 O—O, P—QR4; 10 B—K3?, Kt—Kt5; 11 B—Q4, KKt—K4; 12 Kt×Kt, Kt×Kt =. Alekhine—Yates, Carlsbad, 1923

(i) Somewhat better than 10 Kt—Q4, Kt—B4; 11 P—K4, P—B4; 12 K Kt—K2, Q—K2; 13 B—K3, P—Kt3; 14 Q—Q2 ±. Grünfeld—Yates, Moscow, 1925.

(j) Grünfeld—Yates, Semmering, 1926

(k) 6 , Kt—Kt3; 7 Kt—K2, B—Kt5; 8 P—B3, B—Q2; 9 QKt—B3, Q—B1; 10 O—O, B—R6; 11 B—K3 ±. Réti—Euwe, Kissingen, 1928.

(l) If 7 Q—R4ch, QKt—Q2; 8 P—Q5, P—QKt4; 9 Q×KtP, Kt—B7ch; 10 K—Q1, Kt×R; 11 Q×Ktch, B—Q2+.

(m) Continued 13 , P—B4; 14 P×P e.p., QKt×P; 15 Kt—Q5. Rubinstein—Réti, Semmering, 1926.

(n) Or 8 P×P, Kt—R3; 9 P—B6, P×P; 10 P—QR3, R—Kt1; 11 Q—B7, Q—R4 ∓. Kupchik—Fine, New York, 1938.

(o) Continued 14 P—Kt5, Q—Q2; 15 Q—K2, R—Q1. Alekhine—Mikenas, Kemeri, 1937

KING'S INDIAN DEFENCE
1 P—Q 4, Kt—K B 3 ; 2 P—Q B 4, P—K Kt 3.

	121	122	123	124	125
3	(P—K Kt 3)................			P—B 3	
	P—B 3			B—Kt 2....P—Q 4	
4	B—Kt 2............	............P—Q 5		P—K 4	P×P
	P—Q 4	B—Kt 2 (e)		P—Q 3	Kt×P
5	P×P........	Kt—K B 3	B—Kt 2	Kt—B 3	P—K 4
	P×P (a)	B—Kt 2	P—Q 3	O—O	Kt—Kt 3
6	Kt—KB3 (b)	O—O	Q Kt—B 3	B—K 3	Kt—B 3
	B—Kt 2	O—O	O—O	P—K 4 (i)	B—Kt 2
7	O—O	P—Kt 3	P—K 4 (f)	K Kt—K2 (j)	B—K 3
	O—O	Kt—K 5	P—K 3 ! (g)	Kt—B 3 (k)	O—O
8	Kt—B 3	B—Kt 2	K Kt—K 2	Q—Q 2	P—B 4 ! (m)
	Kt—K 5 (c)	P×P ?	K P×P	Kt—Q 2	P—K B 4 (n)
9	Q—Kt 3	Q—B 2 !	B P×P	P—Q 5	Q—Kt 3 ch
	Kt×Kt	Kt—Q 3	P×P	Kt—K 2	K—R 1
10	P×Kt	P×P	Kt×P	P—K Kt 3	P—K 5
	Kt—B 3	B—B 4	Kt×Kt	P—K B 4	P—K 3
11	Kt—Q 2	Q—B 1	Q×Kt ?	B—Kt 2	Kt—B 3
	P—K 3	Kt—R 3	B—K 3	P×P	Kt—B 3
12	B—R 3	Q Kt—Q 2 ±	Q×Kt P	P×P ± (l)	P—K R 4 ±
	R—K 1 =	(d)	Kt—Q 2 + (h)		(o)

(a) If instead 5 , Kt×P? ; 6 Kt—K B 3, B—Kt 2 ; 7 O—O (but not 7 P—K 4 ?, Kt—Kt 3 ; 8 O—O, B—Kt 5 ; 9 B—K 3, P—Q B 4 ; 10 P—K 5, Kt—B 3 ; 11 P×P, Q×Q ; 12 R×Q, Kt—B 5 ∓. Fine—Reshevsky, Kemeri, 1937), O—O ; 8 Kt—B 3, Kt×Kt ; 9 P×Kt, P—Q B 4 ; 10 B—Q R 3, P×P ; 11 Kt×P !, Q—B 2 ; 12 Q—Kt 3 ± Keres—Flohr, Semmering-Baden, 1937.

(b) Or 6 Kt—Q B 3, Kt—Q B 3 ; 7 Kt—R 3, B—Kt 2 ; 8 O—O, O—O ; 9 Kt—B 4, P—K 3 ; 10 P—K 3, P—Kt 3 =. Stahlberg—Flohr, Kemeri, 1937.

(c) 8 ... Kt—B 3 is also good enough. 9 Kt—K 5, Kt×Kt ; 10 P×Kt, Kt—Kt 5 ; 11 Kt×P, Kt×K P ; 12 Q—Kt 3, Kt—B 3 ; 13 B—K 3, P—K 3 ; 14 Kt—B 3, Kt—Q 5 with a perfectly level position. Samisch—Grunfeld, Carlsbad, 1923. The column is Rabinovitch—Botvinnik, Moscow, 1935.

(d) Continued 12 , Q—B 1 ; 13 R—K 1, Kt—K 5 ; 14 Kt—Kt 3, B—R 6 ; 15 B—R 1, Q—K 3 ; 16 Q—B 4. Bogoljuboff—Euwe, 7th match game, 1928.

(e) Weak is 4 , P×P ; 5 P×P, B—Kt 2 ; 6 B—K 2, O—O ; 7 Kt—Q B 3, P—Q 3 ; 8 Kt—B 3, Kt—R 3 ; 9 O—O, B—Q 2, 10 P—K R 3, Q—Kt 3 ; 11 R—Kt 1, B—B 4 ; 12 B—K 3, Q—R 4 ; 13 R—B 1 ±. Flohr—Koltanowski, Hastings, 1935-36.

(f) If 7 Kt—B 3, P—K 4 ; 8 P×P B P ?, P×P ; 9 O—O, Q—B 2 ; 10 P—Kt 3, R—Q 1 ; 11 B—Kt 2, Q Kt—Q 2 ; 12 Kt—Q 2, B—Kt 2 ; 13 Q—B 2, P—Q 4 ∓. Stahlberg—Flohr, Moscow, 1935.

(g) If 7 , P—K 4 ; 8 K Kt—K 2, P—B 4 ; 9 O—O, Kt—K 1 ; 10 P—K R 3, P—B 4 ; 11 P—B 4, Kt—Q 2 ; 12 K P×P, Kt P×P ; 13 Q—B 2, Q Kt—B 3 ; 14 B—K 3+. Rubinstein—Carls, Baden-Baden, 1925.

(h) Landau—Euwe, Amsterdam, 1935. 10 P×P should have been played.

(i) If 6 , Q Kt—Q 2 ; 7 Kt—R 3, P—K 4 ; 8 P—Q 5, P—Q R 4 ; 9 Kt—B 2, P—R 4 ; 10 Q—Q 2, Kt—B 4 ; 11 B—Kt 5, B—Q 2, 12 P—K Kt 4, Q—B 1 ; 13 P—K R 4+. Nimzovitch—Tartakover, Carlsbad, 1929.

(j) 7 P—Q 5, P—B 3 ; 8 Q—Q 2, P×P ; 9 B P×P, Kt—K 1 ; 10 O—O—O, P—B 4 leads to a wild position with chances for both sides. Alekhine—Euwe, 3rd match game, 1926

(k) 7 , Q Kt—Q 2 ; 8 Q—Q 2, Kt—K 1 ! ; 9 P×P, Kt×P ! ; 10 Kt—Q 4, B—K 3 ; 11 P—Q Kt 3, P—Q B 3 ; 12 B—K 2, P—Q 4 ; 13 B P×P, P×P =. Fine—Tartakover, Warsaw, 1935. 7..,P×P ; 8 Kt×P, P—B 3 ; 9 B—K 2, R—K 1 ; 10 Kt—B 2, P—Q 4 , 11 B P×P, P×P ; 12 P×P, B—B 4. Euwe—Pirc, Hastings, 1939.

(l) Continued 12 , Kt—K B 3 ; 13 P—K R 3, P—Kt 3 ; 14 P—Kt 3, K—R 1 , 15 P—K Kt 4. Botvinnik—Alatorzeff, Moscow, 1931. White's game is much freer

(m) 8 Q—Q 2, Kt—B 3 ! ; 9 P—Q 5, Kt—K 4 ; 10 B—K Kt 5, P—Q B 3 ; 11 R—Q 1, Q P×P ; 12 P×P, B—B 4+. Alekhine—Bogoljuboff, Bled, 1931.

(n) 8.., Kt—B 3 ; 9 P—Q 5, Kt—Kt 1 ; 10 Kt—B 3, P—Q B 3. Euwe—Reshevsky Avro, 1938. Black has provoked an attack in the centre to counter-attack as shown

(o) Rödl—Helling, Bad Pyrmont, 1933.

KING'S INDIAN DEFENCE
1 P—Q 4, Kt—K B 3.

2 P—Q B 4, P—K Kt 3.   2 Kt—K B 3, P—K Kt 3.

	126	127	128	129	130
3	(P—B 3)	B—Kt 5 .	B—B 4		Kt—B 3 (f)
	P—B 4	B—Kt 2	B—Kt 2		P—Q 4 (g)
4	P—Q 5	Q Kt—Q 2	Q—B 1	P—K R 3	B—B 4 (h)
	P—K 3	P—B 4	P—K R 3	P—B 4 (d)	B—Kt 2
5	Kt—B 3	P—K 3 (b)	P—K R 3	P—B 3	P—K 3
	P—Q 3	P—Q Kt 3	P—Kt 3	P—Kt 3	O—O
6	P—K 4	B—Q 3	Kt—B 3	Q Kt—Q 2	B—Q 3
	P×P	B—Kt 2	B—Kt 2	P×P	P—B 4
7	B P×P	O—O	Q—Q 2	P×P	P×P
	B—Kt 2	P—K R 3	P—R 3	B—Kt 2	Q Kt—Q 2
8	B—Kt5 ch	B—K B 4	R—Q 1	P—K 3	O—O
	Q Kt—Q 2	P—Q 3	P—K 3	O—O	Kt×P
9	B—K B 4	P—B 3	Q—B 1	B—Q 3	B—K 5
	Q—K 2	Kt—R 4	P—Q 3	Kt—B 3	B—Kt 5
10	Q—Q 2	Q—Kt 3	P—K Kt 3	O—O	P—K R 3
	P—Q R 3	Kt×B	Q Kt—Q 2	P—Q 3	Kt×B
11	B—K 2	P×Kt	B—Kt 2	Q—K 2	P×Kt
	P—Q Kt4	O—O	Q—K 2	P—Q R 3	B×Kt
12	Kt—R 3	Q R—Q 1	Kt—K R 4	K R—Q 1	Q×B
	O—O =	Kt—B 3 ∓	B×B = (c)	Q—Kt 1 = (e)	P—K 3 = (i)
	(a)				

(a) Chekhover—Alatorzeff, Moscow, 1935. Black's opening play is original and noteworthy.

(b) Or 5 P—B 3, P×P; 6 P×P, Q—Kt 3 (or Kt—B 3; 7 P—K 3, O—O; 8 B—Q 3, P—Q 3; 9 O—O, P—K R 3; 10 B×Kt, B×B. Marshall—Euwe, Kissingen, 1928); 7 Kt—B 4, Q—Q 1; 8 P—K 3, O—O; 9 B—Q 3, P—Q 4; 10 Q Kt—Q 2, Kt—B 3; 11 O—O, Q—Kt 3, 12 Q—Kt 3, Q×Q; 13 Kt×Q =. Vidmar—Bogoljuboff, San Remo, 1930. The column is Vidmar—Euwe, Carlsbad, 1929.

(c) Lasker—Euwe, Mährisch-Ostrau, 1923.

(d) Or 4. , O—O; 5 P—K 3, P—Q 3, 6 Q Kt—Q 2, Q Kt—Q 2; 7 B—B 4, P—K 3 (if 7.., P—B 4; 8 P—B 3, R—K 1?; 9 O—O, P—K 4; 10 P×P, Kt×P; 11 B×Kt, P×B; 12 Kt—Kt 5! ±); 8 P—B 3, Q—K 2; 9 P—K 4, P—K 4; 10 P×P, P×P; 11 B—K 3, P—Q Kt 4; 12 Q—K 2, Q R 3; 13 P—K Kt 4, Kt—B 4; 14 B—K Kt 5, B—Kt 2 ∓. Vidmar—Flohr, Bled, 1931.

(e) Continued 13 B—R 2, Q—R 2; 14 P—R 3, Q R—B 1; 15 Q R—B 1, P—Q Kt 4. Em. Lasker—Alekhine, New York, 1924.

(f) Other variations rarely seen are: (1) 3 Q Kt—Q 2, B—Kt 2; 4 P—K 4, P—Q 3; 5 B—B 4, O—O; 6 O—O, B—Kt 5; 7 P—K R 3, B×Kt; 8 Kt×B, P—Q 4; 9 P×P, Kt×P; 10 P—B 3, Kt—Q B 3 =. Capablanca—Marshall, Lake Hopatcong, 1926. (2) 3 P—K Kt 3, P—Q 4; 4 B—Kt 2, B—Kt 2; 5 P—B 3, O—O; 6 B—Kt 4, B—B 4; 7 Q—R 4, P—K R 1, 8 Q Kt—Q 2, Q Kt—Q 2; 9 Kt—R 4, B—K 3; 10 Q Kt—B 3, Kt—K 5; 11 Kt—Kt 5, Kt×Kt; 12 B×Kt, P—Q B 4. Znosko-Borovsky—Euwe, Scheveningen, 1923. (3) 3 P—K 3, B—Kt 2; 4 B—Q 3, O—O; 5 O—O, P—Q 3; 6 P—K 4, Q Kt—Q 2; 7 P—K R 3, P—B 4; 8 P—B 3, P—K 4; 9 P×K P, P×P; 10 P—Q R 4, Q—B 2; 11 Kt—R 3, P—B 5; 12 Kt×B P, Kt—B 4; 13 Q—K 2, Kt×B ∓. Dus-Chotimirsky—Capablanca, Moscow, 1925 (4) 3 P—K 3, B—Kt 2; 4 B—Kt 2, O—O; 5 P—K 3, P—Q 3; 6 B—Q 3, Q Kt—Q 2; 7 P—K 4, P—K 4; 8 Q Kt—Q 2, P×P; 9 B×P, R—K 1; 10 O—O, P—Q Kt 3; 11 R—K 1, B—Kt 2 ∓. Tirtakover—Euwe, Amsterdam, 1926.

(g) Black cannot afford to play carelessly, e.g. 3.., B—Kt 2; 4 P—K 4, O—O; 5 B—K Kt 5, P—K R 3; 6 B—K B 4, P—Q 3; 7 Q—Q 2, K—R 2; 8 O—O—O, P—Q R 4?; 9 B—Q 3, Kt—R 3; 10 P—K 5, Kt—K Kt 1; 11 P—K R 4, Kt—Kt 5; 12 P—R 5 with a winning attack. Tarrasch—Davidson, Semmering, 1926.

(h) Or 4 P—K R 3, B—Kt 2; 5 B—B 4, O—O; 6 P—K 3, P—B 4; 7 P×P, Q—R 4? (better 7 , Q Kt—Q 2, as in the column); 8 Kt—Q 2, Q×B P; 9 Kt—Kt 3, Q—Kt 3; 10 B—K 5, P—K 3, 11 Kt—Kt 5, Kt—K 1; 12 B×B, Kt×B; 13 P—K R 4 ±. Capablanca—Yates, New York, 1924.

(i) Colle—Euwe, Amsterdam, 1928.

KING'S INDIAN DEFENCE
1 P—Q 4, Kt—K B 3 ; 2 P—Q B 4, P—K Kt 3.

GRUENFELD DEFENCE
3 Kt—Q B 3, P—Q 4.

	131	132	133	134	135
4	P × P...............................			B—Kt 5	
	Kt × P			Kt—K 5	
5	P—K 4 (a)...............		Q—Kt 3	P × P......	Kt × Kt
	Kt × Kt		Kt × Kt (h)	Kt × Kt (j)	P × Kt
6	P × Kt		P × Kt	P × Kt	Q—Q 2
	B—Kt 2.....	P—Q B 4	B—Kt 2	Q × P	P—Q B 4 ! (l)
7	B—R 3 (b)	Kt—B 3 (e)	Kt—B 3	Kt—B 3	P—Q 5
	O—O	B—Kt 2	O—O	B—Kt 2	Kt—Q 2
8	Q—Kt 3	B—Q B 4 (f)	P—K 3	P—K 3	P—B 3
	Kt—Q 2	Kt—B 3	P—B 4	P—Q B 4	Q—Kt 3
9	Kt—B 3 (c)	B—K 3	B—K 2	B—Kt 5 ch	P × P
	P—B 4	O—O	Q—B 2	B—Q 2	B—Kt 2
10	R—Q 1	P—K R 3	O—O	P—B 4	O—O—O
	Q—R 4	P × P	P—Kt 3	Q—K 5	Q—R 3
11	B—K 2	P × P	P—Q R 4	O—O	P—Q Kt 3
	P × P	P—Q Kt 4 ?	Kt—B 3	B × B	P—K R 3
12	B—Kt 4	B—K 2	Q—R 3	P × B	B—R 4
	Q—Kt 3	B—Kt 2	Kt—R 4	Kt-Q 2 ∓ (k)	P—Q Kt 4 !
13	P × P ± (d)	O—O	Kt—Q 2		P—K 3
		Kt—R 4 (g)	B—Kt2 ∓ (i)		Kt—Kt 3 +
					(m)

(a) 5 P—K Kt 3, B—Kt 2 ; 6 B—Kt 2, Kt—Kt 3 ! ; 7 P—K 3, O—O ; 8 K Kt—K2,
P—K 4 =. Capablanca—Flohr, Hastings, 1934-35.
(b) 7 P—K B 4 involves some tricky gambit play: 7 ., P—Q B 4 ; 8 B—K 3,
Kt—B 3 (8 , Q—R 4 ? ; 9 K—B 2 !, O—O ; 10 Q—Kt 3, P × P ; 11 P × P, Kt—Q 2 ;
12 P—K R 3 +) ; 9 P—Q 5, B × P ch ; 10 K—B 2, B × R ; 11 Q × B, Kt—Q 5 ;
12 Kt—B 3, Q—R 4 ; 13 Kt × Kt, P × Kt ; 14 Q × P, O—O ; 15 P—K R 4 (Seitz—
P. Johner, Trieste, 1923). White has a strong attack, but it is doubtful whether it is
sufficient compensation for his material disadvantage.
(c) Weaker is 9 B—R 4, P—B 4 ; 10 Kt—B 3, P × P ; 11 P × P, Kt—Kt 3 ;
12 B—K 2, B—Q 2 ; 13 R—Q B 1, R—K 1, 14 O—O, P—K 3 ; 15 B—B 5, B—B 3 =.
Ed. Lasker—Kupchik, Lake Hopatcong, 1926
(d) R. P Michell—Torre, Marienbad, 1925.
(e) If 7 B—Q B 4, B—Kt 2, 8 Kt—K 2, O—O, 9 B—K 3, Q—B 2 ; 10 R—Q B 1,
Kt—Q 2 ; 11 O—O, R—Kt 1 ; 12 B—B 4 ?, P—K 4 ; 13 B—K Kt 3, P—Q Kt 4 ∓.
Stoltz—Kashdan, Bled, 1931.
(f) Or 8 B—K 3, Kt—B 3, 9 P—K R 3, O—O ; 10 Q—Q 2, Q—R 4 ; 11 B—Q B 4,
P × P ; 12 P × P, Q × Q ch ; 13 K × Q, R—Q 1 =. Vidmar—Alekhine, Nottingham,
1936. The older continuation 8 B—Kt 5 ch, B—Q 2 ; 9 B × B ch, Q × B ; 10 O—O,
P × P ; 11 P × P, Kt—B 3 ; 12 B—K 3, O—O (Kostich—Grunfeld, Teplitz-Schonau,
1922 and Kashdan—Alekhine, London, 1932) is disadvantageous for White, although
he need not necessarily lose.
(g) Continued 14 Q—Kt 1, P—Q R 3 ; 15 R—B 1, P—B 4 ; 16 P × P ±. Engels—
Alekhine, Dresden, 1936. Black's 11th move was premature, and compromised his
position.
(h) If 5 , P—Q B 3 ? ; 6 P—K 4, Kt × Kt ? ; 7 P × Kt, B—Kt 2 ; 8 B—R 3 !,
Kt—Q 2 ; 9 Kt—B 3, P—Q B 4 ; 10 B—K 2 ±. Alatorzeff—Lilienthal, Moscow, 1938
(i) Goglidse—Botvinnik, Moscow, 1935.
(j) Or 5 , Kt × B, 6 P—K R 4, Kt—K 5 ; 7 Kt × Kt, Q × P ; 8 Kt—Q B 3,
Q—Q R 4, 9 P—K 3, B—Kt 2 ; 10 P—R 5, Kt—B 3 ; 11 Q—Q 2, B—B 4 ∓. Kashdan
—Fine, New York, 1938
(k) Alekhine—Grünfeld, Vienna, 1922.
(l) A valuable improvement upon 6 B—Kt 2 ; 7 O—O—O, Kt—B 3 ; 8 P--K 3,
B—B 4 ; 9 P—B 3 ±. Lundin—Spielmann, Stockholm, 1933.
(m) Spielmann—Van den Bosch, 4th match game, 1934. B'ack has a winning
attack. The continuation was 14 P × P, Q—R 6 ch ; 15 K—Kt 1, Kt × P ! ; 16 Kt—K 2
O—O ; 17 Q—B 1, Q—Kt 5 ; 18 Q—B 4, Q × Q ; 19 P × Q, Kt × P . etc.

KING'S INDIAN DEFENCE
1 P—Q 4, Kt—K B 3; 2 P—Q B 4, P—K Kt 3.

GRUENFELD DEFENCE
3 Kt—Q B 3, P—Q 4.

	136	137	138	139	140
4	B—B 4				P—K 3
	B—Kt 2 (a)				B—Kt 2
5	P—K 3 (b)				Kt—B 3
	O—O				O—O
6	Q—Kt 3 (c)			Kt—B 3 ?	Q—Kt 3
	P—B 3		P×P (h)	P—B 4 !	P—B 3
7	Kt—B 3		K B×P (i)	P×Q P	B—Q 2
	P×P (d)		Q Kt—Q 2	Kt×P	P—Kt 3 (l)
8	B×P		Kt—B 3	B—K 5	P×P
	Q Kt—Q 2	...P—Q Kt 4 ?	Kt—Kt 3	Kt×Kt	P×P
9	O—O	B—K 2	B—K 2	P×Kt	Kt—K 5
	Kt—Kt 3	B—K 3	B—K 3	P×P	B—Kt 2
10	B—K 2	Q—B 2	Q—B 2	B×B	B—Kt 5
	B—K 3	P—Kt 5	K Kt—Q 4	K×B	P—Q R 3 (m)
11	Q—B 2	Kt—Q R 4	B—K 5	B P×P	B—K 2
	Q Kt—Q 4 (e)	Q—R 4	R—B 1	Q—R 4 ch	Q Kt—Q 2
12	B—K 5	Kt—B 5 !	Kt×Kt	Q—Q 2	Kt×Kt
	B—B 4	B—B 1	Q×Kt	Kt—B 3	Kt×Kt
13	Q—Kt 3	O—O + (g)	B×B (j)	B—K 2	P—B 4
	Q—Kt3 = (f)		Q—R 4 ch =	R—Q 1 ∓ (k)	P—K 3 = (n)

(a) If 4.., Kt—R 4?; 5 B—K 5, P—B 3, 6 B—Kt 3, Kt×B; 7 R P×Kt, P—Q B 3; 8 P—K 3, B—Kt 2; 9 B—Q 3+. Euwe—Alekhine, 14th match game, 1935 Or 4 ., P×P; 5 P—K 3 (5 Q—R 4 ch, P—B 3; 6 Q×B P, Q—Kt 3 =), Kt—Q 4; 6 B—K 5, P—K B 3; 7 B—Kt 3, Kt×Kt; 8 P×Kt, P—Q Kt 4; 9 P—Q R 4 !+, for if 9... P—B 3?; 10 P×P, P×P; 11 Q—B 3+ (Euwe).

(b) 5 B—K 5, P×P; 6 P—K 3, O—O 7 K B×P. Q Kt—Q 2; 8 Kt—B 3, P—B 4; 9 O—O ±. Colle—Grunfeld, Baden-Baden 1925. 5.., P—B 3 followed by 6.. O—O is better here, and sufficient for equality.

(c) Winning the Pawn leads to no lasting advantage for White. After 6 P×P, Kt×P; 7 Kt×Kt, Q×Kt; 8 B×P, there can follow either (1) 8 , Kt—R 3; 9 B—Kt 3, B—B 4; 10 P—Q R 3, Q R—B 1; 11 Kt—B 3, B—B 7; 12 B—O 3 R×Kt P; 13 O—O =. Kashdan—Santasiere, Milwaukee, 1935. (Flohr—Botvinnik, Avro, ran 9 B×Kt, Q×Kt P; 10 Q—B 3, Q×Q; 11 Kt×Q, P×B; 12 O—O, B—Kt 2; 13 Kt—K 5, P—B 3; 14 Kt—Q 3.) Or (2) 8.., Kt—B 3; 9 Kt—B 3, B—Kt 5; 10 B—K 2, Q R—B 1; 11 B—Kt 3, Q—R 4 ch; 12 Kt—Q 2, B×B; 13 Q×B, P—K 4 ! with sufficient compensation for the Pawn. Gilg—Helling, Leipzig, 1928.

(d) An unusual alternative is 7 , Q—R 4; 8 Kt—Q 2, Q Kt—Q 2; 9 B—K 2, R—K 1; 10 P×P, Kt×P; 11 Kt—B 4, Q—Q 1; 12 Kt×Kt?, P×Kt; 13 Kt—Q 2, P—K 4 ! =. Lisitzin—Romanovsky, Moscow, 1935.

(e) Better than 11 , K Kt—Q 4; 12 B—Kt 3, R—B 1; 13 P—K 4, Kt—B 2; 14 K R—Q 1, P—K R 3; 15 Kt—K 5, Q—K 1; 16 P—Q R 4 ±. Fine—Keres, Semmering-Baden, 1937.

(f) Capablanca—Flohr, Semmering-Baden, 1937.
(g) Euwe—Mikenas, Stockholm, 1937.
(h) But not 6 , P—B 4?; 7 B P×P, P×P; 8 P×P, Q Kt—Q 2; 9 B—K 2, Kt—Kt 3; 10 B—B 3+. Lovenfisch—Botvinnik, 1937. Or 7 Q P×P, Kt—K 5; 8 P×P, Q—R 4; 9 Kt—K 2, Kt×Q B P; 10 Q—B 4, Q Kt—R 3. Capablanca—Flohr, Avro, 1938. Flohr says 10 ., P—K 4 was better; if 11 P—Q Kt 4, Q×Kt P!.

(i) Better than 7 Q×P, P—B 3; 8 Kt—B 3, B—K 3; 9 Q—Q 3, Kt—Q 4; 10 B—K 5. B×B, 11 Kt×B, Kt—Q 2; 12 Kt×Kt, Q×Kt; 13 B—K 2, K R—Q 1 = Euwe—Flohr, Semmering, 1937.

(j) Reshevsky—Santasiere, New York, 1938. Continued 13.., K×B?; 14 P—Q Kt 4 ±.
(k) Eliskases—Flohr, Semmering-Baden, 1937.

Notes ctd. on p. 217.

KING'S INDIAN DEFENCE
1 P—Q 4, Kt—K B 3; 2 P—Q B 4, P—K Kt 3.

GRUENFELD DEFENCE
3 Kt—Q B 3, P—Q 4.

	141	142	143	144	145
4	P—K 3 B—Kt 2	....	....	P—B 3 (g)	
5	Kt—B 3 O—O			Kt—B 3 B—Kt 2	
6	Q—Kt 3 P—B 3		P—K 3 (e)	B—Q 3 O—O (h)	
7	B—Q 2 P—Kt 3	P—K 3	B—K 2 P—Q Kt 3	O—O P—K 3 (i)	...B—B 4
8	B—K 2 B—Kt 2	B—Q 3 Q Kt—Q 2	O—O B—Kt 2	P—Q Kt 3 Q Kt—Q 2	P×P (k) B×B
9	O—O Q Kt—Q 2	O—O P—Kt 3 (c)	R—Q 1 Q Kt—Q 2	Q—K 2 R—K 1	Q×B P×P
10	K R—Q 1 (a) P×P	P×P K P×P	B—Q 2 P—B 4	B—Kt 2 P—Kt 3	Q—Kt 5 Q—Q 2
11	B×P Kt—K 1 !	P—K 4 P×P	P×Q P Kt×P	Q R—Q 1 B—Kt 2	Q×Q Q Kt×Q
12	Q R—B 1 Kt—Q 3	Kt×P P—B 4 !	P×P Kt×B P	Kt—K 5 Kt×Kt	P—Q Kt 3 K R—B 1
13	B—K 2 P-Q B 4 = (b)	Kt×Kt ch Kt×Kt (d)	Q—R 3 Q—Kt 1 = (f)	P×Kt Kt—Q 2 = (j)	B—Kt 2 P—K 3 = (l)

(a) Or 10 P—Q R 4, P×P; 11 B×P, Kt—K 1; 12 P—R 5, P—Q Kt 4; 13 P—R 6, B—B 1; 14 B—K 2, Kt—B 2; 15 Kt—K 4, Kt×P =. Ragosin—Spielmann, Moscow, 1935.

(b) Bogatyrchuk—Spielmann, Moscow, 1935

(c) Weaker is 9 , Kt—Kt 3; 10 K R—Q 1, P×P; 11 B×B P, Kt×B; 12 Q×Kt, Kt—Q 2?; 13 P—K 4, Q—B 2; 14 P—K 5 ±. Fine—Lilienthal, Moscow, 1937.

(d) 14 P×P, P×P; 15 K R—Q 1, B—K 3; 16 Q—R 3, Kt—Q 4!. Fine—Mikenas, Kemeri, 1937. Black's weak Pawn-position is sufficiently counterbalanced by the aggressive placement of his pieces.

(e) Inferior is 6. , P×P; 7 B×P, Q Kt—Q 2; 8 Kt—K Kt 5! (8 O—O, Kt—Kt 3; 9 B—K 2, B—B 4; 10 B—Q 2, Kt—K 5 =. Eliskases—Keres, Semmering-Baden, 1937), P—K 3 (8 ., Q—K 1; 9 Kt—Kt 5+); 9 B×P, P×B, 10 Kt×P, Q—K 2; 11 Kt×P dis ch, K—R 1; 12 Kt×R, Kt—Kt 5!; 13 P—K R 3!, Kt×B P; 14 R—B 1, Q—R 5; 15 K—K 2+. since the complications are in White's favour.

(f) Flohr—Botvinnik, 12th match game, 1933.

(g) The Schlechter Variation. The position can also arise from the Slav Defence: 1 P—Q 4, P—Q 4; 2 P—Q B 4, P—Q B 3; 3 Kt—K B 3, Kt—B 3; 4 Kt—B 3, P—K Kt 3. For variations with Q—Kt 3 see cols 141—142.

(h) If 6 .., Q Kt—Q 2?; 7 P×P, Kt×P; 8 Kt×Kt, P×Kt; 9 O—O, O—O; 10 Q—Kt 3, Kt—B 3 (or 10 , Kt—Kt 1; 11 B—Q 2, Kt—B 3; 12 K R—B 1, B—B 3; 13 R—B 5+. Flohr—Sultan Khan, 6th match game, 1931); 11 B—Q 2, Kt—K 5; 12 K R—Q 1, Kt×B; 13 R×Kt, Q—Q 3; 14 R—Q B 1 ±. Rubinstein—Bogoljuboff, Vienna, 1922.

(i) On 7 , P—Kt 3; 8 P—Q Kt 3, P—B 4; 9 P×B P? (9 B—Kt 2 is preferable), Kt—K 5; 10 B×Kt, P×B; 11 Q×Q!, R×Q; 12 Kt—Q 4, P×P; 13 K Kt—K 2, B—Kt 5 ∓. Botvinnik—Lövenfisch, 10th match game, 1937.

(j) Botvinnik—Lövenfisch, 12th match game, 1937.

(k) Better than 8 B×B, P×B; 9 P×P, P×P; 10 Q—Kt 3, P—Kt 3; 11 B—Q 2, Kt—B 3; 12 K R—B 1, Q—Q 2; 13 B—K 1, P—K 3 ∓. W. A. Fairhurst—Flohr, Folkestone, 1933.

(l) Euwe—Flohr, Zurich, 1934.

KING'S INDIAN DEFENCE
1 P—Q 4, Kt—K B 3 ; 2 P—Q B 4, P—K Kt 3.

GRUENFELD DEFENCE
3 Kt—Q B 3, P—Q 4.

	146	147	148	149	150
4	Q—Kt 3			Kt—B 3	
	P×P ....P—B 3			B—Kt 2 .....P—B 3	
5	Q×B P	Kt—B 3 (f)	. . B—B 4	P×P (j)	P×P (m)
	B—K 3 (a)	B—Kt 2	P×P	Kt×P	P×P (n)
6	Q—Kt5ch(b)	P×P (g)	Q×B P	P—K Kt 3	Q—Kt 3
	Kt—B 3	P×P	B—K 3	O—O	B—Kt 2
7	Kt—B 3	B—Kt 5	Q—Q 3	B—Kt 2	B—B 4
	Kt—Q 4 ! (c)	Kt—B 3 !	Kt—Q 4	P—Q B 4	O—O
8	Kt×Kt (d)	P—K 3 !	Kt×Kt	O—O	P—K 3
	B×Kt	Kt—Q R 4	P×Kt	Kt×Kt	Kt—B 3
9	P—K 3	B—Kt 5 ch	Q—Kt 5 ch	P×Kt	P—K R 3
	P—K 3 !	K—B 1	Q—Q 2	Kt—B 3 (k)	Kt—Q R 4
10	B—Q 2	Q—B 2	P—K 3	P—K 3	Q—R 3
	P—Q R 3	B—B 4	Q×Q	Q—R 4	B—B 4
11	Q—R 4	B—Q 3	B×Q ch	Q—Kt 3	B—K 2
	B—Q 3	B×B	B—Q 2	R—Kt 1	P—Q R 3
12	B—K 2	Q×B	B—Q 3	B—R 3 (l)	O—O
	O—O	Kt—B 5	Kt—B 3	P—B 5	P—Q Kt4 ∓
13	Q—B 2	P—Q Kt3 ±	Kt—K2 ± (i)	Q—Kt 2	(o)
	Kt—Kt5 ∓ (e)	(h)		B—B 4 =	

(a) 5 ., B—Kt 2 leaves White in command of more space, but this advantage may easily prove to be of ephemeral value. E.g., 6 P—K 4, O—O; 7 Kt—B 3, P—Kt 3; 8 B—B 4, P—B 4 !, 9 P×P, B—R 3; 10 Q—Q 4, Q×Q; 11 Kt×Q, B×B; 12 R×B, Kt×P ! ∓. Botvinnik—Lovenfisch, Russian Championship, 1933.

(b) An alternative is 6 Q—R 4 ch, B—Q 2 ; 7 Q—Kt 3, B—B 3; 8 Kt—B 3, B—Kt 2 ; 9 P—K 3, O—O ; 10 B—K 2, Q Kt—Q 2 ; 11 O—O, Kt—Kt 3; 12 Q—B 2, Q Kt—Q 4 , 13 Kt—K 5 ±. Fine—Flohr, Semmering-Baden, 1937.

(c) Not 7 ., R—Q Kt 1 ? ; 8 Kt—K 5, B—Q 2 ; 9 Kt×B, Q×Kt; 10 P—Q 5 ±. Euwe—Alekhine, 2nd match game, 1935.

(d) This is weak. 8 P—K 4, Kt—Kt 5 ; 9 Q—R 4, B—Q 2 ; 10 Q—Q 1 is slightly in White's favour.

(e) Feigin—Flohr, Kemeri, 1937.

(f) If 5 P×P, Kt×P ! ; 6 P—K 3, Kt—Kt 3 ; 7 Kt—B 3, B—Kt 2 ; 8 B—K 2, B—K 3 ; 9 Q—B 2, B—B 5 ; 10 O—O, O—O ; 11 R—Q 1, B×B =. Lovenfisch—Spielmann, Moscow, 1935. 5 B—Kt 5 allows Black to obtain a strong initiative by 5 .., P×P ! (inferior is 5 , B—Kt 2 ; 6 P—K 3, O—O ; 7 P×P, Kt×P ; 8 Kt×Kt, P×Kt ; 9 Kt—K 2, Q—R 4 ch ; 10 Kt—B 3, P—K 3 ; 11 B—K 2, Kt—B 3 ; 12 O—O ±. Lövenfisch—Flohr, Moscow, 1935); 6 Q×B P, P—Q Kt 4 ; 7 Q—Q 3, B—B 4 ; 8 Q—Q 1, P—Kt 5 ; 9 Kt—R 4 (9 B×Kt, P×Kt ! +), Kt—K 5, etc.

(g) 6 P—K 3, O—O ; 7 B—Q 2, P—K 3 ; 8 B—Q 3, P—Kt 3 ; 9 O—O, B—Kt 2 ; 10 Q R—Q 1, Q Kt—Q 2 ; 11 P×P, K P×P ; 12 P—K 4. Reshevsky—Flohr, Avro, 1938.

(h) Petrov—Landau, Kemeri, 1937.

(i) Reshevsky—Mikenas, Hastings, 1937–38.

(j) Alternatives are: (1) 5 B—Kt 5, Kt—K 5 ; 6 P×P, Kt×B ; 7 Kt×Kt, P—K 3 ; 8 Kt—B 3, P×P ; 9 P—K 3, O—O ; 10 B—K 2, P—Q B 3 ; 11 O—O, Q—K 2 =. Lasker—Botvinnik, Nottingham, 1936. (2) 5 P×P, O—O ; 6 B—Q 3, P—B 4 ; 7 O—O (7 P×B P, P×P, 8 B×P, Q×Q ch ; 9 K×Q was better), P×Q P ; 8 Kt×P, Kt—B 3 ; 9 Kt×Kt, P×Kt ; 10 P—K R 3, B—K 3, 11 P×P, P×P =. Flohr—Bogoljuboff, Bled, 1931. (3) 5 Q—Kt 3, P—B 3 ; 6 B—B 4, P×P ; 7 Q×B P, B—K 3, 8 Q—Q 3, Kt—Q 4 ; 9 B—Q 2, Kt—Kt 5 ; 10 Q—Kt 1, P—Q B 4 ; 11 P×P, Q Kt—R 3 ; 12 P—K 4. Euwe—Botvinnik, Avro, 1938. Euwe—Landau, Hastings, 1938-39, ran 5 , P×P ; 6 Q×B P, B—K 3 ; 7 Q—Kt 5 ch, Kt—B 3 ; 8 Q×P, B—Q 2 ; 9 Q—Kt 3, R—Q Kt 1 ; 10 Q—Q 1, B—B 4 ; 11 Q—R 4, Q—Q 2. Here 6 ., O—O ; 7 B—B 4, P—B 3 ; 8 Q—Kt 3, Kt—Q 3 ; 9 P—K 3, B—K 3 ; 10 Q—R 3, P—Q R 4, is Klein—Szabo in the same tournament.

(k) Better than 9 ., P×P ; 10 Kt×P !, Q—B 2 ; 11 O—Kt 3, Kt—B 3 ; 12 Kt×Kt, P×Kt ; 13 B—B 4 P—K 4 ; 14 B—K 3 ±. Keres—Mikenas, Hastings, 1937–38.

Notes ctd. on p. 218

TCHIGORIN'S DEFENCE
1 P—Q 4, Kt—K B 3; 2 P—Q B 4 (a), P—Q 3.

	151	152	153	154	155
3	Kt—Q B 3............................Kt—K B 3				
	Q Kt—Q 2...P—K 4.....B—B 4			B—B 4......B—Kt 5	
4	P—K 4	P—K 4! (c)	P—K Kt 3	Kt—B 3	Kt—B 3 (j)
	P—K 4	Q Kt—Q 2 (d)	P—B 3	Q Kt—Q 2 (h)	Q Kt—Q 2
5	P—Q 5	Kt—B 3	B—Kt 2	Kt—K R 4	P—K 4
	Kt—B 4	B—K 2	Q Kt—Q 2 (g)	B—Kt 3	P—K 4
6	P—B 3	P—K Kt 3 (e)	P—K 4	Kt×B	B—K 2
	B—K 2	O—O	B—Kt 3	R P×Kt	B—K 2
7	B—K 3	B—Kt 2	K Kt—K 2	P—K Kt 3	O—O (k)
	O—O	P—B 3	P—K 4	P—K 4	O—O
8	P—Q Kt 4!	O—O	P—K R 3	B—Kt 2	B—K 3
	Q Kt—Q 2	Q—B 2	Q—Kt 3	P—B 3	P—B 3
9	B—Q 3	P—K R 3	O—O	P—Q 5	Kt—K 1
	Kt—K 1	R—K 1	O—O—O	P—B 4	B×B
10	K Kt—K 2	B—K 3	P—Q 5	P—K 4	Q×B
	P—K Kt 3	B—B 1	Kt—B 4	B—K 2	R—K 1
11	O—O	K—R 2	B—K 3	O—O	R—Q 1
	P—Q R 4 ?	P—Q Kt 3	P×P	P—R 3	B—B 1
12	P-QR3 ± (b)	R-QB1 ± (f)	B P×P ±	B—K 3	P—B 3 ± (l)
				Q—R 4 = (i)	

(a) 2 Kt—K B 3, P—Q 3; 3 Kt—B 3, B—B 4, 4 Kt—K R 4, P—K 3; 5 Kt×B, P×Kt; 6 Q—Q 3, Q—Q 2, 7 P—K Kt 3, P—Q 4; 8 B—Kt 2, P—B 3 =. Sämisch—Réti, Pistyan, 1922. Another possibility here is 3 P—K 3, P—B 3; 4 B—Q 3, P—K 4; 5 Q Kt—Q 2, Q—B 2; 6 O—O, B—Kt 5; 7 P—Q Kt 3, B—K 2 =. Flohr—Sämisch, Swinemünde, 1930.
(b) Continued 12.., Kt—Kt 2; 13 B—R 6, P—B 3; 14 Q—Kt 3!. Capablanca—Rumin, Moscow, 1936.
(c) Weak is 4 P×P?, P×P; 5 Q×Q ch, K×Q; 6 Kt—B 3, K Kt—Q 2; 7 P—K Kt 3, P—K B 3; 8 B—Kt 2, P—B 3; 9 O—O, K—B 2; 10 P—Q R 3, Kt—Kt 3; 11 P—Kt 3, B—K B 4 ∓. Ragosin—Kan, Moscow, 1936. And 4 Kt—B 3 is too passive: 4.., Q Kt—Q 2; 5 P—K Kt 3, P×P; 6 Kt×P, P—B 3!; 7 B—Kt 2, Kt—Kt 3, 8 Q—Q 3, P—Q 4 ∓. Euwe—Réti, Mährisch-Ostrau, 1923.
(d) Or 4.., P×P; 5 P—K Kt 3, P×P; 6 Kt×P, P—B 3!; 7 K Kt—K 2, B—Kt 2; 8 P—B 3 ±. Alatorzeff—Rumin, Leningrad, 1934.
(e) Equally good is 6 B—K 2, O—O; 7 O—O, R—K 1; 8 B—K 3, Kt—Kt 5; 9 B—Q 2 ±.
(f) Rubinstein—Przepiorka, Marienbad, 1925.
(g) 5.., P—K 4 is playable. If 6 P×P, P×P; 7 Q×Q ch, K×Q; 8 Kt—B 3, Q Kt—Q 2 =. Rabinovitch—Capablanca, Moscow, 1925.—The column is Alekhine—Janowski, New York, 1924.
(h) Or 4.., P—K R 3; 5 P—K 3 (after 5 P—K Kt 3, P—B 3; 6 B—Kt 2, Q—B 1; 7 P—K R 3, Q Kt—Q 2; 8 Kt—Q 2, P—K 4; 9 P—Q 5, B—K 2; 10 P—K 4, B—R 2; 11 Q—K 2, O—O; 12 Kt—B 1, P×P Black has a strong initiative. Grunfeld—Réti, Pistyan, 1922), Q Kt—Q 2; 6 B—Q 3, B×B; 7 Q×B, P—K 4 =. Grunfeld—Réti, Carlsbad, 1923.
(i) Grunfeld—Lasker, Mährisch-Ostrau, 1923.
(j) Weaker is 4 Q—Kt 3, B×Kt! (or 4.., Q—B 1; 5 P—K R 3, B—B 4; 6 Kt—B 3, Q Kt—Q 2; 7 P—Kt 4, B—Kt 3; 8 B—B 4 =. Alekhine—Réti, Margate, 1923); 5 Kt P×B, Q—B 1; 6 P—B 4, P—K Kt 3; 7 B—Kt 2, P—B 3; 8 Kt—Q 2, B—Kt 2; 9 O—O, O—O; 10 Kt—B 3 Q Kt—Q 2; 11 B—K 3, P—K 3; 12 Q R—B 1, R—Q 1 ∓ Appel—Tartakover, Lodz, 1938.
(k) More aggressive than 7 B—K 3, O—O; 8 P—K R 3, B×Kt; 9 B×B, R—K 1; 10 P—Q 5, Kt—B 1; 11 P—K Kt 3, K Kt—Q 2; 12 Q—Q 2, Kt—Kt 3 =. Grünfeld—Lasker, Moscow, 1925.
(l) Continued 12 , Q—R 4; 13 Kt—B 2, Q R—Q 1; 14 P—Q 5, P×P; 15 Kt×P, R—B 1; 16 Kt—B 3, P—Q R 3. Keres—Tartakover, Ostend, 1937. White's advantage is difficult to maintain.

BUDAPEST DEFENCE
1 P—Q4, Kt—KB3; 2 P—QB4, P—K4; 3 P×P.

	156	157	158	159	160
3	Kt—Kt5..				Kt—K5 (k)
4	P—K4..................		B—B4 (f)		Kt—Q2 (l)
	Kt×KP (a)		Kt—QB3		Kt—B4
5	P—B4......	Kt—QB3	Kt—KB3		K Kt—B3
	K Kt—B3 (b)	B—Q Kt5	B—Kt5 ch		Kt—B3
6	Kt—KB3 (c)	Kt—B3	Q Kt—Q2...	Kt—B3	P—K Kt3
	B—B4	B×Kt ch	Q—K2 (g)	Q—K2	Q—K2
7	Kt—B3	P×B	P—QR3	Q—Q5	B—Kt2
	P—Q3	Q—K2	K Kt×P!	B×Kt ch	P—K Kt3
8	P—QR3	B—K2	Kt×Kt!	P×B	Kt—QKt1!
	P—QR4?	O—O	Kt×Kt	Q—R6 (i)	Kt×P
9	B—Q3	Kt—Q4	P—K3	R—B1 (j)	O—O
	O—O	P—Q3	B×Kt ch	P—B3	Kt×Kt ch?
10	Q—K2	O—O	Q×B	P×P	P×Kt!
	B—K Kt5	Kt—R3	O—O	Kt×P (B3)	B—Kt2
11	B—K3	P—B4	B—K2	Q—Q2	R—K1
	Kt—Q5	Kt—B3	P—Q3	P—Q3	Kt—K3
12	Q—KB2	R—K1	O—O	Kt—Q4	Kt—B3
	B×Kt	Kt×Kt	B—B4	O—O	O—O
13	B×Kt ± (d)	P×Kt ± (e)	Q R—B1	P—B3! ±	Kt—Q5 +
			QR—Q1=(h)		(m)

(a) Best. If instead 4.., P—KR4; 5 Kt—QB3, Kt—QB3 (or 5.., B—B4; 6 Kt—R3, Kt—QB3; 7 Kt—Q5, K Kt×KP; 8 B—Kt5, P—B3; 9 B—K3, P—Q3; 10 K Kt—B4+. Euwe—Mieses, Hastings, 1924); 6 Kt—R3, K Kt×KP; 7 B—K2, P—Q3; 8 Kt—B4, P—KKt3; 9 O—O ±. Sämisch—Spielmann, Copenhagen, 1923. Or 4 , P—Q3; 5 P×P, B×P; 6 B—K2, P—KB4; 7 P×P, Q—K2; 8 Kt—KB3 (8 P—B5 wins a piece, but exposes White to a strong attack), B×P; 9 B—K Kt5, Kt—KB3; 10 Kt—B3, Kt—B3; 11 Kt—Q5 ±. Capablanca—Tartakover, Kissingen, 1928.

(b) Superior to the alternative 5.., Kt—Kt3; 6 Kt—KB3, B—B4; 7 P—B5, Kt—R5?; 8 Kt—Kt5!, Q—K2; 9 Q—Kt4+. Alekhine—Rabinovitch, Baden-Baden, 1925. Playable is 6 , B—Kt5 ch, 7 Kt—B3 (7 Kt—Q2, Q—K2; 8 B—Q3?, Q—Q3! wins a Pawn for Black), Q—K2; 8 B—Q3, B×Kt ch; 9 P×B, P—Q3; 10 O—O, O—O.

(c) 6 B—K3, P—QR4; 7 Kt—KB3, Kt—R3; 8 Kt—B3, B—B4; 9 Q—Q2 is also in White's favour.

(d) Yates—Spielmann, Carlsbad, 1923.

(e) Continued 13 , Q×P; 14 B—B3, Q—Kt3; 15 B—R3, Q—B3; 16 Q—Q2, P—B3; 17 P—Q5, P—B4; 18 B—Kt2. Tartakover—Tarrasch, Semmering, 1926. In the column 8.., Kt×Kt ch was better.

(f) 4 Kt—KB3, B—B4; 5 P—K3, Kt—QB3; 6 B—K2, K Kt×KP; 7 Kt×Kt, Kt×Kt; 8 O—O, O—O leads to a level position, while 4 Q—Q4 is too impetuous. After 4 , P—Q3! (4 , P—KR4?); 5 P—KR3, Kt—QB3; 6 Q—Q4, K Kt×KP; 7 P—B4, Q—R5 ch; 8 K—Q1++); 5 P×P, B×P; 6 Kt—KB3, O—O; 7 Kt—B3, Kt—B3; 8 Q—Q1, B—K3; 9 P—K3, Q—K2; 10 B—K2, Q R—Q1 Black has a powerful attack.

(g) If instead 6.., P—B3; 7 P×P, Q×P; 8 P—KKt3, Q×Kt P; 9 B—Kt2, P—Q3; 10 O—O, O—O; 11 Kt—Kt3, Q—Kt3; 12 Kt—R5, P—KR3; 13 Kt—K4, Q—K4, Q—B2; 14 P—QR3+. Rubinstein—Tartakover, Kissingen, 1928.

(h) White's advantage is negligible.

(i) If 8 , P—B3; 9 P×P, Kt×P (B3); 10 Q—Q1, Kt—K5; 11 P—K3, P—Q3; 12 B—Q3, Kt—B4; 13 B—B2, O—O; 14 O—O+. Simonson—Kevitz, 2nd match game 1936

continued on p 218

1 P—Q 4, Kt—K B 3.

BLUMENFELD COUNTER GAMBIT

	161	**162**	**163**	**164**	**165**
2	P—Q B 4 / P—K 3	....		Kt—K B 3 / P—B 4	
3	Kt—K B 3 / P—B 4			P—Q 5 (j) / P—Q 3 (k)	
4	P—Q 5 / P—Q Kt 4			P—B 4 / P—K 4	Kt—B 3 / B—B 4 (m)
5	B—Kt 5 (a) / K P×P	P—K R 3	Q—R 4 ch	Kt—B 3 / B—B 4	Kt—Q 2 / P—K Kt 4
6	P×Q P / P—K R 3	B×Kt / Q×B	Q—Q 2 / Q×Q ch	P—K Kt 3 / P—K R 3	P—K 4 / B—Kt 3
7	B×Kt / Q×B	Kt—B 3 / P—Kt 5	Q Kt×Q / P×Q P (h)	B—Kt 2 / P—K Kt 4	B—K 2 / B—Kt 2
8	Q—B 2 (b) / P—Q 3	Kt—Kt 5 / Kt—R 3	B×Kt / P×B	Kt—Q 2 / B—Kt 2	O—O / Q Kt—Q 2
9	P—K 4 / P—R 3	P—K 4 / P—K 4 (f)	P×Q P / B—Q Kt 2	P—K 4 / B—Q 2	R—K 1 / O—O
10	P—Q R 4 / P—Kt 5	P—K Kt 3 / P—Kt 4	P—K 4 ! / P—Q R 3	Kt—B 1 / Kt—R 3	B—B 1 / Kt—K 4
11	Q Kt—Q 2 (c) / B—Kt 5	B—R 3 / B—K Kt 2	Kt—R 4 / P—Q 3	Kt—K 3 / Q—B 2	Kt—B 3 / Kt×Kt ch
12	B—K 2 (d) / Kt—Q 2 = (e)	Kt—Q 2 / Q—Q Kt 3 (g)	P—R 4 + (i)	Q—K 2 ± (l)	Q×Kt / P—K R 3 = (n)

(a) Undoubtedly strongest Alternatives are: (1) 5 P×K P, B P×P; 6 P×P, P—Q 4; 7 P—K 3, B—Q 3; 8 Kt—B 3, O—O; 9 B—K 2, B—Kt 2; 10 P—Q Kt 3, Q Kt—Q 2; 11 B—Kt 2, Q—K 2; 12 O—O, Q R—Q 1; 13 Q—B 2, P—K 4 $\mp$. Tarrasch—Alekhine, Pistyan, 1922. (2) 5 Kt—B 3, P—Kt 5!; 6 Kt—Q R 4, P×P; 7 P×P, P—Q 3; 8 B—Kt 5, B—K 2; 9 P—K 3, O—O; 10 B—Q B 4, Q Kt—Q 2; 11 O—O, B—Kt 2; 12 P—K R 3, Kt—Kt 3 $\mp$. H Steiner—Samisch, Berlin, 1930. (3) 5 P—K 4, Kt×K P; 6 Q P×P, B P×P; 7 B—Q 3, Kt—K B 3; 8 Kt—Kt 5; Q—K 2; 9 P×P, P—Q 4; 10 O—O, P—K Kt 3; 11 R—K 1, K B—Kt 2 =. Rubinstein—Tartakover, Teplitz-Schonau, 1922.

(b) If 8 Kt—B 3, P—Kt 5, 9 Kt—Kt 5, Q—Q Kt 3; 10 Q—R 4, P—R 3; 11 P—K 4, B—Kt 2, and the White Kt has no escape.

(c) 11 P—K R 3 is superior, and sufficient to give White an advantage.

(d) If 12 P—K 5, Q—K 2! (but not 12 , P×P; 13 Kt—K 4, Q—K 2, 14 P—Q 6 +); 13 Q—K 4, B×Kt; 14 Kt×B, Kt—Q 2 =.

(e) Kmoch—Spielmann, Semmering, 1926. 13 Kt—K Kt 1 is now best.

(f) If 9 , Q×Kt P; 10 B—Q 3, P—Q 3; 11 O—O, B—Q 2; 12 Q—R 4, Q—R 6; 13 Q×Kt, Q×Q; 14 Kt—B 7 ch +. Helling—Leonhardt, Berlin, 1928.

(g) 13 Q—R 4 +. M. E. Goldstein—G. E. Smith, London, 1922.

(h) Or 7 , P×B P, 8 B×Kt, P×B; 9 P—K 4, P—B 4; 10 B×P +. Grünfeld—Rabinovitch, Baden-Baden, 1925.

(i) Continued 12 , P—Kt 5; 13 Kt—B 4, K—Q 1; 14 B—K 2, P—K R 4; 15 Kt—B 5. Marshall—Hanauer, New York, 1937.

(j) This position can also arise from the Benoni Counter-Gambit: 1 P—Q 4, P—Q B 4; 2 P—Q 5, Kt—K B 3; 3 Kt—K B 3.

(k) If 3 , P—Q Kt 4, 4 P—B 4!, B—Kt 2 (for 4 ., P—K 3 se cols. 161—163), 5 P—Q R 4!, P×B P; 6 Kt—B 3, P—K 3; 7 P—K 4, Kt×h ; 8 Kt×Kt, P×P; 9 K—B 3, P—Q 5; 10 B×P, P×Kt; 11 B×P ch, K× 12 Q—Kt 3 ch +. Rubinstein—Spielmann, Vienna, 1922.

(l) Bogoljuboff—Hromadka, Pistyan, 1922.

(m) Or 4.., P—K Kt 3; 5 P—K Kt 3, B—B 4; 6 B—Kt 2, Kt—R 3; 7 O—O, Q—Q 2; 8 R—K 1, Kt—K 5; 9 Kt—Kt 1, B—R 6, 10 B—R 1, B—Kt 2; 11 K Kt—Q 2, Kt—B 3 with a good position. Euwe—Mieses, Scheveningen, 1923.

(n) Grünfeld—Spielmann, Pistyan, 1922

1 P—Q 4.

	166	167	168	169	170
1	Kt—K B 3				.P—K 3
2	Kt—K B 3				Kt—Q 2 (i)
	P—K 3 (a)				P—Q B 4
3	P—K 3	B—Kt 5			P × P
	P—B 4 (b)	P—Q Kt 3 (d)	.P—B 4		Q—R 4
4	P—Q Kt 3	P—K 3	P—K 3 (f)		P—Q B 3
	P × P	B—Kt 2	Q—Kt 3	....P × P	Q × P (B 4)
5	P × P	B—Q 3	Q—B 1	P × P	P—K Kt 3
	P—Q Kt 3	B—K 2	Kt—K 5	B—K 2	Kt—K B 3
6	B—Kt 2	Q Kt—Q 2	B—K B 4	Q Kt—Q 2	B—Kt 2
	B—Kt 2	P—Q 3	P—Q 4	P—Q 3	P—Q 4
7	Q Kt—Q 2	O—O	B—Q 3	P--B 3	K Kt—B 3
	B—K 2	Q Kt—Q 2	Q Kt—Q 2	Q Kt—Q 2	Q—B 2
8	P—B 4	P—K 4	O—O	B—Q 3	O—O
	O—O	P—K 4 ?	B—Q 3	P—Q Kt 3	Kt—B 3
9	B—Q 3	R—K 1	B × B	Kt—B 4	P—K 4 ! ?
	P—Q 3	Kt—Kt 5	Q × B	B—Kt 2	B—K 2
10	O—O	B × B	P—B 4	Q—K 2	P × P
	Q Kt—Q 2	Q × B	O—O	Q—B 2	Kt × P
11	R—K 1	Kt—B 4	Q—B 2	O—O	Kt—B 4
	R—K 1	O—O	K Kt—B 3 .	O—O	O—O
12	Kt—B 1 (c)	Q—Q 2 + (e)	B P × P	K R—K 1	Kt—K 3
	P—Q 4 =		K P × P (g)	KR-K1 = (h)	Kt-B3 ∓ (j)

(a) 2 ., P—Q Kt 4 (the Polish Defence); 3 P—K 3 (or 3 B—B 4, B—Kt 2;
4 P—K 3, P—Q R 3; 5 Q Kt—Q 2, P—K 3; 6 B—Q 3, P—B 4. Torre—Dus-
Chotimirsky, Moscow, 1925), P—Q R 3; 4 B—Q 3, B—Kt 2; 5 Q Kt—Q 2, P—K 3;
6 O—O, P—B 4; 7 P—B 4, Kt P × P; 8 Kt × P, Kt—B 3, 9 P—Q Kt 3, Q—B 2;
10 B—Kt 2, P × P; 11 P × P, Kt—Q Kt 5 =. Sir G. A. Thomas—Sämisch, Marienbad,
1925. Or 2 ., Kt—K 5 (sometimes called the Dory Defence); 3 K Kt—Q 2, P—Q 4;
4 Kt × Kt, P × Kt; 5 Kt—B 3, B—B 4; 6 P—K Kt 4!, B × P; 7 Kt × P, P—K 4;
8 P × P, Q × Q ch; 9 K × Q, Kt—B 3; 10 P—K B 4, O—O—O ch; 11 B—Q 2, Kt—Q 5;
12 Kt—B 2 ±. Keres—Becker, Vienna, 1937
(b) 3 .., P—Kt 3 transposes into the Colle System, cols. 5—6.
(c) Better 12 Q—B 2, Q R—B 1; 13 Q R—Q 1, P—Q 4, 14 Q—Kt 1 (Tartakover).
The column is Rubinstein—Spielmann, Kissingen, 1928.
(d) Or 3 ., P—K R 3; 4 B—R 4, P—Q Kt 3; 5 Q Kt—Q 2, B—Kt 2; 6 P—K·3,
B—K 2, 7 B—Q 3, P—Q 3; 8 P—B 3, O—O, 9 P—K R 3, P—B 4; 10 O—O, Kt—B 3:
11 Q—K 2, Kt—K R 4; 12 B × B, Q × B; 13 B—R 6, Kt—B 3 =. Capablanca—
Nimzovitch, New York, 1927.
(e) Keres—Petrov, Semmering-Baden, 1937.
(f) Alternatives are (1) 4 P—B 3, Q—Kt 3 (4.., P—K R 3?; 5 B × Kt, Q × B;
6 P—K 4, Q—Q 1, 7 P—Q 5, Q—B 2; 8 Kt—R 3!+. Alekhine—A. Steiner, Kemeri,
1937); 5 Q—B 2, P × P; 6 Kt × P, Kt—B 3; 7 P—K 3, P—Q 4; 8 Kt—Q 2, B—Q 2,
9 Q Kt—B 3?, Kt—K 5; 10 B—KB 4, P—B 3+. Marshall—Capablanca, New York,
1927. (2) 4 P—K 4, P—K R 3; 5 B × Kt, Q × B; 6 P—K 5, Q—Q 1; 7 Kt—B 3,
P × P; 8 Kt × P, Kt—B 3; 8 Kt × Kt, Kt P × Kt =. Torre—Sämisch, Marienbad,
1925.
(g) Continued 13 P × P, Kt × P; 14 Kt—B 3, B—K 3 =. Alekhine—Spielmann,
Semmering, 1926. The isolated Pawn is no handicap in this position.
(h) Torre—Lasker, Moscow, 1925.
(i) 2 Kt—K B 3, P—Q B 4; 3 P—B 4, P × P; 4 Kt × P, P—K 4 ! ?; 5 Kt—B 2,
Kt—Q B 3; 6 Kt—B 3, Kt—B 3, 7 P—K Kt 3, B—B 4; 8 B—Kt 2, P—Q 3; 9 O—O,
O—O; 10 B—K 3, B × B; 11 Kt × B, B—Q 2; 12 Q—Q 2 ±. Grünfeld—Alekhine,
Amsterdam, 1936. Or 2 P—Q B 4, B—Kt 5 ch; 3 Kt—B 3, P—K B 4; 4 Q—Kt 3,
Q—K 2, 5 P—Q R 3, B × Kt ch; 6 Q × B, Kt—K B 3; 7 P—K Kt 3, P—Q 3. Euwe---
Keres, Avro, 1938.
(j) Mikenas—Alekhine, Warsaw, 1935.

BENONI COUNTER GAMBIT
1 P—Q 4, P—Q B 4.

	171	172	173	174	175
2	P—Q 5 (a) P—K 4 (b)				
3	P—K 4 .... P—Q 3			P—Q B 4.... P—Q 3	Kt—K B 3 P—Q 3
4	Kt—Q B 3 B—K 2 (c)	B—Q 3 P—Q R 3	P—K B 4 P×P	Kt—Q B 3 Kt—K B 3 (k)	P—K Kt 3 P—K Kt 3
5	B—Q 3 B—Kt 4	P—Q R 4 Kt—K 2	B×P Q—R 5 ch (f)	P—K Kt 3 (l) P-K Kt 3 (m)	B—Kt 2 B—Kt 2
6	Kt—B 3 B×B	Kt—K 2 Kt—Kt 3	P—Kt 3 Q—K 2	B—Kt 2 B—Kt 2	Kt—B 3 Kt—K 2
7	Q×B Kt—K R 3	Kt—R 3 B—K 2	Kt-K B 3! (g) Q×P ch (h)	P—K 4 O—O	O—O O—O
8	P—K R 3 P—B 4	Kt—Q B 4 O—O	K—B 2 Kt—K B 3 (i)	K Kt—K 2 Q Kt—Q 2	Kt—Q 2 P—B 4
9	Q—Kt 5 ! O—O	O—O Kt—Q 2	B—R 3 ! K—Q 1	O—O Kt—K 1	Kt—B 4 P—Q R 3
10	Q×Q R×Q	B—Q 2 P—Q Kt 3	Kt—B 3 Q—Kt 3	B—K 3 R—Kt 1	P—Q R 4 P—Kt 3
11	Kt—K Kt 5 P—K Kt 3	P—Q B 3 R—Kt 1	B×B K×B	Q—Q 2 P—Q R 3	B—Kt 5 R—R 2
12	P—B 4! + (d)	P—Q Kt 4 ± (e)	R—K 1 + (j)	P—Q R 4 ± (n)	Q—Q 2 ± (o)

(a) The most aggressive reply. 2 P—K 3, P—Q 4 transposes into other variations of the Queen's Gambit or Queen's Pawn Game, 2.., P×P, 3 P×P, P—Q 4 into a variation of the Caro-Kann Defence.

(b) 2.., Kt—K B 3; 3 Kt—K B 3 transposes into cols. 164—165.

(c) 4 , P—B 4; 5 B—Kt 5 ch, K—B 2! (5.., B—Q 2?; 6 P×P+) merits consideration.

(d) Alekhine—Tartakover, Dresden, 1926.

(e) Kmoch—Alekhine, Amsterdam, 1936.

(f) 5.., Kt—K 2, 6 Kt—K B 3, Kt—Kt 3; 7 B—Kt 3, Kt—Q 2; 8 Q Kt—Q 2, B—K 2; 9 Kt—B 4, Kt—Kt 3; 10 Kt—K 3, O—O; 11 B—Q 3 ±. Fine—Santasiere, Milwaukee, 1935.

(g) If instead 7 Kt—Q B 3?, P—K Kt 4!; 8 B—K 3, Kt—Q 2; 9 Kt—B 3, P—K R 3, 10 Q—Q 2, K Kt—B 3; 11 O—O—O, Kt—Kt 5, 12 B—K 2, B—Kt 2; 13 K R—B 1, Kt×B ∓. Bogoljuboff—Alekhine, 9th match game, 1934.

(h) Black has no good continuation. If 7.., B—Kt 5, 8 Kt—B 3, P—Q R 3; 9 P—K R 3, B×Kt; 10 Q×B, Kt—Q 2; 11 P—K R 4, Kt—K 4; 12 B×Kt, Q×B; 13 B—R 3, B—K 2; 14 O—O, B—B 3; 15 Kt—Q 1!+. Eliskases—Krogius, Munich, 1936. Or 7 ., Kt—K B 3; 8 Kt—B 3, Kt×K P; 9 Kt×kt, Q×Kt ch; 10 K—B 2, B—Kt 5, 11 B—Kt 5 ch, K—Q 1; 12 R—K 1, Q×Kt ch; 13 Q×Q, B×Q; 14 R×B ch+. White has a paralysing grip.

(i) Or 8 ., B—Kt 5; 9 B—Kt 5 ch, K—Q 1; 10 R—K 1, Q×Kt ch; 11 Q×Q, B×Q; 12 R—K 8 ch, K—B 2; 13 R×B, B×P, 14 Kt—B 3, with a winning position. (j) 12 ., P—Q R 3; 13 Kt—Q R 4, K—B 2 (13 , Q Kt—Q 2?; 14 Kt—R 4, Q—Kt 5; 15 R—K 8 ch+ +); 14 Kt×P. Enevoldsen—Winz, Warsaw, 1935.

(k) 4.., P—B 4; 5 P—K 4, Kt—K B 3; 6 B—Q 3, P—B 5; 7 Kt—B 3, B—Kt 5; 8 B—K 2, B—K 2; 9 B—Q 2, Q Kt—Q 2; 10 P—K R 3 ±. Belson—Santasiere, Milwaukee, 1935.

(l) Another good continuation is 5 P—K 4, B—K 2; 6 K Kt—K 2, O—O; 7 Kt—Kt 3, P—Q R 3; 8 B—Q 3, Kt—K 1; 9 P—K R 4!, P—Q Kt 3; 10 B—K 3, Kt—B 2; 11 Q—K 2, R—K 1; 12 Kt—R 4, Bastrikoff—Panoff, 1938.

(m) Or 5.., B—K 2; 6 B—Kt 2, O—O; 7 P—K 4, Kt—K 1; 8 K Kt—K 2, P—B 4; 9 O—O, P×P; 10 Kt×P, B—B 4; 11 P—B 4+. Becker—Grunfeld, 1922

(n) Rabinovitch—Miss Menchik, Moscow, 1935.

(o) Bolbochan—Grau, 7th match game, 1935.

DUTCH DEFENCE

1 P—Q 4, P—K B 4 ; 2 P—K Kt 3, Kt—K B 3 ; 3 B—Kt 2, P—K 3 , 4 Kt—K B 3, B—K 2 ; 5 P—B 4, O—O.

	176	177	178	179	180
6	O—O (a)				
	P—Q 3...............		Kt—K 5 (f).	P—Q 4	
7	Kt—B 3		P—Q 5 ! (g)	Kt—B 3	
	Q—K 1		B—B 3	P—B 3	
8	R—K 1.....	P—Kt 3 (c)	Q—B 2	R—Kt 1....	Q—Q 3
	Q—R 4	Q—R 4	P—Q R 4	Q—K 1	Kt—K 5
9	P—K 4	B—Q R 3 (d)	Q Kt—Q 2	P—B 5	Kt—K 5
	P×P	Q Kt—Q 2	Kt—B 4	Q—R 4	Kt—Q 2
10	Kt×P	Q—B 2	P—K 4	P—Q Kt 4	K Kt×Kt
	Kt×Kt	Kt—Kt 5	Kt×P	Kt—K 5	B×Kt
11	R×Kt	Q R—Q 1	Kt×Kt	Q—B 2	P—B 3
	Kt—B 3	P—Q R 3	P×Kt	Kt—Q 2	Kt×Kt
12	B—B 4	K R—K 1	Q×P	P—Kt 5	P×Kt
	B—B 3	R—Kt 1	P×P	B—B 3	P×P
13	P—K R 4	P—K 4	Q×Q P ch	B—B 4	Q×Q B P (l)
	P—K R 3	P×P	K—R 1	Q—K 1 ! (i)	Q—Kt 3 =
14	R—B 1	Kt×P	Kt—Kt 5	B—B 7 !	
	P—R 3	P—Q Kt 3	Q—K 1	R—B 2 (j)	
15	P—B 5! ± (b)	P—R 3 + (e)	B—B 4 ± (h)	B—R 5	
				P—K 4 = (k)	

(a) 6 P—K 3, P—Q 3 ; 7 Kt—B 3, Q—K 1 ; 8 Q—K 2, Kt—B 3 ? ; 9 P—Q 5, Kt—Q 1 ; 10 Kt—Q Kt 5, Q—Q 2, 11 Kt—Kt 5, P—K 4 ± Grob—Flohr, Rosas, 1935. Weaker is 6 Kt—B 3, P—Q 3, 7 B—B 4, Q—K 1 ; 8 Q R—B 1, Kt—B 3 ; 9 P—Q 5, Kt—Q 1 ; 10 Kt—Q Kt 5, Q—Q 2, 11 Q—Kt 3, P—Q R 3 ; 12 P×P, Kt×P. Bogoljuboff—Alekhine, 11th match game, 1934.

(b) Winter—Mikenas, Lodz, 1935.

(c) The position is decidedly in White's favour, and the various alternatives are of approximately equal value. Besides the two lines given White can play (1) 8 Q—B 2 Kt—B 3 ? (8 , Q—R 4 ; 9 P—K 4, P×P is better) ; 9 P—Q 5 (this is important, if, instead 9 P—K 4, P×P; 10 Kt×P, P—K 4 ; 11 P×P, P×P ; 12 B—K 3, Q—R 4 ; 13 Kt×Kt ch, B×Kt ; 14 Kt—Q 2, B—Kt 5 =. Herzog—Flohr, Bad Liebwerda, 1934), Kt—Q Kt 5 ; 10 Q—Kt 3, Kt—R 3 ; 11 P×P, Kt—B 4 ; 12 Q—B 2, B×P, 13 P—Kt 3+. Fine—Bogoljuboff, Nottingham, 1936. (2) 8 Q—Kt 3, K—R 1; 9 B—B 4, Q Kt—Q 2 ; 10 Q R—K 1, Kt—R 4 ; 11 B—Kt 5, P—B 3, 12 P—K 4, P—B 5 ; 13 B×B, Q×B ; 14 P—K 5 ±. Pirc—Flohr, Ujpest, 1934.

(d) Weaker is 9 B—Kt 2, Q Kt—Q 2 ; 10 Q—B 2, Kt—Kt 5 ; 11 P—K R 3, Kt—R 3 ; 12 P—K 3, P—K Kt 4 ; 13 Kt—K 2, P—B 3 ; 14 K R—Q 1, Kt—B 3 =. Grünfeld—Bogoljuboff, Zandvoort, 1936.

(e) Alexander—Tartakover, Nottingham, 1936.

(f) A variation introduced and recommended by Alekhine See also col. 187

(g) Probably best. Alternatives that have been tried are · (1) 7 Q—Kt 3, B—B 3, 8 R—Q 1, Q—K 1 ; 9 Kt—B 3, Kt—B 3, 10 Kt—Q Kt 5, B—Q 1 ; 11 Q—B 2 (11 P—Q 5 was better), P—Q 3 ; 12 P—Q 5, Kt—Kt 5, Kt—R 3 ∓. Capablanca—Alekhine, Nottingham, 1936. (2) 7 Kt—K 1, P—Q 4 ; 8 P—B 3, Kt—K B 3 ; 9 P×P, P×P ; 10 Kt—Q 3, P—Q Kt 3, 11 B—K 3, B—Q 3 ; 12 Kt—B 3, P—B 3, 13 R—B 1, Q—K 2 =. Flohr—Alekhine, Podebrady, 1936. (3) 7 Q—Kt 2, B—B 3 ; 8 Q—B 2, P—Q 4 ; 9 P—Kt 3, P—B 4 ; 10 B—Kt 2, B P×P ; 11 Kt×P, Kt—B 3 ; 12 Q Kt×Kt, B P×Kt ; 13 Q R—Q 1, Q—Kt 3 ! =. Fine—Alekhine, Amsterdam, 1936

(h) Reshevsky—Suesman, New York, 1938.

(i) If 13 , Q Kt×P ? ; 14 Kt×Kt, Kt×Kt ; 15 P×P+ ; or 14.., B P×Kt ; 15 Q×Kt, P×Kt ±.

(j) Again not 14 , Q Kt×P ? because of 15 Kt—Q 1 !, Kt—Q 2 : 16 P×P+

(k) Reshevsky—Botvinnik, Nottingham, 1936.

(l) Grunfeld—Tartakover, Teplitz-Schonau, 1922.

DUTCH DEFENCE
1 P—Q 4, P—K B 4; 2 P—K Kt 3 (a), Kt—K B 3 (b); 3 B—Kt 2.

	181	182	183	184	185
3	(P—K 3)				P—K Kt 3
4	(Kt—KB3)..Kt—K R 3				Kt—K R 3
	(B—K 2)	P—Q 3	P—Q 4	P—B 4	B—Kt 2
5	(P—B 4)	O—O	O—O	P—Q 5 (i)	P—Q B 4 (k)
	(O—O)	B—K 2	B—Q 3	P—K 4	O—O
6	(O—O)	P—Q B 4	P—Q B 4 (g)	Kt—B 3	Kt—B 3
	(P—Q 4)	O—O	P—B 3	P—Q 3	P—Q 3
7	(Kt—B 3)	Kt—B 3 (e)	Kt—B 3	P—K 4	O—O
	(P—B 3)	Q—K 1	Q Kt—Q 2	B—K 2	Kt—B 3
8	Q—Kt 3 (c)	Kt—B 4	Q—Q 3	P—B 4	P—Q 5
	K—R 1	B—Q 1 !	Kt—K 5	Kt—Kt 5	Kt—K 4
9	Kt—K 5	P—K 4	P—B 3	B P×P	Q—Kt 3
	Q Kt—Q 2	P—K 4 !	Kt×Kt	Kt×K P	K Kt—Q 2
10	Kt×Kt	P×K P	P×Kt	O—O	B—K 3
	Kt×Kt	Q P×P	B—K 2	O—O	Kt—Kt 5
11	R—Q 1	Kt—Q 3	P—K 4	Kt—B 4	B—Q 2
	Kt—Kt 3	P×P	Kt—Kt 3	P×P	Kt—B 4
12	P×P	Q Kt×P	B P×P	B×P	Q—B 2 ± (l)
	K P×P	Kt—B 3	Q B P×P	B—Kt 5	
13	Kt—R 4	R—K 1	P×B P+ (h)	Q—K 1 + (j)	
	Kt—B 5 = (d)	Q—Kt 3 = (f)			

(a) Some continuations seldom encountered are: (1) 2 Kt—Q B 3, P—Q 4 (2..,
Kt—K B 3; 3 P—K Kt 4?, P—Q 4; 4 P—Kt 5, Kt—K 5; 5 Kt×Kt, B P×Kt;
6 P—K B 3,B—B 4; 7 B—Kt 2, P—K 3+); 3 B—Kt 5, P—B 3; 4 P—K 3, P—K Kt 3;
5 P—K R 4, P—K R 3; 6 B—K B 4, B—Kt 2; 7 Kt—B 3, Kt—Q 2; 8 B—Q 3,
K Kt—B 3; 9 Kt—K 5, Kt×Kt ∓. Opocensky—Tartakover, Pistyan, 1922.
(2) 2 Kt—K B 3, Kt—K B 3; 3 P—Q 5, P—K Kt 3, 4 P—K Kt 3, B—Kt 2; 5 B—Kt 2;
O—O; 6 O—O, Kt—R 3; 7 P—B 4, Kt—B 4; 8 B—K 3, Q Kt—K 5; 9 Q Kt—Q 2,
P—B 4; 10 Kt×Kt, Kt×Kt; 11 Q—B 2 ±. Reshevsky—Hasenfuss, Kemeri, 1937.
(b) An unusual defence is 2 ., P—Q Kt 3; 3 B—Kt 2, Kt—Q B 3; 4 Kt—K B 3,
P—K 3; 5 O—O, B—Kt 2; 6 P—B 4, B—Q 3; 7 Kt—B 3, B—Kt 5; 8 P—Q R 3,
P—Q R 4; 9 Kt—Q Kt 5, O—O; 10 Q—B 2, Kt—R 2; 11 Kt×B, P×Kt; 12 B—B 4+.
Spielmann—Mieses, Teplitz-Schönau, 1922.
(c) This position is approximately even, and other continuations yield just as little
advantage as the text. E.g., (1) 8 Q—B 2, Q—K 1; 9 B—B 4 (or 9 B—Kt 5, Q—R 4;
10 B×Kt,B×B; 11 P×P, K P×P?; 12 P—K 3, Kt—Q 2; 13 P—Q Kt 4, Kt—Kt 3;
14 P—Kt 5 ±. Chekhover—Rumin, Leningrad, 1936. 11. , B P×P = should have
been played), Q—R 4; 10 P—B 5 (weaker is 10 P—K 3, Q Kt—Q 2; 11 Q R—Q 1,
K—R 1; 12 K—R 1, R—K Kt 1; 13 P—K 3, P—K Kt 4 with a dangerous attack.
Yudovitch—Botvinnik, Leningrad, 1934), Q Kt—Q 2; 11 P—Q Kt 4, Kt—K 5;
12 Kt×Kt, B P×Kt =. Flohr—Rumin, Moscow, 1936. (2) 8 P—Kt 3,
Q Kt—Q 2; 9 B—Kt 2, Q—K 1, 10 Q—Q 3, K—R 1; 11 P×P?, K P×P,
12 Kt—Q 2, Kt—K 5; 13 P—B 3, Kt×Kt (B 6) ∓. Flohr—Botvinnik, 10th match
game, 1933.
(d) Capablanca—Botvinnik, Moscow, 1936.
(e) Or 7 Q—Kt 3, P—B 3; 8 Q—Q 2, K—R 1; 9 Q—Q B 3, Kt—R 3;
10 P—Q Kt 4, Kt—B 2; 11 P—R 4?,P—K 4!, 12 P×P, P×P; 13 P—Kt 5, P—K 5 =.
Eliskases—Rumin, Moscow, 1936.
(f) Lövenfisch—Rumin, Leningrad, 1934.
(g) Weaker is 6 B—B 4, O—O; 7 Kt—Q 2, P—B 3; 8 Kt—B 3, Q—B 2; 9 B×B,
Q×B; 10 Kt—B 4, P—Q Kt 3; 11 Kt—K 5, Q Kt—Q 2; 12 K Kt—Q 3, B—R 3 =.
Alekhine—Tartakover, London, 1922
(h) Continued 13 , P×P; 14 R—K 1, O—O; 15 Kt—B 4. Grünfeld—Mieses
Teplitz-Schonau, 1922.

Notes ctd. on p. 218.

Notes ctd. on p. 218.

H

DUTCH DEFENCE
1 P—Q 4, P—K B 4; 2 P—Q B 4, P—K 3.

	186	187	188	189	190
3	P—K Kt 3 Kt—K B 3	. . .	. . .	. . .	P—K 3 (l) Kt—K B 3
4	B—Kt 2 B—Kt 5 ch				Kt—KB3 (m) P—QKt3 (n)
5	B—Q 2 B×B ch (a)	..B—K 2 (d)	Kt—Q 2 O—O	Kt—B 3 O—O	B—Q 3 B—Kt 2
6	Q×B O—O	Kt—Q B 3 O—O (e)	Kt—B 3 Kt—B 3	Kt—R 3 P—Q 4 (i)	Kt—B 3 B—Kt 5
7	Kt—Q B 3 P—Q 4 ! (b)	Kt—B 3 Kt—K 5	O—O B×Kt	O—O P—B 3	B—Q 2 (o) O—O
8	Kt—B 3 Kt—B 3 !	O—O P—Q Kt 3 (f)	B×B P—Q 3	Q—Kt 3 Kt—R 3	Q—B 2 K B×Kt
9	P×P ? P×P	Q—B 2 B—Kt 2	B—B 3 Q—K 2	Kt—B 4 B—Q 3	B×B Kt—K 5
10	Kt—K 5 Kt—K 2	Kt—K 5 Kt×Kt	P—Q 5 ! Kt—Q 1	Kt—Q 3 Kt—B 2	O—O—O P—Q R 4
11	O—O P—B 3	B×Kt B×B	P×P Kt—K 5	P—B 5 (j) B—K 2	K R—Kt 1 Kt—R 3
12	Q R—B 1 Q—K 1 = (c)	K×B Q—B 1 (g)	Q—B 2 ± (h)	B—B 4 ± (k)	B×Kt P×B (p)

(a) Weak is 5.., Q—K 2; 6 Kt—K R 3, Kt—K 5?; 7 B×Kt, P×B; 8 O—O, B×B, 9 Kt×B, P—Q 4; 10 Kt—B 4, P—B 3; 11 Q—Kt 3!, O—O; 12 P—B 3!, K P×P; 13 R×P+. Landau—Tartakover, Rotterdam, 1932.

(b) Best. If instead 7.., P—Q 3; 8 Kt—R 3 (equally good is 8 Kt—B 3, Kt—B 3; 9 R—Q 1, Kt—K 2; 10 O—O, Kt—Kt 3; 11 Q—B 3, P—B 3; 12 P—K 4 +. Euwe—Alekhine, 10th match game, 1927), Q—K 2; 9 O—O, P—B 3; 10 P—K 4, P×P; 11 Kt×P, Kt×Kt; 12 B×Kt, P—K 4; 13 Kt—Kt 5 ±. Euwe—Yudovitch, Leningrad, 1934.

(c) Stahlberg—Alekhine, Zürich, 1934.

(d) Another Alekhine idea.

(e) If 6., Kt—B 3?; 7 P—Q 5, Kt—K 4; 8 Q—Kt 3, O—O; 9 Kt—R 3, Kt—Kt 3, 10 P×P, P×P; 11 R—Q 1, P—B 3; 12 O—O, P—K 4; 13 P—B 5 dis ch, K—R 1; 14 Kt—K Kt 5+. Fine—Alekhine, Margate, 1937.

(f) Or 8., B—B 3; 9 Kt×Kt, P×Kt, 10 Kt—K 1, B×P; 11 B×P, B×P; 12 B×P ch, K×B; 13 Q—B 2 ch ±. Euwe—Alekhine, 24th match game, 1935.

(g) 13 P—Q 5 ! ±. Euwe—Alekhine, 26th match game, 1935.

(h) Flohr—Keres, Kemeri, 1937.

(i) Inferior is 6., P—B 4; 7 P—Q R 3, B—R 4; 8 O—O, P×P; 9 Kt—Kt 5!, P—Q 4; 10 P—Q Kt 4, B—Kt 3; 11 P—B 5+. Petrov—Keres, Kemeri, 1937.

(j) Better than 11 P—B 3, K—R 1; 12 B—Q 2, P—Q Kt 3; 13 P×P, K P×P; 14 Kt—K 5, P—B 4; 15 P—K 3, Q—K 1; 16 P—B 4, P—B 5. Grau—Alekhine, Warsaw, 1935.

(k) Capablanca—Botvinnik, Hastings, 1934-35.

(l) 3 Kt—Q B 3, Kt—K B 3, 4 B—Kt 5, B—K 2; 5 Kt—B 3, O—O; 6 P—K 3, P—Q Kt 3; 7 B—Q 3, B—Kt 2; 8 O—O, Q—K 1; 9 Q—K 2, Kt—K 5; 10 B×B, Kt×Kt; 11 P×Kt, Q×B; 12 P—Q R 4. Capablanca—Tartakover, New York, 1924.

(m) An unusual line here is 4 P—K B 4, Kt—K 5; 5 Kt—K B 3, B—Kt 5 ch; 6 Q Kt—Q 2, O—O; 7 B—Q 3, B×Kt ch; 8 B×B, Kt×B?; 9 Q×Kt, P—Q Kt 3; 10 O—O, B—Kt 2; 11 Q R—K 1, Q—B 3; 12 P—K 4 ±. Rubinstein—Tartakover, Budapest, 1926.

(n) 4., P—K Kt 3; 5 B—K 2, B—Kt 2; 6 O—O, O—O; 7 P—Q Kt 4, P—Q 3; 8 Q Kt—Q 2, Q Kt—Q 2; 9 B—Kt 2, Q—K 2; 10 P—B 5, P—Q R 4; 11 B P×P ±. Nimzovitch—Tartakover, Gothenburg, 1920.

(o) 7 O—O, B×Kt; 8 P×B, O—O. Rubinstein—Maróczy, Teplitz-Schönau, 1922. The doubled Pawn is not necessarily disadvantageous for White in such positions.

(p) 13 P—Q 5. Lövenborg—Marchand, Stockholm, 1916. If Black captures the Kt White has a winning attack.

DUTCH DEFENCE
1 P—Q 4, P—K B 4.

STAUNTON GAMBIT (a)
2 P—K 4.

	191	192	193	194 ₁	195
2	P×P...				P—Q 3 (m)
3	Kt—QB3 (b)				Kt—QB3 (n)
	Kt—KB3 (c)				Kt—KB 3
4	B—KKt5 (d)........................P—B 3				P×P (o)
	Kt—B 3.....P—KKt3	...P—QKt3 (i)	P—Q 4		B×P
5	P—Q 5	P—KR4 (g)	B—QB4 (j)	B—K Kt 5	B—Q 3
	Kt—K 4	P—Q 3 (h)	P—K 3	Kt—B 3	Q—Q 2
6	Q—Q 4	P—R 5	B×Kt	B×Kt	B×B
	Kt—B 2	B—Kt 5	Q×B	K P×B	Q×B
7	B×Kt	B—K 2	Kt×P	P×P	Q—B 3
	K P×B	P×P	Q—K 2	P×P	Q×Q
8	Kt×P	B×Kt	B—Q 3	P—Q 5	Kt×Q
	B—Q 3 (e)	P×B	Kt—B 3	Kt—K 4	Kt—B 3
9	Kt×B ch	B×B	P—Q B 3	Kt×P	B—B 4
	Kt×Kt	P×B	B—Kt 2	Q—K 2	P—K 3
10	B—Q 3	Q×P	Kt—B 3	Q—K 2	O—O—O
	Q—K 2 ch	Q—Q 2	O—O—O	B—Kt 5	P—K Kt 3
11	K—Q 2	Q—R 5 ch	O—O	Kt—K B 3	K R—K 1 ±
	O—O	K—Q 1	R—Kt 1	B×Kt	(p)
12	R—K 1	O—O—O +	Q—K 2	P×B	
	Q—B 2		K—Kt 1	P—KB4 ∓ (l)	
13	Kt—B3+ (f)		P—Q R 4		
			P—QR4 ∓ (k)		

(a) Also known as the Blackmar Attack.
(b) A novel line is 3 P—K B 3 !, P—K 3 ; 4 Kt—Q 2, P × P ; 5 K Kt × P, Kt—K B 3 ; 6 B—Q 3, P—B 4 ? ; 7 O—O, P × P ; 8 Kt—Kt 5, P—Q 4 ; 9 Kt × R P ! +. Denker—Dake, Syracuse, 1934.
(c) Playable is 3 , P—K Kt 3 !, e.g., 4 Kt × P, P—Q 4 ; 5 Kt—Kt 3, B—Kt 2 ; 6 P—K R 4, Kt—Q B 3 ; 7 B—Q Kt 5 ?, Q—Q 3 ; 8 B × Kt ch, P × B ; 9 P—R 5, P—K 4 ; 10 P × P, Q × P ch ; 11 K Kt—K 2, Kt—K 2 ∓. Marshall—Tartakover, Liège, 1930.
(d) On 4 P—K Kt 4 ! ? Black's best reply is 4 , P—K R 3 ; 5 P—Kt 5, P × P ; 6 B × P, P—Q 4. If, however, 4 , P—Q 4 ; 5 P—Kt 5, Kt—Kt 1 ; 6 P—B 3, P × P ; 7 Q × P, P—K 3 ; 8 B—Q 3, P—K Kt 3 ; 9 K Kt—K 2, B—Kt 2 ; 10 O—O, Q—K 2 ; 11 B—K B 4, P—B 3 ; 12 Q—Kt 3 with a powerful attack. Tartakover—Mieses, Baden-Baden, 1925.
(e) Nimzovitch suggested 8 ., P—K B 4 ; 9 Kt—Kt 3, P—K Kt 3 ; 10 O—O—O, B—R 3 ch ; 11 K—Kt 1, O—O.
(f) Réti—Mieses, Berlin, 1920.
(g) If 5 P—B 3, P × P ; 6 Kt × P, P—Q 4 ; 7 B—Q 3, Kt—B 3 ; 8 O—O, B—Kt 2 ; 9 Q—Q 2, O—O ; 10 Q R—K 1, Kt—Q Kt 5 ; 11 Kt—K 5, Kt × B +. Euwe—Tartakover, The Hague, 1921. The column is N. P. Zelikoff—N. M. Zubareff, 1922, and illustrates Alekhine's Attack (5 P—K R 4).
(h) If 5. , B—Kt 2 ; 6 P—R 5, Kt × P ; 7 R × Kt +. The crucial variation 5 .., P—Q 4 ; 6 P—R 5, B—Kt 2 ; 7 P—R 6, B—B 1 ; 8 P—B 3, P × P ; 9 Kt × B P, Kt—B 3 has yet to be tested in practical play.
(i) After 4 .., P—Q B 3 White gets too strong an attack by 5 P—B 3 (but not 5 B × Kt, K P × B ; 6 Kt × P, Q—Kt 3 ; 7 R—Kt 1, P—Q 4 =), P × P ; 6 Kt × P, P—K 3 (or 6 . , Q—Kt 3, 7 Q—Q 2, P—Q 3 ; 8 O—O—O); 7 B—Q 3, B—K 2 ; 8 Kt—K 5, O—O ; 9 B × Kt !, B × B ; 10 Q—R 5, P—K R 3 ; 11 Kt × Kt P ! +. Lasker—Pillsbury, Paris, 1900. Better for Black is 5 ., Q—R 4 ; 6 Q—Q 2, P—K 6 ; etc.
(j) Or P—B 3, P—K 6 (best), 6 B × P, P—K 3 ; 7 Q—Q 2, P—Q 4 ; 8 O—O—O, P—B 4 =. P. Johner—Nimzovitch, Carlsbad, 1929.

Notes ctd. on p. 218.

Notes for cols. 1 to 5 ctd.

(m) Or (1) 8 .., P—K 4?; 9 P—K 4!, K P×P; 10 B P×P, Q P×P; 11 Kt×P, Kt×Kt; 12 B×Kt, P×P; 13 Q×P, Q—B 3; 14 B—K Kt 5 ±. Colle—Sir G. A. Thomas, Paris, 1929. (2) 8. , R—K 1; 9 P—K 4, Q P×P; 10 Kt×P, Kt×Kt; 11 B×Kt, P×P?; 12 B×P ch ¹, K×B; 13 Kt—Kt 5 ch, K—Kt 3; 14 P—K R 4, R—R 1; 15 R×P ch ¹! + +. Colle—O'Hanlon, Nice, 1930. (3) 8. , Q—Kt 3, 9 P—Q Kt 3, P—K 4; 10 P—K 4, B P×P; 11 B P×P, Q P×P; 12 Q Kt×P, Kt×Kt=. Fine—Keres, Kemeri, 1937.

(n) 15 Q—R 5 ¹ with a strong attack. Landau—Boóh, Kemeri, 1937.

(o) 6 P—Q Kt 3 ?, B—Kt 2; 7 B—Kt 2, O—O; 8 P—K R 3, P×P, 9 Kt×P, Kt—R 4 ¹; 10 P—Kt 3, Q—B 2; 11 Q—K 2, Kt—B 4 ! +. Relstab—Petror. Kemeri, 1937.

(p) Prins—Landau, Zandvoort, 1936.

Notes for cols. 31 to 35 ctd.

(n) If 10 Kt—B 5, B×Kt; 11 Q×B, Kt—B 3; 12 P—K 3, O—O; 13 B—K 2. Q—K 5; 14 Q—B 3 (Capablanca—Euwe, "Avro," 1938), Q×Q; 15 B×Q, P—K 5 =. The column is Lövenfisch—Botvinnik, 7th match game, 1937.

(o) 6 P—K 3, O—O; 7 B—Q 3, P—Q Kt 3; 8 Kt—K 2, P—B 4; 9 P×P, P×P is a good alternative.

(p) Or 7 B×Kt, Q×B; 8 P—Q R 3, B×Kt ch; 9 Q×B, O—O; 10 P—K 3, P—B 3; 11 Kt—B 3, B—B 4; 12 B—K 2 with a minimal advantage. Capablanca—Euwe, 1st match game, 1931.

(q) If 8 . , Q—K Kt 3; 9 P—Q R 3 !, B×Kt ch; 10 P×B, B—B 4; 11 Q—Kt 3, O—O; 12 P—B 3 !, Kt—Q 3; 13 P—Kt 4, B—Q 6; 14 Q×Q P+. Capablanca—Euwe, 3rd match game, 1931. The column is Stahlberg—Alekhine, Prague, 1931.

Notes for cols. 36 to 40 ctd.

(j) 5 P—K 3, Kt—B 3; 6 Kt—B 3. O—O; 7 P—Q R 3, B×Kt ch; 8 Q×B, P×P; 9 P×P, P—Q 4; 10 B—Kt 5, P×P; 11 B×P, Kt—K 5 =. Vidmar—Alekhine, Hastings, 1926.

(k) 7 . , B—K 2; 8 O—O—O ? (8 R—Q 1 or 8 P—K 4), Q—R 4; 9 P—Q R 3, P—Q R 3; 10 P—K 3, P—Q Kt 3; 11 B—K 2, B—Kt 2, 12 Q Kt—Kt 1, P—Q Kt 4+, Euwe—Colle, Amsterdam, 1926. If 7 , P—K R 3; 8 B—R 4, B—K 2; 9 R—Q 1, O—O; 10 P—K 3, P—Q 4, 11 B—K 2, Q—R 4; 12 Kt—Q 2 !, K R—Q 1, 13 O—O ±. Rubinstein—Ahues, Berlin, 1926.

(l) Or 11 K R—Q 1, P—Q R 3; 12 Q R—B 1, Kt—Q R 4 ?; 13 Kt—K 5 !, Q—B 2; 14 P—Q Kt 4 !, K B×P; 15 B×Kt, P×B; 16 Kt×Q P+. Euwe—Sämisch, German Quadrangular Tournament, 1937.

(m) 13 , Q—B 2; 14 B—B 4 !, Kt—K 4; 15 Kt×Kt, P×Kt; 16 B—Kt 3 ±. Keres—Samisch, Dresden, 1936.

(n) Rubinstein—Samisch, Berlin, 1926. White stands slightly better.

(o) Eliskases—A. Steiner, Ujpest, 1934.

Notes for cols. 51 to 55 ctd.

(k) 7 ., B×P is simpler and safer.

(l) Botvinnik—Savitzky, Leningrad, 1932.

(m) 4 ., Q—K 2 ?; 5 P—Q R 3, B×Kt ch; 6 Q×B, P—Q Kt 3; 7 P—B 3. P—Q 4, 8 P×P, Kt×P; 9 Q—B 2 !, Q—R 5 ch; 10 P—Kt 3, Q×Q P; 11 P—K 4+. Bogoljuboff—Alekhine, 6th match game, 1929.

(n) Or 5 P—K 3, P—Q R 4; 6 B—Q 2 (6 B—Q 3 ?, P—R 5; 7 Q—Q 1, P—R 6 ∓), P—K 4, 7 P—Q 5, Kt—K 2; 8 B—Q 3, P—Q 3, 9 Kt—K 2, Kt—Q 2; 10 Q—Q 1, Kt—Q B 4; 11 B—B 2, B—Kt 5 =. Stahlberg—Nimzovitch, 7th match game, 1934.

(o) For 5 , P—Q 3; 6 P—Q R 3 see cols. 44—46.

(p) Fine—Reshevsky, New York, 1938.

Notes for cols. 56 to 60 ctd.

(m) Or 7.., Kt×P; 8 Kt×Kt, P×Kt; 9 P—K Kt 3, Kt—Q 2; 10 B—Kt 2, Kt—B 3; 11 O—O =. Reshevsky—Botvinnik, Avro, 1938.

(n) 9 P×P, B×P; 10 P—Q Kt 4 ?, P—Q 5!; 11 P×B, P×Kt; 12 Q—B 2, Q—R 4, 13 R—Q Kt 1, B—Q 2 ∓. Euwe—Alekhine, 25th match game, 1937.

(o) 14.., Q Kt—Kt 5; 15 B—Kt 2 with a strong attack. Flohr—Lisitzin, Moscow, 1935.

(p) 5 B—Q 3, P—Q 4 transposes into col. 56.

(q) 6 , O—O; 7 P—Q R 3, B—K 2; 8 Kt—B 4, P—Q 4; 9 P×P, Kt×P; 10 K Kt×Kt, P×Kt; 11 Q—Kt 3, Kt—B 3; 12 B—K 3, B—B 3; 13 R—Q 1, B—Kt 5; 14 B—K 2, B×B; 15 K×B. Capablanca—Keres, Avro, 1938.

(r) If 7 P—Q R 3, B×Kt ch (but not 7 , B—K 2; 8 P—B 5, P—Q Kt 3; 9 P—Q Kt 4, P×P; 10 Q P×P, P—K 4; 11 P—B 4!+. Rubinstein—Maróczy, Hamburg, 1930); 8 Kt×B, P×P; 9 B×P, O—O; 10 O—O, Kt—B 3; 11 B—K 3, P—Q Kt 3 =. Rubinstein—Ahues, Liège, 1930.

(s) Rubinstein and Colle—Tartakover and Landau, Rotterdam, 1932.

(t) Rubinstein—Colle, Liège, 1930.

Notes for cols. 61 to 65 ctd.

(n) If 5.., Kt—K 5; 6 Q—B 2, P—K B 4; 7 P—K 3 (7 Kt—R 3, P—Q Kt 3; 8 P—B 3, Kt—K B 3; 9 P—K 3, O—O; 10 B—Q 3, Q—K 2; 11 O—O, P—Q 3; 12 Kt—B 2, P—B 4 ∓. Eliskases—Pleci, Warsaw, 1935), P—Q Kt 3, 8 B—Q 3, B—Kt 2; 9 Kt—K 2, Q—R 5?; 10 O—O, O—O; 11 P—B 3 +. Fine—Araiza, Chicago, 1934.

(o) 6 Q—B 2, P—Q 4; 7 B—Kt 5, P—B 4; 8 P—K 3, B P×P; 9 K P×P, Kt—B 3; 10 Kt—B 3, R—K 1; 11 Kt—K 5, P×P =. Winter—Alexander, Nottingham, 1936.

(p) Bogoljuboff—Reshevsky, Nottingham, 1936.

(q) B×Kt ch is too dogmatic, e.g., 5 P×B, O—O; 6 B—K Kt 2, P—Q 3; 7 Kt—B 3, Kt—B 3, 8 O—O, Kt—Q R 4; 9 Q—Q 3, Q—K 2; 10 Kt—Q 2, P—K 4; 11 R—Q Kt 1, R—Kt 1; 12 B—R 3 ±. Grau—Fine, Warsaw, 1935.

(r) 14 Q—Kt 2. Alekhine—H. Golombek, Margate, 1938. 14.., R—Kt 1 now equalises (Alekhine).

Notes for cols. 66 to 70 ctd.

(m) There is nothing better. If 4.., B—Kt 2; 5 B—Q 3, P—Q 4; 6 B P×P, P×P; 7 P—K 5+; or 4 , B—Kt 5; 5 P—K 5, Kt—K 5; 6 Q—Kt 4, Kt×Kt; 7 P×Kt, B×P ch; 8 K—Q 1, K—B 1 (best), 9 R—Kt 1, Kt—B 3; 10 B—R 3 ch, K—Kt 1; 11 R—Kt 3, B×P; 12 Q×P ch !! with mate to follow (a game between two Russian players). If Black plays 11.., P—K R 4; 12 Q—Kt 3, B×P; 13 Q×P ch, etc.

(n) Bogoljuboff—Opocensky, Pistyan, 1922.

Notes for cols. 136 to 140 ctd.

(l) Weaker is 7.., P×P; 8 B×P, Q Kt—Q 2 (more aggressive but still of doubtful value is 8 , P—Q Kt 4; 9 B—Q 3, B—K 3; 10 Q—B 2, P—Q R 4; 11 O—O, Q—Kt 3; 12 Kt—K Kt 5, B—Q 2; 13 Q Kt—K 4, Kt—R 3. Van den Bosch—Sultan Khan, Cambridge, 1932); 9 O—O, Kt—K 3, 10 B—K 2, B—K 3; 11 Q—B 2, B—B 5; 12 P—K 4, R—K 1; 13 Q R—Q 1 ±. Reshevsky—Santasiere, Syracuse, 1934.

(m) Inferior is 10 , K Kt—Q 2; 11 Kt×Kt, Kt×Kt; 12 P—B 4 ±. Alatorzeff—Lilienthal, 4th match game, 1935.

(n) 14 O—O, P—B 4. Botvinnik—Winter, Nottingham, 1936.

Notes for cols. 146 to 150 ctd.

(*l*) 12 Kt—Q 2 ?, Q—B 2 ; 13 B—R 3, P—Kt 3 ; 14 P × P, B—R 3 ; 15 K R—Q 1, P × P ∓. Kashdan—Bogoljuboff, Bled, 1931.

(*m*) Simpler is 5 P—K 3. If 5 B—B 4, P × P ; 6 B—K 5 ! (6 P—Q R 4, Kt—Q 4 ; 7 B—Q 2, Kt—Kt 5 ; 8 R—B 1, B—Kt 2 ; 9 Kt—Kt 1, P—Q R 4 ; 10 Kt—R 3, P—Q B 4 +. Euwe—Flohr, 6th match game, 1932. Here 7 B—K 5, P—B 3 ; 8 B—Kt 3, B—Kt 2 ; 9 P—K 4, Kt × Kt ; 10 P × Kt, P—Q Kt 4 ; 11 B—K 2, with excellent attacking prospects, should have been played—Euwe), Q Kt—Q 2 ; 7 P—K 3, Kt—Kt 3 ; 8 Kt—Q 2, B—K 3 ; 9 B—K 2, B—Kt 2 ; 10 Q Kt—K 4, O—O ; 11 Kt—B 5 =. Enevoldsen—Fine, Folkestone, 1933

(*n*) 5 ., Kt × P ; 6 P—K 4, Kt × Kt ; 7 P × Kt, B—Kt 2 ; 8 B—Q B 4 ± (Spielmann —Flohr, Moscow, 1935) is bad for Black, since after the eventual P—Q B 4 he will be playing the variation in col. 132 with a tempo behind.

(*o*) If instead 12 ., R—B 1 ? ; 13 K R—B 1, Kt—B 5 ; 14 Q—Kt 3, Kt—Q R 4 : 15 Q—Kt 4, P—Q Kt 4 ; 16 Kt—K 5 ±. Reshevsky—Mikenas, Kemeri, 1937. The text is suggested by the Tournament Book.

Notes for cols. 156 to 160 ctd.

(*j*) On 9 Q—Q 2, Q—K 2 White has nothing better than 10 Q—Q 5. But Black, also has no alternative to 9 , Q—K 2, for if 9 , Q—B 4 ; 10 P—K 3, Q—R 4 (10 ., K Kt × P (K 4) ; 11 Kt × Kt, Kt × Kt ; 12 Q—Q 4 +) ; 11 R—Q Kt 1, P—Q R 3 ; 12 P—B 5 Q × P (B 4), 13 P—K R 3, Kt—R 3 ; 14 B—Q 3 +. Bogoljuboff—Tartakover, Kissingen, 1928.

(*k*) The Fajarowicz Variation.

(*l*) Simplest. If 4 Q—B 2, P—Q 4 ! ; 5 P × P *e.p*, B—K B 4 ; 6 Q—R 4 ch, Kt—Q B 3 ; 7 Kt—K B 3, B × P ; 8 P—Q R 3, Q—B 3 followed by O—O—O ∓. H. Steiner—Fajarowicz, Wiesbaden, 1928.

(*m*) Alekhine—Tartakover, London, 1932.

Notes for cols. 181 to 185 ctd.

(*i*) Also strong is 5 P × P, B × P, 6 O—O, P—Q 4 ; 7 P—B 4, O—O ; 8 P × P. Kt × P ; 9 Kt—B 4, Kt × Kt, 10 B × Kt, Q—Kt 3 ; 11 Kt—B 3, R—Q 1 ; 12 Q—B 2 + Grünfeld—Tartakover, Pistyan, 1922.

(*j*) Eliskases—Alekhine, Hastings, 1936–37.

(*k*) If 5 Kt—B 4, Kt—B 3 (not 5 ., O—O ; 6 P—K R 4, Kt—B 3 ; 7 P—R 5, Q—K 1 ; 8 P × P, P × P ; 9 Kt—B 3 +. Alekhine—Tartakover, Carlsbad, 1923) ; 6 P—Q 5, Kt—K 4 ; 7 Kt—B 3, P—B 3 ; 8 Kt—Q 3, Kt—B 2 ; 9 O—O O—O ; 10 P—B 4, P × P =. Rubinstein—Bogoljuboff, Carlsbad, 1923.

(*l*) Bogoljuboff—Tartakover, Carlsbad, 1923.

Notes for cols. 191 to 195 ctd.

(*k*) Brinckmann—Nimzovitch, Copenhagen, 1924.

(*l*) Teichmann—Mieses, Teplitz-Schönau, 1922.

(*m*) The Balogh Defence.

(*n*) Alternatives that have been tried are : (1) 3 P—K 5, P × P ; 4 P × P, Q × Q ch ; 5 K × Q, P—K 3 ; 6 B—K 3, Kt—Q 2 ; 7 Kt—K B 3, B—B 4 ; 8 B × B, Kt × B, 9 Kt—B 3, B—Q 2 ; 10 B—B 4, P—B 3 ; 11 P—Q Kt 4 ±. Grunfeld—S. R. Wolf, 1914. (2) 3 P × P, B × P ; 4 Q—B 3, Q—B 1 ; 5 B—Q 3, B × B ; 6 Q × B, Kt—Q B 3, 7 Kt—K B 3, P—K 3 ; 8 O—O, Q—Q 2 ; 9 P—B 4, O—O—O ; 10 R—K 1, Kt—B 3 ; 11 B—Q 2, R—K 1 ; 12 Kt—R 3 !, B—K 2 ; 13 P—Q Kt 4 ! ±. Euwe—Weenink, Amsterdam, 1923.

(*o*) Weaker is 4 B—Q 3, Kt—Q B 3 ; 5 P × P, Kt × P ; 6 P—K Kt 4, P—K R 4 ; 7 P—K B 3, P × P ; 8 P × P, Q—Q 2 ! ; 9 P—K R 3, Q—B 3 ; 10 R—R 2, Q—B 4 ! ; 11 B—K B 4 ? (11 K—B 1), P—K 4 + +. Dührssen—Balogh, 1929.

(*p*) Ahues—Brinckmann, match, 1930.

RÉTI OPENING.

THE characteristic moves of this for White are Kt—K B 3, P—Q B 4,* P—K Kt 3, B—Kt 2; and Kmoch prefers to call the opening the King's Indian Attack, as he calls Nimzovitch's the Queen's Indian Attack. In our last edition this opening was named the Réti-Zukertort; we have dropped the "Zukertort" because the characteristic King's Fianchetto is purely modern. In Réti's opening position judgment of a very high order is called for, and the ordinary amateur would be prudent not to adopt it unless he has a wide knowledge of the theories underlying the close game.

The most usual reply to 1 Kt—K B 3 is P—Q 4; after 2 P—B 4 Black can then branch off into four possible lines : (i) P×P; (ii) P—Q 5; (iii) P—Q B 3; (iv) P—K 3. These four continuations are all equally good, so that the choice of defence is largely a matter of taste.

(i) 2..., P×P (cols. 1 to 5). White can play to re-capture the Pawn by either 3 Kt—R 3 (cols. 1 to 3), which leaves Black with a tangible positional superiority after P—Q B 4; or 3 P—K 3, which leads to approximate equality. If possible, White should transpose into the Queen's Gambit Accepted. Black can, however, avoid this by the relatively unknown line in col. 5.

(ii) 2..., P—Q 5 (cols. 6 to 10) was formerly thought to be inferior, but has since been hailed by some as the refutation of Réti's Opening. White is really playing a Benoni Counter Gambit with a move in hand, but this move weighs heavily. By attacking Black's centre immediately

*But P—Q B 4 is not essential.

White can certainly avoid a disadvantage; the line in col. 6, due to Alekhine, shows that the variation is full of pitfalls for the second player.

(iii) 2..., P—Q B 3. This, coupled with a development of his Queen's Bishop at B 4 or Kt 5, is one of Black's most promising counter-attacks. In the line in col. 11, where the manœuvres of the White Rooks and Queen appeared so startling at the time the game was played, Black's position is quite solid and can effectively withstand all attacks. 4..., B—Kt 5 (col 15) is a welcome departure from routine.

(iv) 2..., P—K 3. At first sight this continuation appears to be inferior to the others, since it shuts in the Black Queen's Bishop. But tournament experience has shown that this objection is not serious, since Black can usually manage to fianchetto this piece. In col. 16 Black defers P × P to the 3rd move; in col. 17 he defers P—Q 5 to the 3rd, with satisfactory results in both cases. Cols. 18 to 22 exemplify the variations where White avoids an early advance in the centre. Here Black has nothing to fear; on the contrary, White often finds his game beset with difficulties.

CATALAN SYSTEM.

The Catalan System is by far the most important addition to opening theory since our last edition. It is a combination of the King's Indian Attack (P—K Kt 3) and the Queen's Gambit (P—Q 4 and P—Q B 4). Essentially the opening is one of transposition, into either a pure Réti Opening, a Queen's Gambit, or a Queen's Pawn Game. We have deemed it most convenient to include it under the Réti Opening, although the most usual order of moves is by way of the Queen's Gambit. See p. 227, note (A).

After the customary moves 1 P—Q 4, Kt—K B 3; 2 P—Q B 4, P—K 3; 3 Kt—K B 3, P—Q 4; 4 P—K Kt 3, B—K 2; 5 B—Kt 2, O—O; 6 O—O Black has the choice of three main defensive systems. 6..., Q Kt—Q 2 (cols. 23 to 25) is a passive continuation, but Black cannot be prevented from gradually freeing his game and securing adequate scope for his pieces. 6..., P—B 4 (cols. 26 to 29) is the most aggressive continuation. Against the advance of White's King's Pawn the retreat to Kt 3 is best for Black (col. 26). However, in all these columns the second player is continually faced by difficulties in development, and the slightest misstep is fatal. 6..., P—Q B 4 before Castling (col. 30) is the simplest for Black to equalise.

Instead of maintaining his centre Black can also choose to accept the Gambit Pawn on his 4th move. This too leads to positions of great complexity, where the advantage of the move sometimes proves decisive. An excellent defence for Black is C. H. Alexander's line (col. 35), where Black plays P—Q B 4 as soon as White adopts the Catalan formation. The idea is to post Black's King's Bishop at Q B 4; this considerably enhances the mobility of Black's pieces. White can also, as in cols. 36 to 40, try the Catalan System on his 3rd move, but then Black has the strong defence 3..., B—Kt 5 ch at his disposal, which assures him complete equality.

Cols. 41 to 45 exemplify variations where the struggle in the centre is not paramount. In col. 41 White omits P—Q B 4; in cols. 42 to 44 Black omits P—Q 4. The absence of a sharply defined attack and counter-attack makes these lines very drawish. In col. 45 White obtains a superior position against Black's Dutch Defence formation.

.

RETI OPENING.

1 Kt—K B 3, P—Q 4; 2 P—B 4.

1	2	3	4	5
2 P×P (a)				
3 Kt—R 3 ……………………			P—K 3	
P—Q B 4 ……………		P—K 4 (h)	Kt—K B 3 ..	Kt—Q B 3
4 Kt×P	‘K Kt×P	B×P	B×P	
Kt—Q B 3	B×Kt	P—K 3	P—K 4	
5 P—K Kt 3 …	P—Q Kt 3 (e)	Q—R 4 ch	O—O	Q—Kt 3
P—B 3	P—K 4	P—Q Kt 4	P—B 4	Kt—R 3
6 B—Kt 2	B—Kt 2	Q×B	P—Q Kt 3 (k)	P—Q 4
P—K 4 (b)	P—B 3	Q—Q 4 (i)	Kt—B 3	P—K 5
7 P—Q 3	P—Kt 3 (f)	Q—K B 3	B—Kt 2	K Kt—Q 2
B—K 3	K Kt—K 2	Kt—K B 3	P—Q R 3	P—B 4
8 O—O	B—Kt 2	Q×Q	P—Q R 4	Kt—Q B 3
K Kt—K 2	Kt—B 4! (g)	Kt×Q	B—K 2	B—Q 2
9 K Kt—Q 2!	O—O	P—K Kt 3	Kt—K 5	Q—Q 1 (m)
Kt—Q 4 (c)	B—K 2	P—K B 3	Kt—Q R 4	Q—Kt 4
10 Kt—K 4	R—B 1	B—Kt 2	P—Q 4	O—O
B—K 2	B—K 3	B—Kt 2	Kt×B	O—O—O
11 Kt—K 3	P—Q 3	Kt—Kt 4	Kt×Kt	P—Q R 3
Q—Q 2	O—O	P—K R 4	O—O	Kt—K Kt 5
12 Kt—B 3	K Kt—Q 2	Kt—K 3	Q Kt—Q 2	Q—K 1
Kt—B 2 = (d)	Q—Q 2 ∓	Kt×Kt (j)	B—Q 2 = (l)	P—K R 4 ∓

(a) The Réti Gambit Accepted.

(b) Inferior is 6., Kt—R 3; 7 O—O, P—K 4; 8 P—Q 3, Kt—B 2? (best is 8.., Kt—Q 5 as in the next column), 9 B—K 3, B—K 2; 10 R—B 1, O—O; 11 Q Kt—Q 2, Kt—Q 5; 12 Kt—Kt 3, Q—Kt 3; 13 K Kt—Q 2 ±. Réti—Havasi, Budapest, 1926.

(c) Again 9., Kt—B 4 is best. It is more important for Black to control the square Q 4 than to occupy it.

(d) 12., Kt—Kt 3 (Kashdan—Nimzovitch, Bled, 1931) is somewhat weaker.

(e) 5 Q Kt—K 5, Kt×Kt; 6 Kt×Kt, Kt—B 3, 7 P—K 3, P—K 3; 8 P—Q Kt 3, Kt—Q 2; 9 B—Kt 5, B—Q 3; 10 B—Kt 2, O—O; 11 Kt×Kt, B×Kt; 12 Q—Kt 4, P—B 3 =. Keres—Fine, Semmering-Baden, 1937.

(f) White's position must be handled with care. If 7 Q—B 2?, B—Kt 5; 8 R—B 1, Q—Q 2, 9 Kt—K 3, B—K 3, 10 Q—Kt 1?, Kt—R 3; 11 P—K R 3, Kt—Q 5; 12 P—Q 3, B—K 2; 13 Kt—Q 2, O—O; 14 Kt—K 4, K R—B 1+. Réti—Nimzovitch, Semmering, 1926.

(g) If instead 8., Kt—Q 4; 9 O—O, B—K 2; 10 Kt—R 4!, O—O; 11 Q—Kt 1!, R—B 2; 12 Kt—B 5, B—K 3 (12, B—B 1??, 13 Kt (B 5)—Q 6! and wins); 13 P—B 4!, P×P; 14 P×P, Kt—Kt 3, 15 B—K 4, B×Q Kt=. Botvinnik—Fine, Nottingham, 1936.

(h) A continuation leading to equality is 3.., P—Q B 3; 4 Kt×P, P—Q Kt 4; 5 Kt—K 3, B—Kt 2; 6 P—K Kt 3, P—K 3; 7 B—Kt 2, Kt—K B 3; 8 O—O, Q Kt—Q 2; 9 P—Q 3, B—Q 3; 10 B—Q 2, O—O; 11 P—Q R 4, P—B 4; 12 Q—Kt 1, Q—K 2=. Bogoljuboff—P. Johner, Berlin, 1926.

(i) Or 6, B—Kt 2; 7 P—K 3, Q—Q 3; 8 Q×Q, P×Q; 9 Kt—B 3, Kt—Q B 3; 10 P—Q Kt 3, P—Q 4; 11 P×P, Q P×P; 12 P—Q R 4+. Tartakover—Spielmann, Moscow, 1925. On 6.., Q—Q 3; both 7 Q×Q and 7 Q—K Kt 3 are strong.

(j) 13 B×B, Kt—B 7 ch; 14 K—Q 1, Kt×R; 15 B×R+. Euwe—Spielmann, Wiesbaden, 1925.

(k) 6 P—Q 4 transposes into regular variations of the Queen's Gambit Accepted.

(l) Keres—Fine, Zandvoort, 1936.

(m) If 9 Q×P, R—Q Kt 1; 10 Q—R 6, R—Kt 3; 11 Q—R 4, Kt×P+ (Kmoch). The column is Bogoljuboff—Leonhardt, Magdeburg, 1927.

1 Kt—K B 3, P—Q 4 ; 2 P—B 4, P—Q 5.

	6	7	8	9	10
3	P—K 3...........................			...P—Q Kt 4	
	Kt—Q B 3..............	...P—Q B 4		P—K B 3!....P—Q B 4 (*m*)	
4	P×P........P—Q Kt 4?		P×P (*f*)	B—Kt 2 (*k*)	B—Kt 2
	Kt×P	P×P (*c*)	P×P	P—K 4	P—K Kt 3
5	Kt×Kt	B P×P	P—K Kt 3	P—Q R 3	P—K 3
	Q×Kt	Kt×P	Kt—Q B 3	P—Q B 4	B—Kt 2
6	Kt—B 3	P—Q 4	B—Kt 2	P×P	Kt P×P
	B—Kt 5 (*a*)	P—K 4 !	P—K Kt 3	B×P	P—K 4
7	Q—R 4 ch	P—Q R 3	P—Q 3	P—Q 3	P×P
	P—B 3	Kt—Q B 3 (*d*)	B—Kt 2	Kt—B 3	P×P
8	P—Q 3	P—Q 5	O—O	Q Kt—Q 2	P—Q 3
	Kt—B 3	P—K 5 !	P—K 4	P—B 4 !	Kt—Q R 3
9	B—K 3	K Kt—Q 2	R—K 1	P—Kt 3	Q Kt—Q 2
	Q—Q 2	Kt—K 4	P—B 3 ! (*g*)	Kt—B 3	Kt×P
10	P—Q 4	Kt×P	P—Q Kt 4 (*h*)	B—Kt 2	Kt—Kt 3
	P—K 3	Q—R 5 ch	Kt×P	O—O	Kt—K 3
11	P—B 3	Kt—B 2	Q—R 4 ch	O—O	P—Kt 3
	B—K B 4	B—Q B 4	Kt—B 3	Q—K 1	Kt—K 2
12	O—O—O	Kt—B 3	Kt×Q P (*i*)	Kt—Kt 3	B—Kt 2
	B—Q 3	Kt—K B 3	Q×Kt	B—Q 3	O—O
13	P—K Kt4 ±	P—Kt 3	B×Kt ch	P—K 3	O—O
	(*b*)	Q—R 3 ∓ (*e*)	B—Q 2 = (*j*)	P×P+ (*l*)	Kt-B 3 = (*n*)

(*a*) If instead 6. , Kt—B 3 (or 6. ., P—Q B 3 ; 7 P—Q 3, B—Kt 5 ; 8 Q—R 4 ±) ; 7 P—Q 3, P—B 3 ; 8 B—K 3, Q—Q 2 ; 9 P—Q 4, P—K Kt 3 ; 10 B—K 2, B—Kt 2. 11 P—K R 3, O—O ; 12 O—O, P—Kt 3 ; 13 B—B 3 ±. Alekhine—Euwe, 22nd match game, 1937.

(*b*) 13. ., B—Kt 3 ; 14 P—K R 4, P—K R 3. If here 14. , P—K R 4 ? ; 15 P—Kt 5, Kt—R 2 ; 16 P—B 5 !, B—K 2 ; 17 P—Q 5 !+. Keres—Euwe, Noordwijk, 1938.

(*c*) Another good reply is 4 , Kt×P ; e.g. 5 P×P, P—K 4 ! ; 6 P—Q R 3 (6 P×P, B—K B 4+), P—K 5 !, 7 P×Kt, P×Kt ∓. Keres—Flohr, Pernau, 1937.

(*d*) Better than 7. , P—K 5 ; 8 K Kt—Q 2, Kt—Q 6 ch , 9 B×Kt, P×B ; 10 O—O, Kt—B 3 ; 11 Q—Kt 3, B—K 2=. Takacs—Rubinstein, Meran, 1924.

(*e*) Keres—Stahlberg, 7th match game, 1938.

(*f*) 4 P—Q Kt 4, P—B 3 (for 4. ., P—K Kt 3 see col.10) ; 5 Kt P×P, P—K 4 ∓. If now 6 Kt×P !?, P×Kt ; 7 Q—R 5 ch, K—K 2 ; 8 Q×P ch, K—B 2 ; 9 Q×P, Q—B 2 ; 10 Q—Q 5 ch, B—K 3 ; 11 Q—B 3 ch, Kt—B 3 ; 12 P—Q 4, B—B 3 ; 13 B—Q 2, R—K 1 +. Capablanca—Schenk, simultaneous exhibition, Prague, 1935.

(*g*) 9. , K Kt—K 2 is weak : 10 P—Q Kt 4 !, Q—B 2 ; 11 P—Kt 5, Kt—Q 1 ; 12 P—Q R 3, O—O ? (Lisitzin—Stahlberg, Moscow, 1935) ; 13 Kt×Q P. P—K 5 ; 14 R×P, Kt—K 3 ; 15 Kt×Kt, B×Kt, 16 P—Q 4 !.+

(*h*) In view of Black's threatening majority in the centre, White cannot afford to develop quietly.

(*i*) If 12 B—Kt 2, B—Q 2+, but not 12. ., Kt—K 2 ? ; 13 Kt×Q P, P×Kt ; 14 B×Kt ch, P×B ; 15 B—B 3+.

(*j*) 14 B×B ch, Q×B ; 15 Q—Kt 3, Kt—K 2 ; 16 P—Q 4, O—O ; 17 P×P, P×P ; 18 B—K 3. If 13. , K—Q 1 ; 14 Q—R 5 ch, Q—Kt 3 (14. ., P—Kt 3 ; 15 Q—R 3+) ; 15 Q—Q 5 ch, K—B 2 ; 16 Q—B 7 ch+.

(*k*) Or 4 P—K 3, P—K 4 ; 5 P×P, P—K 5 ! ; 6 Q—K 2, Q—K 2 ; 7 Kt—Kt 1 Kt—B 3 ; 8 Q—K 3, Kt×KtP+. Lokvenc—Addicks, Prague, 1931.

(*l*) 14 P×P, Kt—K Kt 5 ; 15 Q—Q 2, Q—R 4. Kleefstra—Euwe, Amsterdam, 1933.

(*m*) The alternative 3. ., P—K Kt 3 is inferior, because of 4 P—Kt 3 (or even 4 P—K 3, P—Q R 4 ? ; 5 P—Kt 5, P—Q B 4 ; 6 P×Q P, P×P ; 7 P—Q 3, B—Kt 2 ; 8 P—Kt 3, Kt—Q 2 ; 9 Q Kt—Q 2, Kt—B 4 ; 10 Kt—Kt 3+. Euwe—Alekhine, 8th match game, 1927), B—Kt 2 ; 5 B—Kt 2, Kt—K B 3 ; 6 P—Q 3, O—O ; 7 Q Kt—Q 2, P—B 4 ; 8 P—Kt 3, P×P ; 9 B—Kt 2, Kt—B 3 ; 10 Q Kt×P+. Réti—Rubinstein, Carlsbad, 1923

(*n*) Tarrasch—Alekhine, Semmering, 1926.

1 Kt—K B 3, P—Q 4; 2 P—B 4, P—Q B 3; 3 P—K Kt 3, Kt—B 3.

	11	12	13	14	15
4	B—Kt 2				
	B—B 4				B—Kt 5 (m)
5	P—Kt 3				Kt—K 5
	Q Kt—Q 2				B—R 4
6	B—Kt 2				P—Kt 3
	P—K 3				Q Kt-Q 2 (n)
7	O—O				Kt×Kt
	B—Q 3			P—K R 3	Q×Kt
8	P—Q 3		P—Q 4	P—Q 3 (i)	B—Kt 2
	O—O (a) ....P—K R 3	P—K R 3	P—K R 3	B—K 2 (j)	P—K 3
9	Q Kt—Q 2 (b)	Q Kt—Q 2	Q Kt—Q 2	Q Kt—Q 2 (k)	O—O
	P—K 4 (c)	O—O	O—O (g)	O—O	B—Q 3
10	P×P (d)	P×P	Kt—R 4	R—B 1	P—Q 3
	P×P	K P×P	B—R 2	P—Q R 4	Q—K 2
11	R—B 1	P—K 4	B—K R 3	P—Q R 3	Q—B 2
	Q—K 2	B—K Kt 5	Q—K 2	R—K 1	O—O
12	R—B 2	P—K R 3	P—K 3	R—B 2	P—K 4
	P—Q R 4 !	B×Kt	B—R 6	B—R 2	P×K P
13	P—Q R 4	Kt×B	B—B 3	Q—R 1	P×P
	P—R 3	R—K 1	P—Q Kt 4	B—B 1 ⇌ (l)	B—B 4
14	Q—R 1	Kt—R 4	P×Kt P		Kt—Q 2
	K R—K 1 ∓	P×P= (f)	P×P ∓ (h)		Q R—Q 1 ⇌
	(e)				(o)

(a) If 8.., P—K 4?; 9 P—K 4!, B—K 3 (9.., P×K P?; 10 P×P, Kt×P; 11 Kt—R 4++); 10 K P×P, B P×P, 11 P—Q 4, P—K 5; 12 Kt—Kt 5, O—O; 13 P×P+. Romanovsky—Rabinovitch, Moscow, 1924.

(b) Or 9 Kt—B 3, Q—K 2 (if now 9 , P—K 4; 10 P×P, P×P; 11 P—K 4! ±); 10 R—K 1, P—K 4, 11 P×P, P×P; 12 P—K 4, P×P; 13 P×P, B—Kt 3; 14 Kt—K R 4 (H. Muller—Lilienthal, Budapest, 1933), B—R 6!=.

(c) Inferior is 9 , Q—K 2; 10 R—K 1, P—K 4; 11 P×P, P×P; 12 P—K 4, P×P; 13 P×P, B—K 3; 14 Kt—R 4 ± (14 Q—K 2, Kevitz—Capablanca, New York, 1931, is also good). Capablanca—Santasiere, New York, 1931.

(d) 10 Kt—R 4, B—K 3; 11 P—K 4?, P—Q 5!; 12 Kt—B 5, B×Kt; 13 P×B, Q—K 2; 14 R—K 1, B—R 6; 15 B×B, Q×B; 16 Q—B 1, Q—K 2; 17 P—Q R 3, P—Q R 4 ∓.

(e) 15 K R—B 1, B—R 2; 16 Kt—B 1, Kt—B 4. Réti—Em. Lasker, New York 1924. White now sacrificed the Exchange, by 17 R×Kt, but against best play can hope at most for a draw.

(f) 15 P×P, B—K 4. Bogoljuboff—Staehelin, Zurich, 1934.

(g) Weaker is 9 ., Q—B 2, 10 Kt—R 4, B—R 2; 11 P×P, K P×P; 12 B—K R 3 O—O; 13 Kt—B 5 ±. Kashdan—Santasiere, 1928.

(h) 15 Kt—Kt 1, B—Q 3. Flohr—Thelen, 1931-32.

(i) Or 8 P—Q 4, B—K 2; 9 Kt—B 3, O—O; 10 Kt—Q 2, Q—R 4; 11 P—Q R 3, Q R—Q 1; 12 P—Q Kt 4, Q—B 2; 13 Q—Kt 3, P—R 3=. Van Hoorn—Kmoch, 1934.

(j) Or 8. , B—K 4; 9 Q Kt—Q 2, O—O (9.., Q—K 2?; 10 P—K 4., P×K P; 11 P×P, B—R 2; 12 P—K 5, Kt—K 5; 13 Kt×Kt, B×Kt; 14 Q—K 2, B—R 2; 15 P—Q R 3, P—Q R 4; 16 P—Q Kt 4! +. Simonson, Newman and Phillips—Capablanca, New York, 1936); 10 R—B 1, B—K R 2; 11 P—Q R 3, P—Q R 4; 12 P—Q 4, B—K 2; 13 Kt—K 1, P—Q Kt 4!; 14 P—B 5, Kt—K 5=. Capablanca and Kmoch—Euwe and Lilienthal, 1935.

(k) 9 Kt—B 3, O—O; 10 Q—B 2, B—R 2; 11 P—K 4, P×K P; 12 P×P, Kt—B 4; 13 Q R—Q 1, Q—B 2; 14 Kt—B 2, Q R—Q 1=. Euwe—Kmoch, Leningrad, 1934.

(l) Capablanca—Lilienthal, Moscow, 1936.

(m) For 4 , P—K 3, see cols. 19, 20, 23 and 25.

(n) Equally good is 6 , P—K 3; 7 B—Kt 2, B—K 2; 8 O—O, Q Kt—Q 2; 9 Kt×Kt, Q×Kt; 10 P—Q 3, O—O; 11 Kt—Q 2, Q—B 2; 12 R—B 1, K R—Q 1; 13 Kt—B 3=. Réti—Capablanca, Moscow, 1925.

(o) Réti—Torre, Moscow, 1925.

1 Kt—K B 3, P—Q 4 ; 2 P—B 4, P—K 3.

	16	17	18 .	19	20
3	P—K Kt 3				
	P×P........	P—Q 5......	Kt—K B 3		
4	Q—R 4 ch (a)	B—Kt 2	B—Kt 2		
	B—Q 2	Kt—K B 3	B—K 2 (g)...	Q Kt—Q 2...	B—Q 3
5	Q×B P	P—Q 3	P—Kt 3	P—Kt 3	P—Kt 3
	P—Q B 4 (b)	P—B 4 (d)	O—O	P—B 3	O—O
6	Kt—K 5	O—O	B—Kt 2	B—Kt 2	O—O
	Kt—Q B 3	Kt—B 3	P—Q R 4 !	B—Q 3	Q Kt—Q 2
7	Kt×B	P—K 4 (e)	O—O	O—O	B—Kt 2
	Q×Kt	P—K 4 (f)	P—R 5	O—O	P—B 3
8	B—Kt 2	Kt—K 1	Kt P×P (h)	Kt—B 3	P—Q 4 (j)
	Kt—B 3	P—K Kt 3	Q Kt—Q 2	P—Q Kt 3	Kt—K 5 (k)
9	P—Q 3	P—B 4	P×P	P—Q 3	Q Kt—Q 2
	B—K 2	B—Kt 5	P×P	B—Kt 2	P—K B 4
10	O—O	Kt—K B 3	Q—B 2	P—K 4	Kt×Kt
	Kt—Q 5	Q—B 1	Kt—Kt 3	P×K P	B P×Kt
11	Kt—B 3	Q—K 1	B—K 5	P×P	Kt—K 1
	R—Q 1	B—Kt 2	Kt—B 5	Q—B 2	Kt—B 3
12	P—Q R 4	Kt—R 3	P—Q 4	Q—K 2	P—B 3
	Kt—Q 4	O—O	Kt—K 5	K R—Q 1	B—Q 2
13	P—K 3	Kt—B 2	K Kt—Q 2	Q R—Q 1 (i)	P×P
	Kt-Kt 3 = (c)	Kt—K R 4 =	Kt(B5)×Kt	P—K 4 =	Kt×P= (l)
			=		

(a) Or 4 B—Kt 2, Kt—K B 3; 5 O—O, Q Kt—Q 2; 6 Kt—R 3, Kt—Kt 3; 7 Kt×P, Kt×Kt; 8 Q—R 4 ch, B—Q 2; 9 Q×Kt, B—B 3; 10 P—Kt 3, B—Q 3; 11 B—Kt 2, O—O=. Réti—Kmoch, Budapest, 1926.

(b) Inferior is 5. , B—B 3; 6 B—Kt 2, Kt—B 3; 7 O—O, B—K 2; 8 Q—B 2, O—O ; 9 Kt—B 3, Q Kt—Q 2; 10 R—Q 1, P—K 4; 11 P—Q 4 ±. Réti—Vidmar, London, 1927.

(c) Réti—Tartakover, Semmering, 1926.

(d) 5.., B—Kt 5 ch ; 6 Q Kt—Q 2, O—O; 7 P—Q R 3, B—K 2; 8 P—Q Kt 4, P—Q R 4 ; 9 B—Kt 2, P×P; 10 P×P, R×R; 11 Q×R, B×P; 12 B×P, Kt—B 3; 13 B—B 3 ±. C. H. Alexander—P. S. Milner-Barry, Brighton, 1938.

(e) 7 P—K 3 ?, P—K 4 ; 8 P—K 4, P—K Kt 3; 9 Kt—K 1, B—Kt 2; 10 P—B 4, B—Kt 5; 11 Kt—K B 3, Q—B 1; 12 Kt—R 3, O—O; 13 Q—K 1, Kt—K R 4 ∓. Kevitz—Kashdan, New York, 1931.

(f) 7.., P×P e.p. is inferior. Compare col. 22, note (d).

(g) 4.., P×P transposes into col. 16; 4.., P—Q 5 into col. 17.

(h) 8 P—Q 3, P—B 3, 9 Q Kt—Q 2, Kt—R 3; 10 P—Q 4, P—R 6; 11 B—B 3, P—Q Kt 4 ∓. Lovenfisch—Bogoljuboff, Moscow, 1924. The column is Rabinovitch—Marshall, Moscow, 1925.

(i) Kashdan—Horowitz, New York, 1931.

(j) Or 8 Q—B 2, R—K 1; 9 Kt—B 3, B—B 1; 10 P—Q 4, P—Q Kt 3; 11 P—K 4, P×K P; 12 Kt×P, B—Kt 2=. Bogoljuboff—Gygli, Zürich, 1934.

(k) If 8.., R—K 1 ?; 9 Q Kt—Q 2, Kt—K 5; 10 Kt×Kt, P×Kt; 11 Kt—K 5, P—K B 4; 12 P—B 3, P×P; 13 B×P, Q—B 2; 14 Kt×Kt, B×Kt; 15 P—K 4 ±. Réti—Bogoljuboff, New York, 1924.

(l) Réti—Vajda, Semmering, 1926.

1 Kt—KB3, P—Q4; 2 P—B4, P—K3; 3 P—K Kt3, Kt—KB3; 4 B—Kt2, B—K2; 5 O—O, O—O.

	21	22	CATALAN SYSTEM 23	24	25
6	P—Kt3 .... / P—B4 !		P—Q4 (e) / Q Kt—Q2 (f)		
7	P×P .... / Kt×P (a)	P—Q3 / Kt—B3	Kt—B3 .... / P—B3	P×P	Q Kt—Q2 / P—B3
8	B—Kt2 / Kt—QB3	B—Kt2 / P—Q5	P—Kt3 / P—QR3 ! (g)	P—K4 / P—B3	Q—B2 / P—QKt3 (l)
9	P—Q4 (b) / P—QKt3	P—K4 / P—K4 (d)	B—Kt2 / P—QKt4	P—QR4 / P—QR4 (i)	P—Kt3 (m) / B—Kt2
10	Kt—B3 / Kt×Kt	Q Kt—Q2 / B—K3	Kt—K5 / Kt×Kt	Q—K2 / Kt—Kt3	B—Kt2 / R—B1
11	B×Kt / B—Kt2	P—KR3 / Kt—K1	P×Kt / Kt—Q2	R—Q1 / B—Kt5	Q R—B1 / P—B4
12	P×P / B×P	Q—K2 / Q—Q2	P×QP / BP×P	Kt—K5 / Q—K2	Q—Kt1 / R—B2
13	Q—Kt1 / Q—K2	K—R2 / P—K Kt3	P—K4 / P—Q5 !	B—K3 / B—Q2	Q—R1 / Q—R1
14	R—Q1 / K R—Q1	Kt—K1 / Kt—Kt2	Kt—K2 (h) / Kt×P	Kt×P (B4) / Kt×Kt	K R—Q1 / R—K1
15	Q—B2 / QR-B1 = (c)	P—B4 / P—B4 ∓	Kt×P / Q—Kt3 =	Q×Kt (j) / P—K4 ! = (k)	B P×P / B×P= (n)

(a) Best, but 7 Q×P is also playable, e.g. 8 B—Kt2, Q—R4; 9 P—Q3, Kt—B3; 10 Q Kt—Q2, R—Q1; 11 Kt—B4, Kt—Q4=. Sorokin—Rauser, Tiflis, 1934.

(b) An alternative is 9 Kt—B3, B—B3 (or 9 ., Kt×Kt; 10 B×Kt, B—Q2; 11 Q—Kt1, B—B3; 12 Q—Kt2, R—B1; 13 K R—Q1, B×B; 14 P×B, Q—K2=. Takacs—Capablanca, Hastings, 1929-30); 10 Q—B1, P—QKt3; 11 Kt×Kt, P×Kt; 12 P—Q4, B—R3; 13 R—K1, Kt×P; 14 Kt×Kt, P×Kt; 15 Q—Q2, R—K1=. Flohr—Stoltz, 6th match game, 1931. Weak, however, is 9 Kt—R3, B—B3; 10 B×B, Kt×B; 11 R—B1, Q—K2; 12 Q—B2, Kt—Q2; 13 Kt—B4, R—Kt1; 14 K R—Q1, P—B4 ∓. Réti—Honlinger, Trentschin-Teplitz, 1928.

(c) Euwe—Flohr, 16th match game, 1932.

(d) 9.., P×P e.p.?; 10 P×P, Kt—K Kt5; 11 Q—K2, B—B3; 12 Kt—B3, Q—R4; 13 Q R—B1, R—Q1; 14 P—K R3+. Capablanca—Marshall, Moscow, 1925.

(e) Now generally known as the Catalan System.

(f) If 6 , P×P; 7 Q—B2 (7 Q Kt—Q2?, P—QKt4!; 8 Kt—K5, Kt—Q4; 9 P—K4, Kt—Kt3; 10 P—Q5, P—KB3; 11 Kt—Kt4, P—K4; 12 P—Q R4, P—B6!; 13 Kt P×P, Kt×P+. Bogoljuboff—Pirc, Noordwijk, 1938), P—B4; 8 P×P, Q—B2; 9 Kt—R3!, Q×BP; 10 B—K3, Q—K R4; 11 Kt×P, Kt—B3; 12 B—B4 ±. Ragosin—Ilyin-Zhenevsky, Tiflis, 1937.

(g) Inferior is 8.., P—QKt3; 9 B—Kt2, P—QR4?; 10 Kt—Q2!, B—R3; 11 P—K4, P×BP; 12 P—K5!, Kt—Q4; 13 P×P+. Keres—Böök, Kemeri, 1937.

(h) If 14 Q×P, B—B4=. The column is Keres—Bogoljuboff, Noordwijk, 1938

(i) Another good reply is 9 , P—QKt3; 10 Q—K2, B—R3; 11 P—QKt3, B—Kt5!, 12 B—Kt2, P—B4; 13 KtP×P, P×P; 14 Kt×P, B×Kt; 15 B×B, R—B1; 16 Kt—Kt5, B×Kt; 17 R P×B, Q—B2= (Botvinnik).

(j) Botvinnik—Lasker, Moscow, 1936.

(k) 16 P×P, Kt—Kt5! (Euwe).

(l) 8 , P—QKt4?; 9 P—B5!, Q—B2; 10 Kt—Kt3, P—K4; 11 Kt×P, Kt×Kt; 12 B—B4, K Kt—Kt5; 13 P—K4!+. Botvinnik—Rabinovitch, Leningrad, 1938.

(m) If 9 P—K4, B—Kt2!; 10 P—Kt3, R—B1; 11 P—K5, Kt—K1; 12 B—Kt2, P—Q B4=.

(n) Flohr—Ragosin. Semmering-Baden, 1937.

CATALAN SYSTEM

1 P—Q 4, Kt—K B 3; 2 P—Q B 4, P—K 3; 3 Kt—K B 3, P—Q 4;
4 P—K Kt 3, B—K 2; 5 B—Kt 2 (A).

	26	27	28	29	30
5	O—O				P—B 4
6	O—O				P×Q P
	P—B 4 (a)				Kt×P
7	P×Q P				O—O
	Kt×P (b)				Kt—B 3
8	P—K 4.............................			Kt—B 3	Kt—Q B 3
	Kt—Kt 3 .... Kt—B 2 ..... Kt—K B 3			Kt×Kt (i)	P×P
9	Kt—B 3	Kt—B 3	Kt—B 3	P×Kt	Kt—QKt5(k)
	P×P	P×P	P×P	P×P	O—O
10	Kt×P	Kt×P	Kt×P	P×P	Q Kt×Q P
	Kt—B 3! (c)	P—K 4	Kt—B 3 (f)	B—Q 2	Q—Kt 3
11	Kt×Kt (d)	Kt—B 5	Kt×Kt	Kt—K 5	P—K 4
	P×Kt	Kt—B 3	P×Kt	Kt—B 3	Kt—B 3
12	Q—K 2	B—K 3	Q—B 2 (g)	Kt×B	Kt×Kt
	P—K 4	B—K 3	B—R 3	Q×Kt	Q×Kt!
13	B—K 3	Kt—Q 5!	R—Q 1	P—K 3	P—K 5
	B—K 3	Kt×Kt	Q—R 4	K R—Q 1	Kt—Q 4
14	K R—Q 1	Kt—R 6 ch!	B—Q 2	R—Kt 1	B—Kt 5
	Q—B 2	P×Kt	Q—R 4	Q R—B 1	Q—Kt 3
15	Q R—B 1	P×Kt ± (e)	Q—R 4	B—Q 2	Q—Q 3
	Q—Kt 2 =		B—Kt 4 (h)	P-QKt3=(j)	R—Q 1 =(l)

(A) The Catalan System can arise from either a pure Réti Opening (cols. 23-25), or a Queen's Gambit. Since the latter is the more usual order of moves, we have adopted it in cols. 26-40.

(a) 6. , P—Q Kt 3; 7 P×P, Kt×P; 8 P—K 4, Kt—K B 3; 9 Kt—B 3, B—Kt 2; 10 Kt—K 5, P—B 4; 11 P—Q 5! ±. Ragosin—Rabinovitch, Leningrad, 1934.

(b) 7.., K P×P is weak, since it transposes into the disadvantageous Tarrasch Defence in the Queen's Gambit Declined.

(c) If instead 10 ., B—B 3?; 11 K Kt—Kt 5!, Kt—B 3; 12 B—K 3, Kt—B 5; 13 B—B 5, Q×Q; 14 Q R×Q, R—Q 1; 15 R×R ch, B×R; 16 P—Kt 3+. Fine—Kashdan, New York, 1938.

(d) 11 B—K 3?, Kt—B 5 ∓.

(e) 15 ., B×P; 16 B×B. Alekhine—P. S. Milner-Barry, Margate, 1938.

(f) If 10.., P—K 4; 11 K Kt—Kt 5, Kt—B 3; 12 Kt—Q 5 ±.

(g) Better than 12 Q—R 4, Q—Kt 3; 13 R—Kt 1 (after 13 P—K 5, Kt—Q 4; 14 Q—K Kt 4, K—R 1!—not 14 , P—K B 4; 15 P×P e.p., Kt×P; 16 Q—K 2, K—R 1; 17 B—K 3+—15 Kt—K 4, B—R 3, Black has excellent counterplay. Ragosin), B—R 3; 14 B—K 3, Q—Kt 2; 15 K R—K 1, P—K 4; 16 P—Q Kt 4, B—Q 6; 17 Q R—Q 1, K R—Q 1=. Ragosin—Eliskases, Moscow, 1936.

(h) 16 Kt×B, P×Kt; 17 Q—Kt 3, B—B 4 (Keres—Stahlberg, 5th match game 1938); 18 B—K B 3!+ (Keres).

(i) An improvement upon 8 , Kt—Q B 3; 9 Kt×Kt, P×Kt; 10 P×P, B×P (Keres—Stahlberg, 1st match game, 1938); 11 Q—B 2, Q—K 2; 12 R—Q 1 ±.

(j) Keres—Stahlberg, 3rd match game, 1938.

(k) Or 9 Kt×P, Kt×Q Kt; 10 P×Kt, B—Q 2= (Ragosin).

(l) Ragosin—Lasker, Moscow, 1936.

CATALAN SYSTEM

1 P—Q4, Kt—KB3; 2 P—QB4, P—K3; 3 P—KKt3, P—Q4.

	31	32	33	34	35
4	Kt—KB3 PxP				P—B4
5	Q—R4 ch Q Kt—Q2				BPxP KtxP
6	B—Kt2 P—QR3 (a)			QxBP P—B4	B—Kt2 PxP
7	Kt—B3 R—QKt1	...P—B4 (c)	QxBP P—QKt4	B—Kt2 Kt—Kt3 (i)	O—O B—B4
8	QxBP P—QKt4	O—O B—K2	Q—B2 (g) B—Kt2	Q—Q3 PxP	KtxP O—O
9	Q—Q3 B—Kt2	PxP BxP (d)	P—QR4 P—Kt5	O—O B—K2	Kt—Kt3 (m) B—Kt3
10	O—O P—B4	QxBP P—QKt4	O—O P—B4	KtxP O—O	B—Q2 Kt—Q B3
11	PxP KtxP	Q—KR4 B—Kt2	PxP BxP	Kt—Q B3 P—K4 (j)	Kt—R3 Q—K2 (n)
12	QxQ ch RxQ	B—Kt5 O—O (e)	Q Kt—Q2 R—B1	Kt—B5 B—Q Kt5	Kt—B4 B—B2
13	B—B4 P—Kt5 (b)	QR—Q1 Q—B2 (f)	Q—Q3 O—O= (h)	Q—B2 (k) Q—B2= (l)	P—K4 KKt—Kt5=

(a) 6 .., P—B3; 7 QxP (B 4), B—Q3; 8 Kt—B3, O—O; 9 O—O, Q—K2; 10 P—K4, P—K4; 11 P—KR3, Kt—Kt3; 12 Q—K2 ±.

(b) 14 Kt—Q1, Kt—Q4, 15 R—B1 ±. Petrov—Alekhine, Margate, 1938.

(c) If 7 , B—Q3?; 8 P—K4!, Black must embark on the speculative sacrifice 8 .., P—QKt4; 9 KtxP, PxKt; 10 QxR, Kt—Kt3 (10 .., B—Kt5 ch; 11 B—Q2, Kt—Kt3; 12 Q—R7, BxB ch; 13 KtxB, QxP; 14 QxP, P—O; 15 O—O¹+); 11 Q—R7 (11 Q—R5?, Q—K2 ∓), KtxP; 12 O—O, O—O; 13 Kt—K5, when his compensation for the material sacrificed is insufficient.

(d) If 9 . O—O; 0 P—B6, P—QKt4; 11 Q—B2, Kt—B4; 12 R—Q1, Q—Kt3; 13 P—QR4, P—Kt5; 14 P—R5+.

(e) 12 , P—Kt5; 13 Kt—R4, B—K2; 14 KR—Q1, Q—R4; 15 P—Kt3, R—Q1; 16 Kt—Kt2, Kt—Kt3; 17 RxR ch, BxR, 18 Kt—Q3 ±. Fine—Dake, New York, 1938.

(f) 14 R—B1!, Q—Kt3; 15 P—Q Kt4, B—K2; 16 KR—Q1 ±. Alekhine—Euwe, 16th match game, 1937. If here 13 , Q—K2, 14 RxKt!, QxR; 15 Kt—K5 (not 15 BxKt, PxB; 16 QxP, Q—K2+), Q—B2; 16 BxKt, PxB (BxB?; 17 Kt—Kt5 +); 17 Kt—Kt4, B—K2, 18 BxB, QxB; 19 Kt—K4!!, KR—Q1; 20 K Ktx Pch+.

(g) Or (1) 8 Q—Q3, B—Kt2; 9 Kt—B3, P—B4; 10 O—O, P—B5; 11 Q—B2, P—Kt5; 12 Kt—Q1, R—B1; 13 B—Kt5, Q—R4; 14 BxKt, KtxB; 15 Kt—K3, P—B6 ∓. Reshevsky—Fine, Nottingham, 1936. (2) 8 Q—B6?, R—R2!; 9 B—B4, B—Kt2; 10 Q—B1, P—B4; 11 PxP, BxP; 12 O—O, O—O; 13 Q Kt—Q2, Q—K2; 14 Kt—Kt3, B—Kt3; 15 B—K3, R—B1 ∓. Capablanca—Reshevsky, Nottingham, 1936.

(h) Flohr—Fine, Kemeri, 1936.

(i) 7.., P—Q R 3 transposes into col. 33.

(j) 11.., Q Kt—Q 4 was good enough for equality: 12 R—Q1, KtxKt; 13 QxKt, Kt—Q4; 14 Q—Kt3, Q—Kt3! and White cannot accept the sacrifice (15 BxKt, PxB; 16 QxP, R—Q1; 17 Q—K4, B—B3; 18 P—K3, B—K3 ∓).

(k) Alekhine—Euwe, 14th match game, 1937 which continued 13.., BxKt; 14 PxB, BxKt; 15 QxB, Q—B2; 16 B—R6!?, Q Kt—Q2; 17 Q—Kt5, Kt—K1; 18 Q R—Kt1, when Black's position is not easy to defend. The text is simpler.

(l) 14 B—Kt5, K Kt—Q4; 15 Q R—B1, BxKt; 16 PxB, P—B3.

(m) Weaker is 9 P—Q R3, B—Kt3; 10 Kt—B2, Kt—B3; 11 P—K4, Kt—B2; 12 Kt—Q4, Kt—R4; 13 Kt—R4, Kt—K3; 14 QxQ, BxQ; 15 B—K3, Q Kt—Q5 ∓. Fine—C. H. Alexander, Hastings, 1937-38.

(n) Best. If instead 11 , P—Q R3; 12 Kt—B4, B—R2; 13 Kt (B 4)—R5, KtxKt; 14 BxKt, Q—K2; 15 R—B1, B—Q2; 16 P—K4 ±. Simonson—Fine, New York, 1938.

CATALAN SYSTEM
1 P—Q 4, Kt—K B 3; 2 P—Q B 4, P—K 3; 3 P—K Kt 3.

	36	37	38	39	40
3	(P—Q 4)................		B—Kt 5 ch		
4	B—Kt 2	..... Kt—Q B 3	B—Q 2		
	P×P	P×P	B×B ch................		Q—K 2
5	Q—R 4 ch	Q—R 4 ch	Q×B......	Kt×B......	B—Kt 2
	Q Kt—Q 2	Kt—B 3 (d)	Kt—K 5 (g)	Kt—B 3!	O—O (j)
6	Kt—QB3 (a)	B—Kt 2	Q—B 2	K Kt—B 3	Kt—K B 3
	P—B 3 (b)	B—Q 2	P—Q 4	P—Q 3	P—Q 4
7	Q×P (B 4)	Q×B P	B—Kt 2	B—Kt 2	Q—B 2
	P—K 4	Kt—Q Kt 5	Q—K 2	P—K 4	Kt—K 5
8	Kt—B 3	Q—Kt 3	P—Q R 3	P—Q 5	O—O
	P×P	P—B 4	P—K B 4	Kt—K 2	Kt×B
9	Q×Q P	Kt—B 3	Kt—K B 3	O—O	Q Kt×Kt
	B—B 4	B—B 3	O—O	O—O	P—Q B 3
10	Q—Q 3	O—O !	O—O	P—K 4	P—K 4
	O—O	P×P P (e)	P—B 3	Kt—Q 2	B×Kt
11	O—O	R—Q 1	Kt—B 3	Kt—K 1	Kt×B
	Kt—Kt 3	Q—R 4	Kt—Q 2	P—K B 4	P×K P (k)
12	Q—B 2	Kt×P	P—Q Kt 4	Kt—Q 3	Kt×P
	P—K R 3	B×B	Kt—Q 3!	P—B 5	Kt—Q 2
13	Kt—Q2 ± (c)	K×B ± (f)	P—B 5!	P×P	P—B 5 (l)
			Kt—B 5 (h)	P×P= (i)	Kt—B 3 (m)

(a) Again the immediate capture of the Q B P is inferior: 6 Q×B P, P—B 4; 7 P×P, B×P; 8 Kt—K R 3, Q—B 2; 9 Kt—Q 2, R—Q Kt 1; 10 O—O, P—Q Kt 4; 11 Q—Kt 3, B—Kt 2; 12 B×B, Q×B; 13 Kt—K B 4, O—O and Black's position is somewhat more comfortable. Flohr—Reshevsky, Hastings, 1937-38.

(b) Best is 6.., P—Q R 3, transposing into cols. 31-32.

(c) Flohr—W. A. Fairhurst, Hastings, 1937-38.

(d) Better is 4.., Q Kt—Q 2, with variations similar to those in cols. 31-35.

(e) If 10.., B×Kt; 11 B×B, P×P; 12 R—Q 1, Q—Kt 3; 13 Kt—R 4 ±.

(f) Keres—Ragosin, Semmering-Baden, 1937.

(g) Better 5.., P—Q 3 as in the next column.

(h) 14 K R—K 1, P—Q Kt 3; 15 Kt—Q 2! ±. Belavenetz—Lövenfisch, Tiflis, 1937.

(i) Alatorzeff—Lövenfisch, Tiflis, 1937.

(j) 5. , Kt—B 3; 6 K Kt—B 3, B×B ch; 7 Q Kt×B, P—Q 3 is similar to col. 39 If here 6 ., P—K 4?; 7 P×P, Kt×P; 18 Kt×Kt, B×B ch; 9 Q×B, Q×Kt; 10 Kt—B 3, O—O; 11 O—O, P—Q 3; 12 K R—K 1±. Alatorzeff—Chekhover, Tiflis, 1937.

(k) If 11. , P×B P; 12 Kt×P, P—Q B 4; 13 P—Q 5!, P×P; 14 P×P, Kt—Q 2; 15 K R—K 1, Q—B 3, 16 P—Q 6+ (Reshevsky).

(l) Reshevsky—Treysman, New York, 1938, which continued 13.., P—K 4??; 14 P×P, Kt×K P; 15 K R—K 1, Kt—Kt 3; 16 Kt—Q 6, Q—B 2; 17 P—B 4+.

(m) White has a slight positional advantage.

1 Kt—KB3.

	41	42	43	44	45
1	(P—Q4)....Kt—KB3				P—KB4
2	P—KKt3 (a) / Kt—KB3	P—B4 / P—B4	P—K3	P—KKt3 (h)	P—K Kt3 / P—Q Kt3
3	B—Kt2 / P—B4	P—KKt3 (e) / P—K Kt3	P—K Kt3 / P—Q Kt3	P—Q Kt4 (i) / B—Kt2	B—Kt2 / B—Kt2
4	P—Q4 (b) / P—K3 (c)	B—Kt2 / B—Kt2	B—Kt2 / B—Kt2	B—Kt2 / O—O	O—O (l) / Kt—KB3
5	O—O / Q—Kt3	O—O / O—O	O—O / B—K2	P—Kt3 / P—Kt3 (j)	P—Q3 / P—K3
6	P—K3 / Kt—B3	Kt—B3 / Kt—B3	Kt—B3 / P—B4	B—Kt2 / B—Kt2	P—K4 / PxP
7	P—Kt3 / B—K2	P—Q3 / P—Q3	P—Q Kt3 / P—Q4 !	O—O / P—Q3	Kt—Kt5 / B—K2
8	B—Kt2 / PxP	B—K3 / B—Q2	Kt—K5 / Q Kt—Q2	P—Q3 / Q Kt—Q2	Kt—QB3 / O—O
9	PxP / O—O	Q—B1 / R—K1	P—B4 / B—Q3	Q Kt—Q2 / P—K4	Q KtxP / KtxKt
10	Q Kt—Q2 / B—Q2	P—KR3 / R—B1	PxP / BxP	Q—B2 / R—K1	KtxKt / Kt—B3
11	P—B4 / PxP (d)	P—R3 / P—QR3=(f)	Kt—B4 / Q—Kt1=(g)	K R—Q1 / P—QR4=(k)	B—Q2 ± (m)

(a) P—Q B4 at any one of White's first six moves would transpose into better-known variations.

(b) White is now playing the Grünfeld Defence to the Queen's Pawn Game with a move in hand.

(c) 4.., B—B4; 5 P—B4 ±, for if 5. , Q PxP; 6 O—O, Kt—B3; 7 Q—R4, PxP; 8 KtxP, QxKt; 9 BxKtch, B—Q2; 10 R—Q1, QxRch (10., BxB; 11 QxBch, PxQ; 12 RxQ with the better ending); 11 QxQ, BxB; 12 Kt—B3 and White should win.

(d) 12 KtxP, Q—R3; 13 K Kt—K5, K R—Q1; 14 KtxB, KtxKt; 15 Q—B3 (Santasiere—Fine, New York, 1938), Kt—Kt3=.

(e) 3 P—Q4 at an early stage is best, and would transpose into either the English Opening, Queen's Gambit, or Queen's Pawn Game.

(f) Réti—Grünfeld, Mährisch-Ostrau, 1923.

(g) Alekhine—Nimzovitch, New York, 1927.

(h) Two alternatives are : (1) 2. , P—Q Kt3; 3 P—K Kt3, B—Kt2; 4 B—Kt2, P—K4; 5 Kt—B3, B—Kt5; 6 O—O, K Bx Kt; 7 Kt Px B, P—Q3; 8 P—Q4, P—K5; 9 Kt—R4, O—O; 10 P—B3, PxP; 11 BxP. Kevitz and Pinkus—Alekhine, New York, 1929. (2) 2. , P—Q3; 3 P—K Kt3, B—B4; 4 B—Kt2, P—B3; 5 P—Kt3, Q—B1; 6 P—KR3, P—K4; 7 B—Kt2, Kt—R3; 8 Kt—B3, P—R3; 9 P—Q3, B—K2; 10 Q—Q2, Kt—B2; 11 Kt—Q1, O—O=. Réti—T. Gruber, Vienna, 1923.

(i) 3 P—Q Kt3, B—Kt2; 4 B—Kt2, O—O; 5 P—Kt3, P—Q3; 6 B—Kt2, Kt—B3; 7 O—O, P—K4; 8 P—Q4, Kt—Q2; 9 PxP. Capablanca—Yates, Barcelona, 1929.

(j) 5.., P—Q4; 6 PxP, KtxP; 7 BxB, KxB; 8 Q—Kt3, Kt—KB3; 9 B—Kt2, Kt—B3; 10 O—O, P—K4=. Réti—Pokorny, Mährisch-Ostrau, 1923.

(k) Réti—Capablanca, New York, 1924.

(l) Or 4 P—Kt3, Kt—KB3; 5 O—O, P—K3; 6 B—Kt2, B—K2; 7 P—Q3, O—O. 8 Q Kt—Q2, Q—K1; 9 P—QR4, P—QR4; 10 Kt—B4, Q—R4; 11 Q—Q2, P—R3. Réti—Fick, Scheveningen, 1923. 4 P—Q4, at an early stage transposes into the Dutch Defence to the Queen's Pawn Game.

(m) Euwe—Tartakover, Kissingen, 1928.

RUY LOPEZ

THIS opening comes nearer than any other to conferring a winning advantage with the move; and its popularity for match and tournament play (when White is allowed the choice of playing it) is by no means surprising. White controls the centre, his pieces have greater mobility than those of his adversary, and the opening accordingly yields him an immediate and enduring attack. Against the passive defences such as the Berlin, Steinitz, and Steinitz Deferred, White's grip is extremely cramping; nor can Black try a more enterprising defence (*e.g.*, the Classical, Cozio, or Schliemann) without the risk of finding White's superiority in development speedily decisive.

The principal defences, in alphabetical order, are as follows :—

The Berlin Defence, 3..., Kt—K B 3 (cols. 1 to 20) is a solid form of the close game, which leaves Black with a dangerously backward development. This is the reason why it has fallen out of favour in modern days and has received exceedingly few illustrations since the fourth edition of this work. In the customary variations of the attack, illustrated in cols. 1 to 7, the substitution of 10 Kt—Q 4 for 10 R—K 1, strengthened by Schlechter's move 14 P—Q Kt 4 (col. 1) enables White to avoid the drawing possibilities of the Rio de Janeiro variation (col. 3). Against 5..., Kt—Q 3 (cols. 6 and 7) P—Q R 4, followed by P—K 6, gives White a strong attack at the cost of a Pawn. As to the relative merits of the two moves 4 O—O and 4 P—Q 4 there is no general agreement, but we feel that the reply 4..., Kt × K P to the latter is an adequate defence.

Bird's Defence, 3..., Kt—Q 5 (cols. 21 to 25), is theoretically unsound and has been abandoned in serious chess.

The Classical Defence, 3..., B—B 4 (cols. 26 to 35) is also out of fashion. Against the strongest reply 4 P—B 3,

4..., P—B 4 gives rise to an exceedingly complicated position, where only P×P (col. 29) yields White the superiority. Should White seek safety, the simple developing move 4 O—O (cols. 33 to 35), which has the additional merit of avoiding prepared variations, assures him of a slight positional advantage.

The Cozio and Fianchetto Defences (cols. 36 and 37, and 38 to 40) have both been practically abandoned by the masters, the " Lopez grip " being too strong in both for Black's hopes of success against a player of approximately equal class.

The Morphy Defence, 3..., P—Q R 3, under which heading one could also include the Steinitz Defence Deferred, is now practically the only defence ever played. This is due to the fact that the additional tempo is always desirable for the second player. After the customary moves 3..., P—Q R 3; 4 B—R 4, Kt—B 3; 5 O—O Black has the choice of two widely differing systems of defence, 5..., Kt×P (cols. 41 to 75) and 5..., B—K 2 (cols. 76 to 114).

The former is the more aggressive line, by which Black obtains a free, open game, but at the expense of some insecurity of position. It has lost popularity with the great masters, with the notable exception of Euwe, who continues to play it with success. Apparently the other masters instinctively distrust the infraction of sound opening principles which the line involves. White's Pawn at K 5 exercises a restraining influence on Black's game and can serve as a basis for a vigorous King-side attack by P—K B 4 at a later stage. Moreover, Black's Pawn-formation on the Queen's wing is early left ragged, his Queen's Bishop's Pawn being frequently kept backward on the open file when White can force an exchange of Knights by Kt—Q 4 at a suitable moment. As compensation for these weaknesses Black's minor pieces are aggressively placed and, if he can succeed in playing P—Q B 4, he will have a formidable

" Pawn-roller." In the normal variation (cols. 41 to 62) White, on his 10th move, has a choice of (i) Q Kt—Q 2; (ii) B—K B 4; (iii) B—K 3; (iv) R—K 1; (v) P—Q R 4; or (vi) Kt—Q 4.

(i) 10 Q Kt—Q 2 (cols. 41 to 48) is the move most frequently seen. After 10..., O—O, White's best continuation is 11 Q—K 2 (cols. 41 to 43), when the line in col. 41, played by Dr. Euwe in an important encounter, solves Black's opening problems. Of the two other possibilities on White's 11th move B—B 2, with the continuation in col. 45, is worthy of attention.

(ii) 10 B—K B 4 (cols. 49 and 50) is an old move revived by Hungarian analysts. The complicated line in Col. 50 is very trappy, but with best play leads to an even ending.

(iii) 10 B—K 3 (cols. 51 to 55) is a more logical move than the foregoing, and confronts Black with a serious problem about his Queen-side Pawns. In the main variation in col. 52 White's King-side attack was formerly thought to be quite sufficient for the Pawn sacrificed, but in the light of the innovation on Black's 17th move, shown in the column, Black must be given the better chances in this particular line and consequently in the whole variation.

(iv) 10 R—K 1 (cols. 56 to 60) is the introduction to the sparkling Breslau Variation, in which White gains a piece at the expense of a fierce attack, which is at least good enough to draw for Black.

(v) 10 P—Q R 4 (col. 61) has been revived by Alekhine, who has demonstrated that it is at least as good as the other variations.

(vi) 10 Kt—Q 4 (col. 62) is a line of recent origin where White sacrifices a Pawn to prevent Black from Castling.

The older defence, 9..., B—Q B 4 (cols. 64 and 65) is now not often encountered, as it is found that this square is better left available for Black's King's Knight when

driven from K 5. Nevertheless, Black can attain theoretical
equality. Neither side is well advised to vary from the
moves in the normal variation. Alternatives for White on
his 8th and 9th moves are illustrated in cols. 66 to 70; they
are not nearly as dangerous for Black as the main line.
Of the alternatives for Black the Riga Variation (col. 73)
is the most interesting. Here Capablanca's line is still considered the refutation.

The move 5..., B—K 2 (cols. 76 to 114), much more
popular now than 5..., Kt × P, is played with a view to
maintaining Black's centre Pawn at K 4 and following up
with a counter-action on the Queen's wing. The bad
feature of this defence is that it leaves Black with a
cramped game, and recent master-practice consistently
prefers White.

On his 6th move White has the choice of (i) R—K 1;
(ii) Q—K 2; or (iii) P—Q 4.

(i) 6 R—K 1 (cols. 76 to 100) is the older line, played
with a view to defending the King's Pawn and leaving the
square K B 1 free for the Queen's Knight. In Tchigorin's
Defence, where Black sets up his Pawns at Q Kt 4, Q B 4,
Q 3, and K 4, White can branch off into three lines of play
on his 11th move. 11 P—K R 3 (cols. 76 to 86) is preferred
by most masters. In the traditional line, where White
locks the centre and plays for a King-side attack, it is
difficult to find anything new for either side before the 20th
move. Black's position remains exceedingly cramped, but
it is by no means certain that White's King-side manœuvres
should lead to a win. With best play, however, White
leaves his opponent without any counter-play whatsoever
(col. 76), so that this variation should be avoided by Black.
The variations where White keeps his Pawn at Q 4 are
generally much easier for Black; in col. 81, e.g., the Pawn-
sacrifice involved is unsound. An exception to this rule is
the attack on Black's Queen-side Pawns in col. 84, which has
l⌐d to some brilliant wins in Keres's hands. 11 Q Kt—Q 2

(cols. 87 and 88) is a stronger alternative, since it saves a valuable tempo for the attack.   11 P—Q R 4 (col. 89) is much weaker than the same move after White has played P—K R 3 (col. 84), for White cannot afford to accept the Pawn-sacrifice involved.

Bogoljuboff's idea of exchanging the centre Pawns in order to obtain a majority of Pawns on the Queen's side is no longer held in such high esteem as was formerly the case. By P—Q 5, closing the centre, White can, if he wishes, maintain a slight positional advantage (col. 94).

A weaker alternative for Black is the omission of the counter-attack on the Queen's side by P—Q Kt 4 (cols. 97 to 100).   These variations are no longer popular because modern masters distrust the cramped positions which they involve on general principles.   The Kecskemét Variation (cols. 98 and 99) is an example of this.

(ii) 6 Q—K 2 (cols. 101 to 114), the Worrall Attack, is coming more and more into the limelight.   A good many authorities, notably Alekhine, believe that it is at least as good as 6 R—K 1 and recent tournament practice certainly confirms this contention.   Black cannot, as against R—K 1, force the Tchigorin defensive set-up.   In the gambit defence, where Black sacrifices his King's Pawn to cramp White's development, some notable improvements were found in the American Championship Tournament of 1936.   If White accepts the Pawn, as in col. 108, he is exposed to a severe attack, which can prove fatal.   The variations where Black omits P—Q Kt 4 (cols. 110 to 113) are even more unfavourable than the corresponding lines after 6 R—K 1.

(iii) 6 P—Q 4 (col. 114) is an indifferent continuation for White.

5..., B—B 4 (cols. 117 to 119), formerly played by Alekhine, has since practically disappeared from tournament chess, White obtaining a clear advantage with both 6 P—B 3 (col. 117) and 6 Kt × P (col. 119).

The remaining columns, 120 to 135, exhibit lines of play diverging at an earlier stage. They all permit Black to equalise with comparative ease and are for that reason of infrequent occurrence.

The Exchange Variation (cols. 136 to 140) is of the greatest theoretical importance, since if it were good for White the other variations of Morphy's Defence would be of no consequence. It is played with a view to establishing a majority of four Pawns to three on the King's side and utilising this theoretical advantage in the ending; but Black always finds more than sufficient compensation in his two Bishops and freer development.

The Steinitz Defence, 3..., P—Q 3 (cols. 141 to 160), has had the approval of not only Steinitz himself, but also his successors in the championship, Lasker and Capablanca. It gives a solid positional game, such as Steinitz loved, and, like the Berlin Defence, demands unlimited patience on Black's part. It has strong tendencies towards a draw, Black's game being very compact and not as a rule open to direct attack. The characteristic positions commencing with 7 R—K 1 (cols. 141 to 148) are now more generally reached by transposition from the Berlin Defence, the troublesome attack based on 6 B × Kt and O—O—O (cols. 154 and 155) being thereby avoided. By the substitution of 7 B × Kt for 7 R—K 1 Black is hard taxed to equalise the game.

The Steinitz Defence Deferred, 3..., P—Q R 3; 4 B—R 4, P—Q 3 (cols. 161 to 190) has gained in popularity since our last edition, chiefly because it avoids most of the bad features of the Steinitz Defence, and retains most of the good ones. White has the choice of five continuations :

(i) 5 B × Kt ch (cols. 161 to 167) is played with a view to taking advantage of White's superior development. The second player must be very careful, but if he supports his centre by P—K B 3 (cols. 161 to 164) his two Bishops and his command of the open Q Kt file frequently tell in his favour.

(ii) 5 P—Q 4 (cols. 168 and 169) can be either a dull drawing line as in col. 168, or a sparkling gambit as in col. 169.

(iii) 5 P—B 4 (cols. 170 and 171) has attracted attention because of Keres's adoption of it against Alekhine at Margate, 1937. Where Black maintains his King's Pawn at K 4 (col. 170) Lajos Steiner's move leads to an overwhelming position for White; Black should exchange his King's Pawn early, as in col. 171, since White is forced to exchange two minor pieces, when a draw is practically unavoidable.

(iv) 5 O—O (cols. 171 to 176), formerly thought to be inferior because of Rubinstein's analysis in the *Lärobok,* has been rehabilitated. On his 6th move White has the choice of 6 B × Kt ch (cols. 172 to 174), where the interesting line in col. 174 is hard for Black to meet, or 6 P—Q 4 (col. 175), an enterprising sacrificial line, which Yates handled with great skill.

(v) 5 P—B 3 (cols. 177 to 190) is the main variation. Where Black plays B—Q 2 and B—K 2, contenting himself with simple developing moves, White's hold on the centre and freer development give him a clear superiority (cols. 177 and 178). The stronger continuation for Black is 6..., P—K Kt 3, and this line has often been adopted by Capablanca, Alekhine, and Rubinstein. Black can develop his King's Knight at either K 2 or B 3; the latter is stronger because it avoids the dangerous attack in col. 183. The Siesta Variation (cols. 186 to 190) is no longer seen; according to present analysis 6 P × P (cols. 186 to 188) gives White an overwhelming attack, to which no satisfactory defence has been found.

The Unusual Defences (cols. 191 to 200) are of no great theoretical importance. Schliemann's Defence (cols. 191 to 194) is the only one which is occasionally played : it is refuted by 4 Kt—B 3. Alapin's Defence Deferred (col. 200) merits interest because no theoretical refutation is known.

1 P—K 4, P—K 4 ; 2 Kt—K B 3, Kt—Q B 3 ; 3 B—Kt 5.

BERLIN DEFENCE

3.., Kt—B 3 ; 4 O—O, Kt×P ; 5 P—Q 4, B—K 2 ; 6 Q—K 2 (*a*).

	1	2	3	4	5
6	Kt—Q 3..				P—B 4 (*h*)
7	B×Kt				P×P (*l*)
	Kt P×B (*b*)				O—O
8	P×P				Kt—B 3
	Kt—Kt 2				Kt×Kt
9	Kt—B 3.............................		P—Q Kt 3		P×Kt
	O—O			O—O	P—Q 4
10	Kt—Q 4!....	R—K 1		B—Kt 2	R—Q 1
	B—B 4 (*c*)	Kt—B 4.....	R—K 1 (*g*)	P—Q 4	Kt—Q R 4
11	R—Q 1	Kt—Q 4	Q—B 4	P×P e.p.	P—B 4
	B×Kt	Kt—K 3	Kt—B 4	P×P	P—B 3
12	R×B	B—K 3	Kt—K Kt 5	Q Kt—Q 2	P×P
	P—Q 4	Kt×Kt	B×Kt (*h*)	B—B 3	P×B
13	P×P e.p.	−B×Kt	B×B	B×B	P—Q 6
	P×P	P—Q B 4 (*e*)	Q×B	Q×B	Kt—B 5
14	P—Q Kt 4 !	B—K 3	Q×Kt	K R—K 1	P—Q R 4 +
	Q—B 3	P—Q 4	R—K 3	Kt—B 4	(*m*)
15	B—K 3	P×P e.p.	Q—Q 4	Kt—K 4	
	B—B 4	B×P	B—Kt 2	Kt×Kt	
16	Q R-Q 1+ (*d*)	Q R-Q 1 ± (*f*)	Q—Q Kt 4	Q×Kt	
			B—B 1 (*i*)	B—Q 2 = (*j*)	

(*a*) The most energetic continuation. Some alternatives are : (1) 6 P—Q 5, Kt—Q 3 ; 7 Kt—B 3, Kt×B ; 8 Kt×Kt, P—Q R 3 ; 9 Kt—B 3, Kt—Kt 1 ; 10 Kt×P, P—Q 3 ; 11 Kt—B 3, O—O=. (2) 6 P×P, O—O ; 7 Q—Q 5, Kt—B 4 ; 8 B—K 3, P—Q R 3 ; 9 B—Q B 4, Kt—Kt 5 ; 10 Q—Q 1, P—Q Kt 4 ; 11 B—K 2, B—Kt 2=. Or (3) 6 R—K 1, Kt—Q 3 ; 7 B×Kt (7 P×P, Kt—B 4 ; 8 Kt—B 3, O—O ; 9 Kt—Q 5. Charousek—Tarrasch, Budapest, 1896), Q P×B ; 8 P×P, Kt—B 4 and Black has a good enough game.
(*b*) Forced, for if 7 , Q P×B ? ; 8 P×P, Kt—B 4 ; 9 R—Q 1, B—Q 2 ; 10 P—K 6 (if 10 P—K Kt 4, Kt—R 3 but not Kt—R 5 ; 11 Kt×Kt, B×Kt ; 12 P—Kt 5!+ +), P×P ; 11 Kt—K 5, B—Q 3 ; 12 Q—R 5 ch, P—Kt 3 ; 13 Kt×Kt P, Kt—Kt 2 ; 14 Q—R 6+ (*Lärobok*).
(*c*) 10 ., Kt—B 4 ; 11 R—Q 1, Q—K 1 ; 12 Kt—B 5, P—B 3 ; 13 B—R 6, Kt—K 3 ; 14 Q—Kt 4, R—B 2 ; 15 B—Q 2+. W. H. S. Monck—J. J. O'Hanlon, correspondence, 1903.
(*d*) 16.., P—Q R 3 ; 17 P—Kt 4. Schlechter—Réti, Vienna, 1914.
(*e*) The Rio de Janeiro Variation, originated by the late Dr. Caldas Vianna. If 13.., P—Q 4 ; 14 Q—K 3, followed by Kt—R 4+.
(*f*) 16.., Q—R 5 ; 17 P—K R 3, Q—Q Kt 5 (better B—Kt 2) ; 18 B—B 1. Tarrasch—Lasker, 14th match game, 1908. In the 10th game the continuation was 16 Kt—K 4, B—Kt 2 ; where Hoffer pointed out a probable draw by 16.., B×P ch ; 17 K×B, Q—R 5 ch ; 18 K—Kt 1, Q×Kt.
(*g*) Or 10 ., P—Q 4 ; 11 Kt×P, B—Q 2 ; 12 Kt—K 4 ±.
(*h*) 12.., R—B 1 ; 13 Q Kt—K 4, B—R 3 ; 14 Q—B 3, Kt×Kt ; 15 Kt×Kt, P—K B 4 ; 16 Kt—B 5, B×Kt is better.
(*i*) 17 Kt—K 4 +. Schlechter—Janowski, Paris, 1900.
(*j*) Pillsbury—Lasker, St. Petersburg, 1895.
(*k*) 6 , P—Q 4 ; 7 Kt×P, B—Q 2 ; 8 B×Kt, P×B ; 9 R—K 1, Kt—B 3 ; 10 B—Kt 5, Kt—Kt 1 ; 11 Kt×B+. Analysis by Max Lange.
(*l*) If 7 P—Q 5, Kt—Kt 1 ; 8 Kt×P, O—O ; 9 P—Q 6, Kt×Q P ; 10 B—B 4 ch, K—R 1 ∓.
(*m*) *Lärobok.*

1 P—K 4, P—K 4 ; 2 Kt—K B 3, Kt—Q B 3 ; 3 B—Kt 5.

BERLIN DEFENCE
3.., Kt—B 3 ; 4 O—O, Kt×P.

	6	7	8	9	10
5	(P—Q 4)...................................				R—K 1 (m)
	Kt—Q 3.................		P—Q R 3 (h)		Kt—Q 3
6	P×P........	B×Kt (d)	B—Q 3 (i)	...B×Kt	Kt×P
	Kt×B	Q P×B (e)	P—Q 4	Q P×B	B—K 2
7	P—Q R 4	P×P	P—B 4	R—K 1 (k)	B—Q 3
	P—Q 3	Kt—B 4	Kt×Q P (j)	Kt—B 3	O—O
8	P—K 6 ! (a)	Q×Q ch (f)	Kt×Kt	Kt—B 3	Kt—Q B 3
	B×P (b)	K×Q	P×Kt	B—K 2	Kt×Kt (n)
9	P×Kt	R—Q 1 ch	P×P	B—Kt 5	R×Kt
	Kt—K 4	K—K 1	Kt—B 3	O—O	P—Q B 3
10	Kt—Q 4	Kt—B 3	R—K 1 ch	P×P ± (l)	P—Q Kt 3
	B—Q 2	P—K R 3	B—K 2 ∓		Kt—K 1
11	Kt—Q B 3	P—Q Kt 3			B—Kt 2
	B—K 2	B—Kt 5			P—Q 4
12	P—B 4	B—Kt 2			Q—R 5
	Kt—Kt 5 (c)	B×Kt= (g)			Kt—B3 = (o)

(a) 8 P×Kt, Kt×P; 9 R—K 1, B—K 2; 10 Kt×Kt, P×Kt; 11 Q×Q ch, K×Q; 12 R×P, B—Q3=.

(b) If 8.., P×P; 9 P×Kt, Kt—K 2; 10 Kt—B 3, Kt—Kt 3; 11 Kt—Kt 5, B—K 2; 12 Q—R 5, B×Kt; 13 B×B, Q—Q 2; 14 P—Kt 6 ! with a strong attack. Halprin—Pillsbury, Munich, 1900.

(c) 13 Kt—Q 5, O—O; 14 P—B 5, Kt—B 3; 15 Kt×B ch, Q×Kt; 16 R—K 1, Q—Q 1; 17 B—Kt5 + ; Didier—Pillsbury, Paris, 1900.

(d) 6 B—R 4, P×P; 7 P—B 3, B—K 2 !; 8 P×P, P—Q Kt 4; 9 B—Kt 3, Kt—R 4 ; 10 B—B 2, B—Kt 2; 11 Kt—K 5, O—O is a gambit alternative.

(e) Much weaker is 6 ., Kt P×B; 7 P×P, Kt—Kt 2; 8 B—Kt 5, B—K 2; 9 B×B, Q×B; 10 Kt—B 3, O—O; 11 R—K 1, Kt—B 4; 12 Q—Q 2+. A. Steiner—Treybal, Ujpest, 1934.

(f) Or 8 Q—K 2, Kt—Q 5; 9 Kt×Kt, Q×Kt; 10 Kt—B 3, B—K Kt 5; 11 Q—K 3, Q×Q=.

(g) Maróczy—Pillsbury, Paris, 1900.

(h) Or 5. , P×P; 6 R—K 1, P—K B 4 (or 6.., P—Q 4; 7 Q×P, Q—Q 2; 8 B×Kt, Q×B; 9 P—B 4+. Compare Riga Variation, col. 73); 7 Kt×P, Kt×Kt; 8 Q×Kt, P—B 3; 9 P—K B 3, P×B; 10 P×Kt+. Or 5.., P—Q 4?; 6 Kt×P, B—Q 2; 7 Kt×P, K×Kt; 8 Q—R 5 ch, K—K 3; 9 Kt—B 3, or 9 P—Q B 4+.

(i) For 6 B—R 4 see col. 41 ff.

(j) Weaker is 7.., B—K Kt 5; 8 B P×P, Q×P; 9 R—K 1, Kt—B 3; 10 Kt—B 3, Q—Q 2; 11 Kt×P, Kt×Kt; 12 R×Kt ch ±.

(k) 7 Q—K 2, B—K B 4; 8 R—Q 1, B—K 2; 9 P×P, Q—B 1; 10 Kt—Q 4, O—O; 11 P—K B 3, Kt—B 4; 12 Kt—B 3, B—Kt 3. Spielmann—Bogoljuboff, Stockholm. 1919.

(l) Analysis by Svenonius.

(m) 5 Q—K 2, Kt—Q 3; 6 B×Kt, Q P×B; 7 Kt×P, B—K 2; 8 R—K 1, B—K 3; 9 P—Q 4, Kt—B 4; 10 P—Q B 3, O—O=.

(n) 8.., Kt—K 1; 9 Kt—Q 5, B—B 3; 10 Kt—K Kt 4, P—Q 3; 11 R×Kt?, R×R; 12 K Kt×B ch, P×Kt; 13 P—Q Kt 3, Kt—K 4+. Janowski—Lasker, Nuremberg, 1896.

(o) Janowski—Burn, Cologne. 1898.

1 P—K 4, P—K 4 ; 2 Kt—K B 3, Kt—Q B 3 : 3 B—Kt 5.

BERLIN DEFENCE

3.., Kt—B 3

	11	12	13	14	15
4	(O—O)......P—Q 4 P—Q 3	P×P.......................................Kt×K P (*m*)			
5	P—Q 4 (*a*) B—Q 2 (*b*)	Q—K 2...... B—K 2 (*e*)	O—O (*g*) B—K 2.....P—Q 3		P—Q 5 (*n*) Kt—Q 3
6	R—K 1 P×P (*c*)	O—O O—O	P—K 5 (*h*) Kt—K 5	Kt×P B—Q 2	Kt—B 3 Kt×B
7	Kt×P B—K 2	P—K 5 Kt—K 1	Kt×P O—O	B×Kt P×B	Kt×Kt P—Q R 3
8	P—Q Kt 3 Kt×Kt	R—Q 1 P—Q 4 (*f*)	Kt—B 5 ! P—Q 4	Q—B 3 ! P—B 4 (*j*)	Kt—B 3 Kt—Kt 1
9	B×B ch Kt×B	P—B 3 ! B—K B 4	Kt×B ch Kt×Kt	Kt—B 5 B—K 3 (*k*)	Kt×P P—Q 3 =
10	Q×Kt B—B 3	P×P Kt—Kt 5	P—K B 3 Kt—Q B 4 (*i*)	Kt—B 3 Q—Q 2	
11	P—K 5 (*d*)	Kt—R 3 P—Q B 3	P—Q Kt 4 Kt—K 3	Kt—Q 5 ± (*l*)	
12		B—R 4 ±	P—K B 4 ± P—K B 4		

(*a*) 5 R—K 1, B—Q 2 ; 6 P—B 3, B—K 2 ; 7 P—K R 3, O—O ; 8 B—R 4, Kt—Q Kt 1 ; 9 B—B 2, P—B 3 ; 10 P—Q 4, Q—B 2. Kmoch—Orbach, Giessen, 1928, a curiously dilatory opening, which led to a draw. With 5.., P—K Kt 3 ; 6 P—B 4 it transposes into a variation similar to that in col. 18, note (*d*) and to the Duras Variation, cols. 121—122.

(*b*) For 5.., B—Q 2 in normal variations and for 5.., P×P, see Steinitz Defence cols. 141 ff. If 5., Kt—Q 2 ; 6 P×P (weaker is 6 Kt—B 3, B—K 2 ; 7 B—K 3, O—O ; 8 Q—K 2, P—Q R 3 ; 9 B×Kt, P×B ; 10 Q R—Q 1, P—Q R 4. Engels—Richter, Bad Nauheim, 1935), Q Kt×P (6.., P×P is playable, but leaves Black with a cramped position) ; 7 Kt—Q 4, P—Q R 3 ; 8 B—K 2, Kt—K B 3 ; 9 P—K B 4, Kt—B 3 ; 10 B—B 3 ±.

(*c*) 6.., B—K 2 ; 7 Kt—B 3 transposes into Steinitz Defence, cols. 141 *ff.* Here 7 P—B 3, O—O ; 8 B—R 4, R—K 1 ; 9 P—Q 5 again leaves Black cramped. (Cp. also col. 177.)

(*d*) 11.., P×P (if Kt or B×P, 12 P—K B 4 ; if Q—K 2, 12 B—R 3, Kt×P ; 13 Q—Q 1) ; 12 B—R 3, B—K 2 ; 13 Q—K Kt 4, O—O ; 14 R—Q 1. Znosko-Borovsky— A. Eva and W. A. Fairhurst consulting, 1926 (*British Chess Magazine*, 1926, p. 750).

(*e*) Black's safest line is P—Q 3 ; 6 P—K 5, P—Q 6 ! transposing into col. 16.

(*f*) 8.., P—B 3 ? ; 9 B×Kt, Kt P×B ; 10 Kt×P, P—Q 3 ; 11 Kt×P, Q—Q 2 ; 12 Q—B 4 ch, R—B 2 ; 13 P—K 6 ! +. Sir G. A. Thomas—Yates, Hastings, 1922.

(*g*) If 5 Kt×P, Kt×P ; 6 O—O, Q—B 3 ! ; 7 Kt—K B 3, B—B 4 ! ; 8 Q—Q 5, Q—K 3 ; 9 Q—R 5, O—O ; 10 B—Q 3, P—Q 3 ; 11 Kt—B 3, Kt—B 3 +.

(*h*) 6 Kt×P, O—O ; 7 Kt—Q B 3, Kt×Kt ; 8 Q×Kt ± is an alternative.

(*i*) Or 10.., P—Q B 3 ; 11 P×Kt, Q—Kt 3 ch ; 12 K—R 1, Q×B ; 13 Kt—B 3, Q—B 4 ; 14 P×P, P×P.

(*j*) 8., B—K 2 ; 9 P—K 5, Kt—Q 4 ; 10 P—B 4, P×P ; 11 Kt—B 5, B×Kt ; 12 Q×B, Kt—Kt 3 ; 13 Q×K P ±.

(*k*) 9., P—K Kt 3 ; 10 B—Kt 5 !, P×Kt ; 11 P—K 5 + (Bogoljuboff).

(*l*) Nyholm—Harald, 1920.

(*m*) Weak for Black are : (1) 4., Kt×Q P ; 5 Kt×Kt, P×Kt ; 6 P—K 5, P—B 3 ; 7 Q×P, Kt—Q 4 ; 8 B—Q B 4, Kt—B 2 ; 9 B—B 4 !, Kt—K 3 ; 10 B×Kt, B P×B ; 11 Kt—B 3, B—Q 3 ; 12 O—O—O + and (2) 4., P—Q R 3 ? ; 5 B×Kt, Q P×B ; 6 Kt×P, Kt×P ; 7 Q—K 2, Q×P ; 8 Kt—K B 3, Q—Q 4 ; 9 K Kt—Q 2 +. Bogoljuboff—J. S. Morrison, London, 1922.

(*n*) For 5 O—O, B—K 2 ; 6 Q—K 2, see cols. 1 to 5. 5 P×P, P—Q 4 and 5 Q—K 2, Kt—Q 3 have been tried.

1 P—K 4, P—K 4 ; 2 Kt—K B 3, Kt—Q B 3 : 3 B—Kt 5.

BERLIN DEFENCE
3.., Kt—B 3.

	16	17	18	19	20
4	Q—K 2..... P—Q 3 (a)	P—Q 3 P—Q 3	....	B—B 4......	P—Q 4 (i)
5	P—Q 4 P×P (b)	P—B 3...... P—K Kt 3	Kt—B 3 (d) B—Q 2	B—K 3 ! B×B (f)	Kt×P Q—Q 3
6	P—K 5 P—Q 6 !	.Q Kt—Q 2 B—Kt 2	O—O P—K Kt 3	P×B P—Q 3 (g)	B—K B 4 P—Kt 4 (j)
7	B P×P P×P	Kt—B 1 O—O	B—Kt 5 P—K R 3	O—O P—Q R 3	B×Kt ch P×B
8	Kt×P B—Kt 5 ch	Kt—K 3 Kt—K 2	B×K Kt Q×B	B—R 4 P—Q Kt 4	B—Kt 3 Q—Kt 5 ch
9	B—Q 2 O—O	B—R 4 P—Q 4	P—Q 4 B—Kt 2	B—Kt 3 Kt—Q R 4 (h)	Kt—Q 2 Q×Kt P
10	B×Kt B×B ch=	Q—B 2 Kt—Kt 5	P×P Kt×P		Kt×Q B P B—K Kt 2
11		B—Kt 3 P—Q B 3	Kt×Kt Q×Kt		O—O Q—B 6
12		P—K R 3 Kt×Kt	B×B ch (e)		P×P Kt×P
13		B×Kt= (c)			R—K 1 ch+ (k)

(a) 4.., B—K 2; 5 P—Q 3 (5 P—Q B 3, P—Q 3; 6 P—Q 4, P×P; 7 P×P, or P—K 5 can be played), P—Q 3; 6 Q Kt—Q 2, O—O; 7 Kt—B 1, Kt—Q 5; 8 Kt×Kt= Or 4 , P—Q R 3; 5 B×Kt (5 B—R 4 transposes into cols. 76 ff), Q P×B; 6 Kt×P, Q—Q 5=. 4.., B—B 4 is inferior. 5 B×Kt, Q P×B, 6 Kt×P, Q—Q 5; 7 Kt—Q 3, B—Kt 3; 8 P—K B 3, B—K 3; 9 Kt—B 2+.

(b) 5.., Kt—Q 2; 6 B×Kt, P×B; 7 P×P, Kt×P; 8 Kt×Kt, P×Kt; 9 O—O, P—Q R 4; 10 R—Q 1, Q—B 3 (Dr. Fick—Maróczy, Scheveningen, 1923). 11 B—Q 2 followed by B—B 3 and Kt—Q 2—B 4+. Or 5 ., B—Q 2; 6 B×Kt, B×B; 7 P×P Kt×P; 8 Kt—Q 4!, P—Q 4; 9 Kt×B, P×Kt.

(c) Steinitz—Rosenthal, London, 1883.

(d) 5 P—B 4 (Duras's variation, see also cols. 121—122), P—K Kt 3!; 6 P—Q 4, P×P; 7 Kt×P, B—Q 2; 8 Kt—Q B 3, B—Kt 2; 9 B×Kt, P×B; 10 B—Kt 5, P—K R 3 ∓. Duras—Bernstein, St. Petersburg, 1909. Or 5 P—K R 3, P—K Kt 3; 6 B—K 3, B—Kt 2; 7 Q—Q 2, O—O; 8 B—K R 6, Kt—K R 4; 9 Kt—B 3 (Duras—Süchting, Prague, 1908), P—B 4∓.

(e) W. Cohn—Lasker, London, 1899.

(f) This exchange is best, for if 5.., B—Kt 3; 6 B×B followed by B×Kt and Kt×P +, and if 5 ., Q—K 2; 6 Kt—B 3, Kt—Q 5; 7 B—Q B 4 ±.

(g) 6 ., Q—K 2; 7 Kt—B 3, O—O; 8 O—O, P—Q 3; 9 Q—K 1 (Romanovsky—Malyutin, St. Petersburg, 1906) 9. , Kt—K 1 followed by P—K Kt 3, Kt—Kt 2 and P—B 4.

(h) Analysis by Schlechter

(i) 4 ., Kt—K 2 (Mortimer's Defence); 5 Kt—B 3 (not 5 Kt×P, P—B 3; 6 B—B 4, Q—R 4 ch++. Mortimer's Trap), P—B 3; 6 B—Q B 4, Kt—Kt 3; 7 P—K R 4!, P—K R 4; 8 Kt—K Kt 5, P—Q 4; 9 P×P, P×P; 10 Kt×Q P, Kt×Kt; 11 Q—B 3+.

(j) 6.., Q—Kt 5 ch, 7 Kt—B 3, P—Q 5; 8 P—Q R 3, Q×Kt P; 9 Kt—B 4, Q×Kt ch; 10 B—Q 2+ +.

(k) Nyholm—Moller, match, 1917

1 P—K4, P—K4; 2 Kt—KB3, Kt—QB3; 3 B—Kt5.

BIRD'S DEFENCE
3.., Kt—Q5.

	21	22	23	24	25
4	Kt×Kt............................				B—B4 (g)
	P×Kt				Kt×Kt ch
5	O—O				Q×Kt [(h)
	P—K Kt3...		P—QB3....B—B4		Q—B3
6	P—Q3		B—K2 (d)	P—Q3	Q—K Kt3
	B—Kt2		P—K Kt3	Kt—K2	B—B4
7	Kt—Q2....	P—QB3 (b)	P—Q3	B—Kt5 (f)	Kt—B3
	Kt—K2	Kt—K2	B—Kt2	O—O	Kt—K2
8	P—KB4	P×P	P—KB4	Q—R5	P—Q3
	P—QB3	B×P	P—Q4	P—QB3	P—KR3
9	B—B4	Kt—B3	Kt—Q2	B—QB4	Kt—Kt5
	P—Q4	P—QB3	Kt—K2	P—Q3	B—Kt3
10	B—Kt3	B—QB4	Q—K1	Kt—Q2	B—K3
	O—O	P—Q3 (c)	Q—B2	B—K3	P—R3
11	Kt—B3	B—K3	Kt—B3 ± (e)	P—B4	Kt—B3
	P—QB4	B—Kt2		B×B	B—R4
12	P—K5	Q—B3		Kt×B	O—O
	P—QKt4	O—O		P—B3	B×Kt
13	P—B3	B—Kt3 ±		B—R4 ±	P×B ±
	P—B5				
14	B—B2+ (a)				

(a) Capablanca—Blackburne, St. Petersburg, 1914.

(b) 7 P—KB4, P—QB3; 8 B—B4, P—Q4; 9 P×P, P×P; 10 B—Kt5ch, K—B1 (Alekhine—Blackburne, St. Petersburg, 1914); 11 B—R4±. 7 B—KB4, Kt—K2; 8 Kt—Q2, O—O; 9 Kt—B3, P—Q4; 10 Q—Q2, followed by B—K5 or B—KR6 has been suggested.

(c) If 10 , P—Q4; 11 P×P, P×P; 12 Q—R4ch, B—Q2; 13 B—QKt5, B—Kt2; 14 B—Kt5+. The column is Tarrasch—Blackburne, St. Petersburg, 1914.

(d) Or 6 B—B4, Kt—B3; 7 P—Q3, P—Q4; 8 P×P, Kt×P; 9 R—K1ch, B—K3; 10 Q—Kt4, Q—B3; 11 B—KKt5, Q—Kt3; 12 Q—R4±. If here 6.., P—Q4; 7 P×P, P×P; 8 Q—K2ch, Kt—K2; 9 B—Kt5ch, B—Q2; 10 R—K1, B×B; 11 Q×Bch+. Panoff—Freymann, Leningrad, 1934.

(e) Yates—A. Louis, Chester, 1914.

(f) Or 7 Kt—Q2,O—O; 8 P—KB4,P—QB3; 9 B—R4,P—Q4; 10 K—R1±.

(g) Recommended by Em. Lasker. 4 B—R4 (weaker is 4 B—K2, Kt×B; 5 Q×Kt, P—Q3; 6 P—B3, P—QB3; 7 P—Q4, Q—B2. Dr. Olland—Alekhine, Scheveningen, 1913), B—B4; 5 O—O, Kt×Ktch; 6 Q×Kt, Kt—K2; 7 P—Q3, O—O; 8 B—K3, B—Kt3 (Réti—Spielmann, Budapest, 1914); 9 P—B3±.

(h) Or 4.., B—B4; 5 O—O (if 5 Kt×P?, Q—Kt4+), P—Q3.

1 P—K 4, P—K 4 ; 2 Kt—K B 3, Kt—Q B 3 ; 3 B—Kt 5.

CLASSICAL DEFENCE
3.., B—B 4.

	26	27	28	29	30
4	P—B 3				
	P—B 4.....	.....	.....	.....	.....Q—B 3
5	P—Q 4.....		B×Kt.....	P×P (h)	P—Q 4
	K P×P.....	.....B P×P (f)	Q P×B	P—K 5 (i)	P×P
6	B P×P (A)	K Kt—Q 2 !	Kt×P	P—Q 4	P—K 5 !
	B—Kt 5 ch	B—K 2	B—Q 3	B—Kt 3	Q—Kt 3 (l)
7	Kt—B 3 (a)	P—Q 5	Q—R 5 ch	Kt—K 5	P×P
	P×P	Kt—Kt 1	P—Kt 3	Kt—B 3	B—Kt 5 ch
8	Kt—K 5 (b)	Q—R 5 ch	Kt×Kt P	P—K Kt4 (j)	Kt—B 3
	Kt—B 3	P—Kt 3	Kt—B 3	O—O	P—Q 4
9	O—O	Q×K P	Q—R 4	P—Kt 5 (k)	O—O
	Q—K 2 !	Kt—K B 3	R—K Kt 1	Kt×Kt	Kt—K 2
10	B×Kt (c)	Kt×P	P—K 5	Q P×Kt	Q—Kt 3
	Q P×B (d)	O—O	R×Kt	Kt—K 1	B×Kt
11	B—Kt 5	B-KR6+ (g)	P×Kt	P—B 6	P×B ± (m)
	B—K B 4 (e)		B—K 3	P—B 3	
12	P—B 3		P—B 7 ch	B—K 2	
	P—K 6		K×P	P—Q 3	
13	B×P		Q×Q	B—K 3 ±	
	O—O—O=		R×Q ∓		

(A) 6 O—O, B P×P; 7 P×P, P×Kt?; 8 P×B, Q—B 3; 9 Kt—B 3; K Kt—K 2; 10 Kt—Q 5, Kt×Kt; 11 Q×Kt+. Sir G. A. Thomas—J. Montgomerie, City of London championship, 1938.

(a) Or 7 B—Q 2, B×B ch; 8 Q Kt×B, P×P; 9 Kt×P, Kt—B 3; 10 Kt×Kt ch, Q×Kt; 11 O—O, O—O.

(b) 8 Kt—Kt 5?, Kt—B 3; 9 P—B 3, P—K 6; 10 O—O, P—Q 4; 11 R—K 1, O—O; 12 B×P, P—K R 3; 13 Kt—R 3, B×Kt+. Yates—C. B. Heath, Tenby, 1928.

(c) 10 B—Kt 5, Kt×Kt; 11 Kt—Q 5, Q—Q 3; 12 B×Kt, Kt—B 6 ch!; 13 P×Kt, Q×Kt; 14 P×P, Q×B; 15 P—K 5, P×B; 16 Q—R 5 ch, K—Q 1!+. Or 10 P—B 4, Kt×P+.

(d) 10.., Kt P×Kt; 11 B—Kt 5, B×Kt; 12 P×B, O—O; 13 P—B 3+.

(e) 11.., B×Kt; 12 P×B, O—O (or 12., B—B 4; 13 Q—Kt 3) 13 Q—Kt 3 ch, K—R 1; 14 Q R—K 1+ for if 14 , R—Kt 1?; 15 Kt×P. The column is N. J. Roughton—C. B. Heath, Scarborough, 1930.

(f) 5.., B—Kt 3?; 6 B—Kt 5, Kt—B 3; 7 Q P×P, P—K R 3; 8 B×K Kt, P×B; 9 Kt—R 4+. Sir G. A. Thomas—R. C. J. Walker, City of London championship, 1913.

(g) Analysis by Sir G. A. Thomas.

(h) 5 Kt×P (or 5 Q—K 2, Q—K 2), Kt×Kt; 6 P—Q 4, P×P; 7 P×B, Kt—K B 3; 8 Q—Q 4 ±. Or 5 O—O, P×P; 6 B×Kt, Q P×B; 7 Kt×P, Kt—B 3; 8 P—Q 4, P×P e.p.; 9 Kt×Q P, B—K 2; 10 R—K 1, O—O; 11 Q—Kt 3 ch, K—R 1; 12 Kt—K 5, Kt—Q 4=.

(i) If 5.., Q—B 3; 6 P—Q 4, P×P; 7 O—O, K Kt—K 2; 8 B—Kt 5+.

(j) After 8 B—Kt 5, O—O; 9 Q—Kt 3 ch, P—Q 4; 10 Kt×Kt, P×Kt; 11 B×P, R—Kt 1; 12 B×Kt, Q×B; 13 B×P ch, K—R 1; 14 O—O, B×B P. Black has attacking possibilities.

(k) 9 Q—Kt 3 ch, P—Q 4; 10 Kt×Kt, P×Kt; 11 B×P, R—Kt 1; 12 P—Kt 5 Q—Q 3; 13 P×Kt, Q×B is inferior.

(l) 6.., Kt×P?; 7 Q—K 2, B—Q 3; 8 P×P costs Black a piece.

(m) Blackburne and Pillsbury—Schiffers and Steinitz, Nuremburg, 1896.

1 P—K 4, P—K 4 ; 2 Kt—K B 3, Kt—Q B 3 ; 3 B—Kt 5.

CLASSICAL DEFENCE
3 . ., B—B 4.

	31	32	33	34	35
4	(P—B 3)		O—O		
	B—Kt 3 (a)	.. K Kt—K 2	P—Q 3	Kt—Q 5	K Kt-K 2 (j)
5	O—O (b)	P—Q 4	P—Q 4	Kt × Kt	P—B 3
	P—Q 3	P × P	P × P	B × Kt	B—Kt 3
6	P—Q 4	P × P	Kt × P	P—Q B 3	P—Q 4
	B—Q 2	B—Kt 5 ch	B—Q 2	B—Kt 3	P × P
7	Kt—R 3	B—Q 2	Kt—B 5 (g)	P—Q 4	P × P
	K Kt—K 2	B × B ch	Q—B 3 (h)	P—Q B 3	P—Q 4
8	Kt—B 4	Q × B	Kt—B 3	B—Q B 4	P × P
	O—O	P—Q R 3	K Kt—K 2	P—Q 3	Kt × P
9	P—Q R 4	B—R 4	Kt × Kt	B—K 3	R—K 1 ch
	P × P (c)	P—Q 4	Kt × Kt	Kt—B 3	B—K 3
10	P × P	P × P	B × B ch	Kt—Q 2	B—Kt 5
	B—Kt 5	Q × P	K × B	O—O	Q—Q 3
11	P—Q 5 (d)	Kt—B 3	Q—Q 3	P—K R 3	Kt—B 3
	B × Kt	Q—K 3 ch	P—B 3	Q—K 2	O—O
12	P × B	K—B 1 !	B—K 3	Q—B 3 ± (i)	Q—Q 2
	Kt—Kt 1	Q—B 5 ch	B × B		Kt × Kt
13	Kt × B	K—Kt 1	Q × B ±		P × Kt
	R P × Kt (e)	O—O (f)			B—Q 4 = (k)

(a) Charousek's Variation. If 4. , P—Q 3 (4 ., Q—B 3 or Q—K 2 is met by 5 P—Q 4+); 5 P—Q 4, P × P ; 6 P × P, B—Kt 5 ch ; 7 K—B 1 +, since Black must lose a Pawn.

(b) Or 5 P—Q 4, P × P ; 6 P × P, Q Kt—K 2 ! ; 7 Kt—B 3, P—Q B 3 ; 8 B—Q 3 (8 B—Q B 4, P—Q 4 ; 9 P × P, Kt × P ; 10 Kt × Kt, P × Kt=. Maróczy—Charousek, 1898), P—Q 4 ; 9 P—K 5, B—Kt 5 ; 10 B—K 3, Kt—Kt 3 ; 11 P—K R 3, B × Kt ; 12 Q × B, K Kt—K 2 ; 13 O—O—O ±.

(c) 9 ., P—Q R 3 ; 10 Kt × B, P × Kt. Metger, Schiffers and Teichmann—Charousek, Marco and Suchting, 1897. 11 B—Q 3 !

(d) If 11 P—R 5, Kt × R P ; 12 R × Kt, P—Q B 3+.

(e) 14 B—Q 2+. Cambridge Town—Hampstead, correspondence, 1918.

(f) 14 P—Q 5, R—Q 1 ; 15 Q—K 1 !, B—Kt 5 ; 16 B—Kt 3+. Alekhine—Bogoljuboff, St. Petersburg, 1914.

(g) Best. If 7 B—K 3, Kt—B 3 ; 8 Kt × Kt, P × Kt ; 9 B × B, P × K B ; 10 B—Q 4, O—O ; 11 P—K B 3, B—B 3 ; 12 Kt—B 3, P—Kt 5 ; 13 Kt—K 2, R—K 1 ; 14 Q—Q 2, B—Kt 4=. Or 7 B × Kt, P × B ; 8 B—K 3, Kt—B 3 ; 9 Kt—Q 3, O—O ; 10 B—Kt 5, P—K R 3 ; 11 B—R 4, P—Kt 4 ; 12 B—Kt 3, R—Kt 1 ; 13 P—K 5, Kt—Kt 5 ; 14 P—K 6, R—Kt 5 ! ∓. H. J. Stephenson—R. F. Goldstein, 1923.

(h) 7. ., B × Kt ; 8 P × B, Q—B 3 ; 9 R—K 1 ch, Kt—K 2 ; 10 B × Kt ch, P × B ; 11 Kt—B 3, Q × P ; 12 Kt—K 4 with a strong attack for the Pawns. G. J. van Gelder—R. Loman, match, 1919.

(i) S. Rotenstein—H. v. Hennig, Frankfurt, Haupt tourney, 1930.

(j) 4.., P—B 4 ; 5 P × P !, Kt—B 3 ; 6 Kt × P, O—O ; 7 P—Q B 3, Kt × Kt ; 8 P—Q 4+. Sheffield—Manchester, correspondence, 1917. Or 4 .., Q—B 3 ; 5 Kt—B 3, K Kt—K 2 ; 6 Kt—Q 5, Kt × Kt ; 7 P × Kt, Kt—Q 5 ; 8 Kt × Kt, B × Kt ; 9 P—B 3, followed by P—Q 4, R—K 1 and B—K 3+. Or 4 ., Kt—B 3 ; 5 Kt × P, Kt × Kt ; 6 P—Q 4, B—Q 3 ; 7 P—K B 4, Kt—Kt 3 ; 8 P—K 5, B—K 2 ; 9 P—B 5 ±.

(k) Chajes—Bogoljuboff, Carlsbad, 1923. Compare col. 32.

1 P—K4, P—K4; 2 Kt—KB3, Kt—QB3; 3 B—Kt5.

COZIO DEFENCE 3.., KKt—K2.		FIANCHETTO DEFENCE 3.., P—KKt3.		
36	37	38	39	40
4 Kt—B3..... P—KKt3 (a)	P—Q4 (e) PxP	Kt—B3..... B—Kt2 (h)	P—Q4 (j) PxP.......	Ktᴜ×P!
5 P—Q4 (b) PxP (c)	B—Kt5 (f) P—KR3	P—Q3 KKt—K2	B—Kt5! (k) P—B3 (l)	KtxKt PxKt
6 Kt—Q5 B—Kt2	B—KR4 P—Q4!	B—Kt5 P—B3	B—KR4 Kt—R3 (m)	QxP Q—B3
7 B—Kt5 P—KR3	KtxP P—Kt4	B—K3 P—QR3	KtxP KtxKt	P—K5 Q—Kt3
8 B—B6 BxB (d)	B—Kt3 B—Kt2	B—R4 P—QKt4	QxKt B—Kt2	QxQ RPxQ
9 KtxB ch K—B1	Kt—QB3 O—O	B—Kt3 Kt—R4	Kt—B3 O—O	B—KB4 R—R4!
10 KKtxP K—Kt2	BxKt PxB	Q—Q2 KtxB	O—O K—R1	B—Q3 P—KB3
11 Kt—Q5 KKtxKt=	PxP B—R3!	RPxKt B—Kt2	Q—Q2 P—Q3	PxP Q—Q3
12 (A)	Q—Q2 KtxP (g)	B—R6+ (i)	QR—Q1 ±	Kt—B3 KtxP= (n)

(A) After 12 PxKt, R—K1 ch; 13 B—K2, Q—Kt4 Black has perhaps a slight advantage (C. D. Locock).

(a) For 4 , P—Q3 see Steinitz Defence, col. 157.

(b) 5 P—Q3, transposing into col. 38, is stronger.

(c) If 5.., B—Kt2?; 6 PxP, KtxP; 7 KtxP, BxKt; 8 B—KR6+ Compare col. 196.

(d) 8.., K—B1; 9 BxB ch, KxB; 10 O—O, P—Q3; 11 KtxKt, QxKt; 12 BxKt, PxB; 13 QxP ch ±. Sterk—Réti, Debreczen, 1914.

(e) 4 P—B3, P—Q4; 5 PxP, QxP leads to a form of the Ponziani favourabl for Black. An alternative is 4 O—O, P—KKt3; 5 P—Q4, PxP; 6 KtxP, B—Kt2 7 P—QB3 (weaker is 7 B—K3, O—O; 8 P—QB3, P—Q4; 9 PxP, QxP; 10 KtxKt, PxKt; 11 QxQ, KtxQ; 12 BxP, KtxB; 13 PxKt, R—Kt1+), O—O; 8 B—Kt5!, KtxKt; 9 PxKt, P—KB3; 10 B—K3, P—B3; 11 B—Q3, P—Q4; 12 P—B3, B—K3. V. Buerger—R. F. Goldstein, match, 1921.

(f) Or 5 KtxP, P—Q4; 6 Kt—QB3, PxP; 7 O—O, P—B4; 8 B—Kt5, Q—Q3; 9 QBxKt, KxB; 10 BxKt, PxB; 11 P—B3, P—Kt3; 12 PxP, B—RKt2; 13 KKt—K2 ±.

(g) 13 O—O—O, KtxKt. Perlis—Tartakover, 1913.

(h) Somewhat better is 4 , Kt—Q5; 5 B—R4 (5 KtxKt, PxKt; 6 Kt—K2, Q—Kt4; 7 KtxP?, B—Kt2, 8 P—Q3, Q—QB4+), KtxKt ch; 6 QxKt, B—Kt2.

(i) 12.., O—O; 13 P—R4, P—Q3; 14 O—O—O, with a winning attack. Tchigorin—Pillsbury, St. Petersburg, 1896.

(j) Less good are 4 O—O and 4 P—B3 (B—Kt2; 5 P—Q4, PxP; 6 PxP, KKt—K2; 7 Kt—B3, O—O, 8 O—O, P—Q4; 9 PxP, Kt—Kt5).

(k) Inferior is 5 KtxP, P—Kt2; 6 KtxKt (6 B—K3, Kt—B3; 7 Kt—QB3, O—O), KtPxKt; 7 B—QB4. Lasker—Pillsbury, Hastings, 1895. With the opening cp. col. 157, note (e).

(l) 5.., B—K2; 6 BxB, QxB; 7 O—O, Kt—B3; 8 BxKt, QPxB; 9 QxP, O—O; 10 Kt—B3, R—Q1; 11 Q—K3, P—Kt3; 12 P—KR3, B—Kt2; 13 Q—R6 ±. M. E. Goldstein—P. Wilson, correspondence, 1922.

(m) 6.., B—Kt2; 7 KtxP, KKt—K2 (7.., Kt—R3 transposes back to the column); 8 B—B4, Kt—K4 (8.., Kt—R4; 9 P—K5+); 9 B—QKt3 +.

(n) 13 Kt—Kt5, B—Q2!

1 P—K 4, P—K 4 ; 2 Kt—K B 3, Kt—Q B 3 ; 3 B—Kt 5.

MORPHY DEFENCE

3..., P—Q R 3 ; 4 B—R 4 (a), Kt—B 3 ; 5 O—O, Kt×P ; 6 P—Q 4,
P—Q Kt 4 ; 7 B—Kt 3, P—Q 4 ; 8 P×P, B—K 3 ; 9 P—B 3,
B—K 2 ; 10 Q Kt—Q 2, O—O.

	41	42	43	44	45
11	Q—K 2..............................			B—B 2	
	Kt—B 4 (b)			P—B 4 (j)	
12	Kt—Q 4 (c)			Kt—Kt 3 (k)	
	Kt×B !.....Q—Q 2......Kt×Kt ?			Q—Q 2	
13	Q Kt×Kt (d)	B—B 2	P×Kt	Q Kt—Q 4...	K Kt–Q 4 (n)
	Q—Q 2	P—B 3	Kt—Kt 2 (h)	Kt×Kt	Kt×Kt (o)
14	Kt×Kt	P×P	P—B 4	Kt×Kt (l)	Kt×Kt (p)
	Q×Kt	B×P	Q—Q 2	P—B 4	P—B 4
15	B—K 3 (e)	Kt(Q2)–Kt3	B—B 2	Kt×B	Kt—K 2 (q)
	B—K B 4	Kt×Kt (Q5)	P—K B 4	Q×Kt	Q R—Q 1
16	K R—Q 1	Kt×Kt (Q 4)	Kt—B 3 (i)	P—B 3	Kt—B 4
	K R—Q 1	B—Kt 5	P—B 4	Kt—Kt 4	Q—B 3
17	P—B 3	P—B 3	P×P	B×Kt	Q—R 5
	B—K B 1	Q R—K 1	Kt×P	B×B	B—B 1
18	Q—K B 2	Q—B 2	Kt—Q 4	P—K B 4	P—Q R 4
	P—Q R 4	B—R 4	P—Kt 3	B–Q 1! ∓ (m)	P—Kt 5=
19	R—Q 2 (f)	Kt—K 2	R—Q 1 ±		
	P—Kt 5=	Q—Q 3 (g)			

(a) After 4 B—B 4, B—B 4 Black has a very favourable position in the Giuoco Piano.

(b) 11.., B—K B 4 ; 12 R—Q 1, Kt—R 4 ; 13 Kt—Q 4, B—Kt 3 ; 14 Kt×Kt, B×Kt ; 15 B—B 2 ± is inferior for Black.

(c) Best, for if 12 B—B 2, P—Q 5 ! ; 13 P×P, Kt×P ; 14 Kt×Kt, Q×Kt ∓.

(d) If 13 Kt×Kt (B 6), Kt×B ; 14 Q R×Kt (not Kt×Q ?, Kt×Q ch++) Q—Q 2, Black has improved his position considerably.

(e) Or 15 P—K B 4, B—K B 4 ; 16 Kt—Q 4, B—B 4 ; 17 B—K 3, B×Kt ; 18 P×B, Q—K Kt 3 ; 19 Q—B 3, P—Q B 3=. Sir G. A. Thomas—Tartakover, London, 1932.

(f) Euwe suggests 19 Q R—B 1. The column is Botvinnik—Euwe, Leningrad, 1934.

(g) 20 B—K 3, Kt—Q 2=. If, however, 20 Kt—Kt 3 ?, B—Kt 3 ; 21 B×B, P×B ; 22 B—K 3, P—Q 5 ! ; 23 B×P, Kt—Q 6 ; 24 Q—B 2, B×B ch+. M. Seibold—B. Ohls, correspondence, 1929-31.

(h) If 13 , Kt—Q 2 ; 14 P—B 4, P—K B 4 ; 15 P×P e.p., R×P ; 16 P—B 5, B—B 2 ; 17 P—Kt 4+. Znosko-Borovsky—Euwe, Broadstairs, 1921. A playable alternative for Black is 13 , Kt×B ; 14 Kt×Kt, Q—Q 2 ; 15 B—K 3, P—Q R 4 (15.., P—Q B 4? ; 16 P×P, P—Q 5 ; 17 P—B 6, Q—B 2 ; 18 Kt×P, B—B 5 ; 19 Q—Kt 4, B×R ; 20 Kt—B 5+. Analysis by Sir G. A. Thomas) ; 16 Q R—B 1, P—R 5.

(i) If instead 16 Kt—Kt 3, P—Q R 4 ! ; 17 B—K 3, P—R 5 ; 18 Kt—Q 2, P—B 4 ; 19 Kt—B 3, P—B 5=. R. P. Michell—P. W. Sergeant, 1923. The column is Sir G. A. Thomas—J. H. Blake, Weston, 1924.

(j) 11.., Kt—B 4? ; 12 Kt—Q 4 !, Kt×P ; 13 Q—R 5 ! (13 P—K B 4?, B—Kt 5 !), Kt—Kt 3 ; 14 P—B 4, B—Q 2 ; 15 P—B 5, Kt—R 1 ; 16 P—B 6++.

(k) Or 12 P×P e.p., Kt×P (B 3) ; 13 Kt—Kt 3 (weaker is 13 Kt—Kt 5, B—K Kt 5 !), Q—Q 2 =.

(l) 14 P×Kt, P—B 5 !=.

(m) Chajes—Tarrasch, Carlsbad, 1923.

(n) Or 13 R—K 1, P—Q R 4 ; 14 B—Q 3, Kt—Q 1 ; 15 K Kt—Q 4, P—Kt 5 ; 16 P—B 3, Kt—B 4 ; 17 Kt×Kt, B×Kt ; 18 P—K B 4, B—R 2=. Balogh—Rey, correspondence.

(o) If 13 ., Q Kt×P ; 14 P—B 3, B—B 4 ; 15 R—K 1, Kt—Kt 3 ; 16 Q—K 2+.

(p) Better than 14 P×Kt, P—Q R 4 ; 15 P—B 3, P—R 5 ! Bogoljuboff—Rubinstein, Stockholm, 1919.

(q) Better than 15 Kt×B, which would transpose into col. 44. The column is Bogoljuboff—Euwe, 1st match game, 1928.

I *

1 P—K 4, P—K 4; 2 Kt—K B 3, Kt—Q B 3; 3 B—Kt 5.

MORPHY DEFENCE

3.., P—Q R 3; 4 B—R 4, Kt—B 3; 5 O—O, Ktx P; 6 P—Q 4,
P—Q Kt 4; 7 B—Kt 3, P—Q 4; 8 PxP, B—K 3;
9 P—B 3, B—K 2.

	46	47	48	49	50
10	(Q Kt—Q 2) / (O—O)		Kt—B 4 (e)	B—K B 4 / O—O	P—Kt 4
11	R—K 1 (a) / Kt—B 4		B—B 2 ! (f) / P—Q 5 (g)	Kt—Q 4 / Kt—R 4 (i)	B—K 3 (k) / P—Kt 5
12	Kt—B 1 (b) / Kt x B	B—B 2 / P—Q 5 !	Kt—K 4 ! / P x P (h)	P—B 3 / Kt—B 4	K Kt—Q 2 (l) / R—K Kt 1 (m)
13	P x Kt / P—Q 5 ! (c)	P x P / Kt x Q P	Kt x Kt / B x Kt	B—B 2 / Kt—Q 2	Kt x Kt / P x Kt
14	Kt x P / Kt x Kt	Kt x Kt / Q x Kt	B—K 4 / Q—Q 2	Kt—Q 2 / P—Q B 4 !	B x B / P x B
15	P x Kt / P—Q B 4	Q—R 5 (d) / P—Kt 3	P x P / R—Q 1	Kt—B 5 / P—B 3 !	Q x Q ch / R x Q
16	P x P / B x B P	Q—R 6 / Q—K R 5 =	Q x Q ch / B x Q	P x P / B x Kt !	Kt—Q 2 / Kt x P
17	B—K 3 / B—K 2		R—Q 1 / Kt—Kt 1	B x B / R x P	P—Q R 4 ! / Kt—B 5 !
18	B—Q 2 / Q—Q 5 ∓		Kt—Q 4 +	P—K Kt 4 / Kt—B 1 = (j)	Kt x Kt / P x Kt= (n)

(a) 11. Ktx Kt, Px Kt; 12 Bx B, Px Kt!; 13 B—Q 5, Ktx P; 14 Bx P (14 Bx R?, Q x B; 15 P—K Kt 3?, Q—B 1++), Ktx B ch=. Or 11 Kt—Q 4, Q Ktx Kt (not 11 , Ktx K P; 12 Ktx Kt, Px Kt, 13 B x B, P x B, 14 Kt x K P+); 12 Px Kt, P—K B 4 (simpler is 12.., Ktx Kt; 13 Bx Kt, P—Q B 4 with equality); 13 Ktx Kt, B Px Kt; 14 B—K 3, P—B 3; 15 P—B 3, Px P; 16 Rx P, Q—Q 2; 17 B—Q B 2, with a slight advantage. Sir G. A. Thomas—Yates, Southsea, 1923.

(b) 12 Kt—Q 4?, Ktx Kt; 13 Px Kt, Kt—Q 6; 14 R—K 3, Kt—B 5; 15 B—B 2, P—Q B 4!; 16 Kt—Kt 3, P—B 5; 17 Kt—Q 2, P—B 4; 18 Kt—B 1, R—B 2 ∓. Flamberg—Alekhine, Mannheim, 1914.

(c) 13. , P—Kt 5; 14 Q—Q 3, Q—B 1; 15 Kt—Kt 3, P—R 3; 16 B—B 4; Q—Kt 2; 17 Kt—R 5, K—R 1; 18 Q—Q 2, K—R 2; 19 Ktx P !++. Olland—Euwe, Gothenburg, 1920. The column is analysis by Dr. von Claparède.

(d) Weaker is 15 Kt—Kt 3, Ktx Kt; 16 Px Kt?, Q x Q; 17 Rx Q, P—Q B 4; 18 B—Q 2, K R—Q 1; 19 B—R 5, Rx R with the better ending for Black. Lasker—Tarrasch, St. Petersburg, 1914.

(e) 10. , Ktx Kt; 11 Bx Kt, Kt—R 4; 12 Kt—Q 4 is in White's favour.

(f) Now this retreat is quite strong. If instead 11 Kt—Q 4, Ktx Kt; 12 Px Kt, Kt—Kt 2; 13 P—B 4, P—Kt 3; 14 Kt—B 3, P—Q B 4; 15 K—R 1, P—B 5 ∓. J. H. Blake—Znosko-Borovsky, Weston, 1924.

(g) Or 11.., B—Kt 5; 12 R—K 1, O—O (12 ., P—Q 5; 13 Kt—Kt 3 !, Px P; 14 Ktx Kt, K Bx Kt; 15 B—K 4, Q—Q 2; 16 Q—Kt 3 !, Bx Kt; 17 Px B+. Malkin); 13 Kt—Kt 3, Kt—K 5; 14 B—B 4, P—B 4; 15 Px P e.p., Ktx P (B 3); 16 Q—Q 3 ±. Alekhine—Nimzovitch, St. Petersburg, 1914.

(h) If 12 , Q—Q 4; 13 Ktx Kt, Bx Kt; 14 B—Kt 3, Q—Q 2; 15 Bx B, Px B; 16 Px P, Ktx Q P; 17 B—K 3 !, R—Q 1; 18 R—B 1, Ktx Kt ch; 19 Q x Kt, Bx B; 20 Px B+ (Tarrasch). The column is Capablanca—Hodges, New York, 1916.

(i) 11.., Ktx Kt; 12 Px Kt, P—K B 3 (Blackburne—Zukertort, 3rd match game, 1887) is also playable.

(j) Alekhine—Euwe, German Quadrangular tournament, 1937.

(k) Not 11 B—Kt 3?, P—K R 4!+.

(l) If instead 12 Kt—Q 4?, Ktx K P; 13 Ktx B, Px Kt; 14 B—Q 4, Q—Q 3; 15 Bx Kt, Qx B; 16 Q x K P, Ktx K B P! and wins.

(m) The alternative 12 , Ktx Kt is weaker: 13 Ktx Kt, Ktx P; 14 B—Q 4, B—Q 3; 15 P—K B 4, Px P e.p.; 16 Ktx P, Ktx Kt ch; 17 Q x Kt, Q—R 5, 18 P—K R 3, R—K Kt 1 ?; 19 Bx P!+.

(n) Nagy—Dyckhoff, correspondence, 1936.

1 P—K 4, P—K 4 ; 2 Kt—K B 3, Kt—Q B 3 ; 3 B—Kt 5.

3.., P—Q R 3 ; 4 B—R 4, Kt—B 3 ; 5 O—O, Kt×P ; 6 P—Q 4, P—Q Kt 4 ; 7 B—Kt 3, P—Q 4 ; 8 P×P, B—K 3 ; 9 P—B 3, B—K 2.

	51	52	53	54	55
10	B—K 3				
	O—O				Kt—R 4 (h)
11	Q Kt—Q 2				Kt—Q 4
	B—K Kt 5	...Kt×Kt (c)		P—B 4 ?	O—O
12	Kt×Kt	Q×Kt		P×P e.p.	P—B 3
	P×Kt	Kt—R 4		Kt×P (B 3)	Kt—B 4
13	Q—Q 5	B—B 2	Kt—Q 4	Kt—Kt 5	B—B 2 (l)
	P×Kt (a)	Kt—B 5	P—Q B 4 ? (g)	B—B 2 (i)	Kt—B 5
14	Q×Kt	Q—Q 3	Kt×B	Kt×B	B—B 1
	P×P	P—Kt 3	P×Kt	R×Kt	Kt×K P
15	Q×K Kt P	B—R 6 (d)	B—B 2	Kt—B 3	P—Q Kt 4 !
	Q—Q 2	Kt×Kt P	Kt—B 5	Q—Q 2	Kt—Kt 2
16	B—R 6	Q—K 2	Q—Q 3	Q—Q 3	P—K B 4
	P×B	K R—K 1	P—Kt 3	B—Q 3	Kt—B 5
17	P—B 3	Kt—Q 4	B—R 6	B—Kt 5	Q—Q 3
	B—B 4 ch	B—K B 1 ! (e)	R—B 2	Kt—K 2	P—Kt 3
18	K—R 1	B×B	P—Q Kt 3	B×Kt	P—B 5 +
	Q R—K 1 (b)	R×B (f)	Kt×P (h)	P×B (j)	(m)

(a) 13 ., Q×Q; 14 B×Q, P×Kt; 15 B×Kt, P×P; 16 K×P, Q R—Q 1; 17 P—Q R 4+. Alekhine—Teichmann, match, 1921.

(b) 19 Q R—K 1. White stands slightly better.

(c) 11 .., Kt—B 4; 12 B—B 2, Kt—Q 2; 13 B—B 4, P—Kt 4; 14 B—K Kt 3, P—K Kt 5; 15 Kt—Q 4, K Kt×P; 16 P—K B 4, P×P e.p.; 17 Q Kt×P, Kt×Kt ch; 18 P×Kt+. Schlechter—Strobl, Vienna, 1915. 11 ., Kt—R 4 is playable, for if 12 Kt×Kt, Kt×B; 13 Kt—B 6 ch, P×Kt (or K—R 1; P×Kt), P×Kt the open Knight's file is an asset for Black.

(d) 15 B—B 1, B—K B 4; 16 Q—K 2, B×B; 17 Q×B, P—K B 3; 18 B—R 6, R—K 1; 19 P×P, B×P; 20 Q R—Q 1, P—B 3=. Becker—Euwe, The Hague, 1928.

(e) A valuable improvement, after which it is White who must fight to draw. The line previously accepted as best by theory was 17 , Kt—B 5 (or 17 ., P—Q B 4; 18 Kt×B, P×Kt; 19 Q—Kt 4, B—B 1; 20 B×P, P×B, 21 Q×Kt P ch, K—R 1; 22 P—K B 4, R—R 2; 23 B—Kt 5 with a decisive attack); 18 P—B 4, B—Q 2; 19 Q R—Q 1, B—Q B 4; 20 Q—B 2, P—B 4; 21 B—Kt 5, Q—B 1; 22 Q—R 4, B—K 3; 23 R—B 3+. Bergman—Granfeld, correspondence, 1919.

(f) 19 P—K B 4, P—Q B 4!; 20 Kt×B (if 20 P—B 5, P×Kt; 21 P—B 6, Q—Kt 3+; if 20 Kt—Kt 3, P—Q 5+), P×Kt; 21 B×P, P×B; 22 Q×Kt, R—Kt 1 ! with the better ending for Black. Romanovsky—Tolusch, Leningrad, 1938.

(g) 13 ., Kt×B equalises.

(h) 19 Q—Kt 3, with an attack easily worth the Pawn. Romanovsky—Sosin, 1928.

(i) Or 13. , B—K Kt 5, 14 P—K B 3, B—R 4; 15 Q Kt—K 4!, K—R 1; 16 Kt×Kt+. Rosselli—Yates, Trieste, 1923.

(j) 19 Q R—K 1, P—B 3, 20 Kt—Q 4, P—Q B 4; 21 R×Kt!+. Breyer—Tarrasch, Mannheim, 1914.

(k) 10 , Q—Q 2; 11 Q Kt—Q 2, Kt×Kt; 12 Q×Kt, Kt—R 4; 13 Kt—Kt 5, Kt×B; 14 P×Kt, O—O; 15 P—Q Kt 4, B—K B 4; 16 P—K B 4+. Yates—R. P. Michell, Southport, 1924.

(l) 13 P—K B 4?, Kt (B 4)×B!; 14 Kt×Kt (14 P×Kt, P—Q B 4 ∓), Kt—B 5; 15 B—Q 4, B—K 3; 16 R—B 2, P—Q R 4; 17 Kt—B 5, P—R 5; 18 Q—Q B 1, Q—K 1+. Keres—Euwe, Stockholm, 1937.

(m) 18. , B—Q 2; 19 B—R 6. F. Kunert—B. Ohls, correspondence, 1929-30.

1 P—K 4, P—K 4 ; 2 Kt—K B 3, Kt—Q B 3 ; 3 B—Kt 5.

MORPHY DEFENCE

3·.., P—Q R 3 ; 4 B—R 4, Kt—B 3 ; 5 O—O, Kt×P ; 6 P—Q 4,
P—Q Kt 4 ; 7 B—Kt 3, P—Q 4 ; 8 P×P, B—K 3 ;
9 P—B 3, B—K 2.

	56	57	58	59	60
10	R—K 1				
	O—O				
11	Kt—Q 4 (a)				
	Kt×K P (b)				
12	P—B 3				
	B—Q 3 ! (c)				
13	P×Kt..			B—K B 4	
	B—K Kt 5			Kt—B 5	
14	Q—Q 2..............................		Q—B 2	B×B	
	Q—R 5		P—Q B 4	K Kt×B	
15	P—K R 3		B×P (j)	R×B	
	Kt—Q 6.....	P—Q B 4....	B—Q 2	P×Kt	P×R
16	R—K 3	Q—K B 2 (e)	B×P	B×R	Kt×K P
	P×P	Q×Q ch (f)	P—Q B 3	Q—R 5	Q—B 3 !
17	R×P	K×Q	B—Kt 3	R—B 1	Kt×R
	Q—Kt 6	B—Q 2 (g)	P—Q B 4	P—Q 6	R×Kt
18	K—B 1	Kt—B 5	Kt—B 5	Q—B 2	Q×P ch
	Q R—K 1	B×Kt	B×Kt	Q×Q ch	K—R 1
19	R—K 3	P×B	P×B	R×Q	Kt—Q 2
	Q—R 7= (d)	Kt—Q6ch+	Kt—Q 6=(i)	R×B=(k)	Kt—K 6 (l)
		(h)			

(a) For 11 Q Kt—Q 2 see cols. 46 and 47.
(b) If 11.., Q—Q 2 ? ; 12 Kt×B, Q or P×Kt ; 13 R×Kt++ (Tarrasch's Trap).
11.., Kt×Kt ; 12 P×Kt, P—R 3 ; 13 P—B 3, Kt—Kt 4 (Teichmann—Duras,
Hamburg, 1910) ; 14 B—K 3+ is inferior for Black. Playable is 11.., Kt—R 4 ;
12 B—B 2, P—Q B 4 ; 13 Kt×B, P×Kt ; 14 B×Kt, P×B ; 15 Q—K 2, Q—Q 6 ;
16 Q×P, Q×Q ; 17 R×Q, Q R—Q 1 with sufficient compensation for the Pawn
sacrificed (Lárobok, 1921).
(c) The Breslau Variation. If 12.., P—Q B 4 ? ; 13 P×Kt, P×Kt ; 14 K P×P,
B—K Kt 5 ; 15 Q×P, B—B 3 ; 16 R×Kt+. E.g., 16 , R—K 1 ; 17 Q×B, R×R ;
18 Q—Kt 3, Q—Kt 3 ch ; 19 K—R 1, R—K 7 ; 20 B—K B 4, Q R—K 1 ; 21 Kt—Q 2,
Q—B 7 ; 22 Q×B, R×Q ; 23 Kt—B 3 !, Q R—K 7 ; 24 B—Kt 3, R×K Kt P ;
25 Kt—K 1 and wins.
(d) Continued 20 R×Kt, B—B 5 ; 21 P×B, Q—R 8 ch and draws. This column is
the result of exhaustive analysis in the British Chess Magazine, 1921-22.
(e) 16 P×B, P×Kt ; 17 Q—K B 2, Q×P (better than 17.., Q×Q ch ; 18 K×Q,
Kt—Q 6 ch ; 19 K—K 2, Kt×R ; 20 K×Kt, P×K P ; 21 B—Q 5, Q R—Q 1) ;
18 B—Q 1, Q—Kt 3 ; 19 Q×P, B—B 2 ; 20 B—K 3, P×P ; 21 Kt—Q 2, P—B 4.
H. Wolf-Tarrasch, Carlsbad, 1923. The chances are about even.
(f) If 16 ., Q—R 4 ; 17 B—K B 4 !, P×Kt ; 18 Q—Kt 3 repels the attack.
(g) Weaker is 17.., Kt—Q 6 ch ; 18 K—B 1, B—Q 2 ; 19 P—K 5 !, B×K P ;
20 Kt—B 3, Kt×R ; 21 Kt×B, B—B 4 ; 22 K×Kt ±. If here 18.., Kt×R ; 19 P×B,
P×Kt ; 20 K×Kt, P×K P ; 21 P×P ±.
(h) 20 K—B 1, Kt×R ; 21 K×Kt, B—Kt 6 ch ; 22 K—B 1, K R—K 1 ; 23 B—Q 2,
R—K 4.
(i) H. Wolf-Tarrasch, Teplitz-Schönau, 1922.
(j) If 15 Kt×P, P×Kt ; 16 B×P, Q—R 5 ; 17 R—B 1, R—R 3 ! ; 18 B—K B 4,
P—B 5 ; 19 Kt—R 3, B—B 4 ch ; 20 K—R 1, Kt—Q 6 ; 21 Kt×Kt P, P—Kt 4 ;
22 B—B 7, Kt—B 7 ch ; 23 R×Kt, B×R ; 24 B×P, R—Q B 3 ; 25 B—K 2, B×B ;
26 Q×B, R×B+.
(k) Black's position is worth more than the Exchange, but by returning his material
advantage White can draw. The column is Teichmann—John, Breslau, 1913.
(l) 20 Q—Q 3, Q—Kt 4 ; 21 P—Kt 3, Kt (Q 3)—B 4 with a strong attack. Analysis
by Grünfeld.

1 P—K4, P—K4; 2 Kt—KB3, Kt—QB3; 3 B—Kt5.

MORPHY DEFENCE

3.., P—QR3; 4 B—R4, Kt—B3; 5 O—O, Kt×P; 6 P—Q4,
P—QKt4; 7 B—Kt3, P—Q4; 8 P×P, B—K3.

	61	62	63	64	65
9	(P—B3) / (B—K2)		Kt—B4 (g)	B—QB4	
10	P—QR4 / P—Kt5	Kt—Q4 / QKt×P	B—B2 / B—Kt5	QKt—Q2 / O—O	Q—Q3 (m) / O—O
11	Kt—Q4 (a) / Kt×KP	P—B3 / Kt—B4 (A)	R—K1 / P—Q5	B—B2 (i) / P—B4 (j)	QKt—Q2 / P—B4
12	P—KB4 / B—Kt5! (b)	B—B2 / B—Q2 (d)	P—KR3 / B—R4	P×P e.p. (k) / Kt×P (B3)	P×P e.p. / Kt×P (B3)
13	Q—B2 / P—QB4! (c)	P—QKt4 / Kt—R5	P—K6! (h) / BP×P	Kt—Kt3 / B—Kt3	Kt—Kt5 / B—B2 (n)
14	P×Kt / P×Kt	R—K1 / Kt—B5	P—QKt4 / P—Q6	P—QR4 / P—Kt5 (l)	Kt×B / R×Kt
15	P×QP / O—O	Q—K2 / K—B1	P×Kt / P×B	P—R5 / B—R2	Kt—Kt3 / Q—Q3
16	B—K3 / B—K3=	Kt—Q2 / B—KB3 (e)	R×P ch / B—K2	KKt—Q4 / Kt×Kt	Kt—Kt5 / R—Q2!=(o)
17		Kt×Kt / KtP×Kt	Q×P / Q—Q4	Kt×Kt / B—Q2	
18		B×Kt / B×B= (f)	Q—K4+	B—Kt5 / P—B4=	

(a) An ingenious method of revitalising a discredited variation. The older line is 11 R—K1, Kt—B4; 12 B—B2, B—Kt5! ∓. Perlis—Lasker, St. Petersburg, 1909.

(b) Better than 12 , Kt—B5; 13 Q—K2, Kt—R4; 14 B—B2, O—O; 15 Kt—Q2, Kt—KB3; 16 Kt×B+ (Euwe). If here 13 P—B5?, QB—B1; 14 Q—K1, B—Kt2; 15 P×P, P—QB4!; 16 P—B6,B×P+. Alekhine—Euwe, 13th match game, 1935.

(c) Best, for if 13 , Kt—Kt3; 14 P×P! ±.

(A) 11. , Kt—KB3; 12 Q—K2, Kt—B5; 13 B—B2, Q—Q2; 14 P—QKt3, Kt—Kt3; 15 R—K1, O—O; 16 B—Kt5 (16 Kt×B would recover the P), K R—K1; 17 Kt—Q2, Kt—R4; 18 B×B, R×B +. Alekhine—Fine, Avro, 1938.

(d) This leads to equality. The alternative 12 .., O—O; 13 P—QKt4 (13 P—KB4?, B—Kt5!+), Kt—Kt2; 14 P—B4, Kt—B5; 15 Q—Q3+ is bad for Black.

(e) If 16 ., Kt×P; 17 Q—Q3, Kt—R5; 18 B×Kt,P×B; 19 Kt×Kt and White has improved his prospects.

(f) Engels—Kieninger, Barmen, 1938.

(g) If 9.., P—KKt3 (Alapin); 10 P—QR4, R—QKt1; 11 P×P, P×P; 12 QKt—Q2, Kt×Kt; 13 B×Kt, B—Kt2; 14 B—Kt5, Kt—K2; 15 Q—Q4 ±. E. G. Sergeant—A. Louis, Bromley, 1920.

(h) C. Chapman—R. C. Griffith, correspondence, 1915. The later analysis is Burn's.

(i) On 11 P—QR4, P—Kt5 is best. But not 11 , P—R3; 12 Q—K2, Kt×Kt; 13 B×Kt, R—Kt1; 14 P×P, P×P; 15 B—B2, P—B4; 16 R—R6 ±. Bogik—Hasenfuss, Kemeri, 1937.

(j) 11.., Kt×Kt; 12 Q×Kt, P—B3; 13 P×P, R×P; 14 Kt—Q4, Kt×Kt; 15 P×Kt, Kt—Kt3; 16 P—QR4! ±. Lasker—Rubinstein, St. Petersburg, 1914.

(k) 12 Kt—Kt3, B—Kt3; 13 QKt—Q4, Kt×Kt; 14 Kt×Kt, B×Kt; 15 P×B, P—B5; 16 P—B3, Kt—Kt6; 17 R—K2, Q—R5; 18 Q—Q2, Kt—B4; 19 B×Kt, R×B; 20 Q—KB2, Q—R3; 21 K—R1, P—Kt4; 22 P—KKt4, P×P e.p. +. Isbinsky—Vyakhireff, St. Petersburg, 1909

(l) 14 , Kt—KKt5; 15 P×P!, QKt—K4; 16 Kt×Kt, Kt×BP; 17 B×P ch, K×B; 18 Q—R5 ch, K—Kt1; 19 Kt—Q4!+. Palermo—Venice, correspondence, 1923.

(m) The Motzko Variation.

(n) 13 , Kt—K4; 14 Q—Kt3, Q—Q3; 15 R—K1!, K Kt—Kt5 (Black has a draw by 15.., B×P ch; 16 Q×B, Q Kt—Kt5; 17 Q—R4, Q—Kt3 ch; 18 K—R1, Kt—B7 ch, etc.); 16 Q Kt—K4, P×Kt; 17 B×B ch, K—R1; 18 Kt×KP? (much better is 18 B—K3), Q×B; 19 Kt×B, Kt—B6 ch!+. Breyer—Spielmann, Pistyan, 1912.

(o) Analysis by P. Krüger, Ed. Lasker and F. Motzko.

1 P—K4, P—K4; 2 Kt—KB3, Kt—QB3; 3 B—Kt5.

MORPHY DEFENCE

3..., P—QR3; 4 B—R4, Kt—B3; 5 O—O, Kt×P; 6 P—Q4,
P—QKt4; 7 B—Kt3, P—Q4.

	66	67	68	69	70
8	(P×P)................		P—QR4		
	(B—K3) (a)		QKt×P! (f)		
9	QKt—Q2 (b).	Kt—B3 ?	Kt×Kt		
	Kt—B4 (c)	Kt×Kt	P×Kt		
10	Q—K2	P×Kt	Kt—B3 (g)............		P×P
	B—K2	Kt—K2	Kt×Kt.....	Kt—B3 (h)	B—QB4
11	R—Q1	B—R3 (e)	P×Kt	Q×P	P—QB3
	O—O	P—QR4	P—QB4	P—B4	O—O
12	Kt—B1	Kt—Q4	RP×P	Q—K5 ch	BP×P
	Q—Q2	P—R5	B—K2	B—K3	B—Kt3
13	P—B3	P—KB4	BP×P	B×P	Kt—B3 (i)
	Kt×B	P×B	P—B5	Kt×B	B—Kt2
14	P×Kt	B×Kt	B—R4	R—Q1	P×P
	P—B3	B×B	O—O	Q—Q3	R×P
15	B—B4	P—B5	P×P	R×Kt	R×R
	P×P	B—Q2	R×P	Q×Q	B×R
16	Kt×P	P—K6	P—QB3=	R×Q	R—K1
	Kt×Kt	P—Kt7 !		B—Q3	B—Kt2
17	B×Kt	R—Kt1		R—K1	Kt—R4
	B—QB4= (d)	R×P+		P—Kt5=	Q—B3= (j)

(a) 8.., Kt—K2; 9 P—QR4, R—QKt1; 10 P×P, P×P; 11 Kt—Q4, Kt—QB4(if11.,P—QB4?; 12Kt×P,R×Kt; 13B—R4,B—Q2; 14P—KB3+); 12 B—Kt5, Q—Q2; 13 Kt—QB3, P—QB3; 14 Q—R5±. Tarrasch—Tchigorin, match, 1893.

(b) 9 Q—K2, B—K2 (if 9.., Kt—R4; 10 QKt—Q2, Kt×Kt; 11 B×Kt, Kt×B; 12 RP×Kt threatening R×P+; or 9.., B—QB4; 10 B—K3, B×B; 11 Q×B, O—O; 12 QKt—Q2); 10 R—Q1, O—O; 11 QKt—Q2, Kt—B4; 12 Kt—B1, Kt—R4; 13 B—Q2, QKt×B; 14 RP×Kt, Kt—Kt2; 15 P—QKt4. Analysis by C. S. Howell. Better is simply 12.., Q—Q2=.

(c) A variation favoured in the St. Petersburg Tournament of 1914. If 9.,B—K2; 10 P—B3 transposes into the ordinary form of the opening, but White has the option also of 10 Kt×Kt, P×Kt; 11 B×B, P×B; 12 Kt—Kt5, B×Kt; 13 Q—R5ch, P—Kt3; 14 Q×B, O—O.

(d) Réti—L. Steiner, Berlin, 1928.

(e) 11 P—QR4, P—QB4; 12 B—R3, P—B5; 13 B—R2, Kt—B4; 14 B×B, K×B; 15 P×P, P×P+. Bogoljuboff—Tarrasch, Vienna, 1922. The column is Spielmann—Rubinstein, Stockholm, 1919.

(f) The old move 8., R—QKt1 leaves White with complete possession of the QRfileafter9 R P×P, R P×P; 10 P×P, B—K3; 11 P—B3, B—QB4; 12 Q Kt—Q2, O—O; 13 B—B2.

(g) Berger's Variation.

(h) 10.., P×Kt; 11B×P, R—QKt1; 12B×Pch, K—K2; 13B—Q5, B—Kt2; 14 B×Kt, Q×Q; 15 R×Q, B×B; 16 R—K1, P×KtP; 17 R×Bch, K—B2; 18 B×P and 19 B—K5+ (Berger). The column is Maróczy—Tarrasch, San Sebastian, 1911.

(i) 13 Q—Q3, B—K3; 14 P×P, P—QB4 is no better.

(j) Lasker—Schlechter, 8th match game, 1910.

1 P—K 4, P—K 4 ; 2 Kt—K B 3, Kt—Q B 3 ; 3 B—Kt 5.

MORPHY DEFENCE

3.., P—Q R 3 ; 4 B—R 4, Kt—B 3 ; 5 O—O, Kt×P.

	71	72	73	74	75
6	(P—Q 4)............................R—K 1 (f)				
	(P—Q Kt 4)..............P×P (d)		Kt—B 4		
7	(B—Kt 3)...Kt×P (b)	R—K 1	B×Kt......	Kt—B 3	
	P×P	Kt×Kt	P—Q 4	Q P×B	Kt×B (h)
8	R—K 1	P×Kt	Kt×P	P—Q 4	Kt×P
	P—Q 4	P—Q 4	B—Q 3	Kt—K 3	B—K 2
9	Kt—B 3	P×P e.p.	Kt×Kt	Kt×P	Kt—Q 5
	B—K 3	B×P !	B×P ch	B—K 2	O—O (i)
10	Kt×Kt	Q—K 2 (c)	K—R 1	P—Q B 3	Kt×Kt
	P×Kt	B—Kt 2	Q—R 5	O—O	Q P×Kt
11	R×P	Kt—B 3	R×Kt ch	P—K B 4	Kt×B ch
	B—K 2	O—O	P×R	P—B 3	K—R 1
12	B×B	Kt×Kt	Q—Q 8 ch	Kt—B 3	Q—R 5
	P×B	R—K 1+	Q×Q	Q—Q 4	Kt—Kt 3
13	R×K P		Kt×Q ch	P—B 4 (g)	R—K 4
	Q—Q 2 (a)		K×Kt (e)		Q—Q 3 (j)

(a) 14 Q—K 2, O—O ; 15 Q—K 4+. Burn—Tarrasch, Ostend, 1907.

(b) The Friess Attack. An alternative is 7 P—Q 5, Kt—K 2 ? ; 8 R—K 1, Kt—K B 3 (if 8 ., Kt—Q 3 ; 9 B—Kt 3, or 8 ., Kt—B 4, 9 Kt×P, Kt×B?; 10 Q—B 3, P—K B 3 ; 11 Q—R 5 ch++); 9 Kt×P, P—Q 3 (if 9.., P×B?; 10 P—Q 6 !, P×P; 11 Kt—B 4+); 10 Kt—B 6, Q—Q 2 ; 11 B—Kt 3+. 7.., P×B; 8 P×Kt, P—Q 3 ∓ is best.

(c) 10 B×P ch, K—B 1 !; 11 B—Q 3, Q—R 5 ; 12 P—K Kt 3, Kt×Kt P+. Or 10 B—Kt 3, B—Kt 2 ; 11 Q—R 5, O—O+.

(d) 6 ., B—K 2 ; 7 Q—K 2, P—B 4 ; 8 P×P+. Or 6.., P—Q 4 ; 7 Kt×P, B—Q 2 ; 8 Kt×P !+. The column is the Riga Variation.

(e) 14 K×B, B—K 3 ; 15 B—K 3, P—K B 4 ; 16 Kt—B 3, K—K 2 ; 17 P—K Kt 4, P—K Kt 3 ; 18 K—Kt 3+. Capablanca—Ed. Lasker, New York, 1915.

(f) 6 Q—K 2, Kt—B 4 ; 7 B×Kt, Q P×B ; 8 P—Q 4, Kt—K 3 ; 9 P×P, Kt—Q 5 (B—B 4 ; 10 R—Q 1, Q—K 2 ; 11 Kt—B 3, O—O ; 12 Kt—K 4 ±); 10 Kt×Kt, Q×Kt ; 11 P—K R 3, B—K 2 ; 12 Kt—Q 2 ±. A suggestion by Tartakover.

(g) Cambridge Town—Hastings, correspondence, 1921.

(h) Immediate development by 7.., B—K 2 is more prudent, leading by transposition into col. 74.

(i) S. Mlotkowski suggests 9.., K—B 1 ; 10 Kt×Kt, Q P×Kt ; 11 Kt×B, B—K 3 ; 12 P—Q Kt 3, Q×Kt ; 13 P×Kt, P—R 3.

(j) Continued 14 P—Q Kt 3, P—R 3 ; 15 B—Kt 2, Kt—Q 4 ; 16 B—K 5 !+. Yates—Conde, Hastings, 1923.

1 P—K 4, P—K 4 ; 2 Kt—K B 3, Kt—Q B 3 ; 3 B—Kt 5.

MORPHY DEFENCE

3.., P—Q R 3 ; 4 B—R 4, Kt—B 3 ; 5 O—O, B—K 2 ; 6 R—K 1,
P—Q Kt 4 ; 7 B—Kt 3, P—Q 3 ; 8 P—B 3, Kt—Q R 4 ; 9 B—B 2,
P—B 4 ; 10 P—Q 4, Q—B 2 ; 11 P—K R 3, O—O ; 12 Q Kt—Q 2,
Kt—B 3.

	76	77	78	79	80
13	P—Q 5				
	Kt—Q 1				Kt—Q R4 (i)
14	P—Q R 4			Kt—B 1	P—Q Kt 3 !
	R—Kt 1		P—Kt 5 ?	Kt—K 1	B—Q 2
15	P—B 4 !	P×P	Kt—B 4	P—K Kt 4	Kt—B 1
	P—Kt 5	P×P	P—Q R 4 (f)	P—Kt 3	Kt—Kt 2
16	Kt—B 1	P—B 4 ! (c)	K Kt×P !	B—R 6	P—B 4
	Kt—K 1	P—Kt 5	B—R 3	Kt—Kt 2	K R—Kt 1
17	P—Kt 4	Kt—B 1	B—Kt 3	Kt—Kt 3	Kt—K 3
	P—Kt 3	Kt—K 1	P×Kt	P—B 3	P×P
18	Kt—Kt 3 (a)	P—Kt 4	P—Q 6	K—R 2	Kt×B P
	Kt—K Kt 2	P—Kt 3	B×P	Kt—B 2	B—K B 1
19	K—R 2	Kt—Kt 3 (d)	Q×B	B—K 3	P—Q R 4
	P—B 3	Kt—K Kt 2	Q×Q	K—R 1	Kt—Q R4
20	R—K Kt 1	K—R 1	Kt×Q ± (g)	R—K Kt 1	K Kt—Q2 ±
	Kt—B 2 (b)	P—B 3 (e)		B—Q 2 (h)	

(a) Less precise is 18 Kt—K 3, P—B 3 ; 19 K—R 2, Kt—B 2 ; 20 R—K Kt 1, K—R 1 ; 21 P—Kt 3, R—K Kt 1 ; 22 B—Kt 2 ?, B—B 1 ; 23 P—R 4, Q—K 2 ; 24 R—Kt 2, B—R 3 ; 25 Q—K 2, B—B 5 ch, and Black has the initiative. Bogoljuboff—Rubinstein, Breslau, 1925.

(b) Continued 21 P—Kt 3, R—Kt 2 ; 22 B—Q 2, K—R 1 ; 23 Q—K 2, B—Q 1 ; 24 R—Kt 2, Q—Q 2 ; 25 K R—R 1, Q—K 1 ; 26 K—Kt 1. Keres—Vidmar, Nauheim, 1936. White has very slight winning chances, but Black has no counterplay whatsoever.

(c) 16 Kt—B 1, Kt—K 1 ; 17 P—K Kt 4, P—Kt 3 ; 18 Kt—Kt 3, Kt—K Kt 2 ; 19 K—R 1, P—B 3 ; 20 R—K Kt 1, Kt—B 2 ; 21 Q—B 1 ?, B—Q 2 ; 22 B—K 3, R—R 1 ; 23 Q—Kt 2 ?, R×R ; 24 R×R, Q—Kt 2 ; 25 K—R 2 ?, R—R 1 ; 26 Q—B 1, R—R 3. Sir G. A. Thomas—Rubinstein, Baden-Baden, 1925. Because of White's vacillating play Black has the initiative and the better position.

(d) Better than 19 B—R 6, Kt—Kt 2 ; 20 Kt—K 3, Kt—Q 2 ; 21 K—Kt 2, Kt—B 2 ; 22 B×Kt, K×B ; 23 Kt—Q 2, R—K R 1 ; 24 Kt (Q 2)—B 1, P—R 4 ; 25 Kt—Kt 3, P×P ; 26 P×P, Kt—Kt 4, and Black's game is satisfactory. Bogoljuboff—Rubinstein, Berlin, 1926.

(e) If Black operates on the open Q R file, the chances are about even. In the game Réti—Sämisch, Berlin, 1928, after 21 Kt—R 2, Kt—B 2 ; 22 K—R Kt 1, B—Q 2 ; 23 B—K 3, R—R 1 ; 24 Q—Q 2, K—R 1 ; 25 Q R—K B 1, R—K Kt 1 ; 26 P—B 3, Q R—K B 1 ; 27 R—B 2, Q—B 1 ; 28 Q—K 2, Kt—Kt 4 ; 29 Q—B 1 White's attack became steadily stronger. As indicated above, Black should have played 24.., R×R. With fewer pieces White's K-side play cannot become dangerous. In Nillson—Grünfeld, correspondence, 1937, this exchange (of Rooks) led to an early draw.

(f) Better 15 ., Kt—Kt 2 ; 16 P—R 5 ? (16 P×P, P×P ; 16 P—Q Kt 3 ±), R—Kt 1 ! ; 17 B—Q 2, B—Q 2 ; 18 P×P, P×P ; 19 B—Q 3, B—Kt 4 ∓. Rosselli—B. Lasker, Florence, 1927.

(g) Capablanca—Vidmar, New York, 1927.

(h) After 21 Q—K 2, P—B 5 Black has adequate counter-chances on the Q-side. The model game with this line is Chajes—Grünfeld, Carlsbad, 1923, which continued 22 R—Kt 2, Q—B 1 ; 23 Q R—K Kt 1, Q—Kt 2 ; 24 P—R 3, K R—B 1 ; 25 Kt—Q 2, Q—B 2 ; 26 Kt (Q 2)—B 1, B—K B 1 ; 27 P—K R 4, B—K 2 ; 28 K—R 1, R—K B 1 ; 29 K—R 2, Q—B 1 =. The advance P—K B 4 is not good for White ; after K P×P Black can post his Kt strongly at K 4. On the other hand, the attempt to force , P—K B 4 is not advisable for Black ; J. M. Aitken—Reshevsky, Stockholm, 1937, continued 21 Q—K 2 (White's King was at R 1 instead of R 2), P—B 5 ; 22 Kt—Q 2, R—K Kt 1 ; 23 R—Kt 2, Q—K B 1 ; 24 P—B 3, Q—B 1 ; 25 Q R—K Kt 1, P—B 4, 26 Kt×K B P, P×Kt ; 27 K P×P, Kt×P ; 28 P×Kt, B×P ; 29 R×R ch, when the resulting ending was favourable for White.

(i) A novel attempt to obtain a freer game, but it does not work out well. The column is C. H. Alexander—Keres, Hastings, 1937-38.

1 P—K 4, P—K 4 ; 2 Kt—K B 3, Kt—Q B 3 ; 3 B—Kt 5.

3... P—Q R 3 ; 4 B—R 4, Kt—B 3 ; 5 O—O, B—K 2 ; 6 R—K 1,
P—Q Kt 4 ; 7 B—Kt 3, P—Q 3 ; 8 P—B 3, Kt—Q R 4 ; 9 B—B 2,
P—B 4 ; 10 P—Q 4, Q—B 2.

	81	82	83	84	85
11	(P—K R 3)				
	(O—O)				Kt—B 3 (m)
12	(Q Kt—Q 2)			P—Q R 4 !	B—K 3
	(Kt—B 3)	...Kt—Q 2 (d)	..B P×P	P—Kt 5 (i)	O—O
13	Kt—B 1 ? (a)	Kt—B 1	P×P	P×Kt P	Q Kt—Q 2
	B P×P	Kt—Kt 3	Kt—B 3 (f)	P×Kt P	B—Q 2
14	P×P	P—Q Kt 3	P—Q 5	Q Kt—Q 2	R—Q B 1
	P×P (b)	Kt—B 3	Kt—Q Kt 5	B—K 3 (j)	K R—B 1
15	B—Kt 5	P—Q 5	B—Kt 1	Kt—B 1	Kt—B 1
	P—K R 3	Kt—Q 1	P—Q R 4	K R—B 1	Kt—Q R 4
16	B—K R 4	P—K Kt 4	P—Q R 3 (g)	Kt—K 3	K Kt—Q 2
	R—K 1	P—B 3	Kt—R 3	P—Kt 3 (k)	B—K 1
17	R—B 1	Kt—Kt 3	Kt—B 1	P—Q Kt 3	Kt—K Kt 3
	Q—Kt 3	Kt—B 2	Kt—B 4	Kt—R 4	Kt—Q 2
18	Q—Q 2	K—R 2	B—Q 2	B—Kt 2	Kt—B 5
	B—K 3	P—Kt 3	B—Q 2	B—B 3	B—B 1
19	B—Kt 1	B—K 3	Kt—Kt 3	Q R—B 1 ± (l)	Q—Kt 4 ± (n)
	Kt—K 4+ (c)	K—R 1 = (e)	K R—B 1 (h)		

(a) This Pawn sacrifice is unsound. If 13 P—Q R 4, R—Kt 1 is best, but not 13..,
B P×P; 14 B P×P, Kt—Q Kt 5; 15 B—Kt 1, Kt P×P; 16 R×P +. Bogoljuboff—
Rubinstein, Mahrisch-Ostrau, 1923.

(b) Better than 14.., Kt×Q P; 15 Kt×Kt, P×Kt; 16 B—Kt 5 (weaker is
16 Kt—Kt 3, Kt—Q 2; 17 B—Kt 3, Q—Kt 3; 18 Kt—B 5, B—B 3; 19 B—K B 4,
Kt—K 4; 20 B—Q 5, R—R 2; 21 Q—Kt 3, R—B 2 +. Lasker—Tarrasch, 3rd match
game, 1908), P—R 3 ?; 17 B—K R 4, Q—Kt 3; 18 Q—Q 3, P—Kt 4 ?; 19 B—Kt 3,
B—K 3; 20 Q R—Q 1, K R—B 1; 21 B—Kt 1 with a powerful attack. Lasker—
Tarrasch, 5th match game, 1908.

(c) Leonhardt—Rubinstein, San Sebastian, 1911.

(d) An unusual line which has not been given much attention. It is at least as good
as 12.., Kt—B 3 (cols. 76—80).

(e) Tarrasch—Lasker, 5th match game, 1916. Black's K-side is secure and he
has the initiative on the Q-side. The next few moves were 20 R—K Kt 1, R—K Kt 1;
21 Q—Q 2, B—Q 2; 22 R—Kt 2, P—Q R 4; 23 R—K B 1, P—Kt 5; 24 P—B 4,
P—R 5; 25 B—Kt 1, P×P.

(f) An improvement on the older line 13.., B—Q 2; 14 Kt—B 1, K R—B 1;
15 B—Q 3 (15 R—K 2 is also good), Kt—B 3; 16 B—K 3, Q—Kt 2; 17 Kt—Kt 3,
R—B 2; 18 R—Q B 1, Q R—B 1; 19 B—Kt 1, Kt—K 1; 20 Q—Q 2 ±. Maróczy—
Réti, New York, 1924.

(g) Inferior is 16 Kt—Kt 3, P—R 5; 17 B—Q 2, Kt (Kt 5)×Q P!; 18 P×Kt,
P×Kt; 19 Q×P, Q—B 5 ∓. Cohen—Kashdan, New York, 1938.

(h) 20 B—B 2, Kt—R 5; 21 B×Kt, with a minimal advantage for White.
Maróczy—Kashdan, London, 1932.

(i) If 12.., R—Kt 1?; 13 R P×P, R P×P; 14 P×KP, P×P; 15 Kt×Kt,
Q×Kt; 16 R×Kt, P—B 5; 17 B—K 3 +. Note the difference between this
and col. 89. 12.., R—R 2 is playable.

(j) Or 14.., B—Q 2; 15 Kt—B 1, K R—B 1; 16 Kt—K 3, P×P; 17 Kt×P,
Kt—B 3; 18 Kt (K3)—B 5 +. Keres—T. H. Tylor, Margate, 1937.

(k) Or 16.., Kt—K 1; 17 P—Q Kt 3, P—B 3; 18 B—Kt 2, B—B 1; 19 Q—Q 3,
P—Kt 3; 20 K R—B 1 +. Keres—Berg, Kemeri, 1937.

(l) Keres—Reshevsky, Stockholm, 1937.

(m) Or 11.., B—Q 2; 12 Q Kt—Q 2, B P×P; 13 P×P, R—Q B 1; 14 B—Kt 1,
O—O; 15 Kt—B 1, K R—K 1; 16 P—Q Kt 3?, Kt—B 3; 17 B—Kt 2, B—B 1;
18 Kt—K 3, Q—Kt 2; 19 P×P? (White should play 19 P—Q 5, as in col. 83), P×P;
20 Kt—Q 5, B—Q B 4 ∓. Horowitz—Santasiere, New York, 1933.

(n) L. Steiner—Asztalos, Maribor, 1934.

1 P—K 4, P—K 4 ; 2 Kt—K B 3, Kt—Q B 3 ; 3 B—Kt 5.

MORPHY DEFENCE

3.., P—Q R 3; 4 B—R 4, Kt—B 3; 5 O—O, B—K 2; 6 R—K 1,
P—Q Kt 4; 7 B—Kt 3, P—Q 3; 8 P—B 3, Kt—Q R 4; 9 B—B 2,
P—B 4.

	86	87	88	89	90
10	(P—Q 4)				P—Q 3 (*l*)
	(Q—B 2)				O—O
11	(P—K R 3)..	Q Kt—Q 2		P—Q R 4 (*h*)	Q Kt—Q 2
	(Kt—B 3)	O—O	Kt—B 3	R—Q Kt 1 (*i*)	Kt—B 3
12	P—Q 5	Kt—B 1	P—Q R 4 (*e*)	R P×P	Kt—B 1 (*m*)
	Kt—Q 1	B—Kt 5	R—Q Kt 1 (*f*)	R P×P	R—K 1
13	Q Kt—Q 2	Kt—K 3 (*c*)	R P×P	P×K P	Kt—Kt 3
	P—Kt 4 (*a*)	B×Kt	R P×P	P×P	Q—B 2
14	Kt×Kt P	Q×B	P×K P	Kt×P ?	P—K R 3
	R—K Kt 1	B P×P	P×P	Q×Kt	P—Q 4
15	P—K B 4 !	Kt—B 5	Kt—B 1	R×Kt	P×P
	P—R 3	P×P	B—K 3	Kt—Kt 5	Kt×P
16	P×P	Q×P !	Kt—K 3	P—K B 4 (*j*)	B—Kt 3
	P×P	K R—Q B 1	O—O	Q—B 2	B—K 3
17	K Kt—B 3	Q—K Kt 3	Kt—Kt 5	R—R 1	Kt—Kt 5
	B×P	B—B 1	K R—Q 1	P—B 5 !+ (*k*)	B×Kt
18	R—K 2	B—Q 3	Q—B 3		B×B
	B—Kt 5	Kt—B 3	R—Q 3		P—B 3
19	K—B 2 + (*b*)	B—Kt 5	Kt—B 5 ± (*g*)		B—Q 2
		Kt—K 1 (*d*)			Q R—Q 1 = (*n*)

(*a*) Leonhardt's move, as in Teichmann—Leonhardt, Carlsbad, 1911, which continued 14 Kt—R 2, P—K R 4 ; 15 P—K Kt 4, P×P; 16 P×P, R×Kt 1 ?; 17 K×R, B×P; 18 P—B 3 +.

(*b*) L. Steiner—Asztalos, Debreczen, 1925.

(*c*) Sacrificing a Pawn for a powerful attack. If 13 P×K P, P×P; 14 Kt—K 3, K R—Q 1 (B—K 3; 15 Q—K 2, K R—K 1; 16 Kt—Kt 5. Alekhine—Flohr, 1938); 15 Kt—Q 5, Q—Kt 2 = ; or 13 P—Q 5 with variations similar to those in cols. 76—80.

(*d*) Alekhine—Fine, Hastings, 1936—37. Black's position is theoretically equal, but the defence offers great practical difficulties.

(*e*) Inferior is 12 Kt—B 1, B P×P; 13 P×P, B—Kt 5; 14 P—Q 5, Kt—Q 5; 15 B—Q 3, Kt—R 4 !; 16 B—K 3, B×Kt; 17 P×B, Kt—B 5; 18 R—B 1, Q—Q 1 ∓. *Lärobok*, 1921.

(*f*) 12.., P—Kt 5; 13 P—Q 5 (compare col. 78) is weak for Black.

(*g*) Rauser—Rumin, Leningrad, 1934.

(*h*) 11 B—Kt 5, O—O; 12 Q Kt—Q 2, B—K 3; 13 P×P, P×P; 14 Kt×P !, Q×Kt; 15 P—K B 4, Q×Kt; 15 P—K B 4, Q—Q 2; 16 P—B 5, B—Q 3; 17 B×Kt, B×P ch; 18 K—R 1, P×B; 19 Q—Kt 4 ch, K—R 1; 20 P×B =.

(*i*) 11.., P—Kt 5; 12 P×Kt P, P×Kt P; 13 P—R 3 transposes into col. 83.

(*j*) 16 P—K Kt 3, Q—R 4; 17 P—R 4, P—Kt 4 !; 18 B×P, B×B; 19 Q—Q 6, B×P; 20 Q×R, B—Q 1; 21 K—B 1 (the subsequent analysis is S. Mlotkowski's), Q—R 7; 22 Q×P ch, B—Q 2; 23 Q×P, B×R; 24 Kt—R 3 !, B—B 2; 25 P—K 5, K—Q 1 (or Kt×B P), with at least a draw.

(*k*) Black has a winning attack.   (*l*) One of Schlechter's favourite lines.

(*m*) Or 12 Q—K 2, R—K 1; 13 P—Q R 4, R—Kt 1; 14 P×P, P×P; 15 Kt—B 1, B—Q 2; 16 Kt—K 3, B—B 1; 17 B—Q 2, P—R 3; 18 R—R 6, Q—B 2; 19 K R—R 1, B—Q B 1 =. Ilyin-Zhenevsky—Panoff, Leningrad, 1934. It should be noted that 12 P—K R 3 is superfluous here; there can follow 12.., P—Q 4 (or 12.., Q—B 2; 13 P—Q R 4, B—K 3; 14 Kt—B 1, Kt—Q 2; 15 Q—K 2, Kt—Kt 3; 16 P—K 3, P—Q 4; 18 P×P, B×Q P; 19 Kt—Q 2, R×R; 20 R×R, P—B 4 ∓. Grob—Lasker, Zürich, 1934); 13 Kt—B 1, P×P; 14 P×P, B—K 3; 15 B—Q 2, R—R 2; 16 Kt—K 3, B—B 5; 17 Kt—K 3, B—Q 6 ∓. Maróczy—Capablanca, New York, 1924. 12 P—Q R 4, B—K 3; 13 Kt—B 1, P—Kt 5; 14 P—Q 4, B P×P; 15 P×Q P, B—Kt 5; 16 P—Q 5, Kt—Q 5; 17 B—Q 3, Kt—R 4; 18 B—K 2, Kt×B ch; 19 Q×Kt, P—B 4 ∓. Romanovsky—Reshevsky, Leningrad, 1939.

(*n*) Panoff—L. Steiner, Moscow, 1936.

1 P—K4, P—K4; 2 Kt—KB3, Kt—QB3; 3 B—Kt5.

MORPHY DEFENCE

3..., P—QR3; 4 B—R4, Kt—B3; 5 O—O, B—K2; 6 R—K1, P—QKt4; 7 B—Kt3, P—Q3; 8 P—B3.

	91	92	93	94	95
8	(Kt—QR4)..O—O				
9	(B—B2)	P—Q4..................................			P—Q3 (l)
	(P—B4)	B—Kt5 (c)			B—K3 (m)
10	(P—Q3)	B—K3.................		P—Q5	BxB
	(O—O)	PxP (d)		Kt—QR4	PxB
11	(QKt—Q2)	PxP		B—B2	P—QR4
	(Kt—B3)	Kt—QR4...P—Q4		P—B3	P—Kt5
12	(Kt—B1)	B—B2	P—K5	PxP! (i)	Q—K2
	(R—K1)	Kt—B5 (e)	Kt—K5	KtxBP (j)	Kt—KR4
13	Kt—K3	B—B1	Kt—B3	QKt—Q2	P—Q4
	P—Q4? (a)	P—B4	KtxKt (g)	Q—B2	KtPxP
14	PxP	P—QKt3	PxKt	Kt—B1	KtPxP
	KtxP	Kt—QR4	Kt—R4	KR—K1	PxP
15	KtxKt	QKt—Q2	B—B2	B—Kt5	KtxP
	QxKt	Kt—B3	Kt—B5	P—R3	KtxKt
16	P—Q4!	P—KR3	B—B1	BxKt	PxKt
	KPxP	B—R4 (f)	R—K1	BxB	Kt—B5
17	B—K4++ (b)		P—KR3	Kt—K3	BxKt
			B—K3 (h)	B—K3 (k)	RxB= (n)

(a) In this position a serious mistake. 13.., B—K3 maintains theoretical equality.

(b) 17 , Q—Q2; 18 PxP, B—B3; 19 B—Kt5 and White won quickly. Alekhine—Eliskases, Podebrady, 1936.

(c) Bogoljuboff's idea. Less precise is 9 , PxP; 10 PxP, B—Kt5; 11 Kt—B3!, Kt—QR4; 12 B—B2, P—B4; 13 PxP!, PxP; 14 P—K5, QxQ; 15 RxQ, Kt—Q2; 16 P—KR3! with the better end-game. Lasker—Bogoljuboff, Mährisch-Ostrau, 1923.

(d) If instead 10 ., KtxKP!?; 11 B—Q5, Q—Q2; 12 PxP! (not 12 BxK Kt, P—Q4), Kt—Kt4; 13 BxKt, BxB; 14 P—KR3! (in the famous game Capablanca—Ed. Lasker, London, 1913, White played 14 KtxB!?, PxQ; 15 P—K6, PxP? and won; later Spielmann demonstrated that 15 ., Q—Q1! wins for Black), BxKt; 15 QxB, KtxP; 16 RxKt +. Analysis by Alekhine.

(e) 12 , P—B4; 13 Kt—B3, Kt—B5; 14 B—B1, Kt—Q2; 15 Kt—Q5, B—R5; 16 P—QKt3, QKt—Kt3; 17 Kt—K3, BxKt; 18 PxB (Verlinsky—E. Rabinovitch, Moscow, 1914), 18.., R—B1 is good for Black.

(f) Yates—Bogoljuboff, New York, 1924. 17 P—KKt4, B—Kt3; 18 P—Q5 (Rubinstein) is now good for White. 17 B—Kt2, QKtxP; 18 BxKt, PxB; 19 P—KR4 is Ragosin—Lilienthal, Leningrad, 1939.

(g) 13 ., B—Kt5; 14 R—QB1, Kt—K2; 15 P—KR3, B—KR4; 16 B—B2, BxQKt; 17 PxB, P—KB4; 18 PxP e.p., RxP; 19 P—Kt4+. Yates—Bogoljuboff, London, 1922.

(h) 18 Kt—R2, B—KB1; 19 Q—Q3 +. Yates—Rosselli, Trieste, 1923.

(i) Superior to 12 P—KR3, BxKt; 13 QxB, PxP; 14 PxP, Kt—B5. Yates—Rubinstein, Hastings, 1922.

(j) 12 ., Q—B2 is preferable.

(k) 18 B—Kt3! ±. Treybal—Vidmar, Carlsbad, 1929.

(l) 9 P—KR3, Kt—QR4; 10 B—B2, P—B4; 11 P—Q4 transposes into columns 76—84; 11 P—Q3? into col. 90, note (m). 9 P—QR4, P—Kt5; 10 P—Q4, KPxP; 11 PxQP, B—Kt5; 12 B—K3, P—Q4; 13 P—K5, Kt—K5; 14 P—R5 is Ragosin—Keres, Leningrad, 1939.

(m) 9.., Kt—QR4; 10 B—B2, P—B4 transposes into cols. 90 and 91.

(n) Yates—Marshall, New York, 1924.

1 P—K4, P—K4; 2 Kt—KB3, Kt—QB3; 3 B—Kt5.

MORPHY DEFENCE

3.., P—QR3; 4 B—R4, Kt—B3; 5 O—O, B—K2; 6 R—K1.

	96	97	98	99	100
6	(P—QKt4)..P—Q3				
7	(B—Kt3)	P—B3 (d)			
	O—O	B—Q2 (e)			
8	P—B3	P—Q4			P—Q3
	P—Q4	O—O			O—O
9	P×P	Q Kt—Q2			Q Kt—Q2
	Kt×P (a)	P×P ...... K—R1 (h)	.. B—K1		Kt—K1 (n)
10	Kt×P	P×P	P—KR3	Kt—B1 (k)	P—Q4
	Kt×Kt	Q Kt—Kt5	B—K1 (i)	Kt—Q2	P×P
11	R×Kt	P—Q5! (f)	B×Kt	Kt—K3 (l)	P×P
	Kt—B3	Kt—Q6	B×B	P—B3	P—Q4
12	P—Q4	R—K3	P×P	B—Kt3 ch	P×P? (o)
	B—Q3	B×B	P×P	B—B2	Kt—Kt5
13	R—K1 (b)	Q×B	Kt×P	B×B ch	B×B
	Kt—Kt5	Kt—B4	B×P	R×B	Q×B
14	P—KR3	Q—B2	Kt×B	Kt—B5	Kt—K5
	Q—R5	Kt—Kt5	Q×Q	B—B1	Q—Q1
15	Q—B3+ (c)	R—K2± (g)	R×Q	P—KR4	Q—Kt3
			Kt×Kt= (j)	Kt—Kt3 (m)	P-QR4∓ (p)

(a) Or 9.., P—K5; 10 P×Kt, P×Kt; 11 Q×P, B—KKt5; 12 Q—Kt3, R—K1; 13 P—KB4! (weaker is 13 P—B3, Q—Q6!+. Ed. Lasker—Marshall, Chicago, 1926), B—Q3; 14 R—K5!, P—KR4; 15 P—Q4, B×R; 16 BP×B, Kt—R2; 17 P—KR3+. Stoltz—H. Steiner, Hamburg, 1930.

(b) R—K2 is safer, but the text is good enough.

(c) 15.., Kt×P!; 16 R—K2!(16 Q×Kt?, B—R7 ch; 17 K—B1, B—Kt6++; but not 16.., B—Kt6?; 17 Q×P ch!++), B—Kt5; 17 P×B, B—R7 ch; 18 K—B1, B—Kt6; 19 R×Kt, Q—R8 ch; 20 K—K2, B×R (or 20 ., Q×B; 21 Q×B, Q×P ch; 22 Kt—Q2+); 21 B—Q2+. Capablanca—Marshall, New York, 1918.

(d) An alternative is 7 B×Kt ch, P×B; 8 P—Q4, Kt—Q2; 9 P×P, P×P; 10 Q Kt—Q2, O—O? (10.., P—B3; 11 Kt—B4, Kt—Kt3=); 11 Kt—B4, B—B3; 12 Kt—R5±. H. E. Atkins—Yates, 1920.

(e) Or 7 ., O—O; 8 P—Q4, P—QKt4; 9 B—B2, B—Kt5; 10 P—Q5, Kt—QR4; 11 Q Kt—Q2, P—B4; 12 P×P e.p., Kt×BP=. Tarrasch—Selesnieff, Mahrisch-Ostrau, 1923. If 8.., P×P?; 9 P×P, B—Kt5; 10 Kt—B3, B×Kt; 11 P×B, P—QKt4; 12 B—B2±. Verlinsky—Spielmann, Moscow, 1925.

(f) Stronger than 11 B×B, Q×B; 12 Kt—B1, P—B4!; 13 P—QKt3, P—Q4!; 14 P—QR3, Kt—B3; 15 Kt—K5, Q—Q1∓. Yates—Romanovsky, Moscow, 1925.

(g) L. Steiner—Keres, Warsaw, 1935.

(h) 9 ., R—K1; 10 Kt—B1, B—KB1; 11 Kt—Kt3, P—KKt3; 12 B—Kt3, B—Kt2; 13 Kt—Kt5 (better than 13 B—K3, Kt—QR4; 14 B—B2, Kt—B5; 15 B—B1. Sir G. A. Thomas—Yates, Cheltenham, 1928), R—KB1; 14 P—KB4, P×QP; 15 P×P, Q—Q4; 16 P—K5±. Yates—E. Spencer, Canterbury, 1930.

(i) The Kecskemét Variation as first played. The best order of moves is exemplified in the next column and notes (k) and (l).

(j) L. Steiner—Alekhine, Kecskemét, 1927.

(k) 10 P—KR3, Kt—Q2; 11 Kt—B1, P—B3; 12 Kt—R4, K—R1; 13 Kt—B5, B—B2; 14 P—KKt4, Kt—Kt3; 15 B—B2, R—K1; 16 Q Kt—Kt3, B—B1=. L. Steiner—Kmoch, Kecskemét, 1927.

(l) 11 Kt—Kt3, K—R1; 12 B—K3, P—B3; 13 Kt—Q2 (better 13 B—B2 or P—Q5), Kt—Kt3; 14 B—B2, P—Q4!∓. Asztalos—Ahues, Kecskemét, 1927.

(m) White's game is somewhat freer.

(n) Or 9 ., B—K1; 10 Kt—B1, Kt—Q2; 11 Kt—K3, P—B3; 12 P—Q4, B—B3; 13 B—Kt3, Kt—R4; 14 B×B ch, R×B; 15 Kt—B5, B—B1; 16 P—KR4±. Ahues—L. Steiner, Bad Niendorf, 1927. Compare col. 99.

(o) 12 P—K5 was much stronger.

(p) A. Steiner—Keres, Kemeri, 1937.

1 P—K4, P—K4; 2 Kt—KB3, Kt—QB3; 3 B—Kt5.

MORPHY DEFENCE

3.., P—QR3; 4 B—R4, Kt—B3; 5 O—O, B—K2; 6 Q—K2 (a),
P—QKt4; 7 B—Kt3, P—Q3.

	101	102	103	104	105
8	P—QR4!				P—B3
	R—QKt1		B—Kt5 (e)		O—O
9	P×P		P—B3		P—Q4 (m)
	P×P		O—O! (f)		B—Kt5
10	P—B3		P×P	P—KR3 (j)	R—Q1 (n)
	B—Kt5		P×P	B—Q2 (k)	P×P!
11	R—Q1		R×R	P—Q3	P×P
	O—O		Q×R	Kt—QR4	P—Q4
12	P—Q4		Q×P?	B—B2	P—K5
	P×P (b)	R—R1	Kt—R2! (g)	P—B4	Kt—K5
13	P×P	R×R	Q—K2 (h)	P×P	P—KR3
	P—Q4	Q×R	Q×P	P×P	B—R4
14	P—K5	P—Q5	Q×Q	B—K3	Kt—B3 (o)
	Kt—K5	Kt—QR4	Kt×Q	Q—B2	Kt×Kt
15	Kt—B3	B—B2	P—Q4	QKt—Q2	P×Kt
	Kt×Kt	P—B3	B×Kt	P—Q4	Q—Q2= (p)
16	P×Kt ± (c)	Kt-R3! ± (d)	P×B	B—Kt5	
			Kt-K Kt4+	P—Q5 ∓ (l)	
			(i)		

(a) The Worrall Attack.

(b) The threat was 13 P—Q5, winning a piece.

(c) 16 ., Q—Q2; 17 P—R3, B—R4 (weaker is 17.., B—KB4; 18 R—R6, K—R1; 19 Kt—Kt5+. Alekhine—Monticelli, San Remo, 1930); 18 R—R6, Kt—Q1; 19 P—Kt4. Alekhine—Asztalos, Kecskemet, 1927.

(d) 16.., R—Kt1; 17 P—Kt4, Kt—B5; 18 Kt×Kt, P×Kt; 19 P—R3. Alekhine—Euwe, 1st match game, 1926.

(e) A playable line is 8.., B—Q2. If 8.., P—Kt5?; 9 Q—B4 (the simple 9 B×P ch followed by 10 Q—B4 ch and 11 Q×Kt is also strong), P—Q4; 10 Q×Kt ch, B—Q2; 11 Q—Kt7, B—QB4; 12 Kt×P!, R—R2; 13 Kt—B6!, R×Q; 14 Kt×Q, K×Kt; 15 P—K5+. Chistiakoff—Panoff, Moscow, 1937. Or 8 , B—K2; 9 P—B3, P—Q4; 10 P—Q3, QP×P; 11 QP×P, Kt×P?; 12 Q×Kt, Kt—Q5; 13 Q×B, Kt×B; 14 R—R2, Q—Q6; 15 B—K3++. Spielmann—Vidmar, Bled, 1931.

(f) 9.., R—Kt1 transposes into cols. 101—2.

(g) If instead 12 , Kt—QR4?; 13 B—B2, Kt×P; 14 Kt×P? (14 B×Kt, Q×B; 15 Q×Kt, Q×Q Kt; 16 P—Q3, Q×QP; 17 Q×BP, B×Kt =. Reinfeld—Kashdan, Syracuse, 1934), R—Kt1; 15 B×Kt!, R×Q; 16 B×Q+. Böök—C. H. Alexander, Margate, 1938.

(h) 13 Q—R4 (or 5), Q×P∓, while if 13 Q—R6, Kt×P+.

(i) Fine—Keres, Avro, 1938.

(j) Or 10 R—Q1, P—Q4?; 11 P—Q3, Kt—QR4; 12 B—B2, P—Kt5; 13 P—Q4, P—Kt6; 14 B—Q3, P×QP; 15 P—K5, Kt—Q2; 16 P×P ±. Reinfeld—Reshevsky, Syracuse, 1934.

(k) If instead 10.., B—R4; 11 P—Kt4, B—Kt3; 12 P—Q3, Kt—QR4; 13 B—B2, Kt—Q2; 14 P—Kt4!, Kt—Kt2; 15 Kt—R3!, P—QB3; 16 B—Kt3, Kt—Kt3; 17 P—R5 ±. Alekhine—Samisch, German Quadrangular Tournament, 1937.

(l) Lasker—Rabinovitch, Moscow, 1935.

(m) 9 P—QR4, transposing into cols. 101 and 102, is much stronger.

(n) 10 P—Q5, Kt—QR4; 11 B—B2, P—B3; 12 P×P, Q Kt×P; 13 P—KR3, B—Q2; 14 B—K3=. Spielmann—Rubinstein, Berlin, 1928.

(o) Now 14 P—QR4 is weak because of 14.., P—Kt5!; 15 P—R5, K—R1!; 16 P—KKt4, B—Kt3; 17 Kt—R2, B—R5; 18 B—K3, P—B4 ∓. Rumin—Botvinnik, Moscow, 1935.

(p) Réti—Stoltz, Stockholm, 1928.

1 P—K 4, P—K 4 ; 2 Kt—K B 3, Kt—Q B 3 ; 3 B—Kt 5.

MORPHY DEFENCE

3.., P—Q R 3 ; 4 B—R 4, Kt—B 3 ; 5 O—O, B—K 2.

	106	107	108	109	110
6	(Q—K 2) (P—Q Kt4)				P—Q 3 (k)
7	(B—Kt 3) (P—Q 3)		O—O		P—B 3 B—Q 2
8	(P—B 3) Kt—Q R 4		P—B 3 P—Q 4 !		P—Q 4 O—O
9	B—B 2 P—B 4		P×P Kt×P	P—Q 3 B—KKt5 (h)	P—Q 5 Kt—Kt 1
10	P—Q 4 (a) Q—B 2		Kt×P (e) Kt—B 5 !	P—K R 3 B—R 4 (i)	B—B 2 P—Q R 4 (l)
11	R—Q 1 O—O	P—K R 3 (c) Kt—Q 2	Q—K 4 Kt×Kt	P—Kt 4 B—Kt 3	P—B 4 Kt—R 3
12	P—K R 3 B P×P	P—Q 5 Kt—Kt 3	P—Q 4 ! B—Kt 2 ! (f)	P—Kt 5 P×P	Kt—B 3 Kt—B 4
13	P×P B—Q 2	Kt—R 2 O—O	Q×Kt (B 4) Kt—Q 6	P×Kt K P×P	B—K 3 P—Q Kt 3
14	P×P ? P×P= (b)	P—K Kt4 R—K 1= (d)	Q—K 3 Kt×B (g)	Q—K 3 B×P (j)	P—K R 3 P—Kt 3 (m)

(a) 10 R—Q 1, Q—B 2 ; 11 P—K R 3, P—Kt 4 ? ; 12 Kt×Kt P, R—K Kt 1 ; 13 P—Q 4, B P×P ; 14 P×P, P—R 3 ; 15 P×P, P×P ; 16 Kt—K B 3, B×P ; 17 Kt—K 1 +. Sir G. A. Thomas—E. G. Sergeant, City of London Championship, 1932. 10 P—Q 3 is weak ; after 10 , O—O ; 11 Q Kt—Q 2, Kt—B 3 ; 12 R—Q 1, Q—B 2 ; 13 Kt—B 1, P—Q 4 Black has the upper hand.

(b) Fine—Reshevsky, Syracuse, 1934.

(c) 11 P—Q 5, O—O ; 12 Q Kt—Q 2, B—Q 2 ; 13 R—Q 1, P—B 5 (Yates—Kmoch, London, 1927) is also satisfactory for Black.

(d) Réti-Grünfeld, Teplitz-Schönau, 1922.

(e) Safer is 10 P—Q 4, P×P ; 11 P×P=. Yates-Vidmar, Carlsbad, 1929.

(f) 12 , Kt—K 7 ch ? ; 13 Q×Kt, Kt—Kt 3 ; 14 Kt—Q 2 +. Brinckmann—Schlage, Berlin, 1928.

(g) 15 R×Kt, B—Kt 4 ; 16 P—B 4, B—R 5 or B 3 with a strong attack for the Pawn. The column is analysis by Tartakover.

(h) 9 ., P—Q 5 ; 10 P×P, Kt×Q P ; 11 Kt×Kt, Q×Kt ; 12 B—K 3, Q—Q 1 ; 13 Kt—B 3, P—B 4 ; 14 P—B 4 ±.

(i) An unsound sacrificial combination. 10.., B×Kt ; 11 Q×B, P×P ; 12 P×P Kt—Q R 4 ; 13 B—B 2, P—Q B 4 is better.

(j) 15 Q Kt—Q 2 +. Kashdan—Hanauer, New York, 1936.

(k) If 6.., O—O ; 7 B×Kt, Q P×B (7 ., Kt P×B ; 8 Kt×P, P—B 4 is Black's best fighting chance—Alekhine) ; 8 Kt×P, Q—Q 5 ; 9 Kt—K B 3, Q×K P ? ; 10 Q×Q, Kt×Q ; 11 R—K 1 + + (Alekhine).

(l) Weak is 10 ., P—B 3 ; 11 P—B 4, P×P ; 12 K P×P, Kt—K 1 ; 13 Kt—K 1. P—B 4 ; 14 P—B 4, P—K 5 ; 15 B—K 3, B—K B 3 ; 16 Kt—Q B 3, P—Q Kt 4 ; 17 B—Kt 3 +. L. Steiner—Kashdan, Folkestone, 1933.

(m) Kashdan and Phillips—Alekhine and Warburg, New York, 1933. White has a minimal advantage.

1 P—K 4, P—K 4 ; 2 Kt—K B 3, Kt—Q B 3 ; 3 B—Kt 5.

MORPHY DEFENCE

3 .., P—Q R 3 ; 4 B—R 4, Kt—B 3 ; 5 O—O.

	111	112	113	114	115
5	(B—K 2)				P—Q Kt 4
6	(Q—K 2)			P—Q 4 (h)	B—Kt 3
	(P—Q 3)			P×P	B—K 2ₐ(
7	(P—B 3)			P—K 5	P—Q 4
	(B—Q 2)			Kt—K 5	P—Q 3
8	(P—O 4)		P—Q 3	R—K 1	P—Q R 4
	(O—O)		O—O	Kt—B 4	B—Kt 5
9	(P—Q 5)	B—Kt 3 (c)	R—Q 1	B×Kt	P—B 3
	(Kt—Kt 1)	Q—K 1 (d)	Kt—K 1	Q P×B	O—O
10	(B—B 2)	Q Kt—Q 2	B—Kt 3	Kt×P	Q—Q 3
	Kt—K 1	K—R 1	K—R 1	O—O	Q—Q 2
11	P—Q B 4	P×P ? (e)	P—Q 4	Kt—Q B 3	B—Kt 5 (k)
	P—K B 4 (a)	P×P	Q—B 1	R—K 1	B×Kt
12	P×P	Kt—B 4	Kt—Kt 5	B—K 3	Q×B
	B×P	B—Q B 4	Kt—Q 1	B—B 1	K P×P
13	B×B	P—Q R 4	P—K R 3	P—B 4	R P×P
	R×B	P—Q R 4	Kt—K 3	P—B 3	Kt—K 4
14	Kt—B 3 ± (b)	B—Kt 5	Kt×Kt	P×P	Q—Q 1
		Kt—R 4 ! (f)	B×Kt= (g)	Q×P= (i)	P×B P (l)

(a) Premature. 11 .., P—K Kt 3 followed by Kt—Kt 2 should have been played (Alekhine).

(b) 14 .., Kt—Q 2 ; 15 Kt—K 4, Kt—B 1 ! ; 16 B—K 3, Kt—Kt 3 ; 17 P—K Kt 3, P—K R 3 ; 18 Kt (B 3)—Q 2. Alekhine—Tylor, Margate, 1938.

(c) 9 P×P is colourless : 9 ., Q Kt×P ; 10 B×B, Kt×Kt ch ; 11 Q×Kt, Kt×B ; 12 B—B 4, B—Kt 4 ; 13 Kt—Q 2, Kt—B 4=. Euwe—Bogoljuboff, 2nd match game, 1928. If 9 R—Q 1 ?, Kt×P ! +.

(d) A type of defensive position sometimes seen in Steinitz's games. Simpler, however, is 9 ., P×P ; 10 P×P, Kt—Q R 4 ; 11 B—B 2, B—Kt 4 ; 12 B—Q 3, B×B ; 13 Q×B, P—Q 4 ; 14 P—K 5, Kt—K 5=. Horowitz—Fine, New York, 1938.

(e) This is decidedly weak. Both 11 R—K 1 and 11 P—Q 5 were preferable.

(f) L. Steiner—Alekhine, Folkestone, 1933. The game continued 15 Kt—R 4 ?, Kt—B 5 ; 16 Q—B 3, P—B 3 ; 17 B×Kt, P×B ; 18 Kt—B 5, P—K Kt 3 ∓. Best is 15 K Kt×P, Kt×Kt ; 16 Q×Kt (not 16 Kt×Kt, Q×Kt ; 17 Q×Kt, P—K B 3, winning a piece), Kt×Kt (tempting but inferior is 16 , B—K Kt 5 ; 17 Q—R 4, B—K 7 ; 18 Kt×Kt¹, B×R ; 19 Kt—Kt 4, B—Q 6 ; 20 Kt—B 6 ! + +) ; 17 B×Kt, Q×P ; 18 Q—K 2=. Analysis by Tartakover.

(g) A. Steiner—Fine, Kemeri, 1937.

(h) 6 P—B 3 ?, Kt×P ; 7 Q—K 2, Kt—B 4 ; 8 B×Kt, Q P×B ; 9 Kt×P, O—O ; 10 P—Q 4, Kt—Q 2 ; 11 Kt—Q 2, Kt×Kt ; 12 Q×Kt, B—K 3 ; 13 Kt—B 3, B—Q 3 ; 14 Q—R 5, P—B 3 ∓. Sir G. A. Thomas—Reshevsky, Nottingham, 1936.

(i) Alekhine—Keres, Kemeri, 1937. The two Bishops are ample compensation for Black's Pawn majority on the K-side.

(j) 6 .., P—Q 3 is playable, since the tempting 7 Kt—Kt 5, P—Q 4 ; 8 P×P, Kt—Q 5 ; 9 P—Q 6, Kt×B ; 10 P×P, Q×B P ; 11 R P×Kt, P—K R 3 leaves Black with the initiative and a splendid development for the Pawn sacrificed.

(k) Safer is 11 P—Q 5, or 11 Q P×P, but the text is by no means bad.

(l) Tarrasch—Burn, Ostend, 1907. White's position is worth the Pawn.

1 P—K4, P—K4; 2 Kt—KB3, Kt—QB3; 3 B—Kt5.

MORPHY DEFENCE
3.., P—QR3; 4 B—R4, Kt—B3.

	116	117	118	119	120
5	(O—O)				P—Q4
	(P—QKt4)	B—B4 (d)			PxP
6	(B—Kt3)	P—B3		KtxP (i)	Q—K2 (m)
	(B—K2)	B—R2		KtxKt (j)	B—K2
7	P—QR4	P—Q4		P—Q4	O—O
	R—QKt1 (a)	KtxKP		KtxP	P—QKt4 (n)
8	R—K1 (b)	R—K1	Q—K2	Q—K2	B—Kt3
	P—Q3	P—B4	P—B4	B—K2	P—Q3
9	PxP	QKt—Q2	PxP	QxKt	P—QR4
	PxP	O—O (e)	O—O	Kt—Kt3	R—QKt1
10	P—B3	KtxKt	QKt—Q2 (g)	P—QB4 (h)	PxP
	B—Kt5	PxKt	P—Q4	O—O	PxP
11	P—Q4	B—KKt5	PxP e.p.	Kt—B3	P—K5
	Q—Q2	Q—K1	KtxP (Q3!)	P—KB4	PxP
12	B—K3	RxP	B—Kt3 ch	Q—B3	KtxKP
	O—O (c)	P—Q3	K—R1	Kt—R5	KtxKt
13	QKt—Q2	PxP	Kt—B4	Q—Q3 ± (l)	QxKt
	R—R1	Q—Kt3	P—B5!		Q—Q3 =
14	P—Q5 ±	R-KB4+ (f)	QKt—K5		
			KtxKt (h)		

(a) Or 7.., P—Kt5; 8 Q—K2, O—O; 9 P—R5, P—Q3; 10 P—B3, P—R3;
11 P—Q4, KtPxP; 12 KtPxP, R—Kt1; 13 B—QB4, B—Kt5 (KtxRP;
14 RxKt, though losing a Pawn, is preferable); 14 B—K3, PxP; 15 BxQP+.
P.Johner—Teichmann, Berlin, 1925.
(b) 8 Q—K2, transposing into cols. 101 and 102, is even stronger.
(c) Not 12.., KtxKP?; 13 P—Q5, Kt—Q1; 14 B—R7 +. Keres—Zinner,
Prague, 1937.
(d) The Moller Defence. For some years it was championed by Alekhine, but he
has since abandoned it. For 5.., P—Q3 see the Steinitz Defence Deferred, cols.
172—175.
(e) Or 9 .., KtxKt; 10 KtxKt, P—K5; 11 KtxP, O—O (if PxKt; 12 RxP ch,
Kt—K2; 13 B—KKt5+. Or 12.., K—B1; 13 Q—B3 ch, K—Kt1; 14 B—Kt3 ch,
P—Q4; 15 BxP ch, QxB; 16 R—K8 mate); 12 B—KKt5, Kt—K2; 13 Kt—Kt3,
R—B2; 14 Q—K2, resigns. Stahlmann—H. Muller.
(f) Capablanca—P. S. Milner-Barry, Margate, 1935.
(g) 10 B—Kt3 ch, K—R1; 11 Q Kt—Q2, Q—K1? (this blunder deprives the
game of theoretical value: 11.., P—Q4 had to be tried); 12 KtxKt, PxKt;
13 QxKP, P—Q4; 14 BxP, B—KB4; 15 Q—KR4+. Alekhine—H. Steiner,
Pasadena, 1932. If 10 B—K3, P—Q3; 11 R—Q1, Q—K2=, or 10 B—B2, P—Q4;
11 PxP e.p., KtxP(Q3); 12 QKt—Q2, R—K1 ∓. Yates—Rey, Barcelona, 1929.
(h) 15 KtxKt, Q—K4 ∓. Yates—Alekhine, Hastings, 1922.
(i) Inferior is 6 P—Q3, P—Q3; 7 P—Q4, PxP; 8 KtxP, B—Q2; 9 KtxKt,
PxKt; 10 Kt—B3, Kt—Kt5!; 11 Q—B3, O—O; 12 B—K2, Kt—K3; 13 Q R—K1,
Q R—K1; 14 Q—Kt3, P—B4!; 15 P—KR3, P—Kt4! +. Bogatyrchuk—
Savitzky, Leningrad, 1934.
(j) If 6.., KtxP; 7 KtxKt (7 KtxBP?, KxKt; 8 Q—R5 ch, P—Kt3;
9 Q—Q5 ch, K—Kt2; 10 QxKt, P—Q4 ∓—Tartakover), QPxKt; 8 Q—B3 (or
8 Q—K2, Q—K2; 9 R—K1!, BxP ch; 10 QxB, PxB; 11 QxBP ch, B—Q2; 12 R—K1 ch! +);
9 Kt—B3, KtxKt; 10 BxP ch, PxB; 11 QPxKt + (J. H. Blake).
9 Kt—B3, KtxKt; 10 BxP ch, K—B1; 11 QPxKt + (J. H. Blake).
(k) Weaker is 10 P—KB4, O—O; 11 P—B5, P—Q3; 12 Q—Q3, Kt—R5!;
13 B—K3, B—Kt4! ∓. W. P.Shipley and S. T. Sharp—Alekhine, Philadelphia, 1924.
(l) Takacs—Alekhine, Vienna, 1922.
(m) 6 O—O, B—K2; 7 P—K5, Kt—K5; 8 KtxP, Kt—B4; 9 Kt—B5, O—O;
10 Q—Kt4, P—KKt3; 11 BxKt, QPxB; 12 KtxB ch=.
(n) Better than 7.., O—O; 8 P—K5, Kt—K1; 9 R—Q1, P—Q4; 10 P—B3,
P—QKt4; 11 B—Kt3, B—Kt2; 12 PxP, Kt—R4; 13 B—B2 ±. Sir G. A.
Thomas—H. Saunders, Southport, 1924.

1 P—K 4, P—K 4; 2 Kt—K B 3, Kt—Q B 3; 3 B—Kt 5.

MORPHY DEFENCE

3.., P—Q R 3; 4 B—R 4, Kt—B 3.

	121	122	123	124	125
5	P—Q 3 (a)				
	P—Q 3........	....	....	....	P—Q Kt 4 (l)
6	P—B 4 (b)........	....	P—B 3		B—Kt 3
	P—K Kt 3...	B—K 2	P—K Kt 3...	B—K 2	B—B 4 (m)
7	P—Q 4 (c)	Kt—B 3 (e)	Q Kt—Q 2 (g)	Q Kt—Q 2	B—K 3 !
	B—Q 2	O—O	B—Kt 2	O—O	P—Q 3
8	P×P	P—Q 4	Kt—B 1	Kt—B 1	Q Kt—Q 2
	P×P (d)	B—Kt 5 !	O—O	P—Q Kt 4	B—K 3
9	Q—K 2	B×Kt	Kt—Kt 3 (h)	B—B 2	O—O
	B—Kt 2	P×B	P—Q Kt 4	P—Q 4 !	O—O
10	B—K Kt 5	P×P	B—B 2	B—Q 2 (j)	P—B 3
	P—R 3	Kt—Q 2	P—Q 4	R—K 1	Q B×B
11	B—R 4	P×P	Q—K 2	Kt—Kt 3	Q×B
	O—O	B×P	R—K 1	B—B 1	B×B
12	Q Kt—Q 2	B—K 3	O—O	O—O	P×B
	Q—K 1=	R—Kt 1	B—Kt 2	P×P	P—Q 4
13		P—K R 3	B—Kt 5	P×P	Q R—Q 1
		B—R 4 (f)	P—Q 5= (i)	B—K 3 (k)	Q—Q 3= (n)

(a) 5 P—B 3, Kt×P! (P—Q 3 transposes into better-known variations); 6 Q—K 2, Kt—B 4; 7 B×Kt, Q P×B; 8 P—Q 4, Kt—K 3; 9 P×P, Kt—B 4; 10 B—Kt 5, Q—Q 6! ∓. Balogh—Probst, correspondence, 1928-29.

(b) The Duras Variation. For 6 Kt—B 3 see col. 135.

(c) Alternatives are: (1) 7 Kt—B 3, B—Kt 2; 8 B—K Kt 5, P—R 3; 9 B—Q 2, O—O; 10 P—K R 3, Kt—Q 2; 11 B×Kt?, P×B; 12 Q—K 2, Kt—B 4. Duras—Maróczy, Vienna, 1908. 2) 7 P—K R 3, B—Kt 2; 8 B—K 3, O—O; 9 Q—Q 2, Kt—K 2; 10 Kt—B 3, P—B 3=.

(d) 8. , Q Kt×P; 9 Kt×Kt, P×Kt; 10 Kt—B 3, P—B 3; 11 O—O, P—R 3. Duras—Yates, match, 1911.

(e) Or 7 P—K R 3, O—O; 8 B—K 3, B—K 3; 9 Kt—B 3, R—Kt 1; 10 Q—K 2, Kt—Q 2. R. H. V. Scott—Sir G. A. Thomas, match, 1915.

(f) 14 Q—K 2, Kt—K 4; 15 P—K Kt 4, R×P! +. Duras—Vidmar, Carlsbad, 1907.

(g) 7 P—K R 3, B—Kt 2; 8 B—K 3, O—O; 9 Q—B 1, P—Q 4!, with a good game (Leonhardt).

(h) 9 P—K R 3, P—Q 4; 10 Q—K 2, Q—Q 3; 11 P—K Kt 4, P×P; 12 P×P, Kt—Kt 5! +. Treybal—Spielmann, Pistyan, 1922.

(i) 14 Q R—Q 1, Q—Q 3. Treybal—Grünfeld, Teplitz-Schönau, 1922.

(j) 10 Q—K 2, R—K 1; 11 P—K R 3, P—Kt 5; 12 P—B 4?, Kt—Q 5; 13 Kt×Kt, P×Kt; 14 B P×P, Kt×Q P; 15 B—Kt 3, Kt—Kt 3; 16 Q—R 5, R—B 1 ∓. Vajda—Lundin, Folkestone, 1933.

(k) 14 P—Kt 3, B—K Kt 5; 15 Q—K 2. Tartakover—Réti, New York, 1924.

(l) 5 ., B—B 4; 6 O—O, P—Q 3; 7 B×Kt ch, P×B; 8 B—K 3!, B×B; 9 P×B, O—O; 10 Kt—B 3, R—Kt 1. Asztalos—Vidmar, Budapest, 1913.

(m) 6 ., B—K 2; 7 P—Q R 4, P—Kt 5; 8 O—O, P—Q 3; 9 B—Kt 5 (or 9 P—R 5), Kt—Q R 4; 10 B—R 2, P—Kt 6?; 11 P×P, P—B 4; 12 P—Q Kt 4. Canal—Asztalos, Trieste, 1923.

(n) Dyckhoff—Tarrasch, 1916.

1 P—K 4, P—K 4; 2 Kt—K B 3, Kt—Q B 3; 3 B—Kt 5.

MORPHY DEFENCE

3.., P—Q R 3; 4 B—R 4, Kt—B 3.

	126	127	128	129	130
5	Q—K 2				B×Kt (h)
	P—Q Kt 4		B—K 2	B—B 4 !	Q P×B
6	B—Kt 3		P—B 3	P—B 3	Kt—B 3
	B—B 4 (a)		P—Q Kt 4	Q—K 2	B-KKt5!(i)
7	P—Q R 4....	P—B 3	B—B 2	P—Q 3	P—K R 3
	R—Q Kt 1	O—O	O—O	O—O	B—R 4
8	P×P	O—O	P—Q 4	Q Kt—Q 2	P—Q 3 (j)
	P×P	P—Q 3	P—Q 3	K Kt—Kt 5 !	Kt—Q 2
9	P—Q 3 (b)	P—Q 3	P—K R 3	O—O	B—K 3
	O—O	B—KKt5(d)	P×P	P—Q 3	B—Q Kt 5
10	O—O	B—K 3	Kt×P	P—Kt 4	B—Q 2
	P—Q 3	Q—K 2	Kt×Kt	B—R 2	Q—K 2
11	B—K 3	Q Kt—Q 2	P×Kt	B—Kt 3	P—R 3
	B—K Kt 5	Kt—Q 1	B—Kt 2	K—R 1	B—Q 3
12	P—R 3	P—K R 3	O—O	P—K R 3	Kt—K 2
	B×Kt	B—R 4	R—K 1	Kt—B 3	B×Kt
13	Q×B	B×B	R—Q 1 ± (f)	Kt—B 4	P×B
	Kt—Q 5 =(c)	P×B (e)		KKt—R4(g)	Kt—B 4 ∓ (k)

(a) 6.., B—K 2; 7 P—B 3, P—Q 3; 8 P—Q 4, B—Kt 5; 9 B—Q 5?, Kt×B; 10 P×Kt, Kt—R 4; 11 P×P, P×P; 12 Q×P, B×Kt; 13 P×B, Kt—B 5; 14 Q×KtP, B—B 3; 15 Q—R 6, Q—K 2 ch, followed by O—O—O + (Grunfeld). Note the numerous possibilities of transposition into the Worrall Attack (cols. 101—113) from cols. 126—129.

(b) 9 Kt—B 3, O—O!; 10 Kt×KtP (or 10 O—O, P—Kt 5; 11 Kt—Q 5, Kt—Q 5!), P—Q 4; 11 P×P, P—K 5; 12 Kt—Kt 5, R×Kt!; 13 Q×R, B×P ch=. Suchting—P. Johner, Vienna, 1908.

(c) Schlechter—Rubinstein, match, 1918.

(d) If 9.., Kt—K 2, Alekhine suggests 10 P—Q 4, P×P; 11 P×P, B—Kt 3; 12 P—K 5, K Kt—Q 4; 13 B—Kt 5 ±. 9.., K—R 1; 10 B—Kt 5, P—R 3; 11 B—K R 4, P—Kt 4; 12 B—Kt 3 can be played.

(e) 14 Q—K 3, Q—Q 3; 15 Kt—R 4, Kt—K 3; 16 Kt—B 5 +. Sir G. A. Thomas—Spielmann, Carlsbad, 1923.

(f) Tarrasch—Bogoljuboff, Kissingen, 1928.

(g) Continued 14 R—K 1, Q—B 3; 15 K—R 2, Kt—B 5; 16 B×Kt, Q×B ch ∓. Sir G. A. Thomas—Alekhine, Margate, 1937.

(h) The Treybal Variation.

(i) Inferior alternatives are: (1) 6. , B—Q 3; 7 P—Q 3, P—B 4; 8 P—K R 3, B—K 3; 9 B—K 3, P—R 3; 10 P—Q R 4, P—B 5?; 11 P—Q 4, P×P; 12 B×Q P, K B—Kt 5; 13 O—O ±. Bogoljuboff—Alekhine, 16th match game, 1934. (2) 6 B—Q Kt 5; 7 P—Q 3, Q—K 2?; 8 B—Q 2, B—Q 2; 9 Kt—K 2, B×B ch; 10 Q×B, O—O—O; 11 P—K R 3, Kt—K 1; 12 Q—R 5 ±. Flohr—Canal, Rogaska-Slatina, 1929.

(j) If 8 P—K Kt 4, B—Kt 3; 9 Kt×P, Kt×K P!; 10 Kt×Kt (10 Kt×B, Kt×Kt=) B×Kt; 11 Q—K 2, Q—Q 4; 12 Kt×QBP, Q×Kt; 13 P—Q 3, O—O—O; 14 P×B B—Kt 5 ch and Black's position is worth the Pawn.

(k) Flohr—Euwe, Semmering, 1937.

1 P—K 4, P—K 4 ; 2 Kt—K B 3, Kt—Q B 3 ; 3 B—Kt 5.

MORPHY DEFENCE

3.., P—Q R 3 ; 4 B—R 4, Kt—B 3.

	131	132	133	134	135
5	(B×Kt)..... (Q P×B)	Kt—B 3 (b) P—Q Kt4 (c)			P—Q 3
6	P—Q 3 B—Q 3	B—Kt 3 B—K 2.........		B—B 4 (h)	P—Q 3 B—K 2
7	Q Kt—Q 2 B—K 3	O—O P—Q 3 (d)		Kt×K P (i) Kt×Kt	P—K R 3 O—O
8	Q—K 2 Kt—R 4	P—Q 3 B—Kt 5	P—Q R 4 P—Kt 5 !	P—Q 4 B—Q 3	B—K 3 P—Q Kt 4
9	Kt—B 4 B×Kt	B—K 3 Kt—Q R 4	Kt—Q 5 Kt—Q R 4 (e)	P×Kt B×P	B—Kt 3 Kt—Q R 4
10	P×B Q—B 3	Kt—K 2 Kt×B	Kt×B Q×Kt	P—B 4 B×Kt ch	Kt—K 2 (k) P—B 4 !
11	P—K Kt 3 Q—K 3	R P×Kt Q—Q 2	P—Q 4 Kt×B	P×B O—O	O—O (l) P—B 5 !
12	B—K 3 P—Q B 4	Kt—Q 2 B×Kt	P×Kt B—Kt 2 (f)	P—K 5 P—B 4 !	P×P P×P
13	Kt—Q 2 Kt—B 3 = (a)	Q×B Kt—Kt 5 =	B—Kt 5 (g)	B—R 3 Q—R 4 (j)	B—R 4 Kt×P+ (m)

(a) Flohr—Reshevsky, Kemeri, 1937.

(b) A move on which Nimzovitch poured scorn as "colourless." In reply he advocated 5.., B—Kt 5, with the continuation 6 Kt—Q 5, B—K 2; 7 O—O, O—O; 8 R—K 1, P—Q 3; 9 Kt×Kt ch, B×Kt; 10 P—B 3, Kt—K 2; 11 P—Q 4, Kt—Kt 3=.

(c) 5.., B—K 2; 6 O—O, P—Q Kt 4 transposes into the column. 5.., P—Q 3; 6 P—Q 4, P—Q Kt 4 (6.., B—Q 2; 7 B×Kt, B×B; 8 Q—Q 3±); 7 P×P!(7 B—Kt 3, P×P; 8 B—Q 5, not, however, 8 Kt×P?, Kt×Kt; 9 Q×Kt, P—B 4 and 10.. P—B 5++. Noah's Ark Trap), P×P; 8 Q×Q ch, Kt×Q; 9 B—Kt 3, B—Q 3; 10 B—Kt 5, O—O; 11 O—O—O, Kt—K 3; 12 Q B×Kt, P×B; 13 Kt—Q 5, K—Kt 2; 14 Kt—Kt 6! +. Marco—Euwe, The Hague, 1921.

(d) 7.., O—O; 8 B—Q 5 (8 P—Q R 4 ? leads to col. 133 by transposition), P—Kt 5; 9 B×Kt, P×B; 10 Kt—K 2, Kt×P; 11 Kt×P, B—Q 3; 12 Kt—Q B 4!=. Schlechter—Vidmar, Carlsbad, 1911.

(e) 9.., R—Q Kt 1; 10 P—B 3, P×P; 11 Kt P×P, Kt—Q R 4; 12 B—R 2 Kt×Kt; 13 B×Kt, O—O=. Or 9.., Kt×P; 10 P—Q 4, O—O; 11 Kt×B ch, Kt×Kt; 12 R—K 1, B—Kt 2; 13 P×P, P—Q 4; 14 B—Q 2, P—Q B 4=.

(f) 12 , B—Kt 5; 13 B—Kt 5, O—O; 14 P—Q 5, P—R 3. Sir G. A. Thomas—Alekhine, Hastings, 1922.

(g) Sacrificing a Pawn, with the continuation 13.., B×P; 14 R—K 1, B×Kt; 15 Q×B, O—O; 16 P—Q 5. Copenhagen—Leningrad, by telegraph, 1930.

(h) 6.., P—Q 3!?; 7 Kt—Kt 5, P—Q 4; 8 Kt×Q P, Kt—Q 5; 9 Kt×Kt ch (or 9 Kt—K 3?, Kt×B; 10 R P×Kt, P—R 3; 11 Kt—B 3, Kt×P; 12 Kt×P, Q—B 3; 13 Kt—B 3, B—Kt 2; 14 Q—K 2, O—O—O, with a winning attack. Sir G. A. Thomas—Keres, Margate, 1937), Q×Kt; 10 B×P ch, K—Q 1; 11 P—Q 3 (11 P—K R 4, P—R 3; 12 Q—R 5, Q—K 1 wins), P—R 3; 12 B—Q 5, P—B 3; 13 Kt—B 7 ch, K—B 2; 14 Kt×R, P×B with excellent attacking prospects.

(i) 7 P—Q 3, P—Q 3; 8 O—O (or 8 B—K 3), B—K Kt 5; 9 B—K 3, Kt—Q 5; 10 B×Kt, B×B; 11 P—K R 3, P—K R 4; 12 Q—K 2, Kt—Q 2!; 13 Kt—Q 1. Fridlizius—Alekhine, Stockholm, 1912.

(j) 14 O—O, Q×B; 15 P×Kt, P—B 5; 16 Q—Q 5, Q—R 4!; 17 P×P ±. Alekhine—Réti, Vienna, 1922.

(k) 10 Kt—Q 5 is better.

(l) And now 11 P—B 3 is much better.

(m) Tartakover—Alekhine, Bled, 1931.

1 P—K 4, P—K 4 ; 2 Kt—K B 3, Kt—Q B 3 ; 3 B—Kt 5.

MORPHY DEFENCE (EXCHANGE VARIATION)
3.., P—Q R 3 ; 4 B×Kt.

	136	137	138	139	140
4	Q P×B (a)				
5	Kt—B 3			P—Q 4 (g)	
	P—B 3		B—Q B 4 (e)	P×P (h)	
6	P—Q 4	P—Q 3	P—Q 3	Q×P	
	P×P	B—Q 3	P—B 3 (f)	Q×Q	
7	Q×P	Kt—K 2	B—K 3	Kt×Q	
	Q×Q	Kt—K 2	B×B	B—Q 2 !....B—Q 3	
8	Kt×Q	Kt—Q 2 (c)	P×B	B—K 3	Kt-Q B 3 (k)
	B—Q 2	B—K 3	Kt—R 3	O—O	Kt—K 2
9	B—B 4	O—O	O—O	Kt—Q 2	B—K 3 (l)
	O—O—O	Kt—Kt 3	O—O	Kt—K 2	P—B 3
10	O—O—O	Kt—Q Kt 3	Kt—K 2	O—O—O (i)	Kt—Kt 3
	Kt—K 2	O—O	Kt—B 2	R—K 1	P—Q Kt 3
11	Kt—Kt 3	B—K 3	Kt—Kt 3	K R—K 1	O—O—O
	Kt—Kt 3	P—Kt 3	P—Q B 4	Kt—Kt 3	P—Q B 4
12	B—K 3	K—R 1	Q—K 2	Kt—K 2	Kt—Q 2
	P—Kt 3	Q—K 2	Q—K 2	B—Q 3	B—K,3
13	P—B 3	P—K B 4	R—B 2	P—K R 3	P—B 4
	Kt-K 4 ∓ (b)	P—KB4!(d)	B—K 3=	P-KB4 ∓ (j)	O—O—O= (m)

(a) If 4 ., Kt P×B; 5 P—Q 4, P×P; 6 Q×P, P—Q 3; 7 O—O, Kt—K 2 (7.., Kt—B3; 8 P—K 5 +); 8 Kt—B 3, Kt—K 3; 9 R—K 1 ±.

(b) 14 K—Kt 1, P—K R 4; 15 P—K R 4, Kt—B 5. Bernstein—Alekhine, Berne, 1932.

(c) Weaker is 8 B—K 3, P—Q B 4; 9 Kt—Kt 3, B—K 3; 10 P—B 3, Q—Q 2; 11 O—O, O—O; 12 Q—B 2, Kt—B 3 ±. Romanovsky—Botvinnik, Moscow, 1935.

(d) 14 B P×P, Kt×P; 15 P×P, Kt—Kt 5 !. Tartakover—Alekhine, Semmering, 1926. Black's position is more comfortable.

(e) If 5 , Kt—B 3; 6 Kt×P (6 P—Q 3 is also good), Kt×P, 7 Kt×Kt, Q—Q 5; 8 O—O, Q×K Kt; 9 R—K 1, B—K 3; 10 P—Q 4, Q—K B 4; 11 B—Kt 5 ±. Karlin and Tanner—Böok and Salo, 1935.

(f) 6 , B—K Kt 3, B×B; 8 P×B, Q—K 2; 9 O—O, O—O—O ?; 10 Q—K 1!, Kt—R 3; 11 R—Kt 1!, P—B 3; 12 P—Kt 4!, Kt—B 2; 13 P—Q R 4 ±. Capablanca—Janowski, St. Petersburg, 1914.

(g) 5 O—O is weak, for Black can safely reply 5 , B—K Kt 5!. If then 6 P—K R 3, P—K R 4! (but not 6., B×Kt; 7 Q×B, Q—B 3; 8 Q×Q, Kt×Q; 9 P—Q 3, B—B 4 ; 10 Kt—Q 2, O—O; 11 Kt—Kt 3, B—Kt 3; 12 B—Q 2, Kt—Q 2; 13 B—R 5, with the better ending for White Bernstein—Rivier, Berne, 1932), with a strong attack, e.g., 7 P×B, P×P; 8 Kt—Kt 5, Q—B 3; 9 Kt—K R 3, Q—R 5; 10 K—R 2, P×Kt; 11 P—K Kt 3, Q—R 2 ∓.

(h) If 5.., B—K Kt 5?; 6 P×P, Q×Q ch; 7 K×Q, O—O—O ch; 8 K—K 1!, B—Q B 4; 9 P—K R 3, B—R 4; 10 B—B 4, P—B 4, 11 Q Kt—Q 2 (if 11 P×P, B×Kt and 12., Kt—K 2); 12 B—Kt 5, B×Kt; 13 P×B +. Em. Lasker—Marshall, New York, 1924.

(i) Weaker is 10 P—K B 4, P—B 3; 11 Kt—K 2, Kt—Kt 3; 12 P—K R 3, B—Q 3; 13 K—B 2, K R—K 1; 14 Q R—Q 1, P—Q B 4 ∓. Henneberger—Euwe, The Hague, 1928.

(j) Petterson—Alekhine, Orebro, 1935.

(k) Or 8 B—K 3, P—Q B 4; 9 Kt—K 2, P—K B 3; 10 B—B 4, B—K 3; 11 B×B, P×B; 12 Kt—B 4, B—B 2; 13 Kt—B 3, Kt—K 2 =. Mattison—Rubinstein, Carlsbad, 1929.

(l) On 9 O—O, B—Q 2 is the simplest method of equalising, for if 9.., O—O; 10 P—K R 4, R—K 1; 11 Kt—R 3, P—B 3; 12 P—B 5!!, P—Q Kt 3; 13 B—B 4, B—Kt 2; 14 B×B!! ±. Lasker—Capablanca, St Petersburg, 1914. After 9 .; B—Q 2; 10 B—K 3, P—B 3; 11 Q R—Q 1, P—Q B 4; 12 K Kt—K 2, Kt—Kt 3; 13 Kt—Q 5, O—O—O Black stands well. Schlechter—Rubinstein, match, 1918.

(m) Bogoljuboff—Kostich, Gothenburg, 1920.

1 P—K 4, P—K 4 ; 2 Kt—K B 3, Kt—Q B 3 ; 3 B—Kt 5.

STEINITZ DEFENCE

3.., P—Q 3 ; 4 P—Q 4, B—Q 2 ; 5 Kt—B 3, Kt—B 3 ;
6 O—O, B—K 2.

	141	142	143	144	145
7	R—K 1 (a)				
	P × P (b)				
8	Kt × P				
	O—O				
9	B × Kt..........................			Kt × Kt.....	K Kt–K 2 (k)
	P × B			B × Kt (i)	Kt—K 4 (l)
10	B—Kt 5.................		P—Q Kt 3	B × B	Kt—Kt 3
	P—K R 3		P—Q 4 (g)	P × B	B × B
11	B—R 4		P—K 5	Kt—K 2	Kt × B
	R—K 1 (c)		B—Q Kt 5	Q—Q 2	K Kt—Q 2
12	Q—Q 3......	P—K 5	B—Q 2 (h)	Kt—Kt 3	B—Q 2
	Kt—R 2	Kt—R 2	B × Kt	K R—K 1	Kt—Q B 3
13	B × B (d)	B—Kt 3	B × B	P—Kt 3	B—B 3
	R × B	P—Q R 4	Kt—K 5 =	Q R—Q 1	B—B 3
14	R—K 3	Q—Q 3		B—Kt 2 ± (j)	Q—Q 2
	Q—Kt 1 = (e)	B–K B 1 = (f)			P—Q R 3 (m)

(a) Frequently arising by transposition from the Berlin Defence. 7 P—Q Kt 3,
P × P ; 8 Kt × P, Kt × Kt ; 9 Q × Kt, B × B ; 10 Kt × B, Kt—Q 2 transposing into
col. 153.

(b) 7.., O—O ? ; 8 B × Kt, B × B ; 9 P × P, P × P ; 10 Q × Q, Q R × Q ; 11 Kt × P,
B × P ; 12 Kt × B, Kt × Kt ; 13 Kt—Q 3 +.

(c) 11.., Kt—R 2 ; 12 B × B, Q × B ; 13 Q—Q 3, K R—K 1 ; 14 R—K 3,
Kt—B 1 =. O. S. Bernstein—Em. Lasker, game in Russia, 1914.

(d) 13 B—Kt 3, Kt—B 1 ; 14 Q R—Q 1, B—B 3 ; 15 R—Q 2, Q—Kt 1. H. G.
Cole—Capablanca, Hastings, 1919.

(e) 15 P—Q Kt 3, Q—Kt 3. Capablanca—Em. Lasker, match, 1921.

(f) 15 P × P, P × P ; 16 R × R, Q × R. O. S. Bernstein—Em. Lasker, St. Petersburg,
1914.

(g) The alternative defence 10.., R—K 1 ; 11 B—Kt 2, B—K B 1, followed by
P—Kt 3 and B—Kt 2, is less energetic.

(h) If instead 12 P × Kt, B × Kt ; 13 B—Kt 5, R—K 1 ; 14 R × R ch, Q × R ;
15 R—Kt 1, Q—K 5 ; 16 Kt—K 2, B × P +. Balla—Vidmar, Warsaw, 1918. The
column is L. Steiner—S. R. Wolf, Vienna, 1923.

(i) 9.., P × Kt ; 10 B—Q 3, R—Kt 1 ; 11 P—Q Kt 3, Kt—Kt 5 (Schlechter).

(j) Tarrasch—Em. Lasker, match, 1908.

(k) 9 P—K R 3, R—K 1 ; 10 B—K B 4, Kt—K 4 ; 11 B—K B 1, P—Q R 3 ;
12 Q—Q 2, Q—B 1. Schlechter—Réti, Vienna, 1912. 9 P—Q Kt 3 is also playable,
as is 9 B—Kt 5 ; but best is Tarrasch's move 9 B—B 1 (cols. 146–7).

(l) 9.., P—Q R 3 ; 10 B—Q 3, Kt—K Kt 5 ; 11 P—K R 3, K Kt—K 4 ; 12 P—B 4,
Kt × B ; 13 P × Kt, P—B 4 (Tarrasch). Or 11 Kt—Kt 3, B—B 3 ; 12 P—K R 3, B × Kt ;
13 P × B, K Kt—K 4 ; 14 P—K B 4 (Q—R 5 may be better), Q—R 5. Janowski—
Em. Lasker, 8th match game, 1909.

(m) 15 B × B ±. Kostich—Selesnieff, Gothenburg, 1920.

1 P—K 4, P—K 4 ; 2 Kt—K B 3, Kt—Q B 3 ; 3 B—Kt 5.

STEINITZ DEFENCE

3.., P—Q 3 ; 4 P—Q 4, B—Q 2 ; 5 Kt—B 3, Kt—B 3 ;
6 O—O, B—K 2.

	146	147	148	149	150
7	(R—K 1)........................			B×Kt	
	(P×P)			B×B	
8	(Kt×P)			Q—Q 3 !	
	(O—O).................		Kt×Kt	Kt—Q 2.....	P×P (g)
9	B—B 1		Q×Kt	P—Q 5 (f)	Kt×P
	R—K 1 (a)		B×B	Kt—B 4	B—Q 2
10	P—K R 3 (b)		Kt×B	Q—B 4	P—K R 3 (h)
	B—K B 1....	P—K R 3	P—Q R 3 (e)	B—Q 2	O—O
11	B—K Kt 5	K Kt—K 2(A)	Kt—B 3	P—Q Kt 4	B—B 4
	P—K R 3	B—K B 1	O—O	Kt—R 3	Kt—R 4
12	B—R 4	Kt—Kt 3	B—Kt 5	B—K 3	B—R 2
	P—K Kt 4	P—K Kt 3	Kt—Q 2	O—O	K B—B 3
13	B—Kt 3	B—K 3	B×B	P—Q R 4	P—K Kt 4
	Kt×Kt	B—Kt 2	Q×B	K—R 1	B×Kt
14	Q×Kt	Q—Q 2	Kt—Q 5	Kt—Q Kt 5	Q×B ± (i)
	Kt—R 4 (c)	K—R 2 (d)	Q—Q 1 ═	Q—Kt 1 ═	

(A) 11 P—Q Kt 3, B—K B 1; 12 B—Kt 2, Kt—K 4; 13 P—B 4, Kt—Kt 3; 14 Q—B 3, P—B 3. Smysloff—Ragosin, Leningrad, 1939.

(a) 9.., Kt×Kt?; 10 Q×Kt, B—B 3; 11 P—Q Kt 4 +. Capablanca—A. B. Hodges, New York, 1915. Or here 10 ., R—K 1; 11 P—Q Kt 3, B—B 3; 12 B—Kt 2, B—B 1; 13 Kt—Q 5 +. Tarrasch—Vogel, 1910.

(b) 10 P—B 3, Kt×Kt; 11 Q×Kt, B—K 3; 12 Q—B 2, P—B 3; 13 B—Q 2, Q—Kt 3. Euwe—Capablanca, London, 1922. Tarrasch recommends 10 P—Q Kt 3 and 11 B—Kt 2.

(c) 15 B—R 2, B—Kt 2; 16 Q—Q 1, Kt—B 5; 17 B×Kt, P×B; 18 Q—B 3, B×Kt; 19 Q×B, R—K 4. Kashdan—L. Steiner, match, 1930.

(d) 15 Q R—Q 1 +. Treybal—Réti, Pistyan, 1922.

(e) Best. If 10.., O—O; 11 Q—B 3, P—B 3 (better is P—Q 4 !); 12 Kt—Q 4, Kt—Q 2, 13 Kt—B 5, B—B 3 ; 14 Q—Kt 3 and White won brilliantly. Capablanca—Tanaroff. The column is Capablanca—Sir G. A. Thomas, Hastings, 1919.

(f) Or 9 B—K 3, P×P; 10 B×P, O—O; 11 Kt—Q 5, B×Kt; 12 P×B, B—B 3; 13 K R—K 1, B×B; 14 Q×B, Q—B 3 ═. Maróczy—Capablanca, London, 1922. The column is Nimzovitch—Breyer, Gothenburg, 1920.

(g) 8 ., Kt×P?; 9 Kt×Kt, P—Q 4; 10 Kt—Kt 3, P—K 5; 11 Q—K 3 !, P×Kt; 12 R—K 1 +. Maróczy—L. Steiner, Hastings, 1924.

(h) Another strong continuation is 10 P—Q Kt 3, O—O; 11 B—Kt 2, R—K 1; 12 Q R—K 1, B—K B 1; 13 P—B 4, Q—K 2; 14 P—K R 3 ±. Pillsbury—Bardeleben, 1900. Inferior is 10 B—Kt 5, O—O; 11 Q R—K 1, P—K R 3; 12 B—R 4, Kt—R 2; 13 B×B, Q×B; 14 Kt—Q 5, Q—Q 1; 15 P—Q B 4, R—K 1 ═. Lasker—Capablanca, 14th match game, 1921.

(i) 14.., Kt—B 3; 15 Q R—Q 1, B—B 3; 16 P—K 5. Brinckmann—Anderssen, Niendorf, 1934.

1 P—K 4, P—K 4; 2 Kt—K B 3, Kt—Q B 3; 3 B—Kt 5.

STEINITZ DEFENCE

3.., P—Q 3; 4 P—Q 4, B—Q 2; 5 Kt—B 3, Kt—B 3 (a).

	151	152	153	154	155
6	(O—O) (B—K 2)		 P × P	B × Kt B × B	
7	P × P Q Kt × P! (b)	B—Kt 5 P × P	Kt × P B—K 2 (d)	Q—Q 3 P × P (f)	
8	Kt—Q 4 O—O	Kt × P O—O	P—Q Kt 3 Kt × Kt	Kt × P B—Q 2	 P-K Kt 3 (h)
9	P—B 4 Kt—B 3	B × Q Kt P × B	Q × Kt B × B	B—Kt 5 B—K 2	B—Kt 5! (i) B—Kt 2
10	Kt—B 5 R—K 1	Q—Q 3 P—K R 3	Kt × B Kt—Q 2	O—O—O O—O	O—O—O Q—Q 2 (j)
11	B—Q 3 B—K B 1	B—R 4 Kt—R 4	B—R 3 P—Q R 3 (e)	P—B 4 Kt—K 1	P—K R 3 O—O
12	P—Q Kt 3 P—K Kt 3	B × B Q × B=	Kt—B 3 B—B 3	B × B Q × B	K R—K 1 K R—K 1 (k)
13	Kt—K 3 B—Kt 2		Q—K 3 O—O	Kt—Q 5 Q—Q 1	Q—B 3! Kt—R 4
14	B—Kt 2 Kt × P (c)		Q R—Q 1 B × Kt=	P—K Kt4 + (g)	P—K Kt4 + (l)

(a) Also frequently reached by transposition from the Four Knights' Game.

(b) 7.., P × P; 8 R—K 1, B—Q 3 (8.., O—O? transposes into col. 141, note (b)); 9 B—Kt 5, P—K R 3; 10 B—K R 4, P—K Kt 4; 11 B—Kt 3, Q—K 2; 12 Kt—Q 5, Q—Q 1; 13 B × Kt, P × B; 14 Kt—K 3, Q—K 2; 15 Kt—B 4 +. Perlis—H. Wolf, Vienna, 1911.

(c) 15 B × Kt, R × B; 16 Kt × R, B × B; 17 Kt—Q 5!, P—B 4; 18 R—Kt 1 +.

(d) 7.., Kt × Kt; 8 Q × Kt, B × B; 9 Kt × B, B—K 2; 10 P—Q Kt 3 transposes back into the column. Or here 9.., P—Q R 3 transposing into col. 143.

(e) If 11.., B—B 3; 12 Q—B 4 +. The column is Lasker—Capablanca, New York, 1924.

(f) 7.., Kt—Q 2 (Tarrasch suggests 7., Q—K 2); 8 B—K 3, P × P; 9 B × P, Q—K 2; 10 O—O, O—O—O; 11 Kt—Q 5, Q—K 3; 12 B × R P +. Bogoljuboff—Bogatyrchuk, 1924. Nimzovitch recommended 9.., Kt—B 4; 10 Q—K 2, Kt—K 3; 11 O—O—O, B—K 2; 12 Kt—Q 5, O—O; 13 B—B 3, R—K 1 =.

(g) Spielmann—Maróczy, Gothenburg, 1920.

(h) 8., Kt—Q 2?; 9 Kt × B, P × Kt; 10 Q—R 6, Kt—Kt 3; 11 Q—Kt 7, K—Q 2; 12 Q—R 6 +. Bogoljuboff—Balla, Pistyan, 1922.

(i) Less complicated than 9 Kt × B, P × Kt; 10 Q—R 6, Q—Q 2; 11 Q—Kt 7, R—B 1; 12 Q × R P, B—Kt 2 (Nimzovitch—Capablanca, St. Petersburg, 1914), when Black has a strong attack for the Pawn.

(j) Alekhine suggests Q—B 1, leaving Q 2 open to the Kt. If 10.., O—O?; 11 Kt × B, P × Kt; 12 P—K 5, P × P; 13 Q × Q, Q R × Q; 14 R × R, R × R; 15 Kt—K 4 +. Lárobok, 1921.

(k) 12.., K—R 1; 13 P—B 4 ± (Alekhine).

(l) Alekhine—Brinckmann, Kecskemét, 1927.

1 P—K 4, P—K 4; 2 Kt—K B 3, Kt—Q B 3; 3 B—Kt 5.

STEINITZ DEFENCE
3.., P—Q 3.

	156	157	158	159	160
4	(P—Q 4)				P—B 3 (j)
	(B—Q 2)			B—Kt 5 ?	P—K Kt 3
5	(Kt—B 3)		B×Kt	P—Q 5	O—O
	P×P		B×B	P—Q R 3	B—Kt 2
6	Kt×P		Kt—B 3	B—R 4	P—Q 4
	Kt—B 3	KKt—K2 (e)	P×P (g)	P—Q Kt 4	B—Q 2
7	B×Kt	B—Q B 4	Q×P	P×Kt	B—Kt 5
	P×B	Kt×Kt	Kt—B 3	P×B	P—B 3
8	Q—B 3	Q×Kt	B—Kt 5	P—B 4	B—K R 4
	P—B 4 (a)	Kt—B 3	B—K 2	Kt—K 2	Q—K 2
9	Kt—B 5	Q—K 3	O—O—O	Q×R P	Kt—R 3
	B×Kt (b)	B—K 3	O—O	B×Kt	Kt—R 3
10	Q×B	Kt—Q 5	K R—K 1	P×B	Kt—B 2
	Q—Q 2	B	Kt—Q 2	Kt—Kt 3	Kt—Q 1
11	Q—B 3	B—Q 2	B×B	B—K 3	B—B 4
	R—Q Kt 1 (c)	O—O	Q×B	B—K 2	K Kt—B 2
12	O—O ± (d)	O—O + (f)	R—K 3 ± (h)	Kt—B 3+ (i)	Kt—Q 2
					Kt—K 3 (k)

(a) Forced. If 8. , B—K 2; 9 P—K 5, P×P; 10 Kt×P, B×Kt; 11 Q×B ch, Kt—Q 2; 12 O—O, O—O; 13 R—Q 1 +.

(b) Not 9. , P—Kt 3 ?; 10 B—Kt 5!, P×Kt; 11 P—K 5, P×P; 12 B×Kt, P—K 5; 13 Kt×P + +.

(c) After 11.., Q—Kt 5; 12 Q×Q, Kt×Q; 13 Kt—Q 5, White has the better ending.

(d) 12.., B—K 2; 13 P—Q Kt 3, O—O; 14 B—Kt 5, Kt—Q 4; 15 Kt×Kt. Löwenfisch—Dubinin, Leningrad, 1934. Compare col. 14.

(e) If 6. , P—K Kt 3; 7 Kt×Kt (7 Kt—B 3, B—Kt 2; 8 B—Kt 5, Kt—B 3; 9 Q—Q 2, P—K R 3; 10 B—K R 4 is weaker J. S. Morrison—Capablanca, New York, 1918), P×Kt; 8 B—Q B 4, B—Kt 2; 9 Q—K 2, Kt—K 2; 10 P—K R 4, P—K R 3; 11 P—R 5. P—Kt 4; 12 P—B 4 +. Pillsbury—Steinitz, London, 1899.

(f) Lasker– Steinitz, St. Petersburg, 1895-96.

(g) Better is 6.., P—B 3. Compare note (j) and column.

(h) Alekhine—Andersen, Folkestone, 1933. Continued 12.., Q—B 3, 13 Kt—Q 5, B×Kt; 14 P×B, Q×Q; 15 Kt×Q, K R—K 1; 16 Q R—K 1, R×R; 17 R×R, Kt—Kt 3; 18 P—Q B 4 1 with a winning ending.

(i) Réti—Spielmann, Berlin, 1919.

(j) For 4 O—O, Kt—B 3 see Berlin Defence, col. 11. 4 B×Kt ch, P×B; 5 P—Q 4, P—B 3; 6 B—K 3 (Alapin recommended 6 Kt—B 3, P—K Kt 3; 7 B—K 3, Kt—R 3, 8 Q—Q 2, B—K B 2 followed by B—Kt 2), Kt—K 2; 7 Kt—B 3, Kt—Kt 3; 8 Q—Q 2, B—K 2; 9 O—O—O, O—O is a possibility.

(k) Lasker—Speyer, 1909.

1 P—K 4, P—K 4 ; 2 Kt—K B 3, Kt—Q B 3 ; 3 B—Kt 5.

STEINITZ DEFENCE DEFERRED

3.., P—Q R 3 ; 4 B—R 4, P—Q 3 ; 5 B × Kt ch, P × B.

	161	162	163	164	165
6	P—Q 4 / P—B 3				P × P (k)
7	B—K 3 / P—Kt 3	Kt—K 2		O—O (h) / P—Kt 3 (i)	Kt × P / B—Q 2
8	Q—Q 2 / B—K Kt 2	Kt—B 3 / Kt—Kt 3		Kt—K 1 / B—K Kt 2	O—O / P—Kt 3 (l)
9	Kt—B 3 / B—Q 2 (a)	P—K R 4 / Q—Q 2 (c)	.... Q—Q 2 / B—K 2 (e)	P—K B 4 / P × Q P	Kt—Q B 3 / B—Kt 2
10	O—O / Kt—K 2	P—R 5 / Kt—K 2	P—K R 4 / P—K R 4! (f)	Q × P / Kt—K 2	R—K 1 / Kt—K 2
11	P—K R 3 / O—O	Q—K 2 / P—R 4	O—O—O / B—Kt 5	P—Q Kt 3 / P—Q B 4	B—B 4 / O—O
12	Q R—Q 1 / Q—Kt 1	O—O—O / B—R 3	Q—Q 3 / P × P	Q—Q 3 / P—B 4	Q—Q 2 / P—Q B 4
13	P—Q Kt 3 / Q—Kt 2	Q—Q 2 / Q—K 3 ?	B × P / Kt—B 5	P—K 5 / B—Kt 2	Kt—Kt 3 / Kt—B 3
14	B—R 6 / Q R—Q 1 = (b)	P × P + (d)	Q—B 4 / Q—Q 2 = (g)	B—Kt 2 / Kt—B 3 ∓ (j)	B—R 6 ± (m)

(a) An excellent alternative is 9.., Kt—K 2; 10 B—R 6, O—O; 11 O—O—O, B—Q 2; 12 P—K R 3, Q—Kt 1; 13 P—K Kt 4, Q—Kt 5; 14 B × B, K × B; 15 P—R 3, Q—Kt 3=. Bogoljuboff—Sir G. A Thomas, Hastings, 1922.

(b) Romanovsky—Capablanca, Moscow, 1935.

(c) 9.., P—K R 4, transposing into col. 163, is preferable.

(d) 14.., B P × P; 15 Kt—K Kt 5 with a decisive attack. Tartakover—Stoltz, Bled, 1931.

(e) Another possibility is 9. , B—K 3; 10 P—K R 4 (10 P—Q Kt 3?, P—Q 4; 11 O—O, P × K P; 12 Q Kt × P, B—Q 4; 13 Kt—Kt 3, B × Kt; 14 P × B, Kt—R 5 +. Sir G. A. Thomas—Capablanca, Nottingham, 1936), P—K R 4; 11 P—Q 5!, P × P; 12 Kt × Q P, B—K 2; 13 Q—R 5!, R—Q B 1; 14 Q × R P, P—B 3!; 15 Kt × B, Q × Kt. Foltys—Fine, Margate, 1937. Black has excellent counterplay for the Pawn sacrificed.

(f) Another playable line is 10 ., B—Kt 5; 11 P—R 5, Kt—B 1; 12 Kt—K Kt 1, Q—B 1; 13 P—B 3, B—K 3; 14 K Kt—K 2, Q—Kt 2; 15 O—O—O, O—O—O; 16 P—Q 5, P × P; 17 P × P, B—B 2=. Kan—Bogatyrchuk, Leningrad, 1934. Weak, however, is 10.., O—O; 11 P—R 5, Kt—R 1; 12 O—O—O, Kt—B 2; 13 Q R—Kt 1, B—Q 2; 14 P—K Kt 4, P × P; 15 Kt × P, Kt—K 4; 16 Q—K 2, Q—B 1; 17 Kt—B 5, R—K 1; 18 P—B 4, Kt—B 2; 19 P—R 6 +. Sir G. A. Thomas—Monticelli, Folkestone, 1933.

(g) Bogoljuboff—Alekhine, exhibition game, Baden-Baden, 1934.

(h) Or 7 Kt—B 3, R—Kt 1; 8 P—Q Kt 3, P—Kt 3; 9 Q—Q 3, Q—Q 2; 10 B—Kt 2, B—R 3; 11 Kt—K 2, Kt—K 2; 12 P × P, B P × P; 14 O—O. P—B 4=. Sir G. A. Thomas—Alekhine, London, 1932.

(i) Equally good is 7 ., Kt—K 2; 8 Kt—R 4, B—K 3; 9 P—K Kt 3, P—Kt 4; 10 Kt—Kt 2, P—Q B 4; 11 P—Q 5, B—B 2; 12 P—K R 4, P × P; 13 Kt × P, Q—Q 2 ∓. Balogh—Kashdan, Gyor, 1930.

(j) 15 Q—B 4, Q—Q 2. Kupchik—Capablanca, New York, 1931.

(k) If 6.., P—K B 4?; 7 Kt—B 3, Kt—B 3; 8 P × K P, Kt × P; 9 Kt × Kt, P × Kt; 10 Kt—Q 4 ! +. Keres—Andersen, Warsaw, 1935.

(l) Simpler for Black is 8 , Kt—B 3; 9 Kt—B 3, B—K 2; 10 R—K 1, O—O; 11 P—Q Kt 3 (or 11 B—Kt 5, P—R 3; 12 B—R 4, Kt—R 2=), R—K 1; 12 B—Kt 2, B—K B !; 13 P—B 3, P—Kt 3; 14 Q—Q 3, B—Kt 2=. Balla—Réti, Budapest, 1911.

(m) Alekhine—Koltanowski. London. 1932.

1 P—K 4, P—K 4 ; 2 Kt—K B 3, Kt—Q B 3 ; 3 B—Kt 5.

STEINITZ DEFENCE DEFERRED
3.., P—Q R 3 ; 4 B—R 4, P—Q 3.

	166	167	168	169	170
5	(B × Kt ch)............P—Q 4.................P—B 4 (*k*)				
	(P × B)		P—Q Kt 4 (*e*)		B—Q 2
6	(P—Q 4)		B—Kt 3		Kt—B 3
	(P × P)		Kt × P		P—K Kt 3
7	(Kt × P)		Kt × Kt		P—Q 4
	(B—Q 2)....P—Q B 4		P × Kt		B—Kt 2
8	Kt—Q B 3	Kt—K 2	B—Q 5..... P—Q B 3 (*h*)		B—K 3 (*l*)
	Kt—B 3	Kt—B 3	R—Kt 1	B—Kt 2 (*i*)	Kt—B 3
9	Q—B 3 (*a*)	Q Kt—B 3	B—B 6 ch (*f*)	P × P	P × P
	P—B 4	R—Q Kt 1	B—Q 2	Kt—B 3	P × P
10	Kt—B 5	O—O	B × B ch	P—B 3	B—B 5
	B × Kt	B—K 2	Q × B	B—K 2	Kt—K R 4
11	P × B	P—Q Kt 3	Q × P	O—O	Kt—Q 5
	B—K 2 (*b*)	O—O	Kt—B 3	O—O	Kt—B 5
12	Q—B 6 ch	B—Kt 2	Kt—B 3	Kt—B 3	Kt × Kt
	Kt—Q 2	R—K 1	B—K 2	P—B 4	P × Kt
13	Kt—Q 5	Q—Q 3	O—O (*g*)	P—Q 5	O—O ! (*m*)
	R—R 2	B—B 1	O—O	R—K 1 (*j*)	Kt—K 2 (*n*)
14	O—O	Q R—Q 1	B—Q 2		B × B ch
	O—O = (*c*)	B—Q 2 = (*d*)	K R—K 1 =		Q × B (*o*)

(*a*) 9 O—O transposes into col. 165, note (*l*).
(*b*) 11.., R—R 2 ? ; 12 O—O, B—K 2 ; 13 B—Kt 5, O—O ; 14 Q R—K 1, R—K 1 ;
15 R—K 2, P—R 3 ; 16 B—R 4 ±. Horowitz—Fine, 7th match game, 1934.
(*c*) Brinckmann—Yates, Kecskemét, 1927.
(*d*) Dake—H. Steiner, 3rd match game, 1935.
(*e*) 5.., B—Q 2 ; 6 P—B 3 transposes into cols. 177—184.
(*f*) More aggressive is 9 Q × P, B—Q 2 ; 10 P—Q B 3, Kt—B 3 ; 11 O—O, B—K 2 ;
12 P—B 3, O—O ; 13 B—Kt 3, B—B 3 ; 14 Q—B 2. Rivline—Znosko-Borovsky,
Paris championship, 1930.
(*g*) Simpler is 13 P—K 5. The column is Stoltz—Alekhine, Bled, 1931.
(*h*) After 8 P—Q R 4, R—Kt 1 ! (but not 8.., B—Kt 2 ; 9 O—O, Kt—B 3 ;
10 Q—K 2, Q—Q 2 ; 11 P—Q B 3, P × B P ? ; 12 Kt × P, P—K t 5 ; 13 Kt—Q 5, Kt × Kt ;
14 P × Kt dis ch, B—K 2 ; 15 B—Kt 5 +. Treysman—Dake, New York, 1936) ;
9 P × P, P × P ; 10 P—Q B 3 (10 Q × P, P—Q B 4 ∓), P × P ; 11 Kt × P, Kt—B 3 Black's
attack is not as strong as in the column. Of course, if 8 Q × P ?, P—Q B 4—B 5 + +
(Noah's Ark Trap).
(*i*) On 8. , P × P White can play either 9 Q—Q 5, B—K 3 ; 10 Q—B 6 ch, Q—Q 2 :
11 Q—Q 5, drawing by repetition of moves, or simply 9 Kt × P and rely on his superior
development to guarantee sufficient compensation for the Pawn.
(*j*) Yates—Bogoljuboff, San Remo, 1930. The chances are about even.
(*k*) A slightly altered version of the Duras Variation. Compare cols. 121 and 122
(Morphy Defence).
(*l*) A strong alternative is 8 P × P, P × P ; 9 Kt—Q 5, Kt—B 3 ; 10 B—K Kt
(but not 10 Kt × Kt ch ?, Q × Kt ; 11 P—K R 3, P—K R 3 ; 12 B—K 3, O—O—O ;
13 Q—K 2 Q—K 2 ; 14 O—O—O, P—B 4 ∓. Rellstab—Fine, Kemeri, 1937), and
Black's position is difficult.
(*m*) L. Steiner's suggestion. If instead 13 Q—Q 2 ?, P—Q Kt 3 ; 14 B—R 3,
P—Q Kt 4 ! ; 15 P × P ?, P × P ; 16 B × P ; R × B ! +. And if 13 P—K 5, Kt × P ! (Forced,
for if 13. , P—K Kt 4 ? ; 14 Q—Q 5 !, B—K B 1 ; 15 B × B, R × B ; 16 O—O—O,
Q—K 2 ; 17 B × Kt, B × B ; 18 Q—Q 3 +. Keres—Alekhine, Margate, 1937) ; 14 Kt × Kt,
(or 14 Q—K 2, P—K B 3 ; 15 O—O—O, P—B 3 ; 16 B—Q 6, Q—R 4 ; 17 Kt × Kt,
P × Kt ; 18 B × K P, Q × B ; 19 Q × Q, B × Q (Keres), and Black can hold the position),
B × Kt ; 15 Q—K 2, P—K B 3 ; 16 O—O—O, P—B 3 , 17 B—Q 6, Q—R 4 ! and Black's
defensive resources are quite adequate.
(*n*) If 13 ., P—Kt 3 ; 14 Q—Q 5 !, P × B ; 15 B × Kt + +. Or 13 ., Kt—K 4 ;
14 Kt × Kt, B × Kt : 15 Q—Q 5 +. Or 13 ., B × P ; 14 R—Kt 1 +.
(*o*) 15 Q—Kt 3 +

1 P—K4, P—K4; 2 Kt—KB3, Kt—QB3; 3 B—Kt5.

STEINITZ DEFENCE DEFERRED
3.., P—QR3; 4 B—R4, P—Q3.

	171	172	173	174	175
5	(P—B4)....	O—O			
	(B—Q2) (a)	Kt—B3			
6	P—Q4 (b)	B×Kt ch			P—Q4 (m)
	P×P	P×B			P—QKt4 (n)
7	Kt×P	P—Q4			B—Kt3 (o)
	Kt×Kt!	Kt—Q2	Kt×P!		QKt×P
8	B×B ch	P—QKt3!	Q—K2	R—K1!	Kt×Kt
	Q×B	B—K2	P—KB4	P—KB4	P×Kt
9	Q×Kt	B—Kt2	QKt—Q2 (f)	P×P	P—QB3 (p)
	Kt—B3 (c)	P—B3	Kt×Kt	P—Q4	P×P
10	O—O	Kt—R4	Kt×Kt	Kt—Q4!	Kt×P
	B—K2	P—Kt3	B—K2 (g)	Q—R5 (i)	B—K2
11	Kt—B3	Q—K2	P×P	P—KKt3	Q—B3
	O—O	P—KB4?	P×P	Q—R6	B—Kt2
12	P—QKt3	QP×P!	Kt—B4	Kt-QB3! (j)	Q—Kt3
	KR—K1	B×Kt	Q—Q4	Kt×Kt (h)	O—O
13	B—Kt2	P—K6+ (e)	Kt×P	P×Kt	B—R6
	B—B1= (d)		O—O (h)	B—Kt2 (l)	Kt—K1 (q)

(a) 5 .., P—B4!?; 6 P—Q4!, BP×P; 7 Kt×P, P×Kt; 8 Q—R5 ch, K—K2; 9 B×Kt, Kt—B3! (9 , Q×P??; 10 Q—K8 ch, K—Q3; 11 B—K3, Q×BP; 12 Kt—B3, B—Kt5; 13 R—Q1 ch, resigns. Book—Andersen, Warsaw, 1935. Or 9 , P×B, 10 B—Kt5 ch, Kt—B3; 11 P×P +); 10 Q×P ch! (10 B—K Kt5 now is a *Fata Morgana*. 10 , Q×P; 11 Q—K8 ch, K—Q3; 12 B×Kt, Kt—Kt5!; 13 B×P ch, Q×B; 14 Q×Q ch, K×Q; 15 B×KP, B—Kt5 ch; 16 Kt—B3, B×Kt ch +. Michel—Czaya, Berlin, 1937), K—B2, 11 B—Q5 ch (Necessary; if 11 B—R4, B—Q3; 13 Q—Q2, B—Q2 with a powerful attack), Kt×B; 12 Q×Kt ch, Q×Q; 13 P×Q, B—KB4; 14 B—B4, R—B1; 15 O—O, followed by P—B3 +.
(b) 6 Kt—B3, B—K2. If White delays P—Q4, Kt—Q5 will give Black a satisfactory game.
(c) Or 9 ., Kt—K2; 10 O—O, Kt—B3; 11 Q—B3, Q—Kt5; 12 P—B3, Q—Kt3; 13 Q—Kt3 (Eliskases—Sir G A. Thomas, Hastings, 1936-37), O—O—O!=.
(d) Keres—Sir G. A. Thomas, Hastings, 1937-38.
(e) 13 ., Kt—B3; 14 Q—B4 with an overwhelming position. C. H. Alexander—Kashdan, Stockholm, 1937.
(f) Inferior is 9 P×P, P—Q4; 10 Q Kt—Q2, B—B4; 11 Kt—Kt3, B—Kt3; 12 K—B3, P—B4!; 13 K Kt—Q2, Kt×Kt; 14 Kt×Kt, O—O; 15 P—KB4, P—QR4! ∓. Dake—Reshevsky, New York, 1938. Or here 10 R—Q1, P—B4; 11 P—B4, P—B3. H. Wolf—Rubinstein, Vienna, 1922.
(g) If 10 ., P—K5; 11 P—KB3, P—Q4; 12 P×P, QP×P; 13 Kt×P! +.
(h) 14 R—Q1, Q—K3. C. H. Alexander—Reshevsky, Hastings, 1937-38. White stands slightly better.
(i) A critical position. If 10. , B—B4; 11 B—K3 ±, while if 10. , P—B4; 11 Kt—K2, P—B3; 12 Kt—B4, P—Kt3; 13 P—KB3, Kt—Kt4; 14 P—K6 because of 14.., B—Q3; 15 P—KR4, Q—B2!+), P—Q5; 14 Q—R4, B—Kt2; 15 P—B3, Kt—Kt4; 16 P—R4, Kt—B2; 17 P—K6 +. Keres—Reshevsky, Avro, 1938.
(j) Better than 12 Kt×BP, B—B4; 13 B—K3, P—B5!; 14 B×B, B—Kt5!; 15 Q—Q3, Kt×B; 14 Q—B1, Q—R3 with a strong counter-attack.
(k) Or 12 , B—Kt2; 13 Q Kt—Q2 ±. Or 12 , B—B4; 13 Q Kt—K2 ±. After 12 ., Kt×BP; 13 K×Kt, Q×RP ch; 14 K—B3 Black has no good continuation because his Queen is threatened by R—R1.
(l) 14 Kt—K6 +.
(m) 6 R—K1, B—K2 transposes into cols. 97—100; 6 Q—K2, B—K2 into cols. 110—113; 6 P—B3, B—K2; 7 P—Q4 into cols. 177 and 178.
(n) 6.., B—Q2 transposes into better-known variations.
(o) Accepting the challenge. 7 P×P, P×P; 8 Q×Q ch, Kt×Q; 9 B—Kt3, B—Q3; 10 B—Kt5, O—O; 11 B×Kt, P×B; 12 Kt—B3= is colourless.
(p) 9 Q×P?, P—B4 and 10 , P—B5+ +. Noah's Ark Trap again.
(q) 14 P—B4, with sufficient compensation for the Pawn. Yates—Rubinstein, Carlsbad, 1923.

1 P—K 4, P—K 4; 2 Kt—K B 3, Kt—Q B 3; 3 B—Kt 5.

STEINITZ DEFENCE DEFERRED
3.., P—Q R 3; 4 B—R 4, P—Q 3.

	176	177	178	179	180
5	(O—O) ..... P—Q Kt4 (A)	P—B 3 B—Q 2			
6	B—Kt 3 Kt—R 4	P—Q 4 Kt—B 3................		P—K Kt 3	
7	P—Q 4 P×P	O—O B—K 2		O—O B—Kt 2	
8	Kt×P B—Kt 2	P—Q 5 Kt—Q Kt 1		B—K 3 K Kt—K 2	
9	P—Q B 4 Kt×P	B—B 2 B—Kt 5.....	P—R 3	P—B 4 !.... P×P	R—K 1 (f) O—O
10	P—Q R 4 P—Q B 3	P—B 4 Q Kt—Q 2	P—B 4 Q—B 1	Kt×P O—O	P×P Kt×P
11	Q—K 2 Kt—K 2	P—K R 3 (b) B—R 4	Kt—K 1 P—K Kt 4	Kt—Q B 3 Kt×Kt	Kt×Kt B×Kt
12	B—Kt 5 P—R 3 = (a)	Kt—B 3 O—O	Kt—Q B 3 Kt—R 4 !	B×Kt Q B×B	B—Kt 3 Kt—B 3
13		P-K Kt4 ±	Kt—K 2 (c) Kt—B 5 (d)	Kt×B B×B (e)	Kt—Q 2 B-Kt2 = (g)

(A) 5.., B—Q 2; 6 P—B 3, P—K Kt 3; 7 P×Q 4, B—Kt 2 (the same position as in cols. 179—83); 8 P×P, Kt×P (for P×P see col. 183, note (f)) ; 9 Kt×Kt, P×Kt; 10 P—K B 4, B×B; 11 Q×B ch, Q—Q 2; 12 Q×Q ch, K×Q; 13 P×P, K—K 3; 14 B—B 4, R—K B 1; 15 Kt—Q 2, B×P; 16 Kt—Kt 3, B×B; 17 R×B, P—Kt 3; 18 P—Q R 4 +. Fine—Alekhine, Avro, 1938.

(a) Leonhardt—Schlechter, Ostend, 1906.

(b) An improvement on 11 Kt—B 3, Kt—B 1; 12 P—K R 3, B—Q 2; 13 Kt—K 1, P—K Kt 4!; 14 B×P, R—K Kt 1; 15 P—B 4 (15 B×Kt, B×B; 16 K—R 2 leaves Black with a strong attack), P×P; 16 B×P, B×P; 17 P—B 5, Kt—Kt 3 with a satisfactory position for Black. Bogoljuboff—Alekhine, 20th match game, 1929. After the text-move the retreat 11 , B—Q 2 is not at Black's disposal; as a result the Bishop is forced out of play and White assumes control of more space.

(c) 13. , B—Kt 3; 14 Q—K 2, Kt—K 1; 15 B—Q 2, P—R 3; 16 K—Kt 2, B—R 2; 17 R—R 1, P—K Kt 4; 18 P—K R 4. White won quickly. Alekhine—P. Johner, Zurich, 1934. The variation is similar to Queen's Pawn Game, Tchigorin's Defence, col. 151.

(d) 14 Kt—Kt 3, P—Q B 3; 15 Kt—B 5, P×P; 16 B×Kt, Kt P×B=. Alekhine—Keres, Warsaw, 1935. Black's opening play is very original.

(e) 14 Q×B, Kt—B 3; 15 Q—Q 2, Q—B 3; 16 Q R—Q 1, with a minimal advantage. Yates—Capablanca, Hastings, 1929.

(f) 9 P×P, P×P? (9 ., Kt×P; 10 Kt×Kt transposes back into the column), 10 B—B 5!, O—O; 11 B×Q Kt, P×B; 12 Kt—R 3, R—K 1; 13 Kt—B 4, P—B 3; 14 Kt—R 5 ±. Maróczy—A. J. Mackenzie, Weston, 1922.

(g) R. P. Michell—Capablanca, Hastings, 1919.

1 P—K 4, P—K 4 ; 2 Kt—K B 3, Kt—Q B 3 ; 3 B—Kt 5.

STEINITZ DEFENCE DEFERRED

3 .., P—Q R 3 ; 4 B—R 4, P—Q 3.

#	181	182	183	184	185
5	(P—B 3) (B—Q 2) (A)				O—O
6	(P—Q 4) (P—K Kt 3)			K Kt—K 2	K Kt—K 2
7	(O—O) (B—Kt 2)		B—Kt 3 ! (i) P—R 3 (j)	P—Q 4	P—Q 4 Kt-Kt 3 (m)
8	(B—K 3) Kt—B 3	R—K 1 Kt—B 3 (d)	B—K Kt 5 (f) K Kt—K 2	B—K 3 P—K Kt 4	R—K 1 B—K 2
9	P×P Q Kt×P (a)	Q Kt—Q 2 O—O	P×P (g) P×P	B×Kt P ! P×B	Q Kt—Q 2 O—O
10	Kt×Kt P×Kt	Kt—B 1 P—R 3	Q—Q 3 P—K R 3	Kt×Kt P P—Q 4	Kt—B 1 Kt—R 5 (n)
11	B—B 2 O—O	Kt—Kt 3 R—K 1	B—K 3 B—Kt 5	K P×P Kt—R 4	P—Q 5 Kt—Kt 1
12	Kt—Q 2 Q—K 2	P—K R 3 R—K 2	Q—K 2 O—O (h)	P—Q 6 ! (k) Kt×B	B×B Kt×B
13	P—K R 3 (b) Kt—K 1	B—B 2 Q—K 1	B—B 5 ! ±	Q×Kt Kt—Q 4	Kt—Kt 3 K—R 1
14	Q—K 2 Kt—Q 3 = (c)	B—K 3 R—Q 1 = (e)		Kt×P + (l)	Q—K 2 Kt × Ktch＝ (o)

(A) 5. , P—Q Kt 4 ?; 6 B—B 2, Kt—B 3; 7 P—Q 4, B—K 2; 8 O—O, O—O ; 9 R—K 1, P—R 3; 10 Q Kt—Q 2, Kt—K R 2; 11 P—Q R 4! ±. Lasker—Romanovsky, Moscow, 1935.

(a) 9 , P×P, transposing into col. 183, note (f), is simpler.

(b) Or 13 P—B 3, K R—Q 1; 14 Q—B 1, P—R 3; 15 P—Q R 4, K—R 2; 16 Kt—Kt 3. Ahues—Przepiorka, Frankfurt, 1930.

(c) Kashdan—Flohr, Bled, 1931.

(d) Or 8 , K Kt—K 2; 9 B—K 3, O—O; 10 Q Kt—Q 2, P—K R 3; 11 B—Kt 3, K—R 2; 12 P×P, P×P; 13 B—B 5, P—Kt 3; 14 B—R 3, Kt—R 4; 15 B—Q 5, P—B 3; 16 P—Q Kt 4, Kt—Kt 2 =. Rauser—Löwenfisch, Leningrad, 1934.

(e) Panoff—Bogatyrchuk, Leningrad, 1934.

(f) 8 P×P ?, P×P; 9 B—K 3, Kt—B 3 ! (9.., K Kt—K 2 transposes into col. 180, note (f)); 10 Q Kt—Q 2, Q—K 2; 11 P—Q Kt 4, P—Kt 3; 12 P—K R 3, O—O; 13 B—Kt 3, P—Q R 4; 14 P—Kt 5?, Kt—Q 1; 15 P—Q R 4, Kt—Kt 2 ∓. E. G. Sergeant—Alekhine, Margate, 1938.

(g) A strong alternative is 9 Q—Q 2, O—O; 10 B×Q Kt, B×B; 11 P×P, Q B×P; 12 P×P, P×P; 13 R—K 1, P—Q 4; 14 Kt—Q 4, R—K 1; 15 P—B 3, B—B 4; 16 Kt×B +. Sir G. A. Thomas—W. Gibson, Southsea, 1923.

(h) Yates—Alekhine, New York, 1924, which continued 13 Q Kt—Q 2, P—B 4 ! ∓. The text is recommended by Alekhine.

(i) Stronger than 7 O—O, Kt—Kt 3 which transposes into the next column.

(j) Forced, to prevent 8 Kt—Kt 5.

(k) This is even stronger than 12 P×P, Kt×B; 13 Q×Kt, Kt×P; 14 Kt×P, K×Kt; 15 Q×Kt ch, B—K 3; 16 Q—B 3 ch, K—K.1; 17 Kt—Q 2, Q—Kt 4; 18 Q×P, R—Q 1, when Black has dangerous counter-chances. Ahues—Rubinstein, San Remo, 1930.

(l) 14 ., K×Kt; 15 P×B P, Q×P; 16 Q×Kt ch, B—K 3; 17 Q—B 3 ch, with P—Q 5 and Kt—Q 2 to follow. Analysis by A. Becker.

(m) Or 7.., P—R 3; 8 Q Kt—Q 2?, P—K Kt 4. E. G. Sergeant—Rubinstein, Scarborough, 1930.

(n) 10.., Q—K 1, threatening Kt×P; 11 B—B 2 (somewhat stronger than 11 P—Q 5, Kt—Q 1; 12 B×B, Q×B; 13 Kt—Kt 3, P—B 3; 14 Kt—B 5 ±. Asztalos—Stoltz, Bled, 1931), K—R 1; 12 Kt—Kt 3, B—Kt 5; 13 P—Q 5, Kt—Q Kt 1; 14 P—K R 3 +. Lasker—Steinitz, Hastings, 1895.

(o) H. Johner, Michel and Naegeli—Alekhine and O. S. Bernstein, Le Pont, 1930.

1 P—K 4, P—K 4 ; 2 Kt—K B 3, Kt—Q B 3 ; 3 B—Kt 5.

STEINITZ DEFENCE DEFERRED
(SIESTA VARIATION)

3 .., P—Q R 3 ; 4 B—R 4, P—Q 3 ; 5 P—B 3, P—B 4.

	186	187	188	189	190
6	P×P !			P—Q 4 ?	
	B×P			B P×P	
7	P—Q 4			Kt—Kt 5 (h)	
	P—K 5			P×P	P—Q 4
8	Kt—Kt5! (a)		P—Q 5	Kt×K P	P×P
	B—K 2	Kt—B 3 (c)	P×Kt	Kt—B 3 (i)	B—Q B 4 !
9	O—O !	P—B 3	P×Kt	B—K Kt 5	P—K 6 (k)
	B×Kt	P—Q 4	P—Q Kt 4	B—K 2	Q—B 3
10	Q—R 5 ch	O—O	Q×B P	B×Kt (j)	O—O
	B—Kt 3	Q—Q 2	B×Kt !	B×B	P—K 6
11	Q×B	P—Q B 4 ! (d)	B—Kt 3	Q—R 5 ch	Kt—B 7
	Q×Q	P—R 3 (e)	B—Kt 3	K—B 1	P×P ch
12	B×Q	P×Q P	O—O	O—O	K—R 1
	Kt—K 2	P×Kt	Kt—B 3	B—K 3 ∓	B×P
13	Kt—Q 2	P×Kt	B—Kt 5		Kt×R
	P—Kt 4	Kt P×P	B—K 2		Kt—K 2 ∓
14	B—Kt 3	B×Kt P	K R—K 1		(l)
	P—Q 4	B—Q 3	K—B 1		
15	Q R—K 1 +	P—K Kt3+	R—K 3		
	(b)	(f)	P—R 3 (g)		

(a) Much stronger than either 8 Q—K 2, B—K 2 ; 9 K Kt—Q 2, Kt—B 3 ;
10 P—K R 3, P—Q 4 ; 11 Kt—B 1, P—Q Kt 4 ; 12 B—B 2, Kt—Q R 4 ; 13 Kt—K 3,
B—Kt 3 ; 14 Kt—Q 2, O—O= (Capablanca—Marshall, 14th match game, 1909) ; or
8 B—K Kt 5, B—K 2 ; 9 K—R 4, B—K 3 10 B×B, K Kt×B ! ; 11 Q—R 5 ch,
P—Kt 3 ; 12 Q—R 6, Kt—Kt 1 ! ; 13 Q—B 4, Kt—B 3 ; 14 Kt—Q 2, O—O ; 15 O—O,
P—Q 4 ∓. A. Steiner—Capablanca, Budapest, 1928.
(b) 15 ., K—Q 2 ; 16 P—B 3, P×P ; 17 R×P !. Szabo—Znosko-Borovsky,
Tata-Tovaros, 1935.
(c) If 8 .., P—R 3 ; 9 P—Q 5, P—Kt 4 ; 10 B—B 2 + ; or 8 .., P—Q 4 ; 9 P—B 3,
P—K 6 ? ; 10 P—K B 4 +. Horowitz—Fine, Syracuse, 1934.
(d) Weaker is 11 P×P, Kt×K P ; 12 Kt×Kt, B×Kt ; 13 Kt—Q 2, B—Kt 3 ;
14 Kt—B 3, P—Kt 4 ; 15 B—Kt 3, B—K 2 when Black's position is tenable. A. Steiner—
Kashdan, Prague, 1931.
(e) White's threat was 11 P×Q P, Q×P ; 12 Kt—B 3++. 11 ., Q P×P
12 P—Q 5 costs Black a piece, while if 11 .., B—Q Kt 5 ; 12 P—Q R 3, B—R 4 ;
13 P—Q Kt 4, B—Kt 3 ; 14 P—B 5, B—R 2 ; 15 Kt—B 3 +.
(f) 15 .., O—O—O ; 16 Kt—B 3.
(g) 16 B×Kt, B×B ; 17 Q—Q 5, P—K R 4 ; 18 P—Kt 3, Q—B 1 ; 19 R—K 6,
Q—Q 1 ; 20 R—K 3, Q—B 1 ; 21 R—K 6, Q—Q 1. Draw by repetition of moves.
Capablanca—H. Steiner, New York, 1931.
(h) If 7 Kt×P ?, P×Kt ; 8 Q—R 5 ch, K—K 2 ; 9 B—Kt 5 ch, Kt—B 3 ;
10 K B×Kt, P×B ; 11 P×P, Q—Q 4 ; 12 B—R 4, K—Q 2 ! and Black wins (Tartakover).
(i) But not P—Q 4 ? ; 9 Q—R 5 ch, P—Kt 3 ; 10 Q—K 5 ch, Q—K 2 ;
11 Q×P (Q 5), Q—K 3 ; 12 B×Kt ch, P×B ; 13 Q×Q P +. L. Steiner—Boros, 1931.
(j) 10 Q×P ?, P—Kt 4 ; 11 Kt×Kt ch, P×Kt ; 12 Q—Q 5, Kt P×B ! ; 13 B—R 6,
Q—Q 2 + +. Réti—Capablanca, Berlin, 1928. If 10 B×Kt ch, P×B ; 11 Q×P, O—O+.
(k) White's position is already bad. If (1) 9 O—O, Kt—K 2 ; 10 P—K 6, Q—Q ;
11 Q—R 5, P—R 3 ; 12 Kt—B 7, Q—K 1 ; 13 B×P, B×P ; 14 B×P, K×B ;
15 Q—R 6 ch, K×Kt++. Gromer—Znosko-Borovsky, Paris, 1930. (2) 9 P—Q B 4,
P—K 6 ; 10 P—B 4, P—Q 5 ; 11 B—B 2, P—K Kt 3 ; 12 Kt×P, Kt×Kt ; 13 B×P ch,
K—B 1 ; 14 B×P, Q×P—R 5 ch ; 15 P—Kt 3, Q×B +. Analysis by Spielmann.
(3) 9 Q—K 2, Kt—K 2 ; 10 O—O, P—Kt 4 ; 11 B—Kt 3, Kt×P ; 12 K—R 1, P—R 3 ;
13 Kt—K R 3, B×Kt ; 14 Q—R 5 ch, K Kt—Kt 3 ; 15 Q×B, O—O ! +. Vajda—
Znosko-Borovsky, Nice, 1931.
(l) Analysis by Znosko-Borovsky.

1 P—K 4, P—K 4 ; 2 Kt—K B 3, Kt—Q B 3 ; 3 B—Kt 5.

UNUSUAL DEFENCES

	191	192	193	194	195
3	P—B 4 (a)				P—Q R 3
4	P—Q 3	Kt—B 3 !			B—R 4
	P×P	Kt—B 3	Kt—Q 5	P×P	P—B 4
5	P×P	P×P !	B—B 4	Q Kt×P	P—Q 4 !
	Kt—B 3	P—K 5 (c)	P—B 3	Kt—B 3 (A)	B P×P
6	O—O	Kt—Kt 5	O—O	Kt×Kt ch	Kt×P
	P—Q 3	P—Q 4	Kt×Kt ch	P×Kt	Kt—B 3 (h)
7	B—Kt 5	P—Q 3	Q×Kt	P—Q 4	O—O
	B—K 2	B×P	Q—B 3	P—Q 3 (f)	B—K 2
8	B×Kt	P×P	P—Q 4 !	O—O	Kt—Q B 3
	B×B	P×P	K P×P	B—Q 2	O—O
9	Q—Q 5 !	Q—K 2	P—K 5	R—K 1	B—Kt 3 ch
	B—Q 2	B—Q Kt 5	Q—R 5	Q—K 2	P—Q 4
10	Kt—B 3	B—Q 2	Kt—K 2	P×P	B—Kt 5
	Q—B 1	Q—K 2	B—B 4	Q P×P	K—R 1
11	Q R—Q 1	B×Ktch+	P—Q Kt 4+	B×Kt	P—B 4 (i)
	Kt—Q 1 (b)	(d)	(e)	B×B (g)	

	196	197	198	199	200
3	P—Q R 3	P—B 3	B—K 2	B—Kt 5 (m)	P—Q R 3
4	B—R 4	O—O	O—O	P—B 3	B—R 4
	K Kt—K 2	K Kt—K 2	B—B 3	B—R 4	B—Kt 5
5	Kt—B 3 !	P—Q 4	P—B 3	Kt—R 3	O—O
	P—K Kt 3	Kt—Kt 3	K Kt—K 2	B—Kt 3	K Kt—K 2
6	P—Q 4	P—Q R 3	P—Q 4	Kt—B 4	P—B 3
	B—Kt 2	B—K 2	Kt—Kt 3	P—Q 3	B—R 4
7	P×P	B—Q B 4	P×P	P—Q 4	P—Q 4
	Kt×P	P—Q 3	Q Kt×P	P×P	P×P
8	Kt×Kt	B—R 3	Kt×Kt	P—Q R 4 !	P×P
	B×Kt	B—Q 2	B×Kt	P×P	P—Q 4
9	B—R 6	Kt—B 3	P—K B 4	P—R 5	P×P
	P—Q B 4	Q—B 1	B—Q 3 !	B—Q B 4·	Q×P
10	B—Kt 3	K—R 2	B—K 3	P—Q Kt 4+	B—Kt 3
	P—Q Kt 4 (j)	Kt—Q 1 (k)	Q—K 2 (l)		Q—R 4 ! =

(a) The Schliemann Defence, against which 4 P—Q 4 is inferior.
(b) S. R. Wolff—Spielmann, Vienna, 1928. White has a slight pull.
(c) 5 , B—B 4; 6 O—O, O—O; 7 Kt×P', Kt—Q 5; 8 B—R 4, P—Q 4; 9 Kt—K 2!+. E. Cohn—Dus-Chotimirsky, Carlsbad, 1907.
(d) 11 , P×B, 12 Q—B 4. Leonhardt—Spielmann, 1906.
(e) Bogoljuboff—Réti, Stockholm, 1919.
(A) 5 , B—K 2; 6 Q—K 2, Kt—B 3; 7 Kt×Kt, B×Kt; 8 P—Q 4, O—O; 9 B×Kt, Q P×B; 10 P×P, B—K 2; 11 B—K 3, Q—Q 4 (threatening B—K Kt 5); 12 Q—Q 3, Q—B 2, 13 O—O, B—K 3. Budapest—Berlin, correspondence, 1938 Black has compensation for his Pawn.
(f) If 7 , P—K 5, 8 Kt×Kt 5, B—Kt 5 ch; 9 P—B 3, P×Kt; 10 Q—R 5 ch +.
(g) 12 Kt×P!, P×Kt; 13 Q—R 5 ch, Q—B 2 (E. G. Sergeant—Spielmann, Margate, 1938); 14 Q×P ch, K—Q 2; 15 Q—Q 4 ch!, and White wins.
(h) 6 , Kt×Kt; 7 P×Kt, Q—K 2; 8 Q—Q 4, Q—Kt 5 ch; 9 Q×Q, B×Q ch; 10 P—B 3 +.
(i) 11 ., P×P e.p.; 12 R×P, Kt—Q R 4; 13 B×P +. Teichmann—Spielmann, match, 1914. The Schliemann Defence Deferred.
(j) 11 B—Q 5, R—R 2; 12 Q—B 3, Kt×B; 13 Kt×Kt, P—Q 3; 14 O—O—O +. Marco—Alekhine, The Hague, 1921. The Cozio Defence Deferred.
(k) Tarrasch—Steinitz, Nuremburg, 1896. 11 Kt—Q 5 +.
(l) 11 B—Q 3 +. Judd—Showalter, 1890.
(m) Alapin's Defence, a name which is also applied to the next column. Other inferior defences are 3 , P—K Kt 4 (Brentano's); 3. , Q—B 3; and 3.., B—Q 5.

SCOTCH OPENING

This old opening (of which the name dates from the time of a game between Edinburgh and London over a century ago) arises from the moves 1 P—K 4, P—K 4; 2 Kt—K B 3, Kt—Q B 3; 3 P—Q 4. After the usual reply 3..., P × P; 4 Kt × P leads into the Scotch Game, and 4 B—Q B 4 or 4 P—B 3 into the Scotch Gambit.

Of these, the Scotch Game is the more important; and, though the whole opening was condemned by Tarrasch as incorrect, a certain number of examples are still found, if in diminishing quantity, in modern master tournaments. White obtains a free and open development of his pieces, but cannot prevent Black from equalising the game.

There are three lines of defence :—

(i) 4..., Kt—B 3 (cols. 1 to 7), favoured in master play. This defence leads to a positional type of game, which Tarrasch and other authorities consider in Black's favour. Col. 2 shows a variation revived by Mieses with some little success, but inadequate against the best defence. Tartakover has reintroduced an old Steinitz line in col. 3, but Black obtains a slight advantage with 6..., B—B 4. In the Four Knights' form of the Scotch Game (cols. 5 to 7) Black can equalise in various ways, the simplest of which is the line in col. 7, due to Rubinstein.

(ii) 4..., Q—R 5 (col. 8), an inferior line yielding White considerable advantage.

(iii) 4..., B—B 4 (cols. 9 to 20), leading to an intricate and combinational type of game, in which Black obtains an advantage in most variations. The speculative Blumenfeld Attack (col. 10) has been discredited by Bardeleben's

K

investigations. In the older forms (cols. 11 to 20), White has the choice of seven lines on his 7th move, of which only Meitner's suggestion, Kt—B 2 (cols. 14 and 15), seems to give him a reasonably good game.

Scotch Gambit.

This Gambit leads to an open game for White, in which he has little compensation for the Pawn sacrificed and is frequently hard pressed to attain equality.

4 B—Q B 4 (cols. 1 to 3) yields positions similar to the Giuoco Piano, Max Lange, and Two Knights' Defence, into which it may readily transpose. The Göring Gambit (cols. 4 and 5) is similar to the Danish Gambit, with one variation of which it unites on the 6th move in col. 4, but has fewer resources for the attack.

1 P—K 4, P—K 4 ; 2 Kt—K B 3, Kt—Q B 3 ; 3 P—Q 4, P×P ; 4 Kt×P, Kt—B 3.

	1	2	3	4	5
5	Kt×Kt				Kt—Q B 3
	Kt P×Kt				B—Kt 5
6	B—Q 3		Kt—Q 2	P—K 5	Kt×Kt
	P—Q 4 (a)		B—B 4 (f)	Q—K 2	Kt P× Kt
7	P×P (b)	P—K 5 (d)	B—Q 3 (g)	Q—K 2	B—Q 3 (k)
	P×P	Kt—Kt 5	O—O	Kt—Q 4	P—Q 4
8	B—Kt5ch(c)	B—K B 4	O—O	Kt—Q 2 (i)	P×P
	B—Q 2	B—Q B 4	P—Q 4	B—Kt 2	P×P
9.	B×B ch	O—O	Q—B 3	Kt—Kt 3	O—O (l)
	Q×B	P—K Kt 4	Kt—Kt 5	O—O—O	O—O
10	O—O	B—Q 2	P×P	P—Q B 4 (j)	B—K Kt 5
	B—K 2	Q—K 2	Q—Q 3	Kt—Kt 3	B×Kt
11	Kt—Q 2	B—B 3	Q—Kt 3	B—Q 2	P×B
	O—O	B—K 3	Q×Q	R—K 1	Q—Q 3
12	P—Q Kt 3	P—K R 3	R P×Q	P—B 4	Q—B 3 (m)
	K R—K 1	P—K R 4	P×P	P—B 3	B—Kt 5
13	Kt—B 3	Kt—Q 2	Kt—Kt 3	P—Q R 4	Q—B 4
	Kt—K 5	Kt×B P	B—Kt 3	B—R 3	Q×Q .
14	B—Kt 2 =	R×Kt	B—K B 4 (h)	Q—K 4	B×Q
		P—Kt 5 (e)	B—K 3 ∓	Q—B 2 ∓	P—B 3 =

(a) 6.., B—B 4 ; 7 P—K 5, Kt—Q 4 ; 8 O—O, O—O ; 9 Kt—Q 2, P—Q 3 ; 10 Kt—K 4 ± is weaker. The column is Maróczy—Janowski, London, 1899.

(b) Or 7 Q—K 2, P×P ; 8 B×P, Kt×B ; 9 Q×Kt ch, Q—K 2 ; 10 Q×Q ch, B×Q =.

(c) Or 8 O—O, B—K 2 ; 9 Kt—B 3, O—O.

(d) 7 Kt—B 3, B—Q Kt 5 transposes into col. 5.

(e) 15 Kt—Kt 3, B×R ch ; 16 K×B, P×P +. Mieses—Fuchs, 1923.

(f) 6.., P—Q 4 ; 7 P×P, P×P ; 8 B—Kt 5 ch, B—Q 2 ; 9 B×B ch, Q×B ; 10 O—O, B—K 2 ; 11 Kt—B 3, O—O ; 12 B—Kt 5 ±.

(g) 7 P—K 5, Q—K 2 ; 8 Q—K 2, Kt—Q 4 ; 9 Kt—Kt 3, B—Kt 3 ; 10 B—Q 2, P—Q R 4 ; 11 P—Q R 4, O—O ; 12 O—O—O (Tartakover—Ed. Lasker, New York, 1924), P—B 3 ! +.

(h) Tartakover—Jacobson, Copenhagen, 1923.

(i) 8 P—K Kt 3, P—K 3 ; 9 B—K Kt 2, B—K Kt 2 ; 10 P—K B 4, Q—B 4 ; 11 P—B 3, O—O ; 12 B×Kt, Q×B ; 13 O—O, P—B 3 ∓.

(j) If 10 Kt—R 5, Q—Kt 5 ch ; 11 Q—Q 2, Q—K 5 ch + (Kmoch). The column is Mieses—Tarrasch, Metz, 1916.

(k) A novel attempt to get something out of this position for White is 7 B—Q 2, but after 7.., O—O ; 8 B—Q 3, P—Q 4 ; 9 P—B 3 !?, P×P ; 10 Kt×P, Kt×Kt ; 11 P×Kt, B—Q B 4 ; 12 Q—B 3, Q R—Kt 1 Black stands well. Alekhine—Alexander, Margate, 1937. Here Black can force a draw by 9.., B×Kt ; 10 B×B, P×P ; 11 B×P, Kt×B ; etc.

(l) Or 9 B—Kt 5 ch, B—Q 2 ; 10 B×B ch, Q×B ; 11 O—O, O—O ; 12 Q—Q 3, K R—K 1 =. Bogoljuboff—Euwe, Carlsbad, 1929. Or here 10 Q—K 2 ch, Q—K 2 ; 11 B×B ch, Kt×B ; 12 Q×Q ch, K×Q ; 13 B—Q 2, Kt—Kt 3 ; 14 O—O—O, P—Q B 3 =. Sir G. A. Thomas—Alexander, Hastings, 1937-38.

(m) 12 B×Kt, Q×B ; 13 Q—R 5, P—K Kt 3 ; 14 Q×Q P, B—K 3 ; 15 Q—Q 4, Q—K 2 leaves Black with freedom of action to compensate for the doubled Pawn minus (Tartakover). The column is Maróczy—Rubinstein, Carlsbad, 1929.

1 P—K 4, P—K 4; 2 Kt—K B 3, Kt—Q B 3; 3 P—Q 4, P×P ; 4 Kt×P.

	6	7	8	9	10
4	(Kt—B 3)...............		Q—R 5.....B—B 4		
5	(Kt—Q B 3)		Kt—Kt 5 (g)	B—K 3 (h)	
	(B—Kt 5)		Q×K P ch	B—Kt 3.....Q—B 3	
6	(Kt×Kt)		B—K 3	Kt—Q B 3	Kt-Kt 5 ? (j)
	(Kt P×Kt)		K—Q 1	P—Q 3	B×B
7	(B—Q 3)		Kt—Q 2	B—K 2	P×B
	(P—Q 4)		Q—Kt 3	Kt—B 3	Q—R 5 ch
8	(P×P)		Kt—K B 3	Q—Q 2	P—Kt 3
	(P×P)......Q—K 2 ch		P—Q R 3	Kt—K Kt 5	Q×K P (k)
9	(O—O)	Q—K 2	Kt(Kt5)—Q4	B×Kt	Kt×P ch (l)
	(O—O)	Kt×P (e)	K Kt—K 2	B×B	K—Q 1
10	(B—K Kt 5)	Q×Q ch	B—Q 3	P—K R 3	Kt×R
	P—B 3 (a)	K×Q	Q—Q 3	B—Q 2	Kt—B 3
11	Q—B 3	P—Q R 3	O—O ±	Kt—Q 5	Q—Q 6
	B—K 2 (b)	B—R 4		O—O	Q×R
12	Q R—K 1 (c)	B—Q 2		O-O-O ± (i)	Kt—Q 2
	R—Kt 1	Kt×Kt			Kt—K 1
13	Kt—Q 1	B×Kt			Q—B 4
	R—K 1	B×B ch			Q—Q 4
14	P—K R 3	P×B = (f)			B—B 4
	B—K 3 (d)				Q—Q 3 + (m)

(a) A simple reply is 10 ., B—K 3!; 11 Q—B 3 (if 11 B×Kt ?, Q×B; 12 Q—R 5, P—Kt 3; 13 Kt×P ?, Q—Q 1 + +, or 12 Kt×P, B×Kt; 13 Q—R 5, K R—Q 1!+ +), B—K 2; 12 P—K R 3, R—Kt 1; 13 P—Q Kt 3, P—B 4; 14 Q R—Q 1, P—Q 5; 15 Kt—K 4, Kt—Q 4 =. Kan—Goglidse, Moscow, 1925.
(b) Or 11 , R—K 1; 12 B×Kt, Q×B; 13 Q×Q, P×Q; 14 Kt—K 2, B—Kt 5; 15 Kt—Kt 3, R—K 4 =. Spielmann—Balogh, Bucharest, 1934.
(c) Better than 12 K R—K 1, R—Kt 1; 13 Q—Kt 1, P—K R 3; 14 B×P, P×B; 15 Q—K 3, B—Q 3; 16 Q×K R P, R—Kt 5; 17 Q—Kt 5 ch with perpetual check. Romanovsky—Capablanca, Moscow, 1925. Or here 12 Q R—Kt 1, R—Kt 1 (P—Q R 3=), 13 Q—K 3, B—K 3? (R—Kt 2 is necessary); 14 Q×P +. E. M. Jackson—Stoltz, Hastings, 1930.
(d) 15 R—K 2. Spielmann—Yates, Semmering, 1926. White's position is freer.
(e) 9 , Q×Q ch?; 10 K×Q!, P×P? (Somewhat better is 10 ., B×Kt; 11 P×B, P×P; 12 B—R 3 ±); 11 Kt—Kt 5!, K—Q 1; 12 R—Q 1, P—B 3; 13 P—Q B 3 R—K 1 ch; 14 K—B 1, B—B 1; 15 Kt—Q 4 +. Spielmann—Lasker, Moscow, 1935
(f) Spielmann—Rubinstein, Teplitz-Schonau, 1922.
(g) On 5 Kt—K B 3, Q—R 4 reduces Black's disadvantage to a minimum. If however, Q×K P ch?; 6 B—K 2, P—Q 4; 7 O—O, B—K 3; 8 Kt—B 3, Q—B 4. 9 B—Q Kt 5, Kt—K 2; 10 B—Kt 5 +. 5 Q—Q 3?, Kt—B 3; 6 Kt—Q 2, Kt—K Kt 5! 7 P—Kt 3, Q—B 3; 8 Kt—Kt 3, Q Kt—K 4; 9 Q—B 3 (9 Q—K 2, B—B 4), B—Kt 5 and White resigns. W. Prugel—Dr. Dyckhoff, correspondence.
(h) 5 Kt—B 5?, P—Q 4!; 6 Kt×P ch, K—B 1; 7 Kt—R 5, Q—R 5; 8 Kt—Kt 3, Kt—B 3; 9 B—K 2, Kt—K 4!; 10 P—K R 3, R—K Kt 1 +.
(i) Spielmann—Tarrasch, Breslau, 1912.
(j) The Blumenfeld Variation.
(k) Or 8.., Q—Q 1; 9 Q—Kt 4, K—B 1 (better than 9.., P—K Kt 3; 10 Q—B 4, P—Q 3; 11 B—B 4, B—K 3. Spielmann—Rubinstein, Stockholm, 1919); 10 Q—B 4, P—Q 3; 11 B—B 4, Kt—B 3; 12 O—O, P—K R 4; 13 Q Kt—B 3, Kt—K 4; 14 B—Kt 3, P—B 3; 15 Kt—Q 4, P—R 5 +.
(l) Or 9 Q Kt—B 3, Q×R; 10 Kt×P ch, K—Q 1; 11 Q—Q 6, Kt—B 3; 12 Kt×R, Q—B 6; 13 Kt—B 7, Q×K P ch +.
(m) 15 O—O—O, P—B 3. Analysis by Bardeleben and Dr. von Claparède.

1 P—K 4, P—K 4 ; 2 Kt—K B 3, Kt—Q B 3 ; 3 P—Q 4, PxP;
4 KtxP, B—B 4 ; 5 B—K 3, Q—B 3 ; 6 P—Q B 3, K Kt—K 2.

	11	12	13	14	15
7	B—Q Kt 5... O—O	B—K 2..... P—Q 4	P—KB 4 (c).. Q—Kt 3	Kt—B 2 ! BxB......	 P—Q 3
8	O—O BxKt (a)	O—O BxKt	Q—B 3 KtxKt	KtxB O—O (d)	Kt—Q 2 B—K 3
9	PxB P—Q 4	PxB PxP	PxKt B—Kt 5 ch	B—K 2 P—Q 3	B—K 2 BxB
10	Kt—B 3 PxP	P—Q 5 Kt—K 4	Kt—B 3 P—Q 4	O—O B—K 3	KtxB O—O
11	KtxP Q—Kt 3 =	Q—R 4 ch P—B 3	P—K 5 Q—B 7 +	Kt—Q 2 P—Q 4	O—O P—Q 4
12		Kt—B 3 O—O (b)		PxP KtxP (e)	P—K B 4 P—Q 5 ! (f)

	16	17	18	19	20
7	Q—O 2............................ P—Q 4 (g)			Kt—Q 2 KtxKt.....	.....O—O (j) O—O (j)
8	Kt—Kt 5 BxB			P—K 5 Kt—B 7 ch	KtxKt QxKt
9	QxB.................. O—O		PxB O—O	QxKt QxP	BxB QxB
10	Kt—Q 2..... PxP	KtxB P R—Kt 1	KtxB P PxP	Kt—B 4 Q—K 3	B—K 2 P—B 4
11	KtxK P Q—K 4	Kt—Q 2 (h) PxP	KtxR R—Q 1	O—O—O BxB ch	O—O PxP
12	O—O—O	KtxP Q—K 4	Q—B 1 Kt—B 4	KtxB QxP	KtxP Q—K 4
13		Kt—Q Kt 5 Kt—Q 4	P—K Kt 3 Q—Kt 4 (i)	Q—K 4 Q—K 3 +	Q—Q 4 =

(a) 8.., P—Q 3; 9 Kt—R 3, Q—Kt 3; 10 R—K 1, Kt—K 4; 11 Q Kt—B 2, P—B 4; 12 PxP, KtxP; 13 KtxKt, BxKt; 14 BxB ±. Mieses—E. G. Sergeant, Margate, 1935.

(b) Alekhine and Reilly—Stoltz and Monosson, Nice, 1931.

(c) 7 B—Q B 4, Kt—K 4; 8 B—K 2, Q—K Kt 3; 9 O—O, P—Q 4 +. The column is analysis by Steinitz.

(d) 8.., Q—K 4; 9 Q—B 3, O—O; 10 B—B 4, P—Q 3; 11 Kt—Q 2, B—K 3; 12 O—O =. Tartakover—Tarrasch, Vienna, 1922.

(e) 13 KtxKt, BxKt; 14 B—B 3, Q R—Q 1 ∓. Martinez—Zukertort, 1884

(f) Tartakover—Brinckmann, Niendorf, 1927.

(g) 7. , BxKt?; 8 PxB, P—Q 4; 9 Kt—B 3, PxP; 10 P—Q 5, Kt—K 4; 11 Kt—Kt 5!, O—O!; 12 KtxB P +. Kashdan—Reshevsky, New York, 1936.

(h) 11 KtxP, KtxKt; 12 PxKt, Kt—Kt 5; 13 PxKt, QxP; 14 Q—Q B 3, R—K 1 ch +. Von Gottschall's Attack.

(i) 14 K—B 2, Kt—K 4; 15 B—K 2, R—Q 6 +. Analysis by Steinitz.

(j) 7. , BxKt; 8 PxB, P—Q 4; 9 P—K 5, Q—Kt 3 is inferior. The column is Mieses—Spielmann, Gothenburg, 1920.

1 P—K 4, P—K 4 ; 2 Kt—K B 3, Kt—Q B 3 ; 3 P—Q 4, P×P.

	1	2	3	4	5
4	B—Q B 4 (a)			P—B 3 (g)	
	B—B 4		B—Kt 5 ch	P×P (h)	
5	P—B 3 (b)		P—B 3	B—Q B 4	
	P×P (c)	P—Q 6	P×P	Kt—B 3	P—Q 3
6	Kt×P (d)	P—Q Kt 4	O—O	Kt×P	Kt×P
	P—Q 3	B—Kt 3	P—Q 3	B—Kt 5	B—K 3
7	Q—Kt 3 (e)	P—Q R 4 (f)	P—Q R 3	O—O	B×B
	Q—Q 2	P—Q R 3	B—Q B 4	B×Kt	P×B
8	Kt—Q 5	O—O	P—Q Kt 4	P×B	Q—Kt 3
	K Kt—K 2	P—Q 3	P—B 7	O—O	Q—B 1
9	Q—B 3	Q—Kt 3	Q×B P	Q—B 2	Kt—K Kt 5
	O—O	Q—K 2	B—Kt 3	P—Q 3	Kt—Q 1
10	O—O	B—K Kt 5	Q—Kt 3	P—K 5	P—B 4
		Kt—B 3	Q—K 2	Kt×P	B—K 2
11		Q Kt—Q 2	Kt—B 3	Kt×Kt	O—O
		O—O	B—K 3	P×Kt	B×Kt
12		B×P	Kt—Q 5	B—R 3	P×B
		Kt—K 4	B×Kt	R—K 1	Kt—K 2
13		P—B 4	P×B +	QR–Q1 = (i)	Kt— Kt 5
					P—h 4+ (j)

(a) 4 B—Q Kt 5 is the variation called by Blackburne the " Mac-Lopez," best met by B—B 4 and if 5 O—O, K Kt—K 2.

(b) For 5 O—O, P—Q 3 ; 6 P—B 3, B—K Kt 5 see Giuoco Piano, col. 23. For 5 O—O, Kt—B 3 ; 6 P—K 5, see Max Lange. If 5 Kt—Kt 5, Kt—R 3 , 6 Q—R 5, Q—K 2 ; 7 O—O, P—Q 3 ; 8 P—K R 3, B—Q 2 ; 9 P—B 4, O—O—O ∓ (Steinitz). Or here 6 Kt×B P, Kt×Kt ; 7 B×Kt ch, K×B ; 8 Q—R 5 ch, P—Kt 3 ; 9 Q×B, R—K 1 ∓.

(c) 5 .., P—Q 3 ; or 5 ., Kt—B 3 transposing into the Giuoco Piano.

(d) Or 6 B×P ch, K×B ; 7 Q—Q 5 ch, K—B 1 ; 8 Q×B ch, Q—K 2 =.

(e) Or 7 B—K Kt 5, Q—Q 2 ; 8 Q—Q 2, P—K R 3 ; 9 B—R 4, K Kt—K 2 ; 10 O—O—O, Kt—Kt 3 ; 11 B—K Kt 3, P—R 3 ; 12 Kt—Q 5, P—Kt 4 , 13 B—Kt 3, B—Kt 2 ; 14 K—Kt 1, O—O—O ; 15 R—Q B 1 ! (Em. Lasker). The column is Tartakover's analysis.

(f) If 7 P—Kt 5, Kt—R 4 ; 8 B×P, P—Q 4 +. The column is P. Johner—Nyholm, Baden, 1914.

(g) The Göring Gambit. At move 6 in this column cp. Danish Gambit, cols. 6 and 7.

(h) 4.., P—Q 4 ; 5 K P×P, Q×P leads into the Danish Gambit. 4.., P—Q 6 is a safe defence.

(i) Réti—Hromadka, Baden, 1914.

(j) 14 Q—B 4, K Kt—B 3 ; 15 P—Kt 6, P×P ; 16 B—Kt 5. Marco—Spielmann, Gothenburg, 1920.

SICILIAN DEFENCE

The Sicilian has claims to be considered as the best of the irregular defences to 1 P—K 4 at Black's disposal, and has been practised with satisfactory results by the leading players, past and present.   Its characteristic is struggle in the opening, and struggle in the middle-game, so that it is not for those who are contented with a draw.   The chief object of the struggle is the control of the centre, at which Black strikes with his first move 1..., P—Q B 4, and later generally with a fianchetto-development for one or other of his Bishops.

After the customary 2 Kt—K B 3 Black has the choice of four main replies :—

(i) 2..., P—K 3 (cols. 1 to 25) is gradually falling into discredit.   The Scheveningen Variation (cols. 1 to 7) is the most important here; Maróczy's continuation (cols. 1 to 3), which is the introduction to a vigorous King-side onslaught, still holds the field as White's best reply.   It leads to a violent attack and counter-attack, where White generally wins.   The alternative to Maróczy's continuation is 8 B—K 3 (cols. 4 and 5), which is also quite strong.   In the Scheveningen Variation Black's Queen's Knight is developed at Q B 3; some masters, notably Tartakover, prefer the development at Q 2, with the idea of an eventual Kt—B 4, attacking White's King's Pawn, but in the positions reached Black has too little scope for his pieces.

Since the usual position of Black's Pawns—at Q 3 and K 3—condemns Black's King's Bishop to inactivity, the second player sometimes tries to institute a counter-attack by developing this piece at Q Kt 5; this gives rise to wild positions full of brilliant possibilities for both sides.   White has three replies at his disposal :—(i) 6 Kt—Kt 5 (cols 13 and 14), inferior against the surprising rejoinder 6..., P—Q 4 (col. 14); (ii) 6 P—K 5 (col. 15) is the strongest line; White submits to a weakening of his Pawn-position in order to hinder Black's development; (iii) 6 B—Q 3 (cols. 16 and 17), against which Jaffe's Variation equalises (col. 1—)

The Sicilian Four Knights' (cols. 18 and 19) is one of Black's strongest lines. After 6 B—K 2 the counter-attack 6..., B—Kt 5 is more effective than on the previous move.

The Paulsen Defence (cols. 22 to 24) is still occasionally played, notably by Tartakover, but White can secure a clear superiority in a number of different ways. Marshall's Variation 3..., P—Q 4 (col. 25) is theoretically unsound.

(ii) 2..., Kt—Q B 3 (cols. 26 to 47), followed by an early King's Fianchetto, is the line preferred by most masters nowadays. The counter-attack against White's Q 4 is exceptionally strong, and gives Black far more counter-play than (i). The normal continuation is the Dragon Variation (cols. 26 to 36), which gives rise to extremely complex positions, where it is difficult to decide who stands better. White has the choice of simple development, coupled with the advance of his King's Bishop's Pawn, or of delaying Castling and playing for a King-side attack. In the former case White must withdraw his Knight from Q 4 to prevent Black from liberating his game by P—Q 4. The continuation in col. 26, due to Spielmann, gives White a minimal positional advantage, although Spielmann could not turn this to account in the games involved. In the latter case recent tournament play has shown that Black's position can withstand all attacks. The extraordinarily brilliant game Alekhine—Botvinnik, Nottingham, 1936, quoted in col. 33, is still the last word on this crucial variation. The Richter Attack (cols. 37 and 38), which was a mere footnote in our last edition, has considerably enriched the theory of the Sicilian Defence. Its object is to prevent Black from adopting the Dragon formation. In this it is certainly successful; whether it leads to a winning advantage, as some maintain, is doubtful. Most masters pay the sincere tribute to the Richter Attack of avoiding it. It should be noted that the Dragon formation can be reached without submitting to the danger of the Richter Attack; see (iii). Black is not well-advised to vary from the customary order of the moves, as the lines in cols. 41 to 45 indicate. In cols. 42 and 43,

where Black tries the fianchetto before developing his
King's Knight, Maróczy's 5 P—Q B 4 comes very near to
conferring a winning advantage. Attention must be called
to Nimzovitch's line in col. 46. It is practically never seen,
yet no clear refutation is known.

(iii) 2..., P—Q 3 (cols. 48 to 50) can be called the
" modern " variation, adopted chiefly in order to avoid the
Richter Attack. The most important continuation with this
move is the Dragon Variation; in cols. 48 to 50 are shown
attempts by White to avoid the routine lines of this variation. Col. 48 is a complicated game with chances for both
sides. The attack with 5 P—K B 3 (cols. 49 and 50) is
played with the object of substituting P—Q B 4 for Kt—
K B 3, thereby transposing into a kind of Maróczy system
(as in cols. 42 and 43). Black can prevent this by P—K 4,
shown in col. 50.

(iv) 2..., Kt—K B 3 (cols. 51 to 54), introduced by
Nimzovitch, has the same strategical goals as Alekhine's
Defence : Black wishes to provoke the advance of White's
centre Pawns in the hope that these will later become weak.
Innovations since our last edition have shown that this line
is much more dangerous than was formerly thought to be
the case. If White plays 3 P—K 5, Kt—Q 4; 4 Kt—B 3
Black has the choice of 4..., P—K 3, which enables White
to build up a strong attack at the expense of a Pawn (col.
51), or the exchange of Knights, which leads to an even
ending, Against 3..., Kt—B 3 Black does best to transpose
into (iii) by 3..., P—Q 3, because the reply 3..., P—Q 4
gives White the opportunity to force a highly favourable
endgame.

Instead of 2 Kt—K B 3 White has also 2 Kt—Q B 3
(cols. 55 and 56); this move, however, is much too passive.
Cols. 57 to 60 and note (n) give unusual first moves for
White.

The Wing Gambit (col. 57) is unsound, but the Wing
Gambit Deferred (col. 58), an idea of Keres's, abounds in
attacking possibilities for White.

SCHEVENINGEN VARIATION

1 P—K 4, P—Q B 4; 2 Kt—K B 3, P—K 3; 3 P—Q 4, P×P;
4 Kt×P, Kt—K B 3; 5 Kt—Q B 3, P—Q 3; 6 B—K 2, Kt—B 3.

	1	2	3	4	5
7	O—O B—K 2				
8	K—R 1 (a)................ P—Q R 3 (b)			B—K 3 P—Q R 3	
9	P—Q R 4.... Q—B 2 (c)	P—B 4 Q—B 2		Q—Q 2...... O—O	P—Q R 4 (j) Q—B 2
10	P—B 4 O—O	B—B 3...... O—O (e)	B—K 3 O—O	P—B 4 (h) Q—B 2	P—B 4 O—O (k)
11	Kt—Kt 3 Kt-Q R 4! (d)	P—K Kt 4 B—Q 2	Q—K 1 B—Q 2	Q R—Q 1 B—Q 2 (i)	Kt—Kt 3 P—Q Kt 3
12	Kt×Kt Q×Kt	P—Kt 5 Kt—K 1	R—Q 1 P—Q Kt 4	B—B 3 Kt—Q R 4	B—B 3 B—Kt 2
13	Q—K 1 Q—B 2	Kt(Q4)—K2 R—B 1	P—Q R 3 Kt—Q R 4	Q—B 2 Kt—B 5	Q—K 1 K R—K 1
14	B—B 3 B—Q 2	P—K R 4 P—Q Kt 4	Q—Kt 3 Kt—B 5	B—B 1 Q R—B 1	R—Q 1 Kt—Q 2
15	B—K 3 K—R 1	P—Q R 3 Kt—R 4	B—B 1 K R—B 1	P—K K Kt4 ±	Q—Kt 3 B—K B 1
16	Q—B 2 B—B 3 =	Kt—Kt3 ± (f)	P—Kt3 ± (g)		R—B 2 ± (l)

(a) Maróczy's continuation.

(b) 8.., O—O; 9 P—B 4, Q—B 2; 10 Kt—Kt 3, B—Q 2; 11 B—B 3, Kt—Q R 4; Kt×Kt, Q×Kt; 13 P—K 5 (13 Q—Q 2 is somewhat better), P×P; 14 P×P, Q×K P; 15 B×P, Q R—Q 1=. Van Doesburgh—Euwe, Zandvoort, 1936.

(c) Or 9.., O—O; 10 Kt—Kt 3, Kt—Q R 4; 11 Kt×Kt, Q×Kt, 12 P—B 4, R—Q 1; 13 B—B 3, B—Q 2; 14 B—K 3, B—B 3; 15 Q—Q 2, Q—Kt 5 ∓. Asztalos—Bogoljuboff, Bled, 1931.

(d) Stronger than 11 , P—Q Kt 3; 12 B—B 3, B—Kt 2; 13 B—K 3, Kt—Q Kt 5; 14 Q—K 2, P—Q 4; 15 P—K 5, Kt—K 5; 16 B×Kt ±. Maróczy—Euwe, Scheveningen, 1923. The column is Leonhardt—Hilse, Magdeburg, 1927.

(e) If 10 , B—Q 2, 11 P—K Kt 4 is again best, for White must attack on the King's side. Weaker continuations after 10 , B—Q 2 are: (1) 11 Kt—Kt 3, R—Q B 1; 12 B—K 3, P—Q Kt 4; 13 Q—K 1, O—O; 14 Q—B 2, R—Kt 1; 15 Q R—Q 1, P—Q R 4 ∓ (Michell—Botvinnik, Hastings, 1934-35); and (2) 11 K Kt—K 2, R—Q B 1; 12 P—Q Kt 3, P—Q Kt 4; 13 P—Q R 3, P—K R 4; 14 Q—K 1, Kt—K Kt 5; 15 Q—Kt 3, B—B 3=. A. Steiner—Pirc, Ujpest, 1934.

(f) White has a strong attack. Maróczy—Pirc, Shac, 1932.

(g) 16 , Kt×R P; 17 P—K 5!. Yates—Takacs, Kecskemét, 1927.

(h) 10 Kt×Kt?, P×Kt; 11 K R—Q 1, Q—B 2; 12 P—B 3, P—Q 4; 13 P×P, B P×P; 14 Q—K 1, Q R—Kt 1; 15 Q R—Kt 1, B—Q 3 ∓. Spielmann—Euwe, Kissingen, 1928.

(i) If 11 , Kt—Q R 4; 12 Q—Q 3, P—Q Kt 4; 13 P—Q Kt 4!, Kt—Kt 2 (not 13.., Kt—B 5?; 14 K Kt×Kt P!, P×Kt; 15 Kt×P+ +); 14 P—Q R 3 (Sir G. A. Thomas—Euwe, Noordwijk, 1938), R—Q 1 (14 , B—Q 2?; 15 P—K 5!, Kt—K 1; 16 Kt—B 5! +); 15 B—B 3, P—Q 4; 16 P×P ±.

(j) 9 P—B 4, Q—B 2; 10 Kt—Kt 3 (or 10 Q—K 1, B—Q 2; 11 B—B 3, Kt—Q R 4; 12 R—Q B 1, R—Q B 1; 13 Q—R 4; 14 B—B 2, P—Q R 4!; 15 P—K Kt 4, P—R 5 with a satisfactory game for Black. Kan—Goglidse, Moscow, 1931.

(k) Or 10 ., B—Q 2; 11 B—B 3, R—Q Kt 1; 12 Kt—Kt 3, Kt—Q R 4; 13 Kt×Kt, Q×Kt; 14 Q—Q 2, Q—B 2; 15 P—R 5 ±. Kashdan—Samisch, Berlin, 1930.

(l) Löwenfisch—Makagonov, Tiflis, 1937.

1 P—K4, P—QB4; 2 Kt—KB3, P—K3; 3 P—Q4, P×P;
4 Kt×P, Kt—KB3; 5 Kt—QB3, P—Q3.

	6	7	8	9	10
6	(B—K2).........				K Kt—K2
	(Kt—B3).......		P—QR3		Kt—B3
7	(O—O) (a)		O—O (f).....B—K3		Kt—B4 (m)
	(B—K2)....P—QR3		Q—B2	P—QKt4	P—QR3
8	P—QKt3	B—K3	B—K3 (g)	P—B3	B—K2
	O—O	Q—B2	B—K2 (h)	B—Kt2	P—QKt4
9	K—R1 (b)	P—B4 (d)	P—B4 (i)	Q—Q2	P—QR3
	B—Q2	Kt—QR4	O—O	B—K2	B—K2
10	B—Kt2	P—B5	B—B3	P—QR4 !	O—O
	P—QR3	Kt—B5	QKt—Q2	P×P	O—O
11	P—B4	B×Kt	Kt—Kt3 (j)	QKt×P	B—K3
	Q—Kt3 !	Q×B	R—QKt1	QKt—Q2	B—Kt2
12	Kt×Kt	P×P	P—QR4	P—QB4	P—B3
	B×Kt	P×P?	P—QKt3	O—O	Q—B2
13	B—B3	R×Kt	Q—K2	O—O	Q—K1
	KR—Q1	P×R	Kt—B4	P—Q4	QR—Q1
14	Q—K2	Q—R5 ch	KR—B1	KP×P	R—Q1
	Q—B2	K—Q1	B—Kt2	P×P	Kt—K4
15	KR—K1	Q—B7+ (e)	Kt-Q2 ± (k)	Kt-KB5 ± (l)	K—R1
	QR—B1 = (c)				Kt-B5 = (n)

(a) An inferior continuation for White is 7 B—K3, B—Q2; 8 Q—Q2, P—QR3;
9 P—B4, Q—B2; 10 Kt—Kt3, P—QKt4, 11 B—B3, R—QKt1; 12 Kt—K2,
B—K2; 13 O—O, O—O; 14 Kt—Kt3, P—QR4! ∓. Lasker—Capablanca, Moscow,
1936.

(b) 9 B—Kt2, Q—R4; 10 Q—Q2, R—Q1; 11 QR—Q1, Kt×Kt; 12 Q×Kt,
Kt—K1; 13 Q—Q3, B—Q2; 14 P—QR3, B—KB3; 15 P—B4, QR—B1 =.
Alekhine—Euwe, 9th match game, 1926-27.

(c) Kunert—Grunfeld, Vienna, 1931.

(d) Or 9 P—QR4, Kt—QR4, 10 Q—Q3, B—Q2; 11 Kt—Kt3, Kt—B3;
12 P—B4, Kt—QKt5; 13 Q—Q2, B—B3; 14 Kt—Q4, P—Q4; 15 P—K5, Kt—K5
with chances for both sides. Sultan Khan—Pirc, Hastings, 1932-33. If 9 Q—K1,
Kt—K4; 10 P—Q1, P—B4; 11 P—B4, Kt—B5; 12 B—B1, B—Kt2;
13 B—B3, R—QB1; 14 P—B5, P—Kt5; 15 Kt—Kt1, P—K4 ∓. Canal—A.
Steiner, Budapest, 1933.

(e) Lasker—Pirc, Moscow, 1935. If now 15.., B—K2; 16 Kt—B5!, R—K1
(on 16.., Q—B2; 17 Kt—QR4 wins); 17 Kt×P!, B×Kt; 18 B—Kt6 ch, B—B2;
19 Q—QB1 ch and wins.

(f) P—QR4 is not essential in this variation: after 7 P—QR4, P—QKt3;
8 B—K3, B—Kt2; 9 P—B3, B—K2; 10 O—O, O—O; 11 Q—Q2, QKt—Q2;
12 B—Q2, Q—B2; 13 Kt—R2, B—B4; 14 P—QKt4, QKt—Q2; 15 P—QB4;
KR—Q1 (Sir G. A. Thomas—Petrov, Margate, 1938), White must soon weaken his
Pawn position.

(g) If 8 K—R1?, P—QKt4; 9 P—QR3, B—Kt2; 10 Q—K1, QKt—Q2;
11 B—Kt5, P—KR3 (11.., Kt×P?; 12 Kt×Kt, B×Kt; 13 B×P +); 12 B×Kt,
Kt×B; 13 B×P +); 12 B×Kt, Kt×B; 13 P—B4, B—K2 ∓. Vajda—Alekhine, Kecskemét, 1927. Or here 10 P—B3,
B—K2; 11 Q—K1, O—O; 12 B—Kt5, QKt—Q2; 13 P—B4, Kt—Kt3; 14 B—Q3,
P—R3; 15 B—R4, QR—B1; 16 R—B3, Kt—B5 ∓. Réthy—Flohr, Ujpest,
1934.

(h) If 8.., P—QKt4; 9 P—B3, B—K2; 10 Q—Q2, O—O; 11 P—QR4 ±.
Post—Becker, Vienna, 1924.

(i) Or 9 P—QR4, P—QKt3; 10 Kt—Kt3, O—O; 11 P—B4, B—Kt2;
12 B—B3, Q Kt—Q2; 13 Q—K1, P—Q4!?; 14 P×P, Kt×P; 15 Kt×Kt, P×Kt;
16 Q—B2±. Ilyin-Zhenevsky—Alatorzev, Tiflis, 1937.

(j) Or 11 Q—K1, Kt—Kt3; 12 R—Q1, B—Q2; 13 P—Kt4, QR—B1;
14 P—Kt5, Kt—K1; 15 Q—Q3 ±. If instead 15 Q—Kt3, Kt—B5; 16 B—B1,
Q—Kt3; 17 P—Kt3, Kt—K4! =. Kan—Ragosin, Moscow, 1936.

(k) Enoch—Bogoljuboff, Berlin, 1927.

(l) Yates—Noteboom, Prague, 1931.

(m) 7 P—KKt3, B—K2; 8 B—Kt2, P—QR3; 9 O—O, Q—B2; 10 P—QR4,
O—O; 11 P—Kt3, KR—Q1; 12 B—Kt2, Kt—QKt5; 13 Kt—R2, Kt×Kt;
14 R×Kt, P—Q4! ∓. Spielmann—Bogoljuboff, Bled, 1931.

(n) Spielmann—Pirc, 1st match game, 1931.

1 P—K 4, P—Q B 4;   2 Kt—K B 3, P—K 3;   3 P—Q 4, P×P; 4 Kt×P, Kt—K B 3;   5 Kt—Q B 3.

	11	12	13	14	15
5	(P—Q 3)		B—Kt 5		
6	P—K Kt 3	B—Q 3	Kt—Kt 5		P—K 5 !
	Kt—B 3	Kt—B 3 (c)	Kt—B 3 (e)	..P—Q 4 !	Kt—Q 4 (l)
7	B—Kt 2	K Kt—K 2	P—Q R 3 (f)	P×P	B—Q 2
	B—K 2	B—K 2	B×Kt ch	P—Q R 3 !	Kt×Kt
8	O—O	O—O	Kt×B	Q—Q 4	P×Kt
	O—O	O—O	P—Q 4	B—K 2 (i)	B—B 1 (m)
9	Kt×Kt (a)	K—R 1	B—Q 3 (g)	P—Q 6 (j)	B—Q 3
	P×Kt	P—Q R 3	P×P	P×Kt	Kt—B 3
10	P—K 5	P—K B 4	Kt×P	Kt×P	Kt×Kt
	P×P	P—Q Kt 4	Kt×Kt	Kt—B 3	Q P×Kt
11	Q×Q	Kt—Kt 3	B×Kt	Q—Q 1	Q—Kt 4
	R×Q	B—Kt 2	Q×Q ch	B—B 1	P—K Kt 3
12	B×P	Q Kt—K 2	K×Q	B—K 3	B—K Kt 5
	R—Kt 1	R—B 1	B—Q 2	Kt—Q 4	B—K 2
13	R—Q 1	B—Q 2	B—K 3	B—B 5	P—K R 4
	R×R	Kt—Kt 1	O—O—O	P—Q Kt 3	O—O
14	Kt×R	Kt—Kt 1	K—B 1	P—Q B 4	O—O
	Kt—Q 4	Q Kt—Q 2	P—Q Kt 3	P×B	B—Q 2
15	B—R 4 ± (b)	Q—K 2	P—Q R 4 ± (h)	P×Kt	Q R—Q 1 ±
		Kt—B 4 ∓ (d)		Q—R 4 ch ∓ (k)	

(a) 9 P—Q Kt 3, B—Q 2; 10 B—Kt 2, Q—R 4! (10 , P—Q R 3; 11 Q Kt—K 2, Q—R 4, 12 P—Q B 4, Q—R 4; 13 Q—Q 2, K R—Q 1; 14 P—K R 3, Q R—B 1; 15 P—K Kt 4 +. Bogatyrchuk—Rumin, Moscow, 1931); 11 Q—Q 2, Q R—B 1, 12 Q R—Q 1, K—R 1; 13 Q Kt—K 2, Q×B; 14 R—R 1; 15 K R—Kt 1, Q×R ch and Black has excellent prospects. Ilyin-Zhenevsky—Lasker, Moscow, 1925.

(b) Bernstein—Bogoljuboff, Zürich, 1934.

(c) Weaker is 6.., P—Q R 3; 7 O—O, Q—B 2; 8 K—R 1, B—K 2; 9 P—B 4, Q Kt—Q 2 (better 9 , Kt—B 3); 10 Q—K 1, P—Q Kt 4; 11 P—Q R 3, B—Kt 2; 12 Q—Kt 3, P—Kt 3; 13 B—Q 2, P—K R 4; 14 Q R—K 1 ±. Yates—Bogoljuboff, Moscow, 1925.

(d) Yates—Verlinsky, Moscow, 1925.

(e) If instead 6. , O—O; 7 P—Q R 3, B×Kt ch; 8 Kt×B, Q—R 4 (8.., P—Q 4 as in the column, is preferable); 9 B—Q 3, P—Q 4; 10 O—O, P×P; 11 Kt×P, Kt×Kt; 12 B×Kt, Kt—Q 2 ±. Chalupetzky—A. Steiner, Budapest, 1924.

(f) On 7 B—K B 4, Kt×P leads to an even position · 8 Kt—B 7 ch, K—B 1; 9 Q—B 3, P—Q 4; 10 O—O—O, B×Kt; 11 P×B, R—Q Kt 1; 12 Kt×Q P (if 12 Kt—Kt 5, Q—R 4; 13 B×R, Q×R P; 14 B—Q 6 ch, K—Kt 1; 15 Kt—R 3, Kt×B; 16 Kt—Kt 1, Kt—K 4 + +), P×Kt; 13 Q×Kt, P×Q; 14 R×Q ch, Kt×R; 15 B×R, P—Q R 3. Becker—Asztalos, Bad Tüffer, 1929. If 7 Kt—Q 6 ch, K—K 2; 8 B—K B 4, P—K 4; 9 Kt—B 5 ch, K—B 1; 10 B—Q 2, P—Q 4+.

(g) After 9 P×P, P×P; 10 B—Q 3, B—Kt 5; 11 P—B 3, B—K 3; 12 O—O, P—K R 3; 13 Kt—K 2, O—O; 14 Kt—Kt 3, Q—Kt 3 ch; 15 K—R 1, Q R—Q 1 Black's pieces are better developed. Kostich—Wagner, Prague, 1931.

(h) John—Sámisch, Hamburg, 1921.

(i) If 8.., B—B 1; 9 P×P!, P×Kt; 10 P×P ch, K—K 2; 11 Q×Q ch, K×Q; 12 B×P +.

(j) This sacrifice is practically forced, for if 9 Q—R 4, O—O; and if 9 Kt—R 3, P×P! with advantage to Black in both cases.

(k) Szabo—Dake, Warsaw, 1935.

(l) Forced, for if 6 ., Q—R 4 (or 6 ., Q—B 2); 7 P×Kt!, B×Kt ch; 8 P×B, Q×P ch; 9 Q—Q 2!, Q×R; 10 P—B 3, Q—Kt 8; 11 B—Q 3, Q—Kt 3; 12 P×P, R—Kt 1; 13 Q—R 6+ + and if 6 ., Kt—K 5; 7 Q—Kt 4!, Kt×Kt; 8 Q×P, R—B 1; 9 P—Q R 3, Q—R 4; 10 Kt×K 3, Q—Q 4; 11 B—Q 3, Kt—R 7 ch; 12 P×B, Kt×B; 13 R×Kt, Kt—B 3; 14 P—K B 4 +. Koch—Elsner, Berlin. 1932.

(m) Or 8., B—K 2; 9 Q—Kt 4, P—Kt 3 (9.., K—B 1 is no better); 10 B—K R 6 ±.

1 P—K 4, P—Q B 4; 2 Kt—K B 3, P—K 3; 3 P—Q 4, P×P; 4 Kt×P, Kt—K B 3.

	16	17	18	19	20
5	(Kt—Q B 3)..				B—Q 3 (m)
	(B—Kt 5)...............	Kt—B 3			Kt—B 3 (n)
6	B—Q 3 (a)		B—K 2....	Kt×Kt (i)	Kt×Kt
	Kt—B 3....	P—K 4 (d)	B—Kt 5	KtP×Kt(j)	Q P×Kt
7	Kt×Kt	KKt—K2(e)	O—O (g)	B—Q 3 (h)	O—O (o)
	Q P×Kt! (b)	P—Q 4	B×Kt	P—Q 4	P—K 4
8	P—K 5	P×P	P×B	O—O	Kt—Q 2
	Kt—Q 2	Kt×P	Kt×P	B—K 2	Q—B 2
9	Q—Kt 4	O—O	B—B 3	Q—K 2	P—Q Kt 3
	Q—R 4	Kt—Q B 3	P—Q 4	O—O	B—Q B 4
10	O—O	Kt×Kt	Kt×Kt	P—Q Kt 3	B—Kt 2
	B×Kt	Q×Kt	P×Kt	Kt—Q 2	B—K Kt 5
11	P×B	P—Q R 3	B×Kt	Kt—R 4	B—K 2
	Q×K P	B—R 4	P×B	B—B 3	B—K 3 (p)
12	B—R 3	P—Q Kt 4	Q×Q ch	R—Kt 1	Kt—B 3
	P—Q B 4	B—B 2	K×Q	Kt—Kt 3	B—Q 3
13	Q R—Kt 1	R—K 1	R—K 1	P—K 5	Q—Q 3
	O—O	P—B 4	P—K B 4	B—K 2	O—O
14	KR-K1 ± (c)	P—Q B 4	B—Kt 5 ch	Kt×Kt	Q R—Q 1
		Q—B 2 = (f)	K—K 1 = (h)	P×Kt = (l)	Q R—Q 1 =

(a) If 6 B—K 2?, Kt×P; 7 O—O, Kt—K B 3 +, or 7.., Kt×Kt; 8 P×Kt, B—K 2 +.

(b) Better than 7.., Kt P×Kt; 8 P—K 5, Kt—Q 4; 9 Q—Kt 4, P—K Kt 3; 10 O—O, B×Kt, 11 P×B, P—Q B 4; 12 B—R 3 +.

(c) Yates—Atkins, London, 1922.

(d) Jaffe's Variation. 6.., P—Q 4; 7 P—K 5, Kt—K 5 (not 7.., Q—B 2; 8 P×Kt, B×Kt ch; 9 P×B, Q×P ch; 10 Q—Q 2, Q×R; 11 P—Q B 3+ +); 8 B×Kt, P×B; 9 O—O, B×Kt; 10 P×B, Q—Q 4; 11 Q—R 5, Kt—Q 2; 12 P—K B 4, Q—B 4; 13 Q—R 3, Kt—Kt 3; 14 B—K 3 ±. Perlis—Jaffe, Carlsbad, 1911.

(e) 7 Kt—B 5, O—O; 8 Kt—K 3, B×Kt ch; 9 P×B, P—Q Kt 3 =.

(f) Yates—Alekhine, The Hague, 1921

(g) If 7 Kt×Kt, Kt P×Kt, 8 O—O, P—Q 4; 9 B—K Kt 5, P—K R 3; 10 B×Kt, Q×B; 11 P×P, K P×P; 12 Q—K 1 (threatening Kt×Q P), B—K 2 ∓. A. Steiner—Walter, Gyor, 1924.

(h) Igel—Beutum, Vienna, 1928.

(i) On 6 K Kt—Kt 5, Black should play either 6.., B—Kt 5, transposing into col. 13, or 6.., P—Q 3, but not 6.., P—Q R 3?; 7 Kt—Q 6 ch, B×Kt; 8 Q×B; Q—K 2; 9 B—K B 4, Kt—K R 4; 10 Q×Q ch, K×Q; 11 B—K 3, P—Q Kt 4, 12 O—O—O +. Kashdan—Vidmar, Prague, 1931.

(j) 6.., Q P×Kt; 7 Q×Q ch, K×Q; 8 P—K 5, Kt—Q 2; 9 P—B 4, B—Kt 5; 10 B—Q 2, P—Q Kt 3; 11 O—O—O, B—K 2; 12 Kt—K 4, B—K 2; 13 B—K 3, K—B 2 ±. Opocensky—Hasenfuss, Folkestone, 1933

(k) Or 7 P—K 5, Kt—Q 4; 8 Kt—K 4, Q—B 2 (8.., P—K B 4; 9 P×P e.p., Kt×P; 10 Kt—Q 6 ch, B×Kt; 11 Q×B, Q—R 4 ch; 12 B—Q 2, Q—Q 4 = is also good. Yates—Em. Lasker, New York, 1924. Or here 11.., Q—Kt 3; 12 B—Q 3, P—B 4 =); 9 P—K B 4, P—K B 4!; 10 P×P e.p., Kt×P; 11 Kt×Kt ch, P×Kt; 12 Q—R 5 ch, K—Q 1 = (Euwe).

(l) Treybal—Tarrasch, Baden-Baden, 1925.

(m) Or 5 Kt—Q 4, P—Q 4. 6 P—K 5, K Kt—Q 2; 7 Q Kt—B 3, Kt—Q B 3, 8 Kt×Kt; 9 B—Q 3, Kt—B 4; 10 O—O, B—K 2; 11 B—K 3, Kt×B =. Spielmann—List, Berlin, 1926.

(n) Alternatives are: (1) 5.., P—Q R 3; 6 O—O, Q—B 2; 7 Q—K 2, P—Q 4, 8 Kt—Q 2, Kt—B 3, 9 Kt×Kt, P×Kt; 10 P—Q Kt 3, B—Q 3; 11 P—K R 3, O—O = Sir G. A. Thomas—Pirc, Ujpest, 1934. (2) 5.., P—Q 3?; 6 O—O, B—K 2; 7 P—Q B 4, Q Kt—Q 2; 8 Kt—Q B 3, P—Q R 3; 9 B—K 3, Q—B 2; 10 R—B 1, P—Q Kt 3; 11 P—B 3, B—Kt 2; 12 Q—K 1, O—O; 13 Q—B 2 +. Treybal—Flohr, Ujpest, 1934.

(o) Or 7 Kt—Q 2, P—K 4; 8 Kt—B 4, B—Q B 4; 9 B—K 3, B×B; 10 Kt×B B—K 3; 11 O—O, O—O =. Spielmann—Alekhine, New York, 1927.

(p) 11.., P—K R 4?; 12 Kt—B 4, R—Q 1, 13 Q—K 1, Kt—Q 2; 14 B×B!, P×B; 15 P—Kt 4 ±. Sir G. A. Thomas—Botvinnik, Hastings, 1934-35

1 P—K 4, P—Q B 4; 2 Kt—K B 3, P—K 3; 3 P—Q 4 (A).

	21	22	23	24	25
3	(P × P)				P—Q 4 (j)
4	(Kt × P)				K P×P
	(Kt—K B 3).P—Q R 3 (c)				K P×P
5	(B—Q 3)	P—Q B 4 !...	Kt—Q B 3...	B—K 2	B—K 2
	(Kt—B 3)	Kt—K B 3	P—Q Kt 4 (f)	Q—B 2	Kt—K B 3
6	(Kt × Kt)	Kt—Q B 3	B—Q 3	O—O	O—O
	Kt P×Kt	P—Q 3 (d)	B—Kt 2	Kt—K B 3	B—K 2
7	O—O	B—K 2	O—O	B—B 3 (h)	P×P
	P—Q 4	Kt—B 3	P—Q 3	B—K 2	O—O
8	Kt—Q 2 (a)	O—O	K—R 1	P—Q Kt 3	Q Kt—Q 2
	B—K 2	Q—B 2	Kt—K B 3	O—O	B×P
9	Q—K 2	P—Q Kt 3	P—Q R 3	B—Kt 2	Kt—Kt 3
	O—O	B—K 2	Q Kt—Q 2	P—Q 3	B—K 2
10	P—K B 4	B—Kt 2	P—B 4	P—Q B 4	B—K Kt 5
	Kt—Q 2	O—O	B—K 2	Q Kt—Q 2	P—K R 3
11	Kt—Kt 3	Kt—B 2	Q—K 2	Kt—B 3	B—R 4
	P—Q R 4	R—Q 1	Q—B 2	R—Kt 1	Kt—B 3
12	B—K 3	Kt—K 3	B—Q 2	Q—Q 2	P—B 3
	P—R 5	Kt—K 4	O—O	P—Q Kt 3	B—K 3
13	Kt—Q 2	Q—K 1+ (e)	R—B 3 ± (g)	P—Kt 3+ (i)	K Kt—Q4+
	Kt—B 4 = (b)				

(A) 3 B—K 2, Kt—K B 3; 4 Kt—B 3, P—Q 4; 5 P×P, Kt×P; 6 P—Q 4, Kt×Kt; 7 P×Kt, B—K 2 =.

(a) Or 8 P×P, B P×P; 9 Kt—B 3, B—Q 3; 10 P—B 4, B—B 4 ch; 11 K—R 1, O—O; 12 Kt—R 4, B—K 2 =. Spielmann—Sämisch, Vienna, 1922.

(b) Foltys—L. Steiner, Mährisch-Ostrau, 1933.

(c) The Paulsen Defence. On 4.., Kt—Q B 3; 5 Kt—Q B 3 is best. If, however, 5 P—Q B 4 (after 4.., Kt—Q B 3), Kt—K B 3 (5.., Q—R 5; 6 Kt—Q B 3, B—Kt 5; 7 Kt—Kt 5, Q×P ch; 8 B—K 2, Q—K 4; 9 P—B 4, Q—Kt 1; 10 P—Q R 3, B—K 2; 11 Kt—K 4 ±. Spielmann—Tartakover, Vienna, 1928); 6 Kt—Q B 3, B—Kt 5; 7 P—B 3, P—Q 4; 8 B P×P, K P×P; 9 B—K Kt 5, Q—R 4; 10 Kt×Kt, P×Kt; 11 B×Kt, P×B+. Teller—Tartakover, Hastings, 1927.

(d) On 6 , B—Kt 5; 7 B—Q 3 retains the advantage. 6.., Q—B 2, 7 P—Q R 3, B—K 2; 8 B—K 2, O—O; 9 O—O, P—Q 3; 10 B—K 3, Q Kt—Q 2; 11 R—B 1, P—Q Kt 3; 12 P—Q Kt 4, B—Kt 2; 13 P—B 3, Q R—B 1; 14 Q—K 1, Q—Kt 1; 15 Q—B 2+ is Spielmann—Tartakover, Marienbad, 1925.

(e) Alekhine—Erdelyi, Prague, 1931.

(f) Here and in the next column Black should transpose into the Scheveningen, Variation by P—Q 3 and Kt—Q B 3.

(g) Bogoljuboff—Rubinstein, London, 1922.

(h) Or 7 Kt—B 3, B—Kt 5; 8 B—B 3, B×Kt; 9 P×B, Q×B P; 10 R—Kt 1, Q—B 2; 11 B—R 3, Kt—B 3; 12 R—K 1, Kt—K 4; 13 R—Kt 3+. Löwy—H. Wolf, 1902.

(i) Möller—Tartakover, Copenhagen, 1923.

(j) Marshall's Variation. The column is Réti—Kostich, Teplitz-Schönau, 1922.

DRAGON VARIATION

1 P—K 4, P—Q B 4 ; 2 Kt—K B 3, Kt—Q B 3 ; 3 P—Q 4, P×P ;
4 Kt×P, Kt—K B 3 ; 5 Kt—Q B 3, P—Q 3 ; 6 B—K 2, P—K Kt 3 ;
7 B—K 3, B—Kt 2 ; 8 O—O, O—O.

	26	27	28	29	30
9	Kt—Kt 3				P—K R 3
	B—K 3	P—Q R 4	P—Q R 3		P—Q 4 ! (*h*)
10	P—B 4 (*a*)		P—Q R 4	P—B 4 (*h*)	P×P
	Kt—Q R 4 (*b*)		B—K 3	B—Q 2	Kt×P (*l*)
11	P—B 5 ! ..... Kt×Kt		Kt—Q 4	B—B 3	Q Kt×Kt
	B—B 5 !	Q×Kt	P—Q 4 !	R—B 1	Q×Kt
12	B—Q 3 ! (*c*)	B—B 3	P×P	Kt—Q 5 (*i*)	B—B 3
	Kt×Kt	B—B 5 (*e*)	B×P	Kt×Kt	Q—B 5
13	R P×Kt	R—K 1	Kt×B	P×Kt	Kt×Kt
	B×B	K R—Q 1	K Kt×Kt	Kt—R 4	P×Kt
14	P×B	Q—Q 2	Kt×Kt	Kt×Kt	P—B 3
	P—Q 4	Q—B 2	P×Kt	Q×Kt	B-K 3 = (*m*)
15	B—Q 4	Q R—B 1	B—Q 4	P—B 3	
	P×K P	P—K 4 !	P—K 4	K R—K 1	
16	Q P×P ± (*d*)	P×P (*f*)	B—B 5	Q—Q 2	
		P×P =	R—K 1 = (*g*)	P-QKt4 = (*j*)	

(*a*) If 10 P—B 3, P—Q 4 ! equalises at once : 11 P×P, Kt×P; 12 Kt×Kt,, Q×Kt; 13 Q×Q, B×Q, with an even ending. Schonmann—Rellstab, Hamburg, 1932.

(*b*) Best. If instead 10 , Q—B 1; 11 P—K R 3, Kt—K 1; 12 Q—Q 2, P—B 4; 13 P×P, P×P; 14 Q R—K 1, K—R 1; 15 Kt—Q 4, B—Kt 1; 16 P—K Kt 4 !+. Réti—Tartakover, New York, 1924. Or 10 , P—Q R 3; 11 B—B 3, Q—B 2; 12 Kt—Q 5, B×Kt; 13 P×B, Kt—K 1; 14 R—K 1, R—K 1; 15 Q—Q 2, Q Kt—Q 2; 16 R—K 2 ±. Szabo—Gygli, Warsaw, 1935.

(*c*) 12 Kt×Kt, B×B; 13 Kt×P, B×Q; 14 Kt×Q, B×P; 15 Kt—B 6, K R—K 1 =. Lasker—Rumin, Moscow, 1936. If 12 P—K 5 ?, B×B; 13 Q×B, P×K P; 14 Q R—Q 1, Q—B 2 ; 15 Kt—Kt 5, Q—B 5 +.

(*d*) White maintains a slight advantage after both 16. , Q—B 2; 17 P—K 5, Q R—Q 1!; 18 P×Kt, B×P (Spielmann—Petrov, Riga, 1934); 19 R—R 4!, P—Q Kt 4; 20 Kt×P, Q—Q 2; 21 Q—K 2, P—Q R 3; 22 B×B, P×Kt; 23 B×P, P×R; 24 B×K R (analysis by Spielmann), and 16 ., P—Q R 3; 17 P—K 5, Kt—K 1; 18 P—Q Kt 4, Kt—B 2; 19 P—B 6, P×P; 20 P×P, B—R 3; 21 B—Kt 6. Spielmann—Landau, 5th match game, 1938.

(*e*) Or (1) 12 , K R—Q 1; 13 Kt—Q 5, Kt×Kt; 14 P×Kt, B—B 4; 15 P—B 3, Q R—B 1 =. L. Steiner—Becker, Vienna, 1935. (2) 12 ., Q R—B 1; 13 Kt—Q5, B×Kt; 14 P×·B, Kt—Q 2; 15 P—B 3, Kt—Kt 3; 16 B—B 2, R—B 2 =. L. Steiner—Winter, Lodz, 1935.

(*f*) 16 P—Q Kt 3 ?, P—Q 4 !!+. Rauser—Botvinnik, Leningrad, 1933.

(*g*) Spielmann—Alekhine, Margate, 1938.

(*h*) 10 P—Q R 4, B—K 3; 11 P—B 4, R—B 1; 12 B—B 3, Kt—Q 2; 13 K—R 1, Kt—K 3; 14 P—B 5, B—B 5; 15 R—B 2, Kt—K 4 ∓. Sir G. A. Thomas—Petrov, Prague, 1931.

(*i*) 12 P—K Kt 4 is more aggressive.

(*j*) Sir G. A. Thomas—Alekhine, Nottingham, 1936.

(*k*) This is simplest, but 9 , B—Q 2 is also playable, *e.g.* 10 Q—Q 2, R—B 1; 11 Q R—Q 1, P—Q R 3; 12 K R—K 1, P—Q R 3 ; 13 Kt×Kt, B×Kt; 14 P—B 3, Q—B 2; 15 B—B 1, K R—Q 1 and Black's position is satisfactory. Lasker—Ragosin, Moscow, 1936.

(*l*) Or 10., Kt—Q Kt 5; 11 P—Q 6, Q×P; 12 Q Kt—Kt 5 (weaker 12 K Kt—Kt 5, Q—Kt 1; 13 B—B 3, B—K 3; 14 B—B 5, Kt—B 3; 15 Q—K 2, Kt—Q 2 ∓. Treybal—Petrov, Folkestone, 1933), Q—Kt 1; 13 P—Q B 4 =. Weenink—Réti, match, 1928.

(*m*) Tarrasch—Lipke, Vienna, 1898.

DRAGON VARIATION

1 P—K4, P—QB4; 2 Kt—KB3, Kt—QB3; 3 P—Q4, P×P;
4 Kt×P, Kt—B3; 5 Kt—QB3, P—Q3; 6 B—K2, P—KKt3;
7 B—K3, B—Kt2.

	31	32	33	34	35
8	(O—O)		Kt—Kt3	Q—Q2	P—B3 (p)
	(O—O) (a)		B—K3	O—O (m)	O—O
9	P—B4	Q—Q2 (d)	P—B4	Kt—Kt3 (n)	Q—Q2
	Q—Kt3!	B—Q2 (e)	O—O	B—K3	P—Q4
10	Q—Q3!	QR—Q1 (f)	P—Kt4	B—KR6	Kt×Kt
	Kt-KKt5!(b)	P—QR3	P—Q4! (i)	B×B	P×Kt
11	Kt—Q5	P—B3 (g)	P—B5 (j)	Q×B	P—K5
	B×Kt!	R—B1	B—B1!	Q—Kt3!	Kt—Q2
12	Kt×Q	K—R1	P×QP	Q—Q2	P—B4
	B×B ch	Kt—QR4	Kt—Kt5	KR—Q1	P—K3
13	K—R1	B—R6	P—Q6! (k)	P—KR3	O—O
	B×Kt	Kt—B5	Q×P!	P—Q4	Q—R4
14	B×Kt	B×Kt	B—B5	P×P	P—QR3
	B×B	R×B	Q—B5!	B×QP	Q—B2
15	P—B5	B×B	R—KB1	Q—Kt5	P—QKt4
	B—KR4 = (c)	K×B = (h)	Q×RP = (l)	Kt—Q5 ∓ (o)	P—B3 = (q)

(a) If 8. ., P—Q4?; 9 P×P, Kt×P; 10 Q Kt×Kt, Q×Kt; 11 B—B3, Q—B5;
12 Kt×Kt, P×Kt, 13 P—Q Kt3, Q—B6; 14 Q—Q3!, Q×Q; 15 P×Q, B×R;
16 B×P ch+. Or 8.., Kt—KKt5?; 9 B×Kt, B×B; 10 Kt×Kt++.
   (b) Weaker is 10 , Q—B2; 11 P—QR3, B—Q2; 12 Kt(B3)—Kt5, Q—B1;
13 P—B4, B—Kt5; 14 Kt×Kt, P×Kt; 15 Kt—B3 ±. Treybal—Flohr, Munchen-
gratz, 1933. And if 10.., Q×P?, 11 Kt×Kt, P×Kt; 12 QR—Kt1, Q—R6;
13 Kt—Q5!+.
   (c) Ahues—Richter, Berlin, 1930.
   (d) 9 K—R1?, P—Q4!; 10 P×P, Kt×P; 11 Q Kt×Kt, Q×Kt; 12 B—B3,
Q—B5; 13 P—B3?, Kt×Kt; 14 P×Kt, B—K3 ∓. Vajda—Kmoch, Prague, 1931.
Or 9 P—B3?, P—Q4!; 10 P×P, Kt×P; 11 Q Kt×Kt, Q×Kt; 12 Kt×Kt, Q×Kt;
13 P—B3, B—K3 =. Barth—Flohr, Zwickau, 1930.
   (e) 9 , P—Q4 is also playable. Compare col. 30, note (k).
   (f) Or 10 Kt×Kt, P×Kt; 11 B—KR6, B×B; 12 Q×B, R—Kt1; 13 P—Q Kt3,
Q—R4; 14 Q—K3, P—R4 =. Asztalos—Tartakover, Bled, 1931.
   (g) 11 P—KR3 transposes into col. 30, note (k)
   (h) Nimzovitch—Tartakover, Bled, 1931.
   (i) If 10 , Kt—Q5!; 11 Kt—Kt5, Kt—K1; 12 Q—Q2, R—B1; 13 B—Q4,
Kt—B5, 14 B×Kt, R×B; 15 O—O—O, Q—Q2; 16 Q—Q3+. Kan—Botvinnik,
Moscow, 1936.
   (j) 11 P—K5, P—Q5!; 12 Kt×P, Kt×Kt; 13 B×Kt, Kt×P! =, Lovenfisch—
Botvinnik, Moscow, 1936.
   (k) Best. If 13 P×P, RP×P!; 14 B—B3, Kt×KtP!; 15 B×Kt, B×B;
16 Q×B, B×Kt ch; 17 P×B, Kt×P ch; 18 K—K2, Kt×R; 19 R×Kt, Q×P+;
and if 13 B—B3, P×P, 14 P—Kt5, Kt—Kt5! ∓. Bondarevsky—Alatorzeff, Tiflis,
1937.
   (l) 16 B×Kt, Kt×KtP!; 17 B×Kt, Q—Kt6 ch; 18 R—B2, Q—Kt8 ch;
19 R—B1, drawn. Alekhine—Botvinnik, Nottingham, 1936.
   (m) 8 , Kt—KKt5 is weak: 9 B×Kt, B×B; 10 Kt—Q5 (or 10 P—B3, B—Q2;
11 Kt×Kt, P×Kt; 12 B—Q4, P—B3; 13 P—KR4, P—KR4; 14 P—KKt4!,
P×P), O—O; 11 P—QB4, B—Q2; 12 O—O, P—B4; 13 P×P, B×P; 14 Kt×B,
R×Kt; 15 QR—Q1 ±. Bogatyrchuk—Botvinnik, Leningrad, 1933.
   (n) 9 R—Q1, P—Q4!; 10 Kt×Kt, P×Kt; 11 O—O, Q—B2; 12 P×P, P×P;
13 Kt—Kt5, Q—Kt2 ∓. T. H. Tylor—Foltys, Margate, 1938.
   (o) Horowitz—Reshevsky, New York, 1938.
   (p) 8 P—KR3, O—O; 9 Q—Q2, B—Q2; 10 P—KKt4, Kt×Kt!; ¡11 B×Kt,
B—B3 =, for if 12 P—Kt5?, Kt×P; 13 Kt×Kt, B×Kt; 14 B×B, B×R!+.
Straat—Colle, Scheveningen, 1923.
   (q) L. Steiner—Herzog, Mahrisch-Ostrau, 1933.

1 P—K 4, P—Q B 4 ; 2 Kt—K B 3, Kt—Q B 3 ; 3 P—Q 4, P×P ;
4 Kt×P, Kt—B 3 ; 5 Kt—Q B 3, P—Q 3.

	36	37	38	39	40
6	(B—K 2)....B	—KKt5(b)............	....P—B 3	......	B—Q B 4 (h)
	(P—K Kt 3)	P—K 3......Q--R 4		P—K Kt 3	P—K 3 ! (i)
7	O—O	Q—Q 2 (c)	B × Kt	B—K 3	O—O
	B—Kt 2	B—K 2	Kt P × B	B—Kt 2	B—K 2
8	Kt—Kt 3	O—O—O	B—Kt 5	Q—Q 2	B—K 3
	O—O	P—Q R 3 (d)	B—Q 2	O—O	O—O
9	P—B 4	B × Kt	O—O	O—O—O	P—B 3
	P—Q Kt 4 (a)	P × B	O—O—O	Kt × Kt !	P—Q R 3
10	B—B 3	P—B 4	Kt—Kt 3	B × Kt	P—Q R 4
	Q—Kt 3 ch	B—Q 2	Q—Kt 3	B—K 3	B—Q 2
11	K—R 1	P—B 5	P—Q R 4	K—Kt 1	Q—K 2
	P—Kt 5	Kt × Kt	P—Q K 4	R—B 1	Q—B 2
12	Kt—Q 5	Q × Kt	Kt—Q 5	P—K R 4	Kt × Kt
	Kt × Kt	Q—R 4 (e)	Q—R 2	Kt—R 4	B × Kt
13	P × Kt	B—K 2	Q—Q 2	B × B	K R—Q 1
	Kt—R 4	O—O—O	R—Kt 1	K × B	Q R—B 1
14	R—K 1	B—B 5	K—R 1	Kt—Q 5	B—Kt 3
	Kt × Kt	B—K 1	P—B 4	B × Kt	P—Q 4 !
15	R P × Kt	P-K Kt 4 ! ±	P—B 3 + (f)	P × B	P × P
	Q—B 2 =			Kt—Kt6 = (g)	Kt × P ∓ (j)

(a) Rauser's suggestion. If now 10 Kt × P, Kt × P ; and if 10 B × P, Kt × P ; 11 B × Kt, Q—Kt 3 ch and Black stands well in both cases. Some alternatives to the text are. (1) 9. , B—K 3, 10 P—B 5, B × Kt, 11 R P × B, Q—Kt 3 ch ; 12 K—R 1, Kt—K 4, 13 P—K Kt 4, Q—B 3 ; 14 R—R 4 !, P × P ; 15 Kt—Q 5 ! ±. Romanovsky—Rabinovitch, Moscow, 1935. (2) 9 , B—Q 2, 10 P—Kt 4 ! (or 10 B—B 3, R—B 1 ; 11 K—R 1, P—Q R 3 ; 12 P—Q R 4, K—Q R 4 ? ; 13 P—K 5 !, Kt—K 1 ; 14 Kt × Kt+. Alekhine—Desler, Hamburg, 1930), Q—B 1 ; 11 P—Kt 5, Kt—K 1 ; 12 Kt—Q 5, P—B 4 ; 13 P—K 5 !, P × P, 14 Kt—B 5, P—K 3 ; 15 Kt—B 6+. Keres—Grau, Warsaw, 1935 (3) 9 , P—Q R 3 ; 10 B—B 3, Q—B 2 ; 11 R—K 1, P—K 3 ! ; 12 B—K 3, P—Q Kt 4 ; 13 Q—Q 2, B—Kt 2, 14 P—Q R 4, P—Kt 5 ; 15 Kt—K 2, Kt—Q R 4 ! ; 16 Q × Kt P, Kt—B 5 with chances for both sides. Tartakover—Najdorf, 3rd match game, 1935.

(b) The Richter Attack.
(c) Better than 7 Kt × Kt, P × Kt ; 8 P—K 5, P × P (or 8.., Q—R 4 ; 9 B × Kt, P × B ; 10 P × Q P, Q—K 4 ch, 11 Q—K 2, B × P ; 12 O—O—O, R—Q Kt 1 = ; if here 9 B—Kt 5, P × B ; 10 P × Kt, P—Kt 5 ; 11 Q—B 3, Q—Kt 4 ch ! +) ; 9 Q—B 3, B—Q 2 ; 10 O—O—O, B—K 2 ; 11 B × Kt, P × B , 12 Q—Kt 3 = Analysis by Euwe. 7 Kt—Kt 3, B—K 2 ; 8 Q—Q 2, O—O (better was P—K R 3) ; 9 O—O—O, Kt—Q R 4 ; 10 K—Kt 1, Kt × Kt, 11 R P × Kt, Kt—K 1 ; 12 B × B, Q × B ; 13 Kt—Kt 5+ is Alekhine—P. Frydman, Podebrady, 1936.
(d) If 8.., O—O, both 9 K Kt—Kt 5, P—K R 3 ; 10 B—K B 4, P—K 4 ; 11 B—K 3 ± and 9 B—B 4, P—Q 4 ; 10 P—K 5, Kt—K 1 ; 11 Kt—B 3 ± are strong. Bad, however, is 9 B × Kt ?, B × B ! ; 10 Kt × Kt, P × Kt, 11 Q × P, Q—R 4 ; 12 B—B 4, B—R 3 ; 13 B × B, B × Kt ∓. Keres—Heinicke, Bad Nauheim, 1936.
(e) Goglidse—Pirc, Moscow, 1935. The continuation in the column is suggested by the Tournament Book.
(f) Alekhine—Frentz, Paris, 1933.
(g) Rauser—Chekhover, Leningrad, 1936.
(h) Some other continuations seldom encountered are : (1) 6 P—K R 3, P—K Kt 3 ; 7 B—K 3, B—Kt 2 ; 8 P—K Kt 4, O—O ; 9 P—Kt 5, Kt—Q 2 ; 10 P—K R 4, Q—R 4 ; 11 P—B 4, Kt × Kt ; 12 B × Kt, P—K 4 ; 13 P × P, Kt × P ; 14 B—K 2, Q—Kt 5 ; 15 P—Q R 3, Q × B ! ∓. Réti—Sämisch, Kiel, 1921. (2) 6 Kt × Kt, P × Kt ; 7 B—Q3, P—Kt 3 ; 8 O—O, B—Kt 2 ; 9 Q—K 2, O—O ; 10 P—K R 3, P—K 4 ; 11 B—K 3, P—Q 4 ! ; 12 B--B 5, R—K 1 ; 13 P—K Kt 4 ?, P—Q 5+. Henneberger—Flohr, Liebwerda, 1934. (3) 6 B—Q Kt 5, B—Q 2 ; 7 O—O, P—K Kt 3 ; 8 B—K 3, B—Kt 2, 9 Q—K 2, Kt × P ? ?, 10 Q Kt × Kt, Kt × Kt ; 11 B × Kt, K B × B, 12 Kt × P ch, K—B 1 ; 13 Q—B 4, P × Kt ; 14 Q × B, K—Kt 1 ; 15 B—B 4 +. G. Abrahams—Winter, Ramsgate, 1929.
(i) Simplest and best. If instead 6 , P—K Kt 3 ; 7 Kt × Kt, P × Kt ; 8 P—K 5, Kt—Kt 5 ; 9 B—B 4 ! (after 9 P—K 6, P—B 4 ! ; 10 O—O, B—Kt 2 Black has adequate counter-play. Schlechter—Lasker, 7th match game, 1910), Q—Kt 3 ; 10 Q—B 3, B—B 4 ; 11 P × P, P × P ; 12 O—O, O—O—O ; 13 K R—K 1, P—Q 4 : 14 P—K R 3+. Rodl—Engels, 2nd match game, 1930
(j) Spielmann—Euwe. Scheveningen, 1923

1 P—K 4, P—Q B 4; 2 Kt—K B 3, Kt—Q B 3; 3 P—Q 4, P×P; 4 Kt×P.

	41	42	43	44	45
4	(Kt—B 3)...P—K Kt 3................Q—B 2				
5	(Kt—Q B 3)	P—Q B 4 ! (c)		Kt—Kt 5 !...Kt—Q B 3	
	P—Q R 3 (a)	B—Kt 2		Q—Kt 1	P—K 3
6	Kt×Kt	B—K 3.....Kt—B 2 (f)		P—Q B 4	B—K 2
	Q P×Kt	Kt—B 3	Kt—B 3	Kt—B 3	Kt—B 3
7	Q×Q ch	Kt—Q B 3	Kt—B 3	Kt(Kt5)–B 3	O—O (l)
	K×Q	P—Q 3 (d)	P—Q 3	P—K 3 [(j)	P—Q R 3
8	B—K B 4	B—K 2	B—K 2	B—K 3	P—Q R 3
	K—K 1	O—O	Kt—Q 2	B—K 2	P—Q Kt 4
9	P—B 3	O—O	Q—Q 2 (g)	B—K 2	B—K 3
	B—K 3	B—Q 2	Kt—B 4 (h)	O—O	B—Kt 2
10	P—Q R 4	P—K R 3	P—Q Kt 4	O—O	P—B 4
	P—Q R 4	R—B 1	Kt—K 3	R—Q 1	B—B 4
11	Kt—K 2	Q—Q 2	B—Kt 2	P—Q R 3 !	Q—Q 3
	B—B 5	P—Q R 3	O—O	P—Q Kt 3	Q—Kt 3
12	O—O—O	Q R—B 1	O—O	P—Q Kt 4	Q R—Q 1
	P—K 3	Kt×Kt	Kt(B3)—Q 5	B—Kt 2	P—Q 4
13	Kt—Q 4	B×Kt	Kt×Kt	P—B 4	P×P
	B×B	B—B 3	Kt×Kt	P—Q 3	Kt×Kt
14	KR×B± (b)	Q—K 3 ± (e)	B—Q 1 ± (i)	R—R 2+ (k)	B×Kt
					O—O—O! =
					(m)

(a) Two other unusual replies are : (1) 5 ., Q—R 4 ; 6 Kt—Kt 3, Q—B 2 ; 7 B—K 2, P—K 3, 8 O—O, P—Q R 3 ; 9 P—Q R 3, B—K 2 ; 10 P—B 4, O—O ; 11 B—B 3 ±. Maróczy—A Steiner, Budapest, 1932. (2) 5 , P—K 4 !?, 6 Kt×Kt? (6 K Kt—Kt 5, P—Q 3 ; 7 B—Kt 5 ±), Kt P×Kt ; 7 B—K Kt 5 ?, R—Q Kt 1 ; 8 B×Kt??, Q×B ; 9 B—B 4, R×P + +. Mellgren—Alekhine, Orebro, 1935.

(b) Botvinnik—Flohr, Moscow, 1935.

(c) The Maróczy Variation.

(d) 7.., Kt—K Kt 5 ; 8 Q×Kt, Kt×Kt ; 9 Q—Q 1, Kt—B 3 ; 10 Q—Q 2 ±.

(e) Kashdan—Apscheneek, Folkestone, 1933.

(f) 6 Kt—Kt 3 is also quite strong, e.g. 6 Kt—Kt 3, Kt—B 3 ; 7 Kt—B 3, P—Q 3 ; 8 B—K 2, O—O , 9 B—K 3, B—K 3 ; 10 P—B 3, Kt—Q 2 ; 11 Q—Q 2, K Kt—K 4 ; 12 Kt—Q 5, P—B 4 ; 13 P×P, B×P ; 14 O—O±. Tartakover—Rosselli, Baden-Baden, 1925.

(g) After 9 O—O, O—O ; 10 B—K 3, Kt—B 4 ; 11 Kt—Q 4, B—Q 2 ; 12 Q—Q 2, R—B 1 ; 13 Q R—Q 1, R—K 1 ; 14 K—R 1, Q—R 4 Black has excellent counter-chances. Nimzovitch—Capablanca, Carlsbad, 1929.

(h) Or 9 ., O—O ; 10 O—O, Kt—B 4 ; 11 P—B 3, Q—R 4 ? ; 12 P—Q Kt 4 !, Kt×Kt P ; 13 Kt—Q 5 !, B×R ; 14 Kt×B+. Euwe—Landau, 5th match game, 1934.

(i) Flohr—Engels, Sliac, 1932.

(j) Better than 7 Kt—Kt 3, P—B 3, P—Q R 3 ; 8 Kt—R 3 (8 Kt—Q 4 ?, Kt×P !+), P—K 3 ; 9 Kt—B 2, Q—B 2 ; 10 P—B 4, P—Q 3 ; 11 B—Q 3, P—Q Kt 3 ; 12 O—O, B—Kt 2 ; 13 B—Q 2, B—K 2 and Black has counterplay. Rumin—Flohr, Moscow, 1936. Or here 7.., P—K 3 ; 8 B—K 3, P—Q R 3 ; 9 Kt—Q 4, B—Kt 5 ; 10 B—Q 3, Kt—K 4 ; 11 O—O ?, K Kt—Kt 5 !+. Alexander—Flohr, Nottingham, 1936.

(k) Kan—Flohr, Moscow, 1936.

(l) Or 7 B—K 3, P—Q R 3 ; 8 O—O, P—Q Kt 4 ; 9 P—B 3, B—B 4 ; 10 Q—Q 2, Q—Kt 3 ; 11 Q R—Q 1, O—O ; 12 K—R 1, B—Kt 2 ; 13 B—Kt 1, P—Q 4 ; 14 P×P, P×P =. Sir G. A. Thomas—Mikenas, Hastings, 1937-38.

(m) Kan—Flohr, Moscow, 1935.

1 P—K4, P—QB4; 2 Kt—KB3.

	46	47	48	49	50
2	(Kt—QB3)..............		P—Q3		
3	(P—Q4).....	B—Kt5 (c)	P—Q4		
	(P×P)	Q—B2 (d)	P×P		
4	(Kt×P)	B×Kt	Kt×P		
	P—Q4	QP×B	Kt—KB3		
5	B—QKt5 (a)	P—Q3	Kt—QB3	...P—KB3	
	P×P!	Kt—B3	P—KKt3	Kt—B3.....	P—K4!
6	Kt×Kt	Q—K2	B—Kt5 (e)	P—QB4	Kt—Kt5
	Q×Q ch	P—KKt3	B—Kt2	P—KKt3 (j)	P—QR3
7	K×Q	O—O	Q—Q2	Kt—QB3	Kt(Kt5)—B3
	P—QR3	B—Kt2	Kt—B3	B—Kt2	B—K3
8	Kt—Q4 dis ch	R—K1	O—O—O (f)	B—K3	Kt—Q5 (m)
	P×B	O—O	O—O (g)	Kt—Q2 (k)	Kt×Kt
9	Kt×P	Kt—B3	Kt—Kt3 (h)	Q—Q2	P×Kt
	B—Kt5 ch	R—Q1	B—K3	Kt×Kt	B—B4
10	K—K1	P—KR3	K—Kt1	B×Kt	B—Q3
	R—Q1	Kt—Q2	R—B1	B×B	B—Kt3
11	Q Kt—B3	P—K5	P—B3	Q×B	O—O
	P—K4	Kt—B1	R—K1	O—O	B—K2
12	P—KR3	B—B4	P—Kt4	Kt—Q5	P—QB4
	B—R4 = (b)	Kt—K3 =	Kt—K4 (i)	Kt—Kt3! =	Kt—Q2 =
				(l)	(n)

(a) After 5 Kt×Kt, P×Kt; 6 P×P, Q×P; 7 Kt—Q2, Kt—KB3; 8 B—K2, P—K4 White's advantage is negligible.

(b) Von Holzhausen—Nimzovitch, Dresden, 1936.

(c) Some other unusual continuations are: (1) 3 B—K2, Kt—B3; 4 Kt—B3, P—Q4; 5 P—K5, Kt—Q2; 6 Kt×P, K Kt×P; 7 Kt×Kt, Kt×Kt; 8 P—Q4, Q×Kt; 9 P×Kt, Q×Q ch =. Romanovsky—Botvinnik, Leningrad, 1934. (2) 3 P—B4, P—B4; 4 Kt—B3, P—Q3; 5 P—Q3, P—B4; 6 P—K Kt3, B—K2; 7 B—Kt2, P×P; 8 P×P, B—Kt5; 9 P—KR3, B—R4; 10 O—O, Kt—B3; 11 Q Kt—B3, B—B2; 12 P—Kt3, P—KR4; 13 P—Kt5, Kt—R2. Alekhine and Turover—Tartakover and Cukierman, Paris, 1931. (3) 3 Kt—B3, P—K4!; 4 B—QB4, P—Q3; 5 P—Q3, B—K2; 6 Kt—Q5, Kt—B3; 7 P—B3, Kt×Kt; 8 B×Kt, O—O; 9 O—O, K—R1 ±. Yates—Tartakover, Hastings, 1928.

(d) Or 3.., P—KKt3; 4 P—B3, B—Kt2; 5 O—O, Q—Kt3; 6 Kt—R3, Kt—B3; 7 P—K5, Kt—Q4; 8 B—B4, Kt—B2; 9 R—K1, O—O; 10 B—Kt3, Kt—R4; 11 P—Q4, P×P; 12 Kt×P, Kt×B; 13 P×Kt, P—Q4; 14 Q Kt—B2, P—B3. Nimzovitch—Stoltz, 5th match game, 1934. The column is Henneberger—Flohr, Zürich, 1934.

(e) 6 B—K2, Kt—QB3 transposes into the Dragon Variation. The order of moves in the text is often adopted to avoid the Richter Attack.

(f) Safer is 8 Kt—Kt3, O—O; 9 B—K2, B—Q2; 10 O—O, R—K1; 11 Q R—Q1, R—QB1; 12 K—R1, P—QR3; 13 P—B4, K—K3 =. Rabinovitch—Kan, Tiflis, 1937. Or here 9 B—R6, P—QR4; 10 B×B, K×B; 11 P—QR4, B—K3; 12 Kt—Q4 Kt×Kt =. Keres—Reshevsky, Hastings, 1937–38.

(g) 8 Kt×P; 9 Q Kt×Kt, Kt×Kt; 10 Kt—B6 ch, P×Kt; 11 Q×Kt, O—O; 12 B—K B4 ±. Rauser—Ragosin, Leningrad, 1936.

(h) After 9 Kt×Kt, Kt—Kt; 10 P—K5, Kt—K1; 11 P×P, Kt×P; 12 B×P, Q×B; 13 Q×Kt, Q—Kt4 ch; 14 Q—Q2, Q—QR4; 15 B—B4, R—Kt1 Black has a strong attack. Rauser—Kan, Leningrad, 1936.

(i) 13 B—K2, K Kt—Q2; 14 B—KR6, B—R1; 15 P—KR4, Kt—Kt3 with a complicated position and chances for both sides. Panoff—Kan, Tiflis, 1937.

(j) 6.., P—K3?; 7 Kt—B3, B—K2; 8 Kt—B2, O—O; 9 B—K2, Q—B2; 10 O—O, R—Q1; 11 B—B4!, Kt—K4; 12 Kt—Kt5+. Euwe—Winter, Amsterdam, 1937.

(k) Or 8.., O—O; 9 Q—Q2, Q—R4!?; 10 Kt—Kt3, Q—Kt5; 11 Q—B2, Kt—Q2; 12 B—Q2, Kt—B4; 13 Kt×Kt, Q×Kt with chances for both sides. Keres—Capablanca, Semmering-Baden, 1937.

(l) Keres—Landau, Noordwijk, 1938.

(m) Or 8 B—Kt5, B—K2; 9 B×Kt, B×B; 10 Kt—Q5, B—Kt4 = Spielmann—Landau, 1st match game, 1938.

(n) Fine—Eliskases, Semmering-Baden, 1937.

1 P—K 4, P—Q B 4.

	51	52	53	54	55
2	(Kt—K B 3) Kt—K B 3 (a)				Kt—Q B 3 Kt—Q B 3
3	P—K 5 Kt—Q 4			Kt—B 3 P—Q 4 (j)	P—K Kt 3 P—K Kt 3
4	Kt—B 3 P—K 3	...Kt×Kt	P—B 4 (h) Kt—B 2	P×P (k) Kt×P	B—Kt 2 B—Kt 2
5	Kt×Kt P×Kt	Q P×Kt P—Q 4	P—Q 4 P×P	B—Kt5ch(l) B—Q 2	K Kt—K 2 P—K 3
6	P—Q 4 P—Q 3	P×P e.p. (g) Q×P	Q×P Kt—B 3	Kt—K 5 ! B×B	P—Q 3 (n) K Kt—K 2
7	B—Kt 5 ! Q—R4ch(b)	Q×Q P×Q	Q—K 4 P—Q 4	Q—B 3 P—B 3	B—K 3 Kt—Q 5
8	P—B 3 P×Q P	P—B 4 B—B 4	P×P e.p. Q×P	Kt×B P×Kt (m)	Q—Q 2 K Kt—B 3
9	B—Q 3 ! P×B P (c)	B—Q 3 B×B	Kt—B 3 Q—Kt 3	Q×Kt Q×Q	Kt—Q 1 Kt×Kt
10	O—O Kt—B 3 (d)	P×B Kt—B 3	Q×Q R P×Q	Kt—B 7 ch K—Q 2	Q×Kt Q—R 4 ch
11	R—K 1 B—K 3	B—B 4 O—O—O	B—B 4 Kt—K 3	Kt×Q Kt—B 3	Q—Q 2 Q×Q ch
12	Kt P×P (e) P×P (f)	O—O—O B—K 2 =	B—Kt 3 B—Q 2 = (i)	P—Q 3 ±	K×Q P—Q 3 = (o)

(a) Nimzovitch's Variation, resembling Alekhine's Defence.
(b) A simpler reply is 7. , Q—Kt 3; 8 P×B P, P×B P; 9 Q×P, B—K 3;
10 B—Kt 5 ch, Kt—B 3; 11 B×Kt ch, P×B; 12 Q—Q 2, P—K R 3!=. Folttys—
Seitz, Lodz, 1938.
(c) If 9 , P×K P; 10 Kt×K P, Q—B 2 (10.., Kt—B 3; 11 O—O!); 11 O—O,
B—Q 3; 12 P×P, O—O; 13 Q—R 5! (13 R—B 1, Kt—B 3; 14 B—B 6 (Eliskases—
P Frydmann, Lodz, 1938), P×B; 15 Q—R 5, P—B 4 and White must take a draw by
perpetual check), P—B 4; 14 Q R—B 1, Kt—B 3; 15 K R—K 1 with a powerful
attack. Analysis by Eliskases. If here 13 , P—K Kt3; 14 Q—R 4!, B×Kt;
15 P×B, Q×P; 16 Q R—K 1, Q—B 2; 17 B—B 6 +.
(d) 10 , P×Kt P?, 11 R—Kt 1, P×P; 12 Kt×P, B—Q 3; 13 Kt×P!,
K×Kt; 14 Q—R 5 ch, with a winning position. Keres—Winter, Warsaw, 1935.
(e) 12 K P×P, B×P; 13 B—B 5?, O—O+.
(f) 13 Kt×P, Kt×Kt; 14 R×Kt, B—Q 3; 15 R—K 3, O—O and Black's defensive
resources are adequate
(g) For 6 B—K B 4, Kt—B 3 = see Alekhine's Defence, col. 17, note (c).
(h) 4 P—Q 4, P; 5 Q×P (simpler 5 Kt×P, P—K 3; 6 B—Q B 4, Kt—Kt 3;
7 B—Kt 3, Kt—B 3 8 Kt—K B 3, P—Q 4; 9 P×P e.p., B×P; 10 Kt—B 3, O—O=),
P—K 3!; 6 P—B 4, Kt—Q B 3; 7 Q—Q 1?, K Kt—K 2!; 8 B—Q 2, Kt—Kt 3;
9 Q—K 2, Q—B 2, 10 B—B 3, P—Kt 3; 11 P—K R 4, P—Q 3; 12 P×P, B×P∓.
Euwe—Rubinstein, The Hague, 1921.
(i) J. J. O'Hanlon—Kostich, Hastings, 1921.
(j) 3. , P—Q 3; 4 P—Q 4 transposes into more regular variations.
(k) 4 P—K 5 transposes into Alekhine's Defence, col. 19.
(l) Better than either 5 Kt—K 5, Kt×Kt; 6 Kt P×Kt, Q—B 2; 7 B—Kt 5 ch,
Kt—Q 2, 8 Q—B 2, P—K 3; 9 O—O, B—Q 3; 10 R—K 1, O—O; 11 P—Q 4, P×P;
12 P×P, Kt×Kt = (Tarrasch—Tartakover, Berlin, 1928), or 5 P—Q 4, Kt×Kt;
6 P×Kt, P—K 3; 7 B—Q 3, Kt—Q 2; 8 O—O, B—K 2; 9 Q—K 2, Kt—B 3;
10 B—Kt 5 ch, B—Q 2; 11 Kt—K 5, O—O = (Kashdan—A. Steiner, The Hague,
1928).
(m) If 8.., Kt—R 3; 9 Q—R 5 ch, P—K Kt 3; 10 Kt×P+.
(n) Or 6 O—O, K Kt—K 2; 7 P—Q 3, O—O, 8 B—K 3, Kt—Q 5; 9 Q—Q 2,
K Kt—B 3 (9 , P—Q 4?; 10 P×P, P×P; 11 Kt—B 4 ±); 10 Kt—Q 1, Q—R 4;
11 P—Q B 3, Kt×Kt ch; 12 Q×Kt, P—Q 3 =. Rumin—Kyriloff, Moscow, 1931.
(o) Stoltz—Nimzovitch, Berlin, 1928.

1 P—K4, P—QB4.

	56	57	58	59	60
2	(Kt—QB3)..	P—QKt4 (d).	Kt—KB3 ..	P—KKt 3...	P—KB4 (n)
	(Kt—QB3)	P×P	P—Q3	P—Q4	Kt—QB3 (o)
3	(P—KKt3)	P—QR3	P—QKt4	B—Kt2 (h)	P—Q3
	(P—KKt3)	P—Q4 ! (e)	P×P	P×P	P—KKt3
4	(B—Kt2)	P—K5 (f)	P—Q4	Kt—QB3 (l)	P—B4
	(B—Kt2)	Kt—QB3	Kt—KB3	P—B4	B—Kt2
5	KKt—K2 (a)	P—Q4	B—Q3	P—B3	Kt—QB3
	P—Q3	Q—B2	P—Q4	P×P	P—Q3
6	P—Q3	Kt—KB3	QKt—Q2	Kt×P	B—K2
	B—Q2 (b)	B—Kt5	P×P (h)	Kt—QB3	Kt—B3
7	P—KR3	P×P	Kt×P	O—O	Kt—B3
	Q—B1	Kt×KtP	QKt—Q2	P—K4	B—Kt5
8	B—K3	P—B3	Kt(K4)-Kt5	P—Q3	B—K3
	R—Kt1	Kt—QB3	Q—B2	B—K2	O—O
9	Q—Q2	Kt—R3	P—QB4 !	Q—K2	O—O
	P—QKt4	P—QR3	P—KR3 (i)	Kt—B3 (m)	Kt—Q2
10	P—B4	B—K2	Kt—R3	K—R1	KKt—Kt5
	P—Kt5	P—K3	P—KKt4	Kt—Q5 ∓	B×B
11	Kt—Q1	O—O	Kt(R3)-Kt1		Q×B
	P—K4	R—Q1	B—Kt2		Kt—Q5
12	P—B3 [(c)	Q—R4	Kt—K2		B×Kt
	KKt—K2 =	Kt-K2+ (g)	P—K4 (j)		B×B ch ■

(a) 5 — Q3, P—K3; 6 B—K3, Kt—Q5; 7 Q—Q2, Q—R4; 8 P—B4, Kt—K2, 9 Kt—B3, KKt—B3, 10 O—O, O—O; 11 P—K5, P—Q4 =. Sir G. A. Thomas—A. Steiner, Ujpest, 1934.

(b) Or 6 ., Kt—KB3; 7 O—O, O—O; 8 P—KR3, Kt—K1; 9 B—K3; Kt—Q5; 10 P—B4, P—B4; 11 Kt—R2, R—Kt1; 12 P—QR4, Kt—B2; 13 P×P, Kt×P(B4); 14 B—Kt1, P—K4 =. C.H Alexander—Pirc, Hastings, 1932-33. Or 6 ., R—Kt1; 7 O—O, P—QKt4; 8 Kt—Q5, P—K3; 9 Kt—K3, K Kt—K2: 10 P—QB3, P—Kt5; 11 B—Q2, O—O; 12 Q—B1, P×P =. Nilsson—Euwe, The Hague, 1928.

(c) Von Nuss—V. Buerger, 1927. (d) The Wing Gambit.

(e) Best. Inferior alternatives are: (1) 3 , P×P; 4 Kt×P, P—Q4; 5 P×P, Q×P; 6 B—Kt2, Kt—QB3; 7 Kt—Kt5, Q—Q1; 8 Q—B3, P—K4; 9 B—B4, Kt—B3 10 Q×Kt3+. Spielmann—Sämisch, Carlsbad, 1923. (2) 3.., P—K4; 4 P×P, B×P; 5 P—QB3, B—B4; 6 Kt—KB3, Kt—QB3; 7 B—B4, P—Q3; 8 P—Q4, P×P; 9 P×P, B—Kt3; 10 O—O, B—Kt5; 11 Q—Kt3+. Marshall—Verlinsky, Moscow, 1925. (3) 3 , P—K3; 4 P×P, B×P; 5 P—QB3, B—K2; 6 P—Q4, P—Q3; 7 P—KB4, P—Q4, 8 P—K5, Kt—KR3; 9 B—Q3, P—B4; 10 P×P e.p. ±. Spielmann—König, Vienna, 1922

(f) Or 4 KP×P, Q×P, 5 B—Kt2, P—K4; 6 P×P, B×P; 7 Kt—QB3, R×Kt; 8 B×B, Kt—QB3; 9 Kt—B3, K Kt—K2; 10 B—K2, O—O; 11 O—O, P—B3+. Spielmann—Sämisch, Marienbad, 1925.

(g) Yates—V. Buerger, London, 1926.

(h) After 6 ., P—K3; 7 O—O, Kt—B3; 8 R—K1, B—K2; 9 P—K5, Kt—Q2; 10 Kt—B1, O—O; 11 Kt—Kt3 Black's position remains cramped.

(i) If 9 ., P×P e.p.?, 10 Q—Kt3!, P—K3, 11 Kt×BP!! and wins.

(j) Keres—Eliskases, Semmering-Baden, 1937. White won, but Black's conduct of the defence was far from faultless.

(k) 3 P×P, Q×P, 4 Kt—KB3, B—Kt5; 5 B—Kt2, Kt—QB3 (or 5 ., Q—K5 ch =); 6 P—K3, B—B4; 7 O—O, Q—Q2; 8 K—R2, O—O—O; 9 P—Q3, P—K4; 10 Kt—B3, P—B3. Tartakover and others—Alekhine and others, Paris, 1933.

(l) 4 B×P, Kt—KB3; 5 B—Kt2, B—Kt5; 6 Kt—K2, Kt—B3 ∓.

(m) Better than 9 , B—B3?; 10 B—K3, Q—Q3?; 11 Kt—QKt5, Q—K2; 12 Q—B2, Kt—Q5; 13 Q Kt×Kt, B P×Kt; 14 B×P!+. Spielmann—Bogoljuboff, 7th match game, 1932.

(n) Or 2 P—Q3, P—K3; 3 P—QB3, P—Q4; 4 Kt—Q2, Kt—QB3; 5 P—KB4, B—Q3; 6 Q—B3, K Kt—K2, 7 Kt—K2, O—O; 8 P—KKt4, P—B4!, 9 KtP×P B—Q3; (9 P—K5 is better), QP×P; 10 QP×P, P×P; 11 Kt—KKt3, P×P +. S R. Wolf—Spielmann, Vienna, 1932. Or 2 P—QB3, P—K3; 3 P—Q4, Kt—KB3; 4 P—K5, Kt—Q4; 5 Kt—B3, P×P; 6 P×P, B—K2; 7 Kt—B3, Kt×Kt; 8 P×Kt, P—Q4; 9 P×P e.p., Q×P; 10 B—K2, O—O =. Nimzovitch—Vidmar, New York, 1927. 2 P—QB4, Kt—QB3; 3 P—Q3, B×P, 4 P—B4, P—Q3 transposes into the column.

(o) Black can also play 2.., P—K 3, followed by P—Q4, leading to a French Defence. The column is Nimzovitch—Capablanca, Berlin, 1928.

THREE KNIGHTS' GAME

THIS comparatively safe way of avoiding the many drawing variations of the Four Knights' Game is barren of resources for the second player, whose chances of winning are small. Yet we find it occasionally adopted even by the greatest masters in modern tournament play.

The opening arises from either 2..., Kt—Q B 3 (cols. 1 to 8) or 2..., Kt—K B 3 (cols. 9 and 10), the latter form producing immediate equality of position. On the former line the attack by 4 Kt—Q 5 (cols. 1 to 4) still holds the field, Black's best answers being 4..., B—K 2 (the line in col. 1 showing the soundest form of the defence), and 4..., Kt—B 3, recommended by Schlechter.

White appears to retain better chances with 4 B—Kt 5 (col. 5), the reply K Kt—K 2 being of doubtful value. In the Fianchetto Defence (col. 7) Tartakover's suggestion in note (e) is worthy of attention. Col. 8 shows an important line, which had the advantage of two high tests in 1931.

Col. 10 gives an improvement in the 2..., Kt—K B 3 form of the Three Knights'.

1 P—K 4, P—K 4 ; 2 Kt—K B 3, Kt—Q B 3 ; 3 Kt—B 3.

	1	2	3	4	5
3	B—Kt 5				
4	Kt—Q 5 (a)				B—Kt 5
	B—K 2	Kt—B 3		B—R 4 (j)	KK—K2 (l)
5	P—Q 4	Kt×B (d)...B—B 4 (g)		B—B 4	P—Q 4 ! (m)
	P×P (b)	Kt×Kt	O—O	P—Q 3	P×P
6	Kt×P	Kt×P (e)	P—B 3	P—B 3	Kt×P
	Kt×Kt	P—Q 3	B—K 2	Kt—B 3	O—O
7	Q×Kt	Kt—B 3	Kt×Ktch (h)	P—Q 3	O—O
	Kt—B 3	Kt×P	B×Kt	Kt×Kt (k)	P—Q R 3
8	Kt×B	P—B 3	P—Q 3	B×Kt	Kt×Kt
	Q×Kt	Kt—Q B 3	P—Q 3	Kt—K 2	Kt P×Kt
9	B—Q 3	P—Q 3 (f)	P—Q R 3	B—Kt 5	B—Q 3
	P—B 4	Kt—B 3	P—Q R 3	P—Q B 3	B×Kt
10	Q—K 3	P—Q 4	O—O	B—Kt 3	P×B
	P—Q 4		B—Q 2	P—B 3	P—Q 3
11	P×P ± (c)		B—Kt 3	B—K 3	R—Kt 1
			Kt—K 2 (i)	P—Q 4 =	R—K 1 (n)

(a) 4 P—Q R 3, B×Kt; 5 Q P×B, P—Q 3; 6 B—Q B 4, Kt—B 3; 7 Q—Q 3, B—K 3; 8 P—R 3, P—Q R 3; 9 Kt—Kt 5, B×B; 10 Q×B, P—Q 4; 11 P×P, Q×P; 12 Q×Q, Kt×Q ∓. Flohr—Alekhine, Prague, 1931. Or 4 B—B 4, Kt—B 3; 5 O—O, O—O, 6 P—Q 3, B×Kt; 7 P×B, P—Q 4; 8 P×P, Kt×P; 9 P—K R 3. Kt×P; 10 Q—Q 2, Kt—Q 5; 11 Kt×P, Kt (B 6)—K 7 ch; 12 K—R 2, Kt×B =. Leonhardt—Schlechter, San Sebastian, 1911.

(b) If 5.., P—Q 3; 6 B—Q Kt 5, P×P; 7 K Kt×P, B—Q 2; 8 O—O, Kt—B 3; 9 R—K 1, O—O; 10 B×Kt, P×B; 11 Kt×B ch, Q×Kt; 12 B—Kt 5 ±. Znosko-Borovsky—Alekhine, London, 1922.

(c) Alekhine—Tartakover, New York, 1924.

(d) For 5 B—Kt 5, Kt×Kt see Four Knights' Game, col. 30. 5 P—B 3, B—K 2; 6 B—B 4, P—Q 3; 7 P—Q 3, Kt×Kt; 8 B×Kt, O—O has been played.

(e) 6 P—Q 4, P—Q 4; 7 Kt×P, P×P; 8 P—Q B 3, Q Kt—Q 4; 9 B—Q B 4, O—O =. Forgacs—Schlechter, San Sebastian, 1912. Or 6 P—B 3, Kt—B 3; 7 Q—B 2, O—O; 8 B—K 2, P—Q 3; 9 O—O, Q—K 2; 10 P—Q 3 =. Maróczy—Alekhine, London, 1932.

(f) Or 9 P—Q 4 at once. The column is suggested by Tartakover.

(g) Playing the Rubinstein Defence to the Four Knights' Game with a move in hand. If 5.., Kt×P; 6 O—O, O—O; 7 Q—K 2 ±.

(h) Or 7 Kt×B ch, Q×Kt; 8 O—O, P—Q 3; 9 Q—K 2, Kt—Q R 4; 10 B—Q 3, Kt—R 4; 11B—B 2, Kt—K B 5; 12Q—Kt 5, Kt—B 3. T. H. Tylor—Alekhine, Hastings 1933-34.

(i) 12 P—Q 4. Maróczy—Grünfeld, Vienna, 1920.

(j) 4.., B—B 4; 5 B—B 4, P—Q 3; 6 P—B 3, P—Q R 3; 7 P—K R 3, P—R 3 (if 7.., Kt—B 3; 8 P—Q 4 and 9 B—K Kt 5); 8 P—Q 4, P×P; 9 P×P, B—R 2; 10 O—O, Kt—B 3; 11 B—Kt 3, O—O; 12 Kt—B 3 !, Kt—K 2; 13 B—K 3.± Maróczy—Chajes, Carlsbad, 1923.

(k) If 7.., P—K R 3; 8 O—O, O—O; 9 P—Q R 4, P—Q R 3; 10 P—Q Kt 4, B—Kt 3; 11 Kt×B +. Alekhine—Cohn, Carlsbad, 1911.

(l) For 4.., Kt—B 3 see Four Knights' Game. If 4.., P—Q R 3; 5 B×Kt, Q P×B; 9 Kt—K 2 ! ±.

(m) Forcing exchange of centre Pawns. If instead 5 O—O, O—O; 6 P—Q 4, P—Q 3; 7 P—K R 3, P—Q R 3; 8 B—K 2, P×P; 9 Kt×P, Kt×Kt; 10 Q×Kt, B—Q B 4=. Schlechter—Tarrasch, Hamburg, 1910.

(n) 12 P—K B 4. P—B 3; 13 Q—R 5! ±. Treybal—Réti, Teplitz-Schónau, 1922.

1 P—K 4, P—K 4 ; 2 Kt—K B 3.

	6	7	8	9	10
2	(Kt—Q B 3).........................Kt—K B 3				
3	(Kt—B 3)			Kt—B 3 (j)	
	B—B 4......P—K Kt 3 (c)	.P—Q 3		B—Kt 5	
4	Kt×P (a)	P—Q 4 (d)	P—Q 4	Kt×P......B—B 4	
	Kt×Kt (b)	P×P (e)	B—Q 2	O—O	P—Q 3 (l)
5	P—Q 4	Kt×P (f)	B—Q B 4	B—K 2	Kt—Q 5
	B—Q 3	B—Kt 2	P×P	R—K 1	Kt×Kt
6	P×Kt	B—K 3	Kt×P	Kt—Q 3	B×Kt
	B×P	K Kt—K 2	Kt—B 3	B×Kt	O—O
7	P—B 4	Q—Q 2 !	O—O	Q P×B	P—B 3
	B×Kt ch	P—K R 3	B—K 2	Kt×P	B—R 4
8	P×P	O—O—O	Kt—B 5	O—O	P—Q 3
	P—Q 3	P—Q 3	B×Kt	P—Q 3	P—B 3
9	Q—Q 4	B—K 2	P×B	Kt—B 4	B—Kt 5
	Q—B 3	B—Q 2	Q—Q 2 (h)	Kt—Q 2	Q—K 1
10	B—B 4 ±	P—K R 3	P—K Kt 4	B—K 3	B—Kt 3
		Kt×Kt (g)	Kt—K 4 (i)	Kt—K 4 (k)	K—R 1 (m)

(a) For 4 B—Kt 5, Kt—B 3 see Four Knights', cols. 31-35.

(b) 4.., B×P ch; 5 K×B, Kt×Kt; 6 P—Q 4, Q—B 3 ch; 7 K—Kt 1, Kt—Kt 5 ; 8 Q—Q 2, Kt—K 2; 9 P—K R 3+.

(c) 3 , B—K 2 transposes into the Ruy Lopez (Steinitz Defence) by 4 B—Kt 5, Kt—B 3; 5 O—O, P—Q 3 or into the Hungarian Defence, p. 83, by 4 B—B 4, Kt—B 3. If 3. , P—B 4?; 4 P—Q 4, B P×P; 5 Kt×P, Kt—B 3; 6 B—Q B 4, P—Q 4; 7 Kt×Q P!, K Kt×Kt; 8 Q—R 5 ch, P—Kt 3; 9 Kt×P, P×Kt; 10 Q×P ch+ +. Breyer—Balla, Pistyan, 1912.

(d) 4 B—Kt 5, B—Kt 2; 5 O—O, K Kt—K 2; 6 P—Q 3, O—O; 7 B—B 4? (better R—K 1). V. Marin—Capablanca, Barcelona, 1929.

(e) Or 4.., B—Kt 2; 5 P×P, Kt×P; 6 Kt×Kt, B×Kt (Tartakover).

(f) 5 Kt—Q 5, B—Kt 2; 6 B—K Kt 5, P—-B 3; 7 B—K B 4, P—Q 3; 8 Kt×Q P, K Kt—K 2; 9 B—B 4, Kt—R 4; 10 B—K 2 ±.

(g) 11 B×Kt, O—O; 12 B×B, K×B; 13 P—K B 4 +. Weenink—Kmoch, London, 1927.

(h) 9.., O—O; 10 P—K Kt 4. Kt—Q 2; 11 P—B 4, Kt—Kt 3; 12 B—Q 3, P—B 3; 13 P—Q R 3 ±. Mattison—Alekhine, Prague, 1931.

(i) 11 B—K 2, P—K Kt 4 ! =. Riga Chess Club—Riga Seniors (Behting and Mattison), correspondence, 1931.

(j) This position may be reached through Vienna Game, Alekhine's Defence or Petroff Defence. For 3 B—B 4, Kt×P; 4 Kt—B 3, Kt×Kt; 5 Q P×Kt see Boden-Kieseritzky Gambit, p. 14, col. 6.

(k) 11 P—B 3, Kt—K B 3; 12 B—B 2. Tarrasch—Grünfeld, Vienna, 1922.

(l) 4.., O—O; 5 P—Q 3, P—B 3; 6 O—O, P—Q 4; 7 B—Kt 3, B—Kt 5; 8 P—K R 3, B—K R 4 (simplest is P×P); 9 Q—K 2, P—Q 5; 10 Kt—Kt 1, Q Kt—Q 2; 11 P—B 3. Yates—Olland, Hastings, 1919.

(m) 11 Q—K 2, Kt—R 3!; 12 Kt—R 4 (better 12 O—O), Kt—B 4; 13 B—K 3 (13 B—B 2, Kt—K 3; 14 B—K 3, Kt—Q 5), Kt×B; 14 P×Kt, B—Q 1; 15 Kt—B 5, Q—K 3; 16 P—Q Kt 4. Becker—Euwe, Carlsbad, 1929.

TWO KNIGHTS' DEFENCE

THIS defence, sometimes called in German-speaking countries the *Preussisch* (Prussian), is an effective method of avoiding the dangerous attacks in the Giuoco Piano and Evans Gambit, arising from the substitution of Kt—B 3 for B—B 4 on Black's 3rd move. It is still frequently adopted with satisfactory results by enterprising players, and indeed has attracted some little attention from the modern school.

For his 4th move White has the choice of :—

(i) 4 Kt—Kt 5 (cols. 1 to 15), entailing upon Black the necessity of sacrificing a Pawn, for which he obtains control of the centre and a strong and enduring attack. The old form 6 P—Q 3 (cols. 1 to 7), favoured by Morphy, has again come into favour through the influence of Tartakover's analysis of the opening in *Die Hypermoderne Schachpartie*. Black obtains a powerful attack with 9..., B—Q B 4 (cols. 1 to 3), but both 9..., B—Kt 5 ch (cols. 4 and 5) and Maróczy's 9..., B—K 2 are unsatisfactory. The form with 6 B—Kt 5 ch (cols. 8 to 10) has seen some important improvements since our last edition. On his 11th move White can play either P—Q 4, which is inferior against P × P *e.p.*, and P—K B 4, which is advantageous for the first player, according to recent analysis.

(ii) 4 P—Q 4 (cols. 16 to 28), an aggressive continuation which retains the initiative for White at the temporary expense of a Pawn. Since our last edition it has been shown that in the usual lines Black can obtain a clear superiority with 12.... B—Q 3 (col. 19), so that he has no reason to adopt the simplifying variations given in col. 16 and col. 17 note (*b*). Canal's Variation (cols. 20 to 23) may involve Black in considerable difficulties, but here too recent analysis indicates that it is unsound against the line given in col 23. The counter-attack in col. 28 has been strengthened by a recent test.

(iii) 4 P—Q 3 (cols. 29 and 30), played on the authority of Charousek, Tarrasch, and Tartakover, but leading to a slight positional advantage for Black when correctly countered.

1 P—K 4, P—K 4; 2 Kt—K B 3, Kt—Q B 3; 3 B—B 4, Kt—B 3.

4 Kt—Kt 5, P—Q 4; 5 P×P, Kt—Q R 4; 6 P—Q 3, P—K R 3;
7 Kt—K B 3, P—K 5; 8 Q—K 2, Kt×B; 9 P×Kt.

	1	2	3	4	5
9	B—Q B 4.............................				B—Kt 5 ch
10	K Kt—Q 2.. O—O	P—K R 3 O—O	P—B 3 (d) P—QKt4!(e)	P—B 3 B—Q 3 (g)...O—O	
11	Kt—Kt 3 B—Kt 5 !	Kt—R 2 P—Q Kt 4	P—Q Kt 4 B—K 2	Kt—Q 4 O—O	P×B (i) P×Kt
12	Q—B 1 B—Kt 5 ch	P×P Kt×P	K Kt—Q 2 B—K Kt 5	P—K R 3 R—K 1	Q×P Q—K 2 ch
13	Kt—B 3 (a) P—Q Kt 4	O—O Q—K 2	P—B 3 K P×P	B—K 3 Kt—Q 2	Q—K 3 Q×P ch
14	P—K R 3 B—K R 4	P—R 3 P—B 4	Kt P×P B—R 4	Kt—Q 2 Kt—B 4	Q—B 3 R—K 1 ch
15	P—K Kt 4 P—Kt 3	P—B 4 P—K 6 ∓ (c)	P×P O—O	O—O—O P—B 4	.B—K 3 Q—Q 3
16	B—Q 2 B×Kt (b)		O—O R—K 1+ (f)	P—K Kt 3 P—B 3 (h)	O—O P-QKt4!(j)

(a) If 13 P—B 3, B—K 2 l (weaker is 13.., B—Q 3; 14 P—K R 3, B—R 4; 15 P—Kt 4, B—Kt 3; 16 B—K 3, Kt—Q 2; 17 Q Kt—Q 2, P—K B 4; 18 P×P, B—R 4; 19 Kt×P!+. Tartakover—Bogoljuboff, Bad Homburg, 1927); 14 P—K R 3, B—R 4; 15 P—Kt 4, B—Kt 3; 16 B—K 3, Kt—Q 2; 17 Q Kt—Q 2, Kt—K 4; 18 O—O—O, P—Kt 4!; 19 P×P, Kt—Q 6 ch; 20 K—Kt 1, Q×P+. Salwe—Marshall, Vienna, 1908. If 13 P—Q 2, B×B ch; 14 Q Kt×B, R—K 1; 15 P—K R 3, P—K 6!+.

(b) 17 B×B, P×P; 18 Q×P, Q×P; 19 Q×Q, Kt×Q=. Analysis by Tartakover in *Die Hypermoderne Schachpartie.*

(c) Grob—Euwe, Zürich, 1934.

(d) If 10 P—K R 3, O—O; 11 Kt—R 2, P—K 6!; 12 B×P, B×B; 13 P×B, Kt—K 5; 14 Kt—B 1, Q—R 5 ch; 15 P—Kt 3, Q—B 3; 16 P—B 3, B—B 4+ (Steinitz).

(e) Or 10 .., O—O; 11 Kt—Q 4, B—K Kt 5; 12 Q—B 2, B×Kt; 13 P×B, P—Q Kt 4; 14 P—Q Kt 3, P×P; 15 P×P, P—B 3; 16 P—K R 3, B—R 4; 17 B—K 3, P×P; 18 P—B 5, Kt—R 2; 19 P—Kt 4, B—Kt 3; 20 Kt—B 3, Kt—Kt 4 (W. Koch—Schlage, Berlin, 1929); 21 Q—Kt 3, R—Kt 1; 22 Q×P, Q—R 4; 23 R—Q B 1, K R—Q 1+.

(f) 17 Q—B 4, B—Q 3; 18 Q—K R 4, R—K 7. Grob—Keres, Dresden, 1936.

(g) 10 .., B—K 2; 11 Kt—Q 4, B—K Kt 5; 12 Q—B 2, O—O; 13 B—K 3, R—K 1; 14 Kt—Q 2, B—K B 1; 15 O—O+. Tartakover—Teichmann, Berlin, 1921.

(h) 17 Q—R 5, Kt—Q 6 ch; 18 K—Kt 1, R—B 1; 19 P—K Kt 4+. Tartakover—Yates, The Hague, 1921.

(i) 11 Kt—Q 4 is necessary.

(j) 17 P—Q Kt 3, P×P; 18 P×P, P—B 3; 19 P×P, Kt—Kt 5+. W. Koch—Dr. R. Dührssen, Berlin, 1923.

1 P—K 4, P—K 4; 2 Kt—K B 3, Kt—Q B 3; 3 B—B 4, Kt—B 3.

4 Kt—Kt 5, P—Q 4; 5 P×P, Kt—Q R 4.

	6	7	8	9	10
6	(P—Q 3) (a)		B—Kt 5 ch		
	(P—K R 3)		P—B 3		
7	(Kt—K B 3)		P×P		
	(P—K 5)		P×P		
8	(Q—K 2)		B—K 2 (g)		
	(Kt×B)		P—K R 3		
9	(P×Kt)		Kt—K B 3 (h)		
	B—K 2 (b)		P—K 5		
10	K Kt—Q 2 ..	Kt—Q 4 (d)	Kt—K 5		
	B—K Kt 5	P—B 3	B—Q 3 (i)		
11	Q—K 3	Kt—Q B 3	P—Q 4 (j)		P—K B 4
	O—O	B—K Kt 5	P×P e.p.!...Q—B 2		O—O
12	P—K R 3	P—B 3 !	Kt×Q P	B—Q 2 ! (m)	O—O ! (o)
	B—K B 4	K P×P	Q—B 2	O—O	B×Kt
13	P—K Kt 4	Kt P×P	Kt—R 3 (k)	Kt—R 3 !	P×B
	B—R 2	B—R 6 (e)	B—R 3 !	B—K 3	Q—Q 5 ch
14	Kt—Q B 3	R—K Kt 1	P—K Kt 3	O—O	K—R 1
	P—Q Kt 3	Q—Kt 3	O—O	Kt—Kt 2	Q×K P
15	Kt—Kt 3	Q—Q 3	O—O	K—R 1 (n)	P-Q 4 ! ± (p)
	R—K 1 (c)	O—O—O (f)	Q R—Q 1+ (l)		

(a) 6 P—Q Kt 3 is a suggestion by S. Mlotkowski.

(b) Maróczy's Variation. 9 , B—Q 3; 10 P—K R 3, O—O; 11 Kt—Q 4, R—K 1; 12 B—K 3, B—K 4; 13 Q—Q 2, B—Q 2; 14 Kt—Q B 3, P—B 3; 15 P×P, P×P; 16 O—O, Q—K 2 is Grob—Lundin, Ostend, 1936.

(c) 16 B—Q 2+. Analysis by Tartakover.

(d) 10 Kt—K 5, O—O; 11 O—O, R—K 1; 12 P—K R 3, B—Q 3; 13 Kt—Kt 4, Kt×Kt; 14 P×Kt, Q×Q; 15 P—B 4, P—K 6+. Analysis by Dr. v. Claparède.

(e) 12.., B—R 4?; 13 P—Q 6 followed by Kt—B 5+.

(f) 16 R—Kt 3, B—Q B 4; 17 B—K 3, K R—K 1; 18 O—O—O, resigns (if B—Q 2; 19 Kt—R 4++). Dührssen—Demetriescu, Berlin, 1924.

(g) On 8 B—Q 3, Kt—Q 4; 9 Kt—K 4, B—K 2; 10 O—O, O—O ∓ is best for Black. If, however, 8.., Kt—Kt 5?; 9 Kt—K 4!, P—K B 4; 10 B—K 2, P×Kt (Kt—B 3; 11 Kt×Kt ch, Q×Kt; 12 P—Q 3+. Bertrand—Beuter, correspondence, 1930); 11 B×Kt, Q—Kt 4; 12 B—R 3!, B×B; 13 P×B, P—R 4; 14 Q—K 2+ (analysis by Dr. Dührssen, or 8 Q—B 3, Q—B 2; 9 B—R 4, B—Q 3; 10 P—Q 3, O—O; 11 O—O, P—K R 3; 12 Kt—K 4, Kt×Kt; 13 Q×Kt, P—K B 4+.

(h) 9 Kt—K R 3 (Steinitz), B—Q B 4!; 10 O—O, O—O; 11 P—Q 3, Kt—Kt 2!; 12 K—R 1, P—Kt 4; 13 P—Q B 3, B—Kt 3; 14 B—K 3, Kt—Q 4+. Makovetz—Charousek, 1896.

(i) 10.., Q—Q 5; 11 P—K B 4, B—Q B 4; 12 R—B 1, B—Kt 3; 13 P—B 3, Q—Q 3; 14 P—Q 4 ±.

(j) 11 Kt—Kt 4, Kt×Kt; 12 B×Kt, Q—R 5; 13 B×B, R×B; 14 Q—K 2, O—O; 15 Kt—B 3, Q R—K 1; 16 Q—Q 3, P—K B 4 ∓.

(k) Or 13 B—K 3, P—B 4; 14 Kt—B 3, Kt—B 5; 15 Q—B 1, O—O; 16 B—B 4, Kt×P; 17 B×B, Kt×Kt ch; 18 P×Kt, Kt×Q B+. Rödl—Bogoljuboff, 5th match game, 1931. If 13 P—K R 3, O—O; 14 O—O, B—R 3 with variations similar to the text should be played, but not 14 .., B—K B 4?; 15 R—K 1, Q R—Q 1; 16 B—B 1!, B—K 5?; 17 Kt—B 3, Q R—K 1?; 18 Kt×B, Kt×Kt; 19 P—Q Kt 3, Kt—B 6; 20 Q—Q 2+. Dührssen—Demetriescu, Berlin, 1927.

(l) Spielmann—Eliskases, 7th match game, 1936.

(m) Dr. Knorre's old move. If 12 B—K B 4, O—O; 13 B—Kt 3, R—Kt 1; 14 P—Kt 3, P—B 4; 15 P—Q B 3, P×P; 16 P×P, Kt—Q 4+. Demeter—Kostich, Gyula, 1921.

(n) Capablanca suggests 15 P—K B 4 (to which P—B 4 is a good reply) and Duhrssen 15 B—Q B 4. The column is Becker—Vidmar, Carlsbad, 1929. Continued 15 ., Q R—Q 1? (B×Kt is necessary); 16 Q Kt—B 4, Q B×Kt; 17 Kt×B, B×P (Black's only resource); 18 P—K Kt 3+.

(o) 12 P—Q 4?, P×P e.p.; 13 Q×P, Kt—Kt 2; 14 B—K 3, Q—B 2; 15 Kt—Q 2, R—Q 1+. Spielmann—Pirc, Noordwijk, 1938.

(p) Analysis by Euwe.

1 P—K 4, P—K 4; 2 Kt—K B 3, Kt—Q B 3; 3 B—B 4, Kt—B 3;
4 Kt—Kt 5.

	11	12	13	14	15
4	(P—Q 4)			B—B 4 (g)	...Kt×P!?
5	(P×P) / Kt×P?	.....Kt—Q 5 (b)		B×P ch (h) / K—K 2	B×P ch / K—K 2
6	P—Q 4! (a) / B—K 3	P—Q B 3.... / P—Kt 4	P—Q 6? / Q×P	B—Kt 3 / R—B 1	P—Q 4! / P—Q 3
7	Kt×B / P×Kt	B—B 1 (c) / Kt×P	B×P ch / K—K 2	O—O / P—K R 3	B—Kt 3 / Kt—B 3
8	P×P / Kt×P	Kt—K 4! (d) / Kt—K 3 (e)	B—Kt 3 / Kt×B	Kt—K B 3 / P—Q 3	Kt—B 7 / Q—K 1
9	Q—R 5 ch / Kt—B 2	B×P ch / B—Q 2	R P×Kt / P—K R 3	P—K R 3 / Kt×P	P×P / P×P
10	O—O / B—K 2	B×B ch / Q×B	Kt—K B 3 / P—K 5	P—B 3 / Q—K 1	Kt×R+
11	R—K 1 / Q—Q 2	O—O / B—K 2	Kt—Kt 1 / K—B 2	P—Q 4 / B—Kt 3	
12	Q—Kt 4+	P—Q 4 / P×P	Kt—Q B 3 / Q—B 3	Q—K 2+	
13		P×P / O—O	Q—K 2 / B—Q B 4		
14		Q Kt—B 3+	Q—Kt 5 / P—K 6!+ (f)		

(a) 6 Kt×B P (the Fegatello Attack), K×Kt; 7 Q—B 3 ch, K—K 3; 8 Kt—B 3, Kt—Kt 5 (8.., Kt—K 2; 9 P—Q 4, P—B 3; 10 B—K Kt 5, K—Q 2; 11 P×P, K—K 1; 12 O—O—O, B—K 3; 13 Kt×Kt, B×Kt; 14 R×B, P×R; 15 B—Kt 5 ch++); 9 Q—K 4, P—B 3; 10 P—Q R 3, Kt—R 3; 11 P—Q 4, Kt—B 2; 12 B—B 4, K—B 2; 13 B×P. White has a powerful attack, but Black has excellent counter-chances.

(b) Fritz's Variation.

(c) Better than 7 P×Kt, P×B; 8 P×P, Q×P; 9 O—O, B—Kt 2; 10 Kt—K B 3, Kt—Q 2, 11 P—Q 4, P×P e.p.; 12 Kt—B 3, Q—B 3; 13 Q×P, O—O—O.

(d) T. Gruber's suggestion. If 8 P×Kt, Q×Kt; 9 B×P ch, K—Q 1; 10 O—O, B—Kt 2; 11 P—B 3, Kt—B 5; 12 P—K Kt 3, Kt—R 6 ch; 13 K—R 1, P×P; 14 B—K 2 =.

(e) 8. , Q—R 5; 9 Kt—Kt 3, B—K Kt 5; 10 P—B 3, Kt—B 4; 11 Q—K 2!!++.

(f) 15 Kt—B 3, P×Q P ch: 16 B×P, R—K 1 ch; 17 K—B 1, B—K Kt 5. Bogoljuboff—Rubinstein, Stockholm, 1919.

(g) The Wilkes-Barre Variation, so-called because it has been played and analysed by the Wilkes-Barre C C. of Pennsylvania.

(h) Best. If 5 P—Q 4?, P—Q 4!!; 6 K P×P, Kt×P; 7 P—Q 6, O—O ∓. An alternative is 5 Kt×B P, B×P ch; 6 K—B 1, Q—K 2; 7 Kt×R, P—Q 4; 8 B—K 2, B—Kt 3 with counter-play for the Exchange. If here 6 K×B??, Kt×P ch; 7 K—Kt 1, Q—R 5; 8 Q—B 1, R—B 1; 9 P—Q 3, Kt—Q 3; 10 Kt×Kt ch, P×Kt; 11 Q—K 2, Kt—Q 5; 12 Q—Q 2, Q—Kt 5; 13 White resigns. G. H. Perrine—Wilkes-Barre C.C., correspondence, 1931.

1 P—K 4, P—K 4 ;   2 Kt—K B 3, Kt—Q B 3 ;   3 B—B 4, Kt—B 3.

4 P—Q 4, P×P ;   5 O—O, Kt×P ;   6 R—K 1, P—Q 4.

	16	17	18	19	20
7	B×P...				Kt—B 3 (j)
	Q×B				P×B
8	Kt—B 3				R×Kt ch (k)
	Q—Q 1	Q—Q R 4 (b)			B—K 3
9	R×Kt ch	Kt×Kt (c)			Kt×P
	B—K 2	B—K 3			Kt×Kt
10	Kt×P	Q Kt–Kt5 (d)			R×Kt
	P—B 4 !	O—O—O			Q—B 1 ?
11	R—B 4 (a)	Kt×B			B—Kt 5
	O—O	P×Kt			B—Q 3
12	Kt×Kt	R×P			Kt—K 4
	Q×Q ch	Q—K B 4...Q—Q 4......B—Q 3 ! (h)			O—O
13	Kt×Q	Q—K 2	Q—K 2	Q—K 2	Kt—B 6 ch !
	P×Kt	P—K R 3	P—K R3!(f)	Q—R 4	P×Kt
14	R—Q B 4	B—Q 2	B—B 4	P—K R 3	B×P
	R—K 1	Q×P	P—K Kt 4	Q R—K 1	B—K 4
15	B—B 4	R—Q B 1	B—Kt 3	B—Q 2	B×B
	B—R 3	Q×P	P—Q 6	Kt—K 4 !	P—K B 3
16	R×P	K R×Kt	P×P	R×R ch	B—Kt 3
	B—Kt 2=	P×R (e)	P—Kt 5 (g)	R×R (i)	R—Q 1 ? (l)

(a) 11 B—R 6 ? (Dr. Hartlaub), P×R ; 12 B×P, Kt×Kt ; 13 Q—R 5 ch, K—Q 2 ; 14 B×Kt, R—B 1 ; 15 R—Q 1, B—Q 3 ; 16 Q—Kt 4 ch, K—K 1+. Analysis by Tarrasch in *Kagan's Neueste Schachnachrichten*, 1921.

(b) 8.., Q—B 5 ; 9 Kt—Q 2 !, Q—R 3 ; 10 Kt—Q 5, Q—R 4 ; 11 P—Q B 4+ Analysis by Schlechter in *Deutsche Schachzeitung*, 1916. Or 8 ., Q—K R 4 ; 9 Kt×Kt B—K 3 ; 10 B—Kt 5, B—Q Kt 5 ; 11 Kt×P, Q×Q ; 12 K R×Q, Kt×Kt =.

(c) 9 R×Kt ch (or 9 Kt×P ?, Kt×Kt ; 10 Q×Kt, P—K B 4+), B—K 3 ; 10 Kt×P, O—O—O ; 11 B—K 3, B—K B 4+.

(d) 10 B—Q 2, B—Kt 5 ; 11 B×B, Q×B ; 12 Kt (K 4)—Kt 5, O—O—O ; 13 Kt×B, P×Kt ; 14 Kt—Kt 5, Q R—K 1 ; 15 Kt×K P, R—K 2 = (Euwe). Or 10 B—Kt 5, B—Q Kt 5 ; 11 R—K 2, O—O ; 12 P—Q R 3, B—Q 3 ! ; 13 Kt×B, P×Kt ; 14 B—B 4, B—Kt 5 ∓. Cortlever—Euwe, Amsterdam, 1938.

(e) 17 Q—K 6 ch (17 Kt—K 5 ?, R—K 1 ; 18 Q—R 6 ch, Q—Kt 2 ; 19 Q—K 2, B—R 6 ; 20 R—K 1, Q—Kt 4+. Kostich—Vidmar, Bled, 1931), K—K 1 ; 18 Q—K 4, P—Q 6 ; 19 Kt—K 5, Q—Kt 2 ; 20 Kt×P ch, K—R 1 ; 21 Q—Q R 4, with a strong attack (Tartakover).

(f) 13.., P—Q 6 ; 14 P×P, Q×P ; 15 B—Kt 5 ! ±.

(g) 17 R×Kt!, P×R ; 18 Kt—K 5, P—K R 4 ; 19 P—Q 4, K—Kt 2 ; 20 R—Q B 1, R—K 1 ; 21 R—B 3. Tartakover—A. Steiner, Budapest, 1921.

(h) 12.., B—K 2 ; 13 Kt—K 5!, Kt×Kt ; 14 R×B, Q—K 2 ; 15 R×R, Kt×R ; 16 B—B 4, R—K 1 ; 17 P—K R 3, Q—K B 4 ; 18 B—Kt 3, Q—K 5 ; 19 Q—Q 2, P—Q Kt 3 ; 20 P—Kt 4, Kt—B 3 ; 21 R—Q 1 ±. Tartakover—Tarrasch, Gothenburg, 1920.

(i) 17 R—Q 1, Kt×Kt ch ; 18 Q×Kt, Q×Q ; 19 P×Q, P—B 4 +. Tartakover and others—Oskam and others, Rotterdam, 1933.

(j) Canal's Variation.

(k) If 8 Kt×Kt, B—K 2+.

(l) 17 B—R 4, P—Q B 4 ; 18 R×R ch, Q×R ; 19 Q—B 3 + +. Canal—P. Johner, Trieste, 1923. Better was 16 ., R—B 2 ; 17 Q—K 2 !, P—B 3 (Tartakover).

1 P—K 4, P—K 4; 2 Kt—K B 3, Kt—Q B 3; 3 B—B 4, Kt—B 3.

4 P—Q 4, P×P (a).

	21	22	23	24	25
5	(O—O) (Kt×P)				P—Q 3 (i)
6	(R—K 1) (P—Q 4)			B—K 2 ·	Kt×P B—K 2
7	(Kt—B 3) (P×B)		P×Kt! (f)	R×Kt P—Q 4	Kt—Q B 3 O—O
8	(R×Kt ch) (B—K 3)	B—K 2	B×P B—K 3 !	R×B ch Kt×R	P—K R 3 (j) Kt×Kt
9	(Kt×P) (Kt×Kt)	Kt×P P—B 4	B×Kt ch (g) P×B	B—Kt 3 P—Q B 4	Q×Kt B—K 3
10	(R×Kt) B—Q 3	R—B 4 B—Kt 4 (c)	Q×Q ch R×Q	P—B 3 P×P	B×B P×B
11	B—B 4 O—O	Q—K 2 ch Kt—K 2	R×Kt R—Q 8 ch	Kt×P P—Q 5	P—K 5 Kt—Q 2
12	B×B P×B	R×P! ·B—B 3 (d)	R—K 1 R×R ch	Kt—K 4 Q—B 2	P×P P×P
13	R×Q P Q—K 2	R—Q 5 B—Q 2	Kt×R P×P	K Kt—Kt 5! O—O	B—K 3 P—Q 4
14	Q—Q 4 K R—Q 1	B—B 4 P—B 3	B×P P—B 3	Q—R 5 B—B 4	K R—K 1 ±
15	R×R ch Q×R (b)	R—Q 6 (e)	Kt—Q 3 B—Q 3 +	B×P ch (h)	

(a) 4.., K Kt×P; 5 P×P, Kt—B 4 (if B—B 4?; 6 Q—Q 5++).

(b) 16 R—Q 1, Q×Q; 17 R×Q. Analysis by Tartakover in *Neue Weiner Schachzeitung*, 1923. White's advantage is negligible.

(c) 10.., O—O, transposing into col. 16, is best.

(d) If B×R; 13 B×B threatening Kt—Q 5 and R—K 1. If Q×Kt; 13 B×B with the same threats. If B×B; 13 R—Q 5, B—Q 2; 14 Q R×B+. Analysis by M. Frh. von Feilitzsch.

(e) 15 ., P—Q Kt 4; 16 Kt×B P++. Von Feilitzsch—Dr. Kreyher, correspondence, 1928. If 15.., B×Kt; 16 R×K B, O—O; 17 Q R—Q 1+.

(f) 7.., B—K 3; 8 Kt×Kt, P×B; 9 K Kt—Kt 5, B—K 2; 10 Kt×B, P×Kt; 11 Q—R 5 ch, P—Kt 3; 12 Q—Q Kt 5, O—O; 13 Q×B P, Q—Q 4; 14 Q—K 2, Q R—K 1 =.

(g) 9 R×Kt, Kt—K 2!!+. Or 9 B×Kt, B—Q Kt 5 + (Euwe).

(h) 15.., K—R 1 (R×B would have prolonged the game); 16 K Kt×P, resigns. Von Feilitzsch—F. Eschrich, correspondence, 1930.

(i) Giving a cramped game. The column is Tarrasch—Taubenhaus, Ostend, 1905. With this column compare Three Knights' Game, col. 8.

(j) 8 P—Q Kt 3, Kt—K 4; 9 B—Q 3, R—K 1; 10 B—Kt 2, P—B 3; 11 Q—Q 2, Q—B 2; 12 Q R—Q 1, B—Q 2; 13 P—B 4+. Cancelliere—Asztalos, Trieste, 1928. 8 B—B 4, Kt—K 4; 9 B—Q Kt 3, R—K 1; 10 P—K Kt 3, B—B 1 =. Becker—Vidmar, Graz, 1929.

1 P—K 4, P—K 4; 2 Kt—K B 3, Kt—Q B 3; 3 B—B 4, Kt—B 3

	26	27	28	29	30
4	(P—Q 4) .... Kt—B 3 (h)				
	(P × P)			Kt × P	
5	(O—O)	P—K 5	Kt—Kt 5	Kt × Kt (l)	
	B—K 2 (a)	P—Q 4	P—Q 4 (g)	P—Q 4	
6	Kt × P	B—Q Kt 5 (d)	P × P	B—Q 3	
	Kt × P (b)	Kt—K 5 (e)	Q—K 2 ch! (h)	P × Kt	
7	Kt—B 5	Kt × P	K—B 1 (i)	B × P	
	P—Q 4	B—Q 2 (f)	Kt—K 4	B—K Kt 5 . . B—Q 3 (n)	
8	Kt × P ch	Kt—Kt 3	Q × P	P—K R 3	P—Q 4
	K—B 1	Q—R 5	Kt × B (j)	B × Kt	Kt × P (o)
9	B—K R 6	O—O	Q × Q Kt	Q × B	Kt × Kt
	K—Kt 1	O—O—O	Q—B 4	Q—Q 2	P × Kt
10	Q × P	B × Kt	Q × Q	B × Kt	Q × P
	Q × Q	B × B	B × Q	P × B	O—O
11	B × Q	Kt—B 3	P—Q B 4	O—O	B—K 3
	Kt—B 3	P—B 3	B—B 4	B—B 4	Q—K 2
12	B × Kt	Kt × Kt	K—K 2	Q—K Kt 3	O—O—O
	P × B	P × Kt	O—O	P—B 3	R—K 1
13	R—K 1	Q—K 2	R—Q 1	P—Q 3	B—Q 5 (p)
	B—B 1	R—Q 4	K R—K 1 ch	O—O	B—K 4
14	Kt–K 8!+ (c)	P—K 6	K—B 1	B—K 3	Q—Q R 4
		B—Q 3+	Kt—K 5 ∓	B–Kt 3 = (m)	P—Q B 3 ∓

(a) For 5.., B—B 4 see Max Lange, pp. 107–9.

(b) 6 , O—O; 7 Kt—Q B 3, P—Q 3 transposes into col. 25.

(c) Dr. Krause's analysis.

(d) 6 P × Kt, P × B; 7 Q—K 2 ch, B—K 3; 8 P × P, B × P; 9 Kt—Kt 5, Q—Q 4 +

(e) The column is Tartakover—Réti, Baden, 1914. White may answer 6.., Kt—K 5 by 7 O—O, transposing into the Max Lange.

(f) 7.., B—Q B 4; 8 B—K 3!+. Not, however, 8 Kt × Kt, B × P ch; 9 K—B1, Q—R 5!; 10 Q—K 2, O—O; 11 B—K 3, P × Kt; 12 B × B P, B—Kt 5; 13 Q—Q 3, Q R—Q 1+ (Dr. Keidanzki).

(g) 5.., Kt—K 4; 6 Q × P, Kt × B; 7 Q × Q Kt, P—Q 4; 8 P × P, Q × P =. Torre—Marshall, New York, 1925. If here 6 B—Kt 3, P—K R 3; 7 P—K B 4, P × Kt; 8 P × Kt, Kt × P; 9 O—O, P—Q 4; 10 P × P e.p., Q × P; 11 B × P ch, K—Q 1+. Kan—Löwenfisch, Leningrad, 1933.

(h) 6.., Kt—K 4; 7 Q × P, Kt × B; 8 Q × Q Kt, Q × P; 9 Q × Q =.

(i) If 7 Q—K 2, Kt—K 4; 8 B—Kt 5 ch, P—B 3; 9 P × P, P × P; 10 B—Q 3, Kt × B ch+.

(j) Or 8 .., P—K R 3; 9 Kt—K 4, Kt × B; 10 Kt × Kt ch, Q × Kt; 11 Q × Kt, B—Q 3; 12 Q—K 2 ch, K—B 1 ∓. Szabo—Kostich, Lyublyana, 1938.

(k) 4 O—O, Kt × P; 5 B—Q 5, Kt—B 3; 6 B × Kt, Q P × B; 7 Kt × P, B—Q 3 =. 4 P—Q 3, B—B 4 transposes into the Giuoco Piano. If 4 P—Q 3, P—Q 4?; 5 P × P, Kt × P; 6 O—O, B—K 2; 7 R—K 1+.

(l) 5 B × P ch (for 5 O—O, Kt × Kt; 6 Q P × Kt see Boden-Kieseritzky Gambit, p. 14, col. 6), K × B; 6 Kt × Kt, P—Q 4; 7 Q Kt—Kt 5 ch, K—Kt 1+.

(m) Analysis by Dr. Krause.

(n) 7.., Kt—K 2; 8 P—B 3, P—K B 4; 9 B—B 2, Kt—Kt 3. G. Haglund—W. Edman, Ljusne (Sweden), 1927.

(o) Or 8 ., P × P; 9 B × Kt ch, P × B; 10 Q × P, O—O; 11 O—O, P—Q B 4; 12 Q—B 4, B—Kt 2; 13 P—Q Kt 3, Q—Q 2; 14 B—Kt 2, P—K B 3; 15 Q R—Q 1, Q—B 4; 16 Q—B 4 ch, K—R 1; 17 Kt—R 4 (Tartakover—Bogoljuboff, Pistvan, 1922), Q—K 5! =.

(p) 13 B—B 3 is probably stronger (Tartakover). The column is Tartakover—Atkins, London, 1922.

VIENNA GAME

THE very complex opening arising from 1 P—K 4, P—K 4;
2 Kt—Q B 3, a great favourite with the master Rudolf
Spielmann, diverges into three branches by the replies 2...,
Kt—K B 3, 2..., B—B 4, and 2..., Kt—Q B 3, and in each
immediately sub-divides again. The play, which may in
general be summed up as counter-attack with a move in
hand, abounds in opportunities for brilliant combinations,
but exhaustive analysis has shown that the opening is on the
whole advantageous for Black.

In the first group play branches into three sections :—
(i) 3 B—B 4 (cols. 1 to 10), with which the name of
J. H. Blake is closely associated, both in theory and practice.
Black's most usual answer is 3..., B—B 4 (cols. 1 to 5),
though this allows White by the advance of 6 P—B 5 (cols.
1 and 2) to cramp Black's development.   With correct play,
however, White is unable to prevent the equalising move
of P—Q 4, except at the cost of a total disruption of his
Queen's side.

Black has at his disposal three main alternatives : 3...,
Kt—B 3 (cols. 6 and 7), enabling White to defend a Ruy
Lopez with a valuable move in hand, the line of play in col.
7 being simplest for both sides; 3..., P—B 3 (col. 8), also
leading to equality; and 3..., Kt × P (cols. 9 and 10), when
Black can either play for an attack at the expense of the
Exchange (col. 9, note (h)), or adopt the simplifying lines
shown in cols. 9 and 10, which give him complete equality.
The first alternative (col. 9, note (h)), has never been
subjected to an exact analysis, but is apparently a win for
White.

(ii) 3 P—K Kt 3 (p. 306, note (A)), which is less
effective against 2..., Kt—B 3 than against 2..., Kt—Q B 3
(col. 23).

(iii) 3 P—B 4 (cols. 11 to 21), giving rise to extremely critical positions, tending on the whole in favour of the second player if he is prepared to risk the ensuing complications.

In the most usual variation, beginning with 5 Kt—B 3, Black has the choice of five moves :—

(i) 5..., B—Q Kt 5 (cols. 11 to 13), which is advantageous for Black after 6 B—K 2, for he can then either obtain a more solid Pawn position (col. 11), or even play for an attack (col. 11, note (e)), but is of questionable value after Spielmann's recommendation 6 Q—K 2 (col. 13). In col. 12 White sacrifices the Exchange for so strong a position that no satisfactory defence has been found for Black.

(ii) 5..., B—Q B 4 (col. 14) is Marshall's idea (which was still earlier Marco's) of playing B—Q Kt 5 in two stages, to provoke P—Q 4.

(iii) 5..., B—K 2 (cols. 15 and 16), which has now generally come into recognition as Black's soundest policy, avoiding the complications of the other variations, and against any but the best play by White leading to a positional superiority.

(iv) 5..., B—K Kt 5 (col. 17), leading to approximate equality.

(v) 5..., Kt—Q B 3 (col. 18) has been analysed least. The reply in the column is definitely weak, but it is not easy to see how White can obtain a satisfactory game with any other continuation.

The attack with 5 Q—B 3, favoured for some time by Spielmann, should occasion the second player no difficulties. Both 5..., P—K B 4 (col. 19), and 5..., Kt—Q B 3 (col. 20) are strong replies, where no continuation is known in which White can as much as equalise.

The second form of this opening diverges at 2..., B—B 4 (col. 22), a move which usually transposes into variations dealt with under the first and third groups.

The third group diverges at 2..., Kt—Q B 3 (cols. 23 to 25), a move from which the Gambit also springs. Against this move White has more chance to obtain a promising attack.

VIENNA GAMBIT.

This arises from White's sacrifice of the King's Bishop's Pawn on the 3rd move, and leads to positions akin to those of the King's Gambit; it is therefore too speculative in character for match use. The Pierce Gambit (cols. 1 and 2) provokes sparkling sacrifices, frequently turning out in favour of White in over-the-board play, although analytically unsound. The Hampe-Allgaier Gambit (cols. 3 and 4) yields an attack perhaps surpassing in violence the ordinary Allgaier Gambit, but Black should survive the storm. In the Steinitz Gambit (col. 5), White allows his King to be driven about the board in the early stages of the game in the hope of obtaining positional superiority. The simple continuation 5..., P—Q 3, is advantageous for Black; the sacrifice of the Knight in note (i) is not sound.

1 P—K 4, P—K 4 ; 2 Kt—Q B 3, Kt—K B 3 ; 3 B—B 4, B—B 4 ;
4 P—Q 3, P—Q 3.

	1	2	3	4	5
5	P—B 4				B—K 3
	Kt—B 3 (a)		Kt—Kt 5 ?	..B—K 3	Kt—B 3
6	P—B 5 (b)		P—B 5	B×B (g)	B×B
	Kt—Q 5 (c)		P—K R 4 (f)	P×B	P×B
7	Kt—B 3	B—Kt 5	Kt—R 3	P×P	K Kt—K 2
	P—B 3	P—B 3	Q—R 5 ch	P×P	Kt—QR4(i)
8	Kt×Kt	P—Q R 3	K—B 1	Q—K 2	B—Kt 3
	B×Kt	P—Kt 4	B—K 6	Kt—B 3	Kt×B
9	Q—B 3	B—R 2	Kt—Q 5	B—K 3	R P×Kt
	P—Q Kt 4	Q—Kt 3	B×B	B×B	O—O
10	B—Kt 3	Kt—B 3	Q×B	Q×B	O—O
	P—Q R 4	P—Q R 4	K—Q 2	O—O	Kt—Kt 5 (j)
11	P—Q R 3	R—K B 1	Q—Kt 5	Q—R 3	P—K R 3
	P—R 5	P—R 5	Q×Q	Kt—Q 5	Kt—R 3
12	B—R 2	Kt×Kt	Kt×Q	O—O—O	P—B 4
	B×Kt ch	B×Kt	P—Q B 3	Q—Q 3	P×P
13	P×B	B×Kt	P—K R 3	Kt—B 3	Kt×P
	B—Kt 2	P×B	Kt—K R 3	P—Q R 4	P—K B 3
14	B—Q 2	Q—R 5	Kt—K 3	K R—B 1	Q—B 3
	P—Q 4 (d)	R—K B 1	K—K 2	Q R—Kt 1	Kt—B 2
15		Kt—Q 1	P—K Kt 4 ±	P—K Kt 4 (h)	R—B 2 ±
		P—Kt 5 + (e)			

(a) For 5.., B—K Kt 5 ; 6 Kt—B 3 see King's Gambit Declined.

(b) For 6 Kt—B 3 see King's Gambit Declined.

(c) If 6.., Kt—Q R 4 ; 7 Q—B 3, Kt×B ; 8 P×Kt, B—Q 2 ; 9 K Kt—K 2, B—B 3 ; 10 P—Q R 3, P—Q R 4 ; 11 P—K Kt 4, Q—K 2 ; 12 B—Q 2, Kt—Q 2 ; 13 P—K R 4, B—Q 5 ; 14 R—Q Kt 1, P—Q Kt 3. J. H. Blake—R. T. Black, cable match, 1910.

(d) J. H. Blake—R. P. Michell, City of London championship, 1921.

(e) Spielmann—P. Johner, Vienna, 1908.

(f) If 6.., Kt—B 7 ; 7 Q—R 5, O—O (or 7.., Q—Q 2 ; 8 P—B 6 ; or 7.., P—K Kt 3 ; 8 Q—R 6) ; 8 B—K Kt 5, Q—Q 2 ; 9 Kt—Q 5+. Or 6.., Q—R 5 ch ; 7 P—Kt 3, Q—R 4 ; 8 P—K R 3, B×Kt ; 9 Q×Kt, Q×Q ; 10 P×Q, B—Kt 3 ; 11 P—Kt 5 and P—Kt 6+.

(g) If 6 B—Kt 3, Kt—B 3 ; 7 P—B 5, B×B ; 8 R P×B, P—K R 3 ; 9 B—Q 2, P—Q 4 ; 10 P×P, Kt×P ; 11 Q—Kt 4, K—B 1 =. Mieses—von Scheve, Monte Carlo, 1901. If 6 P—B 5, B×B ; 7 P×B, Q Kt—Q 2 ; 8 Q—B 3, P—B 3 ; 9 K Kt—K 2, Kt—Kt 3 ; 10 P—Q Kt 3, P—Q 4 ; 11 B P×P, P×P ; 12 B—Kt 5, P—Q 5 ∓. Spielmann—Eliskases, 9th match game, 1932.

(h) Spielmann—Tarrasch, Bad Kissingen, 1928. Tartakover suggests the continuation 15.., P—Q Kt 4 ; 16 P—Kt 5, P—Kt 5 ; 17 P×Kt, P×Kt ; 18 Kt P×P, Kt—K 7 ch ; 19 K—Q 2, Kt—B 5.

(i) 7.., O—O followed by an eventual Kt—Q 5 was better (Bogoljuboff). The column is Tartakover—Rubinstein, Moscow, 1925.

(j) Better 10.., Kt—Q 2 against which 11 Kt—Kt 3, followed by Q—Q 2, is stronger than 11 P—B 4, P×P ; 12 Kt×P, Kt—K 4 (Tartakover).

L ?

1 P—K4, P—K4; 2 Kt—QB3, Kt—KB3.

	6	7	8	9	10
3	B—B4				
	Kt—B3		P—B3	Kt×P	
4	P—Q3 (a)		Q—K2 (g)	Q—R5	
	B—Kt5		B—B4	Kt—Q3	
5	B—KKt5 ...Kt—K2 (d)		P—Q3	B—Kt3.....Q×KP ch	
	P—KR3	P—Q4	P—Q3	B—K2 (h)	Q—K2
6	B×Kt	P×P	P—B4	Kt—B3	Q×Q ch
	B×Kt ch	Kt×P	B—KKt5	Kt—QB3	B×Q
7	P×B	B×Kt	Kt—B3	Kt×P	B—Kt3
	Q×B	Q×B	Q Kt—Q2	O—O (i)	Kt—B4 (j)
8	Kt—K2	O—O	P—B5	Kt—Q5	Kt—B3
	P—Q3	Q—R4 (e)	Q—K2	Kt—Q5	P—QB3
9	O—O (b)	P—QR3	P—KR3	O—O	O—O
	P—KKt4	O—O	B×Kt	Kt×B	P—Q4
10	P—Q4	B—K3	Q×B	RP×Kt	R—K1
	P—KR4	B×Kt	P—KR3	Kt—K1	O—O (k)
11	P—B3 (c)	Kt×B	P—QR3	P—Q4	P—Q4
	P—R5	Kt—Q5 = (f)	Kt—Kt3	P—Q3	B—B3
12	Q—Q3	B—R2	Kt—KB3	Kt—K2	
	B—Q2 ∓	P—Q4 =	B—K3 =	B—K3 =	

(a) 4 P—B4, Kt×P; 5 Kt—B3, Kt—Q3 (5. , Kt×Kt; 6 QP×Kt, P×P; 7 B×P, with a fine attack); 6 B—Kt3, P—K5; 7 Kt—KKt5, P—KR3; 8 KKt×KP, Kt×Kt; 9 Q—K2. Bogoljuboff—Romanovsky, match, 1924. 9.., Kt—Q5; 10 Q×Kt ch, Q—K2 ∓.

(b) 9 Q—Q2, P—KKt4; 10 P—Q4, Kt—K2; 11 P×P, P×P; 12 R—Q1, Kt—Kt3; 13 B—Kt5 ch, P—B3; 14 B—B4, Kt—R5∓. P.S. Milner-Barry-Alekhine, London, 1932.

(c) 11 R—Kt1, P—R5; 12 Q—Q3, Kt—K2; 13 B—Kt5 ch, K—B1; 14 P×P, P×P; 15 Q—Q8 ch, K—Kt2; 16 Q×P, P—R6+. Spielmann—Bogoljuboff, Berlin, 1920.

(d) Or 5 B—Q2, O—O; 6 KKt—K2, P—Q3; 7 O—O, B—K3; 8 P—B4, B×B; 9 P×B, P×P=.

(e) Or 8. , Q—Q1; 9 P—B4, P—B4; 10 P×P, Kt×P; 11 P—Q4 ± Spielmann—Ahues, Berlin, 1926. Here 9.., B—Kt5 was better (Spielmann).

(f) Spielmann—Réti, Dortmund, 1928.

(g) Weaker is 4 P—Q4, B—Kt5; 5 P×P, Kt×P; 6 Q—Q4, P—Q4; 7 P×P e.p., O—O; 8 Kt—B3, Kt×Kt ∓. Tartakover—Réti, 1919. The column is J. H. Blake—J. A. J. Drewitt, Hastings, 1923.

(h) 5 ., Kt—B3 involves Black in the promising but highly speculative sacrifice: 6 Kt—Kt5, P—KKt3; 7 Q—B3, P—B4; 8 Q—Q5, Q—K2; 9 Kt×P ch, K—Q1; 10 Kt×R, P—Kt3; 11 P—Q3, B—QKt2; 12 P—KR4, P—KR3; 13 Kt×P, P×Kt; 14 Q—B3, Kt—Q5; 15 Q—Kt3+.

(i) 7 , Kt×Kt?; 8 Q×Kt, O—O; 9 Kt—Q5!, R—K1; 10 O—O, B—B1; 11 Q—B4, P—QB3; 12 Kt—K3, Q—R4; 13 P—Q4, Q—R4; 14 P—QB3 !. Alekhine—Euwe, 27th match game, 1935. The continuation in the column is suggested by Alekhine.

(j) 7.., O—O; 8 P—Q4, with a view to B—KB4 and O—O—O.

(k) Sämisch—Rubinstein, Hanover, 1926. If now 11 P—Kt4?, Kt—R5; 12 R×B, Kt×Kt ch; 13 K—Kt2, Kt—Q5 ∓ (Kmoch).

1 P—K 4, P—K 4; 2 Kt—Q B 3, Kt—K B 3; 3 P—B 4 (A), P—Q 4; 4 B P×P, Kt×P; 5 Kt—B 3.

	11	12	13	14	15
5	B—Q Kt 5			B—Q B 4	B—K 2
6	B—K 2		Q—K 2	P—Q 4 (g)	P—Q 4
	O—O	P—Q B 3	Kt×Kt (e)	B—Q Kt 5	O—O
7	O—O	O—O	Q P×Kt	Q—Q 3 (h)	B—Q 3
	Kt—Q B 3	Q—Kt 3 ch	B—K 2	P—Q B 4	P—K B 4
8	Q—K 1	P—Q 4	B—B 4	P×P	P×P e.p.
	B—Kt 5 (a)	Kt×Kt (c)	P—Q B 4	Kt×P	B×P! (j)
9	P—Q 3	P×Kt	O—O—O!	Q—K 3	O—O
	P—Q 5	B×P	Kt—B 3	Kt—B 3	Kt—B 3
10	P×Kt	B—R 3	Q—B 2	B—Kt 5	Kt×Kt (k)
	P×Kt	B×R	B—K 3	Kt—K 3	P×Kt
11	P×P	Q×B	Q—Kt 3	P—Q R 3	B×P
	B—B 4 ch	B—K 3 (d)	P—K Kt 3	B—R 4	Kt×P
12	K—R 1	B—Q 6	Kt—Kt 5	P—Q Kt 4	Kt—Kt 5
	B×Kt	Q—Q 1	Q—Kt 3	B—Kt 3	B—B 4
13	B×B	Q—K 1+	Kt×B	Q—Q 3	P—B 3
	Kt×P		P×Kt	O—O	B×Kt
14	Q—Kt 3		B—K 2	Q×P (i)	Q B×B
	Kt—Kt 3 (b)		Kt—Q 1	K Kt—Q 5	Q×B
15	B—Kt 5		P—K R 4 ±(f)	Q×Q	Q×Kt
	B—K 2 ∓			R×Q =	B×B =

(A) 3 P—K Kt 3 ?, P—Q 4; 4 P×P, Kt×P; 5 B—Kt 2, B—K 3; 6 K Kt—K 2, Kt—Q B 3; 7 O—O, B—K 2; 8 P—Q 4, Kt×Kt; 9 P×Kt, B—Q 4; 10 P—B 3, O—O; 11 B—K 3, Q—Q 3; 12 Q—Q 3, Q—K 3 ∓. O. C. Muller—Grunfeld, Margate, 1923. Here 7 P—Q 3, B—K 2; 8 O—O, P—K R 4!; 9 P—R 3, Q—Q 2; 10 K—R 2, P—B 4 is Mieses—Asztalos, Kassa, 1918.

(a) Or 8.., P—B 3; 9 Kt×Kt, P×Kt; 10 B—B 4 ch, K—R 1; 11 Q×P, B—B 4 ch; 12 K—R 1, P×P; 13 P—Q 3, B—B 4; 14 Q—Q 5, Q— 3 15 B—Q 2=. If here 13 Kt×P?, R×R ch; 14 B×R, Q—B 3; 15 B—Q 3, P—h Kt 3 16 Kt×Kt, P×Kt; 17 Q—B 3, Q—Q 5; 18 Q—K 3, B—Q 2; 19 Q×Q ch, ⌐ ×Q; 20 P—B 3, R—K 1; 21 P—K R 3, R—K 8 ch+. W. E. Bonwick—M. E. Goͮ.. .in, London 1923. Another alternative to the text is 8.., B—B 4 ch; 9 K—R 1, Kt—Q 5; 10 B—Q 1, P—B 4; 11 P—Q 3, Kt×Q Kt; 12 P×Kt, Kt—K 3; 13 P—Q 4, B—K 2; 14 B—K 2, P—K Kt 4; 15 B—Q 3, P—Kt 5 with attacking possibilities.

(b) Analysis by S. Mlotkowski.

(c) If 8.., B×Kt; 9 P×B, Kt×P; 10 Q—K 1, Kt×B ch; 11 Q×Kt, Q—R 3, 12 Q—Q 2, O—O; 13 P—Q R 4+.

(d) 11.., P—K R 3; 12 B—Q 6, Kt—R 3; 13 Kt—R 4, Kt—B 2; 14 P—R 4, Kt—K 3; 15 Kt—B 5+. Flamberg and Rabinovitch—Bogoljuboff and Vainstein, 1915.

(e) 6.., B×Kt; 7 Kt P×B, O—O; 8 Q—K 3, P—K B 4 (8.., Kt—Q B 3, 9 B—Kt 5! ±); 9 P—B 4, P—B 3; 10 P—Q 3, Q—R 4 ch (10 ., Kt—B 6 ?, 11 Q—Q 4+); 11 B—Q 2, Kt×B; 12 Q×Kt, Q×Q ch; 13 Kt×Q, B—K 3; 14 P×P ±.

(f) Spielmann—Yates, Prague, 1931.

(g) Also good is 6 Q—K 2, B—B 4; 7 Kt—Q 1, followed by P—Q 3 (Alekhine).

(h) If 7 B—Q 2, P—Q B 4 is best. A curious variation is 7 B—Q 3, Kt×Kt, 8 P×Kt, B×P ch; 9 B—Q 2, B×R; 10 Q×B, White having prospects of an attack, but not enough to compensate him for so heavy a sacrifice.

(i) 14 Kt×P, Kt×K P; 15 Kt×Kt, B—Q 5+ (Alekhine). The column is Spielmann—Marshall, New York, 1927.

(j) Much better than 8 , Kt×P; 9 O—O, Kt—B 3; 10 B—K Kt 5, B—K Kt 5, 11 Q—K 1, P—K R 3; 12 B—Q 2, B×Kt, 13 R×B, Kt×P; 14 R—Kt 3, B—B 4, 15 K—R 1 ±. Spielmann—Maróczy, Teplitz-Schönau, 1922.

(k) Or 10 Kt—K 2, Kt—K 2; 11 P—B 3, Kt—Kt 3; 12 Kt—B 4, Kt×Kt. Spielmann—Loman, Scheveningen, 1923. 10 B—K 3, B—B 4; 11 Q—K 1, B—Kt 3; 12 Kt—K 2, Q—K 2; 13 Kt—B 4, B—B 2 =. Spielmann—von Holzhausen, Berlin, 1926. The column is Spielmann—Réti, Vienna, 1922.

1 P—K 4, P—K 4; 2 Kt—Q B 3, Kt—K B 3; 3 P—B 4, P—Q 4; 4 B P×P, Kt×P.

	16	17	18	19	20
5	(Kt—B 3)............................			Q—B 3 (h)	
	(B—K 2)....B—K Kt 5..Kt—QB3(e)			P—K B 4...	Kt—Q B 3
6	Q—K 2 (a)	Q—K 2	Q—K 2 ?	P—Q 3	B—Kt 5 (j)
	P—K B 4	Kt×Kt (c)	B—KB4!(f)	Kt×Kt	Kt×Kt
7	P—Q 3	KtP×Kt(d)	Q—Kt 5	P×Kt	KtP×Kt
	Kt—B 4	P—Q B 4	P—QR3!(g)	P—Q 5	Q—R 5ch(k)
8	P—Q 4	Q—B 2	Q×Kt P	Q—Kt 3 (i)	P—Kt 3
	Kt—K 5	Kt—B 3	Kt—Kt 5 !	Kt—B 3	Q—K 5 ch
9	B—B 4	B—Kt 5	Kt×Kt	B—K 2	Q×Q
	O—O	B—K 2	P×Kt	B—K 3	P×Q
10	P—K R 4	O—O	Kt—Q 4	B—B 3	B×Kt ch
	P—B 3 (b)	O—O	R—Q Kt 1	Q—Q 2	P×B
11	Q—K 3	P—Q 4	Q—R 7	Kt—K 2	Kt—K 2
	B—Kt 5	P×P	B—B 4 !	B—B 4	B—K 2 !
12	Kt—Q 2	B×Kt	Q×B	P—B 4	R—B 1
	B—K 3	P×B	Q×Kt	O—O	O—O
13	Q Kt×Kt	P×P	Q×Q	O—O	R—B 4
	B P×Kt	P—B 3	Kt×P ch	B×P	P—B 3+ (l)
14	B—K 2	Q—Kt 3	K—B 2	Kt—B 4	
	P—B 4 ∓	Q—Q 2 =	Kt×Q ∓	B—K 3 ∓	

(a) Alternatives are : (1) 6 B—K 2, O—O; 7 O—O, Kt—Q B 3; 8 P—Q 3, B—B 4 ch; 9 P—Q 4, B—Kt 3; 10 Kt—Q R 4, B—K B 4 ∓. Marotti—Réti, London, 1927. (2) 6 P—Q 3, Kt×Kt; 7 P×Kt, O—O; 8 B—K 2, P—K B 3; 9 P×P, B×P; 10 P—Q 4, B—R 5 ch; 11 P—Kt 3, B—K 2; 12 O—O, B—K R 6; 13 R—B 2, Kt—Q 2 ∓. Sultan Khan—Weenink, Liège, 1930.

(b) Or 10 ., B—Kt 5; 11 Q—K 3, P—B 4 (Grünfeld). The column is Spielmann—Teichmann, Teplitz-Schönau.

(c) If 6.., Kt—QB3; 7 Kt×Kt, Kt—Q5; 8 Q—Q3, B×Kt; 9 Kt—Kt3+.

(d) Or 7 Q P×Kt, P—Q B 3; 8 B—B 4, Kt—Q 2; 9 O—O—O, Q—R 4; 10 K—Kt 1, O—O—O.

(e) 5 ., P—K Kt 4 (Locock's Counter Attack); 6 P—Q 3, Kt×Kt; 7 P×Kt, P—Kt 5; 8 Kt—Q 4, P—Q B 4; 9 Kt—K 2, P—Q 5; 10 Kt—B 4+.

(f) Better than 6.., Kt—B 4; 7 P—Q 4, Kt—K 3; 8 B—K 3, P—Q R 3; 9 Kt—Q 1, B—K 2; 10 P—B 3, O—O; 11 Q—Q B 2 ±. Mattison—Rubinstein, Prague, 1931.

(g) Simpler than 7.., Kt—B 4; 8 P—Q 4!, P—Q R 3; 9 Q—K 2, Kt—K 5; 10 Q—K 3, Kt×Kt; 11 P×Kt, B×P!; 12 Q—B 2!, B—K B 4; 13 Kt—R 4, B—K 3; 14 B—Q 3, Q—Q 2; 15 O—O with a strong attack for the Pawn sacrificed. Kan—Botvinnik, Moscow, 1935. The column is analysis by Rabinovitch.

(h) Other continuations are. (1) 5 B—Kt 5 ch (the Schräder Variation), P—B3 ; 6 Kt×Kt, P×Kt; 7 B—B 4, P—Q Kt 4; 8 B—Kt 3, B—K B 4 followed by 9.., B—B 4 ∓. (2) 5 P—Q 3, Kt×Kt; 6 P×Kt, P—Q 5; 7 Kt—B 3, P—Q B 4; 8 B—K 2, B—K 2; 9 O—O, O—O; 10 Q—K 1, P—B 3; 11 Q—Kt 3, B P×P; 12 B—R 6, B—B 3. Milner-Barry—Alexander, Worcester, 1931. Here 5. , Q—R 5 ch; 6 P—Kt 3, Kt×P; 7 Kt—B 3, Q—R 4; 8 Kt×P+ is Würzburger's Trap. If now 8.., B—K Kt 5; 9 Kt—B 4, B×Kt; 10 Kt×Q, B×Q; 11 P×Kt, B×P?; 12 P—Kt 3!, and the B cannot escape (Milner-Barry).

(i) Or 8 Q—B 4, Kt—B 3; 9 Kt—B 3, B—B 4; 10 B—Kt 2, P×P; 11 B×P, B—K 3; 12 P—Q R 3, Q—K 2; 13 B—Kt 2, O—O—O ∓. E. Schräder—Ed. Lasker, Chicago, 1916. If 8 Q—B 2, P×P; 9 P—Q 4, B—K 3; 10 B—Q 3, B—K 2; 11 Kt—K 2, O—O; 12 O—O, Kt—B 3; 13 B—K 3, Kt—Kt 5; 14 Kt×P, Kt×B; P—B 5! ∓. Tartakover—Lilienthal, Paris, 1933. The column is Spielmann—Romanovsky, Moscow, 1925.

(j) 6 Kt×Kt?, Kt—Q 5; 7 Q—B 4, P×Kt; 8 B—B 4, B—K B 4; 9 P—B 3, P—K Kt 4; 10 B×P ch, K×B; 11 Q—B 2, P—K 6!+. Boros—Lilienthal, 1933.

(k) 7 , B—K 2; 8 P—Q 4, O—O; 9 B—Q 3, P—B 3; 10 Q—R 5, P—K Kt 3; 11 B×P, leading to perpetual check. Hromadka—Em. Lasker, Mährisch-Ostrau, 1923.

(l) Hromadka—Spielmann, Trentchin-Teplitz, 1928. If 14 R×K P, B—K B 4; 15 R—Q B 4, P×P; 16 R×P, B—Q 3+. Or 14 P×P, B×P; 15 R×P, B—B 4; 16 R—Q B 4, Q B×P; 17 R×P, Q R—K 1+ (Kmoch).

1 P—K 4, P—K 4 ; 2 Kt—Q B 3.

	21	22	23	24	25
2	(Kt—K B 3).	B—B 4	Kt—Q B 3		
3	(P—B 4)	Kt—B 3 (e)	P—K Kt 3 ...	B—B 4	P—B 4 (m)
	(P—Q 4)	P—Q 3	B—B 4	B—B 4 (j)	B—B 4
4	P—Q 3 (a)	P—Q 4 ! (f)	B—Kt 2	Q—Kt 4	P × P (n)
	P × B P (b)	P × P	P—Q 3	P—K Kt3 (k)	P—Q 3 !
5	P × P (c)	Kt × P	Kt—R 4 (h)	Q—Kt 3	P × P
	B—Q Kt 5	Kt—K B 3	Kt—B 3	P—Q 3	Q × P
6	B × P	B—K Kt 5	Kt × B	P—Q 3	Kt—B 3
	Kt × P	P—K R 3	P × Kt	Kt—Q 5	B—K Kt 5
7	B—Q 2	B—R 4	P—Q 3	B—Kt 3	Kt—K 2
	B × Kt	Kt—B 3	O—O	B—K 3	O—O—O
8	P × B	Kt × Kt	Kt—K 2	B—Kt 5	P—B 3
	O—O	P × Kt	B—K 3	Q—Q 2	P—B 4
9	Kt—B 3	B—Q 3	P—Kt 3	O—O—O	P—Q 4
	R—K 1 ch	Q—K 2	Q—Q 2	B × B	P × P
10	B—K 2	O—O	O—O	R P × B	Kt—Kt 5
	Q—K 2	Q—K 4	B—R 6	P—K B 3	Q—K 2
11	P—B 4 (d)	Kt—R 4	P—K B 4	B—K 3	Q—B 2
	Kt—K B 3 ∓	B—Kt 3	B × B	O—O—O	P—K 6
12		B—Kt 3 ± (g)	K × B	K Kt—K 2	Q—K 4
			Kt—K 1 = (i)	Kt—K 2 (l)	Q × Kt+ (o).

(a) Steinitz's Variation. If 4 K P × P, Kt × P ; 5 Kt × Kt, Q × Kt, 6 P × P, Kt—B 3 ; 7 Kt—B 3, B—K Kt 5 ; 8 B—K 2. For 4 K P × P, P—K 5 see Falkbeer Counter-Gambit.

(b) Or (1) 4 .., Kt—B 3 ; 5 P × K P, Q Kt × P ; 6 P—Q 4, Kt—B 3 ; 7 P—K 5, Kt—K 5 ; 8 Kt × Kt, P × Kt ; 9 B—K 3, B—K 2 ; 10 Kt—K 2, O—O ; 11 Kt—B 4, B—Kt 4 ; 12 P—B 3, Kt—K 2 ; 13 B—B 4 ±. Horowitz—Maderna, Warsaw, 1935. (2) 4.., P—Q 5 ; 5 Q Kt—K 2 (Steinitz recommended 5 Kt—Kt 1), Kt—B 3 ; 6 Kt—K B 3, B—Kt 5 ; 7 Kt × P, Kt × Kt ; 8 P × Kt, Kt—Q 2 ; 9 P—K R 3, B × Kt ; 10 Q × B, Q—R 5 ch ; 11 K—Q 1, Kt × P ∓. (3) 4 ., B—Q Kt 5, 5 B P × P, Kt × P ! ; 6 P × Kt, Q—R 5 ch ; 7 K—K 2, B × Kt ; 8 P × B, B—Kt 5 ch , 9 Kt—B 3, P × P ; 10 Q—Q 4, B—R 4 ; 11 K—K 3, B × Kt ; 12 P × B, Q—K 8 ch ; 13 K—B 4, Q—R 5 ch with a draw by perpetual check.

(c) If 5 P—K 5, P—Q 5 !+.

(d) Spielmann—Lasker, St. Petersburg, 1909.

(e) For 3 B—B 4, Kt—K B 3 see cols. 1-5. For 3 P—K Kt 3, Kt—Q B 3 see col. 23. For 3 P—B 4, Kt—Q B 3 see col. 25.

(f) Weaker is 4 Kt—Q R 4, B—Kt 3 ; 5 Kt × B, R P × Kt ; 6 P—Q 4, P × P ; 7 Q × P, Q—B 3 ; 8 B—K Kt 5, Q × Q ; 9 Kt × Q, B—Q 2 ; 10 B—Q B 4, Kt—K 2 ; 11 O—O, Kt—Kt 3 =. Kan—Capablanca, Moscow, 1936.

(g) Horowitz—Kupchik, Syracuse, 1934.

(h) Or 5 P—Q 3, P—K R 4 ; 6 P—K R 3, B—K 3 ; 7 Kt—B 3, Q—Q 2 ; 8 Kt—K Kt 5, Kt—Q 5 ; 9 B—K 3, Kt—K 2 ; 10 Q—Q 2, P—K B 3 ; 11 Kt × B, Kt × Kt ; 12 O—O—O. J. H. Blake—H. Saunders, London, 1921.

(i) Mieses—Alapin, Vienna, 1908.

(j) For 3 .., Kt—B 3 see cols. 6-7.

(k) If 4 .., Q—B 3 ; 5 Kt—Q 5, Q × P ch ; 6 K—Q 1+. An alternative is 4 .., K—B 1 ; 5 Q—Kt 3, P—Q 3, 6 K Kt—K 2, Kt—K B 3. Rosselli—Yates, Semmering, 1926.

(l) Spielmann—Tarrasch, Vienna, 1922. The position is even.

(m) 3 P—Q 4 (Fyfe Gambit), Kt × P ; 4 P—B 4, B—Kt 5 ; 5 Kt—B 3, B × Kt ch +.

(n) White should transpose into the King's Gambit Declined by Kt—B 3 The column is Spielmann—Schlechter, Vienna, 1914.

(o) 13 B × P, Q—R 5 ch.

1 P—K4, P—K4;   2 Kt—QB3, Kt—QB3;   3 P—B4, P×P.

	1	2	3	4	5
4	Kt—B3				P—Q4 (h)
	P—K Kt4				Q—R5 ch
5	P—Q4 (a)	....P—Q3 (c)	P—KR4		K—K2
	P—Kt5		P—Kt5		P—Q3 (i)
6	B—B4	P—Q5	Kt-KKt5 (d)		Kt—B3
	P×Kt	Kt—K4	P—KR3		B—Kt5
7	O—O	B—Kt5 ch	Kt×P		B×P
	P—Q4	B—Q2	K×Kt		P—B4
8	KP×P	B×B ch	P—Q4		P—K5
	B—K Kt5	K×B	P—B6......P—Q4 (f)		B×Kt ch
9	Q—K1 ch (b)	P—K Kt3	B—B4 ch	B×P	K×B
	B—K2	P—KR4	P—Q4	B—Kt5	Q—Kt5 ch
10	B×P	P×P	B×P ch	P—K5 (g)	K—K3
	Kt×P	Kt×Kt ch	K—K1	B—K3	P×P+ (j)
11	B—K5	Q×Kt	P×P	B—K2	
	Kt—K7 ch	P—Kt5	B—K2	Q—Q2	
12	Kt×Kt	Q—Q3	B—K3	O—O	
	P×Kt	Q—R5 ch	B×P ch	K—Kt2+	
13	K B×P	K—K2+	K—Q2		
	B×B		B—Kt4		
14	Q×B		P—B4 .		
	P—KB3+		B—B3 (e)		

(a) Pierce Gambit.

(b) If 9 P×Kt (the Rushmere Attack), P—B7ch; 10 R×P, B×Q; 11 P×P, B—KKt5; 12 B—Kt5 ch, B—Q2; 13 Kt—Q5, R—Kt1; 14 B×P, R×P; 15 R—K1 ch, B—K2; 16 R×B ch, Q×R+ (Analysis by S. Mlotkowski and W. T. Pierce), or 9 R—K1 ch, K Kt—K2; 10 P×P, B—R6; 11 B×P, B—Kt1 ch; 12 B—Kt3, Kt—R4; 13 B—Kt5 ch, P—B3; 14 Kt—K4, B—Kt2; 15 K—R1, Q×P, 16 P—QB4, Q—Q2+. P. S. Milner-Barry—C. H. Alexander, Cambridge, 1932. The only tournament example of the Pierce Gambit for almost fifty years!

(c) 5 , B—Kt2; 6 P—Q5, Kt—K4; 7 P—Q6, Kt×Kt ch (if 7 , P×P; 8 P—KR4, Kt×Kt ch; 9 Q×Kt, P—Q4; 10 Kt×P +); 8 Q×Kt, P—QB3; 9 P—KR4, B—K4; 10 P×P, Q×P; 11 R—R5, Q—B3; 12 R×B, Q×R; 13 B×P+.

(d) Hampe-Allgaier Gambit.

(e) 15 P—K5, B—Kt2; 16 Q—K2, K Kt—K2+.

(f) 8.., P—Q3; 9 B×P, B—Kt2; 10 B—B4 ch, K—Kt3; 11 P—K5 is weaker.

(g) If 10 B—QKt5 (Lärobok, 1921), K Kt—K2.

(h) Steinitz Gambit.

(i) 5.., P—Q4; 6 P×P, B—Kt5 ch; 7 Kt—B3, O—O—O; 8 P×Kt, B—QB4; 9 Q—K1, B×Kt ch (or 9.., R—K1 ch; 10 K—Q2, Q—Q1; 11 Q—B2+); 10 P×B, R—K1 ch, 11 Kt—K4, Q—R4; 12 K—Q2, P—KB4; 13 B—R3+.

(j) Analysis by Dr. E. von Schmidt.

INDEX

	Page	Col. or note
RUY LOPEZ	231–76	....
Alapin's Defence	276	199–200
Berlin Defence	238–41	1–20
Duras Variation	241	n. (d)
Mortimer's Defence and Trap	241	n. (i)
Nyholm's Variation	240	14
Rio de Janeiro Variation	238	2
Schlechter's Variation	238	1
Znosko-Borovsky's Variation	240	11
Bird's Defence	242	21–5
Brentano's Defence	276	n. (m)
Classical Defence	243–4	26–35
Charousek's Variation	244	31
Cozio Defence	245	36–7
Cozio Defence Deferred	276	196
Fianchetto Defence	245	38–40
Morphy Defence	246–65	41–140
Berger's Variation	251	68–9
Bogoljuboff's Defence	256	92–4
Breslau Variation	249	56–60
Duras Variation	262	121–2
Exchange Variation	265	136–40
Friess Attack	252	72
Giuoco Piano Deferred	246	n. (a)
Howell's Variation	251	n. (b)
Kecskemét (Alekhine's) Variation	257	98–9
Leonhardt's Counter-Attack	255	86
Marshall's Variation	257	96
Möller Defence	261	117–9
Motzko Variation	250	65
Noah's Ark Trap	264	n. (c)
Riga Variation	252	73
Schlechter's Variation	255	90
Tarrasch's Trap	249	n. (b)
Tartakover's Variation	252	n. (f)
Treybal's Variation	263	130
Worrall Attack	258–60	101–13
Schliemann Defence	276	191–4
Schliemann Defence Deferred	276	195
Steinitz Defence	266–9	141–60
Nimzovitch's Attack	268	154–5
Steinitz Defence Deferred	270–5	161–90
Capablanca's Defence	273	179–80
Exchange Variation	270–1	161–7
Keres Variation	273	178
Noah's Ark Trap	{ 271 / 272 }	n. (h), / n. (p)
Siesta Variation	275	186–90
L. Steiner's Variation	271	170
Unusual Defences	276	191–200
SCANDINAVIAN DEFENCE, see Centre Counter Game		
SCOTCH OPENING	277–82	....
Scotch Gambit	282	1–5
Göring Gambit	282	4–5
" Mac-Lopez "	282	n. (a)
Scotch Game	279–81	1–20
Blumenfeld Variation	280	10

CHESS BOOKS

Chess the Easy Way. *By Reuben Fine* $1 50
Hoffer's Chess. *By L. Hoffer* 1 50
Chess: An Easy Game. *By R. E. Kemp and W. H.*
Watts 75
Chess for Fun and Chess for Blood. *By Edward Lasker* 2 50
Common Sense in Chess. *By Emanuel Lasker* 50
Lasker's Chess Primer. *By Emanuel Lasker* 1 00
A Guide to the Game of Chess. *By David A. Mitchell*
             Paper 35
             Cloth 75
The Beginner's Book of Chess. *By Frank Hollings* .. 75
Principles of Chess in Theory and Practice. *By James*
Mason 2 50
How Not to Play Chess. *By Eugene A. Znosko-*
Borovsky 1 25
Chess Mastery by Question and Answer. *By Fred*
Reinfeld 2 00
Chess Cameos. *By F. Bonner Feast* 1 25
The Art of Chess. *By James Mason* 2 50
The Game of Chess, Popular Edition. *By Dr. S. Tar-*
rasch .... NOW 2 50
The Ideas Behind the Chess Openings. *By Reuben Fine* 2 00
Modern Chess Openings. *By Griffith and White* 2 50
White to Play and Win. *By Weaver W. Adams* 75
Imagination in Chess. *By C. D. Locock* 1 00
Instructive Positions from Master Chess. Collected
and annotated *by J. Mieses* 1 00
Basic Chess Endings. *By Reuben Fine* 3 50
An Introduction to the End-Game at Chess. *By Philip*
W. Sergeant. 3 00
How to Play Chess Endings. *By Eugene A. Znosko-*
Borovsky. Translated *by J. Du Mont* 4 00
Practical End-Game Play. *By Fred Reinfeld* 2 00
Modern Chess Endings. *By Barnie F. Winkelman* 1 50
Chess Studies. *By A. A. Troitsky* 3 00

CHESS BOOKS

1234 Modern End-Game Studies. Compiled *by M. A. Sutherland* and *H. M. Lommer* 5 00

The Golden Treasury of Chess. *By Francis J. Wellmuth* 3 00

The Immortal Games of Capablanca. *By Fred Reinfeld* 3 00

Fifty Great Games of Modern Chess. Chosen and annotated *by H. Golombek* 1 25

Every Game Checkmate. Compiled *by W. H. Watts* and *Philip Herford* 1 25

Keres' Best Games of Chess. Annotated *by Fred Reinfeld* 3 00

Rubinstein's Chess Masterpieces. Translated *by Barnie F. Winkelman* 2 50

One Hundred-and-One of My Best Games of Chess. *By F. D. Yates*, British Champion, 1913, 1914, 1921, 1926, 1928, 1931. Edited *by W. H. Watts* 3 00

One Hundred Chess Gems. *By P. Wenman* 1 50

200 Miniature Games of Chess. *By J. Du Mont* 3 00

Morphy Gleanings. *By Philip W. Sergeant* 2 50

My Fifty Years of Chess. *By Frank J. Marshall*.... 3 00

Modern Chess. *By Barnie F. Winkelman* 1 00

A. Alekhine vs. E. D. Bogoljubow. World's Chess Championship, 1934. Annotated *by Fred Reinfeld* and *Reuben Fine* 1 25

Nottingham Tournament Book. Annotated *by Dr. A. Alekhine* 5 00

The World's Chess Championship. Official Account of the Games *by Dr. A. Alekhine*. With annotations *by the author* and *Dr. Max Euwe* 2 00

Comparative Chess. *By Frank J. Marshall* 1 00

Chess and Its Stars. *By Brian Harley* 2 00

A copy of our latest catalogue of Chess books sent post free on request.

DAVID McKAY COMPANY

604–608 So. Washington Square, PHILADELPHIA, PA.

CPSIA information can be obtained
at www.ICGtesting.com
Printed in the USA
LVHW11*0224251018
594770LV00005B/29/P